THE TALMUD

THE STEINSALTZ EDITION

A REFERENCE GUIDE

RANDOM HOUSE

NEW YORK

THE TALMUD

THE STEINSALTZ EDITION

A REFERENCE GUIDE
BY
RABBI ADIN STEINSALTZ

TRANSLATOR AND EDITOR:
Rabbi Israel V. Berman

MANAGING EDITOR:
Baruch Goldberg

ASSOCIATE EDITORS AND TRANSLATORS:
Dr. Jeffrey M. Green
Rabbi Moshe Sober
Rabbi Eli Touger

COPY EDITOR
Alec Israel

PRODUCTION MANAGER:
Meir Hanegbi

BOOK DESIGNER:
Ben Gasner

GRAPHIC ARTIST:
Michael Etkin

TECHNICAL STAFF:
Moshe Greenvald
Michael Plotkin
Chana Lawrence
Rachel Lichtenstein

This is an English translation of *A Reference Guide,* one volume of a work originally published
in Hebrew by The Israel Institute for Talmudic Publications, Jerusalem, Israel in 1988. Copyright
by The Israel Institute for Talmudic Publications.

Library of Congress Cataloging-in-Publication Data

Talmud. English.
The Talmud : the Steinsaltz edition / the Talmud with commentary by
Adin Steinsaltz
p. cm.
ISBN 0-394-57666-7 (v. 1)
ISBN 0-394-57665-9 (a reference guide)
I. Talmud—Commentaries I. Steinsaltz, Adin. II. Title.
BM499.5.E4 1989 296.1'250521—dc20 89-42911

Manufactured in the United States of America
98765432
First American Edition

כרך זה מוקדש
על ידי בני משפחתו בלונדון, פריז ורעננה
לזכרו של יוסף בן ישראל שולדנפריי ז״ל
נולד בראש חודש ניסן תרצ״ז
נפטר ביום ט״ו באייר תשמ״ז

Dedicated
in loving memory of
Joseph Schuldenfrei
by his family in London, Paris and Raanana

Preface

This *Reference Guide* was conceived as a tool to facilitate the study of the Talmud, both for the beginner and the more advanced student; it was not designed to be used only with the present edition of the Talmud. Students ought to find helpful information in this *Guide*, whether they are learning in a formal framework or on their own. As much as possible, we have used non-technical language while striving for the greatest precision.

One of the principal difficulties in studying the Talmud is that it is not written in a systematic fashion; it does not move from simple to weighty material, from the definition of terms to their use. In almost every passage of the Talmud, discussion is based on ideas that have been discussed elsewhere, and on terms that are not necessarily defined on the page where they appear. The Sages themselves said, "The words of Torah are poor in one place and rich in another" (Jerusalem Talmud, *Rosh HaShanah* 3:5). This *Guide* has been written to help the student understand concepts that are not explained in a particular passage and are therefore not clear in their limited context.

The *Guide's* main aims are to foster the understanding of principles and ways of study; to clarify and provide precise understanding of a wide range of concepts; and to summarize general conceptual structures.

Those beginning their study of the Talmud can turn first to the introductory and background chapters and the guidelines to Talmudic study. If they are studying from a traditional edition of the Talmud, they can consult the explanation of the structure and content of the traditional page. If they want to learn the rudiments of Aramaic, they can make use of the chapter on that language. If they want to learn Rashi script, a chapter on the subject is available to them.

The student already familiar with the Talmud should find the extensive glossaries useful. They explain the terminology of Talmudic discourse and the terms and concepts of the Halakhah, as well as provide information on the weights and measures used.

The chapters dealing with Mishnaic and Talmudic terminology and with Halakhic concepts can help both the beginner and anyone else who is seeking a more profound understanding of the principles whereby issues and problems are interpreted and resolved.

Although the *Guide* is mainly intended for the the study of the Babylonian Talmud, it also contains material useful for the study of the Jerusalem Talmud and Halakhic and Aggadic Midrashim.

While this book is primarily meant to serve as a study-aid, many of its chapters may be read on their own for general background concerning the world of Judaism; the entries in the glossaries also clarify matters beyond their strictly utilitarian function.

For the sake of brevity and clarity we have included relatively few references to sources or authorities. Naturally scholars have different approaches to the various matters discussed in this book; in general, we have presented only one approach, which we took to be the most representative.

Contents

THE TALMUD

THE STEINSALTZ EDITION

A REFERENCE GUIDE

Introduction:
The Essential Nature
of the Talmud

Torah and
Talmud

Just as the Bible is the foundation of Judaism, the Talmud is the central pillar supporting the entire spiritual and intellectual edifice of Jewish life. The Talmud, in the broader sense of the term, is made up of two components: the Mishnah, which is the first written summary of the Oral Law, and the Gemara (called Talmud in the more restricted sense of the term), which is formally an explanation and commentary on the Mishnah. The legal and practical value of the Talmud is obvious, but this does not explain its centrality and vital importance for Judaism.

In order to understand and appreciate the unique nature of the Talmud, one must first have a clear understanding of the unique Jewish concept of Torah study, of which studying the Talmud is a distinctive and characteristic part.

Specifically, the study of Torah (the Written and Oral Law) can be viewed as a means to an end. The Torah consists primarily of laws and commandments, not all of them easily understandable. They require elaboration, commentary, and explanations as to how to fulfill them. According to this perspective, Torah study provides the means for learning the principles and details necessary to fulfill the commandments.

In reality, however, this view of Torah fails to convey its true purpose and leaves many things totally unexplained. In particular, it does not explain why Judaism developed such great veneration for the study of Torah, a veneration expressed throughout Rabbinic literature:

"'All things that may be desired are not to be compared to it [the study of Torah]' (Proverbs 8:11). This means that even the desires of heaven [the commandments] cannot be compared to it." (Babylonian Talmud: *Moed Katan* 9b.)

"These are the things, the fruits of which man enjoys in this world, while the reward remains for him in the World to Come: honoring one's father and mother, performing deeds of kindness, making peace between man and his fellowman. And the study of Torah is equal to all of them." (Mishnah: *Pe'ah* 1:1.)

To say that "the study of Torah is equal to all of them" implies that Torah study is on a higher level than performing the commandments. It shows that the importance of Torah study transcends that of an aid to the fulfillment of the commandments. Otherwise, we would be faced with a strange contradiction: If the study of Torah is merely an aid, a guide to fulfilling the commandments, how can it be more important than actual performance of the commandments themselves?

In reality Torah and its study must be seen in an entirely different light.

Torah, as its Hebrew root implies, is a form of הוֹרָאָה — teaching. It teaches man the path he should follow, and is indeed a guide to fulfilling the commandments. Yet it is also far more than that. It is a comprehensive guide, the expression of Judaism's conception of everything in the world. Every subject lies within the compass of Torah, and Torah tells us how every subject is to be understood, how we should relate to it and act toward it. Hence, whether the subject is concrete and practical or abstract and spiritual, whether it expresses an immediate and living need or is entirely theoretical and without practical application, since it is related to Judaism's world view it is related to Torah, and Torah does indeed deal with it.

Establishing Halakhah (practical law) and providing guidance in fulfilling the commandments are only part of Torah. Torah seeks the essence of all things, in every area of life. It embraces the entire world and what lies beyond it. The ultimate purpose of Torah is not, then, only to scrutinize the commandments and reach practical conclusions regarding them; it is, rather, to provide a comprehensive world view, bringing out both the essential relationship of Torah to every subject and also the subjects' connections with each other.

If we understand the overall nature and purpose of the Torah, we can then understand and appreciate the special nature of that portion of it known as the Talmud.

The Mishnah and the Talmud

The Mishnah (the scholars of which are called Tannaim) is written in a precise and very terse Hebrew style, presenting complex subject matter in concise form. Although the text of the Mishnah is itself usually clear, it does not cover every possible case, and many problems and questions arise whose solution cannot be found in the wording of the Mishnah alone. For three centuries (c. 200 C.E.–500 C.E.) after the compilation and editing of the Mishnah, the Rabbis (called Amoraim) and their students discussed and analyzed the Mishnah. Their questions, discussions, and solutions make up the Talmud.

Understandably, since the Mishnah deals mainly with Halakhic matters, many of the issues and problems that arise in the study of the Mishnah are Halakhic ones. Nevertheless, the solution of Halakhic problems, and in particular the finding of definitive Halakhic rulings, is not the main purpose of the Talmud. Halakhic rulings and the practical application of Torah laws are subordinate to the quest for the underlying truth of things. The ultimate purpose of the Talmud is not in any sense utilitarian — its sole aim is to seek out the truth.

Accordingly, it is immaterial whether the subject under investigation is practical or theoretical, whether the conclusions reached in the investigation ever yield material benefit or forever remain no more than an abstract, conceptual achievement. The Talmud's purpose is to seek out the exclusive Torah connection with any given subject, whether it be legal, ritual, historical, philosophical, or in any other area of inquiry. The truth is the objective toward which the Talmud strives.

In this way we can explain the extraordinary fact that the Talmud attaches equal weight to the study of both practical and theoretical issues, and, similarly, to the study of opinions that are Halakhically binding and those that are not binding and were in fact rejected generations earlier. Since the aim is to know the truth, it makes no difference whether a subject does or does not have a practical application. Many subjects — perhaps a majority — do not. The investigation, for example, of the authorship of the various Mishnayot is not always of practical importance, but it is nevertheless of major concern to the Talmud.

The Talmudic Dialectic

The non-utilitarian nature of the Talmud also helps explain another of its characteristics, one that may initially deter the student considerably — the Talmudic dialectic. This dialectic is unique in taking nothing for granted. It is only satisfied with proofs that approach absolute certainty. It constantly tries to sharpen the proofs, cull the evidence, and reach the very essence of the problems, with the greatest possible precision. This dialectic and the high level of exact distinctions it draws are not always appropriate to the practical requirements of everyday life. But where the purpose of the inquiry is truth for its own sake, one must use the most sensitive and acute instruments to analyze the issues, to verify inferences, and to differentiate between cases, so as to arrive at a correct understanding of every matter. Thus a proof that would normally be accepted as self-evident may be rejected in the Talmud because it contains some exceedingly subtle flaw in its argumentation. Only the most logical and convincing argumentation is accepted by the Talmud.

The Talmudic dialectic can be compared to an inquiry in pure science, particularly in the sphere most closely resembling Talmudic study — that of mathematics. Where one wants to know the truth, one cannot rely on inaccurate measurements or on evidence that is not completely certain. One has to prove the matter conclusively point by point. The entire structure is not acceptable until it is completely sound. The authority of the Talmud lies in its use of this rigorous method in its search for truth with regard to the entire Torah — in other words, with regard to all possible subjects in the world, both physical and spiritual.

When studying the Talmud, we must identify with its spirit. We must not approach matters from the point of view of their outward value or practical use, but rather in terms of their intrinsic importance, based on our need to arrive at a true understanding of things.

The Spiritual Foundations of the Talmud

Although the Talmud is a most varied and discursive work, dealing with many aspects of Judaism and life in general (the Talmud contains, among other things, medical cures, commercial advice, tales about individuals, philosophical and historical inquiries), it is nevertheless based on a fundamentally coherent plan — the Mishnah.

The Mishnah is the foundation of the Talmud, and the Talmud is first of all an explanation and expansion of the Mishnah. It is organized around the Mishnah, interpreting and analyzing it. But the Mishnah's relationship to the Talmud is not merely organizational. The Mishnah is not just the text of which the Talmud is a commentary. The Mishnah provides the Talmud with both its conceptual and its factual foundation. All the provisions and laws in the Talmud are laid down in accordance with the Mishnah. Every Halakhah has a source — and this source is generally the Mishnah. In every discussion or argument, there are factors that determine its correctness — and these, too, are found in the Mishnah.

The Talmud accepts the contents of the Mishnah as incontrovertible facts. The Talmud can find interrelationships and connections among the subjects, it can draw attention to problems, it can reconcile apparent contradictions — but it cannot disagree with the Mishnah. The Talmud looks to the Mishnah as the source for the certainty of its findings. The Mishnah serves as the ultimate arbiter of every problem and provides final proof for every assertion or theory.

This special authority and importance is not accorded solely to the Mishnah, but also to the other collections of the statements of the Tannaim — the Tosefta, Baraitot, Sifra,

Principles of Talmudic Inquiry

The basis of the Talmud is, as we have said, the Mishnah. The Talmud approaches the Mishnah and conducts its inquiries and investigations in characteristic ways. If we do not understand the fundamental principles on which these inquiries are based, the Talmud will remain an impenetrable maze.

The first principle of Talmudic inquiry into the Mishnah has already been mentioned: the acceptance of the Mishnah and the teachings of the early Amoraim as incontrovertible and unchallengeable facts. As we have said, this esteem is not attached to the mere opinions of scholars, but rather to facts that were attested and established by divine revelation.

The second principle is the premise that every word of the Mishnah, of the Tannaim and of the Amoraim, was precisely weighed and measured, as was their every action, and hence even the most far-reaching conclusions may be drawn from them. Lessons are drawn not only from the wording of the Mishnah but also from the way it uses language, from expressions that the Mishnah could have used but did not use, and from the order in which things are mentioned. All these elements comprise the basis for the characteristic Talmudic study called דִּיּוּק — "precision." The fundamental idea here is that a true scholar, in the Talmudic sense, is a person embodying general perfection and not just intellectual excellence. Such a scholar expresses and embodies God's word as revealed in the Torah. Therefore his conduct, including his every statement, is marked by absolute precision and divine guidance, and serves as an authoritative source for binding Halakhic decisions: "Even the mundane conversation of scholars deserves study" (*Avodah Zarah* 19b).

The third principle is that there is a common, shared basis to all the opinions expressed in the Mishnah, and that in seeking to understand the words of the Mishnah or of the Amoraim one should always seek elements that reconcile the parties to the dispute and not those that divide them. Many of the most searching and significant questions and discussions in the Talmud derive from the desire to resolve differences. The goal is not to accentuate the division between opinions and principles and thus form separate groups and trends, but rather to uncover the affinities between the various opinions, bringing out what they have in common and what unites them. This principle finds expression in two basic ways. Firstly, in differentiating between the sources, the Talmud seeks to restrict the points at issue between the disputants as narrowly as possible, and when the inquiry reaches the source of their dispute we are made aware that the difference is based on an extremely subtle point that can be understood in two different ways. Secondly, the Talmud seeks to explain that the words of the Mishnah or of the Amoraim do not represent the specific viewpoint of a single scholar, but rather that they are consistent with all the opinions (אַלִּיבָּא דְּכוּלֵי עָלְמָא — "according to everyone" [lit., "the whole world"]). Only in special cases does the Talmud classify opinions according to preexisting, differing viewpoints.

The fourth principle is that everything found in the sources has significant meaning. Points already made are not repeated without reason; nothing is stated which could simply and logically be deduced from known facts; nor are well-known things recorded unless they contain some new or unusual feature. Apparent tautologies prompt queries such as פְּשִׁיטָא — "Surely this is obvious?!" Or מַאי קָמַשְׁמַע לָן — "What is he trying to tell us?" The answer to such questions is usually צְרִיכָא — "It was necessary to teach this...," proving that a seemingly superfluous addition was, in fact, important and necessary. The Talmud explains and defines the cases and the special circumstances requiring just that repetition, or it shows that, were it not for the special emphasis in the phraseology, we would have arrived at different, and erroneous, conclusions.

A similar sort of question frequently arises when the Talmud finds that a difference of opinion between Amoraim seems to be no more than a repetition of the identical difference of opinion between Tannaim. The question לֵימָא כְּתַנָּאֵי — "Must we say that this difference is like that between Tannaim?" — is one which the Talmud does its utmost not to answer affirmatively. It tries to show that the differences of opinion of the Tannaim and of the Amoraim are not the same by pointing out the subtle distinctions between them.

These basic principles, which form a set of axioms of Talmudic inquiry, may be summarized as follows: (1) The Mishnayot and other Tannaitic statements are the source material in the Talmud's search for the truth. (2) The sources are precise and accurate in every detail. (3) One must find what differing views have in common and what unites them. (4) All statements in the sources have independent and significant meaning.

The Structure of the Talmud

Viewed superficially, the Talmud seems to lack inner order. The order of the Talmud is not that commonly found in standard textbooks. The arrangement of the Talmud is not systematic, nor does it follow familiar didactic principles. It does not proceed from the simple to the complex, or from the general to the particular. Nevertheless, the Talmud does have an inner order, different from the kind with which we are familiar. Textbooks deal with specific material, and it is therefore easy to present that material in a clearly defined order. The Talmud, by contrast, deals with an overwhelmingly broad subject — the nature of all things according to the Torah. Therefore its contours are a reflection of life itself. It has no formal external order, but is bound by a strong inner connection between its many diverse subjects.

The structure of the Talmud is associative. The material of the Talmud was memorized and transmitted orally for centuries. Its ideas are joined to each other by inner links, and the order often reflects the needs of memorization. Talmudic discourse shifts from one subject to a related subject, or to a second that brings the first to mind in an associative way.

There are, of course, a number of features characteristic of the way the Talmud is organized. First, it is very rare for the Talmudic discussion of any given subject to begin with a detailed definition of the subject. The vast majority of concepts discussed throughout the Talmud are not defined in the Talmud itself. They have to be known and understood before one begins to study them in the Talmud, and a person who does not succeed somehow in imbibing the atmosphere of Talmudic study and its fundamental concepts will make no headway in understanding the subject.

A second feature of Talmudic organization is that subjects are arranged so as to stimulate interest. Tractates usually open with a somewhat puzzling introduction, taken from the very depths of the subject, and only afterwards does the discussion return to its original starting point.

In general the Talmud starts from the Mishnah (whose structure is based on similar principles), and, after explaining it, the Talmud continues to develop themes connected with it. The sources bearing on these themes are quoted and discussed in detail. Sometimes, however, when a source connected to the central theme is quoted, a detailed discussion of that source ensues. The Talmudic expression for this is גּוּפָא (see entry in section on Talmudic terminology).

Sometimes, too, the Talmud passes from one subject to another in an associative way. After the statement of a certain scholar is cited, a whole series of his statements may be presented. Hence the Talmud may drift away from the first, central topic. Sometimes in discussions of this kind the focus of attention may shift from subject to subject until we find ourselves far from the original starting point. However, not only does the Talmud ultimately return to the original subject, but it is also guided by an inner connection — sometimes very subtle, but often very strong — between all the subjects discussed. This connection is never merely superficial, and the seemingly wayward digressions in fact add substance and interest to the central theme.

Aggadah in the Talmud

It is difficult to define Talmudic Aggadah. Generally, Aggadah is taken to include all parts of the Talmud which are non-normative in nature and which are therefore not subject to any final, definitive ruling. Thus all the theological and philosophical discussions, stories about individuals, ethical guidance and other such subjects are included in a category which is by no means homogeneous — Aggadah.

There is no fundamental distinction between Halakhah and Aggadah. In fact, Halakhah and Aggadah are so intimately intertwined as to blur distinction between them. They resemble each other closely in method and in their ways of thought, and the transition from one to the other is generally so handled in the Talmud as not to emphasize any practical distinction. The subject of the Talmud is reality in its entirety, including both those things regarding which it is possible to define specific obligations, and these are called Halakhah, and those things regarding which it is impossible to define such obligations, and these are called Aggadah.

The Halakhic and Aggadic elements in the Talmud are not contradictory, but complementary. If the basic subject is normative, obliging everyone to act in a certain way, then the basis of the tractate will be Halakhic. If the tractate deals with ethical and spiritual issues, the Aggadic part will be correspondingly greater. The great abundance of Aggadic material in tractates such as *Berakhot* or *Sotah* and its absence in *Eruvin*, for example, can be easily understood in the light of the general nature of the subjects of these tractates. Since the topics discussed in *Berakhot* are general moral and religious issues, extensive space will naturally be given over to Aggadah. The same is true of tractate *Sotah*, because of the religious and moral aspects of marital infidelity. In tractate *Eruvin*, on the other hand, where moral and spiritual considerations do not occupy a central place, Halakhah predominates.

Even if the Aggadic elements are not directly connected with the subject of the tractate (as is frequently the case), there is often an implicit connection between the Aggadic and the Halakhic elements in their relationship with the central theme of that tractate.

The Development of the Talmud

Many of the difficulties encountered by the student of the Talmud are caused by the special structure of the book, which itself derives from the way it came into being. Although we do not possess abundant historical material about the development of the Talmud, from what we do have (for example, the letter of Rav Sherira Gaon) the following picture emerges: Talmudic scholars would gather together at fixed times of the year, or might meet by chance. Their conversations, their teachings and their conduct were committed to memory (and sometimes recorded in writing in brief notes). This material makes up the Talmud. An eminent scholar had to be completely proficient in the Written Torah and equally knowledgeable about the entire Mishnah. Only a scholar who had mastered these two areas was considered sufficiently advanced to enter the deeper area of Torah study — the Talmud.

Talmudic study was thus a higher level, a deeper area of specialization. The foundation was the Mishnah, but the statements of the Mishnah were also the basis for more profound understanding of all Halakhic statements and the Torah in general. Each Mishnah was the source for several standard, almost routine questions, such as מַתְנִיתִין מַאן תַּנָּא or מַנִּי — "Which Tanna is the author of the opinion expressed in our Mishnah?" Sometimes the answers to these preliminary questions were clear to everyone with the necessary knowledge. In such cases both the question and the answer would remain the anonymous collective contribution of all the scholars. Sometimes, however, more complicated problems would arise, but these too became, as it were, common property, as each scholar tried to the best of his ability to contribute something to their solution. Occasionally, problems such as these were left unresolved, occupying scholars for generations. In science, too, one encounters questions that do not yield a satisfactory answer despite generations of effort. There are also cases in the Talmud where, after the combined effort of generations, an individual scholar would succeed in finding a solution to a problem. This solution would then be attributed to him and recorded in the Talmud as his personal discovery.

In this way the Halakhic rulings of various scholars were transmitted. Some of them were stated publicly, so that every scholar knew them and also knew which scholar was their author. There were, however, other statements known only to very few scholars who had themselves received them by tradition. When these later scholars made such statements known in the Academy, their name would be attached to the statement which they transmitted in the name of an earlier scholar.

Thus the Talmud was created from generation to generation. Certain questions, either collective or raised by an individual scholar and cited in his name, together with the answers to them, became part of the treasure-house of knowledge of every scholar. He had to remember the questions raised regarding particular Mishnayot and their answers. These questions and answers and their study in one generation were passed on to the next. Later, other problems would arise and be transmitted to the following generation as the remembered tradition of the previous one.

The Talmud in its present form is the "freezing," as it were, of the Torah of a particular generation. Towards the end of the fourth century C.E., the Babylonian scholar Rav Ashi decided that it was necessary to collect and summarize all the known Halakhah and Aggadah in order to prevent them being forgotten. This final editing of the Talmud, which began under his supervision, was completed during the following century-and-a-half.

All the questions, answers, and discussions of the Sages of Rav Ashi's generation and previous generations were recorded for posterity.

The Talmud is thus the recorded dialogue of generations of scholars. It has all the characteristics of a living dialogue. Freshness, vivid spontaneity, and acute awareness of every subject permeate every argument and discussion. The spirit of life breathes on every single page.

Historical Background:
Life in the Talmudic Period

Most of the issues with which the Talmud deals are abstract, and their significance and concern are not restricted to a particular period or way of life. Nevertheless the Talmud is very closely connected with real life, since the subjects and issues raised in the Talmudic discussion and Halakhic debate frequently derive from specific problems of everyday life. On a more general level, historical events and developments are referred to in the Talmud and provide background to the Talmudic discussion, to the relations between the various personalities, and even to the Halakhic debate. The following sections throw light on certain aspects of the background against which the Talmud was created — those aspects that have a direct connection with the Talmud itself.

During the entire Mishnaic and Talmudic period (approximately 30 B.C.E.–500 C.E.) Eretz Israel was ruled in fact, if not always in name, by the Romans. Roman rule in general, and the problems Roman government and its representatives posed for the Jewish community in particular, provide the political background of the period. From a political-historical point of view the Mishnaic period (c. 30 B.C.E.–200 C.E.) and the Talmudic period (200 C.E.–500 C.E.) coincide with two distinct eras of Roman rule, and can therefore be regarded as two distinct periods.

The Political Background
Eretz Israel

During the Mishnaic period Roman imperial power was at its height. As a rule, the Roman emperors exercised their power vigorously and effectively, and their authority was felt throughout the Empire. Internal public order was well maintained, and the Romans imposed international order as well — the Pax Romana. During most of the period relations between the Jewish community in Eretz Israel and the Romans were bad. Nevertheless, short intervals of tranquillity did provide opportunities for such important events as the building of the magnificent Temple by Herod, the participation of Herod's grandson Agrippa in the life of the people, and the editing of the Mishnah in the days of Rabbi Yehudah HaNasi. Most of the time, however, the Jewish community was in conflict with the Roman overlord and his local representatives. The tense relationship with the House of Herod and the Roman governors of Judea led to the great Jewish revolt, which the Romans crushed, destroying the Second Temple (70 C.E.). A number of other uprisings occurred after the destruction (the "wars" of Quietus and Trajan), culminating in the Bar Kokhba revolt, the failure of which brought ruin upon Judea. The centers of Jewish life and culture were then transferred northward to Galilee.

During the Talmudic period (approximately 200 C.E.–500 C.E.) Roman authority was shaken. The central government of the Empire disintegrated, giving rise to periods of anarchy and wars between rival claimants to the imperial throne, and bringing about economic collapse. Simultaneously, the power of Christianity increased, and by the end of the fourth century it had become the official religion of the Empire. Because of international developments, pressure from the authorities on the Jewish community in Eretz Israel constantly increased. To maintain itself, the government imposed crippling taxes on the population, which undermined the economy (there were instances when the scholars permitted working the land during the Sabbatical Year in order to alleviate the burden of taxation). Local security was adversely affected, and toward the end of the period the Christian minority also exerted pressure, which went beyond tale-bearing and petty persecution and extended to the systematic suppression of Jewish life. The scope of internal Jewish self-government was gradually reduced, and the Jewish community declined in numbers because of emigration to other countries, either to the center of the Roman Empire or to the Persian Empire. These developments brought about a decline in Torah study in Eretz Israel, compelling the scholars to undertake a hasty summary and incomplete editing of the Jerusalem Talmud, with no possibility of completing it. Political pressures and persecution severely weakened the remaining Jewish community. Lacking leadership and central direction they devoted their creative efforts to the area of Aggadah and piyyutim (liturgical poetry).

Babylonia

The beginning of the Amoraic period in Babylonia also coincides with a division between two periods in Babylonian political history. Until this period Persia was ruled by the Parthians, an Iranian people who established a quasi-feudal regime, leaving very broad powers in the hands of the local rulers. The central government scarcely intervened in the lives of the various peoples living in the country. Culturally, the country experienced considerable Hellenistic influence (יְוָנָאֵי — Greek — is the expression used by the Amora, Rav). In 226 C.E., however, the Parthian kingdom was conquered by the Sassanids. Unlike the Parthians, the Sassanids strengthened and promoted the Zoroastrian religion and its priests (מְגוּשִׁים or אַמְגוּשִׁים — "magi"), and strengthened the power of the country's central government. The wars with the Roman Empire, which had subsided at the end of the Parthian period, now flared up again, affecting the border regions. The centers of population moved eastward. At first the Sassanids were rather hostile to the Jews, but with the passage of time good and even cordial relations developed between the leaders of the Jewish community and the Persian government. As a result of the increased centralization of government power, the power of the Jewish Exilarch (the "Resh Galuta," head of the Jewish community) likewise increased.

The relative calm within the kingdom and its stable economic situation both enabled the Jewish community to grow and encouraged immigration of Jews from other countries, mainly from Eretz Israel. Despite friction with the Persian priests (the *habbarim*), the Jewish community developed almost undisturbed.

In the time of Rav Ashi (toward the end of the fourth century C.E.) relations with the Persian government were excellent, enabling the Sages to undertake the great project — the fundamental general editing of the Babylonian Talmud. In the next generation, however, a period less favorable to the Jews began. Decrees, mainly religious restrictions, were enacted against the Jews during the reigns of Jezdegerd II and Peroz (described in our sources as רְשִׁיעָא — "the wicked"), reaching their climax with the ascent of Mazdak. In response, a Jewish revolt broke out at the beginning of the sixth century under the leadership of the Exilarch, Mar Zutra. The final years of this period also reflect a major decline in spiritual creativity, which was limited to the final editing of the Talmud. Only after the Persian kings relaxed their religious extremism was stability restored to the Babylonian Jewish community, bringing about a renewed spiritual renaissance during the period of the Geonim.

Internal Administration
Eretz Israel

The Roman emperors generally did not involve themselves deeply in the internal administration and local affairs of the Jews, nor did their representatives in Eretz Israel, the House of Herod. Later Tannaim, such as Rabbi Yose, draw an idyllic picture of Roman indifference to local affairs and of Jewish self-rule during the Second Temple period. However, as early as Hasmonean times, this picture had ceased to be accurate. The later Hasmonean kings, and certainly the Herodian kings and the Roman governors, deprived the Sanhedrin of most of its authority to decide national issues, and ultimately also of its jurisdiction over capital offences. According to tradition, "forty years before the destruction of the Temple the Sanhedrin was exiled from it and met in the markets" (*Avodah Zarah* 8b). This was in reality a voluntary exile, in which the Sanhedrin relinquished its right to judge capital cases because it lacked the authority to implement its decisions. However, the Rabbinical Courts and the scholars did retain jurisdiction over ritual matters, and also the power of decision in monetary disputes and local affairs.

Since most of the Jewish community was concentrated in towns and villages entirely populated by Jews, the forms of Jewish local administration were still preserved. The affairs of the town were managed by a committee, most probably elected, of the שִׁבְעָה טוֹבֵי הָעִיר — "the seven elders [lit., 'best men'] of the city" — and decisions of especial importance were most likely reached by public voting, "with all the men of the city present" (בְּמַעֲמַד אַנְשֵׁי הָעִיר; see *Megillah* 26a). The local Rabbinical Courts, consisting of three judges, received their authority from the Nasi, the head of the Sanhedrin. They decided all matters of a ritual nature, and Rabbinic scholars were appointed as the leading scholars or spiritual heads of the locality.

After the destruction of the Temple, the Jewish High Court (the Great Sanhedrin) — commonly referred to then as "the Great Council" (בֵּית הַוַּעַד הַגָּדוֹל) since the Sanhedrin had ceased to operate with its full authority — became the recognized center of Jewish life. The head of the Sanhedrin, who was always chosen from among the descendants of Hillel the Elder, was recognized as the head of the Jewish community of Eretz Israel not only by the Jewish community, who gave him the title of Nasi, but also by the Roman authorities, who called him the Ethnarch. The scholars and the head of the Sanhedrin still retained the authority to fix the date of each new month (and thus the dates of the Festivals), to intercalate the years, and to ordain Rabbis (סְמִיכַת זְקֵנִים). Ordination was only recognized when carried out by scholars of Eretz Israel (and, according to an ancient agreement, only with the authorization of the Nasi). The importance of these functions was so great that the Nasi was considered the spiritual leader not only of the Jews in Eretz Israel, but of all Jewry.

Nevertheless, as political pressure on the Jews of Eretz Israel increased, many attempts were made to diminish the status of the Nasi and interfere with the relationship between him and the Jewish Diaspora in Babylonia. In 358 C.E., the head of the Sanhedrin, Hillel II, fixed the Jewish calendar by calculation for all future generations, renouncing the Nasi's right to perform this act and thus his authority throughout the Jewish world. The position of Nasi was abolished early in the fifth century (429 C.E.). In the larger towns Jewish affairs were administered by an official institution, the Boule ("the council," in Greek), which for a certain period was the decisive power in every town.

A turning point in internal administration took place during the time of Rabbi Yehudah

HaNasi (c. 200 C.E.). In his will he divided into two parts the role of Nasi, which had been spiritual, educational, and administrative. The title and the political authority remained in the hands of his descendants until the end of the period of the Nesi'im, but after his death scholars from other families headed the Great Council. As a consequence, the spiritual and cultural power of the heads of the academies greatly increased; from an administrative point of view most of the Nesi'im, with the exception of individuals such as Rabbi Yehudah Nesi'a I and Hillel II, were leaders in name only. Because of the increasing burden of taxation imposed on the community leaders, the members of the Boule, and the extortion of "contributions" and "gifts" of every kind, everyone sought to avoid these communal positions, until in the end they had no importance whatever.

The local administration seems to have been run, on the one hand, by the Rabbinical Court, and, on the other, by "the heads of the synagogues" ("archisynagogos" in Greek). These already existed in the Temple period, but their importance as leaders of the Jewish community increased in the course of time. The weakness of the independent central authority also forced certain leaders to take upon themselves the burden of representing the Jews to the authorities, although they had not been chosen for this role. For example, Rabbi Abbahu of Caesarea was the decisive political personality of his generation, although he had not been formally appointed.

The erosion of the power of the central government and the decline of the Great Council accompanied the general decline of the Jewish community in Eretz Israel.

Babylonia In practice the Jewish community in Babylonia enjoyed extensive internal autonomy for centuries. The decentralized structure of the Parthian kingdom and the lack of interest in internal problems shown by its rulers enabled the Jews to live almost independently. In addition, the Jewish community was largely concentrated in certain areas; in some cities the majority of the inhabitants were Jews, and there were whole regions whose administration was in practice in the hands of Jews.

It is not certain when the special status of the Exilarch was recognized by the authorities. The Exilarch, who was descended from the House of David (a descendant, in fact, of King Jehoiachin), was recognized by the Jews as the heir to "the scepter from Judah" and was entrusted with wide official powers. It would seem that in the Sassanid period his position was already fairly well defined. He was the leader of the Jews of the Persian kingdom and their representative to the authorities, who regarded him as belonging to a princely house. Hence he held a very high position within the Persian court. At various periods he was considered third in the royal hierarchy. He was responsible for the collection of a major portion of the taxes for the government, and he could appoint leaders and judges whose powers included the imposition of corporal, and sometimes capital, punishment. Near the Exilarch's home was a special Rabbinical Court appointed by him to deal in particular with cases involving money and property. He also seems to have had the authority to make certain appointments throughout the country, though most of them were made in consultation with the heads of the great academies. The Exilarchs themselves were referred to in the Talmud by the honorific title מָר — "Sir" — before or after their name, and were steadfastly devoted to Torah. Some of them were, indeed, important scholars in their own right.

In every generation the Exilarch's family contained prominent scholars. In the Tannaitic period Rabbi Natan the Babylonian was the son of the Exilarch, and in the Amoraic period there was the famous Amora, Rabbah bar Avuha, among others. Rabbana Neḥemyah, too, was a member of the Exilarch's family and the grandson of the Amora, Rav, and Rav Naḥman bar Ya'akov was "the son-in-law of the Exilarch." Nevertheless, friction frequently developed between the Exilarch and the leading scholars of the generation, who did not always accept his authority. Despite that friction a well-established structure of relations evolved between the scholars and the Exilarch, reaching its height in the period of the Geonim. The Exilarch's supreme political leadership was recognized by all, and he also received religious respect since he was a scion of the House of David;

however, the leadership in the cities and towns was in the hands of the local scholars, who were mainly appointed by the heads of the great academies.

Appointments to public offices in the Jewish communities, many of which were connected with local government, such as inspection of the markets, allocation of water from the rivers, and supervision of the large irrigation network, were made in part by the Exilarch and his Rabbinical Court and in part by the local scholars. In contrast to Eretz Israel, in Babylonia there seems to have been no official title of "seven elders of the city"; the administration of the city was generally in the hands of one man, sometimes the most prominent local scholar, who was called "master of the place" (מָרָא דְאַתְרָא), or sometimes a lay leader, who would leave Halakhic issues in the hands of a Rabbinical scholar while he dealt with administrative matters.

The Rabbinical Courts seem to have enjoyed the exclusive right to adjudicate matters among Jews, and great care was taken not to involve the courts of the secular authorities (עַרְכָּאוֹת שֶׁל נָכְרִים) except in disputes with non-Jews. In general the heads of the great academies were highly respected by the non-Jewish authorities and sometimes very close relations developed between the scholars and the Persian kings.

Culture and Language
Eretz Israel

Throughout the Talmudic period the language and culture of Eretz Israel were under Greek influence. Even the imposition of direct Roman rule did not materially change the situation. Although the Hasmonean war began as a war against Hellenism, it does not seem to have achieved much change in the relationship with that culture. During the Second Temple period and in Talmudic times the Jews of Egypt were extremely well-versed in all aspects of the general Greek culture. However, the relationship of the Jews of Eretz Israel (with the exception of active assimilationists) toward this culture is not clear. On the one hand, the Jews of Eretz Israel seem to have avoided contact with the general Greek culture, particularly bearing in mind the Rabbinical ban forbidding Jews from studying "Greek wisdom." This ban was not, however, total. Jews, such as the members of the family of the Nasi, who had close connections with the ruling power, were permitted to study Greek philosophy. Nor is it clear what the purpose of the ban was. Some modern scholars maintain that the scholars of Eretz Israel in every generation were well-versed in Greek philosophy and culture, though they refrained from drawing attention to the matter, a hypothesis which is difficult to either prove or refute. What is clear is that in certain areas of life no Greek influence was felt, whereas in others, despite the lack of specific quotations or cross-references, there were many parallels between the two civilizations.

Although the influence of Greek culture in its broadest sense is uncertain, there is no doubt that the Greek language was enormously influential. In the Mishnaic period, and in many places even in the Talmudic period, the language of the common people was probably Hebrew. They spoke and wrote it. Gradually, however, Hebrew was replaced by Aramaic or, as it was called in Eretz Israel, "Syriac" (סוּרְסִית), which was also spoken by many non-Jews and served as the common language of all the inhabitants of Eretz Israel. Rabbi Yehudah HaNasi continued to fight against the use of Aramaic, and said: "Why use Syriac in Eretz Israel? Speak either Hebrew or Greek" (*Bava Kamma* 82b–83a). It would seem, however, that once the center of the Jewish community moved to Galilee, the use of Hebrew as a spoken language radically declined and the use of Aramaic grew. Everybody, including the common people, of course understood a little Hebrew from studying the Bible and other sources, and it is certain that all the Rabbinical scholars knew Hebrew. It is possible that, in areas where large numbers of Jews were concentrated, Hebrew continued to be spoken for many years, even during the period of Muslim rule.

But whatever language the Jews spoke, the influence of Greek was very great. Many words, concepts and definitions, measures, and technical terms were borrowed from Greek. Many of these borrowed words have remained part of the Hebrew language to this day: אֲלַכְסוֹן — "diagonal"; פְּרוֹזְדוֹר — "corridor"; סִינָר — "apron"; סוּדָר — "scarf"; פְּנָס — "lamp," to mention only a few. The number of words borrowed from Greek that appear in the Jerusalem Talmud and in the Aggadic Midrashim of Eretz Israel is very great, running into many hundreds. By contrast, the number of words borrowed from Latin is very small, and some of these appear not in their original Latin form but in a Greek variant. It should also be remembered that the translations of the Torah into Greek, both the Septuagint and the later translations by Aquila and Symmachus, helped strengthen the relationship between the Greek language and the world of Judaism. In the Mishnaic period there were scholars who permitted the use of Torah scrolls written in Greek. On this the Rabbis of Eretz Israel commented: Different languages are good for different things — Hebrew for speech, Aramaic for lamentation, Greek for song, Latin for military matters.

Babylonia

Since most of the Jews in the Persian Empire lived in the geographical region of Babylonia, between the Tigris and Euphrates Rivers, their cultural and linguistic contacts were mainly with its Babylonian inhabitants and only to a limited extent with the Persians. The language spoken in Babylonia was a dialect of Aramaic very close to that spoken by the Jews. Even though there were minor differences of accent and dialect, the basic language spoken by Jews and non-Jews alike was the same Aramaic. In Babylonia, Hebrew was the language of scholars only — the common people did not understand it. As for Persian, it would seem that cultural and linguistic contact between Jews and Persians was superficial. It seems clear from several sources that a large majority of the Jews did not understand Persian at all, and if they absorbed a few Persian words over hundreds of years of contact, these generally had very limited application. We should also bear in mind that the Persians themselves used Aramaic as their written language, so that they were more influenced by Aramaic than Aramaic was by them. The Persian masters of Babylonia ruled the country in a feudal manner and mainly from a distance, and they had only slight contact with the local inhabitants. Jewish contact with Babylonian culture was also very limited. Babylonian influence can be detected in the spheres of astronomy, astrology, popular remedies, and superstitions. But in general it would seem that the scholars did their best to avoid cultural contact with Babylonian sages, although Shmuel, for example, did have a friend, Ablat, who was one of them.

With regard to the Persians and their religion, we find that in general the Rabbis avoided debates with them, and only rarely is it possible to find references, sometimes critical, to the dualistic religion of the Persians and other related matters. From time to time the Persian priestly sect did indeed interfere with the lives of the Jews. But apart from periods of religious persecution, even this contact was limited and unimportant. The Jewish scholars possessed superficial knowledge of Babylonian and Persian customs, and of the customs and beliefs of those Arabian tribes which reached certain regions of Babylonia — but in no area can their influence be detected in any substantial way.

The Economy

In the Mishnaic and Talmudic periods, both in Eretz Israel and in Babylonia, the Jewish economy was based primarily on agriculture. The wage earners were mainly farmers, whether estate owners, tenant farmers or agricultural workers. The wealthy Jews, especially in Eretz Israel but also in Babylonia, were generally owners of great estates, from which they derived their wealth. In the eyes of the Halakhah the only substantial property was land.

Jews were also found among the artisans, and many scholars worked as carpenters, cobblers, blacksmiths, potters, and tailors — for example, Rabbi Yoḥanan HaSandlar, "the cobbler"; Rabbi Yitzḥak Nappaḥa, "the smith." There were also many weavers (though for some reason this occupation was considered of lower standing), tanners, builders, and architects. Other occupations were also represented, such as goldsmiths and silversmiths, gem piercers, doctors, bloodletters (אוּמָּנִים — "surgeons"), and surveyors.

We find Jewish hunters and fishermen both in Eretz Israel and outside it, as well as ass drivers, camel drivers, and sailors.

There were also some Jews whose occupation was of a more intellectual and spiritual nature. There were many teachers, of whom a majority were also scribes. We know, too, of a "factory" for tefillin and mezuzot in Babylonia. The scribes in the Rabbinical Courts also wrote official documents. Other Jews were employed as beadles in the synagogues, and elsewhere as officials and clerks.

Most of the trade in which Jews were employed seems to have been local and on a small scale. There were many peddlers selling jewelry and spices in the villages. In every community there was, as a rule, a grocer selling flour, oil, and wine. In larger centers there were butchers, who also served as ritual slaughterers, and bakers. Most towns had money changers.

Very few Jews were employed in wholesale trade, although there were already great Jewish merchants in ancient times who traded with distant lands. It seems that the Jews maintained extensive commercial contacts with remote countries in Asia and Africa. Important merchants were involved in the international silk trade with China, and Babylonian Jews apparently conducted regular trade with India — in spices, various fruits, and iron. A number of Babylonian scholars were themselves connected with this commerce, and we find scholars who had business dealings and partnerships in very remote places. In the town of Meḥoza a significant section of the wealthy Jewish community was involved in major commercial dealings. In general, however, until the period of the Geonim the majority of the Jewish population, even in Babylonia, was employed in agriculture and small trade. Only in later generations did the Jewish community become widely involved in commerce.

Education and Study

According to a tradition cited in the Talmud (*Bava Batra* 21a), in the Second Temple period the Jewish people lacked an organized education system for many generations. Even though in all likelihood most of the the population knew how to read and write, they did not have structured educational institutions everywhere at every level. However, the Talmud ascribes the organization of a comprehensive general education system to the High Priest Yehoshua ben Gamla, in the generation preceding the destruction of the Second Temple. This education system, mainly in the large centers of population, was maintained for centuries. The leaders of every community would ensure that their town had a schoolteacher (מַקְרֵי דַּרְדְּקֵי) at least for primary studies. Apparently, the parents and not the community paid the salary of the teacher, and in practice whoever wanted to become a teacher could do so. The teachers were nevertheless under the supervision of the Rabbinical Court or of the scholars of the community, with regard to their professional competence and to the number of pupils and their age. More than one story is told in the Talmud of a schoolteacher who was removed from his position for various reasons (erroneous teaching, excessive use of corporal punishment, etc.).

Sometimes the children were taught in the teacher's home, but more often in the synagogue, where special rooms were set aside for this purpose. Only boys were sent to school, but in certain places some girls, at least, received a basic education at home from private teachers. The size of a normal class was twenty-five children, and if there were more the teacher was provided with an assistant (רֵישׁ דּוּכָנָא — lit., "superintendent of the platform") until the size of the class reached forty. Studies started at the age of five or six. Sometimes even younger children were sent to school to spend time in class and to absorb something by listening to the lessons.

The basic text studied at the elementary level was the Bible. The children learned to read, understand, and memorize chapters of the Bible, mainly from the Torah (the Five Books of Moses). It was also customary for the children to memorize a verse each day (hence the expression in the Talmud [*Ḥagigah* 15a] used by Rabbis to children: פְּסוֹק לִי

פְּסוּקֶךְ — "Recite your verse to me!"). Other subjects taught in school were writing, blessings, and prayers. Although not all the children continued their studies, it is probable that the ability to read and write was universal among men. The Talmud describes a Jew who did not know how to write as a תִּינוֹק שֶׁנִּשְׁבָּה בֵּין הַנָּכְרִים — "a child taken into captivity by non-Jews." Knowledge of the Bible was widespread and everyone was expected at least to know how to read it. The sarcastic expression זִיל קְרֵי בֵּי רַב — "Go, read [study the Bible], at the Rabbi's house!" — refers to the most elementary thing all Jewish men were expected to know. This elementary period of study lasted about five years, and afterwards the majority of children do not seem to have continued to study in any organized way. Care was taken, however, to ensure that every child received at least this minimal level of education.

The next stage of education was, as outlined in tractate *Avot,* the study of the Mishnah. This stage of study was not available to all, and only those children who were outstandingly gifted and supported by others, or whose parents were especially interested, continued with it. The study of Mishnah was based on memorizing all or part of the six orders of the Mishnah, and this study also lasted about five years. Boys of about fifteen who displayed special talent or desire would then continue their studies at the Academy or attend the lectures of Rabbis at various yeshivot. This group of students of Gemara was small and in effect comprised the nucleus of the תַּלְמִידִים — the disciples of the scholars who continued their studies indefinitely. Some studied until they married and established a home, others continued to study in various ways all their life, combining their studies with their regular occupation. We can estimate the proportion of pupils at the various levels from the following statement: "A thousand enter to study the Bible, a hundred to study Mishnah, ten to study Gemara, and one to teach" — one out of a thousand reaches the level of a scholar worthy to teach others.

The Synagogue

In the Second Temple period there were already synagogues both in Eretz Israel and outside it, wherever there was a Jewish community. In large communities there were a number of synagogues. Some synagogues were attended by members of a particular profession, others by people who shared a common country of origin. Some of the synagogues were originally private houses, but as a rule they were public buildings, constructed, maintained, and owned by the community.

The synagogue served not only as a place for communal prayer but also as a meeting-place where community needs were discussed. It also usually served as a school for children and occasionally for adults as well.

In many small towns the synagogue was built well outside the town boundary, perhaps in order to involve several villages in the joint effort of building it. In some cases it contained living quarters for the ḥazan (beadle). These synagogues far from the town did not usually have a fixed אֲרוֹן קוֹדֶשׁ — "holy ark" — but kept one room locked in which they placed the Torah scrolls. From this room they would bring out the ark for the Torah reading.

The Torah reading in the synagogue was not only a ceremonial matter but also served a practical educational purpose. For many generations it was customary to translate the weekly portion as it was recited aloud, generally verse by verse, into Aramaic. Usually the translators used a well-known Aramaic translation of the Torah, such as that of Onkelos. In Eretz Israel at the end of the Amoraic period the translators often added explanations and Aggadic material, and these served as the basis for the Jerusalem Targum (Translation) of the Torah, erroneously called תַּרְגוּם יוֹנָתָן — "Targum Yonatan."

In the synagogues the scholars would regularly give sermons. Sometimes scholars would speak on Friday evenings, but the regular time for delivering public discourses was on Sabbath afternoons, and the whole congregation, including the women, would assemble in the synagogue and listen. This discourse was called the סִידְרָא — *sidra,* the regular weekly discourse — and it could touch upon various subjects. Some Rabbis would send a young scholar to deliver a preliminary sermon, usually on an Aggadic theme, until the whole congregation had assembled to listen to the main lecture by the town's Rabbi.

The main subject of the *sidra* was a Halakhic matter which the Rabbi would explain in detail. In order to capture the interest of the congregation he would begin with an Aggadic theme taken from the subject matter of that week's Torah reading. These introductions and parts of the Aggadic material used in the sermons on these occasions provided the material from which the Aggadic Midrashim were later compiled. The Halakhic themes of the *sidra* were of various kinds, chosen by the scholar. However, about a month before each of the Pilgrim Festivals and the High Holy Days, they made it a point to begin teaching about them and explaining their themes and special laws.

The *sidra* was usually delivered in the following manner: The scholar would sit on a raised platform and quietly give a summary of what he wanted to say to a young man, his מְתוּרְגְּמָן — "translator" or "interpreter" (in Aramaic, אָמוֹרָא — "Amora," "speaker"). The latter would repeat the scholar's words aloud, and expand them in a manner understood by the congregation. If a large congregation was present, more than one interpreter was sometimes chosen.

Something like the *sidra,* but on a far more imposing scale, was the Festival sermon in Babylonia. This was called פִּירְקָא — *pirka,* "the periodic session." It was delivered at a great public ceremony, frequently attended by the Exilarch and the most prominent scholars. Sometimes, scholars of the Exilarch's house were given the honor of delivering such a sermon. They would receive the basic themes for the sermon from the great scholars of the generation.

Since the *sidra* and *pirka* were intended for the general public, the scholars limited themselves to Halakhic matters of a clear, incontrovertible nature. There are various Halakhot referred to as הֲלָכָה וְאֵין מוֹרִין כֵּן — "Halakhah, but we do not rule this way [publicly]" — even though scholars would occasionally be willing to give such a ruling on an individual question. Generally it was considered discourteous to interrupt the scholar during these public lectures by asking questions, and if there were scholars who had comments or criticisms they would express them afterwards in a more private setting.

The synagogue, as mentioned above, was used for public prayer and as a meeting-place where community needs were discussed. Although public prayer also took place in many Batei Midrash, the Bet Midrash served mainly as a fixed place for the study of Torah, in particular the study of Talmud. The Bet Midrash, sometimes called בֵּי רַבָּנָן — "the house of the scholars" — was where scholars spent their time in study, either alone or, as was customary, in small groups. These studies which private individuals attended were not part of the official, regular curriculum; the official order of studies in the Bet Midrash was more structured and formal, and remained substantially unchanged for many generations in Eretz Israel and Babylonia.

Initially, the order of study in the Bet Midrash was more formal in Eretz Israel than in Babylonia. The great academies, in particular the בֵּית הַוַּעַד, which was the appointed place for meetings of the Sanhedrin or its equivalent, served as general teaching institutions, and to a considerable degree their curriculum was designed to arrive at Halakhic conclusions binding on everyone. In later generations the Batei Midrash of the great Babylonian academies also became more formal, and we have several descriptions of the curriculum of the Babylonian academies in the period of the Geonim, which give us a general idea how the Batei Midrash were organized in previous generations.

At the front of the hall, on a chair or on cushions, sat the head of the yeshivah. Opposite him, in rows, sat the students. Generally everyone had a fixed place. In the front

The Bet Midrash (Torah Academy)

row would sit the great scholars, including distinguished students of the head of the yeshivah, who sometimes also became his colleagues. Less important students occupied the other rows. As a student advanced in his studies, he would be brought closer to the head of the yeshivah.

The standard procedure of teaching was as follows: A particular tractate was studied, for which everyone had prepared in advance. Sometimes the head of the yeshivah would himself begin the explanation of the Mishnah, and sometimes he would permit one of the more important students to begin the Mishnah, and he himself would add explanations as the need arose. When necessary they would invite one of the תַּנָּאִים — "Tannaim," the men who knew many Baraitot by heart — to provide quotations from one of the Baraitot relating to the subject, and the head of the yeshivah would add explanations and commentary where needed. Although this was the standard form of teaching, it seems that only rarely were the studies conducted in precisely this way. Usually the students would raise a series of questions before the assembled gathering, questions of interpretation, Halakhic questions, difficulties in various sources, or other problems of logical analysis. These questions would be answered by the head of the yeshivah, but every one of the students had the right to take part in the debate, to raise objections, and answer them, according to his ability. Usually the discussions continued until the problem was clarified or until the assembled scholars decided that they did not have sufficient information to solve it. Questions such as these were sometimes passed from one yeshivah to another, and sometimes from Babylonia to Eretz Israel and back.

Since the purpose of study in the Bet Midrash was mainly to discuss and solve questions and problems as they were raised, it was not really the place for an individual to reflect upon a particular problem and fully clarify it. Whoever wanted to probe more deeply into a single subject would leave the Bet Midrash and delve into that subject. He would then return and pursue the subject alone or with the help of colleagues.

This was the fixed pattern of study throughout the year. But usually only a limited number of students participated all year long. These were young people with means of their own or whose parents provided for their needs, adults of means who devoted themselves to their studies, and also the permanent staff of the yeshivot. There was, however, a tendency — more pronounced and better organized in Babylonia — for the studies to be most concentrated and best-attended during the יַרְחֵי כַלָּה — "the months of the general assembly." These general assemblies, known themselves by the name יַרְחֵי כַלָּה, took place during two months of the year, Adar and Elul, when agricultural work was less pressing and many people could find time for study. Each time the students gathered for the יַרְחֵי כַלָּה, many scholars would convene in the central yeshivah. They would occupy themselves with one tractate, or part of it, which everyone had been preparing during the previous six months.

During the יַרְחֵי כַלָּה the central educational events in the yeshivah were the lectures given by the leading scholar, who would go through the tractate, beginning with the Mishnah. He would explain and comment on the text, and discuss the main topics with the resident scholars and the guests. This presentation by the head of the yeshivah was very concentrated. In order to ensure that everyone understood him, the students were required to prepare in advance. Afterwards they would also review his words under the supervision of scholars who acted as deputies of the head of the yeshivah and were called רֹאשׁ לִבְנֵי כַלָּה or רֹאשׁ כַלָּה — "the head(s) of the assembly." In large yeshivot this function would be carried out simultaneously by several scholars, depending on the size of the gathering. The רֹאשׁ כַלָּה would also expound on the מַסֶּכְתָּא דְּכַלָּה, the tractate that had been chosen for study on that occasion, but he would do so in a less formal manner than the head of the yeshivah. His role was that of a teacher on an advanced level rather than a profound scholar offering his own specialized, original explanations of the Torah. The רֹאשׁ כַלָּה was usually a younger man, and he would often become the head of the yeshivah after the head of the yeshivah died. At the end of יְמֵי כַלָּה, "the days of the assembly," the head of the yeshivah would decide which tractate would be studied during the next period, and he would מְגַלֶּה אֶת הַמַּסֶּכֶת — "reveal the tractate" — to the students, i.e., explain the basic principles and subjects of the tractate to be studied. At the end of the יַרְחֵי כַּלָּה most of the students would return to their homes to study the tractate by themselves or with partners, according to the principles that the head of the yeshivah had "revealed."

Despite their fixed pattern, the studies in the Bet Midrash were very open, as the Talmud itself reveals. Everyone was permitted to ask questions and raise objections, although there were yeshivah heads who acted on the principle of לִזְרוֹק מָרָה בַּתַּלְמִידִים — "rebuking the pupils" — and dealt sternly with those whose questions were not pertinent to the subject. Nevertheless, there was a general principle that all discussions in the Bet Midrash were secret. No one was allowed to publicize remarks that had been made in the course of the discussions. Sometimes harsh words or sharp expressions were used, and occasionally the discussions involved matters of a private nature, the actual problems of individual families and even political issues. The knowledge that what was said within the Bet Midrash would not be mentioned outside gave the students greater freedom to express their opinions in every sphere. The story is told of a student who revealed something that had been said in the Bet Midrash twenty-two years earlier, and as a punishment was no longer permitted to take part in any discussions.

These fixed arrangements applied mainly to the great central yeshivot; the yeshivot of scholars who did not gather such a large audience around them were less formal, and study there more closely resembled that of the יַרְחֵי כַּלָּה.

The Rabbinical Courts

The Torah scholars were generally also judges in their communities. They decided cases of civil law (דִּינֵי מָמוֹנוֹת), served as arbitrators in private suits, and were regarded as authorities in laws governing ritual matters (דִּינֵי אִיסּוּר וְהֶיתֵּר). People would often go to the Bet Midrash to raise questions that had been asked in the courts, and sometimes a judge would ask the Bet Midrash a question he had been unable to answer satisfactorily, and the matter would be discussed and decided there.

In Eretz Israel, the Rabbinical Courts consisted of three, twenty-three, or seventy-one judges. There were special procedural arrangements governing the courts of twenty-three judges (the Small Sanhedrin) and of seventy-one judges (the Great Sanhedrin). The members of both Sanhedrins would sit in a semicircle at the center of which sat the president of the court (the Nasi), or his deputy (the Av Bet Din), and the other judges sat around him in a fixed order. At a later period the internal hierarchy was very clearly defined, and we find people signing letters indicating their place in the row — "the fourth," for example, or "the fifth." The sons of the scholars would sit in a row facing the audience in front of the Bet Din. These places were allocated as a mark of respect only, and did not reflect specific scholastic attainment. Facing the judges were three rows of twenty-three seats, and these rows would be occupied by scholars according to a fixed order. If a member was absent, his place would be taken by the scholar immediately below him in rank. These fixed arrangements applied to the Sanhedrin, but were also customary in other Rabbinical Courts, even in Babylonia.

The sessions of the Bet Din were public; all the students would be present and would listen to the judges' discussions. The students had the right, and in some cases even the duty, to express their opinions whenever they felt the need to make an observation or ask a question. This participation was one of the most important ways of studying Torah. Sometimes a session of the Bet Din was transformed into a miniature Bet Midrash, with the main legal themes being the subject of discussion between the scholars and their students.

The scribes sat at the side of the court. In the Small Sanhedrin they had the official task of recording the opinions of the scholars, whereas in the other Rabbinical Courts they would write documents and record the formal decisions of the court. In the

Rabbinical Courts there were also special officers (חַזָּנִים) whose task it was to execute the decisions of the court, applying corporal punishment in cases that carried this penalty. The Amora, Rav, would jokingly say to his attendants before leaving for the Bet Din: "Give me the tools of my trade — the stick and the lash [to flog the transgressors], the sandal [for the ḥalitzah ceremony] and the shofar [for excommunication]." (*Sanhedrin* 7b.)

In addition to the official Rabbinical Courts of recognized scholars, there were other courts of arbitration composed of laymen, where these procedures were not followed. One thing, however, was common to all the courts — the judges did not receive payment for their work. In rare cases judges received an attendance fee to compensate them for the time spent away from their regular work. The only judges who received a salary were those attached to the Temple and to the Great Council in Yavneh, but they worked full-time as judges. However, these cases were exceptional. In the Mishnaic and Talmudic period all Rabbinical functions of elucidating and determining the law were carried out on a voluntary basis.

The Scholars and Their Disciples

During the period of the Mishnah and the Talmud scholars represented a special social stratum, an elite empowered to make the most important decisions in every area of life. This scholarly aristocracy was open to talented outsiders, although it occasionally expressed the desire for exclusivity — as evidenced by the saying that it is a fine and praiseworthy thing for a scholar to marry the daughter of another scholar. But gifted men rose to greatness by virtue of their personal qualities, and lineage counted for little in this respect. Although we do find families in which both the father and the son were well-known scholars, and sometimes there were three generations of exceptional men in a family, in general the leading authorities in each generation were individuals who had risen on their own merit.

The scholars stood out from the mass of the people, and in Babylonia scholars were distinguished by their special clothing. Scholars and their students also received various benefits, such as exemption from certain taxes. Basically, however, they lived among the people. Significantly, most of the scholars did not make their living from their knowledge of Torah but, like the rest of the community, worked in agriculture, at a craft, or in trade. Some scholars were wealthy, like Rabbi Elazar ben Azaryah and members of the House of the Nasi, but the majority belonged to the middle classes, and some were poor. For most of their lives the scholars could only study Torah when they were free from their other work. Only those who inherited or acquired the means, or young men supported by their fathers, could devote most of their time to the study of Torah.

In the first stage of their studies the young men would be taught by a single distinguished scholar. From him they would receive both גְּמָרָא — "gemara," the oral traditions on the Mishnah and Baraitot — and סְבָרָא — *sevara*, analytical explanation and commentary on these traditions. In Eretz Israel it was generally customary for a student to study under one particular scholar for years, actually receiving most of his Torah education from him. Both in their personal relations and also in the eyes of the Halakhah such students forged a very deep bond with their teacher, a relationship of great love and profound respect. The relationship between teacher and student was held to be even deeper and more important than that between father and son. In Babylonia such close relationships were not so common, and students moved more easily from one teacher to another. They also learned Torah from other students by studying together. Even where the bond between student and teacher was very strong, most of the students felt the need to listen to the Torah instruction of another scholar, either regularly or when the opportunity arose. This was not done in the elementary stages of learning, but rather after the student had reached advanced levels, and in order to deepen סְבָרָא — "proficiency in logical argument and analysis."

In Babylonia a student who had studied for some years was called צוּרְבָא מֵרַבָּנָן — "a young man among the scholars"; his fellow townspeople would treat him with respect, but it was very unusual for him to receive an official or permanent appointment. At this stage in their education some of the students would go to other scholars to hear new opinions and theories. Conversely, in some cases a student לִסְבָרֵיהּ לֹא הָיָה צָרִיךְ וְלִגְמָרֵיהּ הָיָה צָרִיךְ — "did not need the teacher's logical acumen, but did need the teacher's knowledge of the oral traditions" (see *Sanhedrin* 36b). After a young scholar had held the title צוּרְבָא מֵרַבָּנָן for some time, he could be considered a full member of the Rabbinical fraternity, חַד מֵרַבָּנָן — "one of the Rabbis" — or הַהוּא מֵרַבָּנָן — "that Rabbi."

During their studies, generally away from home, the visiting students and scholars lived in lodging houses. Landlords apparently supported the lodgers to some extent, though most landlords received payment for the accommodation. In only a few places were buildings specially set aside for students and visitors. The local population would generally give support, particularly to needy students, and the head of the yeshivah would sometimes sponsor them himself, either from his own resources or with the help of the community. In the great, established yeshivot, buildings were set aside for use as the Bet Midrash, and charitable trusts existed to provide funds for the students, in some cases substantial amounts. This system was more established in the great yeshivot, which were major Torah centers, where large sums were contributed to support the permanent staff of teachers, the רָאשֵׁי כַלָּה — "heads of the assembly" — and others like them, and to maintain the head of the yeshivah in a fitting manner. In Babylonia, particularly during the period of the Geonim but apparently also much earlier, the great yeshivot had special "spheres of influence" and received tax revenues, and the local taxes levied on the Jews were transferred to the yeshivot.

The regular course of studies in the yeshivot lasted a number of years. In Babylonia it was customary for students to marry and then study Torah. In Eretz Israel, however, where people generally married later, it was more common for the students to study before marriage.

In Eretz Israel, especially in the period of the Amoraim, Rabbinical ordination was conferred upon a select minority of scholars. Under special circumstances, however, the heads of the yeshivot would decide to bestow the title רַבִּי — "Rabbi" — upon worthy pupils. In the Tannaitic period the authority rested with the Rabbi of each Bet Midrash to ordain his pupils as Rabbis; for this purpose he would co-opt two other scholars to act with him. In the period of the Amoraim it was decided that the official authorization of ordination would be granted by the Nasi alone, in order to enhance the status of the Princely House, which the scholars were anxious to strengthen. As a result scholars worthy of ordination sometimes had to wait a long time before they were ordained. The ordination of an important scholar was a notable occasion, and there are even references in our sources to honorific poems written on such occasions. In the period of the Amoraim an unordained scholar in Eretz Israel was called a חָבֵר — "an associate" — and only one who was ordained was called a חָכָם — "a scholar." Since there was no official ordination in Babylonia, there does not seem to have been any special ceremony or specific time when the title רַב — "Teacher" - was bestowed upon a deserving scholar; the matter was handled in a less formal way, and it is possible that they were not overly concerned about it.

In Eretz Israel, because of the connection with the Sanhedrin, the appointment system was complex. After their ordination some scholars were also admitted to the Sanhedrin at a certain rank. The highest rank was that of scholars who sat on the committee that dealt with the intercalation of the year (בֵּית דִּין שֶׁל שִׁבְעָה — "the Bet Din of seven"), to which only the most eminent scholars were admitted. While the Nasi from Bet Hillel was still the head of the Sanhedrin, his colleagues were the Av Bet Din, who was his deputy, and the third in this hierarchy, the Ḥakham. After the title "Nasi" had taken on political rather than Halakhic significance, the Av Bet Din became the head of the Sanhedrin or the head of the Great Council, and the position of Ḥakham remained vacant.

The status of the head of the yeshivah was the highest of all official appointments anywhere. Heads of the yeshivah were generally named at the initiative of the Nasi, or in Babylonia by the Exilarch, or at least with their approval. Because of the special importance of this post, as early as the Talmudic period when a person was elevated to the position of head of the yeshivah, he was described as מָלַךְ — "he became king." To a considerable degree the various generations of scholars are distinguished chronologically by the "reigns" of the holders of this title. A saying based on the Talmud (*Gittin* 62a) puts it in this way: מַאן מַלְכֵי? רַבָּנָן — "Who are the kings? The scholars."

Jewish Communities

Eretz Israel

אוּשָׁא   *Usha*. A town in Galilee; the seat of the Sanhedrin for a generation (c. 140 C.E.). After the Bar Kokhba revolt (132-135 C.E.), when the Jewish community in Eretz Israel was almost completely destroyed, those scholars who survived the revolt began to congregate in Usha, where the Nasi of the Sanhedrin, Rabban Shimon ben Gamliel II, lived. Around him gathered the surviving students of Rabbi Akiva. Although they were scattered in various places, mainly in Galilee, they accepted Usha as the center of Torah study and as the seat of the Sanhedrin. In Usha the scholars of that generation instituted many important enactments, called תַּקָּנוֹת אוּשָׁא — "the Usha enactments." From there, for what seems to have been a short period, the Sanhedrin moved to Shefar'am.

בֵּית שְׁעָרִים   *Bet She'arim*. A small town in Galilee; seat of the Sanhedrin for most of the life of Rabbi Yehudah HaNasi. He apparently did most of the editing of the Mishnah in Bet She'arim. Toward the end of his life he moved to the town of Tzipori (see צִיפּוֹרִי) for health reasons, but he was buried in Bet She'arim. From that time onwards the cemetery there assumed special importance, and many inhabitants of Eretz Israel and the Diaspora were brought there to be buried near his tomb.

בְּנֵי בְרַק   *Bene Berak*. A small town in Judea; apparently the hometown of Rabbi Akiva, and the seat of his yeshivah.

גָּלִיל   *Galilee*. During the Second Temple period Galilee was cut off from the centers of Jewish culture, which were in Judea, and the inhabitants of Galilee were reputed to be ignorant of Torah learning and uncouth. Galilee was backward because it was separated from Judea by רְצוּעָה שֶׁל כּוּתִים — "the area of Samaritan settlement" (see entry) — which interfered with

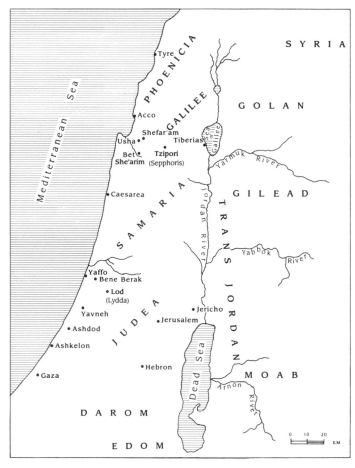

Eretz Israel in the Period of the Mishnah and Talmud

25

regular contact with the South. Only after the destruction of the Temple did the importance of the community in Galilee begin to increase, and following the destruction of Betar and the complete ruin of Judea it became a spiritual center of the first magnitude. In fact, from then until the completion of the Jerusalem Talmud (395 C.E.), Galilee was the center of Jewish culture in Eretz Israel. Typographically, it was divided into two main areas: Lower Galilee, whose northern boundary roughly corresponded with a line drawn between Lake Kinneret and the Mediterranean Sea; and Upper Galilee, to the north.

דָּרוֹם *Darom (South).* The title by which the scholars of Galilee referred to Judea, particularly after the destruction of Betar, when Lod was the main Torah center in Judea. This term was commonly used earlier as well, but then it was used to refer to Southern Judea.

טְבֶרְיָה *Tiberias.* A town on the shore of Lake Kinneret (the Sea of Galilee) founded by Herod Antipas (c. 18 C.E.). It was apparently founded on the site of earlier settlements, and according to some opinions in the Talmud (*Megillah* 6a) this was the site of the Biblical city Rakkat. At the outset Tiberias was a town of mixed Jewish and gentile population. The Jewish population was not distinguished for its Torah scholarship. However, after the destruction of the Temple important Torah scholars, such as Ben Azzai and Rabbi Meir, lived there. Its period of greatness came when the Sanhedrin moved there (c. 235 C.E.) and it became the seat of the בֵּית הַוַּעַד הַגָּדוֹל — "the Great Council" — presided over by Rabbi Yehudah Nesi'a I. After him Rabbi Yoḥanan became its leading spiritual figure, and headed the yeshivah there. From that time Tiberias was the Torah center of Eretz Israel. Most of the disciples of Rabbi Yoḥanan, particularly those who immigrated from Babylonia, lived there, and continued their studies. Resh Lakish lived in Tiberias, as did Rabbi Elazar ben Pedat, Rabbi Ammi, Rabbi Yirmeyah and Rabbi Yonah. It is likely that most of the Jerusalem Talmud was edited there. After the Talmudic period, too, Tiberias remained an important creative religious and spiritual center, and many of the Aggadic Midrashim were composed there, as were many piyyutim (liturgical poems). During the post-Talmudic period the inhabitants of Tiberias were renowned as experts in Hebrew grammar. Indeed, the system of Hebrew vocalization used today is called נִיקוּד טְבֶרְיָנִי — "Tiberian vocalization" — because it was formulated and established there.

יַבְנֶה *Yavneh.* A town in Judea. After the destruction of the Temple it became an important Torah center, and the seat of the Sanhedrin. It seems that Yavneh had been a center of Torah learning even before the Temple was destroyed, but it attained great prominence only after the destruction of the Temple, when Rabban Yoḥanan ben Zakkai reestablished the Sanhedrin there. For a while Yavneh was the spiritual center of the entire Jewish population in Eretz Israel. The Yavneh Yeshivah, כֶּרֶם בְּיַבְנֶה, initially headed by Rabban Yoḥanan ben Zakkai, and later by Rabban Gamliel II (of Yavneh), attracted many of the greatest scholars of that time. At Yavneh many regulations were enacted to rebuild Jewish religious and spiritual life after the destruction of the Temple. Yavneh remained an important center until the time of the Bar Kokhba revolt.

יְהוּדָה *Judea.* The main center of Jewish settlement in Eretz Israel during the Second Temple period, and it continued to be that until the destruction of Betar. During this period most centers of Jewish culture were in Judea, and its inhabitants were famed for their knowledge of Torah and their pure Hebrew. The religious customs of Judea were different from those of Jerusalem, reflecting an independent tradition.

יְרוּשָׁלַיִם *Jerusalem.* The religious and spiritual center of the Jewish people from the time of King David. During the Second Temple period the Great Sanhedrin conducted its proceedings in the Temple, in the Chamber of Hewn Stone (לִשְׁכַּת הַגָּזִית), and was the supreme religious authority of its time. From a cultural and Halakhic point of view Jerusalem was unique, set apart from other places not only by its holiness and the special laws that applied to it, but also in other ways. For example, the people spoke a special Hebrew dialect in Jerusalem, and sections of the Mishnah reflect this dialect. It seems that a small Jewish community continued to live in Jerusalem after the destruction of the Temple, until the city was destroyed in the time of Hadrian; it was later rebuilt as a gentile city to which Jews were forbidden entry.

לוֹד *Lod (Lydda).* One of the oldest towns in Judea. Lod grew in importance toward the end of the Second Temple period, and served as an important cultural center for many generations after the destruction of the Temple. Some of the greatest Tannaim lived there, among them Rabbi Eliezer the Great (ben Hyrcanus), Rabbi Tarfon, and others. Several important enactments were instituted in the "upper chamber of the house of Nitza" in Lod. After the Bar Kokhba revolt the town remained an important Torah center, becoming the center of חַכְמֵי דָרוֹם — "the scholars of the South." Among the great Amoraim who lived there were Rabbi Yehoshua ben Levi, Rabbi Simlai, Rabbi Yitzḥak bar Naḥmani, Rabbi Shimon ben Pazzi, Rabbi Yehudah his son, and Rabbi Aḥa.

צִיפּוֹרִי *Tzipori (Sepphoris).* A large town in Upper Galilee, and the perennial rival of Tiberias for recognition as the religious capital of Galilee. During the Second Temple period it already held a special place among the towns of Galilee because of its large and learned Jewish community. Among the Tannaim who lived there were Rabbi Yoḥanan ben Nuri, Rabbi Ḥalafta and his famous son Rabbi Yose. Rabbi Yehudah HaNasi moved to Tzipori toward the end of his life, and it was the seat of the Sanhedrin for about a generation. Rabbi Yehudah HaNasi's leading disciples lived in Tzipori — Rabbi Yishmael son of Rabbi Yose, Rabban Gamliel son of Rabbi (later appointed Nasi), his brother Rabbi Shimon, Rabbi Ḥanina bar Ḥama (later the head of the Tzipori Yeshivah) and Rabbi Yannai. Even after the Sanhedrin moved to Tiberias, Torah scholars continued to live in Tzipori, among them the important Amoraim of Eretz Israel, Rabbi Ḥanina of Tzipori and Rabbi Mana.

קֵיסָרִי *Kesari (Caesarea).* A coastal settlement originally founded in the fourth century B.C.E. In 30 B.C.E. King Herod developed the site and called it Caesarea. At the beginning of the Common Era (6 C.E.) the Romans established Caesarea as the administrative capital of Eretz Israel. Originally most of

Caesarea's residents were non-Jewish, and even later on, when the Jewish community there expanded and became more established, the town remained fundamentally non-Jewish. Nevertheless, particularly after the Bar Kokhba revolt, it was the home of important Torah scholars and had its own yeshivah. Among the important Tannaim who lived in Caesarea were the disciples of Rabbi Yehudah HaNasi, Bar Kappara and Rabbi Oshayah Rabbah. Important Amoraim also lived there, among them Rabbi Yose son of Rabbi Ḥanina, Rabbi Abbahu and his sons, Rabbi Ḥanina bar Pappa, Rabbi Yitzḥak ben Elazar and Rabbi Ḥizkiyah. Parts of the Jerusalem Talmud were apparently edited in Caesarea.

רְצוּעָה שֶׁל כּוּתִים *The Samaritan zone.* Samaria, the region inhabitated by the Samaritans (כּוּתִים), a district near Biblical Shekhem, was not completely defined politically, and the area densely inhabited by the Samaritans shifted over the generations. Under the Hasmonean monarchy this district was quite small, but later the Samaritans expanded their area of settlement considerably. In certain periods the Samaritan zone actually extended to the Coastal Plain, dividing the area of Jewish settlement in Judea from that in Galilee and severing all direct connection between them.

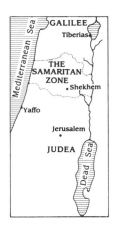

Babylonia

בָּבֶל *Babylonia.* Babylonia's exact borders changed from one period to the next. In the Talmudic period Babylonia was centered in the area between the Euphrates and Tigris Rivers, extending from Biram in the North to Hini and Shili in the South (on the side of the Euphrates), and from Baghdad to Shekanzib on the side of the Tigris. There were, however, Jewish communities in other parts of Babylonia during the Talmudic period.

בַּגְדָּאד *Baghdad.* Baghdad was a small city during the Talmudic period. It had a Jewish community, and a number of scholars were called בַּגְדְּתָאָה — "of Baghdad" — because they came from there.

בֵּי חוֹזַאִי *Bei Ḥoza'i.* A region southeast of the Tigris River; later known as "Ḥuzistan." From the point of view of its Jewish inhabitants it was a distant extension of the main Jewish community in central Babylonia. Because of its great distance from the center of Talmudic activity, its inhabitants were said to be unlearned in Torah. Nevertheless, there were strong commercial links between central Babylonia and Bei Ḥoza'i, in which many Jews, including scholars, were involved.

הוּצָל *Hutzal.* A small town in Babylonia which had a very ancient Jewish community. Its inhabitants were descended from the Tribe of Benjamin, and it was considered one of the most ancient Jewish settlements in Babylonia. Many famous Sages came from this place, and its citizens were known for their independent traditional customs. The Talmud (*Megillah* 29a) says of the ancient synagogue of Hutzal that it was one of the places from which the Divine Presence never departed. According to Rav Sherira Gaon, Hutzal was very close to Neharde'a.

כַּפְרִי *Kafri.* A small settlement apparently located south of Sura, on one of the tributaries of the Euphrates. Its Jewish community dated back to ancient times, and many distinguished families, such as those of Rabbi Ḥiyya and Rav, lived there. The Resh Galuta (the Exilarch) also seems to have lived there.

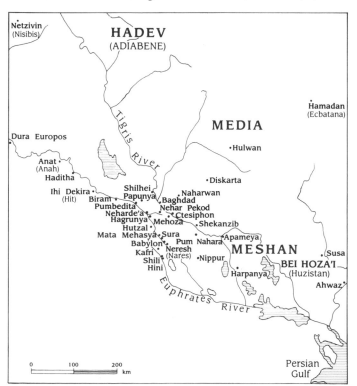

Babylonia in the Period of the Mishnah and Talmud

מְחוֹזָא *Meḥoza.* A city on the Tigris, located near the Malkha River. It was a large commercial city, and most of its inhabitants were Jews. Unlike most other Jewish communities, Meḥoza's Jews generally earned their living from commerce. Jews from different countries lived in Meḥoza, and many converts lived there as well. After Neharde'a was destroyed in 259 C.E. its yeshivah moved to Meḥoza. Meḥoza became the Torah center of leading scholars such as Rav Naḥman, Rav Sheshet, Rava (who later became head of the Meḥoza Yeshivah), Amemar, and Rav Kahana (Rav Ashi's teacher). After the death of Abaye (c. 338 C.E.), the Pumbedita Yeshivah (which was then headed by Rava) also moved for a period to Meḥoza.

מֵישָׁן *Meshan (Mesene).* A region in the southern part of Babylonia, east of the Tigris River. The Jewish community of Meshan was considered inferior to other Jewish communities, both in Torah scholarship and in lineage.

מָתָא מְחַסְיָא *Mata Meḥasya.* A small town near Sura. It was the home of Rav Ashi, and the Talmud was edited there. In later times, Sura and Mata Meḥasya apparently merged, becoming a single town.

נְהַרְדְּעָא *Neharde'a.* A city on the Euphrates, near the Malkha River; one of the oldest Jewish communities in Babylonia. According to tradition, Jews lived in Neharde'a as early as First Temple times (sixth century B.C.E.), beginning with the exile of King Jehoiachin of Judah. Neharde'a was one of the most important Jewish communities in Babylonia. It was a center of Torah learning from an early period and its yeshivah was the oldest in Babylonia. Many of the greatest Tannaim visited Neharde'a, among them Rabbi Akiva, who intercalated the calendar there (*Yevamot* 122b). In Rav's time (the first half of the third century C.E.) the Neharde'a Yeshivah was headed by Rav Shela, and after him by Shmuel. Since the city lay near the border between the Roman and the Persian Empires, it frequently suffered from the wars between the two, and Papa ben Nazer Odonathus, king of Tadmor, destroyed it completely in 259 C.E. Later, however, Jews resettled there, and many Torah scholars remained in Neharde'a even after its yeshivah had moved to Meḥoza and Pumbedita.

נְצִיבִין *Netzivin (Nisibis).* A fortress city in Northern Babylonia; a major Jewish community lived there during the Second Temple period and shortly thereafter. Netzivin's greatest scholar was Rabbi Yehudah ben Betera I, one of the great Torah scholars in the generation preceding the destruction of the Temple. The entire "Benei Betera" family seems to have been connected with the city. The Roman Emperor Trajan destroyed Netzivin at the beginning of the second century C.E., and from then on the Jewish community there ceased to exist.

נֶרֶשׁ *Neresh (Nares).* A town in Babylonia, south of Sura. Several scholars from Neresh are mentioned in the Talmud. The Amora, Rav Pappa, lived in Neresh and was active there (around the middle of the fourth century C.E.). During that time the Sura Yeshivah moved to Neresh (although it later returned to Sura).

סוּרָא *Sura.* A town in Southern Babylonia. Sura was not an important Jewish community until the great Amora, Rav, moved there and established the Sura Yeshivah (c. 220 C.E.). From then on, until the end of Geonic period (c. 1000 C.E.), Sura was a major Torah center. The Sura Yeshivah, under the leadership of Rav and his closest disciples, was influenced by the Halakhic traditions of Eretz Israel, and it was renowned for its unique approach to Torah study. Among the great scholars and leaders of Sura were Rav, Rav Huna, Rav Ḥisda, Ravina, and Rav Ashi. The main editing of the Babylonian Talmud was also done in Sura. There was another town of the same name, and in order to distinguish between them the other town was called סוּרָא דְּפְרָת — "Sura on the Euphrates."

פּוּמְבְּדִיתָא *Pumbedita.* A town on the Euphrates River, northwest of Neharde'a. Pumbedita was an important center of the Babylonian Jewish community for many generations. As early as the Second Temple period Pumbedita was referred to as the גוֹלָה — "the Diaspora" — and it was considered the center of Babylonian Jewry. After the destruction of Neharde'a, its yeshivah moved to Pumbedita, and from then on Torah study continued there uninterruptedly until the end of the Geonic period. The scholars of Pumbedita were particularly famous for their acumen. The most famous heads of the Pumbedita Yeshivah were Rav Yehudah (its original founder), Rabbah, Rav Yosef, Abaye, Rav Naḥman bar Yitzḥak, Rav Zevid and Rafram. The Pumbedita Yeshivah was very prominent in the Geonic period as well, often overshadowing the yeshivah in Sura. The last heads of the Pumbedita Yeshivah were the renowned Geonim Rav Sherira Gaon and his son, Rav Hai Gaon.

The Generations of the Tannaim and the Amoraim

A knowledge of the dates of the Tannaim and the Amoraim, and the chronological order of the generations in which they lived, can frequently be of help in enabling the student to understand different aspects of the Talmudic discussion. This information can help to clarify the relationship between the views of earlier and later scholars. It enables us to know when a scholar is referring to the statements of his predecessors. Chronology shows us which opinions are in conflict with earlier ones or seem to contradict them, and which opinions are in no way connected to those of particular generations. Despite much research in this area, however, much still remains unknown. There are many reasons for this, of which the following are the most important:

(1) We do not possess a full biography of even one of the Sages of this period, which would give his dates of birth and death. What dates we do have merely highlight the period in which certain scholars were active.

(2) Many Sages had identical names, and it is sometimes difficult or impossible to determine whether a statement should be ascribed to the first, second or third scholar bearing a certain name. For example, the Talmud (*Eruvin* 8b) mentions five scholars called Rav Kahana who were active during different generations.

(3) Mistakes by copyists and printers have created serious, and sometimes insoluble, difficulties and confusion in identifying scholars.

We do, nevertheless, have a general picture of the sequence of generations, and the table, lists and charts that follow provide a summary of this subject.

The sequence of generations indicated in the lists, the charts, and the table are obviously intended to give only a general indication of the periods in which the scholars were active. A scholar's "generation" is the period in which he acquired the status of a Rabbinic authority, and from which his main Torah teachings were preserved. Some scholars have been assigned two generations, either because they were active during a transitional period or because they lived to a great age.

In the list appear the names of many important Tannaim and Amoraim, and next to them the following abbreviations:

Z — A scholar before the Tannaitic period.

T — Tanna.

TA — The transitional period between the Tannaitic and the Amoraic periods.

A — Amora.

I — A scholar who was active mainly in Eretz Israel.

B — A scholar who was active mainly in Babylonia.

The numbers indicate the generation(s) in which the particular scholar was active.

The division into generations is as follows:

PRE-TANNAITIC PERIOD:

Zugot, Pairs: 200 B.C.E.–20 C.E.

TANNAITIC PERIOD:

1st generation:	20–40 C.E.
2nd generation:	40–80
3rd generation:	80–110
4th generation:	110–135
5th generation:	135–170
6th generation:	170–200

TRANSITION PERIOD 200–220

AMORAIC PERIOD:

1st generation:	220–250
2nd generation:	250–290
3rd generation:	290–320
4th generation:	320–350
5th generation:	350–375
6th generation:	375–425
7th generation:	425–460
8th generation:	460–500

THE TANNAITIC PERIOD

Dates	Tannaim	Historical events in Eretz Israel		World events
4th century B.C.E.		The conquest of Eretz Israel by Alexander the Great	332 B.C.E.	Greek rule in the East
3rd century B.C.E.	Shimon HaTzaddik Antigonus of Sokho			
2nd century B.C.E.	Yose b. Yoezer Yose b. Yoḥanan Yehoshua b. Peraḥyah Nitai HaArbeli	Hasmoneans		Decline of Seleucid power
1st century B.C.E.	Yehudah b. Tabbai Shimon b. Shetaḥ Shemayah, Avtalyon	Alexander Yannai		
30 B.C.E. – 20 C.E.	Hillel, Shammai	Herodian period	30 B.C.E.	Rise of the Roman Empire in the East. Augustus
20 C.E. – 40 C.E.	1 Gamliel (I) HaZaken			
40 C.E. – 80 C.E.	2 Shimon b. Gamliel (I) Yoḥanan b. Zakkai	Destruction of the Second Temple	70 C.E.	Vespasian, Titus
80 C.E. – 110 C.E.	3 Gamliel (II) of Yavneh Eliezer b. Hyrcanus			
110 C.E. – 135 C.E.	4 Akiva	Bar Kokhba revolt	135 C.E.	Hadrian
135 C.E. – 170 C.E.	5 Shimon b. Gamliel (II) Shimon (b. Yoḥai) Meir			
170 C.E. – 200 C.E.	6 Yehudah HaNasi	Final redaction of the Mishnah	200 C.E.	Caracalla, Alexander Severus

THE AMORAIC PERIOD

Dates	Eretz Israel	Babylonia		World events
Transitional period 200 C.E. – 220 C.E.	Oshaya Rabbah Bar Kappara Ḥiyya			
220 C.E. – 250 C.E.	1 Ḥanina (b. Ḥama), Yannai, Yehoshua b. Levi	Rav, Shmuel	226 C.E.	The Sassanid kingdom in Babylonia
250 C.E. – 290 C.E.	2 Yoḥanan (b. Nappaḥa) Resh Lakish	Huna, Yehudah (b. Yeḥezkel)		
290 C.E. – 320 C.E.	3 Ammi, Assi, Zera	Rabbah (b. Naḥmani) Yosef (b. Ḥiyya)		
320 C.E. – 350 C.E.	4 Hillel (II), Yonah, Yose (b. Zevida)	Abaye, Rava, Rami b. Ḥama	313 C.E	Christianity becomes an officially recognized religion in the Roman Empire
350 C.E. – 375 C.E.	5 Mana (II) Tanḥuma b. Abba	Pappa		
375 C.E. – 425 C.E.	6	Ashi, Ravina (I)	395 C.E.	Final redaction of the Jerusalem Talmud
425 C.E. – 460 C.E.	7	Mar b. Rav Ashi		Roman Empire divided into East and West
460 C.E. – 500 C.E.	8	Rabbah Tosafa'ah Ravina (II)	476 C.E.	Fall of the Roman Empire in the West
			C. 500 C.E.	Final redaction of the Babylonian Talmud

Dates	Nasi	Other principal Tannaim
20 B.C.E.	Hillel	
20 C.E.	Shimon	
20 – 40	1. Gamliel (I) the Elder	Akavyah b. Mahalal'el, Bava b. Buta, Ben He He, Yonatan b. Uziel
40 – 80	2. Shimon b. Gamliel (I)	Dosa b. Harkinas, Ḥanina Segan HaKohanim, Ḥanina b. Dosa, Tzadok (I), Yehudah b. Betera (I), Yoḥanan b. Zakkai
80 – 110	3. Gamliel (II) of Yavneh	Elazar b. Arakh, Elazar b. Tzadok (I), Eliezer (b. Hyrcanus), Eliezer b. Ya'akov (I), Naḥum of Gamzo, Neḥunya b. HaKanah, Shmuel HaKatan, Tarfon, Yehoshua (b. Ḥananyah), Yose HaKohen
110 – 135	4.	*Abba Shaul, Akiva, Elazar b. Azaryah, Elazar of Modi'in, Elisha b. Avuyah, Ḥalafta, Ḥananyah b. Ḥakhinai, Ḥananyah b. Teradyon, Ḥananyah (Nephew of) Yehoshua (b. Ḥananyah), Il'ai, Shimon b. Azzai, Shimon b. Nannas, Shimon b. Zoma, Tzadok (II), Yehudah b. Bava, Yehudah b. Betera (II), Yishmael (b. Elisha), Yoḥanan b. Berokah, Yoḥanan b. Nuri, Yose b. Kisma, Yose HaGelili
135 – 170	5. Shimon b. Gamliel (II)	Elazar (b. Shamu'a), Elazar b. Tzadok (II), Eliezer b. Yose HaGelili, Ḥanina b. Gamliel, Meir, Natan HaBavli, Neḥemyah, Shimon (b. Yoḥai), Yehudah (b. Il'ai), Yehoshua b. Korḥa, Yishmael b. Yoḥanan b. Berokah, Yoḥanan HaSandlar, Yonatan, Yose (b. Ḥalafta)
170 – 200	6. Yehudah HaNasi	Elazar b. Shimon, Ḥama b. Bisa, Pineḥas b. Yair, Shimon b. Elazar, Shimon b. Ḥalafta, Shimon b. Menasya, Shimon b. Yehudah, Summakhos, Yishmael b. Yose, Yose b. Meshullam, Yose b. Yehudah (b. Il'ai)
200 – 220	Gamliel (III) b. Rabbi (Yehudah HaNasi)	Bar Kappara, Ḥiyya, Levi (b. Sisi), Oshaya Rabbah, Shela, Shimon b. Rabbi (Yehudah HaNasi)

Dates	Amoraim in Eretz Israel	Amoraim in Babylonia
220 – 250	1. Ḥanina (b. Ḥama), Yannai, Yehoshua b. Levi, Yehudah Nesi'a (I)	1. Mar Ukva (I), Rav, Shmuel
250 – 290	2. Ḥama b. Ḥanina, Resh Lakish, Yitzḥak (Nappḥa), *Ya'akov b. Idi, *Ulla (b. Yishmael), Yoḥanan (b. Nappḥa), Yose b. Ḥanina	2. Adda b. Ahavah (I), Avimi, Giddel, Hamnuna (I), Ḥisda, Ḥiyya b. Ashi, Ḥiyya b. Yosef, Huna, Kahana (I), Matenah (I), Naḥman b. Ya'akov, Yehudah (b. Yeḥezkel), Yirmeyah b. Abba, Ze'iri
290 – 320	3. Abbahu, Ammi, Assi, Elazar (b. Pedat), *Ḥaggai, Ḥanina b. Pappa, Ḥelbo, Ḥiyya b. Abba, Il'ai, Shmuel b. Naḥmani, *Yirmeyah, Zera	3. Aḥa b. Ya'akov, *Dimi, Ḥisda, *Idi b. Avin (I), Rabbah b. b. Ḥanah, Rabbah (b. Naḥmani), Rabbah b. Rav Huna, *Ravin (Avin), Sheshet, Yosef (b. Ḥiyya)
320 – 350	4. Aḥa, Berekhyah, *Ḥizkiyah, Hillel (II), Huna (b. Avin), Yehudah b. (Shimon b.) Pazzi, Yonah, Yose (b. Zevida)	4. Abaye, Adda b. Ahava (II), *Dimi of Neharde'a, Naḥman b. Yitzḥak, Naḥman b. Ḥisda, Rami b. Ḥama, Rava
350 – 375	5. Avin (II) (b. Ravin), Ḥanina of Tzipori, Mana (II), Tanḥuma b. Abba	5. *Amemar, Ḥama, Huna b. Yehoshua, Kahana (IV), Pappa, Pappai, Zevid
375 – 425		6. *Aḥa b. Rava, Ashi, Geviha of Bei Katil, Mar Zutra, Rafram (I), Ravina (I), *Yeimar
425 – 460		7. Mar b. Rav Ashi, Rafram (II)
460 – 500		8. Rabbah Tosafa'ah, Ravina (II)

*A name marked with an asterisk indicates that the Sage was also active in the following generation.

	Abaye – AB,4		Geniva – AB,1–2
Rabbi	Abba – AI,3	Rav	Geviha of Bei Katil – AB,6
	Abba Arikha (see Rav)	Rav	Giddel – AB,2
	Abba b.Abba (see Avuha Di Shmuel)	Rabbi	Ḥaggai (Rav Ḥagga) – AI,3–4
Rabbi	Abba b. Ḥiyya b. Abba – AI,3	Rabbi	Ḥalafta – T,4
Rabbi	Abbahu (Avahu) – AI,3	Rav	Ḥama – AB,5
	Abba Shaul – T,4–5	Rabbi	Ḥama b. Bisa – T,6
Rav	Adda b. Ahavah (I) – AB,2	Rav	Ḥama b. Gurya – AB,2
Rav	Adda b. Ahavah (II) – AB,4	Rabbi	Ḥama b. Ḥanina – AI,2
Rabbi	Aḥa – AI,4	Rav	Hamnuna (I) – AB,2
Rav	Aḥa b. Rava – AB,6–7	Rav	Hamnuna (II) – AB,3
	Aḥa b. Ya'akov – AB,3	Rav	Ḥanan b. Rabbah (Abba) – AB,2
	Akavyah b. Mahalal'el – T,1		Ḥananyah (Ḥanina) b. Ḥakhinai – T,4
Rabbi	Akiva – T,4	Rabbi	Ḥananyah (Ḥanina) b. Teradyon – T,4
	Amemar – AB,5–6		Ḥananyah (Ḥanina) (Nephew of) Yehoshua (b.
Rabbi	Ammi – AI,3		Ḥananyah) – T,4
	Antigonus of Sokho – Z	Rabbi	Ḥanina (of Tzipori) – AI,5
Rabbi	Aphes – AI,1	Rabbi	Ḥanina b. Dosa – T,2
Rav	Ashi – AB,6	Rabbi	Ḥanina b. Gamliel – T,5
Rabbi	Assi – AI,3	Rabbi	Ḥanina (b. Ḥama) – AI,1
Rav	Assi – AB,1	Rabbi	Ḥanina (Ḥinena) b. Pappa – AI,3
	Avimi – AB,2	Rabbi	Ḥanina (Ḥananyah) Segan HaKohanim (the High Priest's
	Avimi b. Abbahu – AI,4		deputy) – T,2
Rabbi	Avin (see Ravin)	Rabbi	Ḥelbo – AI,3
Rabbi	Avin (II) (b. Ravin) – AI,5		Hillel HaZaken (the Elder) – Z
	Avtalyon – Z		Hillel (II) – AI,4
	Avuha Di (the father of) Shmuel (= Abba b. Abba) –	Rav	Ḥisda – AB,3
	AB,1	Rabbi	Ḥiyya – TA
	Azaryah (Ezra) – AI,5	Rabbi	Ḥiyya b. Abba – AI,3
	Bar Kappara – TA	Rav	Ḥiyya b. Ashi – AB,2
	Bava b. Buta – T,1	Rav	Ḥiyya b. Rav – AB,2
	Ben Azzai (see Shimon b. Azzai)	Rav	Ḥiyya b. Yosef – AB,2
	Ben He He – T,1	Rabbi	Ḥizkiyah – AI,4–5
	Ben Nannas (see Shimon b. Nannas)		Ḥizkiyah (b. Ḥiyya) – AI,1
	Ben Zoma (see Shimon b. Zoma)	Rabbi	Hoshaya Rabbah (see Oshaya)
Rabbi	Berekhyah – AI,4	Rav	Huna (Ḥuna) – AB,2
Rav	Bivi b. Abaye – AB,5	Rav	Huna (b. Avin) – AI,4
Rav	Dimi AB,3–4	Rav	Huna b. Yehoshua AB,5
Rav	Dimi of Neharde'a – AB,4	Rav	Idi b. Avin (I) – AB,3–4
Rabbi	Dosa b. Harkinas – T,2	Rav	Idi b. Avin (II) – AB,5
Rabbi	Elazar b. Arakh – T,3	Rabbi	Il'ai – T,4
Rabbi	Elazar b. Azaryah – T,4	Rabbi	Il'ai (Ia'i, I'la, La) – AI,3
Rabbi	Elazar (b. Pedat) – AI,3		Ishmael (see Yishmael)
Rabbi	Elazar (b. Shamu'a) – T,5		Isaac (see Yitzhak)
Rabbi	Elazar b. Shimon – T,6		Jacob (see Ya'akov)
Rabbi	Elazar b. Tzadok (I) – T,3		Jeremiah (see Yirmeyah)
Rabbi	Elazar b. Tzadok (II) – T,5		Johanan (see Yoḥanan)
Rabbi	Elazar HaKappar – T,6		Jonah (see Yonah)
Rabbi	Elazar HaModa'i (of Modi'in) T,4		Jonathan (see Yonatan)
Rabbi	Eliezer b. Hyrcanus – T,3		Jose (see Yose)
Rabbi	Eliezer b. Ya'akov (I) – T,3		Joseph (see Yosef)
Rabbi	Eliezer (Elazar) b. Yose – AI,5		Joshua (see Yehoshua)
Rabbi	Eliezer b. Yose HaGelili (the Galilean) – T,5		Judah (see Yehudah)
	Elisha b. Avuyah – T,4	Rav	Kahana (I) – AB,1
Rabban	Gamliel (III) b. Rabbi (Yehudah HaNasi) – TA	Rav	Kahana (II) (pupil of Rav) – AB,2
Rabban	Gamliel (I) HaZaken – T,1	Rav	Kahana (III) – AB,3
Rabban	Gamliel (II) of Yavneh – T,3	Rav	Kahana (IV) – AB,5

Rav	Kahana (V) – AB,6	
	Karna – AB,1	
Rav	Ketina – AB,2	
Rabbi	Kohen – AI,3	
	Levi (b. Sisi) – TA	
Rabbi	Mana (Mani) (I) – AI,2	
Rabbi	Mana (II) – AI,5	
	Mar b. Rav Ashi – AB,7	
	Mar Ukva (I) – AB,1	
	Mar Zutra – AB,6	
Rav	Matenah (I) AB,2	
Rabbi	Meir – T,5	
Rav	Mesharshiya – AB,5	
Rav	Naḥman b. Ḥisda – AB,4	
Rav	Naḥman (b. Ya'akov) – AB,3	
Rav	Naḥman b. Yitzḥak – AB,4	
	Naḥum of Gamzo – T,3	
Rabbi	Natan (HaBavli) the Babylonian – T,5	
Rabbi	Neḥemyah – T,5	
Rabbi	Neḥunya b. HaKanah – T,3	
	Nitai HaArbeli – Z	
Rabbi	Oshaya (Hoshaya) Rabbah – TA	
Rav	Pappa – AB,5	
Rav	Pappai – AB,5	
Rabbi	Pineḥas (b. Ḥama) – AI,4	
Rabbi	Pineḥas b. Yair – T,6	
	Rabbah b. Avuha – AB,2	
	Rabbah b. b. Ḥanah – AB,3	
	Rabbah b. Ḥanah – AB,1	
	Rabbah (b. Naḥmani) – AB,3	
	Rabbah b. Rav Huna – AB,3	
	Rabbah Tosafa'ah – AB,8	
	Rabbi (see Yehudah HaNasi)	
	Rafram (I) – AB,6	
	Rafram (II) – AB,7	
	Raḥava (of Pumbedita) – AB,3	
	Rami b. Ḥama – AB,4	
	Rav (= Abba Arikha) – AB,1	
	Rava – AB,4	
	Ravin (Avin, Boon) – AI,3–4	
	Ravina (I) – AB,6	
	Ravina (II) (b. Huna) – AB,8	
	Resh Lakish (see Shimon b. Lakish)	
	Samuel (see Shmuel)	
	Shammai – 1st Century B.C.E	
Rav	Shela – TA	
	Shemayah – Z	
Rav	Shesha (Sheshet) b. Rav Idi – AB, 4–5	
Rav	Sheshet – AB,3	
Rav	Sheshet b. Rav Idi (see Shesha b. Rav Idi)	
Rabbi	Shimon (Shiman) b. Abba – AI,3	
	(Shimon) b. Azzai – T,4	
Rabbi	Shimon b. Elazar – T,6	
Rabban	Shimon b. Gamliel (I) – T,2	
Rabban	Shimon b. Gamliel (II) – T,5	
Rabbi	Shimon b. Ḥalafta – T,6	
Rabbi	Shimon b. Lakish – AI,2	
Rabbi	Shimon b. Menasya – T,6	
Rabbi	Shimon b. Nannas – T,4	

Rabbi	Shimon (Simon) b. Pazzi – AI,2–3
Rabbi	Shimon b. Rabbi (Yehudah HaNasi) – TA
	Shimon b. Shetaḥ – Z
Rabbi	Shimon b. Yehudah – T,6
Rabbi	Shimon (b. Yoḥai) – T,5
	Shimon b. Zoma – T,4
	Shimon HaTzaddik (the Righteous) – Z
	Shmuel – AB,1
Rabbi	Shmuel b. Naḥmani (Naḥman) – AI,3
Rabbi	Shmuel b. Yitzḥak – AI,3
Rabbi	Shmuel b. Yose b. Boon (Avin) – AI,5
	Shmuel HaKatan – T,3
	Simeon (see Shimon)
Rabbi	Simlai – AI,2
	Summakhos – T,6
Rabbi	Tanḥuma (b. Abba) – AI,5
Rabbi	Tarfon – T,3
Rabbi	Tzadok (I) – T,2
Rabbi	Tzadok (II) – T,5
	Ukva, Mar (see Mar Ukva)
	Ulla (b. Yishmael) – AI,2–3
Rabbi	Ya'akov b. Idi – AI,2–3
Rabbi	Yannai – AI,1
Rabbi	Yehoshua (b. Ḥananyah) – T,3
Rabbi	Yehoshua b. Idi – AB,5–6
Rabbi	Yehoshua b. Korḥa – T,5
Rabbi	Yehoshua b. Levi – AI,1
	Yehoshua b. Peraḥyah – Z
Rabbi	Yehudah b. Bava – T,4
Rabbi	Yehudah b. Betera (I) – T,2
Rabbi	Yehudah b. Betera (II) – T,4
	Yehudah (b. Ḥiyya) – AI,1
Rabbi	Yehudah (b. Il'ai) – T,5
Rabbi	Yehudah b. (Shimon b.) Pazi – AI,4
	Yehudah b. Tabbai – Z
Rav	Yehudah (b. Yeḥezkel) – AB,2
Rabbi	Yehudah HaNasi – T,6
Rabbi	Yehudah Nesi'a (I) – AI,1
Rav	Yeimar – AB,6–7
Rabbi	Yirmeyah – AI,3–4
Rav	Yirmeyah b. Abba – AB,2
Rabbi	Yishmael (b. Elisha) – T,4
Rabbi	Yishmael b. Yoḥanan b. Berokah – T,5
Rabbi	Yishmael b. Yose – T,6
Rabbi	Yitzḥak b. Elazar – AI,4
Rabbi	Yitzḥak b. Naḥman (Naḥmani) – AI,3
Rabbi	Yitzḥak (Nappaḥa) – AI,2
Rabbi	Yoḥanan b. Berokah – T,4
Rabbi	Yoḥanan (b. Nappaḥa) – AI,2
Rabbi	Yoḥanan b. Nuri – T,4
Rabban	Yoḥanan b. Zakkai – T,2
Rabbi	Yoḥanan HaSandlar ("the cobbler") – T,5
Rabbi	Yonah – AI,4
Rabbi	Yonatan – T,5
Rabbi	Yonatan b. Uziel – T,1
Rabbi	Yose (b. Ḥalafta) – T,5
Rabbi	Yose b. Ḥanina – AI,2
Rabbi	Yose b. Kisma – T,4
Rabbi	Yose b. Meshullam – T,6

Rabbi	Yose b. Yehudah – T,6		Rabbi	Yoshiyah – T,5
	Yose b. Yoezer – Z			Ze'iri – AB,2
	Yose b. Yoḥanan – Z		Rabbi	Zera – AI,3
Rabbi	Yose (b. Zevida) – AI,4		Rav	Zera – AB,4
Rabbi	Yose HaGelili ("the Galilean") – T,4		Rabbi	Zerika – AI,3
Rabbi	Yose HaKohen – T,3		Rav	Zevid – AB,5
Rav	Yosef (b. Ḥiyya) – AB,3			Zutra, Mar (see Mar Zutra)

The Tractates of the Mishnah and the Talmud

According to tradition there are sixty tractates in the Mishnah, and they are divided into six major sections, called סְדָרִים — "orders." These orders give their name to the entire Talmud: the word ש"ס — *shas* — is an abbreviation of the two Hebrew words שִׁשָּׁה סְדָרִים — "six orders." However, the accepted division comprises sixty-three tractates. Three of them, *Bava Kamma, Bava Metzia,* and *Bava Batra* ("The First Gate," "The Middle Gate," and "The Last Gate"), are really the three parts of a large tractate called *Nezikin* ("Damages"), and the tractate *Makkot* ("Lashes"), seems to have been a continuation of tractate *Sanhedrin.*

The sequence of tractates within the orders is not completely standardized in manuscript and printed editions of the Mishnah and the Talmud. The sequence presented here is that found in most current editions of the Mishnah, but in the course of centuries the tractates were also studied in other sequences. (One unusual variant was the order laid down by the Meiri — Rabbi Menaḥem ben Shlomo — who was born in 1249 and lived in Provence until his death in 1316.) In general, within an order, the tractate with the most chapters is placed first and the tractate with the fewest chapters comes last. In addition, the division of individual tractates into chapters was not entirely standardized, and uncertainty regarding the division into chapters affected the placement of a given tractate in its order. Many scholars, including the Rambam, have sought to explain the arrangement of the tractates and the inner connection between them.

Both the Babylonian Talmud (תַּלְמוּד בַּבְלִי) and the Jerusalem Talmud (תַּלְמוּד יְרוּשַׁלְמִי) contain Gemara text on many, but by no means all, of the tractates of the Mishnah. Some tractates appear with Gemara in both compilations of the Talmud, others appear with Gemara in one but not in the other, and some have no Gemara in either.

In addition to the tractates of the Mishnah there are also מַסֶּכְתּוֹת קְטַנּוֹת — "Minor Tractates" (also called מַסֶּכְתּוֹת חִיצוֹנִיּוֹת — "External Tractates"). These are collections of

---

teaching containing much material from Mishnaic times, though they were not put into their final form until the period of the Geonim.

In the following pages we present short descriptions of the contents of the six orders of the Mishnah and of each individual tractate. We also indicate the number of chapters in each tractate, the number of chapters in the Tosefta on that same tractate, the number of pages in the Babylonian Talmud on that tractate (according to the Vilna edition), and the number of pages in the Jerusalem Talmud (according to the Vilna edition). Each Talmud page is a double-sided folio page, and the numbering traditionally begins with the Hebrew letter ב, corresponding to the number 2. Thus, in practice, the number of pages in each tractate is one less than the final page number in Hebrew would indicate.

First Order

סֵדֶר זְרָעִים   *Zeraim* (Seeds).
Laws relating to agriculture, particularly in Eretz Israel; to contributions to the priests and the Levites; to other things that must be separated from the harvest and given to the poor; and, incidentally, laws concerning blessings.

בְּרָכוֹת   *Berakhot* (Blessings).
In most traditions the first tractate of the Talmud. Laws of reciting the *Shema*, the Amidah prayer (the eighteen benedictions, שְׁמוֹנֶה עֶשְׂרֵה), Grace after Meals (בִּרְכַּת הַמָּזוֹן), blessings for various kinds of food and fragrances (בִּרְכוֹת הַנֶּהֱנִין), blessings for various occasions and things seen (בִּרְכוֹת הָרְאִיָּה).
Mishnah 9; Tosefta 6; Babylonian Talmud 64; Jerusalem Talmud 68.

פֵּאָה   *Pe'ah* (Corner, corner of the field).
Detailed discussion of the laws concerning the harvest of the corner of the field to be given to the poor (פֵּאָה). Laws of the other gifts to which the poor are entitled: gleanings of grain crops (לֶקֶט), forgotten sheaves (שִׁכְחָה), gleanings of grapes (פֶּרֶט), grapes remaining on the vine after picking (עוֹלֵלוֹת), tithes for the poor (מַעֲשַׂר עָנִי). Some treatment of the laws of charity (צְדָקָה).
Mishnah 8; Tosefta 4; Jerusalem Talmud 37.

דְּמַאי   *Demai* (Doubtful, doubtfully tithed).
The laws of doubtfully tithed produce are examined in detail; the produce to which the prohibition of *demai* applies, how it is to be dealt with, and what is to be done to that which is set aside from it.
Mishnah 7; Tosefta 8; Jerusalem Talmud 34.

כִּלְאַיִם   *Kilayim* (Mixtures).
All the laws prohibiting grafting different species of plants, planting together different kinds of plants and trees (כִּלְאֵי זְרָעִים), planting grain or edible plants in a vineyard (כִּלְאֵי הַכֶּרֶם), mixtures of cloth (כִּלְאֵי בְגָדִים, שַׁעַטְנֵז), cross-breeding of animals and yoking animals of different species together (כִּלְאֵי בְהֵמָה).
Mishnah 9; Tosefta 5; Jerusalem Talmud 44.

שְׁבִיעִית   *Shevi'it* (Seventh, the Sabbatical Year).
The laws of the Sabbatical Year (שְׁבִיעִית); leaving fields to lie fallow; those fruits and vegetables that may not be eaten as a result of the Sabbatical Year (בִּיעוּר סְפִיחִים); also the release of debts (שְׁמִיטַת כְּסָפִים) and the prosbul (פְּרוֹזְבּוֹל, a Rabbinical enactment allowing a creditor to claim his debts after the Sabbatical Year).
Mishnah 10; Tosefta 8; Jerusalem Talmud 31.

תְּרוּמוֹת   *Terumot* (Contributions, "the priests' portion of the harvest").
The laws of terumah (תְּרוּמָה, תְּרוּמַת מַעֲשֵׂר); from what terumah is to be separated, and

how ritually impure and pure terumah is to be treated, and what the procedure is when terumah becomes mixed with unconsecrated produce (חוּלִּין).
Mishnah 11; Tosefta 10; Jerusalem Talmud 59.

מַעְשְׂרוֹת Ma'aserot (Tithes).
The laws of tithes (מַעְשְׂרוֹת); particularly the first tithe (מַעֲשֵׂר רִאשׁוֹן), belonging to the Levites, and to some extent the second tithe (מַעֲשֵׂר שֵׁנִי). Who is obliged to give tithes and from when the obligation begins; what is permitted to be eaten before the tithes have been separated.
Mishnah 5; Tosefta 3; Jerusalem Talmud 26.

מַעֲשֵׂר שֵׁנִי Ma'aser Sheni (Second tithe).
The laws of the second tithe (מַעֲשֵׂר שֵׁנִי) — how it is separated, bringing it to Jerusalem, how it is redeemed. The tractate also contains the laws of *neta reva'i* (נֶטַע רְבָעִי — the fruits of the fourth year), the principles of which are similar to those of the second tithe.
Mishnah 5; Tosefta 5; Jerusalem Talmud 28.

חַלָּה Ḥallah (Dough).
The laws of separating ḥallah (חַלָּה) and giving it to the priests; from what dough it is separated, and how it is separated, and how much is to be separated.
Mishnah 4; Tosefta 2; Jerusalem Talmud 28.

עׇרְלָה Orlah (Uncircumcised, "uncircumcised fruit").
The prohibition against the use of fruits of a tree during the first three years after its planting, and to which trees it applies. Most of the tractate is devoted to questions concerning the nullification of various forbidden items that have been blended into a larger quantity of permitted items, and the circumstances in which this nullification takes effect (בִּיטוּל אִיסּוּרִים).
Mishnah 3; Tosefta 1; Jerusalem Talmud 20.

בְּכּוּרִים Bikkurim (First fruits).
First-fruit offerings at the Temple; from which fruits they are to be brought, what the procedure is for bringing them to Jerusalem, and what the ceremony was concerning them in the Temple.
Mishnah 3; Tosefta 2; Jerusalem Talmud 13.

סֵדֶר מוֹעֵד Moed (Appointed time, "Festival").
Second Order

The general subject matter comprises the laws that apply to the Sabbath, Festivals and fasts, and the commandments that are unique to each individual Festival and special occasion. Tractate *Shekalim* falls outside this definition, but since the shekalim tax was collected at regular intervals (appointed times), the tractate was included in *Seder Moed.*

שַׁבָּת Shabbat (Sabbath).
Contains most of the laws governing the Sabbath. It gives a comprehensive explanation of the types of work forbidden on the Sabbath, the sources in the Torah of these prohibitions, the details of their laws, and the Rabbinic enactments connected with them. It also contains material on other commandments that apply to the Sabbath. In the Babylonian Talmud this tractate contains a fundamental discussion of the laws of Ḥanukkah.
Mishnah 24; Tosefta 18; Babylonian Talmud 157; Jerusalem Talmud 92.

עִירוּבִין Eruvin (Mergings).
It constitutes a continuation of tractate *Shabbat* because of its extensive discussion of

the laws concerning the boundaries within which one is allowed to carry and walk on the Sabbath. It deals with the laws of transferring or carrying from one domain to another, and the adjustment of the borders of these domains in order to allow this (עֵירוּב חֲצֵירוֹת — merging courtyards); laws concerning movement beyond the Sabbath boundary, and the merging of boundaries to allow such movement (עֵירוּב תְּחוּמִין — the merging of boundaries); the various Rabbinic enactments relating to the Sabbath domains (רְשׁוּיוֹת הַשַּׁבָּת).

Mishnah 10; Tosefta 8; Babylonian Talmud 105; Jerusalem Talmud 65.

פְּסָחִים Pesaḥim (Paschal lambs, "Passover").
A comprehensive treatment of the laws of Pesaḥ (פֶּסַח — "Passover"): it deals with the laws of matzah (מַצָּה — "unleavened bread") and maror (מָרוֹר — "bitter herbs"), and also with the prohibition of ḥametz (חָמֵץ — "leavened matter") in all its aspects, and also with all the detailed laws of the Paschal sacrifice (קָרְבַּן פֶּסַח). It also deals with the laws of Pesaḥ Sheni (פֶּסַח שֵׁנִי). One chapter is devoted to the order of service on Pesaḥ Eve (לֵיל הַסֵּדֶר).

Mishnah 10; Tosefta 10; Babylonian Talmud 121; Jerusalem Talmud 71.

שְׁקָלִים Shekalim (Shekels).
Deals with a number of interrelated subjects, whose central theme is the contribution of shekalim (מַחֲצִית הַשֶּׁקֶל) that was levied for the Temple service. The analysis of the laws of the shekel levy leads to an explanation of how it was put to use in the Temple, and how the Temple administration was organized, with particular reference to the income from the shekalim and the use made of it.

Mishnah 8; Tosefta 3; Jerusalem Talmud 33.

יוֹמָא Yoma (The Day, "the Day of Atonement").
Deals mainly with the order of service in the Temple on Yom Kippur (יוֹם הַכִּיפּוּרִים). One chapter is devoted to the Yom Kippur fast and the prayers on this day.

Mishnah 8; Tosefta 4; Babylonian Talmud 88; Jerusalem Talmud 42.

סוּכָּה Sukkah (Booth).
The laws of valid and invalid sukkot, and אַרְבָּעָה מִינִים ("the four species" of plants that, when grasped together, constitute the commandment of "taking the lulav" on the Sukkot Festival). It also deals, to some extent, with the special arrangements and ceremonies in the Temple during Sukkot.

Mishnah 5; Tosefta 4; Babylonian Talmud 56; Jerusalem Talmud 26.

בֵּיצָה Betzah (Egg).
The laws that apply to all the Festivals. The types of work prohibited on all Festivals (and also other prohibitions). This tractate was originally called Yom Tov (יוֹם טוֹב — "Festival"), but it later became known as בֵּיצָה, because that is the first word of the tractate.

Mishnah 5; Tosefta 4; Babylonian Talmud 40; Jerusalem Talmud 22.

רֹאשׁ הַשָּׁנָה Rosh HaShanah (New Year).
The laws of fixing the date of Rosh HaShanah, of the calendar in general, and of testimony regarding the New Moon. It also contains the laws regarding the shofar and the prayer service on Rosh HaShanah.

Mishnah 4; Tosefta 2; Babylonian Talmud 35; Jerusalem Talmud 22.

תַּעֲנִית Ta'anit (Fast).
Deals with public fast-days. It is mainly concerned with special prayers for rain, and public fast-days that did not have a fixed date in the calendar but were decreed in periods

of severe drought. It also contains a discussion about the other fixed public fast-days, and about fasts and other special occasions mentioned in *Megillat Ta'anit*.
Mishnah 4; Tosefta 3; Babylonian Talmud 31; Jerusalem Talmud 26.

מְגִילָה   *Megillah* (Scroll).
The various laws concerning the reading of *Megillat Esther* (the Scroll of Esther) and the dates that were fixed for this, and the other commandments connected with the Purim Festival. Also dealt with, incidentally, are the laws of reading the Torah and the Prophets, the laws of prayer, the laws concerning the holiness of synagogues and Torah scrolls, and the laws of writing Torah scrolls, mezuzot, tefillin, and Scrolls of Esther.
Mishnah 4; Tosefta 3; Babylonian Talmud 32; Jerusalem Talmud 34.

מוֹעֵד קָטָן   *Moed Katan* (Minor Festival).
Those acts of work that are forbidden and permitted on חוֹל הַמּוֹעֵד — the intermediate days of Pesaḥ and Sukkot. Because of a similarity in the Halakhic principles involved, the tractate also deals with some of the laws of the Sabbatical Year (שְׁבִיעִית), and — in great detail — with all the laws of mourning (אֲבֵילוּת). In ancient times this tractate was called מַשְׁקִין — *Mashkin* ("to irrigate," "to water") — because that is the first word of the tractate.
Mishnah 3; Tosefta 2; Babylonian Talmud 29; Jerusalem Talmud 14.

חֲגִיגָה   *Ḥagigah* (Festival offering).
Deals with the pilgrimage to Jerusalem (עֲלִיָּה לָרֶגֶל), and the special Festival offerings — the pilgrim's burnt-offering (עוֹלַת רְאִיָּה), the Festival thanks-offering (שַׁלְמֵי חֲגִיגָה), the laws of ritual purity (טָהֳרָה) and impurity (טוּמְאָה) with reference to Festivals and in general. Among the Aggadic matters discussed in the tractate is the subject of the Divine Chariot (מַעֲשֵׂה מֶרְכָּבָה).
Mishnah 3; Tosefta 3; Babylonian Talmud 27; Jerusalem Talmud 22.

סֵדֶר נָשִׁים   *Nashim* (Women).
Third Order
It deals with laws connected with marriage and the obligations resulting from it. There are, however, tractates in this order whose place in it is merely associative (*Nedarim* and *Nazir*).

יְבָמוֹת   *Yevamot* (Sisters-in-law).
The laws of levirate marriage (יִבּוּם) and *ḥalitzah* (חֲלִיצָה — the ceremony whereby a childless widow obtains release from the obligation to perform the levirate marriage). The tractate is the main source for the basic laws of forbidden sexual relationships (עֲרָיוֹת). Also dealt with are the laws of prohibited marriages (פְּסוּלֵי חִיתּוּן), conversion (גִּיּוּר), and the testimony confirming a husband's death that permits his wife to remarry (עֵדוּת אִשָּׁה).
Mishnah 16; Tosefta 14; Babylonian Talmud 122; Jerusalem Talmud 85.

כְּתוּבּוֹת   *Ketubot* (Marriage deeds).
The laws of marriage deeds; and, in general, all the financial and personal obligations pertaining to husband and wife, whether as part of the conditions of the marriage deed itself, or as a result of other special agreements. The tractate also deals with the laws concerning rape and seduction (דִּינֵי הָאֲנוּסָה וְהַמְפוּתָה).
Mishnah 13; Tosefta 12; Babylonian Talmud 112; Jerusalem Talmud 72.

נְדָרִים   *Nedarim* (Vows).
All the laws concerning vows — their definition, the extent to which they are binding, how they take effect, how they may be dissolved by a scholar (חָכָם) or annulled by the wife's father or husband. This tractate is connected to *Seder Nashim* because a woman's

father or husband could annul her vows, a law belonging to the Halakhic network of marital and personal relationships.

Mishnah 11; Tosefta 7; Babylonian Talmud 91; Jerusalem Talmud 40.

נָזִיר   *Nazir* (Nazirite).

The laws of the Nazirite (נָזִיר) — the ways in which a person assumes the status of a Nazir, the various kinds of Nazirite, the prohibitions that apply to a Nazir and the offerings that he brings. The tractate is included in this order because of its connection with tractate *Nedarim*.

Mishnah 9; Tosefta 6; Babylonian Talmud 66; Jerusalem Talmud 47.

סוֹטָה   *Sotah* (A woman suspected of adultery).

The first chapters of the tractate deal with the laws of the *sotah* — when and how the laws of *sotah* apply and what is done to her. Because of a certain Halakhic resemblance this tractate also contains chapters dealing with the Priestly Benediction (בִּרְכַּת כֹּהֲנִים), the laws of *hak'hel* (הַקְהֵל), and the laws of warfare.

Mishnah 9; Tosefta 15; Babylonian Talmud 49; Jerusalem Talmud 47.

גִּיטִין   *Gittin* (Bills of divorce).

The arrangements for writing a bill of divorce, handing it over, and sending it by means of an agent.

Mishnah 9; Tosefta 7; Babylonian Talmud 90; Jerusalem Talmud 54.

קִידּוּשִׁין   *Kiddushin* (Betrothals).

The various ways in which a woman may be betrothed, when, and under what conditions. It also deals with the various genealogical relationships that prohibit marriage. The tractate also deals incidentally with the laws of the Hebrew manservant (עֶבֶד עִבְרִי) and maidservant (אָמָה עִבְרִיָּה), and the distinctions between the mitzvot binding on both men and women and those binding on men alone.

Mishnah 4; Tosefta 5; Babylonian Talmud 82; Jerusalem Talmud 48.

Fourth Order

סֵדֶר נְזִיקִין   *Nezikin* (Damages).

The order of *Nezikin* deals with civil and criminal law, corporal and capital punishment, the composition of Rabbinical Courts, erroneous rulings made by them, and judicial procedure. Incidentally it includes laws regarding idol worship and its avoidance, the personal testimony of Sages with regard to various Halakhic subjects, and matters of ethics and wisdom (*Ethics of the Fathers*, פִּרְקֵי אָבוֹת).

בָּבָא קַמָּא   *Bava Kamma* (The First Gate).

The first part of the larger tractate *Nezikin*, which deals mainly with civil law. It contains the laws relating to the types of damage inflicted by one person on another, whether by his own action or by the action of things in his possession.

Mishnah 10; Tosefta 11; Babylonian Talmud 119; Jerusalem Talmud 44.

בָּבָא מְצִיעָא   *Bava Metzia* (The Middle Gate).

Disputes over financial matters in the course of a person's normal business dealings: laws regarding lost property, deposits, loans, sales, rentals, hiring laborers, contractors, and tenant farmers. Laws of interest.

Mishnah 10; Tosefta 11; Babylonian Talmud 119; Jerusalem Talmud 37.

בָּבָא בַּתְרָא   *Bava Batra* (The Last Gate).

Laws of partnership, problems connected with the preservation of a person's property rights, sales contracts for property of all kinds. Also dealt with extensively are the laws of inheritance, and the laws regarding legal documents and deeds.

Mishnah 10; Tosefta 11; Babylonian Talmud 176; Jerusalem Talmud 34.

סַנְהֶדְרִין *Sanhedrin.*
Laws of capital punishment: those crimes punishable by death and the ways these sentences are carried out. Considerable space is devoted to the composition of the various courts and to judicial procedure. The Aggadic sections contain a broad discussion of the question of man's place in the World to Come and other fundamental tenets of faith.
Mishnah 11; Tosefta 14; Babylonian Talmud 113; Jerusalem Talmud 57.

מַכּוֹת *Makkot* (Lashes).
Continuation of tractate *Sanhedrin,* in which the laws of corporal punishment are clarified, explaining why and how a delinquent is lashed, and giving detailed laws concerning false and conspiratorial testimony. Also discussed is the subject of negligent manslaughter punished by banishment to the cities of refuge.
Mishnah 3; Tosefta 4; Babylonian Talmud 24; Jerusalem Talmud 9.

שְׁבוּעוֹת *Shevuot* (Oaths).
The various types of oaths administered in the course of court hearings concerning monetary matters, as well as private oaths and various oaths instituted by the Rabbis. Two chapters are devoted to a discussion of the laws forbidding a ritually impure person from entering the Temple and from participating in its sacrifices.
Mishnah 8; Tosefta 6; Babylonian Talmud 49; Jerusalem Talmud 44.

עֵדִיּוֹת *Eduyyot* (Testimonies).
A compilation of many testimonies given by different Rabbis on a wide variety of Halakhic subjects. There is also a list of the rare instances when Bet Shammai (the School of Shammai) was lenient and Bet Hillel (the School of Hillel) was strict.
Mishnah 8; Tosefta 3.

עֲבוֹדָה זָרָה *Avodah Zarah* (Idolatry).
Idolatry, in particular how to keep far away from its statues, symbols, and holidays. More broadly the tractate also discusses the whole structure of prohibited contacts between Jews and non-Jews, both those laws directly connected with idolatry (such as יֵין נֶסֶךְ — libation wine made by non-Jews and offered to idols) and those dependent on other factors (such as kashrut and precautionary measures limiting contact with non-Jews).
Mishnah 5; Tosefta 9; Babylonian Talmud 76; Jerusalem Talmud 37.

אָבוֹת *Avot* (Fathers).
A collection of sayings of the Sages extending throughout the Tannaitic period. Distinguished from the other tractates of the Mishnah because it does not discuss specifically defined Halakhic issues, but ethical duties and conduct. Otherwise known as פִּרְקֵי אָבוֹת — *Ethics of the Fathers.*
Mishnah 5.

הוֹרָיוֹת *Horayot* (Decisions, rulings).
Connected to some extent with the tractate *Sanhedrin,* because it also deals with Rabbinical Courts on various levels. Its main concern is the examination of cases in which the Bet Din or the High Priest erred or a King of Israel committed an error, and when and how the special penitential sacrifices for such errors must be brought.
Mishnah 3; Tosefta 2; Babylonian Talmud 14; Jerusalem Talmud 19

סֵדֶר קָדָשִׁים *Kodashim* (Holy things). *Fifth Order*
The order of *Kodashim* is devoted to laws pertaining to the sacrifices and to the Temple (except for the tractate *Ḥullin*). It was already considered a difficult subject of study during the Talmudic period. The Jerusalem Talmud on this order of the Mishnah did at one time exist, but no trace of it has been found.

זְבָחִים   *Zevaḥim* (Animal sacrifices).
In antiquity this tractate was called "The Slaughter of Sacrificial Animals" (שְׁחִיטַת קֳדָשִׁים). It deals with the various animal sacrifices, how they were offered, and under what circumstances they were declared unfit. It contains an exhaustive discussion of the foundations of Halakhic exegesis (מִדְרָשׁ הֲלָכָה) and the laws of forbidden mixtures (דִּינֵי תַּעֲרוֹבֶת).
Mishnah 13; Tosefta 13; Babylonian Talmud 120.

מְנָחוֹת   *Menaḥot* (Meal-offerings).
Laws of the various meal-offerings. It contains the most detailed discussion found in the Talmud on the laws of צִיצִית — tzitzit, ritual fringes — and תְּפִילִין — tefillin, phylacteries.
Mishnah 13; Tosefta 13; Babylonian Talmud 110.

חוּלִּין   *Ḥullin* (Ordinary, unhallowed).
This tractate was called "The Slaughter of Animals Not for the Purpose of Sacrifices" (שְׁחִיטַת חוּלִּין) and it is the only tractate in this order dealing with non-sacrificial regulations, mostly the slaughter of animals for ordinary consumption (דִּינֵי שְׁחִיטָה), the diseases or injuries that render kosher animals unfit to be eaten (טְרֵפוֹת), the laws relating to the prohibition of eating milk and meat together (דִּינֵי בָּשָׂר בְּחָלָב), priestly dues (מַתְּנוֹת כְּהוּנָה), and the duty of setting free the mother bird of a nest of eggs (שִׁילוּחַ הַקֵּן).
Mishnah 12; Tosefta 16; Babylonian Talmud 141.

בְּכוֹרוֹת   *Bekhorot* (Firstlings).
Laws concerning firstborn male animals (בְּכוֹר בְּהֵמָה) and their possible blemishes; also the laws concerning firstborn male human beings (בְּכוֹר אָדָם) and related laws, and the laws of the tithing of animals (מַעְשַׂר בְּהֵמָה).
Mishnah 9; Tosefta 7; Babylonian Talmud 61.

עֲרָכִין   *Arakhin* (Valuations).
Laws regarding dedicatory vows of valuation (עֲרָכִין) and other laws of dedicating objects to the Temple (הֶקְדֵּשׁ); in particular, the dedication of fields. Also laws relating to the Jubilee Year (יוֹבֵל).
Mishnah 9; Tosefta 5; Babylonian Talmud 34.

תְּמוּרָה   *Temurah* (Substitution).
Laws governing the substitution of one sacrifice for another; laws concerning other factors that render animals unfit for the altar — and what is done with them.
Mishnah 7; Tosefta 4; Babylonian Talmud 34.

כְּרִיתוֹת   *Keritot* (Excisions).
Those sins which, if committed intentionally, incur the punishment of excision (כָּרֵת), what sacrifices must be brought if one has committed such sins inadvertently, sin-offerings (חַטָּאת), guilt-offerings (אָשָׁם) or suspensive guilt-offerings (אָשָׁם תָּלוּי).
Mishnah 6; Tosefta 4; Babylonian Talmud 29.

מְעִילָה   *Me'ilah* (Sacrilege).
Laws concerning the unlawful use of objects or property that have been consecrated to the Temple; what constitutes sacrilege; in what circumstances sacrilege is considered to have been committed; laws of agency in committing sacrilege.
Mishnah 6; Tosefta 3; Babylonian Talmud 22.

תָּמִיד   *Tamid* (Daily, "daily sacrifices").
The permanent laws of the Temple, the procedures regarding the regular daily sacrifice

(תָּמִיד) and the other arrangements for the daily service in the Temple, in chronological order from start to finish.
Mishnah 6; Babylonian Talmud 8.

מִדּוֹת *Middot* (Measurements).
The plan of the Temple (mainly the Second Temple), with the measurements of each of its sections, and a description of the functions of its various courtyards and chambers.
Mishnah 5.

קִנִּים *Kinnim* (Birds' nests, "pairs of sacrificial birds").
The sacrifices of birds (mainly in pairs) offered as a sin-offering or burnt-offering for certain offenses or as part of the purification ceremony in certain cases of ritual impurity, and all the laws relating to the problems that arise when birds to be offered up for one sacrifice become mixed up with those of another.
Mishnah 3.

סֵדֶר טָהֳרוֹת *Teharot* (Purity).

Sixth Order

Laws of ritual purity and impurity. Considered even during the Talmudic period an extremely difficult order of the Mishnah. Apparently no Gemara was composed for this order except for the tractate *Niddah*, because of its importance in everyday life.

כֵּלִים *Kelim* (Vessels).
Mainly discusses the various forms of ritual impurity that apply to utensils of all kinds, how they become impure, at what stage in their manufacture they are considered finished articles so that they are liable to ritual impurity, and what parts of them are susceptible to ritual impurity.
Mishnah 30; Tosefta 25.

אֹהָלוֹת *Ohalot* (Tents).
Discusses the ritual impurity of a tent containing a dead body (טוּמְאַת אֹהֶל הַמֵּת), and some other laws regarding the impurity of corpses (טוּמְאַת מֵת).
Mishnah 18; Tosefta 18.

נְגָעִים *Nega'im* (*Tzara'at,* leprosy).
Laws regarding leprosy (צָרַעַת) in people, clothing, and houses — and its purification.
Mishnah 14; Tosefta 9.

פָּרָה *Parah* (Heifer).
Laws regarding the Red Heifer (פָּרָה אֲדוּמָּה) and the ceremony of sprinkling the purifying waters (מֵי חַטָּאת).
Mishnah 12; Tosefta 12.

טָהֳרוֹת *Teharot* (Purifications).
Various laws of ritual impurity, derived both from the Torah and from Rabbinical regulations, and general principles applying to all forms of ritual impurity.
Mishnah 10; Tosefta 11.

מִקְוָאוֹת *Mikvaot* (Ritual baths).
Laws of ritual baths (מִקְוָאוֹת) — how they are to be constructed and how they can be rendered unfit. Laws of ritual immersion (טְבִילָה).
Mishnah 10; Tosefta 8.

נִדָּה *Niddah* (Menstruating woman).
The ritual impurity of a menstruating woman (נִדָּה) and those suffering from uterine

bleeding not connected with their regular period (זָבָה); laws of the ritual impurity of a woman who has given birth (יוֹלֶדֶת).
Mishnah 10; Tosefta 9; Baylonian Talmud 73; Jerusalem Talmud 13.

מַכְשִׁירִין *Makhshirin* (Preparations, predispositions).
How foods become susceptible to ritual impurity by contact with certain liquids.
Mishnah 6; Tosefta 3.

זָבִים *Zavim* (Those suffering from secretions):
Laws of the ritual impurity of those suffering from gonorrheal secretions (זָב); seminal emissions (בַּעַל קֶרִי); transmission of gonorrheal ritual impurity by contact or movement (טוּמְאַת מִדְרָס).
Mishnah 5; Tosefta 5.

טְבוּל יוֹם *Tevul Yom* (Immersed during the day).
Laws governing the ritual impurity of someone who has immersed himself in a ritual bath during the day, but who does not attain ritual purity until the evening.
Mishnah 4; Tosefta 2.

יָדַיִם *Yadayim* (Hands).
Laws regarding the washing of hands (נְטִילַת יָדַיִם) and some of the Rabbinical regulations concerning the ritual impurity of hands. It also contains other Rabbinical regulations on various subjects.
Mishnah 4; Tosefta 2.

עֻקְצִין *Uktzin* (Stems, stalks).
Laws governing the ritual impurity of stems and the fruits attached to them, and in general which inedible parts of fruits are considered parts of the fruit itself when it comes to contracting ritual impurity.
Mishnah 3; Tosefta 3.

The Minor Tractates

מַסֶּכְתּוֹת קְטַנּוֹת (Minor Tractates).
The so-called Minor Tractates, some of which are in fact rather long, were also termed מַסֶּכְתּוֹת חִיצוֹנִיּוֹת (External Tractates) by the Geonim. They deal with many subjects, but what they have in common is that their subject matter does not generally have a specific place in the Mishnah and Talmud, though many of them do refer to Torah laws and major Halakhic principles. These tractates might be an indication that another order of the Mishnah once existed.

אָבוֹת דְּרַבִּי נָתָן *(Avot of Rabbi Natan).*
A supplement and expansion of tractate אָבוֹת *(Ethics of the Fathers)*, consisting mainly of the guidance and ethical sayings of the great Rabbis of the Mishnah. Forty-one chapters.

סוֹפְרִים *Soferim* (Scribes).
A comprehensive collection of laws governing Torah scrolls and how they must be written, laying down the accepted Masoretic text of the Torah, and containing laws of reading the Torah and the Haftarot. Twenty-one chapters.

שְׂמָחוֹת *Semaḥot* (Happy occasions).
The euphemistic name given to the tractate discussing the laws of mourning, its real name being אֵבֶל רַבָּתִי *(Evel Rabbati*, "Great mourning"). It deals with the laws of interment, eulogies, and laws governing mourning in general. Fourteen chapters.

כַּלָּה   *Kallah* (Bride).
Discusses laws of marriage, and modesty in sexual relations. One chapter.

כַּלָּה רַבָּתִי   *Kallah Rabbati* (Long tractate on brides).
Discusses laws of personal behavior and what manners befit a Jew, particularly a scholar. Since it begins with laws of marriage and modesty, it is called *Kallah Rabbati* to distinguish it from the shorter tractate mentioned above. Ten chapters.

דֶּרֶךְ אֶרֶץ רַבָּה   *Derekh Eretz Rabbah* (Long tractate on courtesy).
Deals with the laws of courtesy and with general ethics. Eleven chapters.

דֶּרֶךְ אֶרֶץ זוּטָא   *Derekh Eretz Zuta* (Short tractate on courtesy).
Discusses the manners and behavior appropriate to a scholar. Appended to this tractate is a chapter called *Perek HaShalom* (פֶּרֶק הַשָּׁלוֹם — the chapter of peace), in praise of peace. Eleven chapters including *Perek HaShalom*.

גֵּרִים   *Gerim* (Converts).
Deals with the laws governing converts — the righteous proselyte (גֵּר צֶדֶק) and the resident alien (גֵּר תּוֹשָׁב — a non-Jewish citizen who has renounced idolatry), and general laws regarding conversion. Four chapters.

כּוּתִים   *Kutim* (Samaritans).
The Rabbinical laws applying to the Samaritans, who were viewed as a sect between Jews and non-Jews. Two chapters.

עֲבָדִים   *Avadim* (Slaves).
The detailed laws governing Hebrew slaves. Three chapters.

סֵפֶר תּוֹרָה   *Sefer Torah* (Torah scroll).
The laws of writing a Torah scroll and particular words in the Torah that have to be written in a special way. Five chapters.

תְּפִילִין   *Tefillin* (Phylacteries).
The laws of the head and arm phylacteries (תְּפִילִין) and the laws governing the writing of the parchments they contain. One chapter.

צִיצִית   *Tzitzit* (Fringes).
Laws of ritual fringes (צִיצִית). One chapter.

מְזוּזָה   *Mezuzah.*
Laws of writing the parchment scroll placed on doorposts, and the place and manner in which they must be affixed. Two chapters.

Detailed explanations of these numbers are to be found in the following pages. Large circles indicate the various texts appearing on the Talmud page. Small circles with arrows indicate references to the texts.

1) Page number. 2) Page heading. 3) Talmud text. 4) Indication of the Mishnah and the Gemara. 5) Punctuation. 6) Parentheses and correction of the Talmud text. 7) Rashi's commentary. 8) Tosafot. 9) References in Rashi and in Tosafot. 10) Rabbenu Hananel. 11) *Ein Mishpat Ner Mitzvah.* 12) *Torah Or.* 13) *Masoret HaShas.* 14) *Haggahot HaBah.* 15) *Haggahot HaGra.* 16) *Gilyon HaShas.* 17) *Haggahot Rav B. Ronsburg.*

The Layout of a Talmud Page

The layout of a page of Talmud as we know it today — i.e., the Talmud text running down the center of the page, surrounded by Rashi's commentary and the Tosafot — and the division of the text into numbered pages, was established in the Bomberg edition that was published in Venice between 1520 and 1523. This layout and pagination were later adopted in almost all printed editions of the Talmud, with only minor changes in page numbering.

As new printed editions of the Talmud were produced, additional commentaries, glosses, and reference apparatus were added in the margins. These additions varied considerably from one edition to another. An especially respected edition of the Talmud is that of the Widow and Brothers Romm of Vilna (printed between 1880 and 1886), which was accurately proofread and included many important additions. Most present-day editions of the Talmud are photo-offsets of the Vilna edition.

Since the components of the Talmud page and its reference symbols are important for the understanding of its content, they are explained below.

Page Numbers (1)

The outer upper corner of each page contains its number. On the first side (the front side) of each folio page the number appears in its Hebrew form, using the letters of the alphabet to represent the numerals, in the upper left-hand corner. On the second side (the reverse side) of the folio page, in the upper right-hand (outer) corner, one finds the page number in Arabic numerals and not in Hebrew letters. The numbering in Hebrew letters refers to each folio, both sides of the page. The numbering in Arabic numerals is according to each single page. Thus the Arabic numerals are double the folio number in Hebrew letters. In fact, when referring to the Talmud, the Arabic numeral is generally ignored.

The folio (double page) is the unit on which the numbering of the Talmudic tractates is based. The folio numbers of each tractate always begin with ב, i.e., double-page 2, since double-page 1 is the title page of the tractate. Every folio (in Hebrew, *daf*) has two sides (in Hebrew, *amudim;* sing., *amud*). The first side of the *daf* is called *amud alef* (א), and the second side (the reverse side of the folio), is called *amud bet* (ב). As mentioned above, the Hebrew number of the folio is printed on side *a*, and the Arabic number on side *b*. The standard practice in citing a page of Talmud is to refer to the name of the tractate, the number of the folio, and the side. The sample page would be cited in the following way: מגילה כה ע״א — *Megillah, daf* כה, *amud* א; or *Megillah* 25a. Sometimes a different system of notation is used to identify the sides: a period following the folio number indicates side *a* (כה.), and a colon indicates side *b* (כה:).

The Page Heading (2)

The heading across the top of the page, in large square letters, is composed of three parts: to the right, the name of the chapter; in the center, the chapter number; and to the left, the name of the tractate. The complete heading before us reads as follows: the name of the chapter (הַקּוֹרֵא עוֹמֵד), the chapter number (פֶּרֶק שְׁלִישִׁי, Chapter Three), and the name of the tractate (מְגִילָה, *Megillah*).

The page heading and its form are also a tradition dating from the first printed editions. In most of the manuscript sources before the advent of printing the only way to refer to passages in the Talmud was to give the name of the chapter containing the passage (and, in the case of a Mishnah, the number of the relevant chapter and the number of the paragraph within it). The chapters were usually named after the first word or words in them, and only a few chapters were given names or titles indicating their content.

The Talmud Text [the Mishnah and the Gemara] (3)

The main text of the Mishnah and Gemara is presented in the center of the page, in the traditional "square" typeface. The version of the Talmud in our possession is mainly that of Rashi (Rabbi Shlomo ben Yitzḥak, 1040–1105). He himself studied and compared a great number of manuscripts of the Talmud, and many of his emendations were later included within the text itself, although now, as a result of later editing, some of them may appear superfluous and incomprehensible. Occasionally the authors of the Tosafot defend an earlier reading which Rashi had changed. The text in our possession was also edited by Rabbi Shlomo Luria (מהרש״ל, c. 1510–1574). Many of his corrections were included in the standard printed versions of the text, but without any indication that they were emendations. It should also be noted that there are important variant manuscripts of the Talmud (among the most famous being the Munich manuscript [1334] of the entire Talmud), in which one occasionally finds illuminating variant readings. At the same time it is well known that, despite careful proofreading by generations of printers, the text still contains many mistakes and typographical errors (which, because of the technique of photo-offset reproduction, are perpetuated in new editions). The Talmud was also subjected to government and church censorship, and most present-day editions still contain a considerable number of changes and omissions introduced by censorship. Indeed, almost every passage dealing with non-Jews must be suspected of having undergone some change.

Indication of the Mishnah and the Gemara (4)

When a new Mishnah appears on a page it is preceded by the abbreviation מתני׳ in larger letters, an abbreviation of מַתְנִיתִין, meaning "Mishnah" or "Our Mishnah." The start of the section of Gemara immediately following each Mishnah is indicated by the large letters גמ׳, the abbreviation of גְּמָרָא.

In the editions of the Talmud in our possession the text of the Gemara is presented after every individual Mishnah. In many manuscripts — and also in many editions of the Jerusalem Talmud — all the passages from the Mishnah are presented together at the beginning of each chapter. The division of the Mishnah passages as quoted in the Talmud is not identical with that in separate editions of the Mishnah, and in places the text is slightly different.

The colon (:) is used in the Gemara and in the other sources and commentaries to mark the end of a paragraph (like the period used in standard punctuation today), and the period is used like a comma.

Some manuscripts of the Mishnah and Gemara contain more punctuation marks than the printed editions, and there are also manuscripts containing cantillation marks, like those used in texts of the Bible, which help to punctuate the entire text. In standard editions only traces remain of an ancient four-dot punctuation system, in which a period was a kind of comma, and a colon marked the end of a sentence. Three dots (.:) indicated the end of a passage, and four dots (::) marked a new subject of discussion. Only the first two signs remain in the printed editions. The colon is also found within the text of the Gemara, separating one topic from another. But it does not always indicate a truly significant division.

Parentheses in the Gemara indicate a passage (or word) concerning which there is some doubt, and which according to other sources should be entirely deleted or replaced by another version. Generally, opposite the same line at the side of the page, there is an explanation of the variant or mention of the source according to which the emendation was made in the text.

Square brackets in the Gemara indicate an addition to the text, either according to a manuscript or from another source. Occasionally, at the side of the page and opposite the line in question, there is also an explanation of the source of the addition. Sometimes round and square brackets follow each other, when it is proposed to delete one variant and substitute another for it.

In the body of the text (and sometimes in the commentaries) these parentheses are ordinarily used for a proposed textual emendation, and not for punctuation. In many instances one should view these emendations — both the deletions and the additions — as mere suggestions, since the text may be understood (sometimes using another method of interpretation) in the earlier, uncorrected, version as well. Sets of parentheses (the function of which is not always clear) also separate many of the conventional signs in the Talmud from the rest of the text. These signs, all of which are for mnemonic convenience, vary from manuscript to manuscript. The signs are usually indicated by apostrophes or inverted commas before the final letter of each "word," but they are not always abbreviations. The meaning of the signs is also not always clear. Most of the commentators ignore them, and many of them contain printing errors.

I n all editions Rashi's commentary is found next to the text on the inner side of the page (the one closest to the binding). The commentary is always written in "Rashi script" preceded by a quotation from the Gemara introducing the word or passage to be explained. This quotation is called דִּיבּוּר הַמַּתְחִיל — *dibbur hamat'ḥil,* "the starting word or phrase" — and it is separated from the commentary by a period at its end. The end of the commentary on that word or passage is indicated by a colon (:). In many instances the quotation from the Gemara should be read as an integral part of Rashi's commentary and the two parts should be run together.

Rashi is universally acknowledged as the greatest commentator on the Talmud. He lived in France and spent most of his life in the city of Troyes. Basing himself on the written and oral interpretations of his teachers he composed a commentary on the Talmud which he himself corrected from time to time (the version in our possession is generally a second or third edition of his commentaries). Because Rashi's commentary was copied by his students immediately after it was put in writing by its author and was circulated in the form of booklets, it is occasionally called פֵּירוּשׁ הַקוּנְטְרֵס — *perush hakuntres,* "booklet commentary." Rashi commented on most of the Talmud, but his commentary on certain tractates is incomplete (e.g., *Bava Batra* was mainly interpreted by his grandson, Rabbi Shmuel ben Meir, רשב"ם, c. 1085–1174, and the commentary on

Punctuation
(5)

Parentheses and Corrections of the Text
(6)

Rashi's Commentary
(7)

Makkot was completed by his son-in-law, Rabbi Yehudah ben Natan, ריב״ן, 11th–12th century). In some tractates the commentary attributed to Rashi and printed under his name is not his own but that of one of his students (as in the tractate *Ta'anit*).

Almost all Talmudic commentators after the time of Rashi relate to his commentary, in some way disagreeing with it, defending it, interpreting it, or clarifying it. Books have also been written analyzing his methodology and clarifying and classifying his characteristic expressions.

Tosafot (8)

Tosafot are always printed in the outer column of the page (usually in Rashi script). The quotation from the Gemara text (the *dibbur hamat'hil*) introducing the passage to be explained is found at the beginning of each passage and is set off from the Tosafot proper by a period. The first word of the *dibbur hamat'hil* is printed in large square letters. The end of each Tosafot is indicated by a colon (:).

The Tosafot were the collective creation of Rashi's disciples and their students (including many of his own descendants), and they are a kind of summary of the style of study and inquiry in the yeshivot of France and Germany in the twelfth and thirteenth centuries. They began as additions to and notes on Rashi's commentary; they were subsequently expanded and became a profound and independent interpretation of the Gemara itself. Indeed, in some cases one can view them as an extension of the Talmudic discussion. Among the great authors of the Tosafot were Rabbi Shmuel ben Meir (רשב״ם), Rabbenu Tam (רַבֵּינוּ תָּם), and Rabbi Ya'akov ben Meir (c. 1100–1171) — Rashi's grandsons; also Rabbenu Yitzhak (ר״י, 1115–1184), Rabbi Yitzhak ben Asher (ריב״א), Rabbi Yitzhak ben Avraham (ריצב״א), Rabbenu Hayyim, Rabbenu Peretz, and Morenu (our teacher) Rabbi Meir (מהר״ם) of Rothenberg. The Tosafot were edited in various academies by a number of Sages. The editions of the Tosafot in our possession are mainly those of the Academy of Touques (named after that city in France), but there are some versions of Tosafot from other academies (for example those of Sens and Evreux). These additions sometimes appear as appendices in the outer margins of the page, termed תּוֹסָפוֹת יְשָׁנִים — *Tosafot Yeshanim*. In some tractates only these versions of the Tosafot have been included.

Vernacular Words

Rashi and Tosafot occasionally translated words into Old French or other languages, using the languages they spoke in order to explain obscure concepts when they did not have an appropriate word in Hebrew. Rashi usually accompanies such a translation with the word בְּלַעַז — "in the vernacular" — and the vernacular word is always marked by the insertion of a pair of inverted commas before the last letter of the word. These do not indicate an abbreviation, but simply make the word stand out. The vernacular words are written phonetically, and there are regular rules for transliterating them into Hebrew: ש = s, ק = ch, א at the end of a word = e. In many editions of the Talmud there is a translation appendix after each tractate (פֵּירוּשׁ מְתוּרְגְּמָן) explaining these foreign words (according to their place in Rashi and Tosafot) in Hebrew or in Yiddish-German written in Hebrew letters.

Rashi's vernacular words are usually in Old French or Provencal, and, more rarely, in German and Italian. Many of them were not understood in later generations, so scribal errors were made in copying them. They represent the language at a certain level of historical development and are therefore a valuable source of information for the study of these languages.

References in Rashi and the Tosafot (9)

References in Rashi's commentary and in Tosafot to other Talmudic passages are occasionally included in parentheses or square brackets in Rashi script smaller than the Rashi script of the text. These references are not part of Rashi's commentary or of Tosafot, but rather later additions by other Rabbis.

רַבֵּנוּ חֲנַנְאֵל

In many tractates, but not all, the Vilna edition added the commentary of Rabbenu Ḥananel. In that commentary there is generally no special sign to indicate a quotation from the main body of the text.

Rabbenu Ḥananel, the son of Ḥushiel, lived in North Africa in the eleventh century (990–1055). His is one of the earliest commentaries on the Talmud. His father, who was also his teacher, was a student of the Geonim in Babylonia, and the commentaries of Rabbenu Ḥananel mainly express the exegetical tradition of the Geonim. Unlike Rashi's commentary, Rabbenu Ḥananel deals mainly with the interpretation of whole passages or sections, clarifying the principal contents and not always going into detail. Many of his commentaries appear in the *Arukh* (סֵפֶר הֶעָרוּךְ — Dictionary — by Rabbi Natan b. Yeḥiel of Rome, 11th century) and in the interpretations of the Tosafot.

עֵין מִשְׁפָּט נֵר מִצְוָה

Ein Mishpat provides reference to the primary Halakhic works that treat the subject matter of the Gemara. Reference to *Ein Mishpat* in the text of the Gemara is indicated by a small square letter, generally placed next to the opinion that reflects the ultimately accepted Halakhah. Each entry in *Ein Mishpat* begins with a large square letter followed by a smaller square letter or several small letters, all of which refer to the same topic. The large reference letters run consecutively from the beginning of the chapter to the end, and every chapter starts again from א; that system of reference number, however, no longer has relevance for the user. The smaller square letter following it corresponds to what appears in the body of the text. *Ein Mishpat* usually refers to three works of Halakhah: Rambam's (Maimonides') *Mishneh Torah* (מִשְׁנֶה תּוֹרָה); *Sefer Mitzvot Gadol* (סֵפֶר מִצְוֹת גָּדוֹל) by Rabbi Moshe of Coucy (thirteenth century); and the *Shulḥan Arukh* (שׁוּלְחָן עָרוּךְ) by Rabbi Yosef Caro (1488–1575). The first reference is to Maimonides, generally known by the initials of his name and title as Rambam (רמב"ם = Rabbi Moshe ben Maimon).

His work is indicated by the abbreviation מיי' = מַיְמוֹנִי; then comes the chapter number (e.g., פ"ט = ch. 9); this is followed by the section in which that chapter is found (e.g. הִלְכוֹת תְּפִילָה — the laws of prayer); and finally, the specific Halakhah within the chapter. It should be noted that no explicit reference is made to the book of the *Mishneh Torah* in which the section (e.g. הִלְכוֹת תְּפִילָה) is to be found. The reader is expected to know which of the fourteen books is intended. The second sign is סמ"ג (= סֵפֶר מִצְוֹת גָּדוֹל). This book is arranged in the order of the commandments, positive (עֲשִׂין) and negative (לָאוִין), and the symbols refer to the section of the book and the number of the commandment. The third sign is for the *Shulḥan Arukh*. Since that work is based on the order of the *Arba'ah Turim* (אַרְבָּעָה טוּרִים, an earlier Halakhic work, also known as the *Tur*, טוּר), the reference has two purposes: it refers both to the טוּר and to the שׁוּלְחָן עָרוּךְ and is indicated by the abbreviation טוש"ע (= טוּר שׁוּלְחָן עָרוּךְ). Afterwards the section in which the particular Halakhah appears is indicated, i.e., אֶבֶן הָעֶזֶר — אה"ע; יוֹרֶה דֵעָה — יו"ד; אוֹרַח חַיִּים — או"ח; חוֹשֶׁן מִשְׁפָּט — חו"מ. Then come the numerical letters indicating the sub-sections and paragraphs. There are subjects that are not found in all three of these works. In such cases, only the one or two works where they do appear are indicated.

This important reference tool was created by Rabbi Yehoshua Boaz (author of שִׁלְטֵי הַגִּבּוֹרִים — *Shiltei HaGibborim*), who lived in Italy in the sixteenth century. The author intended to write an even more extensive work. *Ein Mishpat* was to include references to the major Halakhic authorities, whereas *Ner Mitzvah* (indicated by the large square letters) was meant to be a reference to a more extensive and profound discussion of Halakhic issues and the relation between the Talmud and Halakhic decisions. That plan was never carried out, and only the reference marks remain.

תּוֹרָה אוֹר

Torah Or, written mainly by Rabbi Yehoshua Boaz, is a reference apparatus for Biblical quotations. Later Rabbis supplemented his work.

A tiny circle in the Talmud text marks the first word of the Biblical quotation. The reference appears opposite the same line, in the narrow space between the Talmud text and commentaries of Rashi or the Tosafot. It gives the name of the book and the number of the chapter where the quotation is found, but not the number of the verse. If the same book was previously mentioned, it uses only the word שָׁם (= ibid.).

Masoret HaShas (13)

מָסוֹרֶת הַש"ס

Parallel texts and cross-references to identical passages elsewhere in the Talmud are given in the reference apparatus called *Masoret HaShas*. Sometimes the parallel is simply the use of a certain expression, rather than an issue of Halakhah or a whole discussion, or it may also be some parallel linguistic form or topic. Explanations of individual words or expressions are cited from various works, in particular the *Arukh. Masoret HaShas* also frequently contains textual emendations based on the parallel sources. The correction of a text is marked by the abbreviation צ"ל, meaning צָרִיךְ לִהְיוֹת — "it ought to be" — before the emendation. When the correction is not certain, but another significant version exists, there is simply a note that in another source one finds such and such. Parallel sources are cited according to tractate, folio, and page. If the parallel source is from the same tractate, the note says לְעֵיל — "above" — if the parallel is on a previous page, and לְקַמָּן — "in front of us" — if it is on a later page. Not every tractate contains full reference to every parallel of a given subject. Often a reference to one of the sources is given, with the additional abbreviation וש"נ (standing for וְשָׁם נִסְמָן), meaning that the other parallel sources are listed there.

Masoret HaShas is generally printed in small letters in Rashi script in the column headed מסורת הש"ס in the inside margin of the page. Passages cross-referenced by *Masoret HaShas* are marked in the Talmud text by an asterisk before the first word. The reference is printed on the same level as the asterisk. When there is not enough room in that column, some of these references are placed under *Ein Mishpat* on the outer margin of the page. Some of the *Masoret Hashas* references appear in square brackets, meaning that the reference was added by later scholars.

Masoret HaShas was also compiled by Rabbi Yehoshua Boaz. He determined the system and formulation of *Masoret HaShas,* and the main features of this system have been preserved to the present day. Over the generations certain scholars improved *Masoret HaShas,* adding a large number of new sources. Many of the additions were compiled by Rabbi Yeshayahu Pik Berlin, the Rabbi of Breslau during the eighteenth century (1725–1799). Most of his additions are indicated with square brackets in *Masoret HaShas.*

Haggahot HaBaḥ (14)

הַגָּהוֹת הַב"ח (Emendations of the Baḥ)

Haggahot HaBaḥ are generally proposed emendations in the text of the Gemara, in Rashi's commentary and in the Tosafot. When a correction is proposed, the words needing correction are presented in parentheses followed by the letters תא"מ, which stand for תֵּבוֹת אֵלֶּה מֻקָּפוֹת — "these words are circled," after which is written ונ"ב (וְנִכְתַּב בְּצִדּוֹ — "and at its side is written"). Following that abbreviation comes the proposed correction. Sometimes there are explanatory remarks or other comments regarding the contents of the text, but they are always written with great brevity.

The author of *Haggahot HaBaḥ* is Rabbi Yoel Sirkes, who lived in Poland during the seventeenth century. He is famous for his important book, *Bayit Ḥadash* (בַּיִת חָדָש), a commentary on the *Arba'ah Turim*. His textual emendations to the Talmud were written in the margins of the volumes he himself used, and this explains the method adopted to indicate the emendations. He marked dubious words in parentheses, and at their side he wrote his comments. In his editing he seems to have depended greatly on parallel sources and on various manuscripts. Usually, however, his emendations are simple and almost self-explanatory for a scholar expert in the style of the Gemara. Many of them are useful to correct faulty or unclear expressions and replace them with better ones.

Haggahot HaBaḥ are printed either in the outer margin or at the bottom of the page. In the Talmud text, reference to them is made by letter numerals in Rashi script in parentheses; within the commentaries of Rashi and Tosafot these reference numbers do not appear. One must look in the *Haggahot HaBaḥ* to see if there are comments on Rashi or Tosafot. If there are comments, they are indicated by the words רש״י (= Rashi) or תוס׳ (= תּוֹסָפוֹת Tosafot). Immediately following these words appears the abbreviation ד״ה (= דִּיבּוּר הַמַּתְחִיל — the first words of the passage to be commented on) which is concluded by the abbreviation וכו׳ (= etc.). The Baḥ's comments follow this.

הַגָּהוֹת הגר״א   (Emendations of the Vilna Gaon)

This method of emendation is similar to that of the Baḥ, but the language of the author is more vigorous. It often says: "These words are to be erased," or "erased"; and after the correction it adds כצ״ל (= כָּךְ צָרִיךְ לִהְיוֹת — "this is how it should be"). The *Haggahot HaGra* are found in the outer margin of the page and are referred to in the text by a square Hebrew letter enclosed in square brackets.

גר״א are the initials of HaGaon *Rabbi Eliyahu*, known as the Vilna Gaon, who lived in the eighteenth century (1720–1797). Like the Baḥ, he also wrote corrections in the volumes of the Talmud that he used, and these corrections were later copied and printed with the Talmud. *Haggahot HaGra* often suggest radical changes in the standard text, but many of them are generally derived from parallel sources, whether in the Talmud itself or in other books of Talmudic literature and its commentators.

Haggahot HaGra (15)

גִּלְיוֹן הש״ס

The notes in *Gilyon HaShas* refer to the Gemara, to Rashi, and to Tosafot. They may be of various types. Sometimes they merely provide a reference to another source (ע״ש = עַיֵּין שָׁם — "see there") where the same phraseology is found. At other times the references are similar to those of *Masoret HaShas*, but treat a matter not included in that apparatus, either because it was omitted there or because it indicates a similarity not of wording but of a different kind, such as method or approach. Occasionally *Gilyon HaShas* comments on problems and contradictions in the Talmud and its commentators, referring to different interpretations or other sources. The comments are often questions, usually ending in צ״ע (= צָרִיךְ עִיּוּן — "it needs further investigation") or sometimes צע״ג (= עִיּוּן גָּדוֹל — "it needs much further investigation"). The *Gilyon HaShas* is found either in the outer margin or at the bottom of the page, and is referred to in the text by a small diacritical circle: O.

The author of *Gilyon HaShas* is Rabbi Akiva Eger, a famous nineteenth-century scholar (1761–1837) and Rabbi of the city of Posen. He calls the student's attention to a variety of problems, sometimes offering references to sources that are parallel in content but not necessarily in their wording. In general Rabbi Akiva Eger raises questions and points out problems, difficulties, or contradictions in the commentaries accompanying the Talmud or in the remarks of other commentators. Occasionally he also points out difficulties and contradictions in the Talmud itself, but rarely resolves them. Later scholars have written books and hundreds of comments in order to resolve the difficulties he raised.

Gilyon HaShas (16)

הַגָּהוֹת ר״ב רִנְשְׁבּוּרג   (Emendations of Rav B. Ronsburg)

Textual emendations by Rabbi Betzalel Ronsburg (1760–1820), the author of הוֹרָה גָּבֶר. *Haggahot Rav B. Ronsburg* are printed in the inner margin or at the bottom of the page. Reference to them is found in the Talmud text, Rashi and the Tosafot, in the form of a square Hebrew letter with a bracket on the left side of the letter.

Haggahot Rav B. Ronsburg (17)

Summary of Special Signs

The signs listed below are found in the Vilna edition of the Talmud and in other similar editions. These signs, however, are in no way standard, and in some editions different signs are often used to refer to the very same sources.

ASTERISK: An asterisk next to a word in the Talmud text designates a reference to *Masoret HaShas.* The reference is found on the inside margin of the page in the same row as the asterisk. When there is not enough room in that column, some of these references are placed under *Ein Mishpat Ner Mitzvah* on the outer margin of the page.

A SMALL SQUARE LETTER: Indicates a reference to the Halakhah in *Ein Mishpat Ner Mitzvah.* These letters refer, in order, to the small square letters (not the large ones) of the entries on the outer upper margin of the page.

CIRCLE: A circle next to a word designates a reference to a verse in the Bible. The reference itself is found on the same line in the narrow margin between the body of the text and Rashi's commentary or that of Tosafot, on the left or right side of the text, depending on the space available.

A LETTER IN RASHI SCRIPT IN PARENTHESES: Designates a reference to *Haggahot HaBaḥ*, located in the outer or inner margin of the page (depending on the space available), or at the bottom of the page.

A SMALL SQUARE LETTER IN SQUARE BRACKETS: Designates *Haggahot HaGra,* located in the outer or inner margin of the page (depending on the space available), or at the bottom of the page.

A CIRCLE WITH A LINE THROUGH IT: Designates *Gilyon HaShas,* located in the outer or inner margin of the page (depending on the space available), or at the bottom of the page.

Commentaries and Other Additions

Certain tractates in the Vilna edition contain other commentaries and additions, usually printed in the outer margins of the page. These include:

רַב נִסִּים גָּאוֹן   The Commentary of Rav Nissim Gaon. In several tractates there is also the commentary of Rav Nissim Gaon, which explains selected passages only and is not found on every page.

Rav Nissim the son of Ya'akov Gaon (c. 990–1062) lived in North Africa. His commentary, *Mafteaḥ LeManulei HaTalmud* (מַפְתֵּחַ לְמַנְעוּלֵי הַתַּלְמוּד) is only partially extant. His commentaries refer to relatively few passages, and largely express the exegetical methods of the Geonim of Babylonia.

פֵּירוּשׁ רַבֵּינוּ גֵּרְשׁוֹם   The Commentary of Rabbenu Gershom (*Me'or HaGolah — The Light of the Diaspora;* c. 960–1028 C.E.). The style of his commentary bears a certain resemblance to that of Rashi.

תּוֹסָפוֹת יְשָׁנִים   *Tosafot Yeshanim.* A version of the Tosafot containing much new material on the tractates *Yoma* and *Yevamot.* In some editions there are also other versions of Tosafot for various tractates, including material that is not found in the standard version of the Tosafot (תּוֹסְפוֹת הָרִי"ד, תּוֹסְפוֹת חַד מִקַּמָּאֵי, תּוֹסְפוֹת הָרֹא"שׁ and others).

שִׁיטָה מְקוּבֶּצֶת   *Shittah Mekubbetzet.* A collection of emendations and short comments by Rabbi Betzalel Ashkenazi (16th century) on the tractates in the order of *Kodashim.* The emendations are based on many manuscripts and on the commentaries of the Rishonim.

הַגָּהוֹת צֹאן קָדָשִׁים   *Haggahot Tzon Kodashim.* Emendations to the order of *Kodashim* by Rabbi Shmuel Kaidanover (1614–1676), the author of בִּרְכַּת הַזֶּבַח and צֹאן קָדָשִׁים, commentaries on the order of *Kodashim.* Similar to *Haggahot HaBaḥ*.

הַגָּהוֹת הר"י לַנְדָּא *Haggahot HaRi Landau.* The textual emendations of Rabbi Yeḥezkel Landau (1713–1793), the author of נוֹדַע בִּיהוּדָה, and Rabbi of Prague.

In addition to the commentaries "on the page," most editions of the Talmud include appendices presenting the commentaries of several Halakhic authorities and exegetes. The more comprehensive and modern the edition, the more it generally tries to outdo its predecessors by adding commentaries and notes, taken either from manuscripts of the commentaries of the Rishonim or from the textual emendations and interpretations of more recent scholars. Below is a list of some of these additional commentaries, commonly found in most editions.

Additional Commentaries That Do Not Appear on the Page

פִּסְקֵי תּוֹסָפוֹת *Piskei Tosafot* (found in many editions), a summary of the Halakhic rulings and conclusions found in the Tosafot. Traditionally this short book is attributed to the Rosh (see below), and for that reason, though it is only a collection of references, it is considered a book of Halakhic decisions in its own right.

הִלְכוֹת הרא"ש *Hilkhot HaRosh* (found in many editions), Halakhot composed by Rabbenu Asher ben Yeḥiel (1250–1327), who completed his education in Germany, his main teacher being Rabbi Meir of Rothenberg. In later life he settled in Spain. The most important of his works is his book of Halakhot, in which he quotes the Talmud, adds the interpretations (chiefly those touching upon the Halakhah) of the Tosafot and other scholars, and sums up with his own opinion. This book is important as one of the primary sources of Halakhic literature, and it can also serve as a Halakhic commentary on important parts of the Talmud. In most editions *Hilkhot HaRosh* are accompanied by auxiliary commentaries such as *Tiferet Shmuel* (תִּפְאֶרֶת שְׁמוּאֵל) and *Korban Netanel* (קָרְבַּן נְתַנְאֵל), most of which were written in the seventeenth century.

קִיצוּר פִּסְקֵי הרא"ש *Kitzur Piskei HaRosh,* the Halakhic conclusions of the Rosh as found in his book, *Hilkhot HaRosh.* This summary version was composed by his son Rabbi Ya'akov (1270–1343), the author of *Arba'ah Turim* (אַרְבָּעָה טוּרִים). This short work is also used as a Halakhic source.

פֵּירוּשׁ הַמִּשְׁנָיוֹת לרמב"ם *Perush HaMishnayot LaRambam* (in many editions), Rambam's first great Rabbinic work. This commentary, also called סֵפֶר הַמָּאוֹר — *Sefer HaMa'or* — was originally written in Arabic. It appears in regular editions of the Talmud in old, but not necessarily good, Hebrew translations. The commentary is written very succinctly and contains important and original interpretations. The prefaces and introductions are extremely important. In recent years a new Hebrew translation by Rabbi Yosef Kappaḥ has appeared.

מהרש"ל *Maharshal* (in most editions), the work by Rabbi Shlomo Luria, Rabbi in Lublin in the sixteenth century (1510–1573). This is one of the most important and widely used Talmudic reference works. In it the Maharshal succinctly discusses the Talmud and its most important commentators. A major part of the work consists of textual emendations, many of which are now incorporated within the editions of the Talmud itself, often without any indication that they are emendations.

מהרש"א *Maharsha* (in most editions), a combination of two works by Rabbi Shmuel Eliezer Edels (1555–1631), the Rabbi of Ostrog, Poland, in the sixteenth century. Two works, *Ḥiddushei Halakhot* (חִידּוּשֵׁי הֲלָכוֹת) and *Ḥiddushei Aggadot* (חִידּוּשֵׁי אַגָּדוֹת), cover almost the entire Talmud. In most editions the two were combined and printed together, though in two different typefaces. חִידּוּשֵׁי הֲלָכוֹת mainly interprets the Talmud, Rashi, and Tosafot, page by page, whereas חִידּוּשֵׁי אַגָּדוֹת interprets the Aggadic material in the Talmud, both literally and figuratively. For centuries the works of the Maharsha have been considered an essential part of advanced Talmud study.

מהר"ם   *Maharam* (in most editions), a commentary on the entire Talmud written by Rabbi Meir of Lublin (1558–1618). This work is mainly the fruit of the author's teaching experience in his yeshivah, and its didactic nature is evident: the work is quite extensive at the beginning of each tractate but diminishes in extent towards the end. Rabbi Meir's commentaries on the Talmud, Rashi, and Tosafot are considered to be clear and close to the literal meaning of the text.

The study of the המהרש"א, מהרש"ל and מהר"ם was an essential part of Talmud study in almost every yeshivah. Apart from these works, which are printed in many editions, additional commentaries by many later rabbis are found in the large Vilna editions, including comments, emendations, and short explanations. The following are only a few of these many commentaries.

הַגָּהוֹת וְחִידוּשֵׁי הרש"ש   *Haggahot VeḤiddushei HaRashash*, the commentaries of Rabbi Shmuel Strashun of Vilna, a nineteenth-century Rabbinic scholar. They explore the literal meaning of the text, with a critical tendency. Some of these commentaries are also the author's original insights.

חִידוּשֵׁי מהר"ץ חַיּוֹת   *Ḥiddushei Maharatz Ḥayyot*, the commentaries of Rabbi Tzvi Ḥayyot, the Rabbi of Zholkow in Galicia, who lived in the nineteenth century. These commentaries and interpretations include many of the author's original ideas.

הַגָּהוֹת ר' אֶלְעָזָר מֹשֶׁה הוֹרוֹבִיץ   *Haggahot Rabbi Elazar Moshe Horowitz*, original comments and important textual emendations by Rabbi Elazar Moshe Horowitz, the Rabbi of Pinsk in the nineteenth century.

יְפֵה עֵינַיִם   *Yefei Einayim*, by Rabbi Arye Leib Yellin, the Rabbi of Bilsk in the nineteenth century. This work includes many additions to מְסוֹרֶת הש"ס, indicating parallels not only from the Babylonian but also from the Jerusalem Talmud and the Halakhic Midrashim, as well as many quotations from Aggadic Midrashim. It also contains important interpretative comments.

Appended Collections of Halakhic Decisions

The largest and most complete editions of the Talmud also include as appendices certain major works of Halakhic decisions which follow the order of the Talmud.

הִלְכוֹת הרי"ף   *Hilkhot HaRif.* This important book of Halakhah was composed by Rabbi Yitzḥak Alfasi (known as the Rif), who lived in North Africa and Spain in the eleventh century (1013–1103). It is constructed as a kind of Halakhic summary of the Talmud, following the order of discussions in the Talmud but deleting everything that does not touch upon the actual, applicable Halakhah. It shortens the Talmudic debates considerably and leaves out those Halakhot that had no practical application (for that reason it was composed only on the tractates in the orders of *Moed*, *Nashim*, and *Nezikin*, and on the tractates *Berakhot* and *Niddah*). The Rif presents only those Aggadic matters that convey practical lessons, whether in the area of action or of ethics. To this day his work is considered a fundamental source of the Halakhah. Many commentaries have been written on it, some of which are themselves sources for Halakhic decisions and interpretation, and they are important not only for determining the Halakhah but also for understanding the Talmudic text itself. Many of these commentaries, known as נוֹשְׂאֵי כֵּלִים — "armor-bearers" — are printed on the page of standard editions of *Hilkhot HaRif.* Among them should be mentioned an abbreviated version of Rashi's commentary adapted to *Hilkhot HaRif.* Sometimes this commentary reflects a version of Rashi different from that in the Talmud.

הַמָּאוֹר   *HaMa'or* consists of two works, הַמָּאוֹר הַגָּדוֹל (covering the orders of *Nashim* and *Nezikin*) and הַמָּאוֹר הַקָּטָן (on the order of *Moed*). The author is Rabbi Zeraḥyah HaLevi of Lunel in Provence, who lived in the twelfth century. This work mainly contains glosses and criticisms of decisions of the Rif and also the author's original Halakhic conclusions.

הַשָּׂגוֹת הראב״ד   *Hasagot HaRa'avad,* the glosses of Rabbi Avraham ben David of Posquieres (c. 1125–1198), containing sharp criticism of Rabbi Zeraḥyah HaLevi's work and a defense of the Rif, though occasionally also criticizing the latter.

מִלְחֲמוֹת ה׳   *Milḥamot HaShem,* by Rabbi Moshe ben Naḥman (Ramban, also known as Naḥmanides) of Gerona in Spain, who lived in the thirteenth century (1194–1270). Ramban, one of the greatest scholars of the Talmud, wrote this work mainly to defend the Rif from the objections of סֵפֶר הַמָּאוֹר, answering rebuttals and explaining *Hilkhot HaRif.* He also wrote it in response to the *Hasagot HaRa'avad.*

הר״ן   *HaRan,* the interpretation of Rabbenu Nissim ben Reuven of Gerona in Spain, who lived in the fourteenth century. This book is an extensive and exhaustive commentary on *Hilkhot HaRif,* thereby explaining the Talmudic discussion and presenting other authorities as well. The work covers only part of *Hilkhot HaRif* and is generally printed alongside it. It is an extremely important interpretative and Halakhic source.

נִימוּקֵי יוֹסֵף   *Nimukei Yosef,* a commentary on *Hilkhot HaRif,* by Rabbi Yosef Ḥaviva, who lived in Spain in the fifteenth century. His commentaries are usually printed with those tractates on which there is no commentary by Rabbenu Nissim. This work, like that of Rabbenu Nissim, is also a general commentary on the Talmud and the Halakhah, presenting much material from works both by Halakhic authorities and by commentators.

תַּלְמִידֵי רַבֵּינוּ יוֹנָה   *Talmidei Rabbenu Yonah,* a collection of commentaries written by the students of Rabbenu Yonah of Gerona, who lived in Spain in the thirteenth century. This is an extensive and detailed work, and its interpretations are important and interesting. It is printed only on the tractate *Berakhot* (in *Hilkhot HaRif*).

שִׁלְטֵי הַגִּבּוֹרִים   *Shiltei HaGibborim,* the commentary of Rabbi Yehoshua Boaz (the author of מָסוֹרֶת הש״ס and other works), who lived in Italy in the sixteenth century. This book presents supplements to the work of the Rif taken from many other Halakhic authorities.

In addition to those mentioned above, there are a great many additional textual studies and reference works, some of which are printed on the same page as *Hilkhot HaRif.*

סֵפֶר מָרְדְּכַי   *Sefer Mordekhai,* written by Rabbi Mordekhai ben Hillel Ashkenazi, who lived in Germany in the thirteenth century. This book, which follows the order of *Hilkhot HaRif,* is an original work of Halakhic commentary, containing an enormous amount of earlier interpretative and Halakhic material from the Geonim to the great Rabbis of Germany. This work was apparently even more extensive, and what we possess is a kind of summary of it. There are many different manuscripts of this work, which also contain a great deal of additional material. Numerous interpretations, textual emendations, and additions to the *Mordekhai* have been written, some of which are printed on the pages of regular editions of the work. To date no complete edition of this important work has been published.

Aramaic

The Talmud is written in a mixture of Hebrew and Aramaic. A passage of Talmud may be in Hebrew or in Aramaic or in Aramaic and Hebrew. Throughout the Talmud there are also words and expressions in each of these languages that were borrowed from the other. Hebrew and Aramaic are also used together in the Bible (the Books of Daniel and Ezra were written primarily in Aramaic), and this combination continues throughout Talmudic literature and the Midrashim, and extends to Kabbalistic literature and the Siddur. A basic knowledge of Aramaic is therefore necessary if one is to understand classical Jewish literature in general, and the Talmud in particular.

The many similarities between Aramaic and Hebrew are due to the fact that both are northern Semitic languages. Aramaic began as the language of the Aramean tribes; the earliest extant Aramaic inscriptions are about 3,000 thousand years old. With the passage of time, Aramaic became the standard written language of many other peoples as well, and eventually it became an international language, used widely in inscriptions and for international correspondence by the Assyrian kings, as well as by the inhabitants of the Persian Empire. The Aramaic dialect used during this period, Imperial Aramaic, is attested both in contemporary inscriptions and the Books of Ezra and Daniel, and constitutes the first stratum of classical Aramaic. The Persian period marks the golden age of Aramaic as an international language.

The second linguistic stratum of the language, Middle Aramaic, was spoken by the different peoples who lived in Eretz Israel, Syria, and parts of the Persian Empire from the Hellenistic period. Later, Middle Aramaic split into two main branches, each consisting of several dialects: (1) Western Aramaic, whose dialects included the language of the Jews in Galilee (Galilean Aramaic), the Christian inhabitants of Eretz Israel, and Samaritan Aramaic; and (2) Eastern Aramaic, which included the Syriac and Mandaean dialects, as well as the language of the Babylonian Talmud.

After the Arab conquest of the Near East, Arabic replaced Aramaic as the standard language of the region. Aramaic remained a spoken language in only a few places, such as Ma'alula (in Syria), where a dialect of Western Aramaic was spoken, and Kurdistan and the northern parts of Iraq, where a dialect of Eastern Aramaic was spoken by the Jewish inhabitants.

In time, the ties between Hebrew and Aramaic grew stronger, owing to prolonged cultural and social contact between the people who spoke these languages. Borrowed words also strengthened the connection between the languages. This mutual influence and similarity is particularly pronounced in the Talmud. The spoken Aramaic dialects (Eastern Aramaic in the Babylonian Talmud, and Western Aramaic in the Jerusalem Talmud) were influenced and diversified by contact with Hebrew.

Since we do not possess texts of any substantial length written in "pure" Babylonian Aramaic, and since ancient vocalized Aramaic texts are extremely rare, the pronunciation of the language is generally uncertain, and in fact it is vocalized differently by Jews in different communities. As a rule, therefore, it is impossible to determine the correct vocalization of any given Aramaic word, and in attempting to vocalize the language we can rely only on conjecture, based on the few ancient vocalized texts available and comparison with cognate Aramaic dialects.

Roots and Vocabulary

The basic vocabulary of Aramaic is very similar to that of Hebrew, even though not all roots have the same meaning in both languages. Sometimes, indeed, the meaning of an Aramaic root may even be the opposite of its meaning in Hebrew. For example, שכח in Hebrew means "lose," whereas in Aramaic it means "find," and accordingly the Aramaic שְׁכִיחַ, which subsequently entered Hebrew as a loan word, means "frequent." Sometimes a root has similar meanings in both languages, even though the meanings are not identical (e.g., רחם means "have mercy" in Hebrew and "to love" in Aramaic; occasionally, however, this word can mean "love" in Biblical Hebrew as well). Sometimes common Aramaic roots correspond to relatively rare Biblical Hebrew forms (e.g., the Aramaic root חזי — "to see" — is reflected in such Hebrew words as מַחֲזֶה — "scene, sight"; חִזָּיוֹן — "vision"; etc.), while other roots are identical in both languages.

Many words have similar meanings in both languages, although they undergo certain fixed consonantal changes as they pass from the one language to the other. Some of the general principles governing consonantal changes, which are paralleled in other Semitic languages as well, are set forth in the following table:

Hebrew		Aramaic		Example	
ז		ד		דְּהַב = זָהָב	
צ		ט		קַיְטָא = קַיִץ	
צ		ע		בֵּיעָא = בֵּיצָה	
ש		ת		תּוֹר = שׁוֹר	

Certain fixed changes also occur in the vocalization of Aramaic words: for example, the Hebrew וֹ becomes יָ in Aramaic, e.g., the Hebrew שָׁלוֹם, "peace," the Aramaic שְׁלָם.

Thus, the student who encounters an unfamiliar Aramaic word can often guess its meaning by considering the following possibilities:

(1) It is worth checking to see if a similar root exists in Hebrew. Such words might either be loan words from Aramaic, or have a common earlier root.

(2) In Aramaic (particularly in Galilean Aramaic), guttural letters are often dropped or replaced with other letters, e.g., Aramaic אִין "yes" = Hebrew "הֵן".

The following possibilities are also worth investigating:

א is often added to the beginning of a word (both nouns and verbs) in Aramaic; sometimes, however, א is equivalent to the Hebrew עַל, e.g., Aramaic אַיְידֵי, "by way of"

= Hebrew עַל יְדֵי. At the end of a word, א often signifies the definite article, like the prefix ה in Hebrew, e.g., Aramaic גַּבְרָא, "the man" = Hebrew הַגֶּבֶר.

ב occasionally occurs in the Jerusalem Talmud instead of ו (e.g., אֲוִיר = אֲבִיר, "air").

ד sometimes interchanges with the Hebrew ז (e.g., דְּכַר = זָכַר "he remembered").
At the beginning of a word, ד can also mean "who," "of" (= Hebrew שֶׁל, שֶׁ).

ה is occasionally equivalent to the Hebrew ח.

ט is occasionally equivalent to the Hebrew צ (e.g., טִיהֲרָא = צָהֳרַיִם, "midday").

ל at the beginning of a word sometimes interchanges with נ (e.g., נֵימָא = לֵימָא, "let him say," "he will say") or with ר.

ס occasionally interchanges with the Hebrew שׂ (e.g., סָנֵא = שָׂנֵא, "to hate").

ע sometimes interchanges with the Hebrew צ (e.g., עָאן = צֹאן, "sheep").

ק at the beginning of a word is often an abbreviated form of קָא, an auxiliary verb used with the Aramaic participle, which need not be translated in English.

ת interchanges with the Hebrew שׁ (e.g., תְּבַר = שָׁבַר, "to break").

Occasionally the root אמר is conjugated as if its final letter were א or י — e.g., לֵימָא, "he will say," rather than לֵימַר.

A ramaic verbs, like their Hebrew counterparts, generally have three root letters. These verbs may be strong verbs, such as כתב, "write," or defective verbs, such as those with beginning א or נ (e.g., אכל, "eat"; נפק, "go out"), medial ו, א or י (e.g., קום, "rise"; שאל, "ask"; עין, "study"), or final א/י (e.g., שתי, "drink"). In addition, some Aramaic roots have double final letters (e.g., עלל, "come in"), and others are quadriliteral (e.g., גנדר, "roll").

Aramaic verb roots can be conjugated in different conjugations (each conjugation has a different meaning, as in Hebrew). There are six primary conjugations in Aramaic, two secondary conjugations, and isolated remnants of additional conjugations, as shown in the following list.

Verb Forms

1. פְּעַל (also called קַל). This is the main conjugation in Aramaic, and parallels the Hebrew פָּעַל (or קַל) conjugation.

2. פַּעֵל, the intensive, parallels the Hebrew פִּעֵל in both meaning and form (note that, in both conjugations, the second root letter is marked with a *dagesh*).

3. אַפְעֵל, the causative, parallels the Hebrew הִפְעִיל.

4. אִתְפְּעֵל is the passive form of the פְּעַל conjugation, and corresponds to the Hebrew נִפְעַל. (The ת preceding the first root letter is frequently replaced by י. This conjugation, therefore, can also be called the אִיפְּעֵל.)

5. אִתְפַּעַל parallels the Hebrew פֻּעַל, and is the passive of פַּעֵל.

6. אִתַּפְעַל, the passive of אַפְעֵל, parallels the Hebrew הֻפְעַל.
   There are also two secondary conjugations in Aramaic:

7. שַׁפְעֵל, an active form.

8. אִשְׁתַּפְעַל, the passive of שַׁפְעֵל.
   There is no conjugation in Aramaic which exactly parallels the reflexive הִתְפַּעֵל in Hebrew, although the אִתְפְּעֵל conjunction is occasionally used reflexively.

Tenses

Aramaic verbs appear in the same tenses as their Hebrew counterparts: past, participle (both active and passive; the Aramaic participle is approximately equivalent to the present tense in English), and future, as well as imperative and infinitive. The participle can also be used with pronominal suffixes to form a present tense (first and second person, singular and plural); see the tables below.

THE פְּעַל (קַל) CONJUGATION

PAST TENSE

Sing.	1	כְּתַבִי, כְּתַבִית	I wrote
	2m	כְּתַבְתְּ	you wrote
	2f	כְּתַבְתְּ	you wrote
	3m	כְּתַב	he wrote
	3f	כְּתַבָא, כְּתַבַת	she wrote
Pl.	1	כְּתַבַן, כְּתַבְנָא, כְּתַבַן	we wrote
	2	כְּתַבְתּוּן, כְּתַבְתּוּ	you wrote
	3m	כְּתַבוּ כְּתוּב	they wrote
	3f	כְּתַבָן	they wrote

ACTIVE PARTICIPLE

Sing.	Masc.	כָּתֵיב	writing
	Fem.	כָּתְבָא	writing
Pl.	Masc.	כָּתְבִי, כָּתְבִין	writing
	Fem.	כָּתְבָן	writing

PASSIVE PARTICIPLE

Sing.	Masc.	כְּתִיב	written
	Fem.	כְּתִיבָא	written
Pl.	Masc.	כְּתִיבִי, כְּתִיבִין	written
	Fem.	כְּתִיבָן	written

PRESENT TENSE

Sing.	1	כָּתֵבְנָא	I write
	2	כָּתְבַתְּ	you write
Pl.	1	כָּתְבִינַן	we write
	2	כָּתְבִיתוּ, כָּתְבִיתוּן	you write

FUTURE TENSE

Sing.	1	אֶכְתּוֹב	I will write
	2m	תִּכְתּוֹב	you will write
	2f	תִּכְתְּבִי	you will write
	3m	נִכְתּוֹב, לִכְתּוֹב	he will write
	3f	תִּכְתּוֹב	she will write
Pl.	1	נִכְתּוֹב	we will write
	2	תִּכְתְּבוּ, תִּכְתְּבוּן	you will write
	3	נִכְתְּבוּ, לִכְתְּבוּ	they will write

IMPERATIVE

Sing.	Masc.	כְּתוֹב, שְׁמַע, שְׁפֵיל	write, listen, go down
	Fem.	כְּתוֹבִי, שְׁבַקִי	let go, write
Pl.	Masc.	כְּתוֹבוּ, שְׁמַעוּ	write, listen
	Fem.	כְּתוֹבִי, כְּתוֹבִין	write

INFINITIVE   לְמִכְתַּב to write

THE פַּעֵל CONJUGATION

PAST TENSE

Sing.	1	קַבֵּילִי, קַבֵּילִית	I received
		שַׁדַּרִי, שַׁדָּרִית	I sent
	2	קַבֵּילְתְּ	you received
		שַׁדַּרְתְּ	you sent
	3m	קַבֵּל	he received
		שַׁדַּר	he sent
	3f	קַבֵּילַת	she received
Pl.	1	קַבֵּילְנָא, קַבֵּילְנַן	we received
	2	קַבֵּילְתּוּ, קַבֵּילְתּוּן	you received
	3m	קַבֵּילוּ	they received
		שַׁדַּרוּ	they sent
	3f	קַבֵּילָא	They received

ACTIVE PARTICIPLE

Sing.	Masc.	מְקַבֵּל	receiving
	Fem.	מְקַבְּלָא	receiving
Pl.	Masc.	מְקַבְּלִין	receiving
	Fem.	מְקַבְּלָן	receiving

PRESENT TENSE

Sing.	1	מְקַבֵּילְנָא	I receive
	2	מְקַבְּלַתְּ	you receive
Pl.	1	מְקַבְּלִינַן	we receive
	2	מְקַבְּלִיתוּן, מְקַבְּלִיתוּ	you receive

FUTURE TENSE

Sing.	1	אֲקַבֵּיל	I will receive
	2	תְּקַבֵּיל	you will receive
	3m	נְקַבֵּיל, לְקַבֵּיל	he will receive
	3f	תְּקַבֵּיל	she will receive
		תְּשַׁדַּר	she will send
Pl.	1	נְקַבֵּיל	we will receive
		נְשַׁדַּר	we will send
	2	תְּקַבְּלוּן, תְּקַבְּלוּ	you will receive
	3m	לְקַבְּלוּ	they will receive
	3f	לְקַבְּלָן	they will receive

IMPERATIVE

Sing.	Masc.	קַבֵּל	receive
	Fem.	קַבֵּילִי	receive
Pl.	Masc.	קַבֵּילוּ	receive
	Fem.	קַבֵּילִין	receive

INFINITIVE   לְקַבּוֹלֵי to receive

THE אַפְעֵל CONJUGATION

PAST TENSE

Sing.	1	אַדְכֵּירִית, אַדְכֵּירִי	I reminded
	2	אַדְכֵּרְתְּ	you reminded
	3m	אַדְכֵּר	he reminded
	3f	אַדְכֵּירַת	she reminded
Pl.	1	אַדְכֵּירְנָא, אַדְכֵּירְנַן	we reminded
	2	אַדְכֵּירְתּוּן	you reminded
	3m	אַדְכַּרוּ, אַדְכִּירוּ	they reminded
	3f	אַדְכִּירָא	they reminded

ACTIVE PARTICIPLE

Sing.	Masc.	מַדְכַּר, מַדְכֵּיר	reminding
	Fem.	מַדְכְּרָא	reminding
Pl.	Masc.	מַדְכְּרִין	reminding
	Fem.	מַדְכְּרָן	reminding

PRESENT TENSE

Sing.	1	מַדְכַּרְנָא, מַדְכֵּירְנָא	I remind
	2	מַדְכְּרַתְּ	you remind
Pl.	1	מַדְכְּרִינַן	we remind
	2	מַדְכְּרִיתוּ	you remind

FUTURE TENSE

Sing.	1	אַדְכַּר, אַדְכֵּיר	I will remind
	2m	תַּדְכֵּיר	you will remind
	2f	תַּדְכִּירִי	you will remind
	3m	נַדְכֵּיר, לַדְכֵּיר	he will remind
	3f	תַּדְכֵּיר	she will remind
Pl.	1	נַדְכַּיר, נַדְכֵּיר	we will remind
	2	תַּדְכְּרוּ	you will remind
	3	לַדְכְּרוּ	they will remind

IMPERATIVE

Sing.	Masc.	אַדְכַּר, אַדְכֵּיר	remind
	Fem.	אַדְכִּירִי	remind
Pl.	Masc.	אַדְכִּירוּ	remind
	Fem.	אַדְכִּירִין	remind

INFINITIVE

לְאַדְכּוֹרֵי	to remind

THE אִתְפְּעֵל CONJUGATION

PAST TENSE

Sing.	1	אִתְעֲבִידִי(ת)	I became
		אִימְּלִיכִי(ת)	I changed my mind
	2m	אִתְעֲבַדְתְּ	you became
		אִימְּלַכְתְּ	you changed your mind
	2f	אִתְעֲבַדְתְּ	you became
		אִימְּלַכְתְּ	you changed your mind
	3m	אִתְעֲבִיד	he became
		אִימְּלִיךְ	he changed his mind
	3f	אִתְעֲבִידָא	she became
		אִימְּלִיכָא	she changed her mind
Pl.	1	אִתְעֲבִידְנַן	we became
		אִימְּלִיכְנַן	we changed our mind
	2	אִתְעֲבִידְתּוּ	they became
		אִימְּלִיכְתּוּ	they changed their mind
	3m	אִתְעֲבִידוּ	they became
		אִימְּלִיכוּ	they changed their mind
	3f	אִתְעֲבִידָן	they became
		אִימְּלִיכָן	they changed their mind

PARTICIPLE

Sing.	Masc.	מִתְעֲבִיד	becoming
		מִימְּלִיךְ	changing one's mind
	Fem.	מִתְעֲבְדָא	becoming
		מִימַּלְכָא	changing one's mind
Pl.	Masc.	מִתְעֲבְדִי(ן)	becoming
		מִימַּלְכִי	changing one's mind
	Fem.	מִתְעֲבְדָן	becoming
		מִימַּלְכָן	changing one's mind

PRESENT TENSE

Sing.	1	מִתְעֲבִידְנָא	I became
		מִימְּלִיכְנָא	I changed my mind
	2	מִתְעֲבִידְנָא	I became
		מִימְּלִיכְנָא	I changed my mind
Pl.	1	מִתְעֲבְדִינַן	we became
		מִימַּלְכִינַן	we changed our mind
	2	מִתְעֲבִידְתּוּ	you became
		מִימַּלְכִיתוּ	you changed your mind

FUTURE TENSE

Sing.	1	אִתְעֲבִיד	I will become
		אִימְּלִיךְ	I will change my mind
	2m	תִּתְעֲבִיד	you will become
		תִּימְּלִיךְ	you will change your mind
	2f	תִּתְעֲבְדִי	you will become
		תִּימַּלְכִי	you will change your mind
	3m	לִתְעֲבִיד	he will become
		לִימְּלִיךְ	he will change his mind
	3f	תִּתְעֲבִיד	she will become
		תִּימְּלִיךְ	she will change her mind
Pl.	1	נִתְעֲבִיד	we will become
		יִמְּלִיךְ	we will change our mind
	2	תִּתְעֲבְדוּ	you will become
		תִּימַּלְכוּ	you will change your mind
	3m	תֶעֲבְדוּ	they will become
		לִימַּלְכוּ	they will change their mind
	3f	לִתְעֲבְדָן	they will become
		לִימַּלְכָן	they will change their mind

IMPERATIVE

Sing.	Masc.	אִתְעֲבִיד	become
		אִימְּלִיךְ	change your mind
	Fem.	אִתְעֲבְדִי	become
		אִימְּלִיכִי	change your mind

Pl. Masc. אִתְעֲבְדוּ become
אִימְּלְכוּ change your mind
Fem. אִתְעֲבִידִי become
אִימְּלְכִי change your mind

INFINITIVE לְאִתְעֲבוֹדֵי to become
לְאִמְּלוֹכֵי to change one's mind

THE אִתְפַּעַל CONJUGATION

PAST TENSE
Sing. 1 אִתְכַּפְּרִי I was forgiven
אִיעַתְּרִי I became wealthy
2m אִתְכַּפַּרְתְּ you were forgiven
2f אִיעַתַּרְתְּ you became wealthy
3m אִתְכַּפַּר he was forgiven
אִיעַתַּר he became wealthy
3f אִתְכַּפְּרַת she was forgiven
אִיעַתְּרַת she became wealthy

Pl. 1 אִתְכַּפְּרָן we were forgiven
אִיעַתְּרָן we became wealthy
2m אִתְכַּפַּרְתּוּ you were forgiven
2f אִיעַתַּרְתּוּ you became wealthy
3m אִתְכַּפְּרוּ they were forgiven
אִיעַתְּרוּ they became wealthy
3f אִתְכַּפְּרָן they were forgiven
אִיעַתְּרָן they became wealthy

PARTICIPLE
Sing. Masc. מִתְכַּפַּר is forgiven
מִיעַתַּר becomes wealthy
Fem. מִתְכַּפְּרָא is forgiven
מִיעַתְּרָא becomes wealthy
Pl. Masc. מִתְכַּפְּרִי is forgiven
מִיעַתְּרִי becomes wealthy
Fem. מִתְכַּפְּרָן is forgiven
מִיעַתְּרָן becomes wealthy

PRESENT TENSE
Sing. 1 מִתְכַּפַּרְנָא I am forgiven
מִיעַתְּרְנָא I become wealthy
2 מִתְכַּפַּרְתְּ you are forgiven
מִיעַתְּרַתְּ you become wealthy
Pl. 1 מִתְכַּפְּרִינַן we are forgiven
מִיעַתְּרִינַן we become wealthy
2 מִתְכַּפְּרִיתוּ you are forgiven
מִיעַתְּרִיתוּ you become wealthy

FUTURE TENSE
Sing. 1 אֶתְכַּפַּר I will be forgiven
אִיעַתַּר I will become wealthy
2 תִּתְכַּפַּר you will be forgiven
תִּיעַתַּר you will become wealthy
3m לִתְכַּפַּר he will be forgiven
נִיעַתַּר he will become wealthy
3f תִּתְכַּפַּר she will be forgiven
תִּיעַתַּר she will become wealthy

Pl. 1 נִתְכַּפַּר we will be forgiven
נִיעַתַּר we will become wealthy
2 תִּתְכַּפְּרוּן you will be forgiven
תִּיעַתְּרוּ you will become wealthy
3m לִתְכַּפְּרוּ they will be forgiven
לִיעַתְּרוּ they will become wealthy
3f לִתְכַּפְּרָן they will be forgiven
לִיעַתְּרָן they will become wealthy

IMPERATIVE
Sing. Masc. אִתְכַּפַּר be forgiven
אִיעַתַּר become wealthy
Fem. אִתְכַּפְּרִי be forgiven
אִיעַתְּרִי become wealthy
Pl. Masc. אִתְכַּפְּרוּ be forgiven
אִיעַתְּרוּ become wealthy
Fem. Not found

INFINITIVE לְאִתְכַּפּוֹרֵי to be forgiven
לְאִיעַתּוֹרֵי to become wealthy

THE אִתַּפְעַל CONJUGATION

PAST TENSE
Sing. 1 אִתַּכְשְׁרִי I was made fit
2 אִתַּכְשַׁרְתְּ you were made fit
3m אִתַּכְשַׁר he was made fit
3f אִתַּכְשְׁרַת she was made fit

Pl. 1 אִתַּכְשְׁרָן we were made fit
2 אִתַּכְשַׁרְתּוּ you were made fit
3 אִתַּכְשְׁרוּ they were made fit

PARTICIPLE
Sing. Masc. מִתַּכְשַׁר being made fit
Fem. מִתַּכְשְׁרָא being made fit
Pl. Masc. מִתַּכְשְׁרִי being made fit
Fem. מִתַּכְשְׁרָן being made fit

PRESENT TENSE
Sing. 1 מִתַּכְשַׁרְנָא I am (being) made fit
2 מִתַּכְשַׁרְתְּ you are (being) made fit
Pl. 1 מִתַּכְשְׁרִינַן we are (being) made fit
2 מִתַּכְשְׁרִיתוּ you are (being) made fit

FUTURE TENSE
Sing. 1 אִתַּכְשַׁר I will be made fit
2 תִּתַּכְשַׁר you will be made fit
3m נִתַּכְשַׁר, לְתַּכְשַׁר he will be made fit
3f תִּתַּכְשַׁר she will be made fit

Pl. 1 נִתַּכְשַׁר we will be made fit
2 תִּתַּכְשְׁרוּ you will be made fit
3m לְתַּכְשְׁרוּ they will be made fit
3f לְתַּכְשְׁרָן they will be made fit

IMPERATIVE Not found

INFINITIVE לְאִתַּכְשׁוֹרֵי to be made fit

66

Note: Verbs in the three passive conjugations (אִתְפְּעֵל, אִתְפַּעַל and אִתַּפְעַל) whose first root letter is שׁ or ס are conjugated אִשְׁתַּכַּח, אִסְתְּלֵק, like their Hebrew counterparts. Similarly, verbs whose first root letter is ז צ ד or ת are conjugated אִזְדְּבַן (root: זבן), אִצְטַבַּע (root: צבע), אִידְּכַר (root: דכר; note that the ת of the אִתְפְּעֵל form has been replaced by a י) and אִיתַּקַּן (root: תקן; here too the ת of the אִתְפַּעַל has been replaced by י). It should be noted that the ת in the passive conjugations is very frequently replaced by י in other roots as well (e.g., אִיקְלַע rather than אִתְקְלַע, etc.).

Nouns
The Definite Article

As we have explained, the definite article is often represented by the letter א at the end of a word: for example, גְּבַר = "a man," גַּבְרָא = "the man." However, the final א does not necessarily represent the definite article in Babylonian Aramaic (although it usually does in the Aramaic of the Jerusalem Talmud). Thus, the word יַרְחָא in the Babylonian Talmud can mean either "a month" or "the month."

Genders

All Aramaic nouns have genders (masculine or feminine), like their Hebrew counterparts. Most nouns are masculine, although nouns denoting female animals, or bodily organs that come in pairs, are usually feminine. There are also a few other feminine nouns (e.g., אַרְעָא — "land"; שִׁמְשָׁא — "sun").
   Feminine nouns (and adjectives, which resemble the nouns) usually end with the suffix תָּא- or תִי- (e.g., שַׁתָּא = "year"; זוּטַרְתִּי = "small").

Singular and Plural

Aramaic nouns are usually singular or plural; the dual is rare. Various suffixes are used to indicate the plural, the most common of which is י- for masculine nouns (e.g., גַּמְלֵי = "camels"; גַּבְרֵי = "men"). Occasionally the suffix נֵי- is also used (e.g., שַׁקְיָנֵי = drinks). Sometimes the suffix ין- is found (e.g., זִמְנִין = "sometimes," סַגִּיאִין = "numerous"). Nouns with the definite article are changed into the plural by adding the suffix יָא- (e.g., מַלְכַיָּא = "the kings"), but since a distinction between definite and indefinite forms is not always made in Babylonian Aramaic, יָא- can also be used as an indefinite plural suffix (thus, מַלְכַיָּא can also mean "kings").
   As a rule, the plural suffix for feminine nouns is יָתָא- e.g., מַתְנִיתָא = [the] Mishnah; מַתְנִיאָתָא = "Mishnayot"; חוּמְשָׁא = "a fifth"; חוּמְשִׁיָתָא = "fifths"). Occasionally, the suffix ן- is also used (e.g. בְּנָתָן = "daughters"), while other feminine nouns, particularly those ending with וּתָא-, are changed into the plural by adding the suffix וָתָא- (e.g., גָּלְוָתָא = "exiles"; אַרְיְוָתָא = "lions").

Absolute and Construct States

Nouns in Babylonian Aramaic may appear in either the absolute or construct state. Nouns in the absolute state usually end with the letter א, and hence resemble nouns with the definite article (although not every noun that lacks a final א is necessarily in the construct state). Thus, רֵישׁ = "head" or "head of" (c.f., רֵישׁ גָּלוּתָא = "the head of the exile, the Exilarch"); רֵישָׁא = "head" or "the head"; רֵישִׁין (rare!) = "the heads of"; רֵישֵׁי = "heads of"; אִיתְּתָא = "woman" or "the woman"; אִיתַּת = "a woman of, "wife of."

Numbers

As in Mishnaic Hebrew, certain numbers (generally those slightly smaller than a round number) may be expressed as "[round number] minus x," e.g., אַרְבְּעִין נְכֵי חֲדָא (lit., "forty less one") = 39; מְאָה נְכֵי תַרְתֵּי (lit., "one hundred less two") = 98.

		Masc.	Fem.			Masc.	Fem.						
1	חַד	חֲדָא	11	חַדְסַר	חֲדְסְרֵי	20	עֶשְׂרִין		100	מְאָה
2	תְּרֵי	תַּרְתֵּי	12	תְּרֵיסַר	תַּרְתֵּי סְרֵי	30	תְּלָתִין		200	מָאתָן
3	תְּלָתָא	תְּלָת	13	תְּלֵיסַר	תְּלָתֵי סְרֵי	40	אַרְבְּעִין		300	תְּלָת מְאָה
4	אַרְבְּעָא	אַרְבַּע	14	אַרְבְּסַר	אַרְבַּסְרֵי	50	חַמְשִׁין		400	אַרְבַּע מְאָה
5	חַמְשָׁא	חֲמֵשׁ	15	חֲמֵיסַר	חַמְסְרֵי	60	שִׁיתִּין		1000	אַלַף (אַלְפָּא)
6	שִׁיתָּא	שִׁית	16	שִׁיתְּסַר	שִׁיתְסְרֵי	70	שַׁבְעִין		2000	תְּרֵי אַלְפִּי(ן)
7	שַׁבְעָא	שְׁבַע, שַׁב	17	שַׁבְסַר	שַׁבְסְרֵי	80	תְּמָנִין		10000	ריבּוֹיָא, רְבַבְתָא
8	תְּמָנְיָא	תְּמָנֵי	18	תְּמָנֵי־סַר	תְּמָנֵי־סְרֵי	90	תִּשְׁעִין		20000	תְּרֵי רִיבְּבָן
9	תִּשְׁעָה	תְּשַׁע	19	תְּשַׁסַר	תְּשַׁסְרֵי					
10	עַשְׂרָה	עֶשַׂר								

Ordinal Numbers

	Masc. Sing.	Fem. Sing.	Masc. Pl.	Fem. Pl.
First	קַמָּא	קַמַּיְיתָא	קַמָּאֵי	קַמַּיְיתָא
Second	תִּנְיָנָא	תִּנְיָיתָא	תִּנְיָינֵי	
Third	תְּלִיתָאָה	תְּלִיתַיְיתָא	תְּלִתָאֵי	
Fourth	רְבִיעָאָה	רְבִיעַיְיתָא	רְבִיעָאֵי	
Last	בָּתְרָא	בַּתְרַיְיתָא	בָּתְרָאֵי	בָּתְרָיְיתָא

Fractions

	Sing.	Pl.
1/2	פַּלְגָּא (פַּלְגוּ)	פַּלְגֵי
1/3	תִּילְתָא (תּוּלְתָּא)	תִּלְתֵּי
1/4	רִיבְעָא	רִיבְעֵי
1/5	חוּמְשָׁא	חוּמְשֵׁי
1/6	שְׁתוּתָא	
1/10	עִישׂוּרָא	עִישׂוּרְיָיתָא

Personal Pronouns

Sing.		Pl.	
אֲנָא	I	אֲנַחְנָא, אֲנַן	we
אַנְתְּ, אַתְּ	you (masc.)	אַתּוּן, אַתּוּ	you (masc.)
אַנְתְּ, אַתְּ	you (fem.)	אַתּוּן, אַתּוּ	you (fem.)
נִיהוּ, אִיהוּ, הוּא	he	נִינְהוּ, אִינוּן, אִינְהוּ	they (masc.)
נִיהִי, אִיהִי, הִיא	she	נִינְהִי, אִינְהִי	they (fem.)

	Sing.				*Sing.*				*Suffixes*
1	דִּידִי	mine		1	מְנַאי	from me			יּ-, -אי
2m	דִּידָךְ	yours		2m	מְנָךְ	from you			ךָ-, -ךְ
2f	דִּידֵיךְ	yours		2f	מִנֵּיךְ	from you			יִךְ-, -יךְ
3m	דִּידֵיה	his		3m	מִינֵיה	from him			יֵה-, -ֵיה
3f	דִּידָה	hers		3f	מִינָה	from her			ָה-, -ָה

	Pl.				*Pl.*				*Suffixes*
1	דִּידַן	ours		1	מְנָנָא	from us			ַן-, -נָא
2	דִּידְכוּ	yours		2	מְנַיְיכוּ	from you			כוּ-, -כוּ
3	דִּידְהוּ	theirs		3	מְנַיְיהוּ	from them			הוּ-, -הוּ

A Glossary of
Common Verb Forms

אוֹדוּעֵי   "[to] inform" (ידע, conj. אַפְעֵל, infinitive absolute)

אוֹקִים   "he established" (קום, conj. אַפְעֵל, past tense, third person sing. masc.)

אַחֲוֵי   "he showed" (חוי, conj. אַפְעֵל, past tense, third person sing. masc.)

אַחִילוּ   "they defiled" (חלל, conj. אַפְעֵל, past tense, third person pl.)

אִיגַּלְיָא   "it (she) was revealed" (גלי, conj. אִתְפְּעֵל, past tense, third person sing. fem.)

אַיְיתֵי   "he brought" (אתי, conj. אַפְעֵל, past tense, third person sing. masc.)

אִיכַּוֵּן   "he intended" (כון, conj. אִתְפַּעַל, past tense, third person sing. masc.)

אֵימָא   "say!" (אמר, conj. קַל, imperative, masc. sing.)

אִישְׁתַּנִּי   "it (he) changed" (שני, conj. אִתְפַּעַל, past tense, third person sing. masc.)

אִיתְּגַר   "he was hired" (אגר, conj. אִתְפְּעֵל, past tense, third person sing. masc.)

אִיתּוֹתַב   "it (he) was answered, refuted" (תוב, conj. אִתַּפְעַל, past tense, third person sing. masc.)

אִיתַּזַם   "he was proven a false witness" (זמם, conj. אִתְפַּעַל, past tense, third person sing. masc.)

אִיתְּמַר   "it was said" (אמר, conj. אִתְפְּעֵל, past tense, third person sing. masc.)

אִיתְּשִׁיל   "it (he) was asked" (שאל, conj. אִתְפְּעֵל, past tense, third person sing. masc.)

אָמֵינָא   "I say" (אמר, conj. קַל, present tense, with first person sing. pronominal suffix)

אָמְרֵי   "(they) say" (אמר, conj. קַל, active participle, masc. pl.)

אַסִּיק   "he offered" (נסק, conj. אַפְעֵל, past tense, third person sing. masc.)

אַפֵּיק   "he took out" (נפק, conj. אַפְעֵל, past tense, third person sing. masc.)

אִשְׁתַּיַּר   "it (he) was left over" (שיר, conj. אִתְפַּעַל, past tense, third person sing. masc.)

אִשְׁתַּרְבֵּב   "it was extended; moved out of place; dragged down" (שרבב, conj. אִשְׁתַּפְעֵל, past tense, third person sing. masc.)

בָּכֵי	"he is crying" (בכי, conj. קַל, active participle, masc. sing.)
בָּעֵי	"he wants, needs, asks" (בעי, conj. קַל, participle, masc. sing.)
בָּעֵינָא	"I want, need, ask" (בעי, conj. קַל, present tense, with first person sing. pronominal suffix)
בָּעִית	"you want, need, ask" (בָּעֵי, conj. קַל, present tense, with second person sing. masc. pronominal suffix)
גּוּד	"stretch, pull" (נגד, conj. קַל, imperative, masc. sing.)
גְּלֵי	"it is revealed, evident" (גלי, conj. קַל, passive participle, masc. sing.)
גַּלֵּית	"you revealed" (גלי, conj. פַּעֵל, past tense, second person sing.)
דַּיְקָא	"accurate, precise" (דיק, conj. קַל, passive participle, fem. sing.)
דָּק	"he acted meticulously, examined carefully" (דיק, conj. קַל, past tense, third person sing. masc.)
הַב	"give!" (יהב, conj. קַל, imperative, masc. sing.)
הֲווֹ	"they were" (הוי, conj. קַל, past tense, third person pl.)
הֱוֵי	"be!" (הוי, conj. קַל, imperative, masc. sing.)
זִיל	"go!" (אזל, conj. קַל, imperative, masc. sing.)
חָזֵי	"(he) sees" (חזי, conj. קַל, active participle, masc. sing.)
חֲזֵי	"fit" (חזי, conj. קַל, passive participle, masc. sing.)
חָיְשִׁינָן	"we are concerned" (חיש, conj. קַל, present tense, with first person pl. pronominal suffix)
יְדִיעַ	"it (he) is known" (ידע, conj. קַל, passive participle, masc. sing.)
יָזֵיף	"he loans, lends" (יזף, conj. קַל, active participle, masc. sing.)
יֵימָא	"he will say" (אמר, conj. קַל, future tense, masc. sing.)
יָלֵיף	"(he) learns" (ילף, conj. קַל, active participle, masc. sing.)
יָלְפִינָן	"we learn" (ילף, conj. קַל, present tense, with first person pl. pronominal suffix)
כַּיֵּיף	"(he) is subject" (כוף, conj. קַל, active participle, masc. sing.)
לֵימָא	"he will say, "let him (it) say" (אמר, conj. קַל, future tense, third person sing. masc.)
לֵיעוֹל	"he will enter" (עלל, conj. קַל, future tense, third person sing. masc.)
לִיפְּקוּ	"they will leave" (נפק, conj. קַל, future tense, third person sing. masc.)
לֵיתֵי	"he will go" (אתי, conj. קַל, future tense, third person sing. masc.)
לִיתְנֵי	"he will teach" or: "let him teach" (תני, conj. קַל, future tense, third person sing. masc.)
לִיתְּסַר	"it (he) will be forbidden" or: "let it be forbidden" (אסר, conj. אִתְפְּעֵל, future tense, third person sing. masc.)
מוֹדֵי	"he gives thanks, he admits" (ידי, conj. אַפְעֵל, active participle, masc. sing.)
מוֹזֵיף	"he loans" (יזף, conj. אַפְעֵל, active participle, masc. sing.)
מוּכְחָא	"it is proven, it is evident" (יכח, conj. אַפְעֵל, passive participle, fem. sing.)
מוֹקֵי	"he establishes" (קום, conj. אַפְעֵל, active participle, masc. sing.)
מוֹקִים	"he establishes" (קום, conj. אַפְעֵל, active participle, masc. sing.)
מָטוּ	"they reach" (מטי, conj. קַל, active participle, masc. plural)
מִיבָּעֵיָא	"it (she) is required" (בעי, conj. אִתְפְּעֵל, participle, fem. sing.)
מִיהֱוֵי	"(to) be" (הוי, conj. קַל, infinitive absolute)
מִיחֲזֵי	"it (he) appears" (חזי, conj. אִתְפְּעֵל, participle, masc. sing.)

מִיכַּסֵּי   "it (he) is covered" (כסי, conj. אִתְפַּעַל, participle, masc. sing.)

מֵימַר   "(to) say" (אמר, conj. קַל, infinitive absolute)

מִינְּכַר   "it (he) is recognized" (נכר, conj. אִתְפְּעֵל, participle, masc. sing.)

מֵינַם   "(to) sleep" (נום, conj. קַל, infinitive absolute)

מֵיעַל   "(to) enter" (עלל, conj. קַל, infinitive absolute)

מֵיפַּק   "(to) leave" (נפק, conj. קַל, infinitive absolute)

מִית   "he died" (מות, conj. קַל, past tense, third person masc. sing.)

מֵיתִיבֵי   "they object" (תוב, conj. אַפְעֵל, active participle, masc. pl.)

מַסֵּי   "he heals" (אסי, conj. פַּעֵל, active participle, masc. sing.)

מַסְקִינַן   "we conclude" (נסק, conj. אַפְעֵל, present tense, with first person pl. pronominal suffix)

מְעַיֵּיל   "he introduces, puts in" (עלל, conj. פַּעֵל, active participle, masc. sing.)

מְעַלֵּי   "it (he) is lifted up" = "excellent, outstanding" (עלל, conj. פַּעֵל, passive participle, masc. sing.)

מְעַלְיָא   "it (she) is lifted up" = "excellent, outstanding" (עלי, conj. פַּעֵל, passive participle, fem. sing.)

מָצֵינָא   "I find" or: "I am able" (מצי, conj. קַל, present tense, with first person sing. pronominal suffix

מֵקֵיל   "he is lenient" (קלל, conj. אַפְעֵל, active participle, masc. sing.)

מַרַע   "he is evil, he acts badly" (רעע, conj. אַפְעֵל, active participle, masc. sing.)

מְשַׁעְבֵּיד   "he pledges, he mortgages" (עבד, conj. שַׁפְעֵל, active participle, masc. sing.)

מִשְׁתָּעֵי   "he relates, talks" (שעי, conj. אִתְפְּעֵל, active participle, masc. sing.)

מָתֵיב   "he objects" (תוב, conj. אַפְעֵל, active participle, masc. sing.)

מַתְנֵי   "he teaches" (תני, conj. אַפְעֵל, active participle, masc. sing.)

מַתְתִינַן   "we lower" (נחת, conj. אַפְעֵל, present tense, with first person pl. pronominal suffix)

נְהֵי   "it will be, so be it" (הוי, conj. קַל, future tense, third person sing. masc.)

נָח   "he rested" (נוח, conj. קַל, past tense, third person sing. masc.)

נֵיחָא   "it (she) is rested" = "it is acceptable" (נוח, conj. קַל, passive participle, fem. sing.)

נֵיכוּל   "we shall eat" (אכל, conj. קַל, future tense, first person pl.)

נֵימָא   "we shall say" (אמר, conj. קַל, future tense, first person pl.)

נֵיעוּל   "we shall enter" (עלל, conj. קַל, future tense, first person pl.)

נְסִיב   "it (he) is taken" (נסב, conj. קַל, passive participle, masc. sing.)

נָפְקָא   "she leaves" (נפק, conj. קַל, active participle, fem. sing.)

סַק   "go up" (נסק, conj. קַל, imperative, masc. sing.)

עוּל   "they entered" (עלל, conj. קַל, past tense, third person pl.)

עוּלוּ   "enter!" (עלל, conj. קַל, imperative, masc. pl.)

עָיֵיל   "he enters" (עלל, conj. קַל, active participle, masc. sing.)

עָיְילֵי   "they enter" (עלל, conj. קַל, active participle, masc. pl.)

עַל   "he entered" (עלל, conj. קַל, past tense, third person sing. masc.)

פּוּק   "leave!" (נפק, conj. קַל, imperative, masc. sing.)

צַלוּ   "they prayed" (צלי, conj. פַּעֵל, past tense, third person pl.)

צַלֵּי   "he prayed" (צלי, conj. פַּעֵל, past tense, third person sing. masc.)

קָאֵי   "he stands" (קום, conj. קַל, active participle, masc. sing.) This is an alternative form of קָאֵים, see next entry).

קָאֵים   "he stands" (קום, conj. קַל, active participle, masc. sing.)

קִיל   "it (he) is lenient" (קלל, conj. קַל, passive participle, masc. sing.)

קָיְמָא   "it (she) stands" (קום, conj. קל, active participle, fem. sing.)

קָיְמִינָן

     "we are standing" (קום, conj. קל, present tense, with first person pl. pronominal suffix)

קָרוּ   "they call" (קרי, conj. קל, active participle, masc. pl.)

קָרֵי   "he calls" (קרי, conj. קל, active participle, masc. sing.)

קְרֵי   "it (he) is called" (קרי, conj. קל, passive participle, masc. sing.)

שָׁדֵי   "he throws" (שדי, conj. קל, active participle, masc. sing.)

שַׁיּוּלֵי   "(to) ask" (שאל, conj. פַּעֵל, infinitive absolute)

שַׁיַּר   "he left over" (שרר, conj. פַּעֵל, past tense, third person masc. sing.)

שַׁנֵּי   "answer!" (שני, conj. פַּעֵל, imperative, masc. sing.)

שַׁגֵּינָן   "we (have) answered" (שני, conj. פַּעֵל, past tense, first person pl.)

שָׁרֵי   "he begins" or: "he permits" (שרי, conj. קל, active participle, masc. sing.)

תָּא   "come!" (אתי, conj. קל, imperative, masc. sing.)

תּוּב   "return!" (תוב, conj. קל, imperative, masc. sing.)

תֵּימָא   "you will say" (אמר, conj. קל, future tense, second person masc. sing.)

תֵּיקוּ

     "it (she) will stand = let it stand" (קום, conj. קל, future tense, third person fem. sing.)

תֵּיתֵי   "she will come" (אתי, conj. קל, future tense, third person fem. sing.)

תְּנֵי   "he teaches" (תני, conj. קל, active participle, masc. sing.)

תַּנְיָא   "it (she) is taught" (תני, conj. קל, passive participle, fem. sing.)

Glossary of Basic Words

The glossary that follows contains about 200 entries. While the words listed here constitute only a very small percentage of the Aramaic in the Talmud, they may nevertheless serve as a basic Aramaic word list, providing the student with the essentials of Talmudic language and a knowledge of the principal Aramaic expressions used by the classical Talmudic commentators. The entries have been listed according to the forms most frequently encountered in the Talmud; verbs are generally given in the past tense, in the third person singular masculine form.

אַ   as a prefix to a noun, it means "on"

אֲגַר   rent, hire (noun and verb)

אוֹרְחָא   path, way

אוֹרַח אַרְעָא   custom, accepted practice

אוֹרַיְיתָא   Torah

אוּרְתָּא   evening

אֲזַל   went

אַטוּ   could it be that...? Is it possible that...?

אַטוּ   because of (short for אַמְטוּ לְ)

אִי   if (also found as part of other words, e.g., אִילֵימָא — if one says)

אִידִי   this

אִידָךְ   the other

אִיכָּא   there is (short for אִית כָּא — "there is here")

אֵימָא   say!, I can say

אִין   yes

אֵינַש   man, person

אִית   there is

אִיתְּתָא   woman

אִיתְּמַר   it has been said, it has been stated

אַכַּתִּי   yet, still

אַלִּיבָּא   according to the opinion of

אַלִּים   strong

אַלְמָא   therefore

אַמַּאי   why? (= עַל מַאי — "for what?")

אֲנָא   I

אֲנַן   we

אַשְׁכַּח   (he) found

אֲתָא   (he) came (the same root also exists in Hebrew, e.g., Isaiah 21:12: אָתָא בֹקֶר וְגַם לַיְלָה)

אַתְרָא   place

בָּאגָא   field, plain

בָּבָא   gate

בַּהֲדֵי   with

בְּהֶדְיָא   directly, explicitly

בֵּי   (the) house of

בִּיש bad, evil
בְּעָא (1) asked (hence: בָּעְיָא — "a question") (2) needed, required
בַּר son
בָּתַר after
בַּתְרָא the last one

גַּבֵּי by, near, in connection with
גַּבְרָא man (cf. גֶּבֶר in Hebrew)
גּוֹ inside, the middle of (בְּגוֹ — "in the middle of")
גַּוְונָא color; way, manner
גְּמַר learn, study (גְּמָרָא = "Gemara, Talmud").
גְּרַס learn, study

דְּ that, of
דְּבֵיתְהוּ his wife (lit., "of his house")
דַּהֲבָא gold
דּוּכְתָּא place
דּוּמְיָא דְּ similar to
דִּידִי mine (דִּידָךְ — "yours")
דִּילִי mine (דִּילָךְ — "yours")
דְּכֵי clean, pure
דְּכַר remembered
דִּכְרָא ram; male
דִּלְמָא (דִּילְמָא) perhaps
דָּמֵי similar, considered

הָא this; after all (= is it true that...?)
הָאִידְנָא now (short for הָא עִידָנָא — "this time")
הֲדָדֵי each other
הֲדַר returned
הֲוָה was
הַיְינוּ that is (short for הַאי נִיהוּ — "this is it")
הֵיכִי how
הָכָא here
הָכִי thus
הִלְכְתָא Halakhah, law, rule
הָנֵי these
הָשְׁתָּא now
הָתָם there, elsewhere

וְכִי is it true that...?, and when
זַבֵּין sold
זְבַן bought
זוּזָא zuz; dinar; money
זוּטָא small
זוּטְרָא small
זִימְנִין sometimes
זִיקָא wind

חַד one (masc.)
חֲדָא one (fem.)
חַדְתָּא new
חֲזָא saw (cf. Hebrew חָזָה)
חָיֵישׁ is concerned
חֲמָא saw (in Galilean Aramaic)
חַמְרָא wine
חֲמָרָא donkey

טַבָּחָא butcher
טַעֲמָא reason; taste
טְפָא added
טְפֵי more, additional
טָפֵי added

יְהַב gave
יוֹמָא day
יְלִיף learned
יַתְמָא orphan

כּוּלֵי all
כְּוָתֵיה like him (it)
כִּי like, when

לָא not
לַאו (1) not (2) is it not true that...? (3) negative commandment, Biblical prohibition
לֵיכָּא there is not (short for לֵית כָּא — "there is not here")
לִישָׁנָא language, expression, version
לֵית there is not (short for לָא אִית — "there is not")

מַאי what
מַאן who
מְטָא arrived, reached
מִי is it true that...?
מַיָּא water
מִידֵי something, anything
מִיהָא in any case, at any rate
מִיהוּ in any case, at any rate
מִיהַת in any case, at any rate
מִילָא word, thing (cf. Hebrew דָּבָר)
מִילְתָא word, thing
מִכְּדִי now, since
מְנָא from where
מָנָא object, vessel
מְסָאנָא shoe
מֵעֲלֵי evening
מֵעֲלֵי שַׁבְּתָא — Shabbat (i.e., Friday) evening
מְצָא was able to
מָר sir, authority
מָתָא city, place

נְהִי even though
נַהֲמָא bread
נְחַת went down
נְטַר kept, guarded
נַמֵּי also
נְסַב took; married
נְפַק went out
נַפְשֵׁיה himself (נַפְשָׁה — "herself" etc.)
נְקַט took, held

סָבָא old man
סְבַר thought
סַגִּי enough

סַגִי   went (the word סוּגְיָא, which literally means "walking" or "passage," and hence "Talmudic discussion," is derived from this root)

סָהֲדָא   witness

סָהֲדוּתָא   testimony

סֵיפָא   end; last sentence or clause in a Mishnah or a Baraita

סְלֵק   went up

סָלְקָא דַעְתָּךְ   lit., "arises in your mind" = "you may think"

עֲבַד   did

עוּבְדָא   deed, case, incident

עַל   entered

עָלְמָא   world

עַמְרָא   wool

פּוּרְיָא   bed

פְּלַג, פַּלְגָּא   part, half

פְּלוּגְתָּא   controversy, dispute

פְּרַךְ   broke, asked, objected

פְּשִׁיטָא   obvious, self-evident

צְלוֹתָא   prayer

צַלֵּי   prayed

צְרִיכָא   necessary

קָא   an auxiliary verb used with the participle, which need not be translated; sometimes written as part of the next word, e.g., קָאָמַר = קָא אָמַר — "says"

קָאֵי   stands (short for קָאִים; cf. Hebrew קָם)

קוּלָּא   lenient ruling

קוּשְׁטָא   truth

קְטַל   killed

קַמָּא   first

קַמֵּי   before, in the presence of (קַמֵּיה — "before

him", "in his presence")

קְרָא   Biblical verse

קַשְׁיָא   difficult

רַבָּא   great, large (cf. Hebrew רַב)

רַבָּנָן   our Rabbis, the Sages

רְהַט   ran

רְחֵם   loved

רַחֲמָנָא   the All-Merciful, God (often means "the Torah")

רֵישָׁא   head, beginning; first sentence or clause in a Mishnah or a Baraita

רְמֵי   cast; pointed out a contradiction

שָׁאנֵי   different

שְׁבַק   abandoned

שְׁדָא   threw

שַׁוֵּי   treated like

שִׁית   six

שְׁכַב   lay down; died

שְׁמַיָּא   sky, heavens

שַׁפִּיר   good, nice

שְׁרָא   permitted; began

תָּא   come!

תּוּ   furthermore (short for תּוּב)

תְּיוּבְתָּא   reply (usually used in the sense of "refutation")

תְּלָת   three

תְּמָנֵי   eight

תְּנָא   taught (cf. Hebrew שָׁנָה; this verb also occurs in other forms, e.g., תָּנוּ רַבָּנָן — our Rabbis taught)

תְּקֵף   seized

תְּרֵי   two (masc.)

תָּרֵץ   answered, resolved a problem

תַּרְתֵּי   two (fem.)

Guidelines for Talmudic Study

For many generations the Talmud provided both the form and the substance of Jewish study. Children and adults, pupils in school, students in yeshivah, and men throughout their lives devoted their time to the study of the Talmud, and the greatest Rabbinical scholars invested most of their spiritual energy in deepening their knowledge of it. There is obviously no comparison between the level of a beginner in Talmudic study and that of a scholar already well versed in the subject. What is surprising, however, is the ability of students of the most varied levels of understanding and knowledge to study the Talmud endlessly, and with ever-increasing enthusiasm.

There is no single method for studying the Talmud. Throughout the centuries, wherever Jews lived, they developed many systems of study and various styles of commentary. Thoroughness of study also varied widely. In principle it is possible to study the Talmud again and again, constantly finding new insights, but one must distinguish between primary study of the material, necessary for mastering the subject, and all other levels of study, whose purpose is to gain deeper insight and understanding.

Basic Talmudic study is the foundation upon which a vast edifice of profound intellectual understanding and dialectical subtlety can be constructed. This primary stage of learning, practiced in many places, was called the study of the גִּרְסָא — the plain meaning of the text. Only after the student has reached competence at this level can he make significant progress.

The elementary study of the גִּרְסָא has one particular characteristic that distinguishes it from deeper study — it is essentially passive. The student tries to understand the written text, its content and its significance, to the best of his ability. By contrast, deeper Talmudic study, though it may follow any number of intellectual approaches, is essentially active. The student is

The Transition from Passive to Active Learning

not content merely to understand the material before him; he himself raises questions — depending on the intellectual approach he has adopted — and he tries to find solutions to them. His purpose is to continue the Talmudic discussion. He may be seeking Halakhic solutions to unsolved problems, he may be investigating fine points of Jewish law or probing a wide range of possible explanations of the text, or he may be investigating general principles behind the organization and editing of the Talmudic text. All these choices, however, are based on the assumption that the student is already familiar with the material being studied and is capable of grasping its complexities. Advanced study may lead the student to new insights and a deeper understanding of the material. He may discover that the way in which he had previously understood the subject matter was superficial or even mistaken. But he must have a basic grasp of the material before he even begins "active" learning.

The guidelines given below are all intended to help the student during the first, passive stage of his study of the Talmud.

Problems for the Beginner

For centuries the Talmud was usually taught orally, and this method is still used in traditional Jewish education. The classes were usually small, and the pupils could ask questions and receive clarifications of the various problems. This pattern of tuition would continue for several years, and the pupils, even at the elementary stage, memorized huge amounts of material. This intensive study made the Talmudic discourse a language that was readily understood by the pupils. Even if they could not clearly formulate and express what they knew, they were nevertheless able to understand the subject the way a person learns to understand a spoken language.

In our day the situation has changed almost everywhere except in the most Orthodox Jewish communities. Talmud study today cannot be compared to that of earlier periods either in the amount of time devoted to the subject or in the pressure and concentration of effort involved, nor is the amount of material studied comparable. Different methods must, therefore, be employed now in order to achieve results approaching those achieved in the past — the ability to understand the plain meaning of the Talmudic text.

Guidelines: Understanding the Basic Principles of a Subject

Since most tractates of the Talmud do not proceed logically from simple to complex material and do not contain introductions explaining the basic principles underlying the subject, the student must learn these principles before he begins a systematic study of the text. One of the simplest and most natural ways of learning what is at issue is to study, or at least read, the Mishnah of the complete tractate before approaching the Gemara. For more advanced students, reading the appropriate passages in the *Mishneh Torah* of the Rambam can serve as an introduction to the Talmud material being studied. Additional material, dealing with the subject in general terms, may often be found in encyclopedias and other reference works. Between the Mishnah, the Rambam, and these secondary works, the student will familiarize himself with a major part of the Talmudic material to be studied and thus understand the nature of the problems under discussion.

Knowing the Language

Although the Talmud is written in a mixture of Hebrew and Aramaic, the Aramaic will not constitute an insuperable barrier for a student with a basic knowledge of Hebrew if he takes the trouble to learn a relatively small number of key words. (This *Guide* contains a dictionary section with a selection of basic Aramaic words, for this very purpose.) The student will find his path far smoother if he learns these Aramaic terms, most of which are not unfamiliar to a person with some knowledge of Hebrew.

When approaching a particular sentence in the Talmud the student should ask himself — both as a factual question and as a learning technique — what the origin of the sentence is. Is it part of the Talmudic debate among the Amoraim or is it a quotation from an earlier source? What is its function? Is it a question, a statement in support of a previously expressed opinion, a proof, or the beginning of a new subject? Knowledge of some fundamental principles and basic ideas of the Talmudic dialectic will generally be sufficient to provide at least an approximate answer to this question. Once the student has arrived at such an answer, he should check whether it is consistent with what follows in the text. If it is a question — where is the answer? If it is an answer — what question does it answer? And so forth. At first it is enough for the student to try to follow the steps of the Talmudic argument, even if he does not yet have a clear picture of the whole discussion.

The Function of the Various Parts of the Talmudic Text

The student must take as much advantage as possible of the commentaries found on the page of the Talmud. He should turn to the commentaries after reading each sentence. Indeed, Rashi's commentary follows the sequence of sentences in the text. A student beginning to learn Talmud often finds that the commentator has anticipated the question that the student wanted to ask, either by explaining a difficult word or by translating an expression, or by explaining the significance and role of a particular expression.

Commentaries

Easy Talmudic texts are usually those where the argumentation is short, to the point and without digressions. However, only a few tractates or even chapters are constructed in this helpful way. The student must, therefore, expect frequent minor digressions from the subject, regarding them as if they were bracketed off from the main text. If the Talmud goes into an analysis of an expression or subject tangentially introduced into the discussion, or if it pauses to solve a problem that has arisen only incidentally, the student would be well advised initially to omit this additional passage (conceptually at least) and to concentrate on the basic problem. Where the discussion is prolonged, it is helpful to make a note, either in writing or aloud, of the stage the argument has reached at the point of the digression, keeping the basic problem in mind. It is very important to recapitulate and recall who made a particular statement, what the question was, what the answer was, and where the discussion was leading. Wherever the argumentation is complicated, one ought to summarize the points of view bit by bit as one goes along. Only an experienced student can carry in his head a complicated line of thought with its attendant digressions and changes of direction.

Preserving the Line of Thought

Since the Talmud is itself a "language," with a style of its own, there is no better way of understanding it than by extensive reading and study. Even if one does not understand everything, it is of great benefit to persevere and read large amounts of material. By reading, one becomes accustomed to the style of Talmudic thought and expression and gradually learns many new concepts. In Talmudic study quantity rapidly becomes quality. On this point the Talmud itself quotes the advice of one of the Amoraim: "Let a man read the text and afterwards understand its content, even though at first he does not understand and even though he does not at first know what he is saying." (*Avodah Zarah* 19a.) Wide reading is thus an aid to understanding, even if its value is not always immediately discernible.

The More One Reads the Better

After the student has made his way through a particular section and understood it, he is well advised to go over it again to see how he understands it on a second reading. This repetition not only helps the student to retain what he has mastered, but is also of inestimable value in subsequent study of new material, whether on the same subject or a different one.

Repetition

Basic Assumptions and Fundamental Problems

A number of basic asumptions underlie the debates of the Talmud. These assumptions are seldom mentioned explicitly, although they are the axioms upon which the entire Talmud is built. Moreover, the logical principles behind the development of the arguments are not explained by the Talmud itself but brought out later by the commentators, either in special works devoted to general Talmudic principles or, incidentally, in their commentaries.

Just as there are basic assumptions, there are also fundamental problems that occur repeatedly in the Talmudic discussion. These problems have much in common and are arranged according to standard structures. Once a student understands these basic assumptions and problems he will find it much easier to grasp the essential elements of the Talmudic discussion.

Basic Assumptions: The Sanctity and Importance of the Subject Matter

The absolutely basic premise of Talmud study is that the Torah must be fully understood. The Talmud deals with many different subjects. Some are weighty issues of principle; some are fundamental rules upon which the life of every practicing Jew is based; some are practical problems requiring empirical solutions; others appear to be relatively trivial matters of everyday life, insignificant monetary problems or unimportant discrepancies between customs. What they all have in common, however, is that they are "Torah." Consequently every single problem raised in the Talmud, whether fundamental, incidental, or seemingly trivial, is treated with the utmost seriousness and subjected to the most penetrating scrutiny. All the problems arising in the discussion are, in principle, of equal standing and entitled to precise analysis. The search for truth is its own justification.

Reverence for the Sages

The Talmudic Sages do everything in their power to follow the path of truth, both in their Torah teachings and their personal lives. The statements of Sages of all generations are thus entitled to the greatest deference. Most Talmudic discussions are based on the premise that a Sage weighs his words exactly. A Sage is assumed to have made every effort to arrive at correct conclusions and to have expressed them with precision. Every argument and opinion of the Sages, and likewise their actions, merit serious scrutiny. Hence every opinion and argument must be understood and explained, even those ultimately rejected in the formulation of the accepted Halakhah and those that are decisively proven to be incorrect. Clear analysis is always necessary; statements, even erroneous ones, must be properly defined and given the best possible defense. Every stage in the argument must be justified, and error or lack of knowledge are never conceded without conclusive proof.

Clarity and Completeness

The statements of the Sages, in particular those statements that have been carefully edited and organized, such as Mishnayot and important Baraitot, are clear and complete. Therefore, when analyzing the Talmudic text, one must not only consider the content but also pay close attention to the form of the text. The precision of the language used requires the student to understand not only the plain meaning of the words but also what they imply by omission or indirect reference. Statements quoted in the Talmud are assumed to have been formulated as concisely as possible; it is also understood that the Sages did not repeat themselves unnecessarily. Thus, one must explain cases of apparent repetition and, of course, of seeming self-contradiction. Although a number of approaches can be taken in explaining the Rabbis' statements, they must be based systematically upon these fundamental principles.

Narrowing the Differences between Points of View

Although there are many differences of opinion among the Tannaim and Amoraim, nevertheless a constant and consistent effort is made to bring the conflicting points of view as near to each other as possible. This approach is rooted in the assumptions mentioned above, namely that the authors of all statements quoted in the Talmud made every possible effort to ensure the accuracy of their conclusions, and that the differing Sages arrived at their conclusions by using the same logical methods with equal acumen. Thus it is only reasonable that the differences among the disputants ought to be very small, and any interpretive assumption that tends to narrow the gap between conflicting viewpoints is taken to be the most simple and natural one, until the contrary is specifically proved. Hence the Talmud tries to show that apparently contradictory quotations do not necessarily differ from each other, and every effort is made to find common ground between them. All the sources quoted are considered mutually complementary, so that it is permissible to use one source either to challenge or to confirm another (unless it is shown that they are different in context or approach). Therefore, particularly within the dialectic, the Talmud often fuses various lines of thought and Halakhot, even when their internal connection is not immediately obvious. Nevertheless, we seek to accept all the Talmudic material in our possession as a collection of facts, and to unify them all into a single entity.

Every argument put forward in the Talmudic debate is examined minutely and must be proved. Each statement offered as proof of the original argument must also be examined minutely, and it will be rejected if doubts or flaws are uncovered. However, this principle also applies to the refutation itself — it, too, must be well founded and accurate. The purpose of the debate is thus to achieve the highest possible degree of precision in arriving at every proof. *Precise Argumentation*

The criteria for validating an argument are not self-evident. It is indeed possible that an opinion or hypothesis may in itself be likely and reasonable; reasonableness, however, is not conclusive proof, though it is an important consideration in summing up an argument, or where there is a conflict of interpretation, particularly in relation to a Halakhic decision. In the course of the debate, however, before it is resolved, even rather far-fetched objections may be raised, and matters may be explained in a forced manner, as long as these objections and explanations are not self-contradictory.

The principle of the debate is, therefore, as follows: No opinion is considered finally proven if elements of difficulty, however small, remain in it; and conversely no opinion is considered refuted, even if serious difficulties have been revealed in it, as long as some way to defend it, however forced, still remains. A distinction must, therefore, be drawn between the *veracity* of an opinion or point of view, requiring absolute accuracy of proof, and its general *reasonableness,* which is a matter of judgment and is given weight only in the resolution of the argument.

Statements by the Tannaim that appear in the Mishnah, and to a great extent also in Baraitot, are binding upon the Amoraim. An Amora is not permitted, except in rare instances, to disagree with statements of the Tannaim. The Mishnah and the Baraitot, therefore, provide data that the Amoraim use to bring proofs and raise objections. Similar but more limited importance is also extended to the teachings of early Amoraim or of later Sages acknowledged to be the leaders of their generation. This principle is generally applicable in Talmudic debate, although in the area of Halakhic decisions there are several exceptions to it. *General Principles Regarding Statements of the Amoraim: Sources*

Statements by Amoraim are generally expected to be original and not merely to reflect statements by earlier Sages, particularly Tannaim. This is because if something has been said by a previous authority, it is an established, axiomatic truth, and one need not repeat it. Thus the discovery of a statement or dispute between Tannaim parallel to a statement or dispute between Amoraim always poses a problem — if the Tannaim had already said it, why did the Amoraim have to repeat it? *Originality*

Statements by an Amora must be consistent with each other. There must be no contradiction between statements made by an Amora in different contexts. This demand *Consistency* for consistency militates against not only obvious but also implied contradictions. The latter sometimes appear when an Amora's opinion is analyzed and compared to views expressed by him in another context whose ramifications touch upon the problem at hand. There are also cases where a Sage retracts an opinion previously held, thereby obviously creating a contradiction in his expressed viewpoint.

Statements Are Not Repeated

When an Amora makes a statement, he makes it only once. When he formulates a Halakhah or an opinion, he is aware of what he previously said and does not use different words to repeat a statement. Various Sages did, of course, repeat statements they had previously made, before a different audience and in another context, but such repetition was then explicit and deliberate. Whenever an Amora repeats himself without indicating that he is aware of it, the Talmud seeks an explanation.

Consistency with All Views

Given the inner unity of the Halakhah, every Amora sought to keep his teachings and method consistent with all opinions (אַלִּיבָּא דְּכוּלֵּי עָלְמָא). Supporting his views in that way was not necessarily crucial from a Halakhic point of view, since one particular system must necessarily be taken as binding. But in essence each Amora tried to show that his approach did not contradict any opinion expressed by the Tannaim, and as far as possible that it was also consistent with the teachings and interpretations of the Amoraim. Obviously it was not always possible to avoid contradiction. Nevertheless a large part of the Talmudic debate is taken up with attempts to reconcile viewpoints as far as possible (אַלִּיבָּא דְּכוּלֵּי עָלְמָא), despite the very considerable interpretative difficulties frequently entailed in the attempt.

Fundamental Problems

Most of the fundamental questions, answers, objections and solutions found in the Talmudic debate are formulated according to a fixed technical terminology (see more extensively below in the sections on Mishnaic and Talmudic terminology). Many of the basic questions — and their answers — are general in nature and recur frequently.

Fundamental Problems of Interpretation

The fundamental problems of interpretation are the basic questions asked by the Talmud about the sources on which the statements of the Tannaim are based — particularly in the Mishnah. However, the Talmud also frequently examines the sources of statements by Amoraim. Sometimes these problems are raised as independent questions, requiring their own answers, and sometimes they are posed to provide the necessary basis for elucidating another problem.

THE SOURCE IN THE TORAH FOR A PARTICULAR LAW
Such questions are usually introduced by the terms מְנָלָן, מַאי קְרָא, etc., and the answer is given by quoting a specific verse from the Bible or a more complex Midrashic interpretation of various sources.

THE REASON FOR A PARTICULAR LAW
Such questions are usually introduced by the term מַאי טַעְמָא — "What is the reason?" — and their purpose is to find the rationale for a law not found in the Torah, or a law based on logical considerations or on another law.

THE AUTHOR OF A PARTICULAR LAW
Where laws are cited anonymously, the Talmud frequently asks who the author of the law in question is, using the terms מַנִּי, מַאן תַּנָּא, etc. The Talmud answers such questions either by adducing a parallel statement where the author of the statement is named or by trying to infer the authorship in other ways.

FACTUAL CONTEXTS
Sometimes the statement under investigation is phrased generally, and the context in which it was made is not clear. In such cases the Talmud tries to elucidate the precise and practical application of the general statement.

UNCLEAR WORDS AND EXPRESSIONS
The Talmud also offers explanations of difficult and unfamiliar words and unclear or vague sentences and expressions.

After the Talmud has analyzed and clarified the initial, fundamental problems, it turns to secondary difficulties that do not occur in every instance but arise only in particular circumstances. The Talmud sometimes draws attention to contradictions, real or apparent, between sources of equivalent importance — between anonymous Mishnayot or between statements ascribed to the same individual Sage. The terminology used to introduce questions about such seeming contradictions is classified under the general heading רוּמְיָא — "casting" or pointing out of incongruities between statements. Sometimes the contradiction between the sources is immediately apparent, sometimes it is revealed only after lengthy analysis. Two basic solutions are offered by the Talmud to problems of this kind. The first is a form of clarification in which the two statements are shown to have been made by two Sages. In this way the difficulty of discovering an internal contradiction in a single authority's position is avoided. The second is an explanation that the two sources refer to two separate and distinct cases.

Secondary Problems of Interpretation: Contradictions

From a methodological standpoint the Talmud prefers the second type of answer, since it entirely resolves the contradiction rather than pushing it off from one level to another. However, this type of solution sometimes involves a certain degree of forced interpretation. It is specifically preferred when it provides an explanation of a contradiction within one source, but it is also needed when different sources are being compared. There are cases where the difference between the points of view is readily apparent and easily proved. There are also differences between Sages in their approach to this type of problem, some preferring one form of explanation and using it more frequently than others.

Sometimes a particular source appears to be repetitive, and an individual subject seems to recur a number of times in slightly different form. The Talmud investigates the reason for such apparent repetitions, both in Tannaitic and Amoraic sources, using specific terminology classified under the general heading of צְרִיכוּתָא — "necessity." It seeks to show that two seemingly similar statements cannot in fact be inferred from each other, and that each contains some unique nuance. There are, however, other cases where the repetition is ascribed to fixed Mishnaic style or to the way the text was edited.

Repetition

When the Talmud attacks a statement for telling us nothing new, it usually makes use of the expression פְּשִׁיטָא — meaning that the case is obvious, self-explanatory and unnecessary, because it is based either on previously established general principles or on clear and self-evident premises. The Talmud frequently raises this objection to statements by Amoraim and their interpretations of earlier statements. The usual response is once again in the form of a צְרִיכוּתָא — "it is necessary" — showing that the statement is not self-explanatory, either because its purpose is to answer a particular question or because without it we could have arrived at a different and erroneous conclusion. In such circumstances the terminology frequently used is מַהוּ דְּתֵימָא followed by קָא מַשְׁמַע לָן — "You might have supposed X ... therefore the statement teaches Y."

Lack of Originality

Sometimes the Talmud probes a flaw in the sequence of thought in a source where, for example, a conclusion is premature or where an individual case is presented before a fundamental general principle. Occasionally the connection between sentences is not

Incorrect Order

clear or a legal ruling is stated without establishing the necessary foundation and introduction to it. Such problems are sometimes resolved by inserting emendations into the text of the source, or by providing an explanation that brings out the connection between matters that had initially seemed unrelated.

Clarification of Points of Law

The Amoraim constantly seek to clarify the implications of the principles and conclusions that emerge in their discussions. These fall into two main categories: (1) practical problems that arise in everyday life and require practical solutions, and (2) hypothetical problems, many of which are raised only in order to analyze fundamental concepts. The terminology used by the Talmud when introducing problems of either kind is בָּעֵי, אִיבַּעְיָא לְהוּ, etc., which indicate the raising of a בָּעְיָא — "a problem." Of these two main categories the hypothetical problems are the more common.

The Talmud usually approaches these problems by citing a source from the Mishnah or from a Baraita that either provides a specific answer or the basis from which a conclusion regarding the problem may be drawn. Sometimes, rather than refer to an early source, a Rabbi proposes a solution to a problem by applying a solution found by another Rabbi, either in answer to a query or as part of an argument. The raising of problems (בָּעְיוֹת) is one of the most important techniques in the Talmudic dialectic. Not only does it provide solutions to practical, concrete questions, but it also helps to penetrate deeply into the Halakhic and logical apparatus comprising the basis of the Talmudic dialectic.

To understand the way these problems are treated it is important to remember the following general principle: The Talmudic method invariably prefers to pose questions in a concrete rather than an abstract form. However, the concrete cases are chosen so as to be as revealing as possible with regard to the (unstated) principles at issue. This is why problems connected with remote, borderline cases or even seemingly impossible situations (also past and non-recurring events) are discussed with the utmost seriousness. Frequently, a problem is treated in a more abstract way after its various aspects have been analyzed, and once the basis and origin of the Halakhah have been clarified.

Clarification of Points of View

When a difference of opinion between two authorities has emerged, the Talmud will analyze the difference exhaustively. The terminology used varies in accordance with the nature of the analysis. Some discussions begin with the question בְּמַאי קָמִיפַּלְגִי — "What is the basis of the disagreement?" Others begin מַאי בֵּינַיְיהוּ — "What are the practical consequences of the fundamental difference of opinion?" Apart from questions of this kind, the Talmud also attempts to organize the seemingly disparate statements of various scholars in a conceptual structure so that a single fundamental principle can be shown to underlie and explain them all.

One of the most common ways of analyzing conflicting viewpoints is to pursue the debate until all elements have been fully probed. This technique is most frequently applied in disputes between Tannaim. When different opinions are quoted in the Mishnah, they are usually not accompanied by explanations of the reasons for their differing views. Sometimes only one point of view is explained, and sometimes a fragmentary exchange of views is quoted. In such cases and many others the Talmud tries to extend the debate between the Tannaim, and, as it were, to reconstruct what each of the Tannaim would have replied to the objections, claims and arguments of the other. By continuing the analysis of the debate in this manner, whether the subject is a claim presented as a supposition or a Midrashic explanation of a Biblical source, the Talmud provides a much fuller explanation of the differing points of view. Conversely, this method is sometimes used to narrow the difference between the parties, ultimately reducing it to a subtle point of ideological disagreement. The Talmud also applies the technique described above to differences between Amoraim. In some cases the argument is prolonged in an imaginary debate between the disputants (...אָמַר לָהּ... אָמַר לָהּ — "X may reply as follows... Y may reply as follows..."). In other cases the Talmud quotes other sources or raises hypothetical problems and seeks to apply the approaches of the disputants to those sources and problems.

Mishnaic Methodology

Talmudic investigations do not exist in a vacuum. The Mishnah and the Tannaitic literature in general (Toseftot and Baraitot) are the basic source material for the discussions and investigations in the Talmud. The statements and opinions of the Amoraim, which form the Gemara as we know it, follow the teaching of the Tannaim closely in time and in place, and the authors of the Mishnah make use of techniques similar to those found later in the Gemara. Thus a large apparatus of general principles of argument and exegesis had already been consolidated during the Mishnaic period, providing the basis for the debates of the scholars of the Talmud. Some of these principles are explained once, or more frequently, in the Talmud; but others, because of their inherent simplicity (as far as the scholars of the Talmud were concerned) were only explained in the commentaries on the Talmud that appeared during later centuries.

The student of Talmud must know these general principles in order to understand the fundamental axioms of the Talmudic debate. The next section of this Guide contains a selected alphabetical list of these principles. It should be noted that not all of them have a fixed terminology in Tannaitic literature; indeed, some are presented here in later, even modern, terminology, and are expressed in different sources in different ways.

אֶחָד... וְאֶחָד ... *Both* x *and* y. When a Tanna brings several examples demonstrating the categories of people or objects to which a given law applies and uses the terminology אֶחָד... וְאֶחָד ... — "both... and..." (for example, אֶחָד גָּדוֹל וְאֶחָד קָטָן — "both great and small"; אֶחָד אֲנָשִׁים וְאֶחָד נָשִׁים — "both men and women") — he first cites the case that is in his opinion more straightforward and then cites the case that is more unusual or surprising. This usage helps us to understand which subject the Tanna considers more problematic, because he cites it last; we also see that the order in which the cases appear goes from the more to the less obvious.

אֲחֵרִים אוֹמְרִים *Others say.* The Talmud traditionally ascribes the authorship of statements preceded by the words אֲחֵרִים אוֹמְרִים — "others say" — to Rabbi Meir. At one stage in his life Rabbi Meir's colleagues penalized him by not ascribing some of his statements to him directly, introducing them instead by the expression אֲחֵרִים אוֹמְרִים. See יֵשׁ אוֹמְרִים.

אֵין לְמֵדִים מִן הַכְּלָלוֹת *One may not learn from general statements.* When a general statement is made in the Mishnah using the word כֹּל — "all" (for example, כָּל מִצְוֹת עֲשֵׂה שֶׁהַזְּמַן גְּרָמָן נָשִׁים פְּטוּרוֹת — "Women are exempt from all positive commandments limited by time") — it is not to be understood as an all-inclusive general statement without exceptions. It is possible that there are one or more exceptions to a statement phrased in such a way. The reason for this is that general statements of this type were formulated basically as aids to memorization and not as ironclad legal principles.

אֵין סֵדֶר לְמִשְׁנָה Lit., *there is no order in the Mishnah,* i.e., the Mishnah is not sequential. The order of the Mishnayot or the tractates may not be used to establish legal principles. Sometimes a statement appearing in an earlier Mishnah (according to the sequence adopted by Rabbi Yehudah HaNasi) is in fact a later and more authoritative source. Conclusions may likewise not be drawn from the inner arrangement of Mishnayot. On the subject, however, of סְתָם וְאַחַר כָּךְ מַחֲלוֹקֶת — "an anonymous and undisputed Mishnah followed by a difference of opinion" — there are authorities who maintain that the order of Mishnayot in that particular tractate has legal significance, but this certainly does not apply from one tractate to another.

אָמַר ר'... *Rabbi X said.* There is a difference in meaning between the formula אָמַר ר' פְּלוֹנִי — "Rabbi X said" — and ר' פְּלוֹנִי אוֹמֵר — "Rabbi X says." In general the expression אָמַר ר' פְּלוֹנִי — "Rabbi X said" — introduces an undisputed statement by the Sage quoted, whether that particular Sage was the author of the statement, or whether he passed it on as a traditionally accepted statement from a previous generation. On the other hand ר' פְּלוֹנִי אוֹמֵר — "Rabbi X says" — has the connotation that there are those who disagree with him on the matter, even though the statements and arguments of those who disagree with him do not necessarily appear in the same context.

אָסוּר *Forbidden.* When the word אָסוּר appears by itself, it means that something is forbidden, though the prohibition is often of Rabbinic origin (see חַיָּיב). However, when the word אָסוּר appears in combination with the word מוּתָּר ("permitted"), it does not provide new information but is merely used in contrast to the second term. In such a case the prohibition is a Torah prohibition, accompanied by a penalty imposed by the Torah (e.g., an expression frequently used is אָסוּר בַּאֲכִילָה וּמוּתָּר בַּהֲנָאָה — "An object that is forbidden to be eaten but from which benefit is permitted").

בֶּאֱמֶת אָמְרוּ   *Truly they said.* Any law that is preceded by this expression is accepted as Halakhically binding. Some authorities go so far as to say that it represents a Halakhah handed down to Moses on Mount Sinai (הֲלָכָה לְמשֶׁה מִסִּינַי).

בּוֹ בַּיּוֹם   *On that very day.* When this expression is used without specifying the context, it refers to the day when Rabban Gamliel (II) was deposed as president of the Sanhedrin. On that day many changes were made in the organization of the Academy and many laws were reinstituted. Testimony (see below עֵדִיּוֹת) on numerous subjects that had previously been unknown was also given on that day. There are cases, however, where the expression בּוֹ בַּיּוֹם — "on that very day" — refers to the day on which שְׁמוֹנָה עָשָׂר דָּבָר — "the eighteen enactments" — were passed into law (see *Shabbat* 1:4).

בַּמֶּה דְּבָרִים אֲמוּרִים   *In what circumstances does this apply?* When a Mishnaic Halakhah is followed by a statement by a Tanna limiting the application of the law and using the terminology בַּמֶּה דְּבָרִים אֲמוּרִים בְּ... — "In what circumstances does this apply? In the following case..." — it is traditionally maintained that specific Tannaim such as Rabbi Yehudah did not use the expression to register disagreement with the previous statement but only to explain it. This definition is not without exceptions, however, and there are cases where the expression בַּמֶּה דְּבָרִים אֲמוּרִים — "In what circumstances does this apply?" — represents an introduction to another, differing opinion. However, the limiting expression אֵימָתַי — "When is this the case?" — when used by a Tanna does indeed introduce a viewpoint disagreeing with the previous statement in the Mishnah.

בֶּן פְּלוֹנִי   *Ben [= Son of] X.* When a Sage is referred to as בֶּן פְּלוֹנִי, "Ben X" (e.g., Ben Zoma, Ben Azzai) rather than "Rabbi X," it means that the Sage quoted did not receive Rabbinical ordination or that at the time he made the statement quoted he did not yet have the title of "Rabbi."

גּוּזְמָא   *Exaggeration.* The Tannaim sometimes use exaggerated expressions, not intended to be taken literally. Sometimes the exaggeration is understood from the subject matter (e.g., "a fledgling in its shell," *Betzah* 4a); and sometimes an analysis of the real situation reveals the exaggeration. See also מְסַפְּרִים.

דִּיּוּק   *Accuracy, exactness, precision.* The Tannaim are not always particular about the accuracy of small details and sometimes omit a small point or an insignificant number. This occurs especially frequently in arithmetical calculations, which are not invariably precise. This lack of precision is, however, always limited by two general principles: (1) that the portion omitted is insignificant in size, and (2) that the imprecision does

not lead to permitting something that would otherwise be forbidden.

דָּנִין לִפְנֵי חֲכָמִים   *Those who argued before the scholars.* According to a tradition mentioned in the Gemara (*Sanhedrin* 17b), this sentence ("those who argued...") refers to the Sages Shimon ben Azzai, Shimon ben Zoma, Shimon HaTimni, Ḥanan HaMitzri and Ḥananyah ben Ḥakhinai, who were great scholars but were still young (or unordained) when this expression was applied to their legal statements.

וְכֵן   *And likewise.* When a Tanna states an additional Halakhah and precedes it with the word וְכֵן — "and likewise" — it may be inferred that the second Halakhah resembles the one preceding it.

זְמַן דְּקְדּוּקֵי   *The significance of the tense employed by the Mishnah.* Particular attention must be paid in every case to the tense employed by the Mishnah. When the Mishnah expresses something in the past tense, the intention is to show — unless the opposite is clearly indicated by the context — that it is referring to an act already performed and is not giving permission for such an action to be performed *ab initio*. By contrast, when the Mishnah uses the present tense, it is giving permission for such an action to be performed, even *ab initio*. For example, the expression הַכֹּל שׁוֹחֲטִין — "All may perform Sheḥitah" — means that all are permitted to perform Sheḥitah; whereas the expression שָׁחַט — "He performed Sheḥitah" — means that the Mishnah is discussing a case where a person has performed Sheḥitah and the Mishnah has to decide whether the Sheḥitah was valid or not. Wherever the Mishnah deviates from this general principle in the use of tenses, it leaves itself open to the question why it used an unusual and possibly misleading expression, and such a question will almost invariably be asked by the Talmud. Attention should also be paid to sentences beginning with the definite article ה. The definite article followed by the present tense does not necessarily indicate that the case being discussed is permitted *ab initio*. For example, הַלּוֹקֵחַ יַיִן מִבֵּין הַכּוּתִים — "One who buys wine from among the Cuthim" — is the equivalent of מִי שֶׁלָּקַח יַיִן... — "One who bought wine..."; whereas if the Mishnah wished to indicate by its use of the present tense that the case being discussed was in fact permitted *ab initio*, it would use the expression לוֹקֵחַ אָדָם — "A man may buy...."

חֲזָרָה   *Repetition.* We frequently find that a Tanna states a particular Halakhah more than once. He sometimes repeats the statement within its original context, and he sometimes brings it up incidentally in another context. Four reasons have been suggested as to why a Tanna might repeat a particular Halakhah: (1) Where the Halakhah is not self-evident and has some unusual feature. Since the Tanna has a particular affinity to this Halakhah, he likes to repeat it. (2) When the Halakhah is cited a second time, it contains an additional element not mentioned on the first occasion. Since it was necessary to mention this new element, the whole Halakhah is repeated. (3) Sometimes the Tanna repeats a well-known Halakhah for the purposes of comparison — either linguistic or of subject matter — with a series of other Halakhot. Since he is teaching an analogous sequence of

Halakhot, he repeats a subject that has already been stated. (4) The Tanna occasionally repeats a Halakhah where it does not involve him in unduly lengthy exposition; since he needed in any case to mention the subject, he mentions the already known Halakhah.

חִידוּשׁ   *A novel or exceptional case.* It is the practice among Tannaim to place a case of an unusual or anomalous nature at the beginning of their treatment of a given subject. The reason for this is either that the unusual case is derived from the Biblical text by a special kind of exegesis and is not immediately understood from the literal meaning of the text, or because there is some novelty in the particular case mentioned first. Having dealt with the unusual case first, the Tanna frequently then returns to the general principles governing the entire subject under discussion. This technique is especially common at the beginning of a major topic or a new chapter.

חַיָּב   *Liable, guilty, culpable.* This word has a number of meanings, depending on the context. In monetary matters it means that one of the parties to a dispute has been found liable and must pay the sum decided by the court. Where the context is how to fulfill a particular commandment, if a person is said to be חַיָּב to do a certain action it means more than he "needs to" (צָרִיךְ) or "is commanded to" (מְצֻוֶּה). חַיָּב here expresses an absolute obligation to act in a certain way. Where the context is the fulfillment or breach of a commandment, the word חַיָּב means that the person has been guilty of committing a transgression, usually one that involves the bringing of a sin-offering. Sometimes, indeed, the text clearly indicates חַיָּב חַטָּאת — "He must bring a sin-offering." In any case, חַיָּב in this context means "liable to whatever punishment breach of the particular commandment entails," whether the punishment is meted out by a human court or by divine retribution.

חַיָּב מִיתָה   Lit., *deserving death.* In Tannaitic literature this expression is not always meant to be understood literally. It does not necessarily mean that the person has committed an offense carrying the death penalty, but rather that he has committed a very serious transgression and that his punishment will be severe. See מַעֲלֶה עָלָיו הַכָּתוּב.

יֵשׁ אוֹמְרִים   *Some say.* It is traditionally understood that where this expression occurs in the Mishnah or in a Baraita it is to be attributed generally to the statements of Rabbi Natan (the Babylonian), who was punished by the president of the Sanhedrin and whose statements were thenceforth quoted without attribution. See אֲחֵרִים אוֹמְרִים.

כְּלָלִים וּפְרָטִים, פְּתִיחָה וְסִיּוּם   *General statements and particular laws, and their sequence.* When a Tanna begins a Mishnah with a general statement or a series of general statements, he sometimes continues with a detailed exposition of his first general statement, explaining each general principle in turn. Sometimes, however, he reverses the order, giving details of the last principle first and then going back to analyze the details of principles mentioned earlier. These variations of order are without Halakhic significance. Similarly, the Tanna sometimes mentions a specific number before stating a general

principle, as, for example, in the Mishnah that begins אַרְבָּעָה אֲבוֹת נְזִיקִין — "There are four primary categories of damage...." Sometimes, however, he begins by stating the general principle and then mentions the specific number of cases to which the principle applies, as, for example, in the Mishnah that begins הָאִשָּׁה נִקְנֵית בִּשְׁלֹשָׁה דְרָכִים — "A woman is acquired in marriage in three ways." All these variations of order are without Halakhic significance.

לֹא עָשָׂה כְּלוּם   *His act was without effect* (lit., "he did nothing"). There is a difference between the two negative expressions לֹא עָשָׂה כְּלוּם — "His act was without effect" — and פָּסוּל — "It is invalid." Generally speaking, when the expression לֹא עָשָׂה כְּלוּם is used (some scholars distinguish between this and לֹא עָשָׂה וְלֹא כְּלוּם — "His act was completely without effect" — the latter being even more emphatic), the purpose is to maintain that the action under discussion had no Halakhic significance at all and that it is to be completely disregarded. However, the expression פָּסוּל — "It is invalid" — sometimes means that the action under discussion is Rabbinically invalid but may have some Halakhic validity from the point of view of Torah law. An even more emphatic negative than לֹא עָשָׂה כְּלוּם — "His act was without effect" — is the expression אֵינוֹ... — "It is not..." — as, for example, in אֵינוֹ גֵט — "It is no bill of divorce" — which is a total denial of the validity and effectiveness of the divorce and much stronger than הַגֵּט פָּסוּל — "The bill of divorce is invalid." These distinctions of emphasis have very broad implications.

לָשׁוֹן נְקִיָּה   *Refined speech, euphemism.* The Sages of the Mishnah and the Talmud made every effort to use polite and refined language. Some sensitive matters are not mentioned by name, some are referred to by euphemisms, and sometimes these oblique references are themselves disguised. This technique is particularly striking at the beginning of a subject, where emphasis is laid on avoiding a negative presentation. Expressions laying stress on the invalid nature of an act or the guilt of a person are avoided, whereas constructive and positive statements stressing the validity of an action are preferred, even if this makes the statement longer.

לָשׁוֹן אֲרַמִּית וְעִבְרִית   *Aramaic and Hebrew.* There is a fundamental general principle that the language used in the Mishnah and the Baraitot is Hebrew alone, except for verbatim quotations of individual remarks or quotations from documents. Thus almost every Aramaic passage must automatically be part of the Gemara and not a Mishnah or a Baraita. Sometimes the Gemara is written in Hebrew, but Tannaitic sources are *always* in Hebrew.

לְשׁוֹן תּוֹרָה וּלְשׁוֹן חֲכָמִים   *The language of the Torah and the language of the Sages.* Already during the Talmudic period scholars drew attention to the fact that לְשׁוֹן תּוֹרָה לְחוּד וּלְשׁוֹן חֲכָמִים לְחוּד — "The language of the Torah is different from the language of the Sages." Much work has since been done by linguistic scholars in pointing out and explaining the differences between Biblical and Mishnaic Hebrew. It is important to remember that these two developments in the evolution of the Hebrew language differ both in vocabulary and in syntax. As the

Sages of the Talmud pointed out, there are particular differences in grammatical rules and in the formation of words. These differences are especially striking with regard to gender, where the language of the Mishnah is based on principles different from those of Biblical Hebrew. The reader should not, therefore, be surprised to encounter unusual word formations.

מוּתָּר   *Permitted.* The expression מוּתָּר — "permitted" — is to be understood, when it occurs in the Mishnah, as applying only to the particular case being discussed, and not as a general, comprehensive statement of permission. It is possible, therefore, for a particular action to be permissible only in the context of the Sabbath laws but forbidden on other grounds. These limitations are sometimes explained in the Mishnah, but often are left unexplained in the text and must be understood from the context. The expression מוּתָּר — "permitted" — is the converse of the expression אָסוּר — "forbidden." Thus where the Tanna is forced by the subject to declare one aspect of the case to be אָסוּר, he will stylistically be compelled to describe the opposite side of the case as מוּתָּר, even if the expression מוּתָּר is not entirely appropriate there and is not precise. It is also possible that an action described merely as מוּתָּר is indeed positively recommended as praiseworthy — a mitzvah.

מְלִיצָה   *Figurative language.* The Tannaim sometimes make use of Biblical expressions for literary and stylistic reasons. Such expressions should always be understood as being figurative in nature and not taken as fixed Halakhic terminology. For example, in Mishnah *Pe'ah* 2:2, we find the Biblical expression הֶהָרִים אֲשֶׁר בַּמַּעְדֵּר יֵעָדֵרוּן — "The mountains that are cultivated by the hoe." (See Isaiah 7:25.)

מִסְפָּרִים   *Numbers.* Both the Tannaim and the Amoraim tend to use numbers in particular, fixed ways, which need to be understood and carefully differentiated. All small numbers and most larger numbers that are not round numbers should be accepted as being exact, neither more nor less, unless the text specifically says otherwise. If the Tanna uses two numbers together, such as שָׁלֹשׁ אַרְבַּע — "three, four" — or אַרְבַּע חָמֵשׁ — "four, five" — it is appropriate to consider why he used both of them, as this usage creates some kind of contradiction. Usually the two numbers reflect two aspects of the same case. For example, the expression כְּבֶן חָמֵשׁ כְּבֶן שֵׁשׁ — "aged five, aged six" — is explained as referring to a healthy child of five and a sickly child of six, etc. If the Tanna specifies two large numbers, particularly if he first uses the word אֲפִילוּ — "even" — it is necessary to clarify whether he means an infinite number, in which case the numbers he specified are insignificant, or a particular finite number, in which case the purpose behind the use of those particular numbers must be ascertained. There are certain numbers, such as 7 (especially in Biblical usage), 13, 40, 60, 300, 400, etc., which are round numbers and not meant to be taken literally.

מַעֲלֶה עָלָיו הַכָּתוּב   *The verse ascribes to him.* This expression in the Mishnah and the Gemara (מַעֲלֶה עָלָיו הַכָּתוּב כְּאִילוּ — "The verse gives him credit as if he had..."; or מַעֲלֶה... עָלָיו הַכָּתוּב שֶׁ... — "The verse considers that he...") means that in the case under discussion the person performing a certain action

is to be judged in accordance with the Biblical text. Generally, however, the Biblical text is not to be taken literally in such circumstances — it is to be considered as giving general guidance of ethical rather than Halakhic significance.

מַעֲשֶׂה   *An incident, an occurrence.* Tannaim frequently cite incidents or events that occurred, either as a source for a particular Halakhah, or as additional proof of the validity of a logical deduction. The significance of such incidents is very great, bearing in mind the general principle מַעֲשֶׂה רַב — "A practical incident teaches us a precedent." The underlying assumption here is that a Sage would not act in a particular way unless the Halakhah on which his action was based was entirely clear and not dependent on logical reasoning alone. Generally the Halakhah is decided in accordance with the example provided by the particular incident. By contrast, there are occasions when we find the expression מַעֲשֶׂה לִסְתּוֹר — "an incident quoted to disprove a rule" — where the incident seems to testify against the Halakhic principle previously cited. In such cases the Gemara either emends the text of the Mishnah or tries to find circumstances supporting both the incident and the Halakhah.

מִשָּׁם רְאָיָה   *You bring proof from there?!* This expression is usually used in the form of a question: "Do you really seek to bring proof of your point of view from there? Surely the circumstances were different," or "Surely this proof has already been refuted!" The expression is sometimes used as an emphatic statement by the other side: "Yes, indeed, I do bring proof from there," i.e., the very source that you are trying to use as proof of your point of view in fact proves the opposite!

מִשְׁנָה אַחֲרוֹנָה   *The later Mishnah.* This refers to the later views of the Sages of the Mishnah, where their later opinion differs from their earlier opinion, in contrast to מִשְׁנָה רִאשׁוֹנָה — "the earliest Mishnah." See also מִשְׁנָה רִאשׁוֹנָה.

מִשְׁנָה בִּמְקוֹמָה   *A Mishnah in its own context.* There is a general principle that a Mishnah appearing in the context of its main subject has greater Halakhic authority than an opinion expressed in a Mishnah outside its own context. It often happens that a Halakhah on a certain subject, because of the way the Mishnayot were ultimately edited, appears together with Mishnayot that deal with other problems. Sometimes, indeed, a topic is discussed in two different places and two different opinions about it are expressed, or there are alternative readings and differing points of view. In all such cases the authority of a Mishnah cited within its own context is stronger than that of a Mishnah cited outside its own context. The assumption is that the Sages who were dealing with that specific subject were certain to have analyzed it in greater depth than a subject that was not central to their investigation and was only cited incidentally.

מִשְׁנָה רִאשׁוֹנָה   *A Mishnah from the earliest collection.* One occasionally finds in the Mishnah or other Tannaitic sources a comment that certain statements in it agree with the viewpoint of מִשְׁנָה רִאשׁוֹנָה — "a Mishnah from the earliest collection" — and that other views on the subject are held by מִשְׁנַת ר' עֲקִיבָא — "the Mishnah of Rabbi Akiva" — or מִשְׁנָה אַחֲרוֹנָה — "the final

Mishnah." The reason for this is that even before the time of Rabbi Yehudah HaNasi there existed edited collections of the statements of the Tannaim. On more than one occasion the Talmud uses the assumption that there were various levels of earlier editing of the Mishnah in order to explain why the Mishnah contains seeming repetitions of individual Halakhot, often occurring very close to each other, or Halakhot that appear to be contradictory or inappropriately grouped. The explanation may be that one Mishnah is itself part of the מִשְׁנָה רִאשׁוֹנָה — "the original collection" — and a later Mishnah was afterwards added to it. The general principle at work here is מִשְׁנָה לֹא זָזָה מִמְּקוֹמָה — "The Mishnah was not removed from its place," i.e., the later Sages did not delete the earlier Mishnah and left it in its original place. The reason for this was that the students had already become familiar with the earlier Mishnah, and the later Sages then added statements to it to alter its Halakhic and practical conclusions.

סֵדֶר הַדֵּעוֹת
The order in which different opinions are quoted. Where the opinions of individual Sages are quoted in the Mishnah, and also generally speaking in the Talmud, whether the opinions quoted contradict each other or not, the statements are usually cited in chronological order, with the opinion of the earlier Sage appearing before that of the later Sage. This rule is not always observed; but there always has to be a specific reason for its nonobservance. The reason sometimes is that the opinion of the later authority reflects the original opinion of the earlier authority, the circumstances being that the earlier authority changed his view, whereas the later authority continued to maintain his earlier opinion. Sometimes the viewpoint of a later authority is presented first, in order to stress that this viewpoint is to be accepted. There are also occasions where the author of the Mishnah changes the chronological order of statements in order to organize the subject matter in a more coherent way. Also, wherever a difference of opinion is quoted between contemporary Tannaim whose opinions are frequently cited together in the Mishnah, there is a fixed order in which their names appear, either according to importance or to age. In the particular case of disputes between Bet Shammai and Bet Hillel, Bet Shammai is always quoted first because the scholars of Bet Hillel deferred in humility to those of Bet Shammai. Wherever the Mishnah changes the regular order of citing opinions, the Gemara will find occasion to probe the reasoning behind such a change.

סְתַם מִשְׁנָה
An anonymous Mishnah. This expression is used to define a complete anonymous Mishnah, or a part of it that is either preceded or followed by an attributed difference of opinion between individual Sages. The fact that an anonymous Mishnah is quoted in this way does not necessarily prove that it is the viewpoint of all the (other) Sages; sometimes, indeed, it is the opinion of one individual Sage. But in all cases its significance lies in the fact that Rabbi Yehudah HaNasi ascribed particular importance to it, and quoted it anonymously in order to indicate that he himself considered it authoritative. There are, in fact, later authorities — in particular Rambam — who consistently follow the viewpoint of the great Amora, Rabbi Yoḥanan, and almost invariably decide the law in accordance

with the anonymous Mishnah, even in cases where a number of other conflicting opinions exist. The Gemara makes a distinction between an anonymous Mishnah that is uncontested, on the one hand, and — סְתָם וְאַחַר כָּךְ מַחֲלוֹקֶת — "an anonymous Mishnah followed by a difference of opinion." In the latter case some authorities maintain that the Halakhah does not follow the anonymous Mishnah. In the detailed questions of what constitutes "an anonymous Mishnah followed by a difference of opinion," and what constitutes an uncontested anonymous Mishnah, there are a number of different opinions among later authorities.

סְתַם מִשְׁנָה ר׳ מֵאִיר
Anonymous Mishnayot reflect the view of Rabbi Meir. There is a general principle in the Talmud that attributes anonymous Mishnayot to the viewpoint of Rabbi Meir, since Rabbi Yehudah HaNasi tended to rely on the traditions according to their formulation by Rabbi Meir and his school. The commentators on the Mishnah assert that in those frequent instances where the Talmud asks, regarding an anonymous Mishnah, מַנִּי מַתְנִיתִין — "According to whose view is our Mishnah?" — the Sages of the Talmud had a tradition that that particular Mishnah did not reflect the viewpoint of Rabbi Meir.

עֵדוּת
Testimony. The commentators have a general principle that every Halakhic statement cited in the form of "testimony" (...הֵעִיד ר׳ פְּלוֹנִי — "Rabbi X testified that ...") represents the accepted Halakhah, because the Sage bringing the "testimony" had received the statement from authorities who had given these rulings on the authority of earlier tradition. The authority of such a ruling is greater than that of a mere logical inference.

עֵדִיּוֹת
Eduyyot. Testimonies. It is generally held that the Mishnayot in tractate *Eduyyot* are especially authoritative, either because most of them represent personal testimonies of Sages regarding Halakhic rulings they had received from their teachers, or because the tractate was composed at a major assembly of eminent Sages and was unanimously accepted. Some authorities maintain that every statement in this tractate represents binding Halakhah, even where the statement runs counter to other Halakhic general principles. Support for this point of view may be drawn from the alternative title of the tractate, בְּחִירָתָא — "the chosen ones" — which reflects a play on the words עֵדִיּוֹת ("testimonies") and עֲדִיּוֹת ("the choicest ones").

פָּטוּר
Exempt. It is the opposite of the expression חַיָּיב — "liable" — and both expressions appear juxtaposed throughout Mishnaic literature. The word פָּטוּר — "exempt" — has various meanings, depending on the context. In monetary matters it means that the defendant is exempt from payment. In ritual matters it means that a person has no liability, that he is not liable to bring a sacrifice, or that he is not liable according to the laws of a human (rather than divine) tribunal. It should be borne in mind that, particularly in the laws concerning the Sabbath, but sometimes also in other areas, in most of the instances where the word פָּטוּר — "exempt" — is used it means פָּטוּר אֲבָל אָסוּר — "The person is exempt, but the action is forbidden." Only rarely does it mean פָּטוּר וּמוּתָר — "The person is exempt and the action is permitted." The essential nature of

the concept פָּטוּר is that the performance of the given action is not liable to punishment, but not necessarily that the action itself is *ab initio* permissible.

צֵרוּף הֲלָכוֹת שׁוֹנוֹת   *The combination of various Halakhot.*

It is a very frequent practice in the Mishnah that, as a result of a discussion concerning one particular Halakhah, another, unconnected, Halakhah (or occasionally a whole series of such Halakhot) is cited immediately after it. Authorities who have made a study of this tendency state that there are three basic reasons for such combinations of Halakhot: (1) The Halakhot may have one characteristic in common, particularly a Rabbinical enactment. In such a case the Tanna cites various cases only because of this one Halakhic characteristic shared by all the cases. (2) There may be a similarity of language. Sometimes two Halakhot, differing in subject and decision, are nevertheless phrased in very similar language. For this reason alone they are often brought together. (3) Certain Halakhot are linked because their subjects have some outward similarity, and they appear together almost as a form of standard terminology. For example, חֵרֵשׁ שׁוֹטֶה וְקָטָן — "a deaf-mute, an imbecile, and a minor"; or אִשָּׁה עֶבֶד וְקָטָן — "a woman, a slave, and a minor." Sometimes the Mishnah is dealing with Halakhot concerning one of these categories and as a result also brings matters connected with the other categories, even though the subject matter may be quite different.

צָרִיךְ   *It is necessary.*

The word צָרִיךְ — "it is necessary" — expresses an obligation that is placed upon a person *ab initio*. It is not as strong as the expression חַיָּיב — "liable" — and there are cases where, even if a person did not carry out what was צָרִיךְ — "necessary" — he nevertheless did fulfill his obligation. Sometimes the Sages say that צָרִיךְ — "it is necessary" — to perform a certain action, but circumstances prevent it from being performed. In such a case some Sages maintain that, since the action cannot be performed, the necessity to perform it is also cancelled; whereas others maintain that since the action cannot be performed, it is a case of צָרִיךְ וְאֵין לוֹ תַּקָּנָה — "it is necessary but impossible of fulfillment."

שְׁנֵי דְבָרִים הַשְּׁנוּיִים יַחַד   *Two matters taught together.*

If the Tanna teaches two Halakhot together, whether they relate to the same issue or have been brought together for some other reason, it is an accepted principle of study to try to compare them to each other as closely as possible, since the Tanna would not have taught them together if they were not very similar to each other.

שֶׁנֶּאֱמַר   *As it is said.*

Authorities maintain that where the expression שֶׁנֶּאֱמַר — "as it is said" — occurs in the Talmud the intention is to furnish a quotation from the Bible that will serve as a complete proof. On the other hand, when the expression מִשּׁוּם שֶׁנֶּאֱמַר — "since it is said" — is used, the Biblical verse that follows is not intended to provide a complete proof but a less authoritative support.

תְּחִילַת מַסֶּכֶת   *The beginning of a tractate.*

Although the inner order of the various tractates may differ, there are nevertheless certain basic principles governing how tractates begin and the general order they follow. Where the subject under discussion is limited by time, the tractate is usually organized according to time, beginning with what occurs earlier and proceeding to what occurs later. But even in such tractates, and even more so in tractates in which such an inner order is not followed, the Mishnah prefers to begin the tractate with subject matter of especial novelty and interest. Sometimes a tractate begins with an issue that not only appears unconnected with the orderly analysis of the general subject, but is also particularly complicated in its own right; the purpose of this is to arouse interest and curiosity in the student. Some tractates begin with a Halakhah of specific novelty, and not with one that could provide the basis for a systematic and logical study of the subject. Particular care is also taken at the beginning of a tractate to avoid topics of an unseemly or improper nature if a change of language renders such avoidance possible.

תָּנָא וְשַׁיֵּיר   *He taught and left out.*

It is not the practice of the Mishnah to bring all possible examples of a given law. The Mishnah frequently states a whole series of cases yet omits other, equally relevant ones. The Gemara's expression for this practice is אַטּוּ תָּנָא כִּי רוּכְלָא לִיחַשֵּׁב וְלֵיזִיל — "Does the Tanna need to go around like a peddler, enumerating each particular detail?" Indeed, even where the Mishnah's style might lead us to believe that nothing was omitted (e.g., when it says אֵין בֵּין...וּבֵין...אֶלָּא — "There is no difference between X and Y except...") it does not necessarily enumerate all the instances. Furthermore, one may not assume that the Tanna left out one case and not more. If he left out anything, he could well have left out a number of things.

Talmudic Terminology

The Talmud does not give the impression that it underwent strict editing of the subjects that are discussed in it or of the internal connection between those subjects. It did nevertheless undergo the most precise and careful editing with regard to the technical terminology used in it to indicate or introduce questions and answers, observations of surprise and contradictions, problems and solutions. Each term has extremely precise significance and a clearly defined role in the Talmudic debate. One can only understand the Talmud properly if one knows and understands this terminology. The more accurate one's understanding of these terms is, the clearer will be one's understanding of the subject under discussion, the development of the passage, and its exact content.

Most of the dialectical terms found frequently in the Babylonian Talmud have been listed below, together with many key expression from the Jerusalem Talmud and the Halakhic and Aggadic Midrashim. Terms that occur only rarely in the Talmud have generally not been included.

The terminology of the Talmud is discussed extensively in the classical works on Talmudic methodology (כְּלָלֵי הַתַּלְמוּד). (See Bibliography.) Some expressions listed below have been interpreted differently by various scholars. In such cases, only one view has been cited here.

A number of expressions listed below sometimes begin with an additional letter ד or ו. They will usually be classified under the first letter after the ד or ו. In cross-references the additional letter appears in parentheses.

אַבָּא   Lit., *father*. (1) An honorary title given to a number of Tannaitic scholars (e.g., Abba Shaul, Abba Binyamin). (2) The name of several Amoraim, e.g., Rav (see *Ta'anit* 4b), Rabbah (see *Pesahim* 40a).

אֲבָל   Lit., *but*. An expression in Mishnaic literature, meaning: "I accept your argument, but I can nevertheless present an argument against the comparison you are making with the opinion I am expressing." Sometimes, however, אֲבָל means "yes" in Tannaitic literature (see *Eruvin* 30b).

אַגַּב אוֹרְחָא קָא מַשְׁמַע לַן   *He incidentally teaches us.* An expression indicating that a particular subject is not the main purpose of a scholar's argument, although we are able to derive a law relating to it from the way the scholar framed his statement. (See *Berakhot* 2a.)

אַדְּמִיפַּלְגֵי בְּ... לִיפַּלּוֹג בְּ...   *Rather than differing about X, let them differ about Y!* This term introduces an objection to a previously suggested interpretation of a difference of opinion between Tannaim. Such an objection is usually expressed as follows: "Rather than their differing about case X, it would have been more reasonable for these Tannaim to disagree about case Y, and in this way the subject would be better clarified." (See *Betzah* 2b.)

אַדְּרַבָּא   *On the contrary* (lit., "on the greater side"). Where the Gemara presents an argument based on common sense, it sometimes then seeks to refute this argument by showing that

common sense actually tends to support the opposite view, introducing the refutation with this term. (See *Shabbat* 3b.) See also אִיפְּכָא מִסְתַּבְּרָא; (וְ)הוּא דְּרוּבָּה מִינָהּ; כְּלַפֵּי לַיָּיא.

אַהַיָּיא   *To what does this refer?* (Lit., "on which.") Sometimes, when a concluding sentence in a Mishnah, Baraita or Amoraic statement refers to or differs from an earlier statement in the same source, it is not clear to which of the previous statements it is referring. In such cases, the Talmud may ask: "To which statement does this sentence refer?" (See *Kiddushin* 46a.)

אוֹ אֵינוֹ אֶלָּא...   See אַתָּה אוֹמֵר....

וְאוֹמֵר   *And it says.* Sometimes a Mishnah or a Baraita cites two Biblical verses in support of a statement previously made; in such cases the standard usage is שֶׁנֶּאֱמַר... וְאוֹמֵר... — "The Bible says verse A, and it also says verse B." The Gemara may then ask: מַאי וְאוֹמֵר (lit., "What is: 'And it says'?"), i.e., what need is there to cite an additional verse, since the proof from the first verse is sufficient? (See *Berakhot* 2b.) The Gemara usually answers this question by suggesting that one might be able to refute a proof depending on the first verse alone, while the second verse provides an additional element rendering the proof more complete.

אוֹ דִילְמָא...   See מִי אָמְרִינַן... אוֹ דִילְמָא....

אוֹקִימְתָּא   Lit., *establishing*. An interpretation of a Mishnah or a Baraita which "establishes" it as referring to a particular case or following a particular viewpoint is called an אוֹקִימְתָּא.

אוֹרְחָא דְּמִילְתָא קָתָנֵי   Lit., *he teaches the "way of things,"* i.e., the Tanna cited an example from everyday life, and legal inferences cannot, therefore, be drawn from the details specified in connection with this example. (See *Gittin* 29a.)

אָזְדָא לְטַעֲמֵיהּ (אָזְדוּ לְטַעֲמַיְיהוּ)   *He follows his [regular line of] argument (they follow their [regular line of] argument).* The Talmud uses this expression when pointing out that a scholar's statement in the case at hand follows the same principle or line of reasoning that he employs elsewhere. (See *Berakhot* 13b, *Pesaḥim* 29a.)

אַטּוּ   This term has two separate meanings: (1) *Because of,* used in such expressions as אַטּוּ... גָּזְרִינַן — "We make an enactment regarding X because of Y." (See *Gittin* 40b.) (2) *Is it because...? Do you really mean to say that...?* (See *Berakhot* 33b.) In this instance the word expresses spontaneous astonishment. It is frequently used when a reason given for a particular Halakhah does not seem to be logical. See also next entry.

אַטּוּ תַנָּא כִּי רוּכְלָא לִיחֲשֵׁיב וְלֵיזִיל   Lit., *does the Tanna really have to go on reckoning [enumerating cases] like a peddler?* (See *Gittin* 33a.) This is a sarcastic expression, dismissing a demand that the Tanna enumerate every last detail. See also מַאי שַׁיֵּיר דְּהַאי שַׁיֵּיר; תָּנָא וְשַׁיֵּיר.

(אֶלָּא) אִי אִיתְּמַר הָכִי אִיתְּמַר   *If it was said, it was said as follows.* Sometimes, when an objection has been raised against an Amoraic statement, the Talmud resolves this objection by suggesting that the Amora's remark was reported incorrectly, and hence it must be emended: "If such a statement was made, it was made in the following form." (See *Yoma* 28a.)

(דְּ)אִי אָמְרַתְּ...   *(For) if you say....* This expression is used to prove point A by dismissing a counterargument advanced against point A. By proving the counterargument to be false, the Gemara shows that its original proposal must be correct: "If you say the contrary of what I am claiming, you face the following difficulty...." (See *Yoma* 24b.) See also ...(דְּ)אִי לָא תֵּימָא הָכִי.

אִי אָמְרַתְּ בִּשְׁלָמָא...   See בִּשְׁלָמָא.

אִי הָכִי   *If so.* An expression introducing an objection: "If what was just said is in fact so, then the following objection can be raised." See following entries.

אִי הָכִי אַדְתָּנֵי... לִיפְלוֹג וְלִיתְנֵי בְּדִידָהּ   *If so, rather than teaching... let him make a distinction regarding the case itself.* An expression introducing an objection: "If the distinction that you have made is in fact valid, then the Tanna, instead of bringing another ruling from another subject, should have highlighted that distinction by citing various examples from the same subject. Since the Tanna did not do so, it is reasonable to infer that the distinction is not valid." (See *Yevamot* 19a.)

אִי הָכִי אֲפִילוּ... נַמִי   *If so, then even... also.* An expression used by the Gemara to refute an argument by showing that, if it

were accepted, it would be too widely applicable and prove too much: "If the argument just presented were in fact correct, then it should even apply to the following case... but, as we know, it does not." (See *Betzah* 8b.)
See also אִי הָכִי מַאי אִירְיָא... אֲפִילוּ... נַמִי.

אִי הָכִי הַיְינוּ דְּקָתָנֵי...   *If so, is it this that it has taught?!* An expression used by the Gemara to introduce an objection to a proposed explanation or reconciliation of seemingly conflicting Mishnayot or Baraitot. "If what you say is correct, how can we explain the following Tannaitic statement?" (See *Sanhedrin* 85b.)

אִי הָכִי מַאי אִירְיָא... אֲפִילוּ... נַמִי   *If so, why specifically X; even Y too!* An expression used by the Gemara to refute an argument by showing that, if accepted, it would prove too much: "If the argument just presented were in fact correct, why did the text teach case X? It could equally well have taught case Y." (See *Betzah* 8a.) See also אִי הָכִי אֲפִילוּ... נַמִי.

(דְּ)אִי לָא תֵּימָא הָכִי...   *(For) if you do not say so....* An expression used by the Gemara to support an argument by pointing out the undesirable consequences of its rejection: "If you do not accept my argument, then you are faced with the following difficulty." (See *Bava Metzia* 5b.) See also ...(דְּ)אִי אָמְרַתְּ.

אִי מִכְּלָלָא מַאי   Lit., *if from a generalization, so what?* i.e., what difference does it make if a Halakhah transmitted in the name of a certain scholar was not stated by him explicitly, but was inferred from another statement of his or from his conduct? (See *Berakhot* 12a.) See also לָאו בְּפֵירוּשׁ אִיתְּמַר; מִכְּלָלָא אִיתְּמַר.

(דְּ)אִי מִמַּתְנִיתִין, הֲוָה אָמִינָא... קָא מַשְׁמַע לַן   Lit., *if from our Mishnah, I might have said... therefore he tells us.* Sometimes the Gemara asks why a Baraita or an Amora made a certain statement which could have been deduced from the Mishnah. The Gemara may answer thus: "If I knew only what was taught in the Mishnah, I might have made a mistake and interpreted the Mishnah incorrectly. Therefore the Baraita or the Amora teaches us explicitly what was already alluded to in the Mishnah." (See *Shabbat* 108a.)

אִי מִשּׁוּם הָא לָא אִירְיָא   *If because of this, there is no argument,* i.e., your argument is inconclusive, because.... This expression is commonly used when an Amora seeks to prove that the first clause of a Mishnah has to be interpreted in a particular way in order to avoid making the latter clause superfluous. The Gemara answers: "No, this argument is inconclusive and the Mishnah can be interpreted differently." The Gemara often proceeds: תָּנָא סֵיפָא לְגַלוּיֵי רֵישָׁא (see entry). (See also *Gittin* 42a, *Bava Metzia* 100a.)

אִי נַמִי   *Alternatively* (lit., "if also"). This term introduces an alternative suggestion, explanation or answer.

(דְּ)אִי סָלְקָא דַּעְתָּךְ...   *(For) if it should enter your mind.* See ...(דְּ)אִי אָמְרַתְּ; (דְּ)אִי לָא תֵּימָא הָכִי.

אִי קַשְׁיָא הָא קַשְׁיָא   *If there is a difficulty, this is the difficulty.* Sometimes the Gemara raises an objection based on a particular subject, while ignoring a more serious objection that could have been raised. After the Gemara has successfully answered the first objection, it introduces the more serious objection by using this expression. (See *Betzah* 9b, 10a.)

אִי תַּנְיָא תַּנְיָא   *If [this Baraita] was taught, it was taught.* Sometimes an Amora's statement is contradicted explicitly by a Baraita. In such cases the Amora retracts his statement, saying: "If this Baraita was taught, it was taught, and I cannot take issue with it." (See *Moed Katan* 4b.)

אִיבַּעְיָא לְהוּ   *It was asked of them,* i.e., they (the scholars in the Academy) asked. This expression ordinarily introduces a problem raised anonymously in the Gemara. (See *Ketubot* 24b.) The construction of the problem is often in the form of an alternative: "Do we say X, or perhaps Y?" — מִי אָמְרִינַן... אוֹ דִילְמָא.... (See entries.) See also בָּעֵי; בָּעְיָא.

(אִיבָּעֵית אֵימָא) (וְ)אִי בָּעֵית אֵימָא   *If you wish, say....* This expression is used to introduce an additional answer to a question previously asked, or an additional explanation of a problem previously raised. (See *Berakhot* 3a.)

אִיבָּעֵית אֵימָא קְרָא, אִיבָּעֵית אֵימָא סְבָרָא   *If you wish, give a verse; if you wish, give a commonsense argument,* i.e., you may prove your point either by means of a Biblical verse or by using logical reasoning. This expression is used by the Gemara to introduce two proofs of a particular argument, the one from a Biblical verse and the other based upon logic. (See *Berakhot* 4b.)

...אִיהוּ דַּעֲבַד (אִינְהוּ דְּעַבְדוּ) כְּ   *He (they) acted in accordance with [the viewpoint of] Rabbi X,* i.e., the scholar(s) cited acted in accordance with the viewpoint of Rabbi X, whose view was not generally accepted. (See *Yevamot* 121a.)

אַיְּידֵי   *By way of, since.* Sometimes, when part of a Tannaitic source seems irrelevant or superfluous, and an Amora wishes to base an explanation upon this seeming irrelevance or superfluity, the Talmud may answer that the problematic section was included (or worded in its present fashion) in order to maintain stylistic uniformity throughout the passage. Accordingly the Talmud may state that the problematic section was formulated "by way of" (i.e., under the stylistic influence of) another portion of the passage under discussion. אַיְּידֵי in this sense may occur in such expressions as אַיְּידֵי דְּבָעֵי לְמִתְנֵי סֵיפָא... תָּנָא נַמִי רֵישָׁא — "Since the Tanna wanted to teach the latter clause... he also taught the former clause." (See *Shabbat* 30a.)
See also אַיְּידֵי דִּנְסֵיב רֵישָׁא... נָסֵיב סֵיפָא נַמִי....

אַיְּידֵי דְּאָתְיָא מִדְּרָשָׁא חֲבִיבָא לֵיהּ   *Since it comes [i.e., is derived] from exegesis, it is dear to him.* Sometimes a Tanna takes up a minor issue before a major one, and the Talmud wonders why he does so. Often the response is: "Since it [the less important topic] is derived through Midrashic exegesis (and is not explicitly mentioned in the Torah), it is especially dear to the sage who discussed it, and for this reason it was mentioned first." (See *Bava Batra* 108b.)

...אַיְּידֵי דִּנְסֵיב רֵישָׁא... נָסֵיב סֵיפָא נַמִי   *Since he took the first part... he took the end as well....* Where there appears to be an inconsistency between two parts of a Mishnah or a Baraita, the Gemara sometimes explains that the latter part of the Tannaitic statement was not meant to be strictly construed, but was merely a stylistic parallel to the first part: "Since the Tanna needed to teach the first part of his statement, he added the latter part too." (See *Bava Kamma* 71b.) See also אַיְּידֵי.

אִיכָּא בֵּינַיְיהוּ   Lit., *there is between them....* This expression is used by the Gemara when there is a difference of opinion or of explanation between scholars, but the practical consequences of this difference are not clear. The Gemara, in explaining the distinction between the viewpoints, introduces its answer by saying that "the practical difference between the different viewpoints or reasons mentioned in the previous passage is as follows." (See *Bava Metzia* 15b.)
See also מַאי בֵּינַיְיהוּ; ר' פְּלוֹנִי הַיְינוּ תַּנָּא קַמָּא.

אִיכָּא דְּאָמְרִי   *There are [some] who say.* This expression introduces an alternative version of the previous statement or passage. (See *Betzah* 13a.) See also לִישָׁנָא.

אִיכָּא דְּבָעֵי לָהּ מִיבָּעְיָא   *There are [some] who ask it as a question.* This expression (see *Ketubot* 2a) introduces a rephrasing of a Talmudic passage in the form of a problem rather than of a statement: "Some scholars transmit the contents of the previous discussion in the form of a problem and its solution." See also בָּעְיָא.

אִיכָּא דְּמְפָרְשֵׁי הָכִי   *There are [some] who explain thus,* i.e., some scholars suggest the following, alternative reason for a law previously stated. (See *Bava Kamma* 56b.)
See also אִיכָּא דְּאָמְרִי.

...אִיכָּא דְּמַתְנֵי לְהָא דְּר' פְּלוֹנִי אַהָא   *There are [some] who teach the statement of Rabbi X [as referring] to...,* i.e., there is an alternative report, connecting the previously quoted Amoraic statement or interpretation to the following case, rather than to the one mentioned earlier. (See *Sanhedrin* 28b.)

אִיכָּא דְּרָמֵי לְהוּ מִירְמָא   *There are [some] who put it [in the form of] a contradiction.* This term introduces a variant of a previous discussion, in which the discussion is organized in the form of a contradiction between two Tannaitic sources followed by an Amoraic statement resolving the contradiction. (See *Rosh HaShanah* 27b.) See also רָמֵי.

אִיכָּא לְמִפְרַךְ   *It is possible to refute....* An expression used by the Gemara as an introduction to a refutation — in particular of a בִּנְיַן אָב or קַל וָחוֹמֶר (see entries in section on hermeneutics). (See *Bava Kamma* 5b.) See also פִּירְכָא.

אִיכְּפַל תַּנָּא לְאַשְׁמוֹעִינַן   *Did the Tanna take the trouble to teach us...?* An expression used when a Tannaitic source has been interpreted so narrowly as to refer only to a very rare or unusual case (usually in order to resolve an objection). The Talmud may object to this explanation, protesting that the Tanna would not have gone to the trouble of discussing such an unusual case. (See *Bava Metzia* 46a.)

אִילֵימָא *If we say.* An expression used to introduce an assumption or an explanation that is rejected in the subsequent discussion. (See *Bava Metzia* 12b.) See also לֵימָא.

אֵימָא *Say!* An expression used to suggest an explanation or emendation of an unclear statement in the previous passage. (See *Sukkah* 32b.)

אֵימָא אִיפְּכָא *Say the reverse!* This expression is sometimes used when a Mishnah or a Baraita derives two different laws from two Biblical verses dealing with the same subject. The Gemara observes: "Rather than learning Law A from Verse A and Law B from Verse B, it would seem more logical to *say the reverse* and learn Law A from Verse B and Law B from Verse A!" (See *Bava Metzia* 110b.)
See also אִיפּוֹךְ; מוּחְלֶפֶת הַשִּׁיטָה.

אֵימָא סֵיפָא *Say the last clause,* i.e., read the last clause in the source under discussion, and then you will realize that your interpretation of the first clause is incorrect. (See *Betzah* 23b.) Similarly we find: אֵימָא רֵישָׁא — "Say the first clause" (see *Berakhot* 25a); and on rare occasions: אֵימָא מְצִיעָתָא — "Say the middle clause." (See *Yoma* 17b.)

אֵימָא רֵישָׁא *Say the first clause.* See אֵימָא סֵיפָא.

אֵימוֹר (אֵימַר) דְּ... Lit., *say that....* This expression introduces a statement limiting the application of the statement preceding it to special circumstances. (See *Pesaḥim* 25b.) It often appears in the form — אֵימוֹר דְּשָׁמְעַתְּ לֵיהּ לְר'..., ...מִי שָׁמְעַתְּ לֵיהּ "Granted that you heard Rabbi X express this opinion where the following is the case, but where the case is different, did you hear him express this opinion?" (See *Shabbat* 124b.)

אֵימָתַי *When?* This question, used in Tannaitic literature, may be either a straightforward request for information about the time frame for the observance of a particular law — "On what day...?", "At what hour...?" (see *Berakhot* 2a) — or an expression limiting the application of a particular law (see *Megillah* 5a). See also בַּמֶּה דְּבָרִים אֲמוּרִים.

אִין, ...לֹא *[In this case] yes, but [otherwise] no.* An expression introducing an argument (often later refuted) depending on close analysis of a previously quoted passage: "The wording of the passage leads us to infer that in case A the law would be X, but in all other cases the law would not be X." (See *Yoma* 85b.) See also טַעְמָא דְּ... הָא....

אִין הָכִי נַמִי Lit., *yes, so too,* i.e., yes, it is indeed so. An expression used when conceding a point. (See *Eruvin* 93b.)

אִין וְלָאו וְרַפְיָא בִּידֵיהּ *Yes and no and it was unsteady in his hand.* Sometimes a scholar was not certain about the answer to a question; in such cases the Talmud may state that he gave hesitant or even contradictory answers to the question, because the issue was not clear to him. (See *Shabbat* 113a.)

אֵין לִי אֶלָּא א', ב' מִנַּיִן? תַּלְמוּד לוֹמַר... *I have only X, from where [do I have] Y? The Torah says....* An expression used in Halakhic Midrashim. When one law has already been derived from a Biblical verse, and another law remains to be derived through exegesis, the Talmud may state: "I have only law X stated in the text; from where may I derive law Y? The Torah states the following (either from a superfluous expression in the same verse or from another verse). From here I may derive law Y." (See *Shabbat* 27a.)

אֵין צָרִיךְ לוֹמַר Lit., *there is no need to say,* i.e., the matter is self-evident and did not need to be stated explicitly. (See *Moed Katan* 5a.) See also זוֹ וְאֵין צָרִיךְ לוֹמַר זוֹ קָתָנֵי.

אֵינוֹ דִין שֶׁ... *Is it not right that....* An expression used to introduce the conclusion of an *a fortiori* argument: "If the law in case X is A, is it not right that it should be A in case Y?" (See *Bava Metzia* 95a.) See entry קַל וָחוֹמֶר in section on hermeneutics.

אֵינוֹ מְחֻוָּר Lit., *it is not clear.* An expression sometimes found in the Jerusalem Talmud, stating that a law based on a Biblical text is "unclear," i.e., that it is actually a Rabbinic ordinance, even though it seems to be derived from a Biblical verse.

אִינִי *Is that so?* Or: *But that is not so!* A term often used to express astonishment at a previous statement. The Gemara then seeks to show that the Amora previously quoted could not have made the statement attributed to him: "Surely that statement is not correct! Consider the following...." (See *Moed Katan* 20a.)

אִיפּוֹךְ *Reverse!* Sometimes, when certain opinions are attributed to a pair of scholars in one context, and the opposite opinions are attributed to these scholars in another context, the Talmud may attempt to resolve the contradiction by suggesting that the viewpoints attributed to these scholars be "reversed." Subsequently, however, the Gemara may reject this suggestion, saying: לְעוֹלָם לֹא תֵּיפוֹךְ — "In fact do not reverse the opinions, but instead explain as follows...." (See *Shabbat* 120b.) See also חִילּוּף הַדְּבָרִים; מוּחְלֶפֶת הַשִּׁיטָה.

(וְ)אִיפְּכָא אִיתְּמַר *The opposite was stated,* i.e., the original version of this statement is the opposite of what was stated here, and, this being so, the difficulty raised here is resolved. (See *Shabbat* 76a.)

אִיפְּכָא מִסְתַּבְּרָא *The opposite [of what was just stated] is more reasonable!* An expression of astonishment concerning a statement the opposite of which appears to be more reasonable. (See *Kiddushin* 53b.) See also אַדְּרַבָּא.

אִיצְטְרִיךְ, סָלְקָא דַּעְתָּךְ אָמִינָא... *It was necessary [for this statement to be made, for otherwise] it might have occurred to you to say....* This expression is used by the Gemara in answering an objection that a certain provision in a statement is obvious and therefore unnecessary. (See פְּשִׁיטָא.) The Gemara responds by trying to show that there are circumstances where the provision is in fact needed to avoid a possible misunderstanding. (See *Rosh HaShanah* 25b.)

See also ...אָמִינָא דַּעְתָּךְ סָלְקָא ;...דְּתֵימָא מַהוּ ;...אֶלָּא צְרִיכָא לָא.

אִיצְטְרִיךְ קְרָא לְאַשְׁמוֹעִינֶן *The verse was necessary to teach us...,* i.e., the idea just mentioned could not have been understood on its own, without a Biblical verse as its source. (See *Bava Batra* 110b.)

אִיצְטְרִיכָא לֵיה *[Case X] was necessary for him.* Sometimes a case mentioned in a Tannaitic source seems superfluous. The Talmud may explain that this case was included incidentally because another, more important, case had to be mentioned. In such instances the Talmud may justify the inclusion of the incidental case by claiming that the primary case "was necessary for him [i.e., the Tanna]," and the other, seemingly superfluous, case was included because of its close connection with the primary case, although it was not really needed. (See *Menahot* 43a.) See also צְרִיכוּתָא.

אִישְׁתִּיק *He was silent.* Sometimes a scholar is "silent" in the face of an objection raised against his viewpoint, either because he does not have a satisfactory answer to the objection or because he thinks that the answer is so obvious that there is no need to reply. (See *Berakhot* 27a.)

אִישְׁתַּמִּיטְתֵיה הָא דְּ... *It [the statement of Rabbi X] escaped him.* A respectful expression used when suggesting that a scholar may have forgotten or overlooked a Baraita or an Amoraic statement disproving his own opinion. (See *Eruvin* 12b.)

אִית דְּמַחֲלִיפִין *Some reverse.* An expression in the Jerusalem Talmud: "Some scholars transmit the statement under discussion with the sequence of its sentences reversed."

אִית לֵיה Lit., *he has,* i.e., he maintains the following opinion. This expression often appears in the form אִית לֵיה דְּר' פְּלוֹנִי — "He accepts the viewpoint of Rabbi X." (See *Yoma* 58b.)

אִית תַּנָּיֵי תָּנֵי *There is a Tanna who teaches.* An expression in the Jerusalem Talmud introducing a variant version of the previous Tannaitic source or a parallel Tannaitic source discussing a similar theme.

אִיתִּיבֵיה *He objected to him.* An expression used to introduce an objection raised by one Amora, based on a Tannaitic source, to the viewpoint of another Amora. (See *Bava Metzia* 10a.) See also תְּיוּבְתָּא.

(וְ)אִיתֵּימָא Lit., *(and) if you say,* i.e., some say. An expression used to introduce a new opinion regarding the authorship of a statement: "Rabbi X, and some say Rabbi Y, made the following statement...." (See *Yoma* 26b.) See also ...(וְ)אָמְרִי לָה.

אִיתְּמַר *It was said.* An expression used to introduce a difference of opinion between Amoraim (see *Bava Metzia* 21b). (On rare occasions, a difference of opinion between later Tannaim [see *Yoma* 57b].)

אִיתְּמַר הָכִי וְאִיתְּמַר הָכִי *It was said thus and it was said thus.* The Gemara uses this expression when pointing out a

contradiction between two Halakhic rulings made by the same scholar. (See *Pesahim* 108a.)

אִיתְּמַר נַמִי *It was also said.* An expression used to introduce an Amoraic tradition (usually attributed to one of the early Amoraim) in support of a statement (usually by one of the later Amoraim). (See *Gittin* 13b.)

אִיתְּמַר עֲלָה *It was stated regarding it.* An expression used to introduce an Amora's observation on a Mishnah or a Baraita. (See *Megillah* 22a.) See also הָא אִיתְּמַר עֲלָה.

אַל תִּקְרֵי... אֶלָּא... *Do not read X but [rather] Y,* i.e., do not read the verse as it is written; rather, read it as follows (usually, as if one of its words were vocalized differently), and in this way you can derive an important moral lesson from it or explain it in a different way. (See *Berakhot* 64a.) See קְרֵי בֵּיה.

אֶלָּא *But, instead.* This word usually marks a transition in a Talmudic discussion, introducing a new explanation of the subject being discussed. It generally implies that the explanation or statement previously made should be rejected in favor of a new explanation to be offered. See following entries.

אֶלָּא אֶחָד זֶה וְאֶחָד זֶה... *But both this and this....* This term introduces the Gemara's conclusion that two cases, previously thought to differ from each other, are in fact identical: "In fact both case A and case B share the same characteristics...." (See *Bava Metzia* 59b.) See also מַאי שְׁנָא.

אֶלָּא אֵימָא *But say instead....* An expression used by the Gemara to introduce a change in the text of a statement previously made (often as the answer to a question introduced by the term סָלְקָא דַּעְתָּךְ; see entry). "Do not understand the text as saying A, but understand it instead as saying B...." (See *Pesahim* 53a.) See also לָא תֵּימָא...אֶלָּא (אֵימָא).

אֶלָּא אָמַר ר' פְּלוֹנִי *Instead Rabbi X said....* The word אֶלָּא, "but," in this expression indicates that the preceding answer to a question or objection was unsatisfactory and that a new answer is about to be suggested. (See *Pesahim* 9b.)

אֶלָּא הָכִי קָאָמַר *Rather, this is what he said....* This expression introduces a new explanation of a Tannaitic or Amoraic statement, after a more straightforward explanation has been rejected. The new explanation tends to be forced, often involving a change or addition to the original statement. (See *Sanhedrin* 23a.)

אֶלָּא כְּר'... אֶלָּא כְּר'... Lit., *but like Rabbi X... but like Rabbi Y.* This expression, found in the Jerusalem Talmud, means: "If you wish you can explain the case in accordance with the viewpoint of Rabbi X, and if you wish, you may also do so in accordance with the viewpoint of Rabbi Y."

אֶלָּא לָאו... *Is it not [the case]?* i.e., may we not assume that the case being discussed is as follows...? See also next entry.

אֶלָּא לָאו שְׁמַע מִינֵּיה... *Is it not [correct] to conclude* from this...? i.e., may we not conclude from this that the proposition we were seeking to prove is indeed correct? (See *Berakhot* 43b.) See also הָכִי נַמִי מִסְתַּבְּרָא.

(וְ)אֶלָּא מַאי... *But what then?...* This expression is used to introduce a counterargument: "Even if it is as you say, and I accept your proposition, an objection can likewise be raised against this...." (See *Betzah* 13a.) See also (וְ)לִיטַעֲמִיךְ.

אֶלָּא מְחַוַּורְתָּא כִּדְשַׁנֵּינַן מֵעִיקָּרָא *Rather it is clear as we answered originally.* Sometimes, after proposing two answers to a question, the Talmud rejects the second one and states: "Rather it is clear as we answered originally" (i.e., only the first answer is correct). This expression is used when the first answer was given anonymously. (See *Bava Metzia* 3a.) Where, however, the first answer was ascribed to a specific scholar, the expression used is: אֶלָּא מְחַוַּורְתָּא כִּדְר'... — "Rather it is clear as Rabbi X said." (See *Ta'anit* 4b.)

אֶלָּא מֵעַתָּה Lit., *but from now,* i.e., if so. A term used to introduce an objection to what was stated in the previous passage by showing that it leads to an absurd conclusion: "But if what you say is so, then...." (See *Pesaḥim* 5a.) See also אִי הָכִי.

אַלִּיבָּא Lit., *upon the heart,* i.e., according to.... See following entries.

אַלִּיבָּא דְּחַד תַּנָּא *According to [the viewpoint of] one Tanna.* The Talmud uses this expression to explain that two parts of a Mishnah or two Mishnayot represent a single viewpoint but apply to two different sets of circumstances. (See *Bava Metzia* 41a.)

אַלִּיבָּא דְּכוּלֵּי עָלְמָא Lit., *according to the entire world,* i.e., according to all opinions.

אַלִּיבָּא דְּר' פְּלוֹנִי כּוּלֵּי עָלְמָא לָא פְּלִיגִי *According to [the viewpoint of] Rabbi X, everyone [lit., the whole world] does not disagree.* Sometimes, when there is a dispute between two Amoraim, the Talmud seeks to show that the same dispute occurred between two earlier scholars. The Talmud may then reply that the two disputes are not comparable: "With regard to the viewpoint of Rabbi X (one of the two earlier scholars), both the later scholars would agree. The later scholars' dispute can only be understood on the basis of the viewpoint of Rabbi Y." (See *Sukkah* 18b.) See also (וְ)לָא פְּלִיגִי הָא בְּ....

אַלִּיבָּא דְּר' פְּלוֹנִי לָא תִּיבָּעֵי לָךְ, כִּי תִּיבָּעֵי לָךְ, אַלִּיבָּא דְּר' אַלְמוֹנִי *According to Rabbi X you need not ask. When must you ask? According to Rabbi Y!* i.e., the question you are asking or the objection you are raising applies only if you adopt the view of Rabbi Y; if you adopt the view of Rabbi X, there is no basis for the question or objection. (See *Pesaḥim* 38a.)

אַלְמָא *Hence, consequently.* An expression used to introduce a conclusion (דִּיּוּק, see entry) drawn from the previous statement. (See *Yoma* 14b.) See also זֹאת אוֹמֶרֶת; טַעֲמָא דְּ... הָא....; מִכְּלָל דְּ....; שְׁמַע מִינָּה דְּ....

אַלְמָה *Why, for what reason?* (See *Yoma* 2b.)

אַמַּאי (וְהָא...) *Why? (Surely...)* This term introduces an objection to a Tannaitic statement, usually on the grounds that it seems to conflict with an established principle: "Why does the Mishnah rule in this way? Surely this conflicts with the principle...?" (See *Betzah* 31b.)

(וְ)אִם אִיתָא *(And) if it is so,* i.e., if what was stated (previously) by an Amora is correct, then the following difficulty arises (usually, in understanding a Mishnah or a Baraita). (See *Pesaḥim* 25a.) See also (וְ)אִי אָמְרַתְּ...; (וְ)אִי סָלְקָא דַּעְתָּךְ.

וְאִם נַפְשְׁךָ לוֹמַר *And if it is your wish [lit., your soul] to say.* A term used in Halakhic Midrashim to introduce an alternative proof of a particular law (usually because the first proof suggested is problematic). (See *Yoma* 74b.)

וְאִם תֹּאמַר *And if you say....* This expression is sometimes used by the Gemara, when giving an answer or explanation, to anticipate and remove a possible objection. (See *Bava Metzia* 10a.)

וְאִם תִּמְצָא (תִּימְצֵי) לוֹמַר Lit., *if you will be able to say,* i.e., if you say. (1) "If you look into the matter carefully, you will find that...." (See *Nedarim* 73a.) (2) "If you assume that the answer to the previous question is X, then the following question will arise...." (See *Bava Metzia* 24a.) See also כְּשֶׁתִּמְצָא לוֹמַר לְדִבְרֵי ר' פְּלוֹנִי....

אָמוֹרָא *Amora, lecturer, translator.* (1) A lecturer whose function was to listen to the discourse in Hebrew of an eminent scholar and then to translate it into Aramaic and if necessary amplify it to the assembled gathering. (See *Ḥullin* 15a.) (2) A post-Tannaitic Talmudic scholar.

אָמוֹרָאֵי נִינְהוּ וְאַלִּיבָּא דְּר' פְּלוֹנִי Lit., *they are Amoraim, and according to [the viewpoint of] Rabbi X.* Sometimes, when contradictory statements are attributed to a scholar, the Talmud resolves the contradiction by stating that two Amoraim transmitted variant traditions in his name. (See *Shabbat* 112b.)

אָמַר לָךְ *[Rabbi X] says to you,* i.e., Rabbi X can answer you. Sometimes, when an objection is raised against the view of a particular scholar, and the scholar did not respond to the objection himself (e.g., because it was raised by a later authority), the Talmud explains that "Rabbi X could have answered as follows...." (See *Berakhot* 34a.)

אָמַר מָר *It was said above* (lit., "the master said"). A term used to cite a passage from a Mishnah or a Baraita previously mentioned, which will now be elucidated at greater length by the Talmud (usually as a continuation of the previous discussion). (See *Pesaḥim* 5b.) See also גּוּפָא.

אָמַר קְרָא *The verse said.* A term used to introduce a quotation from the Bible. (See *Berakhot* 20b.) See also מְנָא הָנֵי מִילֵּי; מְנָא לַן.

אָמַר ר׳ פְּלוֹנִי   *Rabbi X said.* In this expression the verb אָמַר precedes the name of the scholar cited. The Gemara customarily uses this word order when the statement recorded is an original, undisputed principle, opinion or decision. (See *Berakhot* 5a.) See also ר׳ פְּלוֹנִי אָמַר.

אָמַר ר׳ פְּלוֹנִי אָמַר ר׳ אַלְמוֹנִי   *Rabbi X said in the name of Rabbi Y.* This expression is usually used when Rabbi X reports a tradition which he heard directly from Rabbi Y, his teacher. (See *Berakhot* 5a.) See also next entry.

אָמַר ר׳ פְּלוֹנִי מִשְּׁמֵיהּ (מִשּׁוּם) דְּר׳ אַלְמוֹנִי   *Rabbi X said in the name of Rabbi Y.* This expression, unlike the previous one, introduces a statement which Rabbi X did not hear directly from Rabbi Y; sometimes there may even be a gap of several generations between them. (See *Berakhot* 7a.) See also previous entry.

אָמַר ר׳ פְּלוֹנִי וְתָנֵי כֵּן   *Rabbi X said, and it was taught similarly.* An expression used in the Jerusalem Talmud when an Amoraic statement is corroborated by a Baraita. The Amora's statement then follows (the Baraita, however, is not cited explicitly).

אָמְרוּ דָּבָר אֶחָד   *They said one [i.e., the same] thing.* An expression used to note that two scholars (usually Tannaim) held similar opinions about the subject under discussion. (See *Bava Metzia* 47b.)

אָמְרִי   *They say.* This term introduces an anonymous statement made by scholars of the Academy or by the Gemara itself. (See *Berakhot* 5b.)

אָמְרִי אֵינְשֵׁי   *People say.* A term used to introduce a popular proverb or saying. (See *Bava Metzia* 69a.)

אָמְרִי בְּמַעַרְבָא   *They say in the West.* An expression used to introduce a tradition from Eretz Israel. (See *Bava Metzia* 94b.) According to the Talmud (*Sanhedrin* 17b), such traditions are usually to be ascribed to Rabbi Yirmiyah. (See מַעַרְבָא.)

אָמְרִי לָא   *They say no.* This expression introduces the rejection of a hypothesis, denying the asserted connection betweeen a Tanna's statement and the conclusion drawn from it. The Gemara then proceeds to demonstrate the illogical nature of the proposition and to propose an alternative explanation. (See *Bava Kamma* 62b.)

וְאָמְרִי לָהּ   Lit., *and they say it.* An expression used to introduce the revision of a previous statement. This revision may differ from the original either in content (see *Berakhot* 22a) or in attribution to a different authority (see *Berakhot* 4a.) See also (וְ)אִיתֵּימָא.

לְאָמְרִי לָהּ כְּדִי   *They say it anonymously,* i.e., some auhorities transmit the previous statement anonymously, without ascribing it to a particular scholar. (See *Bava Metzia* 2a.)

אָמְרִי לָהּ לְהַאי גִּיסָא וְאָמְרִי לָהּ לְהַאי גִּיסָא   *Some say it to this side, and some say it to this side,* i.e., there are some who say that Rabbi X made the statement ascribed to him with reference to case A, while with reference to case B he said something else, whereas others say that Rabbi X made the statement with reference to case B, while with reference to case A he said something else. (See *Pesaḥim* 108a.)

(דְּ)אָמְרִי תַּרְוַיְיהוּ   *[X and Y who] both say.* This expression is used to introduce a joint statement by two Amoraim, stressing that they agree about the matter under discussion, though in other matters they usually disagree with each other, e.g., "Rav and Shmuel, who both say..." or "Abaye and Rava who both say...." (See *Berakhot* 36b.)

(דְּ)אָמְרִינַן   *(For) we say....* This term introduces an argument from accepted authority: "For we generally hold the opinion that...." (See *Yevamot* 3b.) See also (דְּ)כְתִיב; קַיְימָא לַן.

אֲנַן כְּר׳ פְּלוֹנִי סְבִירָא לַן   *We think like Rabbi X,* i.e., we follow Rabbi X's opinion, and it would therefore be inappropriate to raise an objection to our viewpoint based on another, different opinion; but even *you,* who follow Rabbi Y's opinion, would agree in this case, because.... (See *Gittin* 38a.)

אֲנַן סַהֲדֵי   *We are witnesses,* i.e., everyone knows that.... This expression is used to introduce a fact known to all and thus needing no special proof. (See *Berakhot* 17b.)

אַסְמַכְתָּא בְּעָלְמָא   *Merely a support* — but not complete proof. (See *Pesaḥim* 81b.) See also entry אַסְמַכְתָּא in section on hermeneutics.

אַף אֲנַן נַמִי תָּנֵינָא   *We, too, have also learned [thus].* This term introduces a quotation from a Mishnah or a Baraita corroborating the previous Amoraic statement. (See *Shabbat* 93a/b.)

אֲפִילוּ לְכַתְּחִילָה   *Even ab initio.* See לְכַתְּחִילָה נַמִי.

אֲפִילוּ תֵּימָא ר׳ פְּלוֹנִי   *You may even say [that the Mishnah is according to] Rabbi X,* i.e., it is possible to explain the Mishnah even in accordance with the viewpoint of Rabbi X, even though in the previous stage of the discussion it had been suggested that the Mishnah was incompatible with his opinion. (See *Bava Metzia* 2b.) See also לֵימָא מַתְנִיתִין דְּלָא כְּר׳ פְּלוֹנִי.

אַשִּׁינוּיֵי לֵיקוּ וְלִיסְמוֹךְ   See (אַ)שִּׁינוּיֵי לֵיקוּ וְלִיסְמוֹךְ.

אַשְׁכַּחַן א׳; ב׳ מְנָלַן   *We have found A; from where [do we find] B?* i.e., we have found a source in the Torah for law A; what is the source for law B? An expression used in the elucidation of Halakhic Midrashim. (See *Pesaḥim* 82b.) See also אֵין לִי אֶלָּא א׳, ב׳ מְנַיִן? תַּלְמוּד לוֹמַר...

וְאַתְּ לָא תִּסְבְּרָא?   *And you?! Do you not understand [the case in this way]?* (See *Yevamot* 89b.) See also (וְ)תִסְבְּרָא.

אָתָא חָמֵי   *Come see.* An expression in the Jerusalem Talmud, used to introduce an observation of astonishment or doubt regarding a statement of one of the scholars. It is followed

105

by an explanation of what the problem is. (See Jerusalem Talmud: *Pe'ah* 3, 17d.)

אֲתָא לְקַמֵּיה דְרַב פְּלוֹנִי   *He came before Rav X.* (1) The claimant in a lawsuit presented his case before the judge, Rav X. (2) The questioner brought his question before the scholar, Rav X. (See *Bava Metzia* 36a.)

אֲתָאן לְר׳ פְּלוֹנִי   *We have come to [the viewpoint of] Rabbi X.* Sometimes, part of a Baraita follows the viewpoint of one scholar, while another follows that of a different scholar. In such cases the Talmud may interject: "We have come to [the viewpoint of] Rabbi X," i.e., the part of the Baraita which follows is in accordance with the viewpoint of Rabbi X, as opposed to the previous part of the Baraita, which follows the viewpoint of Rabbi Y. Similarly, the Talmud sometimes states: אֲתָאן לְתַנָּא קַמָּא — "We have come to the [viewpoint of the] first Tanna," i.e., this part of the Baraita reverts to the view of the anonymous first

Tanna (see תַּנָּא קַמָּא), and is not a continuation of statements by scholars who disagree with it. (See *Pesaḥim* 36a.)

אֲתָאן לְתַנָּא קַמָּא   *We have come to [the viewpoint of] the first Tanna.* See previous entry.

אַתָּה אוֹמֵר א׳, אוֹ אֵינוֹ אֶלָּא ב׳   *You say A; but might it not be B?* An expression used in Halakhic Midrashim to explain why a given verse can only be interpreted as referring to one case and not to another: "You say that the verse refers to case A, but how do you know that it does not refer to case B?" The second proposed interpretation of the Biblical text is usually rejected at once by the Midrash. (See *Menaḥot* 37b.) See also כְּשֶׁהוּא אוֹמֵר.

אַתְקַפְתָּא   *An objection, a refutation.* An objection to an Amoraic statement based on logical reasoning rather than on a Tannaitic source. Such an objection is introduced by the expression מַתְקִיף לָהּ (see entry).

בָּא מִן הַדִּין   *A conclusion drawn [in particular] from an a fortiori inference.* See entry on קַל וָחוֹמֶר in the section on hermeneutics.

בֶּאֱמֶת אָמְרוּ   *In truth they said.* This expression usually introduces an authoritative and uncontested Halakhah, הֲלָכָה לְמשֶׁה מִסִּינַי — a Halakhah handed down to Moses at Sinai. (See *Bava Metzia* 60a.)

בָּאנוּ לְמַחֲלוֹקֶת (פְּלוֹנִי וּפְלוֹנִי)   Lit., *we have come to a difference of opinion between Rabbi X and Rabbi Y,* i.e., the issue being discussed is already the subject of a controversy between Rabbi X and Rabbi Y, and in the same way as they differ in that case they likewise differ in the case we are discussing here. (See *Yoma* 61b.)

בָּבָא דְרֵישָׁא, בָּבָא דְסֵיפָא   *The section [lit., gate] of the first proposition, the section of the latter proposition.* Where a Mishnah contains a series of separate cases or rules, the Gemara often distinguishes between them, using these terms. (See *Shabbat* 3a.) See also סֵיפָא; רֵישָׁא.

בְּדוּתָא   *A fiction, a mistake.* This expression is used when the Talmud claims that a statement attributed to a certain scholar was in fact never made by him and is erroneous. In some texts the reading is בָּרוּתָא — "an external remark," i.e., a remark which was never really made. (See *Bava Metzia* 9a.) See also בּוּרְכָא.

בְּדִין הוּא שֶׁ...   *By right it should have been...,* i.e., justice

and logic demanded that the statement or decision should have been X, but particular circumstances (usually explained in what follows) brought about a different outcome. (See *Berakhot* 14b.) (Similarly, בְּדִין הָיָה... אֶלָּא — "By right it was... only....")

בְּדִיעֲבַד   See דִּיעֲבַד.

בָּדֵיק לַן ר׳ פְּלוֹנִי   *Rabbi X tested us.* An introduction to a statement in which students relate how their teacher asked them a question in order to test their knowledge. (See *Pesaḥim* 55b.)

בִּדְר׳ פְּלוֹנִי קָמִיפַּלְגִי   *They differ with regard to [the ruling of] Rabbi X,* i.e., these Amoraim (or Tannaim) disagree with regard to the ruling of Rabbi X; one of them agrees with it and the other disagrees with it. (See *Eruvin* 11a.)

בְּהֶדְיָא קָתָנֵי לָהּ   *He teaches it explicitly,* i.e., the Tanna makes a certain point explicitly, and not merely by inference. (See *Moed Katan* 5a.) See also מַתְנֵי לָהּ בְּהֶדְיָא.

בּוּרְכָא   *An absurdity.* A term used when the Talmud rejects an earlier statement as being patently absurd. The Talmud then proceeds to clarify where the absurdity lies. (See *Ketubot* 63b.) See also בְּדוּתָא.

בְּמַאי עָסְקִינַן   *With what are we dealing?* This term introduces an investigation of the particular circumstances of a case mentioned in a Mishnah. It is often followed by a suggestion or suggestions which are at once rejected: אִילֵימָא... — "Shall we say...? No," or ...אִי... אִי — "If the case is X, then this problem arises, whereas if the case is Y, then another problem arises." (See *Bava Metzia* 12b.)

בְּמַאי קָמִיפַּלְגִי   *About what do they disagree?* When the practical difference between two conflicting points of view is clear, but the theoretical basis of the dispute is not, the Talmud may use this expression to inquire into the theoretical issue at the basis of the dispute. (See *Bava Metzia* 15b.)
See also ...־דְ פְּלִיגִי לָא ...־דְ הֵיכָא כָּל ;פְּלִיגִי כִּי.

בַּמֶּה דְּבָרִים אֲמוּרִים   *In what [case] are these things said?* An expression used in Tannaitic sources to limit the application of a particular ruling to specific circumstances. (See *Rosh HaShanah* 15b.) See also אֶלָּא שָׁנוּ לֹא ;אֵימָתַי.

בְּמַעֲרְבָא אָמְרִי   See מַעֲרְבָא.

בְּמַתְנִיתָא תָּנָא   *He taught in a Mishnah.* (In fact, usually a Baraita.) This expression introduces a quotation from a Baraita, cited in contradiction to, or as an addition to, an Amoraic statement. (See *Berakhot* 59a.) See also מַתְנִיתָא.

בָּעוּן מֵימַר   *They wished to say.* An expression in the Jerusalem Talmud. Notwithstanding its literal meaning ("they wished to say"), this expression simply means "they said," and the statements it introduces are usually accepted by the Gemara.

בָּעֵי   Lit., *he asked,* i.e., he raised a problem. (1) In the Babylonian Talmud: "He asked, he raised a problem." See אִיבַּעְיָא לְהוּ; בָּעְיָא. (2) In the Jerusalem Talmud: "He asked," but also: "He proposed an argument, he raised a supposition." In most cases the problem raised in this way in the Jerusalem Talmud is not followed by an answer because the argument itself is a form of conclusion.

בָּעְיָא   *Question, problem.* A generic term for one of the basic forms of Talmudic argumentation. The בָּעְיָא is a request for additional information: explanation of an interpretative difficulty, a Halakhic ruling, resolution of a question left unresolved, etc. Among the expressions used to introduce the בָּעְיָא are: בָּעֵי מִינֵּיה — "X asked Y" (a question which one scholar asked another); בָּעֵי מִינַּיְיהוּ — "He asked them" (a question which an individual scholar asked a group of scholars); מִ מִינֵּיה בָּעוּ... — "They asked X" (a question which a group of scholars asked an individual scholar); בָּעוּ מִינַּיְיהוּ — "They asked them" (a question which one group of scholars asked another group of scholars); אִיבַּעְיָא לְהוּ — "They asked" (a question asked by the scholars of the Talmud). The answer to a בָּעְיָא is called a פְּשִׁיטָה ("solution"). In the Jerusalem Talmud the significance of a בָּעְיָא is not always a question, but the expression of an opinion.

בָּעְיָא דָא מִילְתָא   *This thing is uncertain.* An expression in the Jerusalem Talmud used to introduce a question which is left unresolved.

בְּעָלְמָא   Lit., *in the world.* (1) "Merely, only" (when it follows a noun). Occasionally, it has a contemptuous ring. (See *Berakhot* 38a.) (2) "Generally, usually" (at the beginning of a sentence). (See *Sanhedrin* 21a.)

בִּפְלוּגְתָּא   *In a controversy.* Sometimes the Talmud observes that a particular statement is not a matter of unanimous agreement, but instead is "the subject of a controversy between scholars." (See *Shabbat* 19b.)

בִּפְלוּגְתָּא דְּהָנֵי תַּנָּאֵי   *In the dispute between these Tannaim.* Sometimes the Talmud compares Tannaitic differences of opinion, suggesting that the subject of one difference of opinion (at present under discussion) is also in dispute between a second pair of Tannaim who disagree elsewhere about another case, but whose disagreement is based on the same principles. (See *Yoma* 4b.)

בַּר מִינָּה דְּהַהִיא   *Apart from this.* This expression introduces the rejection by the Talmud of an objection based on a Tannaitic source: No proof may be drawn from the Tannaitic source cited, because it refers to a special case or because the text is corrupt. (See *Sukkah* 17a.)

בַּר מִינֵּיה דְּר׳ פְּלוֹנִי   *Apart from Rabbi X,* i.e., no proof can be brought from Rabbi X, as his opinion is based on his own personal experience and was not intended to be binding on others. (See *Berakhot* 43a.)

בְּרִיבִּי   *Son of Rabbi.* (1) Son of Rabbi X (in the form בְּרִיבִּי א׳ = A, the son of B). (2) Specifically, בְּרִיבִּי refers to Rabban Gamliel, the son of Rabbi Yehudah HaNasi. (3) An honorific title bestowed upon Talmudic scholars, even if they were not descended from eminent families. (See *Yevamot* 105b.)

בָּרַיְיתָא   Lit., *external [Mishnah].* A general term for a Tannaitic source which is not part of the Mishnah, the collection of Mishnayot edited by Rabbi Yehudah HaNasi. See also מַתְנִיתָא.

בָּרַיְיתָא לָא שְׁמִיעַ לֵיה   *The Baraita was not known to him.* The Talmud sometimes explains that an Amora ruled against a certain Baraita because he did not know of its existence. Since there were so many Baraitot, not all of which were organized in authoritative collections, it sometimes happened that an Amora was unaware of a particular Baraita.

בִּשְׁלָמָא   Lit., *in peace,* meaning, "granted that...." This term introduces a question in which the element that is understood and acceptable is placed first and the difficulty is placed second. The following are examples of its use: (1) Where one part of a Halakhah is understood and the other presents a problem, we find אֶלָּא... מְשׁוּם... בִּשְׁלָמָא — "Granted case A, because of X, but what about case B?" (See *Berakhot* 52b.) (2) Where a Halakhah is understandable according to the viewpoint of one scholar, but is difficult to understand according to the viewpoint of another scholar: אֶלָּא לְר׳ אַלְמוֹנִי מַאי אִיכָּא ,פְּלוֹנִי לְר׳ בִּשְׁלָמָא לְמֵימַר — "It is all right according to Rabbi X, but according to Rabbi Y what can be said?" (See *Bava Metzia* 13a.) Or in another variation: אִיכָּא מַאי ...אָמְרַתְּ אִי אֶלָּא ,פְּלוֹנִי לְר׳ בִּשְׁלָמָא אָמְרַתְּ אִי לְמֵימַר — "If you accept the viewpoint of Rabbi X it is all right, but if you say Y, how do you explain the difficulty involved?" (See *Bava Metzia* 2b.) Occasionally the case or opinion introduced by בִּשְׁלָמָא may itself be problematic, but this difficulty is usually minor or easily resolved. See also ...־ל הָנִיחָא.

בְּ... שָׁנוּ   *They taught... in....* An expression used when the Talmud suggests that a Tannaitic source is referring to a particular case, even though it does not explicitly say so. (See *Berakhot* 30b.) See also אוֹקִימְתָּא.

בָּתַר דְּבָעֵי הַדַר פַּשְׁטָהּ   *After having raised the question he solved it.* An expression used by the Gemara when the Amora who has raised a problem proceeds to solve it himself. (See *Sanhedrin* 10a.)

גַּבְרָא אַגַּבְרָא קָא רָמֵית   Lit., *are you casting one man against another?* Sometimes, after an objection has been raised to the view of one Amora based on the statement of another Amora, the Talmud asks this question, meaning: "Why do you raise an objection to Rabbi A's viewpoint from a statement by Rabbi B? Surely both have the same authority and are entitled to differ!" (See *Ta'anit* 4b.)

גּוּזְמָא קָתָנֵי   Lit., *he teaches an exaggeration,* i.e., the Tanna's statement is an exaggeration and should not be taken literally. (See *Betzah* 4a.)

גּוּפָא   Lit., *the body, the thing itself.* An expression used to introduce a quotation from a source cited in passing in the previous discussion in the Gemara, which will now be analyzed at length. Generally, גּוּפָא introduces a new theme. (See *Berakhot* 40b.) See also אָמַר מָר.

גּוֹרְעִין וּמוֹסִיפִין וְדוֹרְשִׁין   Lit., *they subtract and add and expound.* A Midrashic device whereby a letter is removed from one word in a Biblical verse and attached to another word in the same verse. The change in meaning caused by the change in the positions of the letters is then used as the basis for a Midrashic exposition. (See *Yoma* 48a.)

גְּזֵירָה   *An enactment, a preventive measure.* A Rabbinic decree enacted in order to prevent people from inadvertently violating a Torah law, or, more generally, the prohibition of something intrinsically permitted, in order to prevent a transgression. (See *Megillah* 4b.) See also next entry.

גָּזְרִינַן... אַטּוּ...   *We prohibit X because of Y,* meaning: the scholars prohibited act X as a גְּזֵירָה (see previous entry), to prevent people from committing transgression Y (= because of Y). (See *Pesaḥim* 58b.)

גַּלֵּי רַחֲמָנָא   *The Torah [lit., the Merciful One] revealed.* This expression usually occurs in the form: גַּלֵּי רַחֲמָנָא בְּ... וְהוּא הַדִּין בְּ... — "The Torah revealed law A in case X, and the law is the same in case Y," i.e., the Torah explicitly stated a certain law in connection with one case, and we may infer that the same law also applies to other, similar cases. (See *Shabbat* 27a.)

גְּמִירִי   *They have learned,* i.e., they have a tradition to the effect that.... The Talmud uses this expression when introducing an argument based on an accepted tradition. (See *Berakhot* 28a.) See also נְקַטִּינַן.

גְּמָרָא   Lit., *study,* i.e., tradition, as opposed to either a Biblical verse or logical reasoning (סְבָרָא = logic). Sometimes the Talmud asks: גְּמָרָא אוֹ סְבָרָא? — "Is this statement based on tradition or logical reasoning?" (See *Eruvin* 60a.)

גְּמָרָא גְּמִירִי לָהּ   *They learned it as a tradition,* i.e., this matter was derived from tradition, rather than from a Biblical verse. (See *Sanhedrin* 22b.)

גְּמְרִינַן   *We have learned,* i.e., we have a tradition. This term usually introduces the exegetical principle known as בִּנְיַן אָב (see entry in the section on hermeneutics). (See *Bava Metzia* 87b.)

דְּאוֹרַיְיתָא   *Of the Torah,* i.e., according to Torah law, as opposed to דְּרַבָּנָן — "of the Rabbis," i.e., according to Rabbinical law. See entry.

דְּאִי לָא קָתָנֵי   Lit, *he does not teach "that if,"* i.e., the Tanna does not discuss exceptional, hypothetical cases (= what would happen if...). (See *Pesaḥim* 105a.)

דְּאָמַר מָר   *For the master said....* This expression is used by the Gemara to introduce a reference to a well-known, anonymous saying. (See *Berakhot* 4a.) See also וְ)הָא אָמַר מָר).

דְּאָמְרִי תַּרְוַיְיהוּ   *[X and Y] who both say.* See אָמְרִי תַּרְוַיְיהוּ.

דְּבֵי   *Of the house of,* i.e., of the school of (Rabbi X). For example: אָמְרִי דְּבֵי רַב — "In the school of Rav they say" (see *Eruvin* 94b), or תָּנָא דְּבֵי ר' יִשְׁמָעֵאל — "The school of Rabbi Yishmael taught" (see *Berakhot* 19a), etc. To be distinguished from דְּבֵיתְהוּ — "The wife of...."

דָּבָר אַחֵר   Lit., *something else.* (1) A term used in Tannaitic literature to introduce an alternative reason or interpretation. (See *Sukkah* 46b.) (2) Sometimes this expression is used as a euphemism for things which the Talmud does not wish to mention explicitly, either for reasons of modesty or because they were considered repulsive. Accordingly דָּבָר אַחֵר can refer to such things as sexual relations, money, pigs, and leprosy (צָרַעַת). (See *Pesaḥim* 76b.)

דְּבַר תּוֹרָה   Lit., *a matter of Torah,* i.e., according to Biblical law. (See *Berakhot* 19b.) See also דְּאוֹרַיְיתָא.

דְּהָא...   *For surely....* This expression is used by the Gemara to introduce an argument based on common sense. (See *Bava Metzia* 8b.)
See also הוֹאִיל וְ...; כֵּיוָן דְּ...; לְפִי...; מִפְּנֵי שֶׁ...; מִשּׁוּם דְּ....

דּוּמְיָא דְּ...   *[This is] similar to the case of....* This expression is used by the Gemara to introduce an argument based on an analogy between cases. (See *Kiddushin* 12a.)
See also הָא לָא דָּמְיָא אֶלָּא לְהָא...; כִּדְאַשְׁכְּחַן; מִידֵי דַּהֲוָה א....

דּוּן מִינָהּ וְאוֹקֵי בְּאַתְרָא   *Deduce from it, and leave it in its place.* An expression used by the Gemara in limiting the application of a גְּזֵירָה שָׁוָה (see entry in section on hermeneutical rules): "Having made the main provision of case A apply to case B, we must recognize that case B has its own character and specific rules that apply to it." (See *Yevamot* 78b.) See also next entry.

דּוּן מִינָהּ וּמִינָהּ   *Deduce from it, and again from it.* This expression is used by the Gemara when it seeks to extend the application of a גְּזֵירָה שָׁוָה (see entry in section on hermeneutical rules): "Deduce B from A, and transfer to B all the characteristics of A." (See *Yevamot* 78b.) See also previous entry.

וְ)דַוְקָא...)   *Only....* This expression is sometimes used by the Gemara before qualifying a statement in a Mishnah and limiting it to particular circumstances: "The statement in the Mishnah applies only to case A, but in case B it does not apply." (See *Yevamot* 98b.) See also לֹא שָׁנוּ אֶלָּא...; וְ)הוּא שֶׁ....)

דִּידֵיהּ אָמַר   Lit., *he said his own.* Sometimes, to distinguish between remarks which a scholar reported in the name of his teacher and a statement which he made on his own, the Talmud states that Rabbi X "said his own" statement. (See *Shabbat* 105a.)

דִּיּוּק   *Inference.* A method of interpretation used to draw conclusions from Tannaitic sources. According to this method of interpretation, inferences may be drawn not only from what is explicitly said in a Mishnah or a Baraita, but also from what is left unsaid. According to the דִּיּוּק method, it may be inferred that anything not mentioned in the text is governed by a different law and is not included in the stated Halakhah (see דַּיְקָא מַתְנִיתִין; דַּיְקָא נַמִי). Tannaitic texts are not, however, always phrased in such a way that a דִּיּוּק inference may be drawn. In such cases the Gemara uses the expression מֵהָא לֵיכָּא לְמִשְׁמַע מִינָה — "From this statement nothing can be proved [either positively or negatively]." See entry.

דִּין   *Law.* (1) A Halakhah, law, judgment. (2) A logical argument, usually an *a fortiori* inference. For example, דִּין הוּא — "It is right that...," i.e., it may validly be inferred that.... (See *Yoma* 45b.)

(בְּ)דִיעֲבַד   Lit., *it having been done.* A situation where the correctness or validity of an action is being considered *after* it has taken place, as opposed to לְכַתְּחִילָה (ab initio), where the correctness or validity of the action is being considered *before* it has taken place. (See *Ḥullin* 2a.) See also following entries and לְכַתְּחִילָה.

(בְּ)דִיעֲבַד אִין לְכַתְּחִילָה לָא   Lit., *it having been done — yes; ab initio — no.* This expression indicates that a certain act, if already done, is considered acceptable and valid, but that one is not directly permitted to perform such an act. (See *Berakhot* 15a.) See also (בְּ)דִיעֲבַד; לְכַתְּחִילָה; לְכַתְּחִילָה לָא דִיעֲבַד שַׁפִּיר דָּמֵי.

דִיעֲבַד נַמִי לָא   Lit., *even if it has been done — no.* This expression indicates that a certain act has no validity whatever: not only is the act forbidden *ab initio*, but "even if it has been done, it is invalid." (See *Berakhot* 15a.)
See also (בְּ)דִיעֲבַד; (בְּ)דִיעֲבַד אִין לְכַתְּחִילָה לָא; לְכַתְּחִילָה.

דַּיְקָא מַתְנִיתִין   Lit., *our Mishnah is precise,* i.e., the precise way in which the Mishnah is phrased supports a particular viewpoint. (See *Yoma* 64b.)

דַּיְקָא נַמִי, דְּקָתָנֵי   Lit., *it is also precise, for it teaches....* An expression introducing a proof in support of the view previously expressed, based on a precise examination of the wording of the Mishnah. (See *Sukkah* 3a.)

דַּל   *Remove.* Sometimes this word means "remove from the discussion," as in the expression דַּל אֲנָא מֵהָכָא — "Remove me from here." This expression may be used by a scholar in response to an objection to his views: "Even if you remove my view from this discussion, in the final analysis the issue will remain problematic." (See *Eruvin* 3a.)

דְּלָא כְּחַד   Lit., *not like one,* i.e., the view just cited is not in agreement with any of the previously expressed opinions. (See *Eruvin* 72b.)

דִּלְכֵן   *For if not so....* An expression in the Jerusalem Talmud used to explain why it is impossible to differ with the ruling or interpretation just cited: "For if you do not say so, the following difficulty will arise...."

(וְ)דִלְמָא   *But perhaps....* This term introduces a mild form of objection to a previously stated argument, indicating that a possibility exists which could invalidate the argument. The Gemara's answer to this suggested refutation often begins with לָא סָלְקָא דַּעְתָּךְ — "You cannot possibly think so, because..." (see entry). (See *Rosh HaShanah* 13a.)

דִּלְמָא   *A story....* An expression used in the Jerusalem Talmud to introduce a story. (See Jerusalem Talmud: *Pe'ah* 3, 17d.)

דָּמֵי הַאי מֵרַבָּנַן כִּדְלָא גָּמְרֵי אֵינָשֵׁי שְׁמַעְתָּא   *This one of the scholars seems like a person who has not studied Halakhah.* This expression indicates that the question just asked

in the Gemara has no basis or relevance. (See *Bava Metzia* 11b.)

דְּרַבָּנַן   *Of our Rabbis,* i.e., a Halakhah of Rabbinic rather than Torah origin. See דְּאוֹרַיְיתָא.

דָּרַשׁ ר׳ פְּלוֹנִי   *Rabbi X expounded.* The Talmud uses this expression to indicate that a scholar stated his views in the presence of the public at large, either in the synagogue or some other public forum, not just in the presence of the scholars of the Academy. (See *Megillah* 16a.)

דְּתָנוּ רַבָּנַן   *For our Rabbis taught.* See תָּנוּ רַבָּנַן.

דְּתַנְיָא   *For it was taught.* See תַּנְיָא.

דִּתְנַן   *For we have learned.* See תְּנַן.

...(וְ)הָא   *But surely....* This term, often joined to the next word (see וְהָתַנְיָא; וְהָתְנַן), introduces a question which challenges a previous argument or statement.

...הָא... הָא   *In this case... but in that case....* This expression introduces the resolution (שִׁינּוּיָא, see entry) of a seeming contradiction between two statements, showing that the circumstances in the two statements are in fact different: "In this case the circumstances are X, but in that case the circumstances are Y." Thus the contradiction is resolved. (See *Bava Metzia* 40b.) See also הָכָא בְּמַאי עָסְקִינַן; שָׁאנֵי.

הָא אִיתְּמַר עֲלָה   *Now surely it was stated concerning it....* The Talmud uses this expression to introduce an Amoraic statement reinterpreting a Tannaitic source, in order to solve problems arising from assumptions previously made in connection with it: "Now surely it was stated by the Amoraim as follows with regard to this Mishnah or Baraita.... (See *Shabbat* 4b.)

וְהָא אָמַר (וְהָאָמַר) מָר   Lit., *but surely the master said....* This expression is sometimes used when the Gemara refers to a well-known saying by an anonymous author. (See *Berakhot* 22b.) See also דְּאָמַר מָר.

הָא אָמְרָה חֲדָא זִימְנָא   *But surely he has said it once...,* i.e., the scholar cited has already voiced his opinion about this matter elsewhere; why, then, did he repeat his views again here? (This question may be asked even if the remarks in question were not repeated verbatim.) (See *Eruvin* 55a.)

וְהָא אָמְרַתְּ רֵישָׁא   *But surely you said in the first part....*

This expression is used by the Gemara to indicate a contradiction within a single paragraph of a Mishnah. (See *Betzah* 31b.) See also הָא גּוּפָא קַשְׁיָא; תַּבְרָא.

הָא אֲנַן תְּנַן   *Surely we have learned....* The Talmud uses this expression to introduce a question from a Mishnah in another context against a Halakhah stated in the current discussion: "But surely we have learned differently elsewhere in a Mishnah...." (See *Sanhedrin* 84a.)

...הָא בְּ... וְהָא בְּ...   *This is in... and this is in....* An expression used to resolve contradictions between two anonymous Mishnayot or Baraitot: "This Mishnah or Baraita is referring to case A, and the other Mishnah or Baraita is referring to case B." (See *Berakhot* 23b.) See also כָּאן בְּ... וְכָאן בְּ....

הָא גַּבְרָא וְהָא תִּיוּבְתָּא   *Here is a [great] man and here is [his] objection.* This expression is sometimes used by an Amora to indicate that a previously stated objection is well founded. In such a situation another Amora sometimes replies: גַּבְרָא קָא חָזֵינָא וּתְיוּבְתָּא לָא קָא חָזֵינָא — "I see the great man, but I do not see the cogency of his argument" (see *Bava Metzia* 16a).

הָא גּוּפָא קַשְׁיָא   *This itself is difficult,* i.e., there is an internal contradiction in this Tannaitic source (between the two parts of the source). (See *Bava Metzia* 31a.) See also (וְ)הָא אָמְרַתְּ רֵישָׁא; תַּבְרָא.

הָא דִּידֵיה וְהָא דְּרַבֵּיה   *This is his and this is his teacher's.* Sometimes the Talmud resolves contradictions between two remarks made by the same scholar by noting that one reflects the scholar's own view, whereas the other reflects his teacher's opinion, which the scholar himself did not accept. (See *Berakhot* 15a.)

הָא דְּרַ' פְּלוֹנִי לָאו בְּפֵירוּשׁ אִיתְּמַר אֶלָּא מִכְּלָלָא אִיתְּמַר *This statement of Rabbi X was not stated explicitly but was implied.* See לָאו בְּפֵירוּשׁ אִיתְּמַר אֶלָּא מִכְּלָלָא אִיתְּמַר.

הָא כִּדְאִיתָא וְהָא כִּדְאִיתָא *This [case] as it is, and this [case] as it is.* An expression used to reject conclusions drawn from the fact that two cases are mentioned together in a single source. The circumstances of each case are held to be different, and hence no inference may be drawn from their juxtaposition. (See *Pesaḥim* 60a.)

הָא לָא דָמְיָא אֶלָּא לְהָא Lit., *this only resembles this.* This expression is used by the Gemara to introduce an argument based on the similarity between two cases, seeking to prove that the law applying to one should likewise apply to the other. (See *Bava Metzia* 30a.) See also דּוּמְיָא דְּ...; כִּדְאַשְׁכְּחַן; מִידֵּי דַּהֲוָה אַ....

הָא לָא קַשְׁיָא *This is not difficult,* i.e., the objection just raised is invalid, and if a difficulty does exist it is of a different kind. (See *Shevuot* 23b.)

הָא לַן וְהָא לְהוּ *This is ours and this is theirs.* Sometimes the Talmud resolves a contradiction between two Halakhot by suggesting that one reflects the Babylonian practice ("this is ours"), and the other reflects the practice followed in Eretz Israel ("this is theirs"). The difference between the two Halakhot reflects the different Halakhic traditions or the different circumstances in the two countries. (See *Berakhot* 44a.)

הָא מָה אֲנִי מְקַיֵּים See יָכוֹל... כְּשֶׁהוּא אוֹמֵר....

הָא מַנִּי *Whose is this?* i.e., in accordance with whose viewpoint is this Mishnah or Baraita? (See *Bava Metzia* 40b.) See also מַאן תָּנָא; מַתְנִיתִין מַנִּי.

הָא קָא מַשְׁמַע לַן *He tells us this.* When the contents of a source seem obvious or repetitive, the Talmud may state: "The scholar cited teaches us the following point," which we would not otherwise have known if not for this scholar's explicit statement. (See *Pesaḥim* 89a.) See also מַאי קָא מַשְׁמַע לַן.

הָא ר' פְּלוֹנִי וְהָא ר' אַלְמוֹנִי *This is [the teaching of] Rabbi X, and this is [the teaching of] Rabbi Y.* Sometimes the Talmud resolves contradictions between anonymous Mishnayot or Baraitot by attributing them to different authorities: "The two sources do not contradict each other, because one is the viewpoint of Rabbi X and the other is the viewpoint of Rabbi Y." (See *Bava Metzia* 90a.)

הָא תּוּ לָמָּה לִי *Why do I need this as well?* i.e., why did the Tanna teach this matter, which is identical with or similar to a subject he has previously dealt with? (See *Shabbat* 19a.) See also הַיְינוּ הַךְ; כָּל הָנֵי לָמָּה לִי; תָּנֵינָא חֲדָא זִימְנָא.

הָא תִּינַח *This may rest,* or *granted.* A formula used to introduce a question: "Granted in case A, but what about case

B?" (See *Sukkah* 48a.) See also תִּינַח; הָנִיחָא לְ...; בִּשְׁלָמָא.

וְהָא תַּנְיָא (וְהָתַנְיָא) *But surely it has been taught.* (1) Usually this expression introduces an objection based on a Baraita: "But surely it has been taught differently in the following Baraita...!" (See *Pesaḥim* 51a. See also next entry.) (2) Occasionally, however, this term introduces a Baraita in support of the previous statement. When it is used in this sense, Rashi usually observes in his commentary that this expression is to be interpreted בְּנִיחוּתָא — "non-interrogatively," "calmly" — or as a סַיַּיעְתָּא — "help," i.e., a support, not an objection. (See *Moed Katan* 19b.)

וְהָא תְּנַן (וְהָתְנַן) *But surely we have learned.* This expression usually introduces an objection based on a Mishnah: "But surely we have learned differently in the following Mishnah...!" (See *Berakhot* 29a.) See also previous entry.

הַאי מַאי *What is this?* A term used to express astonishment at the previous statement, often meaning: "How can you make such a comparison?!" (See *Kiddushin* 18b.)

וְהַאי תָּנָא מַיְיתֵי לָהּ מֵהָכָא *And this Tanna brings it from here.* Where the Gemara wishes to show that two Baraitot contradict each other, it often introduces them as follows: תָּנֵי חֲדָא... תַּנְיָא אִידָךְ — "One Baraita is taught... another Baraita is taught...." If, however, a discussion between Amoraim intervenes between the quotation from the first Baraita and the quotation from the second, the Gemara will introduce the second Baraita with the words: וְהַאי תָּנָא מַיְיתֵי לָהּ מֵהָכָא — "And this Tanna brings it from here." (See *Bava Batra* 109a.) See also תָּנֵי חֲדָא; תַּנְיָא אִידָךְ.

הָבוּ דְּלָא לוֹסִיף עֲלָהּ Lit., *would that one not add to it.* Sometimes a scholar may suggest that a particular prohibition or Rabbinic decree be extended to include a certain case, but the Talmud may reject this suggestion, stating: "Would that one not add to this prohibition," implying that the decree is sufficiently strict as it is. (See *Shevuot* 48b.)

הַגַּע עַצְמְךָ *Put yourself in the position,* or *suppose.* An expression in the Jerusalem Talmud usually used to introduce an explanation of a general principle based on a particular case: "Consider case X" and you will see that the general principle still holds.

הֲדָא אַמְרָה Lit., *this says,* i.e., this implies. An expression used in the Jerusalem Talmud and the Aggadic Midrashim.

הֲדָא הוּא דִכְתִיב (הה"ד) Lit., *this is what is written....* An expression used in the Jerusalem Talmud and the Aggadic Midrashim to introduce a Biblical quotation supporting the previous statement.

הֲדַר בֵּיהּ ר' *Rabbi X retracted [his opinion].* Sometimes the Talmud resolves a contradiction between two statements of the same scholar by suggesting that he changed his mind, and that one of his statements therefore represents his rejection of a view he had previously held. (See *Pesaḥim* 29b.)

הֲדַר(א) קוּשְׁיָיא לְדוּכְתֵּיה Lit., *the question, difficulty, returned to its place.* Sometimes the Gemara raises an objection, solves it, and then rejects the solution; in such cases the Gemara may use this expression. (See *Kiddushin* 15b.)

הַהוּא גַּבְרָא *That man.* This expression is often used by the Gemara to introduce an incident in which an individual claimant appeared before a scholar or before a Rabbinical Court to receive a decision on a point of law. (See *Bava Metzia* 96b.) See also אֲתָא לְקַמֵּיה דְּרַב....

הַהוּא מֵרַבָּנָן *One of the Rabbis,* i.e., an anonymous Talmudic scholar. (See *Berakhot* 6b.)

הַהִיא בְּ... *That one is in...,* i.e., that Tannaitic statement refers to the following specific case.... One of the many expressions used by the Talmud when narrowing the field of reference of a Tannaitic statement in order to resolve an objection. (See *Berakhot* 50b.) See also אוֹקִימְתָּא; בְּ...; שָׁנוּ; מַתְנִיתִין בְּ...; תְּהֵא בְּ....

הוּא דַּאֲמַר כִּי הַאי תַּנָּא *He said like this Tanna.* Sometimes, when an objection to an Amora's viewpoint is based on a Tannaitic source, the Talmud answers the objection and supports the disputed viewpoint with a different Tannaitic source, using this expression to introduce it. (See *Shabbat* 54a.) See also כְּמַאן? כִּי הַאי תַּנָּא... מַאי טַעְמָא....

וְהוּא דְּרוּבָּה מִינָּה Lit., *and this is greater than it.* An expression in the Jerusalem Talmud, meaning: "Logically, the opposite should be the case." See אַדְּרַבָּא.

הוּא הַדִּין Lit., *the same is the law,* i.e., the same law or principle just established applies also in the following case. (See *Bava Metzia* 43a.)

הוּא הוּא *It is the same,* i.e., the law in the two cases is identical, and there is no practical difference between the cases. Sometimes, instead of הוּא הוּא, we find הִיא הִיא or הֵן הֵן. (See *Shabbat* 11b.)

הוּא מוֹתִיב לָה וְהוּא מְפָרֵק לָה *He raised the question and he resolved it,* i.e., the same Amora who raised the objection from a Mishnah or a Baraita, resolved it. (See *Eruvin* 91a.)

וְהוּא שֶׁ.... *Provided that....* This term is used by the Gemara to introduce a limitation to the application of a Mishnah: "The law just stated in the Mishnah is applicable, provided that...." (See *Bava Metzia* 11a.) See also (וְ)דַוְקָא; לֹא שָׁנוּ אֶלָּא.

הוּא תָּנֵי לָה וְהוּא אָמַר לָה *He taught it and he explained [lit., said] it,* i.e., the same Amora who quoted the Baraita explained it. (See *Yoma* 29b.)

הוֹאִיל וְ... *Because, since....* This expression is used by the Gemara to introduce an argument based on common sense. (See *Berakhot* 22b.) See also דְּהָא...; כֵּיוָן דְּ...; לְפִי...; מִפְּנֵי שֶׁ...; מִשּׁוּם דְּ....

הוֹאִיל וַאֲתָא לִידָן נֵימָא בָּה מִילְתָא *Since it has come into our hand, let us say something about it.* Sometimes, after a topic is mentioned in passing during a Talmudic discussion, one of the scholars suggests: "Since this matter has come to our attention [i.e., incidentally], let us discuss it further...." (See *Bava Metzia* 16b.)

הֲוָה אָמִינָא *I would have said.* This expression is used in the Talmud as an introduction to a possible answer which is later found to be incorrect. (See *Pesaḥim* 21b.) The Talmudic commentators, however, use this term as a noun in the sense of "an assumption made at the beginning of a discussion, which is later rejected."

הֲוֵי Lit., *here is, hence,* i.e., you may deduce from here that.... An expression used in the Jerusalem Talmud and the Aggadic Midrashim to introduce a conclusion inferred from the previous discussion. It is also used to introduce a Biblical quotation in support of the previous idea.

וְהָוֵינַן בָּה *We discussed it,* i.e., we discussed the following topic elsewhere in another context. (See *Berakhot* 45b.)

הֲוֵי בָּה ר' פְּלוֹנִי *Rabbi X discussed it,* i.e., he raised a question concerning a subject that came up during the discussion. (See *Ketubot* 58b.) See also הֲוָיָה; (וְ)הָוֵינַן בָּה.

הֲוָיָה, הֲוָיוֹת *Discussions, arguments.* For example, הֲוָיוֹת דְּרַב וּשְׁמוּאֵל — "The [investigative] arguments of Rav and Shmuel." (See *Berakhot* 20a.)

הִיא הֲדָא הִיא הֲדָא Lit., *it is this, it is this,* i.e., this and that are Halakhically identical. An expression used in the Jerusalem Talmud.

הִיא הַנּוֹתֶנֶת Lit., *it is this that gives,* i.e., contrary to your view, the proof you bring to support your argument in fact provides support for our (opposing) argument. (See *Eruvin* 10a.)

הַיְינוּ *This is,* i.e., this is the same as.... A term usually used to express astonishment at the repetition of something which has already been mentioned, either in the previous discussion or by another scholar. For example, הַיְינוּ ר' פְּלוֹנִי — "Surely this is the same as the statement of Rabbi X!" (See *Eruvin* 38b.) Or הַיְינוּ רֵישָׁא — "Surely this is the same as the first part of the Mishnah." (See *Bava Metzia* 93a.)

הַיְינוּ א' הַיְינוּ ב' *A is the same as B.* Sometimes this expression introduces a question: Since cases A and B are identical, why were both mentioned, or why was a distinction made between them? (See *Sukkah* 12a.)

הַיְינוּ הַךְ *This is the same as that,* i.e., this case is identical with that other case; why, then, the repetition? (See *Shabbat* 19a.) See also הָא תּוּ לָמָּה לִי.

הַיְינוּ ר' פְּלוֹנִי See הַיְינוּ.

הַיְינוּ רֵישָׁא See הַיְינוּ.

הֵיךְ מַה דְּאַתְּ אָמַר *As you say,* i.e., as it is written in the

Bible. An expression used in the Aggadic Midrashim to introduce a Biblical quotation in support of the previous statement.

הֵיךְ עֲבִידָא   Lit., *how is it done?* i.e., how so? Or: What are the details of this case? A term used in the Jerusalem Talmud to clarify the circumstances of the case under discussion. See also הֵיכִי דָּמֵי.

הֵיכָא דְּאִיתְּמַר אִיתְּמַר, הֵיכָא דְּלָא אִיתְּמַר לָא אִיתְּמַר   *Where it was said, it was said; where it was not said, it was not said.* The statement just made applies only to the case specified, and no conclusion may be drawn regarding other cases. (See *Berakhot* 24a.)

הֵיכָא קָאֵי   *Where does he stand?* Sometimes, when the basis for a Halakhic detail mentioned in the Mishnah has apparently not been established, the Talmud may ask: "On what does the Tanna base himself?" (See *Berakhot* 2a.)

הֵיכִי דָּמֵי   *What is it like?* i.e., how do we visualize this case? Or: What are the circumstances of the case under discussion? The Gemara usually follows this question by presenting one or more sets of circumstances and showing that the law under discussion cannot refer to them. (See *Bava Metzia* 21a.) The answer to the הֵיכִי דָּמֵי question is usually introduced either by הָכָא בְּמַאי עָסְקִינַן, or לָא צְרִיכָא or לְעוֹלָם (see entries).

הֵיכִי מַשְׁכַּחַת לָהּ   *How can you find it?* Sometimes, when the Gemara finds it difficult to conceive of a real-life situation in which the case under discussion applies, it may ask: "How can you find this case?" i.e., under what circumstances is such a case conceivable? (See *Bava Kamma* 51a.)

הֵיכִי נְדַיְּינוּ דַּיָּינֵי לְהַאי דִּינָא   *How should the judges decide this case?* This expression is used by the Gemara to introduce a legal dilemma: "What should the judges' decision be in such a case?" It usually continues by analyzing the problems caused by each of the possible solutions: נֵימָא... נֵימָא... — "If we decide in this way, the following difficulty arises, and if we decide in another way, then the following difficulty arises...." (See *Bava Metzia* 42a.) See also next entry.

הֵיכִי נַעֲבִיד   *How should we act?* The Gemara uses this expression when confronting a difficult choice between two possible lines of action, both of which are liable to be dangerous or unpleasant. It then suggests that both are to be avoided. (See *Megillah* 12b.)

הֵיכִי קָאָמַר   Lit., *how does he say?* In other words, "To what case precisely is he referring?" (See *Pesaḥim* 28a.)

הָכָא בְּמַאי עָסְקִינַן   *What we are dealing with here is...,* i.e., the case that we are referring to here is.... This expression is used by the Gemara as an introduction to an אוֹקִימְתָּא (see entry), an explanation whose purpose is usually to answer a previously raised objection, and to limit the application of the Mishnah or Baraita under discussion to one particular set of circumstances. (See *Bava Metzia* 10b.) See also מַתְנִיתִין בְּ....

הָכָא רְבוּתָא קָא מַשְׁמַע לַן וְהָתָם רְבוּתָא קָא מַשְׁמַע לַן   *Here he taught us something remarkable, and there he taught us something remarkable.* Sometimes the Gemara questions differences in expression or in Halakhah between different parts of a Mishnah (מַאי שְׁנָא הָכָא דְּתָנֵי..., see entry). In answering a question of this kind the Gemara sometimes explains that the different expressions were intended to bring out new and unexpected features in each of the cases. (See *Kiddushin* 59a.)

הָכָא תַּרְגִּימוּ   *Here they explained.* The Talmud sometimes uses this phrase when a Babylonian interpretation of a Mishnaic expression is cited as differing from an interpretation deriving from Eretz Israel. (See *Rosh HaShanah* 30b.) See also אָמְרִי בְּמַעַרְבָא.

הָכִי הָשְׁתָּא? הָתָם... הָכָא...   *Now is this so? There... here...!* The Talmud uses this expression in rejecting a comparison between two cases which had been suggested previously: "How can you compare? There, in case A, the circumstances are of type X, whereas here, in case B, the circumstances are different!" (See *Shabbat* 81b.) See also מִי דָּמֵי.

הָכִי נַמִי   *So too,* i.e., the same applies in the case under discussion. (See *Bava Metzia* 49a.) However, when this expression appears in the interrogative form הָכִי נַמִי דְּ... — "Is it this way too?" — it means: "Would you say what you have just said even in this case?" (See *Bava Metzia* 8a.)

הָכִי נַמִי מִסְתַּבְּרָא   *So, too, it is reasonable,* i.e., indeed, what has just been stated makes sense (because...). (See *Yoma* 16a.) Arguments introduced by this expression are usually considered conclusive.

הָכִי נַמִי קָאָמַר   *It also said thus.* Sometimes, when the objection is raised that a certain source should have said something other than what is actually stated, the Gemara answers that it should indeed be interpreted this way, even though at first glance it seems to mean something else. (See *Sanhedrin* 41a.)

הָכִי קָאָמַר (ה"ק)   *He says thus,* i.e., his statement should be interpreted as explained below. This term is used to introduce a new explanation or a textual emendation of a difficult passage in a Mishnah or a Baraita, usually proposed in order to resolve a problem raised by the Gemara regarding the passage. (See *Ta'anit* 27a.) See also אֵימָא; מַאי קָאָמַר; תָּנֵי.

הָכִי קָתָנֵי (ה"ק)   *He teaches thus,* i.e., the Tanna's statement should be interpreted as stated below. (See *Berakhot* 50a.) See also הָכִי קָאָמַר.

(וַ)הֲלֹא דִּין הוּא   Lit., *is this not an argument [or: an a fortiori inference]?* An expression used in Halakhic Midrashim when the Midrash asks why the Torah explicitly discussed a certain case, since we could have reached the same conclusion on the basis of *a fortiori* or other logical arguments. (See *Sanhedrin* 4b.) See also אֵינוֹ דִּין שֶׁ...; דִּין שֶׁ....

הֲלָכָה   See מַטִּין; נִרְאִין.

הֲלָכָה וְאֵין מוֹרִין כֵּן *This is the Halakhah, but we do not rule thus,* i.e., this is indeed the Halakhah, but for various reasons it is not made publicly known as a ruling that has practical application. (See *Eruvin* 7a.)

הֲלָכָה לְמשֶׁה מִסִּינַי *A Halakhah handed down to Moses from Sinai.* An authoritative Halakhah handed down from earlier generations. (See *Sukkah* 5b.)

וְהִלְכְתָא *And the Halakhah is....* An expression used to introduce the Talmud's decision about a Halakhic issue which had been left unresolved in the previous discussion. (See *Pesaḥim* 7b.)

הִלְכְתָא גְּמִירִי לָה *They have this Halakhah as a tradition.* Sometimes, when the Gemara asks about the source of a Halakhah under discussion, it answers that there is no reference to this Halakhah in the written text of the Torah, but it is part of accepted tradition handed down orally from generation to generation since the giving of the Torah at Sinai. (See *Shabbat* 97a.)

הִלְכְתָא לִמְשִׁיחָא *A Halakhah for [the time of] the Messiah?* An expression used to express astonishment at a Halakhic ruling that seems to have no practical application, and will be of practical significance only in Messianic times. (See *Sanhedrin* 51b.)

הֵן אִם אָמַרְתָּ Lit., *yes, if you said....* An expression found in the Halakhic Midrashim: "Your statement is correct with regard to A, but with regard to B...."

הָנִיחָא לְ... אֶלָּא לְ... מַאי אִיכָּא לְמֵימַר *It is well according to Rabbi X, but according to Rabbi Y what can be said?* This expression is used to introduce an objection to the view of a particular scholar (usually based on a Baraita), after noting that the view of another scholar, who disagrees with the first scholar, is free of such difficulties. (*Berakhot* 12a.) See also בִּשְׁלָמָא; תֵּינַח.

הָנֵי מִילֵי (ה"מ, הנ"מ) Lit., *these words.* An expression used to limit the application of a foregoing statement: "This statement applies only to certain limited circumstances, whereas in other circumstances the law is different." (See *Pesaḥim* 51a.) See also בַּמֶּה דְּבָרִים אֲמוּרִים; לֹא שָׁנוּ אֶלָּא.

הָנֵי תַּנָּאֵי כְּהָנֵי תַּנָּאֵי *These Tannaim are like those Tannaim,* i.e., this Tannaitic disagreement parallels another Tannaitic disagreement (usually between earlier scholars). (See *Betzah* 19b.)

הֲרֵי אָמְרוּ *Behold they said.* When this expression is used, the Talmud first presents an accepted Halakhah הֲרֵי אָמְרוּ... — "They did in fact lay down the following accepted law" — and then introduces another problem or problems that are similar or connected with it. (See *Yevamot* 52a/b.)

הָשְׁתָּא א', ב' מִיבָּעְיָא *Now [that] A, is B necessary?* Sometimes the Talmud objects to the mention of two cases in a Mishnah, since it seems that the one case can be logically inferred from the other: "Now that case A has been mentioned, is it necessary to mention case B since it follows, *a fortiori,* from case A?" (See *Pesaḥim* 55b.)

הָשְׁתָּא דְּאִיתְּמַר הָכִי וְאִיתְּמַר הָכִי *Now that it has been stated thus, and been stated thus....* When two conflicting statements have been made regarding a Halakhah, and we do not know how to decide between them, the Gemara suggests that, because we are uncertain, we must accept the restrictions of both statements. (See *Pesaḥim* 108a.) See also הָשְׁתָּא דְּלָא אִיתְּמַר הִלְכְתָא לָא כְּ... וְלָא כְּ....

הָשְׁתָּא דְּאָתֵית לְהָכִי *Now that you have come to this.* Sometimes the Rabbis raise a series of objections to a certain viewpoint, and each objection is given a different answer; then a new objection is raised, and someone suggests an answer which resolves not only the new objection but also the previous ones. At that point the Talmud uses this expression, proposing a revision of the solutions first advanced. (See *Berakhot* 15b.)

הָשְׁתָּא דְּלָא אִיתְּמַר הִלְכְתָא לָא כְּ... וְלָא כְּ... *Now that the Halakhah has not been stated either according to Rabbi A or according to Rabbi B,* i.e., since we do not know how to decide between the two conflicting viewpoints previously mentioned, the Gemara may now suggest that we must act in accordance with the restrictions of both statements. (See *Pesaḥim* 115a.) See also הָשְׁתָּא דְּאִיתְּמַר הָכִי וְאִיתְּמַר הָכִי.

הָתָם *There,* as opposed to הָכָא, here, specifically Eretz Israel (when used by Babylonian scholars).

הָתָם קָאֵי *He stands there.* Sometimes the Gemara asks: "What is the basis on which the author of the Mishnah states the details of a particular law?" (הֵיכָא קָאֵי?. See entry.) The answer to this question is introduced by the expression הָתָם קָאֵי — "He bases his ruling on the following passage where the necessary foundation is laid."

וְהָתַנְיָא   See הָא תַּנְיָא(וְ).

וְהָתְנַן   See הָא תְּנַן(וְ).

וַאֲדַיִין אַתְּ לָזוֹ　*Are you still at this?* An expression found in the Jerusalem Talmud, introducing a question of astonishment at a question or doubt raised by a scholar when the conclusive answer on this subject is already well known.

וְאִידָךְ　*And the other one?* i.e., what does the other scholar, holding the conflicting opinion, say to this argument? This expression is used to clarify differences of opinion between scholars, with the Gemara asking each in turn how he will answer the argument brought by the other. (See *Sanhedrin* 25a.) See also אֲמַר לָךְ; (וְ)ר׳ פְּלוֹנִי מַאי טַעְמָא לָא אֲמַר כְּר׳ אַלְמוֹנִי.

וּדְאַתָאַן עֲלָה　*And since we have come upon it,* i.e., since we have reached this particular subject, we will make some observations about it. This expression introduces an observation or question concerning a subject raised incidentally in a discussion. (See *Bava Batra* 9b.)

וּדְקָא אָרֵי (וּדְקָאָרֵי) לָה מַאי קָא אָרֵי (קָאָרֵי) לָה　*And he who asked it — why did he ask it?* An expression of astonishment used after a question has been easily answered. The Gemara then asks: "Why did the questioner cite this particular source to raise an objection from it, when the answer was so overwhelmingly clear?" (See *Yoma* 30b.)

וְהוּא שֶׁ...　*And provided that...,* i.e., the previous statement applies, "provided that" the following conditions are fulfilled. (See *Bava Metzia* 11a.)

וְהָתַנְיָא　See (וְ)הָא תַּנְיָא).

וַיְידָא אָמְרָה דָא　Lit., *and which said this?* An expression in the Jerusalem Talmud, used to cite a new source in support of an opinion mentioned previously.

וְלָא הִיא　*And it is not so.* An expression used when the Talmud rejects a viewpoint cited previously. (See *Berakhot* 36a.)

וְלֵיתָא　*And it is not so,* i.e., there is no validity to the assumption or interpretation just presented. (See *Gittin* 26b.)

וּמְמַאי　*And from where?* This term is used when the Gemara has received a reply to a question, and is seeking further clarification: "And from where do we know that the explanation just given is in fact correct...?" (See *Megillah* 18a.) See also מְמַאי... וְדִלְמָא... לָא סָלְקָא דַעְתָּךְ...

זֹאת אוֹמֶרֶת　*This says.* An introduction to a general conclusion drawn from a previous statement: "From this it follows that...." (See *Shabbat* 21b.)

זֶה הוּא שֶׁאָמַר הַכָּתוּב (זהש"ה)　*This is what the verse said.* An expression found in the Aggadic Midrashim, used to introduce a Biblical verse in support of a previous statement. See also מַאי דִּכְתִיב.

זֶה חוֹמֶר　*This is a stringent feature* — of the case under discussion, meaning that the previously mentioned aspect of the subject is more important, more serious, than what is to follow. (See *Shabbat* 75b.)

זוֹ אֵינָה מִשְׁנָה　*This is not a Mishnah,* i.e., this Baraita (or this variant reading) is not authoritative and hence no proof may be adduced from it. (See *Ketubot* 81b.)

זוֹ אֵינָה צְרִיכָה לִפְנִים　*This [objection] does not need to enter [the Academy].* This expression is interpreted in different ways by the various commentators. Some interpret it as meaning: "This objection is so weak that there is no need to bring it to the attention of the scholars in the Academy." Others, however, interpret it as meaning: "This objection is so strong that there is no point in bringing it up for discussion among the scholars in the Academy, for it cannot be refuted." (See *Bava Metzia* 16a.)

זוֹ וְאֵין צָרִיךְ לוֹמַר זוֹ קָתָנֵי　Lit., *he teaches "this and it is unnecessary to say this."* Sometimes, when the law in the second part of a Tannaitic source seems obvious, the Talmud explains that the source was worded this way for stylistic reasons: First the Tanna taught a case in which it was necessary to discuss זוֹ ("this"), and then he discussed a case which was obvious (וְאֵין צָרִיךְ לוֹמַר זוֹ — "it was unnecessary to say this"). The latter case was not really needed, and was only introduced because of this accepted style of arranging cases in an anticlimactic way. See previous entry. (See *Rosh HaShanah* 32b.) See also לֹא זוֹ אַף זוֹ קָתָנֵי.

זִיל קְרֵי בֵּי רַב הוּא   *It is [a case of] "go, read it in the teacher's house,"* i.e, this matter is so obvious that one can go and learn about it in a children's classroom, and therefore there is no need to state it at all. (See *Sanhedrin* 33b.)

חַד אָמַר... וְחוֹרָנָא אָמַר...   *One said... and the other said...* An expression used in the Jerusalem Talmud and the Aggadic Midrashim when the statements of different scholars are quoted without specifying which scholar was the author of which statement. See next entry.

חַד אָמַר... וְחַד אָמַר...   *One said... and [the other] one said...* An expression used when citing a debate between two scholars, when it is not known which view was held by each scholar. (See *Berakhot* 45a.) See also תִּסְתַּיֵּים.

חַד מִתְּרֵין תְּלָת   *One out of two, three,* i.e., the reason given or the case cited is "one out of two or three" such reasons or cases which could have been cited. (See *Zevaḥim* 94b.)

חֲדָא וְעוֹד קָאָמַר   Lit., *he says one and another one,* i.e., the reason given in the source under discussion is one of two reasons which could have been suggested for this law. (See *Berakhot* 14b.)

חֲדָא מִכְּלַל חֲבֶירְתָּהּ אִיתְּמַר   *One was stated [by implication] from the other.* Sometimes an Amora appears to state a Halakhah in two similar cases, or Amoraim disagree over similar cases. To explain this, the Gemara says: "The scholar in fact stated only one Halakhah [or the Amoraim only disagreed over one matter], and the second Halakhah was inferred from the first." (See *Megillah* 29b.) See also מִכְּלָלָא אִיתְּמַר.

חֵיילֵיהּ דְּר'... מֵהָכָא   *The strength of Rabbi X is from here.* An expression used in the Jerusalem Talmud to introduce support for a certain scholar's opinion from a Mishnah or a Baraita.

חָיישִׁינַן   *We are concerned [lest]...* This expression usually explains a ruling whose source is not known or whose reason is not immediately apparent. The Gemara explains that the scholars made their ruling because they "were concerned" that without it there would be undesirable consequences. (See *Ketubot* 26b.)

חִילּוּף הַדְּבָרִים   *The things are the reverse,* i.e, instead of X applying in case A and Y in case B, as previously stated, the opposite applies. (See *Pesaḥim* 48a.)

חֲכָמִים   *The scholars.* When this term occurs in Tannaitic sources, it describes an anonymous opinion, usually with the implication that it is held by a majority of the scholars or is at all events an accepted viewpoint. (See *Berakhot* 2a.)

חֲכָמִים הַיְינוּ תַּנָּא קַמָּא   Lit., *the scholars are the first Tanna.* An expression of astonishment: "Surely the statement ascribed to 'the scholars' in the latter part of the Mishnah [or other Tannaitic source] is not a new opinion, but merely a repetition in different words of the opinion mentioned at the beginning of the Mishnah [the תַּנָּא קַמָּא = the first Tanna; see entry]. Why, then, did it need to be repeated?" The Gemara usually answers this question with אִיכָּא בֵּינַיְיהוּ (see entry). (See *Berakhot* 61b.)

חַסּוֹרֵי מִחַסְּרָא, וְהָכִי קָתָנֵי   *[The Mishnah] is surely lacking, and it teaches thus.* Sometimes the Talmud resolves a difficulty arising in connection with a Mishnah (or a Baraita) by suggesting that a clause (or an entire sentence) was omitted from the text of the Mishnah: "The Mishnah is lacking the following clause, and it states as follows..." (See *Berakhot* 13b.)

טַעְמָא דְּ... הָא...   *The reason is X; but if...* Sometimes the Talmud raises an objection based on precise analysis of the details specified in a source, asserting that the law is applicable only under certain specifically stated circumstances and that under other circumstances the law would be different. (See *Pesaḥim* 9a.) See also אַלְמָא...; מִכְּלָל...; שְׁמַע מִינָּהּ.

טַעְמָא מַאי *What is the reason?* (1) In the middle of a sentence this expression is used rhetorically, in the sense of "because" (i.e., "Law X — 'what is the reason?' Reason Y"). (See *Betzah* 2b.) (2) At the beginning of a sentence or a clause, this term is used to introduce an observation based on precise analysis of the details specified in the source. (See *Ketubot*

39b.) See also next entry.

טַעְמָא מַאי אָמוּר רַבָּנָן *What is the reason why the Rabbis said...?* An expression used when attempting to determine the reason for a Halakhah, usually in order to draw conclusions based on this reasoning. (See *Yevamot* 90b.)

יֵיבָא כַּחֲדָא *It agrees with this.* An expression used in the Jerusalem Talmud to introduce the answer to a question: "Derive the solution from the following source [or passage]."

יָכוֹל... כְּשֶׁהוּא אוֹמֵר... *I might have thought X... but when it says....* An expression found in Halakhic Midrashim, introducing the possibility of a mistaken interpretation of a Biblical text (...יָכוֹל). If that text were the only one dealing with the subject, we might well have followed such an interpretation. Since, however, there is another text (...כְּשֶׁהוּא אוֹמֵר), we must understand that other text in accordance with our traditional interpretation. The Midrash then reverts to the first text (הָא מָה אֲנִי מְקַיֵּם; see entry), and explains it in a different way. (See *Megillah* 18a.)

יָכוֹל... תַּלְמוּד לוֹמַר... *I might have thought X, therefore the Torah states....* An expression found in Halakhic Midrashim.

Sometimes the Midrash introduces the possibility of a mistaken interpretation of a Biblical verse (...יָכוֹל — "I might have thought..."), before setting forth the correct explanation of the verse, which is based on careful scrutiny of the Biblical text. (See *Pesaḥim* 94a.) See also ...שׁוֹמֵעַ אֲנִי... תַּלְמוּד לוֹמַר.

יְצִיבָא בְּאַרְעָא וְגִיּוֹרָא בִּשְׁמֵי שְׁמַיָּא *The native is on the ground and the stranger is in the sky?!* An expression of astonishment at a statement which seems to be the opposite of what should logically be the case. This expression is derived from the Aramaic translation of Deuteronomy 28:43 ("the stranger in your midst will rise above you higher and higher, and you will descend lower and lower"). (See *Eruvin* 9a.)

יָתֵיב ר'... קַמֵּיהּ דְּר'... *Rabbi X sat before Rabbi Y.* When this expression is used, Rabbi X is usually the student (sometimes, student-colleague) of Rabbi Y. (See *Sanhedrin* 69a.)

כְּאִינִישׁ דְּשָׁמַע מִילָה וּמַקְשֵׁי עֲלֵיהּ *Like someone who hears something and challenges it.* An expression in the Jerusalem Talmud. Sometimes one Rabbi challenges the view of another, but the Talmud then proves that he actually agrees with the view he is challenging. In such cases the Talmud asks why the first Rabbi objected to the opinion of the second, and answers that the questioner was "like someone who hears something and challenges it," i.e., the question was not raised as an objection, but rather to bring out the reasoning behind the expressed view and to analyze it.

כָּאן בְּ... וְכָאן בְּ... *Here [the text refers] to case A, whereas here [the text refers] to case B.* A formula used by the Gemara to resolve a contradiction between two anonymous

Tannaitic statements, the contradiction having been introduced by וּרְמִינְהוּ (see entry) or a kindred term. The Talmud often resolves such contradictions by showing that the seemingly contradictory statements in fact refer to different cases — *"here* the one statement refers to case A, and *there* the other statement refers to case B." (See *Bava Metzia* 15a/b.) See also ...הָא... וְהָא.

כָּאן שָׁנָה רַבִּי *Here Rabbi [Yehudah HaNasi] taught.* When a view found in a Baraita or in an Amoraic statement is corroborated through the careful examination of the language of a Mishnah (which, of course, was edited by Rabbi Yehudah HaNasi), the Talmud notes that our Mishnah alludes to this idea by stating: "Here Rabbi taught...." (See *Bava Kamma* 55a.)

כְּדְאַשְׁכַּחַן... *As we find concerning....* An expression used when the Gemara argues that the similarity between two cases leads to the inference that the law known to apply to the one case should apply also to the other. (See *Berakhot* 20b.)

כְּדִי נָסְבָה *He brought [i.e., cited] it for no reason.* When a Tanna cites a number of cases, one of which is superfluous (for example, because the law in such a case could be deduced from another source), the Talmud remarks on the superfluous case that the Tanna "cited it for no reason, incidentally." (See *Bava Metzia* 27b.)

כְּדְמַחְלִיף ר' פְּלוֹנִי וְתָנֵי *Lit., as Rabbi X reversed and taught.* Sometimes, the Talmud resolves an apparent inconsistency by showing that the names of the disputants in a particular controversy should be reversed. If an extant tradition reports that another Sage had cited this controversy with the names reversed, the Talmud introduces the new, problem-free, version of the dispute by stating: "[The dispute should be reported] as Rabbi X reversed and taught." (See *Bava Metzia* 80b.)

כְּדְתַנְיָא *As it has been taught in a Baraita.* This expression introduces a Baraita in support of the viewpoint of an Amora. (See *Megillah* 14a.) See also next entry.

כְּדְתְנַן *As we have learned.* This expression introduces a Mishnah in support of the viewpoint of an Amora. (See *Berakhot* 50a.) See also previous entry.

כְּהַאי (כִּי הַאי) גַּוְונָא *Like this case,* or *in such a case,* or *in a case like this.* For example (*Bava Metzia* 30b): וּמִי הָוֵי הֶפְקֵר כִּי הַאי גַּוְונָא — "Is the object considered not to have an owner in such a case?"

כּוֹחָה דְּהֶתֵּירָא עָדִיף *The strength of leniency is preferred.* The Talmud frequently explains that the Tannaim chose to highlight a particular case where the law should theoretically have been strict, in order to emphasize that even in such a case one of the Sages was lenient. In these instances, the Talmud remarks that the case was chosen because it is preferable to show where one of the scholars was conspicuously lenient, for no one would be lenient about such a matter unless he was absolutely certain that his opinion was correct. (See *Berakhot* 60a.) See also ...'לְהוֹדִיעֲךָ כּוֹחוֹ דְּר.

כּוּלָהּ ר' פְּלוֹנִי וְהָכִי קָתָנֵי *It is all Rabbi X, and thus he teaches.* Sometimes the Mishnah presents a view anonymously and then cites a Rabbi by name. The impression is thus given that the scholar mentioned disagrees with the first, anonymous, viewpoint. In such cases, the Talmud may argue that even the anonymous part of the Mishnah represents the viewpoint of the scholar mentioned by name. Such an argument is introduced with the formula: "It is all Rabbi X, and thus he teaches," meaning that the entire Mishnah is in accordance with the view of the Rabbi who is mentioned later on in the Mishnah. (See *Nedarim* 11a.) See also חַסּוֹרֵי מִחַסְּרָא וְהָכִי קָתָנֵי; סְתָם מִשְׁנָה.

כּוּלְּהוּ סְבִירָא לְהוּ... *They all hold....* When a viewpoint is attributed to a number of different scholars, the Talmud may state: "They all hold the following opinion...." (See *Sukkah* 7b.)

כּוּלֵי עָלְמָא *The whole world.* Meaning: (1) All the scholars mentioned in the previous passage as disagreeing about a certain subject do nevertheless agree on another subject about to be mentioned. (See *Betzah* 27a.) (2) The general populace, the community at large. See following entries.

כּוּלֵי עָלְמָא אִית לְהוּ דְּר' פְּלוֹנִי וְהָכָא בְּהָא קָמִיפַּלְגִי *Everyone agrees with Rabbi X and here they disagree about this [something else].* Sometimes, in an attempt to explain an argument between Amoraim, the Talmud suggests that one of them agrees with a parallel Tannaitic or earlier Amoraic statement, whereas the other disagrees. In the course of the argument, however, the Talmud may later reject this explanation and instead attempt to resolve the Amoraic controversy by showing that *both* Amoraim could accept the view of one of the Tannaim or earlier Amoraim in question. In such cases, the Talmud states that "everyone [= both Amoraim] agrees with Rabbi X [= the Tanna or early Amora], but here they [= the later Amoraim] disagree about" a different issue. (See *Bava Metzia* 57a.) See אַלִיבָּא דְּר' פְּלוֹנִי כּוּלֵי עָלְמָא לָא פְּלִיגִי; לֵימָא בִּדְר' פְּלוֹנִי קָמִיפַּלְגִי.

(בְּ...) כּוּלֵי עָלְמָא לָא פְּלִיגִי, כִּי פְּלִיגִי בְּ... *Everyone agrees [lit., does not disagree] about X; where they disagree, is about Y.* Sometimes the Gemara attempts to delimit an issue in dispute by first stating which points are agreed upon by both sides: "Everyone agrees [i.e., both parties agree] that the law in case A is such-and-such; the disputants differ about case B...." (See *Bava Metzia* 21b.)

כִּי אֲתָא ר' פְּלוֹנִי *When Rabbi X came [he said]....* This expression introduces a tradition or a new law quoted by a particular scholar when he came to the Academy, usually when he came to Babylonia from Eretz Israel. (See *Betzah* 26b.)

כִּי פְּלִיגִי *They disagree when...* (lit., "when they disagree"). This expression is used where a controversy has been limited to a particular point. "They, the disputants, disagree only when case A is under discussion." Sometimes, this term is found as part of the expression כִּי פְּלִיגִי אַלִיבָּא דְּר' פְּלוֹנִי — "When they disagree, it is according to Rabbi X," i.e., a particular Amoraic controversy obtains only if a certain Tannaitic opinion is assumed. In other words: "They, the Amoraim, disagree only according to [the Tanna] Rabbi X." (See *Pesaḥim* 25b.) See also כּוּלֵי עָלְמָא לָא פְּלִיגִי, כִּי פְּלִיגִי בְּ... (בְּ...).

וְכִי תֵּימָא *And if you say....* This expression introduces a hypothetical answer to an objection which had been raised previously in the discussion; such answers are always rejected later on. The scholar who initially voiced the objection thus strengthens his position by showing that a possible response to it is untenable. The structure of the וְכִי תֵּימָא expression is as follows: (1) The proposed solution is introduced by the words וְכִי תֵּימָא, and (2) the rejection of the proposed solution follows, usually beginning with the interjection וְהָא — "but surely." At the end of this proposed solution and its rejection, the original objection remains to be dealt with. (See *Bava Kamma* 28b.)

כִּי תַּנְיָא הַהִיא   *When that Baraita was taught....* Sometimes an objection based on a Baraita is made to the opinion of an Amora. The Talmud may resolve such an objection by arguing that the Baraita applies only in certain cases. This expression is one of a number of terms used when the Talmud seeks to limit the application of a certain law to specific circumstances. (See *Shabbat* 80a.) See also הָכָא בְּמַאי עָסְקִינַן; הָנֵי מִילֵי.

כִּי תְּנַן נַמִי מַתְנִיתִין   *When we also taught our Mishnah....* Sometimes the Talmud resolves on objection based on a Mishnah by arguing that the law in the Mishnah also applies to the case under discussion: "When we also taught our Mishnah," the Mishnah did in fact refer to this case, although it was not explicitly mentioned. (See *Sukkah* 36a.)

כֵּיוָן דְּ...   *Since....* An introduction to an argument meant to prove a proposition on the basis of sound, commonsense reasoning. (See *Berakhot* 4b.)
See also דְּהָא...; הוֹאִיל וְ...; לְפִי...; מִפְּנֵי שֶׁ...; מִשּׁוּם דְּ...

כָּל הֵיכָא דְּ... (כּוּלֵּי עָלְמָא) לָא פְּלִיגִי דְּ... כִּי פְּלִיגִי...   *Wherever X is the case, everyone agrees that... where they disagree is....* An expression used to limit a difference of opinion between Amoraim on a point of law. The Gemara begins by stating the two conflicting points of view. Then, before analyzing the difference of opinion, the Gemara excludes from the discussion those points on which the Amoraim agree: "With regard to X, both scholars agree... but they disagree with regard to Y." (See *Pesaḥim* 30b/31a.)

כָּל הָנֵי לָמָה לִי   *Why do I need all these [cases]?* When a Mishnah presents a series of apparently similar examples, the Gemara often asks: "Why are they all necessary? They all seem to be based on a single principle, and there seems to be no need to state them all." The Gemara then answers that the cases are indeed necessary (צְרִיכָא or צְרִיכֵי, see entry) and explains the special circumstances justifying their inclusion. (See *Sukkah* 17a.)
See also הָא תּוּ לָמָה לִי; לָמָה לֵיהּ לְמִיתְנֵי... וְלָמָה לֵיהּ לְמִיתְנֵי.

כָּל כְּמִינֵיהּ   *Is this really in his power?* (Lit., "is it all from him?") I.e., is it legally possible for the person in the case under discussion to make the claim he is making, and may he be believed if he makes such a claim? (See *Ketubot* 18b.) See also לֹא הַכֹּל מִמֶּנּוּ; לָא כָּל כְּמִינֵיהּ.

כָּל עַמָּא   Lit., *the whole people.* In the Jerusalem Talmud, this means everyone, all the Sages. See כּוּלֵּי עָלְמָא.

כָּל שֶׁכֵּן שֶׁ...   *All the more so that....* An expression used to introduce the conclusion of an *a fortiori* inference (see קַל וָחוֹמֶר in the section on hermeneutics): "If the law is such-and-such in case A, all the more so [...כָּל שֶׁכֵּן שֶׁ] should the law be the same in case B." (See *Sanhedrin* 32b.)
See also אֵינוֹ דִין; לֹא כָּל שֶׁכֵּן; עַל אַחַת כַּמָּה וְכַמָּה.

כָּלָךְ לַדֶּרֶךְ זוֹ   *Go this way!* An expression used in Halakhic

Midrashim to introduce an alternative interpretation of a Biblical verse or an alternative logical argument, replacing another interpretation or logical argument which had been suggested previously. (See *Pesaḥim* 61b.)

(ו)כְלָלָא הוּא, הֲרֵי...   *But is this a general rule? What about...?* Where a Mishnah lays down a seemingly comprehensive general rule, the Gemara sometimes criticizes the statement, claiming that there is a case (or there are cases) not covered by it. (See *Eruvin* 27a.)

כְּלַפֵּי לַיָּיא   *Just the opposite!* (Lit., "towards where are you facing?") This expression is used to express astonishment at a Halakhic ruling or interpretation which seems totally illogical: "Just the opposite" should be the case! (See *Shabbat* 127a.) See also אַדְרַבָּא.

כְּמַאן? כִּי הַאי תַּנָּא... מַאי טַעְמָא...   *Like whom [i.e., according to whose opinion did the Amora decide the law]? Like this Tanna.... What is the reason?* The Gemara uses this expression when a decision of an Amora has been recorded which appears to run counter to accepted practice. "Upon whom did the Amora base his ruling?" (כְּמַאן.) The Gemara then answers: "He followed the point of view of the following Tanna" (כִּי הַאי תַּנָּא). Or "He followed the point of view of Rabbi X" (הוּא דַּאֲמַר כְּר׳ פְּלוֹנִי). The Gemara then asks: "What was the reason why the earlier scholar decided in the way he did?" (מַאי טַעְמָא.) (See *Megillah* 18b.)

כְּמַאן אָזְלָא הָא דַּאֲמַר ר׳ פְּלוֹנִי   Lit., *according to whom goes what Rabbi X said?* i.e., in accordance with which Tannaitic opinion is Rabbi X's statement? (See *Berakhot* 50b.)

כְּמַאן סְבִירָא לֵיהּ   *According to whom does he hold?* i.e., in accordance with which Tannaitic (or earlier) opinion does the scholar in question rule? (See *Berakhot* 46a.)

כְּמָה דְּאַתְּ אָמַר   Lit., *as you say...,* i.e., as the Bible says. This expression is used in Aggadic Midrashim to introduce a Biblical verse in support of the statement just made.
See זֶה הוּא שֶׁאָמַר הַכָּתוּב.

כְּרַךְ וּתְנִי   *Combine and teach.* Sometimes the Talmud resolves seeming contradictions between two parts of a Mishnah or a Baraita by suggesting that they be combined, making them complementary rather than contradictory. In such cases, the Gemara introduces the resolution of the contradiction with the expression: "Combine the two clauses of the Mishnah or the Baraita and teach...." (See *Shabbat* 34b.)

כְּשֶׁהוּא אוֹמֵר...   *When he says....*
See אַתָּה אוֹמֵר (א׳) אוֹ אֵינוֹ אֶלָּא (ב׳); יָכוֹל... כְּשֶׁהוּא אוֹמֵר...

כְּשֶׁתִּמְצָא לוֹמַר לְדִבְרֵי ר׳ פְּלוֹנִי... לְדִבְרֵי ר׳ אַלְמוֹנִי...   *When you succeed in saying, in analyzing, the matter, you will find that according to Rabbi A the case is X, and that according to Rabbi B the case is Y.* A term used to introduce a conclusion based on a preceding Tannaitic difference of opinion. "When you analyze the matter carefully, you will find that according to Rabbi

A the following must be the case, whereas according to Rabbi B the case must be understood differently." (See *Bava Metzia* 40b.)

כָּתוּב אֶחָד אוֹמֵר... וְכָתוּב אֶחָד אוֹמֵר... *One verse says... and one verse says....* In deriving laws from Biblical texts, a scholar frequently begins by quoting two seemingly contradictory Biblical texts: "One verse says... (A), whereas another verse says... (B). How can they be reconciled?" He then seeks to show that they cannot be understood unless it is assumed, as he proposes, that the two texts refer to two different and separate cases. (See *Ḥagigah* 13b.)

(ד)כְּתִיב *[For] it is written....* An expression used to introduce a quotation from the Bible. When the Gemara proves something using the authority of a Biblical verse, it often introduces the quotation with the word דִּכְתִיב — "for it is written in the Bible..." — followed by the quotation. (See *Berakhot* 2a.)

See also שֶׁנֶּאֱמַר; אֲמַר קְרָא.

כְּתִיב הָכָא... וּכְתִיב הָתָם... *It is written here... and it is written there....* An expression used to support a particular interpretation of a Biblical text, based on a similarity between the expressions used in two Biblical verses. The interpretative principle involved here is the גְּזֵירָה שָׁוָה (see entry in the section on hermeneutics). (See *Megillah* 12a.)

כְּתַנָּאֵי *Like the Tannaim.* When an Amoraic controversy is shown to parallel a Tannaitic dispute, the Talmud states: "This Amoraic controversy is like the dispute of the Tannaim." When the Gemara uses this expression without qualification (i.e., without preceding it with the word לֵימָא — "is it to say") the identification of the Amoraic controversy with a previous Tannaitic controversy is usually accepted. (See *Shabbat* 49b.) See also לֵימָא כְּתַנָּאֵי.

וְלָא? *And is it not so?* Sometimes, when the Gemara reaches a negative answer to a question or problem raised, it refers, as it were in astonishment, to the answer just given and asks: וְלָא? — "Is this really not so?" It then continues by attacking the negative answer. (See *Bava Metzia* 114a.) See also אִינִי; הַאי מַאי; (וְ)תִסְבְּרָא; סָלְקָא דַּעְתָּךְ.

לָא אֲמָרַן אֶלָּא..., אֲבָל... לֵית לַן בָּהּ *We only said... but [about]... we have no problem.* An expression used by the Gemara to limit the application of a previously mentioned Amoraic statement to one particular set of circumstances: "We say that this statement applies only in the following circumstances, but in other circumstances it does not apply." (See *Bava Metzia* 29b.) Where the Gemara seeks to limit the application of a Tannaitic statement, it uses the expression לֹא שָׁנוּ הָכָא בְּמַאי (see entry). For other expressions of limitation, see לֵית לַן בָּהּ. See also עָסְקִינַן; הָנֵי מִילֵי.

לָא בְּדָא *Not in this [case].* An expression used in the Jerusalem Talmud to indicate that a certain law does not apply in a particular case.

לָא דַּיְקָא מַתְנִיתִין אֶלָּא... *Our Mishnah is not exact unless [in accordance with Rabbi X (an Amora)],* i.e., if we analyze the Mishnah closely we will find that its wording or content is understandable only according to the interpretation given to it by a certain Amora. (See *Bava Kamma* 27b.) See also דַּיְקָא מַתְנִיתִין; דַּיְקָא נַמִי; דְּקָתָנֵי; מַתְנִיתִין נַמ דַּיְקָא.

לָא דִּינָא וְלָא דַּיָּינָא *There is no judgment and no judge.* A picturesque expression meaning: "In the particular cir-

cumstances of this case, there is no need for further discussion, since it is perfectly clear that...." (See *Yoma* 72a.)

לָא, דְּכוּלֵי עָלְמָא סָבְרִי... *No, both of them [lit., the whole world] agree that....* When the Gemara investigates a difference of opinion in a Mishnah it often begins by suggesting that the two Tannaim differ with regard to a certain general principle (לֵימָא בְּ..., קָמִיפְּלִיגִי), one scholar holding A and the other holding B. The answer is usually: "No, both of them agree about *this* general principle. They do, however, disagree about *another* principle, namely...." (See *Pesaḥim* 46b.)

לָא הֲוָה בִּידֵיהּ *Lit., it was not in his hand,* i.e., when the scholar was asked, he did not know the answer to the question. He had no tradition about the matter. (See *Yevamot* 105a.)

וְלֹא הִיא *It is not so.* This term is used to reject a Halakhic ruling or interpretation stated in the previous passage. (See *Bava Metzia* 11b.)

לֹא הַכֹּל מִמֶּנּוּ *Not everything is in his power,* i.e., it is not legally possible for him to make that particular claim; an expression in the Jerusalem Talmud. See לָא כָּל כְּמִינֵיהּ.

לֹא זוֹ אַף זוֹ קָתָנֵי *It teaches "not only this but also this."* Sometimes the Mishnah cites a series of cases, the first of which seems superfluous. In such instances, the Talmud may explain the inclusion of the seemingly superfluous first case on stylistic grounds: The Mishnah began by mentioning a simple, relatively obvious matter, and from there it proceeded to a more complicated subject. The expression used in such cases is: "The

Mishnah follows the stylistic principle of teaching not only the simple case [לֹא זוֹ] but also the more complicated case [אַף זוֹ]." (See *Bava Metzia* 38a.) See also זוֹ וְאֵין צָרִיךְ לוֹמַר זוֹ.

לָא כָּל כְּמִינֵיהּ　*It is not all in his power,* i.e., it is not legally possible for a person to make a particular claim or demand. (See *Sanhedrin* 46b.) See also כָּל כְּמִינֵיהּ.

לֹא כָּל שֶׁכֵּן　*How much more so! Is it not true* a fortiori?! This expression is used to introduce the conclusion of an *a fortiori* (קַל וָחוֹמֶר) inference. (See *Yoma* 2b.) See also כָּל שֶׁכֵּן.

לָא מִיבָּעְיָא... אֶלָּא אֲפִילוּ...　*There is no need [to state A,] but even [B].* An expression used by the Gemara to emphasize a new and exceptional feature of a scholar's point of view, when he differs with another scholar. "Not only do the two scholars differ with regard to A, but their dispute is more wide-ranging." In cases of this kind the Gemara goes on to explain the basis for the difference of opinion, and the expression אֶלָּא אֲפִילוּ always introduces a new and somewhat unexpected element. (See *Bava Metzia* 36a.)

לָא מִיבָּעְיָא קָאָמַר, לָא מִיבָּעְיָא... אֶלָּא אֲפִילוּ...　*He is speaking [in the style of] "there is no need." There is no need [to state A,] but even [B].* An expression used to explain the inclusion of a seemingly superfluous case in the Mishnah (or the Baraita) on stylistic grounds: First the Tanna began with an obvious case (a case there is "no need to state"), and from there he proceeded to a more unexpected case. (See *Betzah* 37a.) See also previous entry and לֹא זוֹ אַף זוֹ קָתָנֵי.

לֹא מִן הַשֵּׁם הוּא זֶה　Lit., *this is not from the [same] name,* i.e., this does not fall under the same category. This expression is used when a Rabbi argues that another's conclusion is based on faulty analysis: "The reason you give is inappropriate to the case at hand. The reason there is in fact different...."(See *Shabbat* 116a.)

לָא מְסַיְּימֵי קְרָאֵי　*The verses are not definite.* An expression used when two Biblical verses are cited as sources for different Halakhot, but it is not clear which Halakhah is derived from which verse. (See *Bava Metzia* 31a.)

לָא מִסְתַּבְּרָא דְּלָא חַלִיפִין　*Only the opposite way is reasonable!* An expression found in the Jerusalem Talmud, meaning: "Only the opposite of what has just been stated makes sense!" See אִיפְּכָא מִסְתַּבְּרָא.

לָא נִצְרְכָא אֶלָּא...　*It is only applicable....* See לָא צְרִיכָא אֶלָּא.

לָא סַיְּימוּהַ קַמֵּיהּ　*They did not conclude it before him,* i.e., they did not finish citing the source before one of the Sages, and hence he misinterpreted it. (See *Bava Metzia* 76b.)

לָא סָלְקָא דַּעְתָּךְ　*This cannot enter your mind.* Occasionally the Gemara raises an objection by gently suggesting that an argument might be refuted in a certain way, using such expressions as וְדִילְמָא... or וְאֵימָא... (see entries). The Gemara

often answers this kind of objection by saying: "This cannot enter your mind." In other words, you cannot possibly think so, because.... (See *Rosh HaShanah* 13a.)

לָא פְּלוּג רַבָּנָן　*The Rabbis did not differentiate.* An argument occasionally used by the Gemara to explain why the law is the same in two slightly different situations. "The Rabbis wished to avoid possible confusion and therefore did not differentiate between the cases under discussion." (See *Ketubot* 52b.)

וְלָא פְּלִיגִי, הָא בְּ... וְהָא בְּ...　*And they do not disagree, this applies in X and that applies in Y.* Sometimes, when different scholars make apparently conflicting statements about the interpretation of a Mishnah, the Talmud explains that there is in fact no dispute between them: "They do not disagree; this statement applies in case A, and the other statement applies in case B." (See *Megillah* 30a.)

לָא, צְרִיכָא　*No, it is necessary.* When the Talmud objects to a statement on the grounds that it seems self-evident, using the expression מַאי לְמֵימְרָא or פְּשִׁיטָא (see entries), the Talmud's reply to the objection is often introduced by the expression: "No, the seemingly superfluous statement is necessary," and the Talmud explains why in the following passage. (See *Berakhot* 47b.) See also צְרִיכוּתָא.

לָא צְרִיכָא אֶלָּא　*It is only necessary because of X.* (Lit., "it is not necessary except ....") An expression used to account for the presence of a particular statement in a Mishnah or other authoritative ruling, which otherwise would seem self-evident and hence superfluous: "The statement is only applicable in the following case." The expression is usually preceded by פְּשִׁיטָא or מַאי אִירְיָא (see entries). It is sometimes found in the form: לָא צְרִיכָא אֶלָּא לְר׳ פְּלוֹנִי — "The seemingly superfluous statement is necessary [i.e., relevant or applicable] only according to Rabbi X." (See *Pesahim* 99b.)

לָא צְרִיכָא דְּ...　*It is not necessarily so, for....* Sometimes the Gemara presents an objection in the form of a dilemma, giving two (or more) alternatives and showing that they are both unacceptable. These objections are introduced by various expressions such as בְּמַאי עָסְקִינַן אִי... וְאִי..., מַה נַּפְשָׁךְ אִי... וְאִי... (see entries, and also מַאי קָסָבַר; הֵיכִי דָּמֵי). The Gemara then resolves the dilemma, sometimes showing that the two proposed alternatives are not the only ones available. In such a case the answer is introduced by לָא צְרִיכָא דְּ... — "It is not in fact necessary to choose between the stated alternatives, for another possibility exists which is free from the objections raised against the others." (See *Bava Metzia* 76a.)

לָא צְרִיכָא דְּלָא　*It was only necessary....* An expression used in the Jerusalem Talmud: (1) When a statement is unclear and should have been formulated differently, the Jerusalem Talmud may follow it with: "It was only necessary [to have stated otherwise...]!" (2) Sometimes this term is used to introduce a question following an obvious statement: The law in case A is obvious; "it is only necessary" to ask, what about case B?

לָא קַשְׁיָא   *There is no difficulty.* An expresssion used by the Gemara to introduce a response to the objection that two authoritative sources are in conflict with each other. (Such objections are often introduced by וּרְמִינְהוּ [see entry] or kindred terms.) The Gemara responds: "There is no difficulty, the two sources refer to two different situations." (See *Sukkah* 38a.) The answer often continues: (1) ...וְכָאן... כָּאן — "In the one case the circumstances are X, whereas in the other case the circumstances are Y." Or (2) הָא ר׳ פְּלוֹנִי וְהָא ר׳ אַלְמוֹנִי — "In the one case the view expressed is that of Rabbi X, whereas in the other case the view expressed is that of Rabbi Y."

לֹא רְאִי זֶה כִּרְאִי זֶה וְלֹא רְאִי זֶה כִּרְאִי זֶה, הַצַּד הַשָּׁוֶה שֶׁבָּהֶן שֶׁ...   *The nature of this case is not like the nature of this [other] case and the nature of this [other] case is not like the nature of this [first] case; the common element in the [two cases] is that....* This expression is used in Halakhic Midrashim in formulating a בִּנְיַן אָב (see entry in section on hermeneutics), where a generalization is made on the basis of two cases mentioned in two different verses. First the Midrash points out the difference between the two particular cases. Then it mentions the characteristic they have in common. Any other case with that common feature will then be subject to the same law. (See *Berakhot* 35a.)

לָא שְׁנָא   *There is no difference.* See next entry.

לָא שְׁנָא... וְלָא שְׁנָא...   *No distinction is made between X and Y.* (Lit., "there is no difference... and there is no difference....") This expression is used when the Gemara seeks to show that a Mishnah has applied the same rule to two cases which should in fact be treated differently. "The Mishnah has decided [קָא פָּסִיק וְתָנֵי; see entry] without distinguishing between X and Y. The ruling is appropriate with regard to X, but why should it also apply to Y?" (See *Sukkah* 29b.)

לֹא שָׁנוּ אֶלָּא   *They only taught....* This expression is used by the Gemara to limit the application of a seemingly general law stated in a Mishnah or a Baraita: "They only taught this law in a particular case"; but (...אֲבָל) in other cases this law would not apply. (See *Berakhot* 42b.)
See also the Tannaitic term בַּמֶּה דְּבָרִים אֲמוּרִים.

לֹא תֵּימָא... אֶלָּא (אֵימָא)...   *Do not say... but (say)....* Sometimes, when the Talmud emends the text of a Mishnah or a Baraita (usually in order to resolve an objection), the emendation is introduced by the expression: "Do not say [what is written in the Mishnah or the Baraita], but rather say [the emended version of the text]." (See *Berakhot* 22a.)
See also אֵימָא; תָּנֵי.

לָא תֵּימָא מַתְנִיתִין ר׳ פְּלוֹנִי אֶלָּא...   *Do not say that our Mishnah is [the viewpoint of] Rabbi X, but rather....* The Gemara uses this expression when at first a Mishnah does not appear to reflect accepted Halakhah, and Rabbi Yehudah HaNasi seems to have included the viewpoint to represent a dissenting opinion. "No," says the Gemara, "do not say that our Mishnah is the viewpoint of Rabbi X alone. It is rather the majority viewpoint of the Rabbis as a whole, who maintain...." (See *Bava Kamma* 31a.)

(לְעוֹלָם) לָא תֵּיפוּךְ   *(In fact) do not reverse.* Sometimes the Gemara quotes another Tannaitic source when discussing a difference of opinion recorded in a Mishnah or a Baraita. It does so because there is a contradiction between that source and the Mishnah under discussion: ...לְמֵימְרָא דְּר׳ — "Do we say in our Mishnah that Rabbi A holds X and Rabbi B holds Y? From another Mishnah [or Baraita] we learn that Rabbi A holds Y and Rabbi B holds X!" The Gemara often resolves the contradiction by saying אִיפּוּךְ or מוּחְלֶפֶת הַשִּׁיטָה (see entries), reversing the names of the Rabbis in one of the conflicting sources. But occasionally it rejects this solution, saying לָא תֵּיפוּךְ — "Do not reverse the names in one of the sources," for there is another way of reconciling the contradictory opinions. (See *Bava Metzia* 7b.)

לָא(ו) תָּרוּצֵי מִתְרַצְתְּ לָהּ, תְּרֵיץ נַמֵי הָכִי   *Have you not already corrected [lit., settled] it? Correct [lit., settle], therefore, also thus....* Sometimes, after the Talmud has corrected a problematic text, another objection may be raised in connection with the same text. In such cases the Amoraim may resolve the problem by emending the text once again: "Have you not already emended the text? Emend it again...!" (See *Bava Metzia* 14b.)

לָאו אַדַעְתַּאי (לָאו אַדַעְתֵּיהּ)   *It was not on my (his) mind,* i.e., the matter was not done with my knowledge. I was not aware of the matter which has just been brought to my attention. (See *Betzah* 22a.)

וְלָאו אוֹתְבִינַן חֲדָא זִימְנָא   *Have we not rejected this once?* When an objection appears in the Talmud to an opinion which has already been refuted, the Talmud may object to the unnecessary repetition of the objection: "Have we not already refuted this statement...?" (See *Eruvin* 30a.)

לָאו בְּפֵירוּשׁ אִיתְּמַר, אֶלָּא מִכְּלָלָא אִיתְּמַר   *It was not stated explicitly; rather, it was stated by inference.* Occasionally, a statement attributed to a particular scholar was not made explicitly by him, but was deduced by his students from other statements made by him or from his conduct. In such cases the Talmud may comment that "the remark attributed to this scholar was not stated by him explicitly; rather, it was stated by inference." (See *Berakhot* 9a.) The Talmud then sometimes proceeds to ask וְאִי מִכְּלָלָא מַאי — "And if it was deduced by inference, what difference does it make?"
See אִי מִכְּלָלָא מַאי; חֲדָא מִכְּלַל חֲבֵירְתָּהּ אִיתְּמַר; מִכְּלָלָא אִיתְּמַר.

לָאו מִילְתָא הִיא   Lit., *it is nothing,* i.e., it is incorrect. The Talmud sometimes rejects a statement by saying: "It [= the previous opinion] is incorrect." Sometimes an Amora may use this expression in connection with a statement of his own if he feels he has erred. (See *Rosh HaShanah* 13a.)

לְאַפּוֹקֵי   *To exclude.* Sometimes the Talmud explains that a particular source was worded in order "to exclude" a certain case or situation. (See *Berakhot* 37a.)

לְאַפּוֹקֵי מִדְּרַ׳ פְּלוֹנִי   *To exclude from Rabbi X.* Sometimes the Talmud explains that a source was worded in a particular way in order "to negate Rabbi X's viewpoint." (See *Bava Metzia* 4b.)

לְאַתּוּיֵי מַאי   *To add [lit., bring] what?* The Talmud may ask this question about a word, phrase, or sentence, particularly when a Mishnah introduces a law with a general comprehensive statement: "What was this intended to add?" (See *Pesaḥim* 8a.) See, by contrast, לְמַעוּטֵי מַאי.

לְגַרְמֵיה הוּא דַּעֲבַד   *He acted for himself.* Sometimes the Talmud rejects the actions of a scholar as legal precedent on the grounds that "he acted for himself," meaning that it is not possible to derive a general principle from his action. (See *Berakhot* 48a.)

לִדְבָרָיו דְּ... קָאָמַר   *He stated according to X.* Sometimes, when a contradiction is found between two statements made by the same scholar, the Talmud may resolve the problem by suggesting that in one case the scholar was not expressing his own viewpoint, but simply explaining the viewpoint of another scholar without agreeing with it. (See *Betzah* 40b.) See also (וְ)לֵיה לָא סְבִירָא לֵיה.

לְדִידִי מִיפַּרְשָׁא לִי מִינֵיה דְּר׳ פְּלוֹנִי   *It was explained to me personally by Rabbi X.* An expression sometimes used to introduce an authoritative response to an objection: "I myself personally heard Rabbi X explain this specific law." (See *Berakhot* 34b.)

לְהוֹדִיעֲךָ כּוֹחוֹ דְּר׳...   *To inform you of Rabbi X's strength.* The Talmud sometimes explains that the Tannaim chose a particular case from a wide range of alternatives in order to emphasize the far-reaching consequences of a particular scholar's approach. In such instances the Talmud explains the choice of the case under discussion by saying: "It was chosen 'to inform you of Rabbi X's strength,' i.e., to show us that even here that Rabbi was confident enough to be exceptionally lenient or severe." (See *Betzah* 2b.) See also כּוֹחָא דְּהֶיתֵּרָא עָדִיף.

וְלִיגְמַר מִינָּה   *Let him learn from it!* Why do we not use the particular law just cited as the source for a more comprehensive general principle? (See *Berakhot* 19b.)

וְלֵיה לָא סְבִירָא לֵיה   *He does not agree with it.* In using this expression the Gemara emphasizes that the scholar who reported a statement in the name of someone else did not personally agree with it. (See *Betzah* 40b.) See also לִדְבָרָיו דְּ... קָאָמַר.

וְלִיטַעֲמִיךְ   *And according to your opinion?* This word introduces a counterargument, where the purpose is to refute the reasoning of an objector. "If the reason for the law is as you, the objector, have stated, how do you explain another objection that can be raised? You must agree that there is another underlying reason for the law, not the one you have stated." This form of argument has a dual structure beginning with: (1) The counterargument, to which the objector can have no response, introduced by וְלִטַעֲמִיךְ, and (2) the real reason for the law under discussion, which offers no problem, introduced by אֶלָּא. (See *Yoma* 8b.)

לָיֵיט עֲלָה   *He cursed it.* When an Amora intensely disapproved of a certain custom or Halakhic ruling, the Talmud may note that he "cursed" the author of the ruling or someone who acted in accordance with it. (See *Berakhot* 29a.)

לֵימָא   *Let us say,* or *shall we say?* This expression introduces a suggestion which is almost invariably rejected later on in the discussion. See the following entries and נֵימָא.

לֵימָא בִּדְר׳ פְּלוֹנִי קָמִיפַּלְגִי   *Shall we say that they disagree with regard to Rabbi X?* Sometimes, in an attempt to explain a Tannaitic controversy, the Talmud may suggest that one of the Tannaim is following a certain Amoraic viewpoint parallel to his opinion, while the other Tanna does not accept it. In such cases the Talmud's attempt to explain the dispute between the Tannaim is often introduced by the expression: "Shall we say that they [= the Tannaim] disagree with regard to Rabbi X [= the Amora]?" (Later in the discussion, however, this suggestion is usually rejected; see לֵימָא [above] and next entry.) (See *Nazir* 62b.)

לֵימָא בְּהָא קָמִיפַּלְגִי   *Shall we say that they disagree about this?* Sometimes, in an attempt to explain a Tannaitic controversy, the Talmud may suggest that one of the Tannaim has made a certain basic assumption with which the other Tanna disagrees. In these cases the Talmud's attempt to explain the dispute between the Tannaim is often introduced by the expression: "Shall we say that they [= the Tannaim] disagree about this [point]?" Such a suggestion is usually rejected by the Talmud, using the expression לָא, דְּכוּלֵי עָלְמָא סָבְרִי... — "No. Both scholars accept [or reject] the basic assumption mentioned earlier. But they in fact disagree about another principle...." (See *Pesaḥim* 46b.)

לֵימָא בִּפְלוּגְתָּא דְּ... קָמִיפַּלְגִי   *Shall we say that [these Amoraim] disagree according to the difference of opinion between [Tannaim] A and B.* When there is a difference of opinion between Amoraim, the Gemara often tries to show that the same difference of opinion exists between Tannaim. "Shall we say that these Amoraim in fact disagree about a principle which had previously been the source of a dispute between Tannaim?" (Later on in the discussion, however, this suggestion is usually rejected. See לֵימָא and other entries above.) (See *Eruvin* 68b.) See also לֵימָא כְּתַנָּאֵי.

לֵימָא הָנֵי תַנָּאֵי כְּהָנֵי תַנָּאֵי   *Shall we say that these Tannaim are like those Tannaim?* Sometimes the Talmud attempts to compare two Tannaitic controversies by arguing that each of the viewpoints in the first dispute parallels a corresponding viewpoint in the second dispute, a suggestion that is usually rejected later in the discussion. (See *Sanhedrin* 85b.)

לֵימָא (נֵימָא) כְּתַנָּאֵי   *Shall we say it is like the Tannaim?* Sometimes, in an attempt to understand an Amoraic controversy, the Gemara may suggest that each of the Amoraic viewpoints parallels a corresponding Tannaitic viewpoint. This suggestion is usually rejected by the Gemara, which proceeds to show that the Amoraim are in fact discussing a previously unconsidered aspect of law. (See *Sanhedrin* 27a.)

לֵימָא מְסַיֵּיע לֵיהּ   *Shall we say that it supports him?* The Talmud uses this expression to suggest that a Mishnah supports a particular Amora's view. Suggestions introduced in this way are usually rejected later in the discussion; see above, לֵימָא. (See *Sukkah* 15b.)

לֵימָא מַתְנִיתִין דְּלָא כְּר׳ פְּלוֹנִי   *Shall we say that our Mishnah is not like Rabbi X?* The Talmud uses this expression to suggest that our Mishnah does not agree with the view of a particular Tanna, a suggestion that is usually rejected later on in the discussion. The answer usually takes the form אֲפִילוּ תֵּימָא ר׳ פְּלוֹנִי — "You may even say that our Mishnah does agree with the view of Rabbi X," followed by an explanation showing that the case dealt with by the Mishnah is different from the case dealt with by Rabbi X, and thus the rulings are different. (See *Bava Metzia* 2b.)

לֵימָא תֶּהֱוֵי תְּיוּבְתָּא דְּ...   *Shall we say that it is a refutation of...?* The Talmud uses this expression to suggest that a Mishnah contradicts a particular Amora's view, usually rejecting that idea later in the discussion. (See *Shabbat* 9b.) See also לֵימָא; לֵימָא מְסַיֵּיע לֵיהּ.

לִיעַרְבִינְהוּ וְלִיתְנִינְהוּ   *Let him combine them and teach them!* When a Mishnah (or a Baraita) discusses several cases in separate clauses, and the same law applies in each of the cases, the Talmud may ask why the Tanna did not formulate his statement more concisely. "Let him [= the Tanna] combine them [= the different cases] and teach them as one general principle!" (See *Yoma* 84b.)

לִיפְלוֹג וְלִיתְנִי בְּדִידָהּ   *Let him distinguish and teach it in [this case] itself!* This expression introduces an objection to an explanation previously given by the Gemara of a Mishnaic statement or a Tannaitic difference of opinion: If the principle underlying the statement or difference of opinion is as you have suggested, the Tanna could have illuminated this principle by making a distinction within the Mishnah itself (לִיפְלוֹג וְלִיתְנִי בְּדִידָהּ). Why was he compelled to refer to another case? (See *Yevamot* 19a.)

לִישָׁנָא   *Wording, formulation, version.* This term is found in a number of combinations: לִישָׁנָא אַחֲרִינָא — "another version," i.e., another version of what was stated above [which usually differs substantially from the previous version] (see *Sukkah* 11a); לִישָׁנָא בַּתְרָא — "the latter version" of a statement, question, etc.; לִישָׁנָא קַמָּא — "the former version" of a statement, question etc. (See *Berakhot* 60a.)

לִישָׁנָא מַעַלְיָא (נָקַט)   *[He used] a refined, euphemistic expression.* The scholar (or Biblical verse) quoted used a euphemistic expression, rather than saying something uncouth or unpleasant. (See *Yevamot* 11b.)

לִישְׁנֵי   *Let him answer!* Sometimes, when the Talmud challenges the viewpoint of a certain scholar, it may then suggest the answer he should have given. "Let him [= the scholar whose view was challenged] give the following answer!" (See *Yevamot* 48b.)

לֵית טַעְמָא דְּלָא   *The reason is only....* An expression in the Jerusalem Talmud: The reason for a particular law has to be as stated in the following passage.

וְלֵית לֵיהּ לְר׳ פְּלוֹנִי הָא דִּתְנַן...   *Does Rabbi X not agree with what we have learned [in a Mishnah...]?* An expression of astonishment used by the Gemara when the action of an Amora seems to be in conflict with a clear Mishnaic statement. (See *Pesahim* 51a.)

לֵית לֵיהּ קִיּוּם   *It has no foundation.* An expression in the Jerusalem Talmud. When the objections raised against a certain viewpoint are so strong that they cannot be resolved and the viewpoint is rejected completely, the Jerusalem Talmud may state: "It [= the problematic viewpoint] has no foundation." See תְּיוּבְתָּא.

לֵית לַן בָּהּ   Lit., *we have nothing in it.* An expression limiting the applications of a statement made earlier: "The prohibition, law or ruling stated earlier in general terms does not apply in this case and it poses no problem for us [לֵית לַן בָּהּ]." (See *Bava Metzia* 29b.)

לִיתְנֵי   *Let him teach.* This expression is used by the Gemara to introduce an objection to the language or style of the Mishnah: "Why did the Tanna who taught this Mishnah not teach the Mishnah's contents in another, clearer, way?" (See *Bava Metzia* 31a.)

וְלִיתְנֵי נַמִי   *And let him also teach....* An expression used by the Gemara to introduce a case that should have been included among those dealt with by the Mishnah: "Since the Mishnah is dealing with a whole series of cases, should it not have added the following case as well?" (See *Bava Metzia* 55a.)

לְכַתְּחִילָה   *Ab initio, from the beginning.* An expression used by the Talmud in interpreting the Mishnah to describe a situation where the correctness or validity of an action is being considered *before* the action has been taken, as opposed to דִּיעֲבַד, "after the event" (see entry), where the correctness or validity of an action is being considered *after* it has taken place. (See *Hullin* 2a.) See also following entries.

לְכַתְּחִילָה לָא, דִּיעֲבַד שַׁפִּיר דָּמֵי   *Ab initio no, but after the event it is well.* The Gemara uses this expression in interpreting the Mishnah, arguing that a certain action should not be performed, but conceding that if the action were in fact performed it would be accepted as valid after the event. (See *Berakhot* 15b.) See also (בְּ)דִּיעֲבַד אִין; דִּיעֲבַד נַמִי לָא.

לְכַתְּחִילָה נַמִי   *Also ab initio.* An expression used by the Gemara in interpreting the Mishnah, explaining that the statement in the Mishnah is to be understood as giving direct permission to perform a certain action. (See *Berakhot* 15b.) See also previous entries.

לְמַאי נֵיחוּשׁ לָהּ   *About what do we need to be concerned?* What problem or doubt could exist in such a case? (See *Yevamot* 116a.)

לְמַאי נָפְקָא מִינַהּ   See מַאי נָפְקָא מִינַהּ.

לְמַאן   *According to whom?* According to the opinion of which Tannaitic scholar can the previous statement be understood? (See *Bava Metzia* 39a.)

לְמַאן דַּאֲמַר   *According to the one who says.* Frequently the Talmud uses this expression to refer to the viewpoint of a scholar, which is ascribed to him elsewhere, without mentioning him by name in the present passage. (See *Berakhot* 40b.)

לָמָה   *Why? What is the reason for this law? What is the reason for this custom?* Questions such as these are usually preceded in the Gemara by the Aramaic words מַאי טַעְמָא (see entry). When, however, the reported discussion took place in Eretz Israel, the Hebrew word לָמָה is sometimes used instead. (See *Pesaḥim* 115b.)

לָמָה הַדָּבָר דּוֹמֶה   *To what may the matter be compared?* An expression in the Aggadic Midrashim used to introduce a parable or comparison. (See *Rosh HaShanah* 17b.)

לָמָה לִי   *For what do I need....* A term used when the Talmud objects to the mention of a seemingly superfluous detail. (See *Berakhot* 3a.) See also הָא תּוּ לָמָה לִי; תַּרְתֵּי לָמָה לִי.

לָמָּה לֵיהּ לְמִיתְנֵי... לִיתְנֵי...   *Why does he need to teach... let him teach....* When the Gemara objects to the wording of a Mishnah and suggests a clearer or more concise form of words, it frequently begins: "Why does the author of the Mishnah use this expression? He would make his point more clearly [or more concisely] if he instead said...." (See *Bava Metzia* 2a.)

לָמָּה לֵיהּ לְמִיתְנֵי... וְלָמָּה לֵיהּ לְמִיתְנֵי...   *Why does he teach X, and why does he teach Y?* When the Gemara, in analyzing a Mishnah, finds an unnecessary repetition of seemingly identical cases, it often asks: "Why does the author of the Mishnah need to teach case X, and why does he then need to teach case Y? Surely one of the cases is superfluous!" The Gemara answers, using the expression צְרִיכָא (see entry), showing that the various cases are in fact necessary and going on to explain why. (See *Bava Metzia* 33b.)

לְמֵימְרָא דְּ... וְהָא...   *Do you mean to say that...? After all...!* The Talmud uses this expression when, on occasion, it challenges what seems to be the logical interpretation of a given statement on the basis of another source. In such cases the objection is often introduced: "Do you mean to say that we must interpret this passage as meaning that...? After all we have learned elsewhere that...!" (See *Shabbat* 15b.) See also next entry.

לְמֵימְרָא דְּר' פְּלוֹנִי סָבַר... וְר' אַלְמוֹנִי סָבַר... וְהָא...   *Do you mean to say that Rabbi A holds X and Rabbi B holds Y? Surely....* When analyzing a difference of opinion recorded in a Mishnah, the Gemara sometimes seeks to point out an inconsistency in the viewpoints of both contesting Tannaim: "Do you mean to say that Rabbi A holds X and Rabbi B holds Y? Surely we learn from another Tannaitic source that their opinions are the reverse of those recorded here!" The Gemara often resolves the apparent contradiction by reversing the names of the scholars in one of the conflicting sources. (See *Pesaḥim* 49b.) See also אִיפּוּךְ; לָא תֵּיפוּךְ; מוּחְלֶפֶת הַשִּׁיטָה.

לְמִירְמָא דִּידֵיהּ אַדִּידֵיהּ   Lit., *to cast from him upon him,* i.e., to raise an objection against a certain scholar's ruling based on that very scholar's ruling about something else. (See *Pesaḥim* 107a.)

לְמַעוּטֵי מַאי   *To exclude what?* When the Mishnah states the exact number of cases to which a law applies, or when it uses the expressions: (1) אֵלּוּ... — "these are...," or (2) זוֹ הִיא... — "this is...," the Gemara often asks: "What did the Mishnah intend to exclude when it used a limiting expression of this kind?" (See *Pesaḥim* 76b.) See, by contrast, לְאַתּוּיֵי מַאי.

לְעוֹלָם   *In fact* (lit., "forever"). Sometimes the Talmud may suggest an interpretation and then reject it after finding that it poses problems. Later, however, this interpretation may be reinstated after the difficulties it raises have been resolved. In such cases the Talmud reintroduces the original interpretation by saying: "In fact, despite the difficulties, what was originally stated was correct...." (See *Berakhot* 3a.)

לְפִי שֶׁ...   *Because....* When the Gemara presents an argument in favour of a particular point of view and bases its reasoning on common sense, it often introduces such an argument with the expression לְפִי שֶׁ... — "because...." (See *Gittin* 2b.) See also דְּהָא...; הוֹאִיל וְ...; כֵּיוָן דְּ...; מִפְּנֵי שֶׁ...; מִשּׁוּם דְּ...

וְלִפְלוֹג נַמִי בְּהָא   *Let him also differ with regard to this.* Where a difference of opinion is recorded in a Mishnah with regard to one case, and another case is recorded without a difference of opinion, the Gemara sometimes asks: "Surely Rabbi X ought to differ with regard to the other case as well?" (See *Shabbat* 39a.) See also מַאי שְׁנָא רֵישָׁא דְּלָא פְּלִיגִי וּמַאי שְׁנָא סֵיפָא דְּפְלִיגִי.

לִצְדָדִין קָתָנֵי   *He teaches it as two alternatives* (lit., "to the sides"), i.e., the two clauses in the Mishnah should be treated separately, since they refer to different circumstances, even though this is not stated explicitly in the Mishnah. It is unreasonable, therefore, to subject them to analysis as if they were referring to one case. (See *Shabbat* 60a.)

מַאי   *What is...?* When the Gemara questions the meaning of a word or a phrase in a Mishnah, it frequently poses an anonymous question: "What is the meaning of the word or the phrase...?" This question is usually followed by an explanation given in the name of an individual Amora. (Sometimes two Amoraim give differing answers to such a question.) (See *Pesaḥim* 2a.)

מַאי אִיכָּא בֵּין...   *What [difference] is there between...?* When a Mishnah presents two reasons or two Scriptural derivations for one law, and there does not appear to be any practical difference between them, the Gemara often asks: "What practical difference is there in fact between the two reasons or the two derivations given?" The answer to such a question will begin with the words אִיכָּא בֵּינַיְיהוּ — "There is a difference between them." (See entry.) (See *Ḥullin* 116a.)

מַאי אִיכָּא לְמֵימַר   *What is there to say?* Sometimes, when analyzing a controversy, the Talmud notes that the viewpoint of one of the scholars cited seems reasonable, while the other viewpoint presents difficulties. Sometimes, too, the viewpoint of an individual scholar is found to be acceptable in certain circumstances but not in others. In such cases, the Talmud may state: "The first authority's view is understandable, but according to the second, what is there to say?" Or: "You may be right about X, but what is there to say about Y?" (See *Yoma* 3a.) See בִּשְׁלָמָא; הָנִיחָא לְ...; תֵּינַח; תֵּינַח בְּ..., מַאי אִיכָּא לְמֵימַר.

מַאי אִירְיָא   *Why [this] discussion?* As a rule, statements in a Mishnah or a Baraita are framed to include all relevant cases. If, therefore, a Mishnah or a Baraita links a law to a particular, unusual, set of circumstances when it could have chosen a more common situation, the Talmud may object: "Why [this] discussion?" In other words: "Why was it necessary to specify this particular situation, since the same law would also apply in other cases?" (See *Pesaḥim* 50b.)

מַאי אִירְיָא דְּתָנֵי... לִיתְנֵי...   *Why did he particularly teach X, let him teach Y.* In its analysis of the Mishnah the Gemara sometimes takes exception to an expression or case chosen by the Mishnah and suggests that another — more appropriate or more comprehensive — expression or case could have been chosen. (See *Yevamot* 84a.) See also previous entry.

מַאי אִית לָךְ לְמֵימַר   *What do you have to say?* This expression can be used in two contexts: (1) In introducing the conclusion of a question: "What do you have to say in response to my arguments?" (See *Berakhot* 38a.) (2) In anticipating an argument: "What do you have to say? Will you perhaps say X? If so, I can object to your reasoning." (See *Ketubot* 109b.)

מַאי בֵּינַיְיהוּ   *What is [the difference] between them?* Where

the Gemara records a difference of opinion about the reason for a law or about the definition of a legal concept, it often asks: "What practical difference is there between the different reasons or definitions cited in the previous passage?" The answer to this question is introduced by the expression אִיכָּא בֵּינַיְיהוּ — "[The difference] between them is...." (See entry.) (See *Bava Metzia* 15b.)

מַאי דִּכְתִיב   *What is [it] that is written?* i.e., what is the meaning of the Biblical verse about to be cited? The expression usually introduces an Aggadic interpretation of a Biblical verse. (See *Ḥagigah* 12a.) See also זֶה הוּא שֶׁאָמַר הַכָּתוּב.

מַאי הֲוֵי עֲלָהּ   Lit., *what was there about it?* i.e., what conclusion was reached about the matter? Or: What was the final Halakhic ruling in this case? This question is usually asked at the end of a lengthy discussion of a problem, in which different opinions have been expressed without being either proved or dismissed. (See *Bava Metzia* 7a.)

מַאי וְאוֹמֵר   See (וְ)אוֹמֵר.

מַאי חָזֵית   *What did you see?* i.e., why did you prefer a particular viewpoint over another, conflicting one? (See *Pesaḥim* 25b.) See also מָה רָאִיתָ.

מַאי טַעְמָא   *What is the reason?* The Gemara usually uses this expression to introduce an investigation of an anonymous Mishnah, where the law stated appears to be based on a Rabbinical principle rather than on a Biblical verse. (See *Bava Metzia* 38a.) See also next entry.

מַאי טַעְמָא דְּר' פְּלוֹנִי   *What is Rabbi X's reason?* The Gemara often uses this expression when a Mishnah contains a difference of opinion between a majority of the scholars and a single dissenting Rabbi. (See *Rosh HaShanah* 22a.) See also מַאי טַעְמָא; (וְ)רַבָּנָן; (וְ)תַנָּא קַמָּא.

מַאי (מיי) כְּדוֹן   *What now?* An expression in the Jerusalem Talmud meaning: (1) "What answer can be given to the objection which was just raised?" (See מַאי אִיכָּא לְמֵימַר.) (2) "What is the final conclusion with regard to the Halakhah under discussion?" See מַאי הֲוֵי עֲלָהּ.

מַאי לָאו...   *Is it not...?* This expression is used to propose a suggested interpretation of material found in the preceding passage: "Why not say that the following interpretation is correct?" The reply to such a suggestion usually begins with the word לָא — "This is not the way to interpret the passage under discussion. Rather, the following is the correct interpretation...." (See *Sanhedrin* 24b.)

מַאי לְמֵימְרָא   *What [does it mean] to say?* An expression used by the Gemara following a seemingly superfluous statement (usually in a Mishnah or a Baraita): "Why was this statement made, since it is obvious?" (See *Nazir* 13a.)

מַאי מַשְׁמַע   *What is the meaning?* When a Halakhah is inferred (usually in a Mishnah) from a Biblical verse and the basis of the inference is not fully clear, the Talmud may use this expression to ask how the inference was drawn from the verse cited. (See *Shabbat* 84b.)

מַאי מַשְׁמַע דְּ...   *From where [may we] infer that....* An expression used by the Gemara when interpreting an obscure word or phrase in the Mishnah: "Where in the Bible do we find a similar linguistic usage to that found in our Mishnah, authorizing us to understand the word or phrase in the way proposed?" (See *Rosh HaShanah* 22b.)

(לְ)מַאי נָפְקָא מִינָּהּ   *What difference does it make?* i.e., what practical consequences does it have? This expression is used when a problem raised by the Gemara seems to be merely academic. (See *Shabbat* 14a.)

מַאי עֲבִידְתֵּיהּ   *What is its purpose?* (lit., "its work"). In other words: "What is the relevance here of the item cited in the previous passage?" (See *Shabbat* 120a.) See also מַאן דְּכַר שְׁמֵיהּ.

מַאי פְּסְקָא   *Why the unqualified statement?* Sometimes the Talmud interprets a Mishnah (or a Biblical verse) as applying only under particular circumstances, though they are not specified in the text itself. In such cases, the Talmud may ask: "Why the unqualified, categorical, statement?" i.e., how can you interpret the Mishnah (or Biblical verse) as applying only under the conditions cited above, if this is not explicitly stated in the text? (See *Bava Metzia* 34a.)

מַאי קָאָמַר   *What is he saying?* i.e., what is the meaning of this Tannaitic statement? This expression is used by the Gemara when a complete sentence or statement in a Mishnah or a Baraita appears unclear. The Gemara usually introduces the answer to such a question with the words הָכִי קָאָמַר — "This is what he means...." (See entry.) (See *Shabbat* 41a.)

מַאי קָא מַשְׁמַע לָן (מַאי קמ"ל)   *What is he trying to tell us?* An expression used frequently by the Gemara, generally under the following circumstances: (1) When a Mishnah or a Baraita includes a detail or a story that appears to have no Halakhic significance. (2) When the Halakhah cited has already been stated elsewhere. The Gemara objects: "What has he [= the person who made this statement or related this incident] come to tell us?" The answer to this challenge is usually introduced by the expression מַהוּ דְּתֵימָא..., or ...הָא קָא מַשְׁמַע לָן (see entries). (See *Pesaḥim* 89a.) See also next entry.

מַאי קָמַשְׁמַע לָן תְּנֵינָא   *What is he teaching us? We have [already] learned [this].* Here the Gemara is questioning a Mishnah, a Baraita, or an Amoraic statement on the grounds that it is superfluous, having already been mentioned in a Mishnah. (See *Berakhot* 50a.) See also previous entry.

מַאי קָסָבַר אִי... וְאִי...   *What does he think?* i.e., what is the conceptual basis of his statement? The Gemara uses this expression to introduce a dilemma: "If the authority holds X, then my objection is... and if he holds Y, then my objection is...." (See *Berakhot* 3a.) See also בְּמַאי עָסְקִינַן; הֵיכִי דָּמֵי; מַה נַּפְשָׁךְ.

מַאי קְרָא(ה)   *What is its verse?* i.e., what Biblical verse is the source for this statement or tradition? (See *Berakhot* 3b.) See also מְנָא הָנֵי מִילֵּי; מְנָא לָן.

מַאי רְבוּתָא   *What is the novelty?* (Lit., "greatness," "remarkability.") I.e., what has the statement just cited come to teach us? Why did the scholar make it in that particular context? (See *Bava Metzia* 95b.)

מַאי שַׁיֵּיר דְּהַאי שַׁיֵּיר   *What [else] did he leave out that he left this out?* Sometimes the Talmud suggests that a list given in a Mishnah or a Baraita is incomplete (תָּנָא וְשַׁיֵּיר); however, the Gemara will not accept this suggestion unless it can be shown that at least two items were omitted from the list. Accordingly, if someone argues that a certain item was omitted from a Mishnah or a Baraita, and that the Tanna did not intend to specify all relevant cases, the Gemara will ask: "What other item did he [= the Tanna who compiled the list] omit that you can justifiably claim that he omitted this first item?" (See *Sukkah* 54a.) See also תָּנָא וְשַׁיֵּיר.

מַאי שְׁנָא   *What difference [is there]?* An expression used by the Gemara to express astonishment that, in two seemingly identical cases, a Mishnah or a Baraita lays down different laws. (See *Bava Metzia* 59b.) See also next entries, and אֶלָּא אֶחָד זֶה וְאֶחָד זֶה.

מַאי שְׁנָא דְּתָנָא... בְּרֵישָׁא, לִיתְנֵי... בְּרֵישָׁא   *What is the difference that [the Mishnah] taught X first, let it teach Y first.* The Gemara uses this expression when criticizing the logical order of the cases stated in the Mishnah. (See *Berakhot* 2a.)

מַאי שְׁנָא הָכָא דְּתָנֵי... וּמַאי שְׁנָא הָתָם דְּתָנֵי...   *What is the difference here that [the Mishnah] teaches X, and what is the difference there that [the Mishnah] teaches Y?* This question is asked by the Gemara when it finds two different expressions used in two different Mishnayot to describe the same thing. Surely the same terminology should have been used in both places! (See *Shabbat* 2b.)

מַאי שְׁנָא רֵישָׁא וּמַאי שְׁנָא סֵיפָא   *What is the difference between the first clause and the last clause?* Why does the law stated in the first clause of the Mishnah differ from the law stated in the last clause of the Mishnah, when the two cases appear to be similar? (See *Bava Metzia* 65b.)

מַאי שְׁנָא רֵישָׁא דְּלָא פְּלִיגִי וּמַאי שְׁנָא סֵיפָא דִּפְלִיגִי   *What is the difference between the first case, where they [the Rabbis] do not disagree, and the later case, where they do disagree?* This expression is used by the Gemara in analyzing a Mishnah where a difference of opinion is recorded regarding one case but not another, although the principles involved in both cases seem to be similar. (See *Yevamot* 38a.)

מַאי תַּלְמוּדָא   *What is the Biblical derivation?* (Lit., "learning.") I.e., how is the law or idea mentioned above derived from the verse cited as its source? (See *Shabbat* 149a.)
See also מַאי מַשְׁמַע.

מַאן דְּאָמַר   *The one who says,* i.e., the authority who maintains [the viewpoint cited]. (See *Bava Metzia* 14a.)

מַאן דְּהוּא   *Someone,* i.e., a sage whose remarks were reported anonymously, either because his identity was unknown or because for some reason the Rabbis wished to conceal it. (See *Betzah* 27a.)

מַאן דַּחֲזָא סָבַר: מִשּׁוּם..., וְלָא הִיא...   *The one who saw it thought: because of... but this is not so...,* i.e., the observer misunderstood what he saw, and the conduct of the Rabbi in question can [and should] be explained differently. This expression is used to clarify conclusions based on observation of a scholar's conduct, rather than on his explicit statement of what the law is. (See *Shabbat* 146b.)

מַאן דְּכַר שְׁמֵיהּ   *Who mentioned its name?* When an item is mentioned at the end of a Mishnah without its having been alluded to at the beginning, or when a subject or term mentioned in a Mishnah seems to be out of context, the Gemara may ask: "Who mentioned this item which is being cited now as if it had already been mentioned?" The reply to this question is often introduced by the expressions הָכִי קָאָמַר and חַסּוֹרֵי מְחַסְּרָא וְהָכִי קָתָנֵי. (See entries). (See *Pesaḥim* 8b.)

מַאן דְּתָנֵי... לָא מִשְׁתַּבֵּשׁ, וּמַאן דְּתָנֵי... לָא מִשְׁתַּבֵּשׁ   *He who teaches X is not wrong, and he who teaches Y is not wrong.* When the Gemara records a difference of opinion between Amoraim as to the correct reading of a passage in a Mishnah, the Amoraim usually defend their respective readings as being based on the context of the Mishnah or on some other commonsense argument. Sometimes, however, the Gemara accepts that both readings are in fact possible and reasonable, and uses this expression. (See *Sukkah* 50b.)

מַאן חֲכָמִים, ר' פְּלוֹנִי   *Who are the Sages? Rabbi X.* Sometimes, when a Tannaitic source ascribes a particular viewpoint to "the Sages" (חֲכָמִים), the Talmud may attempt to prove that this is in fact the view of an individual scholar, using this expression. (See *Bava Metzia* 60b.)

מַאן תַּנָּא   *Who is the Tanna?* i.e., who is the author of our anonymous Mishnah [or whose viewpoint is reflected in the Mishnah under discussion]? (See *Megillah* 19b.)

מַאן תָּנֵי לְהָא דְּתָנוּ רַבָּנַן   Lit., *who taught this which our Rabbis taught?* An expression used in introducing a quotation from a Baraita: "Which of the Tannaim cited as disagreeing in the previous Tannaitic passage is the author of the following Baraita?" (See *Shabbat* 18b.)
See also מַתְנִיתִין דְּלָא כְּ...; מַתְנִיתִין מַנִּי.

מְגַדֵּף בָּהּ ר' פְּלוֹנִי   *Rabbi X ridiculed it,* i.e., strongly disapproved of it. An expression used by the Gemara to introduce a strong objection and refutation of an argument previously mentioned. (See *Sanhedrin* 3b.)
See also מְחַכּוּ עֲלָהּ בְּמַעַרְבָא; מַתְקִיף לָהּ.

מַגִּיד שֶׁ...   *It teaches [lit., states] that....* A term used in Halakhic Midrashim to introduce an interpretation of a Biblical text. (See *Pesaḥim* 94b.)

מִדְּקָתָנֵי סֵיפָא... מִכְּלָל דְּרֵישָׁא...   *Since the last [clause] teaches... it may be inferred that the first [clause]....* Sometimes the Talmud interprets the first clause of a Mishnah as referring to a particular case. However, if the final clause of the Mishnah deals specifically with the same case, this interpretation is apt to be challenged, and the inference drawn that the first clause of the Mishnah refers in fact to a different case. In such instances, the Talmud may frame its inference in the following way: "Since the last clause specifically teaches about case A, it may be inferred that the first clause does not refer to case A." The answer frequently given to such an argument is תָּנָא סֵיפָא לְגַלּוּיֵי רֵישָׁא (see entry) — "He taught the final clause to shed light on the first clause," i.e., the final clause of the Mishnah explains the first clause, rather than introducing a new subject. (See *Bava Kamma* 98b.)

וּמָה אֲנִי מְקַיֵּים   *And how do I establish [i.e., explain]?* When a Halakhic Midrash explains a Biblical verse in a certain way, and there is another Biblical verse seemingly in conflict with the explanation offered or rendered superfluous by the explanation, the Midrash sometimes uses this expression to ask what this second verse was intended to teach us according to the explanation just offered. (See *Shabbat* 132a.)

מָה... אַף...   *Just as... so too....* This expression is used to introduce a parallel between two cases: "Just as the law is such-and-such in case A, so too is the law in case B." (See *Nedarim* 37a.)

מָה הֵן קָתָנֵי   Lit., *it teaches [in the style of] "what are they."* Sometimes the Talmud explains that the second part of a passage (e.g., in a Mishnah) was not intended to convey anything new, but rather to explain what the first part of the passage was referring to: "It [= the second part of the passage] teaches the terms of reference of the first part of the passage." (See *Sanhedrin* 2b.)

מָה הֶפְרֵשׁ בֵּין...   *What is the difference between [two similar cases in which different laws apply]?* This expression introduces an explanation of the fundamental difference between two apparently similar cases. (See *Ta'anit* 17b.)

מַה הַצַּד   *The common factor.* This expression describes a method of argumentation in Tannaitic Halakhic exegesis where a third law is derived from two other laws. This method is used when it would not be possible to derive the third law from either of the other laws alone, because of an unusual stringency which applies uniquely to each of the other laws. Since the stringency is not identical in the two laws, it is possible to put aside the unique feature in each of them and to use the "common factor" they share in order to arrive at the third law. See article בְּנְיַן אָב in the section on Talmudic hermeneutics. (See *Bava Metzia* 87b.) See also לֹא רְאִי זֶה כִּרְאִי זֶה.

מָה הָתָם... הָכָא נָמִי *Just as there... so here too.* When the Gemara draws an analogy between a case under discussion and another one and seeks to apply the principle found in the second case to the one under discussion, it often uses this phrase. (See *Sanhedrin* 66b.)

מַה טַעַם קָאָמַר *He is saying: "What is the reason?"* Sometimes the Talmud explains that the latter part of a Mishnah or a Baraita offers the reason for the previous statement, rather than introducing a new case. In such instances, the Talmud interprets the Mishnah or Baraita as if it said: "[Statement A.] What is the reason? — Statement B!" This interpretation is introduced by the expression: "He [= the Tanna who is the author of the latter part of the Mishnah or Baraita] is giving the reason for the law cited in the previous sentence." (See *Berakhot* 52b.)

מַה נַּפְשָׁךְ *In either case, no matter what....* (Lit., "whatever your desire.") The Gemara uses this expression to introduce an objection in a situation where two irreconcilable alternatives exist. The objection is meant to show that both alternatives cannot be accepted, and that it is necessary to choose one of them. (See *Shabbat* 46a.) See also מִמַּה נַפְשָׁךְ; אִם נַפְשָׁךְ לוֹמַר(וְ).

מָה רָאִיתָ *What did you see?* i.e., why did you prefer a particular possibility or interpretation to another, apparently equally plausible, interpretation? (See *Yevamot* 59a.) See also מַאי חָזֵית.

(אֶלָּא) מֵהָא לֵיכָא לְמִשְׁמַע מִינָּהּ *From this it is impossible to learn [anything].* The Talmud may reach this conclusion after it has been shown that the inferences which can be drawn from two clauses of the same Mishnah or Baraita are mutually contradictory. (See *Bava Metzia* 26b.) See also דִּיּוּק.

מַהוּ *Lit., how is it?* In the formulation of a בָּעְיָא (see entry), immediately after the Gemara has set out the essence of the problem to be solved, it often proceeds to ask מַהוּ — "How is the problem to be solved?" The possibilities are analyzed and the answer follows. (See *Shabbat* 3a.)

מַהוּ דְּתֵימָא... קָא מַשְׁמַע לַן *Lit., lest you say... he tells us.* This expression frequently follows the expression פְּשִׁיטָא (see entry). Often the Talmud explains that a seemingly superfluous statement was made to prevent us from reaching an erroneous conclusion. In such cases, the Talmud states: "You might erroneously have said X. Therefore the author of the seemingly superfluous statement teaches us that the law is in fact otherwise." (See *Sukkah* 31b.)

מֵהֵיכָא תֵּיתֵי *From where could you derive [lit. bring] it?* i.e., on what basis could you arrive at the assumption mentioned [or alluded to] previously? Occasionally the Gemara refutes an erroneous conclusion by quoting a Biblical verse and showing that it emphasizes a particular point in order to

forestall that error. Then it sometimes continues by asking how the erroneous conclusion could have been reached in the first place: "How could you have made such a false assumption?" (See *Yevamot* 17b.)

מוּחְלֶפֶת הַשִּׁיטָה *Lit., the view is reversed.* Sometimes a contradiction is found between two scholars' opposed opinions as recorded in one source and their opinions as recorded elsewhere. In such cases the Talmud may propose that the names in one of the sources be reversed. This suggestion is normally introduced by the expression: "The views of the scholars cited should be reversed." (See *Betzah* 3a.) See also אִיפּוּךְ; לָא תֵּיפוּךְ.

מוֹקִים לָהּ... *He establishes it....* This expression introduces the answer to an objection that a certain verse in the Torah, or a ruling in a Mishnah or a Baraita, is superfluous. The answer is that "the text is in fact used in order to establish a different ruling on another subject." (See *Sanhedrin* 3b.)

מְחַוַּורְתָּא כִּדְשַׁנֵּינַן מֵעִיקָּרָא *It is clear as we answered in the beginning.* When two answers are suggested to a question, the Talmud sometimes rejects the second and reverts to the first. (See *Bava Metzia* 3a.)

מְחַכּוּ עֲלָהּ בְּמַעַרְבָא *They laughed at it in the West,* i.e., the scholars of Eretz Israel made fun of, disparaged, a certain viewpoint. (See *Sanhedrin* 17b.)

מַחֲלוֹקֶת בְּ... אֲבָל בְּ... דִּבְרֵי הַכֹּל... *The disagreement is in [the case of X], but in [the case of Y] all agree that....* This formula is used by the Gemara to limit a Tannaitic controversy to a particular case (or group of cases). At first sight the disagreement between the Tannaim seems to be extreme. The Amoraim, however, explain that the disagreement is much more narrow. (See *Betzah* 9a.) See also עַד כָּאן לָא פְּלִיגִי אֶלָּא...; אֲבָל כּוּלֵּי עָלְמָא לָא פְּלִיגִי.

מַחֲלָפָה שִׁיטָתֵיהּ דְּר׳ פְּלוֹנִי *The view of Rabbi X is the reverse!* An expression used in the Jerusalem Talmud to introduce a contradiction between two statements by the same scholar.

מָטוּ בָהּ *They reached up to....* When a statement is reported as having been handed down orally from one scholar to another, the list of scholars may close with the remark: "They reached up to an even earlier scholar as the source of this statement and reported it in his name." (See *Rosh HaShanah* 10a.)

מַטִּין *They incline.* An expression used by the Gemara to indicate that a particular scholar's decision, or a general principle with regard to deciding disputed cases, does not have the full force of a Halakhah, and is not universally accepted, but that an individual judge may decide on the basis of it: "The scholars called upon to render a Halakhic decision in this case incline to rule in a certain way." (See *Eruvin* 46b.) See also נִרְאִין; הֲלָכָה.

מִי אִיכָּא מִידֵּי *Is there anything...?* An expression used to introduce an objection to a Halakhic ruling on the grounds that it is fundamentally illogical, without precedent, or contrary to accepted Halakhic principles: "Is there any case in which the principle you maintain applies? Is there a precedent for this ruling?" (See *Yoma* 2b.)

מִי אַלִּימָא מִמַּתְנִיתִין   *Is it stronger than our Mishnah?* When the Gemara raises an objection to a Baraita, and a similar objection has already been raised and resolved in connection with the Mishnah, the Gemara may answer the new question by saying: "Is the Baraita stronger than our Mishnah?" In fact the objection to the Baraita can be resolved in the same way that the problem with the Mishnah was solved! (See *Shabbat* 12a.)

מִי אָמַר ר' פְּלוֹנִי הָכִי, וְהָא אֲמַר...   *But did Rabbi X say this, surely he said...?* In its analysis of an Amoraic ruling (מֵימְרָא, see entry), the Gemara often questions the authenticity of the ruling by showing that its author elsewhere expressed an opinion that runs counter to the one expressed here. The Gemara then attempts to show that the two seemingly contradictory Amoraic rulings can in fact be reconciled or explained. (See *Yevamot* 42b.)

מִי אָמְרִינַן... אוֹ דִילְמָא...   *Do we say... or perhaps....* In its analysis of a problem, בָּעְיָא (see entry), the Gemara usually sets out the two sides of the problem before proceeding to its solution: "Do we say that X is the case, or do we perhaps hold that Y is the case?" (See *Shabbat* 99b.)
See also אִיבַּעְיָא לְהוּ; בָּעֵי; מַהוּ.

מִי דָּמֵי   *Is it comparable?* i.e., can the two cases be compared, when they are in fact different? Usually, having laid down the basis for rejecting a suggested analogy, the Talmud continues by explaining the difference between the two cases: הָתָם... הָכָא... — "There [in the first case], the situation is as follows, while here [in the second case], the situation is different...." (See *Shabbat* 6a.)
See also הָכִי הַשְׁתָּא.

מִי לָא עָסְקִינַן   *Are we not dealing with...?* An expression used as part of an objection or proof: "In the instance under discussion, are we not dealing with a certain particular case, and even so the law which applies is...?" (See *Berakhot* 11a.)

מִי לָא תְּנַן (תַּנְיָא)   *Have we not learnt in a Mishnah (in a Baraita)?* An expression used to introduce a proof or supporting statement (usually by analogy) from a Mishnah (or from a Baraita). (See *Pesaḥim* 9a.)

מִי לֵימָא   *Shall we say that...?* An expression used to introduce a suggestion which will be rejected later: "Shall we say that the following interpretation holds?" (See לֵימָא.) For example, מִי לֵימָא תַּנָּאֵי הִיא — "Shall we say that this Amoraic controversy parallels a Tannaitic dispute?" (See *Eruvin* 4a.)
See also לֵימָא כְּתַנָּאֵי.

(וּ)מִי מָצֵית אָמְרַתְּ   *Can you say that...?* i.e., how can you make the suggestion you just made, when it is in fact totally unacceptable? (See *Shabbat* 103b.)

מִי סָבְרַתְּ   *Do you think that...?* An expression used by the

Gemara to introduce the refutation of an argument based on a mistaken interpretation of an authoritative text: "Do you really think that such-and-such is the correct interpretation of the text you are quoting, when in fact it is not, because...?" (See *Bava Metzia* 32b.) See also (וְ)תִסְבְּרָא.

וּמִי עֲדִיפָא מִמַּתְנִיתִין   *And is it better than our Mishnah?* (See *Yoma* 80a.) See also מִי אַלִּימָא מִמַּתְנִיתִין.

מִיבַּעְיָא   *Is it necessary?* An expression used when the Talmud objects to a statement which seems superfluous. For a more detailed treatment of the use of this expression, see הַשְׁתָּא...., לָא מִיבַּעְיָא קָאָמַר, and also מִיבַּעְיָא...., וְאֵין צָרִיךְ לוֹמַר זוֹ; זוֹ.

(וְהָא) מִיבַּעְיָא בָּעֵי (לֵיהּ)   *But surely he (already) asked this!* How can the ruling on a certain issue be clear to Rabbi X, when he himself raised a question regarding that very issue, showing he was in doubt as to how to solve the problem. (See *Shabbat* 4b.)

מִידֵי אִירְיָא? הָא כִּדְאִיתָא, וְהָא כִּדְאִיתָא   *Is this an argument? This [case] as it is, and this [case] as it is!* This expression is used when the Talmud rejects a proposed analogy between two cases occurring together in the same passage of a Mishnah: "Is this an argument [i.e., is the comparison between the two cases valid]? This case as it is, and this case as it is [i.e., the particulars of case A do not apply in case B, even though both cases are mentioned together in the same source]!" (See *Bava Metzia* 14b.) See also הָכִי הַשְׁתָּא; מִי דָּמֵי.

מִידֵי גַּבֵּי הֲדָדֵי תַּנְיָא   *Were they taught next to each other?* Sometimes Baraitot seem to deal with similar subjects but are worded differently. The Gemara infers from these differences in phraseology that the Baraitot disagree (or that some other distinction must be drawn between them). However, the Gemara often rejects this inference by asking: "Were they [= the two Baraitot] taught next to each other?" Perhaps the different wording does not indicate substantive disagreement, but rather shows that the Baraitot derive from different compilations, such as those of Rabbi Ḥiyya, Rabbi Oshaya, etc. (See *Shabbat* 18a.)

מִידֵי דַהֲוָה אַ...   *Just as in....* A term used to introduce an argument from analogy: "The principle cited applies here, just as it would in an analogous case." (See *Shabbat* 6a.)
See also הָא לָא דָּמְיָא אֶלָּא לְהָא; דּוּמְיָא דְּ...; כִּדְאַשְׁכְּחַן.

מִידַּת הַדִּין   (1) In the Babylonian Talmud it means *justice, strict logic.* It usually appears as part of a question: "According to justice or strict logic the case should be decided otherwise..." (2) In Aggadic Midrashim it means *heavenly harsh justice.* (3) In the Jerusalem Talmud it means *with regard to monetary matters,* i.e., "this law is limited to monetary matters [דִּינֵי מָמוֹנוֹת] and does not apply to capital cases [דִּינֵי נְפָשׁוֹת] or to ritual matters [דִּינֵי אִיסּוּר וְהֶיתֵּר]."

מַיְיתֵי לָהּ מֵהָכָא   *He adduces it from here.* When one scholar cites a Biblical verse as the source for a law or an idea, and then another scholar cites a different verse as a proof-text for the same idea, the Talmud may remark: "The second scholar adduces this idea from here [i.e., from the verse about to be cited]." (See Ḥagigah 9a.)

מִילְתָא אַגַּב אוֹרְחֵיהּ קָא מַשְׁמַע לַן... *He teaches us something incidentally.* Sometimes the Gemara raises an objection to a certain form of expression used in a Mishnah or a Baraita, claiming that the text could have used a different, clearer, expression. (See entries מַאי אִירְיָא דְּתָנֵי...; לָמָה לֵיהּ לְמִיתְנֵי...) The reply to such an objection may begin as follows: "The Tanna chose to use that particular expression in the Mishnah or the Baraita in order to teach us something else incidentally, namely that...." (See Berakhot 2a.)

See also אַגַּב אוֹרְחָא קָא מַשְׁמַע לַן.

מִילְתֵיהּ אָמְרָה *His statement implies that....* An expression in the Jerusalem Talmud: "The following law can be inferred from the remarks of the scholar cited."

מִילְתֵיהּ דְּר׳ פְּלוֹנִי פְּלִיגָא *The statement of Rabbi X disagrees with what has just been stated.* An expression in the Jerusalem Talmud, used to introduce a different opinion about the subject under discussion.

מֵימְרָא *An Amoraic [as distinct from Tannaitic] statement.* (See Gittin 42b.)

מֵיתִיבֵי (or מֵתִיבֵי) *They object,* i.e., anonymous scholars of the Talmud object to the remarks of an Amora mentioned by name on the grounds that his remarks are in conflict with a Tannaitic statement. The basis for all objections of this kind is the accepted principle that an Amora cannot disagree with a ruling laid down in a Mishnah or a Baraita. (See Berakhot 10b.)

See also אֵיתִיבֵיהּ; מֵתִיב; תְּיוּבְתָא.

מִכָּאן אָמְרוּ *From here they stated.* An expression used in Halakhic Midrashim (and sometimes in the Aggadah) to introduce a Mishnah or other Halakhah based on a Biblical verse: "From here [= the verse mentioned] the Sages stated [= derived] the following law." (See Bava Metzia 56b.)

מִכָּאן סָמְכוּ חֲכָמִים *From here the Sages based....* An expression used to introduce the citation of a Rabbinic statement based to some extent on, or alluded to in, a Biblical verse. (See Ketubot 10a.)

מִכְּדִי *Now since....* An expression used by the Gemara to introduce a Halakhic conclusion indirectly derived from the sources. The Rabbi offering the conclusion must first point out a difficulty in the source. Then he shows how, as a result of this difficulty, he reaches his conclusion. (See Megillah 19a.) See also אַתָּה אוֹמֵר... אוֹ אֵינוֹ אֶלָּא...; כְּשֶׁהוּא אוֹמֵר...; מָה אֲנִי מְקַיֵּים.

מִכְּלָל דְּ... *[This proves] by implication that....* When the Gemara brings an argument for a Halakhic ruling based on an authoritative source (either a Biblical text, a Tannaitic statement, an accepted tradition, or an established legal principle), it often introduces the inference with this expression. (See Ḥullin 37b.) See also אַלְמָא; שְׁמַע מִינָה.

מִכְּלָלָא אִיתְּמַר *It was stated by inference.* The Talmud may use this expression when a statement quoted by the Gemara and attributed to a particular Rabbi was not in fact explicitly made by the Rabbi to whom it is attributed, but was deduced from other statements made by this scholar (or inferred from his conduct). (See Shabbat 29a.)

See אִי מִכְּלָלָא מַאי; חֲדָא מִכְּלָל חֲבֶירְתָּהּ אִיתְּמַר; לָאו בְּפֵירוּשׁ אִיתְּמַר.

מְלַמֵּד שֶׁ... *It teaches that....* A term used in Midrashim to introduce an interpretation of a Biblical text. (See Bava Metzia 39b.)

מִמַּאי... וְדִילְמָא... לָא סָלְקָא דַּעְתָּךְ... *From where... but perhaps... you cannot possibly think so, because....* The Gemara sometimes uses this expression when probing an assumption on which an argument has been based. It often proceeds to suggest an alternative assumption, using וְדִילְמָא (see entry). This alternative is then rejected, using the phrase לָא סָלְקָא דַּעְתָּךְ — "Why [מִמַּאי] do you make assumption X, is it not possible [וְדִילְמָא] that assumption Y is correct? — No, you cannot possibly think so [לָא סָלְקָא דַּעְתָּךְ; see entry]," and the reason for the rejection is given. (See Megillah 18a.)

מִמַּה נַּפְשָׁךְ *In either case, no matter what...* (lit., "from whatever is your desire"). An expression used by the Gemara to indicate an unacceptable dilemma: "No matter which side you take or possibility you favor, the same unacceptable conclusion follows." (See Yevamot 59b.) See also מַה נַּפְשָׁךְ.

וּמִמָּקוֹם שֶׁבָּאתָ Lit., *and from where you came.* An expression used in Halakhic Midrashim, meaning that, from the source cited as the basis for your previous ruling, it is also possible to derive another law (as set forth in the next part of the discussion). (See Gittin 24a.)

מִמַּשְׁמַע שֶׁנֶּאֱמַר... אֵינִי יוֹדֵעַ... אֶלָּא מַה תַּלְמוּד לוֹמַר... *By [logical] deduction from the text... do I not know...? What then does the verse teach?* This expression is part of Midrashic terminology. The author of the teaching begins with a quotation from a Biblical text and questions it (often on the grounds that part of the text is superfluous). He then explains and interprets the text, showing the meaning of the apparently superfluous feature: "From the fact that the text says X, is it not obvious that Y is the case? Why, then, did the text say Y? In order to teach us...." (See Shabbat 22a.)

מִן אוּלְפַּן *From tradition.* An expression in the Jerusalem Talmud: The statement made by a certain Rabbi is "based on a tradition" transmitted from teacher to student, rather than on the Rabbi's own reasoning. See גְּמִירִי; מִן דֵּעָה.

מִן דֵּעָה *From reasoning.* An expression in the Jerusalem Talmud: The statement made by a certain Rabbi is "based on his own reasoning," rather than on a tradition transmitted from teacher to student. See מִן אוּלְפַּן.

מְנָא אָמִינָא לַהּ *From where do I say it?* The Amoraim often use this expression when citing a source from the Bible or early Halakhah for their own statements. (See Shabbat 11b.)

מְנָא הָא מִילְתָא דַּאֲמוּר רַבָּנַן *From where is this matter which the Rabbis said?* What is the source in the Bible or in early Halakhah of the Rabbinic statement cited here? (See *Ḥullin* 10b.)

מְנָא הָנֵי מִילֵי (often abbreviated: מנה״מ). *From where are these things [derived]?* i.e., what verse in the Torah is the source of the statement just made? This question by the Gemara is usually followed either by a specific Biblical text or by a Midrashic interpretation of Biblical verses from which the Halakhic ruling is derived. (See *Berakhot* 30b.) See also next entry.

מְנָא לַן (or מְנָלָן; often abbreviated: מנ״ל) *From where do we [know this]?* i.e., what is the source of the statement just made? Usually the source introduced by this expression in the Gemara is a Biblical verse. (See *Rosh HaShanah* 7a.)
See also מְנָא הָנֵי מִילֵי.

מְנָא תֵּימְרָא *From where do you say it?* i.e., on what basis do you maintain what you are saying? What is the source of this Halakhah? The expression מְנָא תֵּימְרָא is the equivalent of the expression מְנָא הָנֵי מִילֵי (see entry), except that the question מְנָא הָנֵי מִילֵי is asked when the Gemara wants to find the Biblical source for a Tannaitic Halakhic statement, whereas the question מְנָא תֵּימְרָא is asked when the Gemara wants to find a Tannaitic source for an Amoraic Halakhic statement. (See *Bava Metzia* 11a.)

מַנוּ, מַנִּי *Who is it, who is he?* A term used when the Talmud inquires about the identity of the author of a Tannaitic source, as in the expression מַנִּי מַתְנִיתִין — "Who is the author of our Mishnah?" The purpose of this inquiry is usually to find out whether the opinion expressed anonymously in a Mishnah corresponds with the known views of a Tanna in a Baraita. (See *Rosh HaShanah* 16a.)

מִנַּיִן לִיתֵּן אֶת הָאָמוּר לְהַלָּן כָּאן וְאֶת הָאָמוּר כָּאן לְהַלָּן *From where [may we infer that] what is stated below applies here, and that what is stated here [applies] below?* An expression used in Halakhic Midrashim. Sometimes the Talmud compares two cases, each of which is derived from a different verse, and seeks to prove that a law specified in connection with the first case must apply in the second case as well (and vice versa). In such instances the Talmud may use this expression, though the idea may also be phrased מִנַּיִן לִיתֵּן אֶת הָאָמוּר שֶׁל זֶה בָּזֶה וְשֶׁל זֶה בָּזֶה — "From where [may we infer] that what applies in this case applies in that case, and that what applies in that case applies in this case?" (See *Rosh HaShanah* 34a.)

מְסַיִּיעָא לֵיהּ לְ... *It supports [the opinion of] Rabbi X.* When the Gemara wishes to explore the possibility that the Mishnah it is analyzing offers support for the view of a scholar mentioned elsewhere, it often asks נֵימָא מְסַיִּיעָא לֵיהּ... — "May we say that the following expression in our Mishnah supports the opinion of Rabbi X?" (See *Sanhedrin* 71b.) Another phrase of this kind sometimes encountered is מְסַיִּיעָא לֵיהּ לְר׳ פְּלוֹנִי וּתְיוּבְתָּא לְר׳ אַלְמוֹנִי — "Our Mishnah supports the opinion of Rabbi X and refutes the opinion of Rabbi Y." (See *Yevamot* 53a.)

מְסַפְּקָא לֵיהּ *He was in doubt.* Sometimes the Gemara records that an individual Rabbi adopted a practice more stringent than would seem to have been necessary. It explains that he acted in this way because "he was in doubt," i.e., he either lacked the full information on which to base a decision or was in doubt as to the law. The more stringent practice he adopted could be either for himself alone or recommended for others also. (See *Bava Metzia* 18b.)
See also הַשְׁתָּא דְּלָא אִתְּמַר הִילְכְתָא לָא כְ... וְלָא כְ...

מִסְתַּבְּרָא *It is reasonable, it stands to reason.* The Gemara uses this expression to introduce an argument based on common sense. Such an argument is not always accepted ultimately by the Gemara as conclusive. See, however, הָכִי נַמִי מִסְתַּבְּרָא. (See *Shabbat* 25a.)

מֵעִיקָּרָא *From the beginning, at the outset,* i.e., at the beginning of the Talmudic discussion, as in the following expression מֵעִיקָּרָא סָבַר... וּלְבַסּוֹף סָבַר... — "At the outset he thought that X, but in the end he thought that Y." (See *Moed Katan* 16b.) See also next entry.

מֵעִיקָּרָא מַאי סָבַר וּלְבַסּוֹף מַאי סָבַר *In the beginning what did he think, and in the end what did he think?* In cases where a scholar changes his mind, the Talmud may ask what the Rabbi's reasoning was initially, and why he later changed his opinion. (See *Moed Katan* 16b.) See also previous entry.

מַעַרְבָא *The West.* In the Babylonian Talmud, Eretz Israel is called "the West," since it is southwest of Babylonia. Frequently found in the expression בְּמַעַרְבָא אָמְרִי — "In the West they say."

מַעֲשֶׂה לִסְתּוֹר *A story to contradict [what was just stated]?!* Usually, when the Mishnah relates a specific incident (מַעֲשֶׂה) where a celebrated scholar decided the law in a particular way, its purpose is to support a ruling previously laid down in the Mishnah. Sometimes, however, incidents are related in the Mishnah which seem to contradict previous Halakhic rulings. In such cases the Talmud often objects: "Was the story related here in order to contradict the previous statement?!" The answer sometimes given to this question is that something is missing in the text of the Mishnah, and the text in fact reads differently. (See *Bava Metzia* 102b.)
See also חַסּוֹרֵי מְחַסְּרָא וְהָכִי קָתָנֵי.

מַעֲשֶׂה רַב *An act is great,* i.e., actual practice is of critical significance. If a certain Halakhic viewpoint is known to have been followed in actual practice, this sets a legal precedent, as we may assume that a Halakhic opinion was only followed if it had been accepted as binding. (See *Bava Batra* 130b.)

מַעֲשֶׂה שֶׁהָיָה כָּךְ הָיָה *The event which happened, happened that way.* Sometimes, when a case is cited as a legal precedent, the Gemara attempts to draw inferences from the details mentioned in the description of the case. The Gemara may subsequently reject this line of reasoning, on the grounds that these details were not cited in order to provide us with legal inferences, and were no more than an accurate description of what happened. (See *Pesaḥim* 82b.)

מֵעַתָּה *From now.* See אֶלָּא מֵעַתָּה.

מִפְּנֵי הַדִּין *Because of the logical inference.* Sometimes the Talmud explains that a certain expression was used in the Torah in order to prevent us from arriving at an erroneous conclusion which we might otherwise have reached on the basis of "logical inference," e.g., by *a fortiori* (קַל וָחוֹמֶר) or *gezerah shavah* (גְּזֵירָה שָׁוָה) argumentation; see entries in section on hermeneutics. (See *Sanhedrin* 4b.)

מִפְּנֵי שֶׁ... *Because....* An expression used by the Gemara to introduce an argument based on common sense (סְבָרָא). (See *Berakhot* 23b.) See also דְּהָא...; הוֹאִיל וְ...; כֵּיוָן דְּ...; לְפִי...; מִשּׁוּם דְּ....

מְצִיעְתָא *The middle clause* of a Mishnah or other statement, the middle Mishnah in a series. (See *Shabbat* 54a.) See also סֵיפָא; רֵישָׁא.

מָר *Sir, Master.* (1) A title of respect used when a student refers to his teacher, and when one scholar addresses another; also when addressing a stranger. (2) *The scholar* (or one of the scholars) mentioned in the previous discussion; see אָמַר מָר. (3) *An official title* conferred on scholars who did not hold the title "Rav" (e.g., Mar Shmuel). Often such scholars were associated with the House of the Exilarch (e.g. Mar Ukva, who was himself the Exilarch). Sometimes the title "Mar" appears after the scholar's name (e.g., מָרִי מָר, "Mari Mar"). (4) *A title* sometimes given by the scholars to their outstanding teacher. (5) *The first name* (or title that superseded the first name) of some of the Talmudic Rabbis, e.g., Mar, the son of Rav Ashi, Mar Kashisha, the son of Rav Ḥisda.

מָר אָמַר חֲדָא וּמָר אָמַר חֲדָא וְלָא פְּלִיגִי *One scholar said one, and the other scholar said another, and they do not disagree.* Sometimes, when seemingly contradictory statements are made by two scholars, the Talmud explains that there was in fact no dispute between them, since each scholar was discussing a different case. (See *Bava Metzia* 11a.)

מְשַׁבַּשְׁתָּא הִיא *It is [textually] faulty.* Sometimes the Gemara responds to an objection based on a Baraita by showing that the text of the Baraita is faulty and therefore unreliable. (See *Shabbat* 121b.)

מִשּׁוּם דְּ... *Because....* An expression used by the Gemara to introduce an argument based on common sense (סְבָרָא). (See *Bava Metzia* 2b.) See also דְּהָא...; הוֹאִיל וְ...; כֵּיוָן דְּ...; לְפִי...; מִפְּנֵי שֶׁ....

מִשּׁוּם ר׳ פְּלוֹנִי *In the name of Rabbi X.* When one scholar cites a tradition attributed to an earlier scholar which he did not hear personally from that scholar, the Talmud uses the terminology אָמַר ר׳ פְּלוֹנִי מִשּׁוּם ר׳ אַלְמוֹנִי — "Rabbi X said in the name of Rabbi Y." In these cases, there is often a gap of several generations between the scholar being quoted and the scholar quoting him. (See *Berakhot* 7a.) See also אָמַר ר׳ פְּלוֹנִי אָמַר ר׳ אַלְמוֹנִי.

מַשְׁכַּחַת לָה בְּ... *You will find it in [the following case]....*

Sometimes the Gemara lays down a legal principle which seems to have no practical application. The Gemara may then discover a case in which this law applies, introducing the case with the expression: "The legal principle mentioned above applies in the following case...." (See *Bava Metzia* 98a.) See also הֵיכִי מַשְׁכַּחַת לָה.

מִשְּׁמֵיה דְּרַב פְּלוֹנִי *In the name of Rabbi X.* See מִשּׁוּם ר׳ פְּלוֹנִי.

מִשְּׁמֵיה דִּגְמָרָא *In the name of a tradition.* Amoraim sometimes transmit a Halakhic ruling "as an accepted viewpoint, based on tradition," rather than in the name of an individual earlier scholar. (See *Yoma* 33a.) See also גְּמִירִי; נָקְטִינַן.

מַשְׁמָעוּת דּוֹרְשִׁין אִיכָּא בֵּינַיְיהוּ *They disagree about the source from which they derive their interpretations,* i.e., the scholars cited in the passage just mentioned disagree about the source of the law under discussion (in other words, from which verse or word it is derived), but not about the law itself. The choice of source may, nevertheless, according to some commentators, have indirect ramifications regarding other Halakhic issues. (See *Bava Metzia* 27a.)

מְשַׁנֵּי *Answers, resolves [an objection].* See שִׁינּוּיָא.

מִשְׁתָּעֵי *Relates.* This expression usually appears in the form ר׳ פְּלוֹנִי מִשְׁתָּעֵי — "Rabbi X related the following incident...." (See *Ketubot* 27b.) In many cases, the incident related has no direct Halakhic significance.

מְתִיב *Objects* (= raises an objection). See תְּיוּבְתָּא.

מְתִיב ר׳ פְּלוֹנִי לְסַיּוּעֵיה לְר׳ אַלְמוֹנִי *Rabbi A objected [to Rabbi B] in support of Rabbi C.* See תְּיוּבְתָּא.

מַתְלָא אָמַר *The parable states....* An expression used, particularly in Aggadic Midrashim, to introduce a homely parable, sometimes as a means of explaining a more lofty concept.

מַתְנֵי *He teaches.* In other words: (1) He cites Tannaitic sources (see *Shabbat* 129a). (2) He teaches Mishnah, especially to young people (see *Bava Metzia* 44a). (3) He presents a certain version of a tradition, as in בְּסוּרָא מַתְנֵי הָכִי — "In Sura they transmitted the tradition thus...." (See *Sanhedrin* 24b.)

מַתְנֵי לָה אַהָא *He teaches it concerning this.* An expression used to identify the subject or statement to which a Baraita refers, often in contradiction to a previously stated view: "The scholar cited teaches the Baraita with reference to the following statement... and not with reference to the statement previously mentioned." (See *Berakhot* 8b.)

מַתְנֵי לָה בְּהֶדְיָא *He teaches it explicitly.* Sometimes the Gemara cites an unclear statement, which is subsequently emended or interpreted. Then a Rabbi cites an alternative version of this source, which already includes the proposed emendation or interpretation. In such cases the Gemara states: "This scholar teaches a problem-free version of the statement explicitly." (See *Shabbat* 4a.)

מַתְנִיתָא Lit., *Mishnah.* It is to be noted, however, that this expression is generally used to refer to Baraitot ("external Mishnayot"), whereas the Mishnah of Rabbi Yehudah HaNasi is termed מַתְנִיתִין — *"our* Mishnah." (See *Berakhot* 46b.)

מַתְנִיתָא מְסַיְּיעָא לר׳ פְּלוֹנִי *The [external] Mishnah supports Rabbi X,* i.e., the Baraita cited supports the opinion of Rabbi X. (See *Bava Metzia* 48a.)

מַתְנִיתָא פְּלִיגָא עַל ר׳ פְּלוֹנִי *The Baraita disagrees with Rabbi X.* An expression in the Jerusalem Talmud, indicating that a statement made earlier by an Amora or in a Baraita is contradicted by the following Tannaitic source.

מַתְנִיתִין *Our Mishnah.* (1) In general terms, the Mishnah of Rabbi Yehudah HaNasi. (2) Specifically, the Mishnah the Talmud is now discussing (see *Yevamot* 83a).

מַתְנִיתִין ב... Lit., *our Mishnah is in....* An expression used to qualify what is stated in the Mishnah: "The Mishnah refers only to the case specified below." This term is often used to introduce the solution to a problem, in which the application of a Mishnah is limited to one particular case. (See *Pesaḥim* 15a.) See also אוֹקִימְתָּא.

מַתְנִיתִין דְּלָא כִּי הַאי תַּנָּא *Our Mishnah is not like this Tanna.* In editing the Mishnah, Rabbi Yehudah HaNasi often recorded only the majority viewpoint, omitting dissenting opinions. The Talmud, however, sometimes cites the dissenting opinion, using this expression: "Our Mishnah is not in accordance with the following Tanna, who stated...." (See *Yoma* 39a.) See also next entry and הָא מַנִי.

מַתְנִיתִין דְּלָא כר׳ פְּלוֹנִי *Our Mishnah is not like Rabbi X.* After the Talmud has noted this, it then specifies Rabbi X's opinion. (See *Sanhedrin* 34b.) See also previous entry.

מַתְנִיתִין מַנִּי *Who[se] is our Mishnah?* Which Tanna's view does the Mishnah follow? Often the answer to this question is ר׳ פְּלוֹנִי הִיא — "It is Rabbi X," i.e., the Mishnah follows the view of Rabbi X. (See *Yoma* 59a.)

מַתְנִיתִין נַמִי דַּיְקָא *Our Mishnah is also precise.* Sometimes careful reexamination of the wording of the Mishnah reveals that it can be explained as agreeing with the view of an Amora cited earlier. (See *Shabbat* 2b.)

מַתְנִיתִין (מַתְנִיתָא) ר׳ פְּלוֹנִי הִיא *Our Mishnah (the Baraita) is Rabbi X's,* i.e., the Mishnah or the Baraita reflects the viewpoint of Rabbi X. (See *Yoma* 3b.)

מַתְקִיף לָה *He strongly objects to it.* This term is used when an Amora objects to a statement of another Amora on logical grounds rather than on the authority of a literary source (e.g., a Mishnah or a Baraita). (See *Ketubot* 59a/b.) On rare occasions the expression מַתְקִיף לָה is used to indicate an Amora's difficulty with a ruling found in a Mishnah or a Baraita. (See *Bava Metzia* 33b.) See also אַתְקַפְתָּא.

נֶאֱמַר כָּאן... וְנֶאֱמַר לְהַלָּן..., מַה לְהַלָּן... אַף כָּאן... *It states here... and it states below... just as what is stated below... so too what is stated here....* An expression used to introduce a גְּזֵירָה שָׁוָה (see entry in section on hermeneutics).

נִזְרְקָה מִפִּי חֲבוּרָה Lit., *it was thrown out from the group,* i.e., a suggestion was made or an idea was developed by a group of scholars, or by one of the members of this group whose identity was not specified. (See *Shabbat* 3a.)

נֶחֱזֵי אֲנַן *Let us ourselves see.* When the scholars of the Talmud propose to clarify an issue on the basis of their own, independent, reasoning, they may use this expression. (See *Bava Metzia* 8b.)

נִיחָא... *It is right....* An expression in the Jerusalem Talmud like בִּשְׁלָמָא (see entry) in the Babylonian Talmud.

נֵימָא *Shall we say that...?* An expression used to introduce a suggestion which is rejected later on. See לֵימָא.

נֵימָא תֶּהֱוֵי תְּיוּבְתֵּיהּ דְר׳ פְּלוֹנִי *Shall we say that this [Mishnah] is a refutation of Rabbi X?* See לֵימָא תֶּהֱוֵי תְּיוּבְתָּא דְ....

נָסֵיב לָה אַלִּיבָּא דְתַנָּאֵי *He takes it according to [different] Tannaim.* Sometimes the Talmud resolves an internal contradiction in a Mishnah by arguing that the Mishnah's author accepted one Tanna's view regarding the first case discussed in the Mishnah and another Tanna's view regarding the second case. (See *Rosh HaShanah* 7b.)

נָפַק מִילְתָא מִבֵּינַיְיהוּ Lit., *a matter went out from among them,* i.e., a statement was made or a question was asked by a group of scholars, or by a member of that group whose identity was not specified. (See *Moed Katan* 20a.)

נָפְקָא לֵיהּ *He derives* (lit., "it is derived for him"), i.e., he derives the law under discussion from the following Biblical verse.... (See *Berakhot* 13a.)

נָפְקָא מִינָּה *Practical difference* (lit., "goes out from it"). The

Talmud frequently looks for a case in which the practical implications of two different viewpoints, or different explanations of the same law, are clear; such a case is called a "practical difference." (See *Pesaḥim* 53a.)
See also מַאי נָפְקָא מִינָהּ.

נָקְטִינָן *We hold,* i.e., we have it on the authority of tradition that.... This expression introduces an argument based on the

evidence of an accepted tradition. (See *Eruvin* 5a.) See also גְּמִירִי.

נִרְאִין *[The words of Rabbi X] appear [reasonable].* When the viewpoint of a certain scholar is logical but not followed in actual practice, the Talmud may state that his words "appear" correct. In such cases the conduct of a person who follows this Sage's opinion is not deemed improper or legally invalid (at least not *de facto*). (See *Eruvin* 46b.) See also הֲלָכָה; מַטִּין.

סָבוּר מִינָהּ *They understood from it,* i.e., the students of the Academy reached an (erroneous) conclusion from the source cited (which will be rejected in the course of the subsequent discussion). (See *Betzah* 36b.) See also סַבְרוּהָ.

סְבִירָא לִי *I maintain, I hold [the following opinion].* (See *Berakhot* 44b.)

סָבַר לָהּ כְּוָותֵיהּ בַּחֲדָא וּפָלֵיג עֲלֵיהּ בַּחֲדָא *He agrees with him in one [case] and disagrees with him in another [case].* An expression used by the Gemara to describe a situation where Rabbi A made a statement involving two elements, and Rabbi B accepted Rabbi A's ruling in one part but not in the other, maintaining that there was no fundamental logical connection between the two. (See *Bava Metzia* 77b.)

וְסָבַר ר'... וְהָתְנַן (וְהָתַנְיָא)... *But does Rabbi X hold...? Surely in that Mishnah (in that Baraita)....* This expression is used by the Gemara in analyzing the opinion of a scholar cited in a Mishnah, suggesting that he has elsewhere expressed a contrary opinion. "But does Rabbi X in fact hold this opinion? Surely in another Mishnah [or Baraita] he says the opposite." (See *Ketubot* 56a.)

סְבָרָא *Reason.* (1) Halakhic argumentation based on logical analysis, rather than on tradition (see *Yevamot* 25b; see also גְּמָרָא). (2) A sensible and reasonable idea which is not supported by a literary source (e.g., a Biblical verse, a Mishnah or a Baraita). (See *Berakhot* 4b.)

סְבָרָא הוּא *It is a commonsense argument.* An expression used by the Gemara to introduce an argument based on common sense rather than an authoritative source. (See *Bava Metzia* 27b.)

סַבְרוּהָ *They thought, they assumed [that]....* This term introduces an assumption proposed at the beginning of a discussion, but later found to be erroneous. (See *Berakhot* 46a.)

סוּגְיָא *Lit., walk, course.* (1) Talmudic discussion of a given theme (see *Shabbat* 66b). (2) The Halakhic investigation involved

in the analysis by the Gemara of Tannaitic sources. (See *Sanhedrin* 33a.) These investigations were ultimately edited and recorded as the סוּגְיוֹת that make up the bulk of Talmudic literature. (3) סוּגְיָא דִּשְׁמַעֲתָא — "the course of the discussion," i.e., the accepted Halakhic decision. Sometimes this decision is not stated explicitly, but can be derived from the general trend of the discussion.

סוֹף סוֹף *At all events* (lit., "the end," "finally"). In the course of a Talmudic discussion, after an objection has been made to a statement and a response has been offered to that objection, the Gemara may then restate its original objection by pointing out the weak point of the answer: "However much I wish to accept your answer, *nevertheless* my previous objection still stands." (See *Megillah* 3a.) See also הָנִיחָא לְ...; תֵּינַח בְּ....

סַיְיעָתָא *Support.* This term usually refers to supporting statements deduced from Tannaitic sources for Amoraic viewpoints, as opposed to תְּיוּבְתָּא (see entry), refutation of Amoraic viewpoints deduced from Tannaitic sources. (See *Bava Metzia* 48a.)

וְסִימָנֵיךְ *And your sign is....* When the Gemara lists a series of cases or legal decisions on a given topic, it frequently provides a key word or phrase, or a mnemonic word or series of words made up of the initial letters of the various cases to help the student memorize them correctly. The expression used to introduce the key phrase or mnemonic is וְסִימָנֵיךְ — "And your sign is...." (See *Shabbat* 35a.)

סֵיפָא *The last clause* (lit., "end") of a Mishnah, a Baraita, or some other source; sometimes it refers to the next Mishnah, or another Mishnah appearing later in the chapter under discussion. (See *Berakhot* 2a.) See also מְצִיעֲתָא; רֵישָׁא.

סֵיפָא אִיצְטְרִיכָא לֵיהּ *He needed the last clause* (lit., "the end"). Only the last clause of the source cited really neeeded to be mentioned; but since the last clause was mentioned, the first one was also cited. (See *Eruvin* 14a.)
See also הָא קָא מַשְׁמַע לָן; צְרִיכָא.

סָלְקָא דַּעְתָּךְ *Can [this] enter your mind?!* This expression is used by the Gemara when criticizing a word, a phrase, or a statement in a Mishnah which, at face value, appears to be incorrect or imprecise: "Can it enter your mind to imagine that the Mishnah means...?!" The answer will usually begin with the words אֶלָּא אֵימָא (see entry) — "say instead..." — and will suggest an alternative explanation. (See *Pesaḥim* 42b.)

סָלְקָא דַּעְתָּךְ אָמִינָא   *You [might] assume* (lit., "arises in your mind to say"). This expression introduces an erroneous conclusion to which one might have come if a certain word or phrase had been omitted from a source. It often appears in answer to a question in the form !מַאי קָא מַשְׁמַע לָן פְּשִׁיטָא — "What is the scholar trying to teach us? Surely it is obvious!" In answering this question, the Gemara tries to show that the statement is by no means so obvious. It was, in fact, needed to avoid a possible misunderstanding: "You might have thought.... Therefore the text

comes to inform you that the situation is different." (See *Yevamot* 40a.) See also אִיצְטְרִיךְ, סָלְקָא דַּעְתָּךְ אָמִינָא...; הֲוָה אָמִינָא; מַהוּ.

סְמִי   *Remove, delete!* An expression used to suggest that a problematic word or clause be deleted from a Mishnah or, more commonly, from a Baraita, whose text is not always reliable. (See *Pesaḥim* 45b.)

סְתִימְתָאָה   *The anonymous.* An expression used by the Gemara to describe an authoritative Tanna whose view was cited in the Mishnah anonymously. (See *Megillah* 2a.)

סְתָם מִשְׁנָה   *An anonymous Mishnah*, i.e., a Mishnah whose contents are not attributed to a named authority. Such Mishnayot generally reflect the opinion of Rabbi Yehudah HaNasi, the editor of the Mishnah. (See *Bava Metzia* 33a.)

עֲבַד עוּבְדָא   *He acted*, i.e., he followed a particular Halakhic viewpoint in actual practice. (See *Bava Metzia* 18b.)

עַד כָּאן לָא...   Lit., *up to here there is no....* This expression is used by the Gemara to limit a law mentioned earlier or to narrow a difference of opinion between scholars. For more specific applications see following entries. (See *Yoma* 31a.)

עַד כָּאן לָא פְּלִיגִי אֶלָּא... אֲבָל...   *They only differ with regard to A, but with regard to B....* In its analysis of a difference of opinion recorded in a Mishnah, the Gemara often attempts to limit the difference as much as possible, using this expression which is usually the basis for a subsequent question. (See *Bava Metzia* 28b/29a.)

עַד כָּאן לָא קָאָמַר פְּלוֹנִי הָתָם... אֲבָל הָכָא...   *Rabbi X only stated [his opinion] there... but here....* Sometimes the Talmud rejects the comparison of statements made by the same scholar, or of statements made by different scholars, by stating: "Rabbi X only stated his opinion in case A, but in case B, which differs from case A, he would not have maintained this opinion...." (See *Shabbat* 117b.)

עוּבְדָא   *Act, deed, event, precedent.*

עַל אַחַת כַּמָּה וְכַמָּה   *How much more so.* An expression used to introduce the conclusion of an *a fortiori* (קַל וָחוֹמֶר) argument (see entry in section on hermeneutics), e.g.: "If the law is strict in case A, where one would expect it to be lenient, how much more so should the law be strict in case B [where one would expect it to be strict]?" (See *Makkot* 24a.) See also אֵינוֹ דִין; הֲלֹא דִין הוּא; לֹא כָּל שֶׁכֵּן.

עַל דַּעְתֵּיהּ דְּר'... נִיחָא, עַל דַּעְתֵּיהּ דְּר'... קַשְׁיָא   *According to Rabbi A it is satisfactory; according to Rabbi B it is difficult.* A term in the Jerusalem Talmud. Sometimes a Mishnah or a Baraita is cited in support of one scholar's view, but contrary to the view of another; in such cases the Jerusalem Talmud may remark: "According to Rabbi A the Mishnah or Baraita is satisfactory; according to Rabbi B it is difficult."

בְּ... עָסְקִינַן   *We are dealing with X.* An expression commonly used by the Gemara to limit the application of a law to certain specific cases only. (See *Pesaḥim* 51a.) See also הָכָא בְּמַאי עָסְקִינַן.

פּוֹק חֲזֵי מַאי עַמָּא דְּבַר   *Go out [and] see what the people* are doing (i.e., what practice the people are following). If no clear-cut Halakhic ruling has been reached regarding a certain problem, the Talmud may suggest that popular practice serve as the basis for arriving at a decision: "Go out and see what practice the people are following and act accordingly." (See *Berakhot* 45a.)

פּוֹק תְּנֵי לְבָרָא   *Go out [and] teach it outside.* When a Baraita is rejected as being unauthoritative and hence not binding, the Talmud may use this expression, meaning that the Baraita should have no place in the discussion in the Bet Midrash. (See *Shabbat* 106a.)

פֵּירוּקָא   *Answer, solution.* Resolution of an objection or contradiction. (See *Bava Kamma* 117a.)
See also הוּא מוֹתִיב לָהּ וְהוּא מְפָרֵק לָהּ.

פִּירְכָא   *Objection, refutation.* A refutation of an argument based on logical reasoning. Such an objection is usually based on a distinction between two seemingly similar cases or on logical difficulties. (See *Gittin* 83a.)

פִּירְקָא   *Pirka.* The Rabbinic discourse delivered on Shabbat and Festivals at large communal gatherings. (See *Pesahim* 100a.)

וּפְלִיגָא דִּידֵיהּ אַדִּידֵיהּ   *And he disagrees with himself.* An expression used to indicate that one ruling (or action) of an Amora contradicts another of his rulings. (See *Shabbat* 13a.)

וּפְלִיגָא דְּר' פְּלוֹנִי   *And it disagrees with Rabbi X,* i.e., the source just cited disagrees with the view of Rabbi X, which will be cited below. (See *Bava Metzia* 12b.)

פֵּרוּשֵׁי קָא מְפָרֵשׁ   *It [in fact] explains.* Sometimes a seemingly repetitious clause in the Mishnah is interpreted by the Talmud as "explaining" what was stated in a previous clause, rather than introducing a new case. (See *Moed Katan* 13a.) See also תָּנָא וַהֲדַר מְפָרֵשׁ.

פָּרֵיךְ ר' פְּלוֹנִי   *Rabbi X objected.* An expression often used to introduce the objections of certain scholars (in particular Rav Aha). (See *Yevamot* 24a.) See also מְגַדֵּף בָּהּ ר' פְּלוֹנִי; מַתְקִיף לָהּ.

פְּשׁוֹט מִיהָא (מֵהָא) חֲדָא   *Solve from this at least one.* Sometimes, after posing a series of questions, the Gemara cites a source providing an answer to at least one of them. In such cases the Gemara may state: "Solve at least one of the questions just raised on the basis of this source." (See *Bava Metzia* 25a.)

פָּשַׁט   *He solved,* i.e., solved problems, Halakhic questions, or other difficulties arising in connection with the interpretation of sources cited by the Talmud. (See *Yevamot* 122a.)

פְּשִׁיטָא   *It is obvious!* (1) An expression used by the Gemara to express astonishment at the previous statement: "This is obvious!" (Why, therefore, did it have to be stated explicitly?!). When פְּשִׁיטָא is used in this sense, it usually constitutes a sentence unto itself, in contrast to the next meaning. (See *Berakhot* 20b.) The Gemara generally answers this question by showing that the statement was not as obvious as it seemed, or that it was necessary in order to avoid misunderstandings. Such answers usually begin with the expressions אִיצְטְרִיךְ, סָלְקָא דַּעְתָּךְ אָמִינָא...; לָא צְרִיכָא אֶלָּא...; לָא צְרִיכָא דְּ...; מַהוּ דְּתֵימָא... קָא מַשְׁמַע לַן; (see entries). (2) Sometimes פְּשִׁיטָא is used at the beginning of a sentence to introduce a question, first indicating what issues have obvious answers and then setting out those which must be resolved: "It is obvious what the law is in case A; but what about case B?" (See *Berakhot* 12a.)

פָּתַח בְּ... וְסַיֵּים בְּ...   *He began with X and finished with Y!* This expression is used by the Gemara to point out an incongruity in a section of a Mishnah: "Why did the Mishnah begin with case X and then end with case Y?" (See *Moed Katan* 11b.) See also מַאי שְׁנָא הָכָא דְּתָנֵי....

פָּתַח לָהּ פִּתְחָא לְהַאי פַּרְשְׁתָא מֵהָכָא   Lit., *he introduced this section with an introduction from here.* Discourses by Amoraim, which were usually delivered on Festivals or special Sabbaths on themes connected with the occasion being celebrated, were often preceded by a special introduction, the פְּתִיחְתָּא — "proem." This introduction was composed of a series of verses from the later Prophets or Hagiographa (כְּתוּבִים), which the lecturer, through his interpretation, would link to the theme of the occasion. One of the formulae used to introduce such a proem was: "The lecturer introduced his discourse on this section of the Bible from here [i.e., from the verse cited below]." (See *Megillah* 11a.) See also next entry.

פָּתַח ר' פְּלוֹנִי   *Rabbi X introduced....* A formula used in Aggadic Midrashim to introduce the פְּתִיחְתָּא or "proem" (see previous entry). (See *Ketubot* 8b.)

פָּתַר לָהּ   *He explained it.* An expression in the Jerusalem Talmud and Aggadic Midrashim used when a Rabbi explained the verse under discussion as referring to a particular case or incident. See next entry.

פָּתַר קְרָיֵיהּ בְּ...   *He explained the verse in....* An expression in Aggadic Midrashim used when a Rabbi explains a verse under discussion as referring to a particular case or incident. See previous entry.

פָּתְרִיתוּ בָּהּ כּוּלֵי הַאי   Lit., *did you explain it so much?* i.e., did you also arrive at this conclusion regarding the interpretation of the matter under discussion? (See *Eruvin* 32b.)

צוֹרְבָא מֵרַבָּנַן   *Young scholar* (lit., one ablaze from the Rabbis). (See *Megillah* 28b.)

צָרִיךְ וְאֵין לוֹ תַּקָּנָה   *He must, but he has no remedy.* Sometimes a Mishnah or a Baraita states that someone "must" do something which, owing to the circumstances, he cannot actually do. In such cases the Talmud explains that the expression "must" refers to an ideal, theoretical situation, even though as a practical matter the problem is insoluble. (See *Yoma* 61b.)

צָרִיכָא (צְרִיכֵי)   *It is (they are) necessary.* (1) A Mishnah or a Baraita often (and the Torah itself or an Amora occasionally) presents two (or more) seemingly analogous cases. When this apparently unnecessary repetition is challenged, the Gemara points out that the statements are both "necessary." The Gemara justifies the inclusion of the various cases either because each case has a unique feature needing to be stated, or because we might have reached erroneous conclusions if one of the statements had been omitted. (See *Shabbat* 122a.) See also הָא. (2) תּוּ לָמָה לִי; כָּל הָנֵי לָמָה לִי; לָמָּה לֵיהּ לְמִיתְנֵי... In the Jerusalem Talmud this term means "uncertain"; an unresolved issue is thus termed צְרִיכָא.

צְרִיכָא לְמֵימַר   *Need this be said?* Since a similar matter has already been discussed, surely this is self-evident! (See *Bava Metzia* 8a.) See also אֶלָּא לָאו...

צְרִיכוּתָא   Lit., *necessity.* Sometimes an idea is repeated, explicitly or implicitly, in different clauses of the same Mishnah, in different Mishnayot, or by different Amoraim. The Talmud attempts to explain the seemingly unnecessary repetition by arguing that each statement was meant to teach us something which we would otherwise not have known, or to prevent us from reaching erroneous conclusions. Such explanations of seemingly needless repetitions come under the category of צְרִיכוּתָא.

קָא מַשְׁמַע לַן (קמ"ל)   *It tells us.* A term used to introduce the conclusion of a צְרִיכוּתָא (see previous entry). The Talmud explains that an apparently unnecessary source was cited to avoid mistaken conclusions; in such cases the Talmud states that the superfluous source "tells us" not to arrive at such conclusions. (See *Sanhedrin* 18b.)
See also הָא קָא מַשְׁמַע לַן; מַאי קָא מַשְׁמַע לַן.

קָא סָלְקָא (אַ)דַּעְתָּךְ   *It might occur to you....* See סָלְקָא (אַ)דַּעְתָּךְ.

קָא פָּסֵיק וְתָנֵי   *It states categorically [or decisively],* i.e., the Tannaitic source under discussion speaks in general terms, without distinguishing between specific cases where one might have expected the law to be different. These words introduce criticism of a seemingly over-general Mishnaic ruling and are commonly followed by לָא שְׁנָא... וְלָא שְׁנָא... בִּשְׁלָמָא... אֶלָּא... אַמַּאי — "The Mishnah does not distinguish between X and Y; as far as X is concerned, all is well, but as far as Y is concerned, why does it state...?" (See *Sukkah* 29b.)

קוּשְׁיָא   Lit., *difficulty,* i.e., an objection raised against an Amoraic statement, whether on the basis of logical reasoning or a literary source (e.g., a Mishnah or a Baraita contradicting the Amoraic statement). When no solution to this objection is found, the Gemara usually remarks קַשְׁיָא — "It is difficult." (See entry.) This does not necessarily mean that the problematic Amoraic statement is rejected — unless the Gemara remarks תְּיוּבְתָּא (see entry below) — but merely that it is considered difficult. See תֵּירוּץ.

קַיְימָא לַן (קי"ל)   *We maintain,* i.e., it is an accepted view that.... This term is often used to introduce an accepted Halakhic ruling. (See *Yevamot* 6a.)

קִים לְהוּ לְרַבָּנַן   *Our Sages maintain,* i.e., the view stated here was accepted by the scholars. (See *Yoma* 79a.)

קָם ר'... בְּשִׁיטָתֵיהּ דְּר'...   Lit., *Rabbi A stands according to the view of Rabbi B,* i.e., Rabbi A accepted the viewpoint of Rabbi B. This expression is often encountered when Rabbi A originally disagreed with Rabbi B. (See *Shabbat* 92a.)

קְרָא אַשְׁכַּח וְדָרַשׁ   *He found a verse and expounded [it].* Sometimes, when an objection is raised to a seemingly incomprehensible viewpoint, the Talmud may resolve the objection by stating that the scholar who made the problematic statement based his view on an exposition of a Biblical verse, usually one that had hitherto not been understood. (See Ḥagigah 15b.)

קְרָא וּמַתְנִיתָא מְסַיְיעֵי לֵיה   A Biblical verse and a Baraita support him, i.e., support the view of the Amora cited. (See Gittin 48a.)

קְרֵי בֵּיה   Lit., read in it...! i.e., interpret the verse cited in the following manner, usually as if one of its words were vocalized differently. (See Rosh HaShanah 24a.) See also ...אַל תִּקְרֵי.

קְרֵי עֲלֵיה (קְרֵי אַנַּפְשֵׁיה)   Lit., he read [the following verse] concerning him (or himself)..., i.e., one of the Rabbis applied a particular Biblical verse to an actual case, whether involving himself or another person. (See Moed Katan 5a/b.)

קָשׁוּ קְרָאֵי אַהֲדָדֵי   The verses contradict each other. This expression is usually followed by an interpretation resolving the apparent contradiction between the verses cited. (See Kiddushin 2b.)

קַשְׁיָא   It is difficult. At the conclusion of a sugya: the difficulty

mentioned previously remains unresolved. (See Moed Katan 22b.) See also קוּשְׁיָא; תְּיוּבְתָּא.

קַשְׁיָא רֵישָׁא אַסֵּיפָא   Lit., there is a difficulty [from] the first clause to the last clause, i.e., there is a contradiction between the first and last clauses of the same Mishnah, often because the first appears to follow the view of one scholar, while the last appears to follow the view of another scholar, who disagrees. (See Me'ilah 16a.)
See also רֵישָׁא ר' פְּלוֹנִי וְסֵיפָא ר' אַלְמוֹנִי; תְּרֵי תַּנָּאֵי הִיא; תַּבְרָא.

קַשְׁיָין אַהֲדָדֵי   They [the Mishnayot or Amoraic statements] contradict each other. (See Ḥagigah 8b.)

קָתָנֵי   Teaches, i.e., the Tanna teaches a particular Halakhah in a Mishnah or a Baraita. (See Yoma 27b.)

קָתָנֵי מִיהַת   At all events it teaches.... When, as part of an objection, a lengthy Mishnah or Baraita is cited by the Talmud, and only one part of it is actually relevant to the objection being raised, the Talmud may first cite this Mishnah or Baraita in its entirety, and then repeat the relevant section, introducing it with this expression. (See Rosh HaShanah 30a.)

רַב   Rav. (1) The Rabbinical title applied to Babylonian Amoraim. (2) Abba Arikha, the famous first-generation Babylonian Amora.

רַבִּי   Rabbi. (1) The Rabbinical title applied to ordained scholars in Eretz Israel (whether Tannaim or Amoraim). (2) Rabbi Yehudah HaNasi, the editor of the Mishnah.

ר' פְּלוֹנִי אָמַר...   Rabbi [or Rav] X said.... When a statement of an individual scholar is quoted with the name of the scholar preceding the verb אָמַר — "he said" — the statement is usually followed by that of another scholar who holds a different view on the subject under discussion. (See Bava Metzia 21b.)
See also אָמַר ר' פְּלוֹנִי.

ר' פְּלוֹנִי הַיְינוּ תַּנָּא קַמָּא   Rabbi X is the same as the first Tanna! Where a Mishnah contains a series of opinions, those of individual scholars and of the scholars as a whole, it is sometimes difficult to understand the shades of difference between the views. To clarify the situation the Gemara then often asks whether the viewpoint of Rabbi X is identical with that of the first Tanna. The Gemara usually answers such a question with the words אִיכָּא בֵּינַיְיהוּ — "There is a difference between them..." (see entry) — and goes on to explain. (See Berakhot 30a.)
See also חֲכָמִים הַיְינוּ תַּנָּא קַמָּא.

וְר' פְּלוֹנִי מַאי טַעְמָא לָא אָמַר כְּר' אַלְמוֹנִי   And what is the reason why Rabbi X did not explain like Rabbi Y? Where two Amoraim disagree in their interpretation of a term or a passage in a Mishnah, the Gemara often asks why they give different explanations. The argument may then proceed: אָמַר לָךְ — "Rabbi X might reply..." — and the Gemara then analyzes each scholar's point of view in turn. (See Shabbat 19b.)
See also אָמַר לָךְ; וְאִידָךְ.

רַבָּן   Rabban (= our master). The title applied to the head (Nasi) of the Sanhedrin in Eretz Israel.

רַבָּנָא   Rabbana (= our master). The title applied to scholars from the family of the Exilarch (Resh Galuta) in Babylonia. (See Pesaḥim 115b.)

רַבָּנִין (רַבָּנַן) דְּהָכָא   The Sages from here. A term in the Jerusalem Talmud referring to the scholars of Eretz Israel. Sometimes, however, this expression refers specifically to the scholars of Tiberias and Galilee.

רַבָּנִין (רַבָּנַן) דְּתַמָּן   The Sages from there. A term in the Jerusalem Talmud meaning "the Babylonian scholars."

רַבָּנָן   Our Sages. The Rabbis. (1) Sometimes the Talmud uses this term to refer to the "Sages" (חֲכָמִים) or an anonymous opinion cited in the Mishnah. (2) A majority opinion is sometimes called the view of the "Sages" (as opposed to the expressed minority view of an individual scholar). (3) "Scholars," a general term used to refer to the scholars of the Academy.

רוּבָּא דְּר'... וְרוּבָּא דְּר'... *The novelty [lit., greatness, remarkability] of Rabbi A... and the novelty of Rabbi B....* An expression in the Jerusalem Talmud: Rabbi A has come to teach us the following novel or significant point, and Rabbi B has come to teach us another novel or significant point.

רוּמְיָא Lit., *casting.* An objection raised by the Gemara pointing out a contradiction between two sources of equal authority (e.g., two Mishnayot, a Mishnah and a Baraita, two Baraitot, or two Biblical verses), or between two statements made by the same authority. (See *Ketubot* 36a.) See also אִיכָּא דְּרָמֵי לָהּ מִירְמָא; רָמֵי; (וּ)רְמִינְהוּ.

רַחֲמָנָא Lit., *the Merciful One, God.* Generally, however, this term refers to the Torah in which God's commandments were conveyed to man, e.g., אָמַר רַחֲמָנָא — "the Merciful One states" or "the Torah states." (See *Rosh HaShanah* 28a.)

רֵישָׁא *Beginning* (lit., "head"). An expression used by the Gemara to describe the first part of a statement (in a Biblical verse or, most commonly, in a Mishnah). (See *Shabbat* 54a.) See also מְצִיעָתָא; סֵיפָא.

רֵישָׁא ר' פְּלוֹנִי וְסֵיפָא ר' אַלְמוֹנִי *Is the first clause Rabbi A and the last clause Rabbi B?* A formula used to point out an apparent internal contradiction in an anonymous Mishnah, the first clause of which seems to follow one view, while its last clause seems to follow another, contrary one. (See *Eruvin* 99a.) See also תְּרֵי תַנָּאֵי הִיא; קַשְׁיָא רֵישָׁא אַסֵּיפָא.

רֵישָׁא רְבוּתָא קָא מַשְׁמַע לָן וְסֵיפָא רְבוּתָא קָא מַשְׁמַע לָן *The first clause teaches us something significant and the last clause teaches us something significant* — and thus no part of the Mishnah (or the Baraita) is superfluous. (See *Shabbat* 147b.)

רָמֵי Lit., *he casts,* i.e., he raises a contradiction between two sources of equal authority. (See *Pesaḥim* 50b.) See also רוּמְיָא.

רָמֵי דְּר' פְּלוֹנִי אַדְּר' פְּלוֹנִי Lit., *he casts from Rabbi X upon Rabbi X,* i.e., he raises a contradiction between two statements of Rabbi X. (See *Betzah* 3a.) See also רוּמְיָא and next entries.

רָמֵי קְרָאֵי אַהֲדָדֵי Lit., *he casts verses upon each other,* i.e., he raises a contradiction between two Biblical verses. (See *Zevaḥim* 120a.)

(וּ)רְמִינְהוּ Lit., *(and) cast them.* An expression used by the Gemara to introduce a contradiction between the source about to be cited and the source which has just been cited, where both sources are of equal authority. (See *Ta'anit* 4b.) See also רוּמְיָא.

שֶׁאֵין תַּלְמוּד לוֹמַר... וּמַה תַּלְמוּד לוֹמַר *For the Torah does not* [need to] *state... and why does the Torah state...?* An expression used in Halakhic and Aggadic Midrashim to introduce an interpretation of a Biblical verse: "The Torah did not need to state case A here, since it has already stated elsewhere what the law is in such a case.... Why, then, did the Torah state this case here?" I.e., what did the Torah intend to teach us by discussing this case here? Another law or a different principle? (See *Pesaḥim* 41b.) See also תַּלְמוּד לוֹמַר.

שָׁאַל *Asked.* Sometimes used in the Jerusalem Talmud in the sense of "raised an objection." See מְתִיב.

שָׁאנֵי *It is different.* Sometimes the Talmud refutes an objection by distinguishing between two seemingly similar cases, using this term to introduce the distinction: שָׁאנֵי הָכָא — "The case here is different, because..."; שָׁאנֵי הָתָם — "The case there is different, because...." (See *Pesaḥim* 5a.) See also הָכָא בְּמַאי עָסְקִינַן; שִׁינּוּיָא.

שָׁבְקֵיהּ לִקְרָא דְּאִיהוּ דָּחֵיק וּמוֹקִים אַנַּפְשֵׁיהּ *Leave*

the verse alone, because it is difficult and it will have to work itself out in its own way. Sometimes, after the Talmud objects to a certain forced interpretation of a Biblical verse, the objection is resolved: "Leave the verse alone [reconcile yourself to the fact that we have had to interpret the verse as referring to one specific and unusual situation] although it is difficult and the explanation is strained, and the verse itself will, as it were, work out a solution to the problem." (See *Pesaḥim* 59b.)

שֶׁהָיָה בְּדִין... *Because it was fitting that....* In a Halakhic Midrash, when a Biblical verse is cited to rule out an erroneous conclusion based on one of the hermeneutical principles which might otherwise have been drawn, the Midrash may state: "It was fitting that [i.e., we might have thought]... but for the fact that the verse states otherwise."

שׁוֹמֵעַ אֲנִי... תַּלְמוּד לוֹמַר... Lit., *I* [might] *hear... the verse states.* In Halakhic Midrashim this expression is used when part of a verse might lend itself to misinterpretation, were it not for another part of the verse: "I might misinterpret the verse as follows... but another part of the verse states otherwise." (See

Yevamot 5a.) See also ...מִמַּשְׁמַע שֶׁנֶּאֱמַר ; יָכוֹל... תַּלְמוּד לוֹמַר....

שִׁינוּיָא   *Distinction, answer.* The Talmud uses this term to resolve an apparent contradiction between two sources. The contradiction is pointed out by an objection in the category of a רוּמְיָא (see entry) or a תְּיוּבְתָּא (see entry). In response to that objection the Talmud points out a distinction between apparently similar cases. The purpose of the שִׁינוּיָא is to demonstrate that the objection is not necessarily valid, but the שִׁינוּיָא need not represent the final conclusion about the issue under discussion. (See *Shabbat* 3b.) See also next two entries.

שִׁינוּיָא דְּשַׁנֵּינַן, שִׁינוּיָא הוּא   *The answer which we have given is the [correct] answer,* i.e., the answer suggested explains the source being interpreted correctly, and was not intended merely to show that the objection can be rebutted. (See *Pesahim* 12b.) See also previous entry.

(אַ)שִׁינוּיֵי לֵיקוּ וְלִיסְמוֹךְ   *Should we rely on answers [such as these]?* — since they often do not represent the correct interpretation of the source under discussion, and were intended only to show that the Gemara's objection can be rebutted. (See *Yevamot* 91b.) See also שִׁינוּיָא.

שָׁלְחוּ לֵיהּ לְר׳ פְּלוֹנִי, יְלַמְּדֵנוּ רַבֵּנוּ   *They sent to Rabbi X [asking]: Will our teacher instruct us....?* This expression is used by the Gemara to introduce a question regarding the solution of a problem or dispute which was referred to a higher authority — a famous teacher or an academy. The Gemara then introduces the answer שָׁלַח לְהוּ — "He sent them in reply...." (See *Sanhedrin* 24b.) See also next entry.

שָׁלְחוּ מִתָּם   *They sent from there,* i.e., from Eretz Israel to Babylonia. This expression introduces an answer from a scholar or an academy in Eretz Israel to a problem sent by a questioner in Babylonia. (See *Betzah* 4b.) See also previous entry.

שְׁמַע מִינָה (ש״מ)   *Hear from this, learn from this, conclude from this.* (1) At the beginning of an argument: "Draw the [following] Halakhic conclusion" from the previous statement. (See *Berakhot* 13a.) (2) At the end of an argument, this expression is used to confirm that the previous conclusion or explanation is indeed correct. (See *Pesahim* 3a.)

שְׁמַע מִינָה תַּרְתֵּי (תְּלָת)   *Conclude from this two (three) [conclusions],* i.e., the following two (three) conclusions may be inferred from the previous statement (or group of statements). (See *Berakhot* 27a.)

שְׁמַעְתָּא   *Tradition.* An Amoraic Halakhic tradition, as distinct from a Baraita or an Amoraic Aggadic tradition. (See *Berakhot* 33b.)

שְׁמַעְתְּתָא אַהֲדָדֵי אִיתְּמַר   *The traditions were said one upon the other.* An expression used when the statement of a later Amora complements rather than contradicts the statement of an earlier Amora. (See *Kiddushin* 65a.)

שְׁמַעְתִּי   *I heard.* An expression used in Tannaitic literature meaning: "I received this Halakhic tradition from my teacher." This term is often used when the speaker is uncertain about some of the details of the tradition he is reporting. (See *Bava Metzia* 38b.)

שֶׁנֶּאֱמַר   *As it is said.* Introduction to a quotation from the Bible. (See *Berakhot* 8a.) See also (ד)כְּתִיב; אָמַר קְרָא.

שָׁנָה   *He taught* (i.e., Halakhot) — usually Tannaitic Halakhot. (See *Yevamot* 108b.)

שְׁנֵי תַלְמִידִים שָׁנוּ אוֹתָהּ   *Two students taught it.* An expression used in the Jerusalem Talmud when a contradiction is found between two parts of the same Mishnah. The Jerusalem Talmud may resolve the contradiction by suggesting that the different parts of the Mishnah derive from different sources: "Two students taught it." See תַּבְרָא.

שְׁפִיל לְסֵיפֵיהּ דִּקְרָא   *Go down to the end of the verse,* i.e., consider the latter part of the verse you are quoting. There you will find a solution to your problem or an objection to your view. (See *Berakhot* 10a.)

שַׁפִּיר דָּמֵי   Lit., *it seems well,* i.e., it is proper and correct to follow the view just mentioned. (See *Shabbat* 47a.) See also לְכַתְּחִלָּה לָא דִּיעֲבַד שַׁפִּיר דָּמֵי.

שַׁפִּיר קָאָמַר ר׳ פְּלוֹנִי   *Rabbi X said well.* Sometimes, when there is a controversy between Tannaim, one of the scholars gives an explanation of his viewpoint to the other scholar or scholars, and the latter are silent. The Gemara may then probe the position of the latter scholar(s): "Rabbi A [the first scholar] explained his point of view well. What is the reply of Rabbi B [or the Sages]?" (See *Rosh HaShanah* 26a.)

שָׁרַע מִינָּהּ   *He slipped away from it, evaded it,* i.e., gave it up. An expression in the Jerusalem Talmud to indicate that the scholar avoided answering the question, because he was uncertain about its solution.

תָּא שְׁמַע   *Come [and] hear.* An expression used to introduce a source (usually Tannaitic, but sometimes Biblical or Amoraic)

which will be used to support an opinion, prove a point, raise an objection, or resolve a problem. Where תָּא שְׁמַע introduces a suggested solution to a problem, if the solution is rejected, another solution is often introduced by the same expression. When a solution is finally accepted, the concluding expression שְׁמַע מִינָּה (see entry) — "Prove it from this" — is often used. (See *Bava Metzia* 27b/28a.)

תַּבְרָא: מִי שֶׁשָּׁנָה זוֹ לֹא שָׁנָה זוֹ   Lit., *break, fracture* (figuratively, a contradiction: "He who taught this did not teach this"). When an insoluble contradiction is found within a Mishnah, the Talmud may attribute the different parts of the Mishnah to different scholars. (See *Shabbat* 92b.)

תֵּדַע   *Know [that the previous statement is true, because]*.... An expression used to introduce a proof supporting this statement. (See *Bava Metzia* 5b.)

תְּהֵא בְּ...   *Let it be in*.... Sometimes the Talmud resolves an objection by suggesting that the Mishnah refers only to a certain case. (See *Bava Metzia* 35a.) See also אוֹקִימְתָּא; הָכָא בְּמַאי עָסְקִינַן.

וְתוּ   *And furthermore.* When two successive questions (without an intervening answer) are asked by the Gemara on the same point, the second question is often introduced by וְתוּ. (See *Berakhot* 2a.)

(וְ)תוּ לָא מִידֵּי   *(And) nothing more*, i.e., there is no room for further discussion of the matter; the argument that has been presented is convincing. (See *Sukkah* 36b.)

וְתוּ לֵיכָּא   *And is there nothing else?* i.e., is it possible that the previous list is complete, and that nothing was omitted from it? This expression is used when the Gemara is analyzing a Mishnah that contains an expressly limited number of cases, and it often continues ...וְהָא אִיכָּא — "But surely there is the case of... which was not mentioned in the Mishnah!" (See *Eruvin* 27a.)

תִּיבָּעֵי   *Let it be asked.* (1) When used at the beginning or middle of a sentence (usually in the form תִּיבָּעֵי לָךְ — "Ask it") this term proposes that a question should be asked or a problem raised in an alternative form, which then follows. (See *Bava Metzia* 96b.) (2) When used at the end of a sentence this term acknowledges, "It is a problem," i.e., the question raised previously remains unresolved (תִּיבָּעֵי is used in this sense only in certain tractates). (See *Temurah* 13b.) See also תֵּיקוּ.

תְּיוּבְתָּא   Lit., *reply*, i.e., a conclusive refutation of an Amoraic statement, usually on the basis of a Tannaitic source which contradicts the Amora's remarks. (See *Berakhot* 34a.) This is one of a number of expressions based on the Aramaic root תוב, with this connotation of bringing a refutation. Where an Amora objects to the viewpoint of another Amora, citing a Tannaitic source, the expression used is אֵיתִיבֵיהּ — "X raised an objection against Y." Where an Amora raises an objection against an anonymous Amoraic viewpoint, citing a Tannaitic source, the expression used is מְתִיב — "X raised an objection." Where the Gemara itself raises such an objection, the expression used is מֵיתִיבֵי — "An objection was raised." (See under respective

entries.) Where the refutation is conclusive, the expression תְּיוּבְתָּא is often used, bringing the discussion to a close. See next entry. For answers to this form of objection, see שִׁינּוּיָא.

תְּיוּבְתָּא דְּר׳ פְּלוֹנִי תְּיוּבְתָּא   *The refutation of [the viewpoint of] Rabbi X is a [valid] refutation.* When this expression is used, the view of Rabbi X is completely rejected. (See *Pesaḥim* 30b.) See also the previous entry and the next entry.

תְּיוּבְתָּא וְהִלְכְתָא   *A refutation and the Halakhah?* Sometimes, after an Amora's view is rejected (with the expression תְּיוּבְתָּא, see above), the Talmud nevertheless rules that the Halakhah is in accordance with his view. In such cases the Talmud may then ask: "A refutation of this Amora was just offered, yet the Halakhah is in accordance with his viewpoint?!" The Talmud then proceeds to solve this problem. (See *Bava Kamma* 15b.)

תִּינַח   Lit., *let it rest*, i.e., granted, fine. Used to introduce a question which begins by conceding that one kind of case is free of difficulty and then raises a problematic case. (See *Berakhot* 6a.) See also next entry and בִּשְׁלָמָא; הָנִיחָא לְ....

תִּינַח בְּ..., בְּ... מַאי אִיכָּא לְמֵימַר   *Granted in... [but] in... what is there to say?* In the course of Talmudic debate, objection may be made to a statement. Response will then be made to that objection. The Talmud may then acknowledge the validity of that response in part (תִּינַח), but argue that it does not cover all the cases included in the original objection: "Your answer may be satisfactory with regard to case A, but with regard to case B what is there to say?" (See *Bava Metzia* 3a.) See previous entry. See also סוֹף סוֹף; הָנִיחָא לְ....

וְתִיסְבְּרָא   See (וְ)תִסְבְּרָא.

תִּיפּוֹק לֵיהּ   *Let him derive it*.... Sometimes, after the reason for a law has been suggested, the Talmud may object that a more obvious reason could have been proposed. (See *Berakhot* 3a/b.)

תֵּיקוּ   Lit., *let it stand*, i.e., the question raised in the previous passage remains unsolved ("standing").

תֵּירוּץ   *Solution.* The resolution of a difficulty. (See קוּשְׁיָא.) After the Gemara has raised an objection to a statement or an argument, it usually attempts to provide a solution (תֵּירוּץ), either by rejecting the hypothesis on which the objection is based or by some other logical method. See לָא קַשְׁיָא; תְּרֵיץ (וְאֵימָא) הָכִי.

תֵּיתֵי לִי   Lit., *may it come to me*, i.e., I deserve to be rewarded (or punished, as the case may be) for the act that I did. (See *Betzah* 36b.)

תַּלְמוּד לוֹמַר   *The verse states.* An expression used in Midrashic expositions of Biblical texts: "We might have thought that X was the case, therefore the verse came to teach us that..." (i.e., that the situation, law, or interpretation is in fact different). (See *Pesaḥim* 115a.) See also יָכוֹל... תַּלְמוּד לוֹמַר...; מִמַּשְׁמַע שֶׁנֶּאֱמַר....

תַּנָּא   (noun) *Tanna.* (1) A scholar of the Mishnaic period. (See

Berakhot 2a.) (2) During the Amoraic period, a scholar who knew Mishnayot and Baraitot by heart and was called upon to recite these texts before the scholars of the Academy. (See *Berakhot* 16a.)

תָּנָא (verb) *He taught*, i.e., he taught · Halakhot, usually Mishnayot or Baraitot. (See *Bava Metzia* 2a.) This usage sometimes has the specific meaning that the scholar being quoted established a particular textual emendation based on a tradition that he himself had learned.

תָּנָא (occasionally תָּאנָא) Lit., *he taught*, a term used to introduce Baraitot and Toseftot. Usually the Baraitot introduced by this expression are very short (one or two sentences), and they clarify, supplement or limit statements in the Mishnah. (See *Bava Metzia* 28a.)

תָּנָא בָּרָא Lit., *the external Tanna*, i.e., the Tanna who is the author of the Baraita under discussion; as opposed to תַּנָּא דִּידָן — "Our Tanna, the Tanna of our Mishnah" (see entry). (See *Moed Katan* 17b.)

תָּנָא בַּתְרָא *The last Tanna*, i.e., the last opinion to be mentioned in a Tannaitic dispute (see *Bava Batra* 93b); as opposed to תַּנָּא קַמָּא — "the first [anonymous] opinion mentioned in a Mishnah" (see entry).

תָּנָא דְּבֵי ר' פְּלוֹנִי *The [scholar of the] school of Rabbi X taught*. An expression used to introduce a tradition transmitted by one of the scholars of a certain school. (See *Berakhot* 19a.)

תַּנָּא דִּידָן *Our Tanna*, i.e., the Tanna whose view is cited in the Mishnah under discussion, as opposed to the Tanna whose view is cited in another Mishnah, or as opposed to תַּנָּא בָּרָא — "The external Tanna, the author of the Baraita under discussion" (see entry). (See *Moed Katan* 17b.)

תָּנָא הֵיכָא קָאֵי *Where does the Tanna stand?* Sometimes a particular Halakhic ruling is laid down in a Mishnah without any indication of the principle (or source) behind it. In such cases the Talmud may ask: "Where does the Tanna stand?" i.e., on what general principle (or source) does the Tanna base himself? (See *Berakhot* 2a.)

תָּנָא (תְּנֵי) וַהֲדַר מְפָרֵשׁ *He taught [it] and then explained [it]*. Sometimes, when a clause or expression in the Mishnah seems superfluous, the Talmud may suggest that it was included in order to explain a previous clause or expression in greater detail. (See *Bava Kamma* 13b.) See also פְּרוּשֵׁי קָא מְפָרֵשׁ.

תָּנָא וְשַׁיֵּיר *He taught and left over*. An expression used when suggesting that a list given in a Mishnah or a Baraita is incomplete: "The Mishnah taught certain cases, and left other cases to be added." (See *Ta'anit* 13b.)
See also מַאי שַׁיֵּיר דְּהַאי שַׁיֵּיר.

תָּנָא חֲדָא מִינַּיְיהוּ נָקֵט *The Tanna cited one of them*, i.e., the Tanna cited one case out of many which he could have cited, and there is no reason to assume that he was unaware

of these other cases. This expression is used as an answer to a question as to why the Tannaitic source under discussion did not make use of other cases as examples of a general rule. (See *Sotah* 8a).

וְתָנָא מַיְיתֵי לָהּ מֵהָכָא *And a Tanna brings [proof] for it from here*. Sometimes, after the Gemara has presented the Biblical source for a Halakhic or an Aggadic teaching in the name of an individual Amora, it continues by saying that there is a statement by an individual Tanna in which this teaching is derived from a different Biblical source. (See *Betzah* 15b.)

תָּנָא סֵיפָא לְגַלּוּיֵי רֵישָׁא *He taught the last clause to shed light on [lit., reveal] the first clause*. Sometimes the Talmud rejects inferences drawn from the last clause of a Mishnah by suggesting: "The Tanna taught the last clause to shed light on the first clause [and thus the latter part of the Mishnah was never intended to teach us anything new]." (See *Bava Metzia* 100a.) See also אִי מִשּׁוּם הָא לָא אִירְיָא.

תָּנָא קוֹמַיָּא וְתָנָא אוֹחֲרָיָא *The first Tanna and the last Tanna*. Expressions in the Jerusalem Talmud, corresponding to תַּנָּא קַמָּא and תַּנָּא בַּתְרָא in the Babylonian Talmud (see entries).

תַּנָּא קַמָּא *The first Tanna*, i.e., the Tanna whose viewpoint is cited anonymously at the beginning of the Mishnah. This viewpoint is then followed by the viewpoint of a named authority who disagrees. (See *Berakhot* 15a.) See also next entry and תַּנָּא בַּתְרָא.

וְתַנָּא קַמָּא *And the first Tanna?* When a Mishnah contains a difference of opinion between the first, anonymous Tanna (תַּנָּא קַמָּא) and the dissenting viewpoint of a named Tanna, the Gemara frequently begins by probing the viewpoint of the named scholar: מַאי טַעֲמָא דְּר' פְּלוֹנִי — "What is Rabbi X's reason?" (See entry.) Having answered this question, the Gemara then turns to the anonymous holder of the first opinion and asks וְתַנָּא קַמָּא — "And what has the first Tanna to say against the argument just presented?" (See *Pesaḥim* 113b.)

וְתָנָא תּוּנָא *And our Tanna taught it*. An expression used by the Gemara to introduce a Mishnah in support of an Amora's statement. (See *Yevamot* 56b.)

תַּנָּאֵי הִיא Lit., *it is Tannaim*, i.e., the subject under discussion between Amoraim is in fact the subject of a Tannaitic controversy. (See *Berakhot* 24a.) See also כְּתַנָּאֵי; לֵימָא כְּתַנָּאֵי.

תַּנָּאֵי שָׁקֵלְתְּ מֵעַלְמָא? תַּנָּאֵי הִיא Lit., *did you remove Tannaim from the world? It is Tannaim [= a Tannaitic controversy]!* Sometimes a contradiction between similar cases is resolved by distinguishing between them, after which the Talmud suggests: "Did you remove Tannaim from the world [i.e., did you forget about the possibility that this matter might be the subject of a Tannaitic controversy]? In fact it is a Tannaitic controversy, and hence there is no need to differentiate between the two cases!" This expression is uniquely associated with Rav Yosef, who goes on to quote a Mishnah or a Baraita in which the controversy is recorded. (See *Shabbat* 53b.)

תָּנוּ רַבָּנָן (ת״ר)   *Our Rabbis taught.* A term used to introduce a Baraita, usually a longer anonymous passage from the Tosefta, Mekhilta, Sifra or Sifrei. (See *Berakhot* 16a.) See also תָּנָא; תַּנְיָא; תְּנַן.

תָּנֵי   *He teaches.* (1) In general, "he teaches a Halakhah." (2) More particularly, in the form תָּנֵי ר׳ פְּלוֹנִי — "Rabbi X teaches" — this term introduces a Baraita which was not widely known or accepted, and which was taught only by a certain Rabbi and his school. (See *Berakhot* 13a.)

תָּנֵי   *Teach!* A term used to introduce a new interpretation or correction of the text of a Mishnah or a Baraita: "Teach" the text as follows! (See *Bava Metzia* 25a.) See also אֵימָא; הָכִי קָאָמַר.

תָּנֵי וַהֲדַר מְפָרֵשׁ   *He teaches and then explains.* See תָּנָא וַהֲדַר מְפָרֵשׁ.

תָּנֵי חֲדָא   Lit., *one teaches,* i.e., one Baraita teaches — the first of two (usually conflicting) Baraitot about to be cited. (See *Bava Metzia* 106b.) See also תַּנְיָא אִידָךְ.

(וְ)תָנֵי עֲלָהּ   Lit., *it was taught concerning it,* i.e., the following Baraita was taught in reference to the Mishnah. A term used to introduce a Baraita which explains the Mishnah under discussion and in effect forms an integral part of it. (See *Yoma* 14b.)

תָּנֵי ר׳ פְּלוֹנִי   See תָּנֵי.

תָּנֵי תַּנָּא קַמֵּיה דְּר׳ פְּלוֹנִי   *The Tanna taught [a Baraita] before Rabbi X.* This expression describes the situation in which a Baraita was recited in the presence of the head of the Academy, and the latter offered his comments on it. (See *Berakhot* 5a.) See also תַּנָּא (noun, subsection 2).

תַּנְיָא   *It was taught.* A term used to introduce a Baraita citing a named Tanna. (See *Berakhot* 3a.) See also תָּנָא; תָּנוּ רַבָּנָן; תְּנַן.

(וְ)תַנְיָא אִידָךְ   *The other taught,* i.e., the second of two (usually conflicting) Baraitot teaches…. (See *Bava Metzia* 106b.) See also (וְהָא)י תַּנָּא מַיְיתֵי לָהּ מֵהָכָא; תָּנֵי חֲדָא.

תַּנְיָא דִּמְסַיְּיעָא לָךְ   Lit., *[what was] taught supports you.* A term used by one Amora to introduce a Baraita which supports the view of another Amora. (See *Shabbat* 146b.)

תַּנְיָא כְּוָותֵיה דְּר׳ פְּלוֹנִי   *It was taught in accordance with Rabbi X,* i.e., the Baraita that follows supports the view of Rabbi X, an Amora whose view has previously been stated and is the subject of disagreement. (See *Bava Metzia* 34a.)

תַּנְיָא כְּוָותֵיה דְּר׳ פְּלוֹנִי, תַּנְיָא כְּוָותֵיה דְּר׳ אַלְמוֹנִי   *It was taught in accordance with Rabbi X; it was taught in accordance with Rabbi Y.* Where there is a dispute between two Amoraim, this expression is sometimes used by the Gemara to introduce two anonymous Baraitot, one of which agrees with the viewpoint of the one Amora and the other of which agrees with the viewpoint of the second. (See *Berakhot* 24b.) See also previous entry.

תַּנְיָא נַמֵּי הָכִי   *It was also taught thus.* A term used to introduce a Baraita which supports the previous statement by the Gemara or by an individual Amora. (See *Berakhot* 9b.)

תְּנֵינָא   *We have learned.* A term used to introduce an objection based on a statement in a Mishnah or a Baraita which makes a prior statement or question seem superfluous, since it is already covered in a Mishnah or a Baraita. (See *Ta'anit* 10a.) See also אַף אֲנַן נַמֵּי תְּנֵינָא; מַאי קָא מַשְׁמַע לָן תְּנֵינָא.

תְּנֵינָא חֲדָא זִימְנָא   *We have learned it once,* i.e., we have already learned what was just said elsewhere in a Mishnah or a Baraita. Why, therefore, was it necessary to repeat the matter here? (See *Berakhot* 50a.)

תְּנֵינָא לְהָא דְּתָנוּ רַבָּנָן   *We have learned this, as our Sages taught….* An expression used to introduce a Baraita in support of the previous statement, usually a Mishnah or an Amoraic elucidation of a Mishnah. (See *Moed Katan* 8b.)

תְּנֵיתוּהָ   *You have learned it.* Sometimes an Amora may answer a question by noting that the answer is already found in a Tannaitic source. This term was often used by Rav Sheshet, and the sources which it introduces were usually well known (e.g., Mishnayot). (See *Bava Metzia* 23b.)

תְּנַן   *We have learned.* A term used to introduce a quotation from a Mishnah, either in support of an argument or as the basis for an objection. (See *Berakhot* 21b.) See next entry. See also תַּנְיָא and (וְהָא תְּנַן).

תְּנַן הָתָם   *We have learned elsewhere.* A term used to introduce a quotation from a Mishnah which is not at present under discussion (usually, a Mishnah from another tractate or another chapter of the tractate being studied), but which has a bearing on it. (See *Bava Metzia* 9b.)

וּתְנַן נַמֵּי גַבֵּי… כִּי הַאי גַוְונָא וּצְרִיכָא   *And we have also learned similarly regarding… and [both were] necessary.* Where a similar law regarding two different, though comparable, cases is found in two tractates, the Gemara sometimes states directly that both are necessary and does not raise the question of apparently unnecessary repetition. (See *Bava Metzia* 119a.) See also הָא תּוּ לָמָה לִי; מַאי קָמַשְׁמַע לָן תְּנֵינָא; תְּנֵינָא חֲדָא זִימְנָא.

וְתִסְבְּרָא   *And [how] do you understand?* The Gemara uses this expression when seeking to refute an argument based on a particular interpretation of an authoritative (usually Biblical) text, showing that the text upon which the argument is based must anyway (for other reasons) be understood differently or emended. (See *Pesaḥim* 26a.) See also מִי סָבְרַתְּ.

תִּסְתַּיֵּים   *Conclude.* Sometimes the Talmud notes that there was a controversy between two scholars concerning a certain issue, but it is not clear which scholar took what position. In such cases the Talmud's initial attempt to attribute the views correctly is often introduced by the expression תִּסְתַּיֵּים דְּר׳ פְּלוֹנִי הוּא דַּאֲמַר — "Conclude that it was Rabbi X who said… [and that Rabbi B holds the other view]." If this suggestion is confirmed later on in the discussion, the Talmud may close the discussion with the remark תִּסְתַּיֵּים — "Conclude [that the suggested identification was indeed correct]." (See *Berakhot* 45b.) See also חַד אָמַר... וְחַד אָמַר...

תִּפְשׁוֹט   *You may solve, you may answer.* Sometimes, after a certain assumption has been made, the Talmud may suggest that another problem can be "solved" on the basis of this assumption. Usually, however, this suggestion is rejected: לְעוֹלָם לָא תִּפְשׁוֹט — "Do not explain the matter in this way...!" (See *Pesaḥim* 4b.)

תַּרְגְּמָהּ   *He explained it,* i.e., he explained a difficult Tannaitic source, often by suggesting that it refers to a special case or that it follows the view of a particular scholar. (See *Bava Metzia* 80b.) See also next entry.

תַּרְגְּמָהּ אַלִיבָּא דְּ...   *He explained it according to...,* i.e., a certain Amora explained a Tannaitic source according to the view of a certain Amora, frequently the Amora with whom he is in dispute. (See *Pesaḥim* 12b.)

תְּרֵי גַוְונֵי   *Two types, two categories* (lit., "two colors"). Sometimes seemingly superfluous repetition in a Mishnah is explained by suggesting that the clause (or statement) deals with "two similar but different categories" of the item under discussion. (See *Bava Metzia* 8b.)

תְּרֵי תַנָּאֵי הִיא   *It is two Tannaim,* i.e., the two seemingly contradictory parts of the Mishnah reflect the views of two different Tannaim. (See *Pesaḥim* 57a.)
See also קַשְׁיָא רֵישָׁא אַסֵּיפָא; רֵישָׁא ר׳ פְּלוֹנִי וְסֵיפָא ר׳ אַלְמוֹנִי; תַּבְרָא.

תְּרֵי תַנָּאֵי וְאַלִּיבָּא דר׳ פְּלוֹנִי   *Two Tannaim, according to Rabbi X.* Sometimes a contradiction between two statements made by the same Tanna is resolved by suggesting that this Tanna's original statement was reported differently by two other scholars: "Two later Tannaim reported the view of Rabbi X differently." (See *Berakhot* 3a.)

תָּרֵיץ (וְאֵימָא) הָכִי   *Answer (and explain) thus,* i.e., solve the difficulty as follows. Often this solution entails correction of the text that caused the problem. (See *Shabbat* 103b.)

תַּרְתֵּי   *Two?!* An expression indicating astonishment at (1) an internal contradiction within a source (see *Bava Kamma* 21a), and (2) needless repetition within a source (see *Sukkah* 29a).

תַּרְתֵּי לָמָה לִי   *Why do I need two,* i.e., why do I need two statements, each of which teaches the same Halakhah? Or: "Why do I need two statements when one can be inferred from the other?" (See *Eruvin* 49a.)

תַּרְתֵּי מַשְׁמַע   *It means two [things],* i.e., the source under discussion can be interpreted in two ways, and thus two inferences can be drawn from it. (See *Shabbat* 28b.)

תַּרְתֵּי קָאָמַר   *He says two [things],* i.e., the source cited deals with two separate subjects. (See *Bava Metzia* 77b.)
See also סָבַר לָהּ כְּוָותֵיהּ בַּחֲדָא וּפָלֵיג עֲלֵיהּ בַּחֲדָא.

תְּשׁוּבָה   *Response, refutation,* i.e., rejection of the previous viewpoint. The Tannaitic equivalent of תְּיוּבְתָּא (see entry). (See *Bava Metzia* 59b.)

The Principles
of Talmudic Hermeneutics

Much of Talmudic literature is devoted to the exposition of Biblical verses, or Midrash, as it is known in Hebrew. Two types of Midrash are found in the Talmud: Halakhic Midrash, in which the Halakhic contents of the Torah are expounded, and Aggadic Midrash, containing homiletic explanations of the Biblical text, bringing out its moral and theological implications. Outside the Talmud, we find entire works devoted to Halakhic Midrash, the so-called Halakhic Midrashim: Mekhilta on Exodus; Sifra (also known as Torat Kohanim) on Leviticus; Sifrei on Numbers and Deuteronomy. Other works are devoted to Aggadic Midrash; these are called the Aggadic Midrashim, and they include the Midrash Rabbah (on the Five Books of the Torah and the Five Megillot), Midrash Tanḥuma, etc.

Considerable effort has been devoted by Rabbinic scholars to investigating the method by which Halakhic Midrash derives legal rulings from the Biblical text. Were Halakhot actually derived from the Biblical verses, or were these Halakhot originally known independently and only later associated with the Biblical text, in order to make it easier for students to study and memorize them? Differing views may be found both in the works of the classical Talmudic commentators and in those of modern scholars, although in fact this issue remains unresolved, and it is possible that different Halakhot were derived in different ways.

In any event, arbitrary explanations of the Biblical text are not to be found in either the Halakhic or Aggadic Midrashim. All these works follow fixed principles of interpretation, which are known in Rabbinic Hebrew as הַמִּדּוֹת שֶׁהַתּוֹרָה נִדְרֶשֶׁת בָּהֶן — "the principles through which the Torah is expounded." Different lists of such principles are found in Rabbinic literature (e.g., the seven hermeneutic principles of Hillel, the thirteen hermeneutic principles of Rabbi Yishmael, the thirty-two exegetic principles of Rabbi Eliezer the son of Rabbi Yose HaGelili), but none of these lists provides a complete description of all the interpretative principles found either in Halakhic Midrash or in

Aggadic Midrash. Even the Malbim *(Rabbi Meir Loeb ben Yeḥiel Michal [1809–1879]), who compiled a list containing 613 principles of Halakhic Midrash, did not exhaust all the interpretative approaches encountered in Talmudic literature. It should also be noted that many of these approaches were not explicitly formulated as exegetical principles, although their existence can be discerned through careful analysis of the Midrashic texts themselves.*

In the list that follows, we have presented the most frequently encountered principles of Biblical interpretation, together with significant details concerning the way they are used.

אֵין מוּקְדָם וּמְאוּחָר בַּתּוֹרָה *There is no absolute chron-ological order in the Torah* (lit., "there is no earlier and later in the Torah"). In other words, the events and laws contained in the Torah are not necessarily arranged in chronological order. Thus, the narratives in the Torah need not be interpreted as having taken place in the exact order that they are related. This principle applies only to the order in which the different sections (פָּרָשִׁיוֹת) of the Torah are arranged; verses within a given section, by contrast, are assumed to be arranged in exact chronological order. See כְּלָל וּפְרָט.

אֵין מִקְרָא יוֹצֵא מִידֵי פְּשׁוּטוֹ Lit., *a verse does not depart from its literal meaning.* Frequently, the Rabbinic interpretations of Biblical verses (דְּרָשׁוֹת) deviate significantly from the literal meaning of the text; nevertheless, in such cases the literal meaning is also considered a viable approach to interpreting the Torah, and hence both the literal and Midrashic approaches to interpreting the Torah are deemed valid.

אָם אֵינוֹ עִנְיָן... *If it does not refer to....* Or, as this principle is termed in the thirty-two exegetical principles of Rabbi Eliezer the son of Rabbi Yose HaGelili: "Something that was stated in a certain context but does not apply there, but in a different context...." This principle is used in both Halakhic and Aggadic Midrashim. When a law or a verse is discussed by the Torah in a certain context, and it can be shown that there is no need for this verse to appear in this context (or that it is even impossible to interpret the verse in this context), the Talmud may suggest that the problematic verse be interpreted as applying in another, similar, context, where it is relevant. The formula usually used to introduce this idea is אָם אֵינוֹ עִנְיָן לְ... תְּנֵהוּ עִנְיָן לְ... — "If it is not relevant to context X, refer it to context Y." It should be stressed that assumptions of "transferred context" are not made arbitrarily, and as a rule the Talmud uses this principle only if there is support from another source for the idea that the Talmud is trying to prove by invoking the idea of "transferred context." See יִתּוּר.

אַסְמַכְתָּא (also, אַסְמַכְתָּא בְּעָלְמָא) Lit., *(mere) support.* Sometimes, the Rabbis in the Talmud explicitly state that the Biblical verse cited as the basis for a law is merely an allusion to the law rather than its actual source; in such cases, the verse is called an אַסְמַכְתָּא — "support" — for the law. Since laws of this kind do not actually derive from the Biblical text (which serves, instead, as a sort of mnemonic for remembering them), they are generally Rabbinic decrees; in the Talmud's phrase, מִדְרַבָּנָן וּקְרָא אַסְמַכְתָּא בְּעָלְמָא — "the law is Rabbinic, and the verse is a mere אַסְמַכְתָּא".

בִּנְיַן אָב *Analogy, i.e., interpretation based on induction.* בִּנְיַן אָב is one of the fundamental Talmudic principles of Biblical interpretation, and it appears in all the standard lists of exegetical rules. Three types of בִּנְיַן אָב are found in Rabbinic literature: (1) בִּנְיַן אָב מַה מָּצִינוּ — lit., "What do we find with regard to...?" (2) בִּנְיַן אָב מִכָּתוּב אֶחָד — "analogy on the basis of one verse." (3) מִשְׁנֵי כְתוּבִים — "analogy based on two verses." The simplest form of the בִּנְיַן אָב is the מַה מָּצִינוּ — "Just as we find in case A that law X applies, so too we may infer that in case B, which is similar to case A, law X should apply." Thus, the מַה מָּצִינוּ is a generalization from one case, where certain details are specified, applied to a similar case (or series of cases) where such details are not specified.

The בִּנְיַן אָב based on one verse (or two verses) has a more complicated structure than the מַה מָּצִינוּ, even though it follows the same basic principle. This type of בִּנְיַן אָב is used when the two cases being compared are not fully analogous, and so an objection is raised to the comparison. In such instances, the Talmud cites an additional case (C), which, together with the first case (A), may serve as the basis of a viable comparison. The wording usually used to introduce an objection to a בִּנְיַן אָב based on two verses is …שֶׁכֵּן ...לְ ...מַה — "What about case A, on which the original comparison was based, since the following objection applies?" Then case C is introduced, and hence we may infer that just as law X applies in cases A and C, so too it should apply in case B, which is similar to both A and C. However, this new comparison may also be challenged: "What about case C, since...?" After which the Talmud will reply: לֹא רְאִי זֶה כִּרְאִי זֶה וְלֹא רְאִי זֶה כִּרְאִי זֶה הַצַּד הַשָּׁוֶה שֶׁבָּהֶן שֶׁ... — "This aspect is not like that aspect, and that aspect is not like this aspect; the common denominator is...," (i.e., while there may be a certain difference between cases B and C, this difference does not affect the analogy between A and B; thus both A and C have a common denominator making them comparable to B). Even the comparison based on this "common denominator" may be challenged: מַה לְהַצַּד הַשָּׁוֶה שֶׁבָּהֶן שֶׁ... — "What about the common denominator, since...?" And the Talmudic discussion will proceed by citing and refuting additional cases until all the cases from which a comparison could be drawn have been exhausted. See שְׁנֵי כְתוּבִים הַבָּאִים כְּאֶחָד.

גְּזֵירָה שָׁוָה

Gezerah shavah, *verbal analogy*. A fundamental Talmudic principle of Biblical interpretation, appearing in all the standard lists of exegetical rules. If the same word or phrase appears in two places in the Torah, and a certain law is explicitly stated in one of these places, we may infer on the basis of "verbal analogy" that the same law must apply in the other case as well. Thus, the inferences drawn on the basis of גְּזֵירָה שָׁוָה rely on verbal identity, rather than on conceptual similarity, as in בִּנְיַן אָב (see the previous entry). For example, the Torah states concerning those convicted of certain types of sorcery (Leviticus 20:27): "They shall surely be put to death: they shall stone them with stones: their blood shall be upon them." Since this verse uses the expression: "Their blood shall be upon them" when speaking of death by stoning, the Talmud infers by גְּזֵירָה שָׁוָה that in all cases where this expression is used, capital punishment is to be inflicted by stoning. Usually inferences can be drawn through גְּזֵירָה שָׁוָה only if the same word (or phrase) appears in both of the verses being compared, although a גְּזֵירָה שָׁוָה may occasionally be drawn even if the words being compared are not identical, provided that their meanings are similar.

In its simplest form, then, the גְּזֵירָה שָׁוָה is a type of linguistic interpretation by means of which the meaning of an obscure word or phrase is inferred on the basis of another occurrence of the same word or phrase in a clearer context. However, גְּזֵירָה שָׁוָה is often used not only to determine the meaning of obscure words and phrases, but to "transfer" entire Halakhot from one context to another. Accordingly, certain limitations were placed on the use of this principle, to prevent unfounded conclusions from being drawn. Most significantly, "one cannot infer a גְּזֵירָה שָׁוָה on one's own," i.e., only a גְּזֵירָה שָׁוָה based on ancient tradition is valid. However, a difference of opinion exists with regard to the exact nature of the tradition required for making a גְּזֵירָה שָׁוָה. A second condition required for making a גְּזֵירָה שָׁוָה is that at least one of the words on which the גְּזֵירָה שָׁוָה is based

must be מוּפְנֶה (lit., "free, empty"), i.e., unnecessary in its own context. In such cases, we may justifiably assume that this word was included for the express purpose of inferring a גְּזֵירָה שָׁוָה. There are several types of מוּפְנֶה: (1) מוּפְנֶה מִשְּׁנֵי צְדָדִים — "Free on both sides," i.e., the words on which the גְּזֵירָה שָׁוָה is based are unnecessary in both of the places where they appear. In such cases, the גְּזֵירָה שָׁוָה is considered incontrovertible, or, to use the Talmudic expression, לְמֵדִים וְאֵין מְשִׁיבִים — "We can learn, but not refute." (2) מוּפְנֶה מִצַּד אֶחָד — "Free on one side," i.e., only one of the words on which the גְּזֵירָה שָׁוָה is based is unnecessary in its own context. (3) Not מוּפְנֶה at all. Arguments based on these latter types of גְּזֵירָה שָׁוָה can be refuted (לְמֵדִים וּמְשִׁיבִים) by logical proof. Another general rule governing the application of this principle states that אֵין גְּזֵירָה שָׁוָה לְמֶחֱצָה — "There cannot be half a גְּזֵירָה שָׁוָה." In other words, a גְּזֵירָה שָׁוָה must work in both directions, and if an inference is drawn by גְּזֵירָה שָׁוָה from case A to case B, then we may draw conclusions not only from case A to case B, but also from case B to case A. A controversy exists as to the extent of the conclusions that can be inferred through גְּזֵירָה שָׁוָה. According to one opinion, the rule is דּוֹן מִינָהּ וּמִינָהּ — "Learn from it!" (Lit., "deduce from it and again from it.") According to this view, the conclusions that can be drawn from a גְּזֵירָה שָׁוָה extend even to items that were not explicitly included in the original גְּזֵירָה שָׁוָה. Others, however, maintain that the rule is דּוֹן מִינָהּ וְאוֹקֵי בְּאַתְרָא — "Deduce from it and leave it in its place," i.e., no conclusions can be drawn beyond those included in the original גְּזֵירָה שָׁוָה.

גִּילּוּי מִילְתָא

(גִּילּוּי מִילְתָא בְּעָלְמָא sometimes:) *(Merely) revealing something*. Occasionally, the Midrashic explanation of a Biblical verse does not serve as the source for a previously unknown Halakhah or interpretation, but merely brings out with greater emphasis a point that was self-explanatory or was already known from another source (although it had not been made explicit in the Torah). Such Midrashic explanations "merely reveal something," and hence the restrictions that govern the other hermeneutic principles do not apply in these cases, since fully rigorous proofs are not required here.

דִּבֶּר הַכָּתוּב בַּהוֹוֶה

Lit., *the verse speaks about the present*. One of the exegetical principles of Rabbi Eliezer the son of Rabbi Yose HaGelili: Halakhic inferences cannot always be drawn from details specified in the Torah. Such details may have been specified because the Torah was describing a situation encountered in everyday life. For example, the Torah states (Exodus 22:30): "Neither shall you eat any flesh that is torn of beasts in the field." In fact, however, even the flesh of a carcass that was not found in a field is forbidden, and the Torah states "in the field" here because that is where carcasses are usually found.

דָּבָר הַלָּמֵד מִסּוֹפוֹ

Lit., *something learned from its end*, i.e., the interpretation of one verse on the basis of a subsequent verse. One of the hermeneutic principles of Rabbi Yishmael. For example, the Torah states (Leviticus 14:34): "And I shall put the plague of leprosy in the house of the land of your possession." On the basis of this verse, one might think that the laws of house leprosy apply to any kind of house, but in Leviticus 14:45 we read that "...he shall break down the house, its stones, its wood, and all the mortar...," and thus we may infer that the laws of house-leprosy apply only to houses made of stones, wood, and mortar.

דָּבָר הַלָּמֵד מֵעִנְיָנוֹ *Something learned from its context.* One of Rabbi Yishmael's hermeneutic principles. An unclear verse should be interpreted in the light of the context in which it appears. For example, the verse "You shall not steal" in the Ten Commandments (Exodus 20:15; Deuteronomy 5:17) would at first seem to refer to stealing money, but since all the other offenses appearing in this context are capital crimes (e.g., murder, adultery), the Talmud interprets our verse as referring to kidnapping.

דָּבָר שֶׁהָיָה בִּכְלָל *Something that was included in a generalization.* The Torah frequently states a law in general terms and then offers specific instances. What is the relation between the general law and the specific examples? A number of hermeneutical rules to guide us are found in the lists of both Rabbi Yishmael and Rabbi Eliezer the son of Rabbi Yose HaGelili. One such rule is דָּבָר שֶׁהָיָה בִּכְלָל וְיָצָא מִן הַכְּלָל לְלַמֵּד, לֹא לְלַמֵּד עַל עַצְמוֹ יָצָא, אֶלָּא לְלַמֵּד עַל הַכְּלָל כּוּלּוֹ יָצָא — "Something that was included in a generalization, but was explicitly specified to teach something, was intended to teach not just about itself but about the entire generalization." For example, the Torah states that all work is forbidden on Shabbat (a generalization), yet it also states specifically that it is forbidden to kindle fire on Shabbat. From here the Talmud deduces that each category of work is prohibited independently on Shabbat, and thus a person who performs different types of work on Shabbat is punishable for each type of work that he performs.

Another such rule is דָּבָר שֶׁהָיָה בִּכְלָל וְיָצָא לִטְעוֹן טוֹעַן אֶחָד שֶׁהוּא כְעִנְיָנוֹ, יָצָא לְהָקֵל וְלֹא לְהַחֲמִיר — "Something that was included in a generalization, but was specified to discuss a provision similar to those that apply in the generalization [lit., 'like it'], was intended to be lenient rather than strict." If some (but not all) of the restrictions specified in connection with the generalization are mentioned in connection with the specific case, we may conclude that only those restrictions specified in connection with the particular case apply there.

Another, contrasting, application of דָּבָר שֶׁהָיָה בִּכְלָל is דָּבָר שֶׁהָיָה בִּכְלָל וְיָצָא לִטְעוֹן טוֹעַן אַחֵר שֶׁלֹא כְעִנְיָנוֹ, יָצָא לְהָקֵל וּלְהַחֲמִיר — "Something that was included in a generalization, but was specified as containing a provision different from those contained in the generalization, was intended to be both lenient and strict." If a certain rule was mentioned in connection with the specific case, but not in connection with the generalization, we may infer that the law in the specific case may be either stricter or more lenient than that in the generalization, depending on the circumstances.

A broader application of the previous rule is דָּבָר שֶׁהָיָה בִּכְלָל וְיָצָא מִן הַכְּלָל לִדּוֹן בַּדָּבָר הֶחָדָשׁ, אִי אַתָּה יָכוֹל לְהַחֲזִירוֹ לִכְלָלוֹ עַד שֶׁיַּחֲזִירֶנּוּ הַכָּתוּב לִכְלָלוֹ בְּפֵירוּשׁ — "Something that was included in a generalization but was specified as something new, cannot be returned to its generalization until the Torah explicitly returns it to its generalization." Accordingly, if a law that runs counter to a generalization is mentioned in connection with a specific case, we may infer that the laws of the generalization no longer apply to the specific case until the Torah explicitly states otherwise.

For example, after discussing the laws of peace-offerings (שְׁלָמִים) in general terms, the Torah sets forth specific laws pertaining to thanks-offerings (תּוֹדָה), which are actually a kind of peace-offering. Hence, we may conclude that the laws of peace-offerings do not apply to thanks-offerings unless otherwise specified.

דִּבְּרָה תוֹרָה בִּלְשׁוֹן בְּנֵי אָדָם *The Torah spoke in the language of men.* Despite its apparently comprehensive wording, this principle has only narrow and specific application. Frequently, double verbs are used in the Torah (e.g., שַׁלֵּחַ תְּשַׁלַּח — "you shall surely release"). According to Rabbi Yishmael and his school, such verbs have no exegetical significance, as doubling of the verb is simply an ordinary linguistic usage ("the Torah spoke in the language of men"), whereas Rabbi Akiva and his school attempted to draw Halakhic inferences from such verb repetitions. Thus, "the Torah spoke in the language of men" is not a general principle of Biblical exegesis, as its application is limited to cases where a verb form is repeated. Indeed, this formulation of our rule is not found in the Jerusalem Talmud, where the controversy between Rabbi Akiva and Rabbi Yishmael is described thus: לְשׁוֹנוֹת כְּפוּלִין הֵן / לְשׁוֹנוֹת רִיבּוּיִין הֵן — i.e., double verbs are either "repeated expressions" (and hence exegetically insignificant) or "amplificatory expressions" (i.e., exegetically significant).

דִּבְרֵי תוֹרָה מִדִּבְרֵי קַבָּלָה לָא יָלְפִינַן Lit., *we do not learn words of Torah from words of tradition,* i.e., exegetical inferences concerning the Torah cannot be drawn from the Prophets or the Hagiographa. The reason for this is that the Prophets were not permitted to introduce new Halakhot, and hence only the Torah is an authoritative source of Halakhah. Nevertheless, exegetical inferences that are only based on allusion, or that "merely reveal something" (see גִּילּוּי מִילְתָא), may be derived from the Prophets or the Hagiographa. (This principle is not always followed in the Jerusalem Talmud.)

דּוֹרְשִׁין תְּחִילוֹת Lit., *we interpret beginnings.* When a key word appears more than once in the Torah's discussion of a certain law, the Talmud usually draws exegetical inferences from the repetition of this word (since such repetition would otherwise appear superfluous). However, there is a dispute among the Talmudic sages as to whether the first occurrence of a repeated key word is exegetically significant — "we do interpret beginnings" (= first occurrences of a word) — or not (since the first mention of an item can never be considered superfluous, "we do not interpret beginnings").

דַּיּוֹ Lit., *it is sufficient.* This is a shortened form of the expression דַּיּוֹ לַבָּא מִן הַדִּין לִהְיוֹת כַּנִּדּוֹן (lit., "it is sufficient if the conclusion inferred is like the source of the inference") — a principle limiting the applicability of a *kal vaḥomer*. See קַל וָחוֹמֶר.

הֶיקֵּשׁ *Analogy.* An important exegetical principle. When two cases are mentioned together in the same verse (or adjacent verses), the Talmud usually assumes that, since they were juxtaposed, they are analogous. Hence legal inferences may be drawn by comparing the two cases. (On rare occasions, the analogy may even be stated explicitly by the Torah, as in

Deuteronomy 22:26: "But to the girl [who was raped in a field] you shall do nothing; the girl has committed no capital sin, for as when a man rises up against his neighbor to murder him, so too in this case.") For example, the Torah states that a woman being divorced "shall go out of [her husband's] house, and go and marry another man" (Deuteronomy 24:2). Since divorce and marriage are mentioned in the same verse, the Talmud deduces that many of the laws governing divorce apply to marriage and vice versa. הֶיקֵּשׁ is governed by the principle אֵין הֶיקֵּשׁ לְמֶחֱצָה — "there cannot be half a הֶיקֵּשׁ" — and hence the inferences drawn through הֶיקֵּשׁ must be bilateral (cf. גְּזֵירָה שָׁוָה above, where a similar principle is discussed). Accordingly, the cases compared through הֶיקֵּשׁ are considered completely analogous, to the point where occasionally the Gemara sets out to draw an inference from case A to case B, but in the course of the argument we find that the inference actually should be drawn from case B to case A (this phenomenon, known as בָּא לְלַמֵּד וְנִמְצָא לָמֵד — "something that came to teach and was ultimately inferred" — is one of the exegetical principles of Rabbi Eliezer the son of Rabbi Yose HaGelili). See סְמוּכִים.

זֵכֶר לַדָּבָר   Lit., *remembrance of something*, i.e., "allusion." This term is often found in the expression אַף עַל פִּי שֶׁאֵין רְאָיָה לַדָּבָר זֵכֶר לַדָּבָר — "Even though there is no proof of this matter, there is an allusion to the matter." In certain cases, a Biblical verse cannot serve as full-fledged proof of an idea that it has been adduced to support, either because it was interpreted out of context or for other reasons. In such instances, the Talmud may nevertheless cite the verse as a mnemonic aid, to facilitate remembering the idea associated with it (see אַסְמַכְתָּא). Such a mnemonic verse is termed זֵכֶר לַדָּבָר. For example, the Talmud finds an allusion to the practice of tying a strip of red wool to the goat that was sent to Azazel on Yom Kippur (see Leviticus 16:22; Mishnah *Yoma* 6:8) in the verse: "Though your sins be as scarlet, they shall be as white as snow; though they be red as crimson, they shall be as wool" (Isaiah 1:18). This verse is thus a זֵכֶר לַדָּבָר.

חִידּוּשׁ   Lit., *novelty*. A unique law that differs from seemingly comparable laws in the Torah. For example, the law prohibiting the consumption of meat and milk mixtures is a חִידּוּשׁ, since each component of the mixture is itself permitted, and only when these components are mixed is the resulting food prohibited. Other prohibited foods, by contrast, are not produced by mixing permissible foods. And since a חִידּוּשׁ is by definition unique, no exegetical inferences (e.g., *kal vaḥomer, gezerah shavah*) can be drawn from such cases.

טַעֲמֵי הַמִּצְוֹת   *Reasons for the mitzvot*. There is a dispute among the Tannaim as to whether or not legal inferences may be drawn from the reasons for the mitzvot specified in the Torah. Exegesis based on the reasoning behind the law may, at times, even seem to deviate from the plain meaning of the Biblical text. This is termed by the Talmud דָּרְשִׁינַן טַעֲמָא דִּקְרָא — i.e., "we expound the reason for the verse." For example, the Torah states (Deuteronomy 17:17): "[The king] shall not multiply wives, lest his heart be led astray," and from here some of the Sages deduced that a king may marry as many wives as he wishes, provided that they are pious women who will not "lead his heart

astray." Although such exegesis is traditionally associated with Rabbi Shimon bar Yoḥai, it seems that such interpretations were made by other Sages as well, and the dispute between the Tannaim was essentially to what extent it was permitted to rely on such interpretations.

יֵשׁ אֵם לַמָּסוֹרֶת, יֵשׁ אֵם לַמִּקְרָא   *The consonantal text of the Torah is authoritative, the vocalized text of the Torah is authoritative*. Although Hebrew writing does not have vowels, certain letters are occasionally added to words in place of vowels. However, this is not always done, and often a word can be vocalized in two different ways. Usually, one vocalization represents the singular form, and another the plural. Thus, some Sages maintain that words spelled without these vocalized consonants should be interpreted as singular forms (for purposes of Halakhic Midrash), in accordance with the consonantal spelling ("the consonantal text is authoritative"), while other Rabbis, following the traditional Masoretic vocalization, interpret them as plural forms ("the vocalized text is authoritative"). Nevertheless, both sides in this controversy concede that, on certain occasions, it is possible to follow the alternative view.

יִתּוּר   Lit., *superfluity*. This is one of the fundamental principles of Halakhic Midrash, and it is based on the assumption that the wording of the Torah is extremely precise, and hence every word (and even every letter) in the Torah is significant. Thus, if a word in the Torah appears superfluous, we may assume that it was intended to teach us something that we would not otherwise have known. This axiom serves as the basis for many other exegetical principles (e.g., אִם אֵינוֹ עִנְיָן...), and is a cardinal rule of both Halakhic and Aggadic Midrashim. Even where the appearance of a seemingly superfluous expression can be explained on stylistic grounds, the Talmud prefers to draw legal inferences from it, arguing that the unnecessary word was intended to provide special emphasis (see שָׁנָה עָלָיו הַכָּתוּב לְעַכֵּב), or that it alludes to cases not explicitly mentioned in the Biblical text. Often, the Rabbis in the Talmud differed as to precisely what constitutes a superfluous expression, e.g., whether the definite article (the letter ה prefixed to a word) or the word "and" (the letter ו prefixed to a word) should be considered superfluous.

כְּלָל וּפְרָט   *Generalization and detail*. A number of hermeneutic principles deal with the relationship between generalizations and details; some of these are included in Rabbi Yishmael's list of thirteen principles.

(1) כְּלָל וּפְרָט — *Generalization and detail*. When a generalization in the Torah is followed by a detail, we may assume that the generalization refers only to what was specified in the detail. For example, the Torah states that burnt-offerings (קָרְבַּן עוֹלָה) may be brought "from animals, from cattle and from sheep" (Leviticus 1:2). "Animals," a generalization, includes cattle and sheep, but since these were specified separately, after the generalization, we learn that only cattle and sheep may be offered as burnt-offerings, and not other animals. The generalization was included in such cases to prevent us from drawing inferences by analogy (see above, בִּנְיַן אָב) from the details cited.

(2) פְּרָט וּכְלָל — *Detail and generalization.* When a detail cited in the Torah is followed by a generalization, we follow the generalization and do not limit application of the law in question to cases specified in the detail.

(3) כְּלָל וּפְרָט וּכְלָל — *Generalization and detail and generalization.* This principle is, in a sense, a combination of the previous two principles: When a generalization in the Torah is followed by one or more details, and they, in turn, are followed by another generalization, application of the law under discussion is limited to items that resemble the detail (כְּעֵין הַפְּרָט — "like the detail"). For example, the Torah states that money used to redeem the second tithe (מַעֲשֵׂר שֵׁנִי) must be spent as follows: "You shall spend the money on whatever you desire — on cattle, sheep, wine, strong drink, or whatever you wish" (Deuteronomy 14:26). Hence, the Talmud deduces that "tithe-money" may be spent only on things that resemble the details specified in this verse (cattle, sheep, wine, strong drink), i.e., items that derived their sustenance from the ground yet did not actually grow from the ground, but rather underwent some sort of development or processing.

(4) פְּרָט וּכְלָל וּפְרָט — *Detail and generalization and detail.* This principle is, in effect, the inverse of the previous rule: When a detail is followed by a generalization, and this generalization is followed by another detail, the law under discussion applies only to cases that are extremely similar to the detail and that resemble it in a number of respects.

(5) שְׁנֵי כְלָלִים הַסְּמוּכִים זֶה לָזֶה, הַטֵּל פְּרָט בֵּינֵיהֶם וְדוּנֵם בִּכְלָל וּפְרָט וּכְלָל — *If two generalizations are next to each other, place a detail between them and treat them as a generalization and detail and generalization.* In other words, we may apply the rule of "generalization and detail and generalization" even if the detail is not specified between the two generalizations.

(6) כְּלָל וּפְרָט הַמְרוּחָקִים זֶה מִזֶּה — *Generalization and detail that are far from each other.* There is a controversy in the Talmud as to whether or not it is possible to apply the principle of כְּלָל וּפְרָט when the generalization and detail do not appear in the same verse (or in adjacent verses), but only in the same section of the Torah.

(7) כְּלָל הַצָּרִיךְ לִפְרָט וּפְרָט הַצָּרִיךְ לִכְלָל — *A generalization that needs a detail, and a detail that needs a generalization.* Sometimes, a generalization is mentioned in the Torah, yet its meaning cannot be understood without reference to a detail mentioned with it (and vice versa: sometimes the meaning of a detail cannot be understood without reference to the generalization). In such cases, we do not follow the rules of "generalization and detail" or "detail and generalization" discussed above; instead, the detail and generalization are regarded as part of a single, inseparable expression.

לָמֵד מְלַמֵּד בְּקָדָשִׁים   *An inference from what has already been inferred in laws of sacrifices.* As a rule, conclusions drawn on the basis of the exegetical principles are treated as though they were explicitly specified in the Torah, and hence further inferences may be drawn from these conclusions *ad infinitum.* However, this rule has one exception: In the laws of sacrifices, additional inferences cannot be drawn on the basis of conclusions inferred from the exegetical principles (with certain exceptions, which are set forth at length in the fifth chapter of tractate *Zevaḥim*).

מַה מָּצִינוּ   Lit., *what do we find [with regard to...].* An interpretative principle based on inductive reasoning. See בִּנְיַן אָב.

סְמוּכִים   *Juxtaposition.* An exegetical principle used to derive Halakhic conclusions or ethical teachings from the fact that two verses appear next to each other. One of the Tannaim, Rabbi Yehudah, applied this principle only to verses in Deuteronomy, and not to verses in the rest of the Torah. See הֶיקֵּשׁ.

קַל וָחוֹמֶר   An *a fortiori inference.* One of the fundamental principles of Rabbinic exegesis, קַל וָחוֹמֶר is listed in all the standard lists of exegetical rules. In essence, this is a rule of logical argumentation by means of which a comparison is drawn between two cases, one lenient and the other stringent. קַל וָחוֹמֶר asserts that if the law is stringent in a case where we are usually lenient, then it will certainly be stringent in a more serious case; likewise, if the law is lenient in a case where we are usually not lenient, then it will certainly be lenient in a less serious case. A *fortiori* argumentation is already found in the Bible, and lists of Biblical verses containing *a fortiori* arguments were compiled by the Talmudic Rabbis. For example, "If you have run with the foot-soldiers, and they have wearied you, how can you contend with horses?" (Jeremiah 12:5.) This is one of the most commonly encountered exegetical principles, since *a fortiori* inferences can be drawn even without support from tradition (as opposed to *gezerah shavah,* for example). Sometimes, the Sages referred to *a fortiori* inferences as דִּין — "logical argumentation."

Occasionally, formal restrictions limit the use of *kal vaḥomer* argumentation. For example, a קַל וָחוֹמֶר inference can be refuted if it is shown that the lenient case has stringent features that the more stringent case lacks. Another important restriction on the use of *kal vaḥomer* reasoning is called דַּיּוֹ (short for דַּיּוֹ לַבָּא מִן הַדִּין לִהְיוֹת כַּנִּדּוֹן — "It is sufficient if the inference derived from the *kal vaḥomer* is like the source of the inference"). This rule states that if a certain stringent law is found in case A, and a קַל וָחוֹמֶר is drawn from case A to a more stringent case, B, then we may not be more stringent in case B with regard to this law than we are in case A, even though case B is usually stricter than case A. In other words, the stringency of case A is the maximum stringency in respect to this law. In certain cases, דַּיּוֹ can even make it impossible to employ *kal vaḥomer* reasoning in the first place; the Talmud terms this מַפְרִיךְ קַל וָחוֹמֶר — "refuting the *kal vaḥomer*." Yet another restriction set on the use of *kal vaḥomer* is אֵין לְמֵדִים קַל וָחוֹמֶר מֵהֲלָכָה — "We may not derive a *kal vaḥomer* from a Halakhah transmitted to Moses from Sinai." Similarly, *kal vaḥomer* reasoning may not be used to draw inferences from Rabbinic laws concerning Torah laws, or even from one Rabbinic law to another. In addition, there is a controversy in the Talmud as to whether it is possible to inflict punishment on the basis of a law that was inferred through a *kal vaḥomer* but not explicitly stated in the Torah (אֵין עוֹנְשִׁין מִן הַדִּין — "We do not punish on the basis of *kal vaḥomer* argumentation"). However, all authorities agree that אֵין מַזְהִירִים מִן הַדִּין — "We do not warn on the basis of a *kal vaḥomer*," i.e., that we cannot use *kal vaḥomer* reasoning to prove that something is prohibited by Torah law.

רִיבּוּי וּמִיעוּט   *Amplification and restriction.* A series of exegetical principles, somewhat similar to כְּלָל וּפְרָט (see above);

some of these are included in the list of rules of Rabbi Eliezer son of Rabbi Yose HaGelili. In general, these principles were accepted by Rabbi Akiva and his school, although they were also employed by other schools to a certain extent. רִיבּוּי וּמִיעוּט exegesis interprets certain words (such as אֶת — sometimes "with"; גַּם — "also"; and אַף — "also") as amplificatory expressions (רִיבּוּיִים) that allude to items not mentioned explicitly in the Biblical text, even though the use of such words is simply a normal feature of Biblical style. For example, the Torah states: "In the beginning, God created the heavens [אֶת הַשָּׁמַיִם] and the earth [וְאֵת הָאָרֶץ]" (Genesis 1:1). Since the word אֶת appears before both "heavens" and "earth," the Rabbis interpreted this verse as meaning that God created the heavens together with the celestial bodies, and the earth together with the trees and grass. Correspondingly, the words אַךְ ("but"), רַק ("but"), and מִן ("from") are interpreted as restrictive expressions (מִיעוּטִים); as the Talmudic Rabbis put it: אֶתִּין וְגַמִּין רִיבּוּיִים, אַכִין וְרַקִין מִיעוּטִין — "The words et and gam are amplificatory expressions; the words akh and rak are restrictive expressions." רִיבּוּי וּמִיעוּט exegesis in many ways resembles כְּלָל וּפְרָט interpretation, although רִיבּוּי וּמִיעוּט tends to be more inclusive than כְּלָל וּפְרָט. Thus, a מִיעוּט restricts the רִיבּוּי only minimally, and excludes only items that differ radically from itself. Unlike the פְּרָט, a מִיעוּט is not considered an example of the generalization in connection with which it appears, but rather a defining feature which limits the generalization. Thus, when a רִיבּוּי is followed by a מִיעוּט, and these two expressions are then followed by another רִיבּוּי, the only items excluded from the generalization are those that differ totally from the מִיעוּט. For example, the Torah states with regard to money used to redeem the second tithe (Deuteronomy 14:26): "You shall spend the money on whatever you desire — on cattle, sheep, wine, strong drink, or whatever you wish." According to those who interpret this verse through רִיבּוּי וּמִיעוּט, we learn that second tithe money may be spent on all types of food except salt and water, which are excluded because they differ so greatly from the items specified by the מִיעוּט (= cattle, sheep, etc.).

Two other principles of רִיבּוּי וּמִיעוּט exegesis are: (1) אֵין מִיעוּט אַחַר מִיעוּט אֶלָּא לְרַבּוֹת — "One restrictive expression after another amplifies," i.e., when one restrictive expression appears after another, the two expressions cancel each other out, and together they are treated as an amplificatory expression. (2) אֵין רִיבּוּי אַחַר רִיבּוּי אֶלָּא לְמַעֵט — "One amplificatory expression after another restricts," i.e., when one amplificatory expression appears after another, the two expressions cancel each other out, and together they are treated as a restrictive expression. Even though stylistic justification can occasionally be found for these rules, e.g., when a double negative is used (such as לֹא בִלְתִּי), these are essentially formal exegetical principles based on the assumption that nothing in the Torah is superfluous. See כְּלָל וּפְרָט.

שָׁנָה עָלָיו הַכָּתוּב לְעַכֵּב   Lit., *the Torah repeated it to make it necessary.* Generally, if one does not perform a mitzvah exactly as specified in the Torah, one does not fulfill the mitzvah at all. However, this is not the case with regard to the laws of

sacrifices. Details of sacrificial law that were specified only once in the Torah are required only לְמִצְוָה — "for the mitzvah," i.e., for optimum performance of the mitzvah. One who omits these details nevertheless fulfills the mitzvah *de facto*. On the other hand, fulfillment of sacrificial laws that have been specially emphasized by the Torah is necessary even for *de facto* fulfillment of the mitzvah, and one who fails to attend to these details does not fulfill the mitzvah at all. Such emphasis may be provided in the Biblical text either by repeating a particular detail more than once (שָׁנָה עָלָיו הַכָּתוּב לְעַכֵּב — "The Torah repeated the detail to make it necessary"), or by using certain special expressions (e.g., תּוֹרָה — "law"; חוּקָה — "statute"; זֹאת — "this.")

שְׁנֵי כְתוּבִים הַבָּאִים כְּאֶחָד   Lit., *two verses coming together.* One of the principles limiting application of a בִּנְיַן אָב (see above). Ordinarily, a בִּנְיַן אָב may be derived from a law stated in connection with one case in the Torah. However, if such a law appears in connection with two or more cases in the Torah, these cases constitute "two verses that come together," and the rule governing such cases is that שְׁנֵי כְתוּבִים הַבָּאִים כְּאֶחָד אֵין מְלַמְּדִין — "two verses that come together do not teach," i.e., a בִּנְיַן אָב may not be derived from two analogous cases. This is because a law that had to be mentioned in two different places cannot be a general rule, but must instead be an exceptional case. Other Sages, however, maintained that only when a law appears in three places is it impossible to derive a בִּנְיַן אָב: שְׁלֹשָׁה כְתוּבִים הַבָּאִים כְּאֶחָד אֵין מְלַמְּדִין — lit., "three verses that come together do not teach."

שְׁנֵי כְתוּבִים הַמַּכְחִישִׁים זֶה אֶת זֶה   *Two verses that contradict each other.* One of the exegetical principles of Rabbi Yishmael and Rabbi Eliezer the son of Rabbi Yose HaGelili. When two verses seem to contradict each other, the contradiction may be resolved by reference to a third verse, which presents an intermediate position between the contradictory verses.

תָּפַסְתָּ מוּעָט תָּפַסְתָּ   Part of a longer expression, תָּפַסְתָּ מְרוּבֶּה לֹא תָּפַסְתָּ, תָּפַסְתָּ מוּעָט תָּפַסְתָּ — lit., *if you take hold of the larger, you do not take hold; if you take hold of the smaller, you do take hold.* An exegetical principle encountered both in Halakhic and Aggadic Midrashim. This rule is also used to interpret Rabbinic statements. Sometimes, a Biblical verse (or other source) alludes to an item, or group of items, of a certain size or quantity, without explicitly specifying this size or quantity. For example, if a person states: "I undertake to contribute an unspecified 'personal value' [עֵרֶךְ, see Leviticus 27] to the Temple," he is only required to contribute three shekalim, the minimum עֵרֶךְ specified by the Torah, rather than a larger sum (e.g., fifty shekalim, the maximum עֵרֶךְ specified by the Torah). Different explanations of this principle have been suggested, the most important of which is that since a smaller quantity is automatically included in larger quantities, a source that does not specify the quantity must in any case be referring to items of the smallest possible size or quantity.

Halakhic Concepts and Terms

T he largest part of the Talmudic debate centers on various Halakhic problems. However, the discussion of these problems is not always Halakhic. Occasionally we find a fundamental philosophical investigation of a problem and its background. Frequently the discussion inquires into the various systematic approaches of the authors of the Halakhah. Nevertheless, the main concepts discussed in the Talmud are Halakhic.

One of the greatest obstacles to studying the Talmud is that it treats scores — if not hundreds — of terms and topics without first defining them, and occasionally without ever defining them. The student is thus expected to be familiar with the terms and concepts at issue before studying the Talmudic passage. To help overcome this difficulty, we offer the following glossary of Halakhic terms and concepts. It does not include all the terms of the Halakhah, which number thousands, but most of the principal ones are presented, especially those that are not explained where they appear in the text. These terms and concepts are presented in Hebrew alphabetical order, in the form in which they most commonly appear in the Talmud. Every entry contains a brief definition of the concept as well as a short explanation of the contexts in which it appears in the Talmud. In explaining certain fundamental concepts we have expanded the discussion somewhat to present a more general picture or to explain a central point, upon which many details depend and from which they derive. This section contains many cross-references, sometimes because of the connection between the entries, and sometimes because one cannot properly understand a certain term without comparing it to a parallel term on the same topic. Where an asterisk appears next to a Hebrew word or phrase it indicates that this Hebrew word or phrase is itself an entry elsewhere in the section.

The terms found in this section relate to Halakhic questions discussed in the Talmud. We have not presented subjects and topics beyond the area of the Talmud, unless their origin and source lie in the Talmud.

אַב בֵּית דִּין   Lit., *father of the court*. The deputy to the נָשִׂיא*, who was the president of the Sanhedrin. In the absence of the נָשִׂיא, the אַב בֵּית דִּין would frequently preside over the Great Sanhedrin (סַנְהֶדְרִין גְּדוֹלָה*). In later Rabbinic sources the expression אַב בֵּית דִּין refers to the president of a court.

הָאָב קוֹדֵם לְכָל יוֹצְאֵי חֲלָצָיו   *A father takes precedence over all his offspring*. A fundamental principle governing the laws of inheritance. When a person dies without leaving any descendants, the right of inheritance passes to his father (and then to his father's heirs if he too is deceased). If the father of the deceased has no heirs, the right of inheritance passes to the grandfather of the deceased (and then to his heirs). On every level, therefore, the right of inheritance passes first to the father and from him to his heirs.

אָבוֹת   Lit., *fathers*. (1) The first blessing of the Amidah prayer (see שְׁמוֹנֶה עֶשְׂרֵה), which mentions Abraham, Isaac, and Jacob, the Patriarchs of the Jewish people. (2) Primary Halakhic categories from which the Sages derived sub-categories, which are called תּוֹלָדוֹת* — "offspring." For example: אֲבוֹת מְלָאכוֹת* — the primary categories of labor forbidden on the Sabbath; אָבוֹת* נְזִיקִין — the primary categories of damage.

אֲבוֹת הַטֻּמְאוֹת   (sing., אַב הַטֻּמְאָה) Lit., *the fathers of ritual impurities*. The highest category (apart from a human corpse, see אֲבִי אֲבוֹת הַטֻּמְאָה) of persons or objects comprising an original source of ritual impurity and transmitting ritual impurity to other persons or objects. A person or an article rendered ritually impure by contact with an אַב הַטֻּמְאָה is called a רִאשׁוֹן לְטוּמְאָה* or יְלַד הַטּוּמְאָה*. The רִאשׁוֹן, or "first," creates a "second" grade, שֵׁנִי לְטוּמְאָה*, if he touches food or drink. Among the אֲבוֹת הַטֻּמְאוֹת are: שֶׁרֶץ* — the dead body of any of the eight species of reptile or rodent listed in Leviticus 11:29–30; נְבֵלָה* — the corpse of a mammal; שִׁכְבַת זֶרַע — semen; מְצוֹרָע* — a person suffering from leprosy (צָרַעַת*); מֵי חַטָּאת* — the water used in the ceremony of sprinkling the ashes of the Red Heifer (פָּרָה אֲדוּמָה*); בּוֹעֵל נִדָּה* — a person who had sexual intercourse with a menstruating woman; נִדָּה* — a menstruating woman; יוֹלֶדֶת* — a woman after childbirth; זָב* — a man suffering from gonorrhea; זָבָה — a woman who has a menstrual-type flow of blood when she is not menstruating; an article on which a זָב or זָבָה sat or lay (see מִשְׁכָּב מוֹשָׁב וּמֶרְכָּב); טָמֵא מֵת — a person who became ritually impure because of contact with a dead body (see אֲבִי אֲבוֹת הַטֻּמְאָה).

אֲבוֹת מְלָאכוֹת   *Principal labors*. The thirty-nine primary categories of labor that are prohibited on the Sabbath. A person who inadvertently performs one of these labors, or one of the sub-categories (תּוֹלָדוֹת*) derived from them, on the Sabbath is obligated to bring a חַטָּאת*, a sin-offering. See מְלֶאכֶת מַחֲשֶׁבֶת.

אֲבוֹת נְזִיקִין   *Principal damages*. The primary categories of damage inflicted by man or his property (Exodus 21:28–22:5). The Mishnah (*Bava Kamma* 1:1) lists four such primary categories. However, different Baraitot increase this figure until, according to one opinion, there are twenty-four (*Bava Kamma* 4b). See אֵשׁ; בּוֹר; שׁוֹר.

אֲבִי אֲבוֹת הַטוּמְאָה Lit., *the father of the fathers of ritual impurity.* A human corpse — the most severe source of ritual impurity (see חֲלַל חֶרֶב). A person or object which comes into contact with it becomes ritually impure in the category of an אב הַטוּמְאָה (see אֲבוֹת הַטוּמְאוֹת). See also טוּמְאָה בְּחִבּוּרִים.

אֲבֵידָה מִדַּעַת *Conscious, deliberate loss.* An article which is abandoned or left lying where it is very likely to be taken or destroyed. In most cases such an article is assumed not to have an owner (see הֶפְקֵר), and there is no obligation to return it. See יֵאוּשׁ; יֵאוּשׁ שֶׁלֹּא מִדַּעַת.

אֲבֵילוּת *Mourning,* the practices of mourning observed upon the death of a close relative (see קָרוֹב for a precise definition of the term "close relative"). Among these practices are: קְרִיעָה — rending one's garments; שִׁבְעָה — the customs observed during the first week of mourning; שְׁלֹשִׁים — customs observed during the first month after the person's death (see שִׁבְעָה וּשְׁלֹשִׁים). There are additional customs carried out for an entire year after the death of a parent. Certain mourning rites are also practiced for a נָשִׂיא (the president of the Sanhedrin), and for one's Torah teacher.

אֶבֶן מְסָמָא *A very heavy stone.* A situation in which a זָב, a man suffering from gonorrhea; a זָבָה, a woman who has suffered a loss of blood when not menstruating; a יוֹלֶדֶת, a woman who has recently given birth; a נִדָּה, a menstruating woman; and a מְצוֹרָע, a leper, may impart ritual impurity. If one of these persons lies on a very heavy stone, which, because of its size, is not moved or affected at all by the person's weight, the stone itself does not become ritually impure. But any articles found under it do become ritually impure. See הֶיסֵּט; טוּמְאַת מַשָּׂא; מִשְׁכָּב מוֹשָׁב וּמֶרְכָּב.

אַבְנֵט *Girdle, sash.* One of the four priestly garments worn by all priests during their Temple service. The אַבְנֵט was thirty-two cubits (approximately fifteen meters) long and was worn over the heart, slightly above the elbows. It was made of linen and wool. Though this mixture of fabrics is normally forbidden (see שַׁעַטְנֵז), the priestly garments were excluded from this prohibition.

אֲבַק.... *A hint of... [lit., dust].* A transgression which is not explicitly prohibited by the Torah, but which is prohibited by Rabbinic authority because it is a less severe variation of a Torah prohibition. There are four categories of אֲבַק prohibitions: (1) אֲבַק לָשׁוֹן הָרָע — a hint of slander (see לָשׁוֹן הָרָע). (2) אֲבַק עֲבוֹדָה זָרָה — a hint of idol worship (see עֲבוֹדָה זָרָה). (3) אֲבַק שְׁבִיעִית — a hint of interest (see רִיבִּית). (4) אֲבַק רִיבִּית — a hint of the violation of the prohibitions of the Sabbatical Year (see שְׁבִיעִית).

אָבָר See אֵיבָר

אִגְּרוֹת מָזוֹן *Documents concerning food.* A legal document obligating a man to provide for the maintenance of his wife's daughter from a previous marriage (see *Bava Metzia* 20a).

אִגְּרוֹת שׁוּם *Documents of assessment.* A legal document which states that a Bet Din has assessed the property of a debtor

for the purpose of seizing it to pay his debts to his creditor. See שׁוּמָא.

אֲדוֹמִי *An Edomite.* Edom was one of the nations whose territory bordered on Eretz Israel. The Torah forbids an Edomite convert from marrying a native-born Jew. His children are similarly prohibited, and only his grandchildren are permitted to marry Jews (Deuteronomy 23:9). He may, however, marry a convert or a מַמְזֶרֶת. This prohibition is classified as a transgression of a positive commandment of the Torah. See מִצְרִי and אִיסּוּר עֲשֵׂה.

אָדָם חָשׁוּב *An important person.* Someone the public regards as important and whose behavior it emulates. Such a person has to be more careful about his deeds than other people, and has to live by standards stricter than the letter of the law.

אָדָם מוּעָד לְעוֹלָם *A man is always considered forewarned.* A major principle in the laws of damages. A man is held responsible for all damages he causes with his person regardless of whether the damage was caused willfully or inadvertently. Even if he causes the damage unknowingly — for example, while asleep — he is nevertheless liable. See מוּעָד.

אָדָם קָרוֹב אֵצֶל עַצְמוֹ Lit., *a person is close to himself.* A principle in the laws of evidence. The relatives of the litigants or the accused in a lawsuit cannot testify as witnesses. Since a person has no closer relative than himself, an accused man cannot give evidence in his own case — neither in his defense nor to incriminate himself. Thus no one can testify to his own guilt ("אֵין אָדָם מֵשִׂים עַצְמוֹ רָשָׁע"). Only in civil disputes is an admission by one of the litigants accepted, possibly because such an admission is comparable to a gift on the part of the litigant (see הוֹדָאַת בַּעַל דִּין).

אֲדָר רִאשׁוֹן וַאֲדָר שֵׁנִי *The first month of Adar, and the second month of Adar.* According to Rabbinical tradition, the month added in a leap year (see עִיבּוּר הַשָּׁנָה) precedes the month of Adar. The Halakhah regards this extra month as First Adar (אֲדָר רִאשׁוֹן), which always has thirty days. In the second month of Adar (אֲדָר שֵׁנִי), which has twenty-nine days, all the rules that apply in a regular month of Adar in a non-leap year are observed, such as the Festival of Purim, and the reading of the four special portions (אַרְבַּע פָּרָשִׁיּוֹת).

אַדְרַכְתָּא *An authorization.* A legal document written by the court, authorizing a creditor to seek out and take possession of any property belonging to his debtor in order to recover the debt.

אֹהֶל *A tent.* In Halakhic contexts, a reference to any structure with a roof, whether natural or manmade. (1) In connection with the laws of Shabbat, the construction of an אֹהֶל is a derivative (see תּוֹלָדוֹת) of the forbidden category of labor בּוֹנֶה — "building." (2) The term אֹהֶל is also used in connection with the laws of ritual purity (see next entry).

אֹהֶל הַמֵּת Lit., *the tent over a dead body.* A fundamental concept in the laws of ritual impurity. Any structure that has a cavity which is at least a cubic handbreadth in volume (see פּוֹתֵחַ

טְפַח, טֶפַח) and contains a dead body (or part of a dead body: its flesh, bones, or limbs) becomes an אֹהֶל הַמֵּת. Not only do all articles subject to ritual impurity contained within it become ritually impure themselves, but they also become an אַב הַטֻּמְאָה (see אֲבוֹת הַטֻּמְאוֹת), capable of imparting ritual impurity to people and objects (see also צָמִיד פָּתִיל). Conversely, the אֹהֶל הַמֵּת shields people and objects *outside it* against ritual impurity contained within it.

אוֹדִיתָא   *An admission.* The statement made by a person before witnesses, that a sum of money or an object in his possession belongs to another person. Such an admission may also serve as an act of transfer (קִנְיָן), formally transferring ownership of funds or property in a situation where other acts of transfer are not effective.

אֲוִיר   *Air.* Any cavity or space within a container or above a particular circumscribed area. This concept occurs with reference to ritual impurity (see next entry), the Sabbath laws, the laws governing a גֵט (bill of divorce), the laws of damages, and the laws of property.

אֲוִיר כְּלִי חֶרֶס   *The cavity of an earthenware receptacle.* If an article that can impart ritual impurity is contained within an earthenware receptacle, not only does the receptacle itself become ritually impure, but its cavity is also considered filled with ritual impurity. Thus an object which is suspended within that cavity and which does not touch either the source of ritual impurity or the walls of the receptacle nevertheless contracts ritual impurity.

אוֹכֶל נֶפֶשׁ   *Sustenance [lit., food for the soul].* (1) The Torah explicitly prohibits on Festivals all work prohibited on the Sabbath except that of preparing food to be eaten by Jews (see יוֹם טוֹב). (2) It is also forbidden for a creditor to take as security for a loan utensils used by the debtor for the preparation of food (אוֹכֶל נֶפֶשׁ, see מַשְׁכּוֹן).

אוּלָם   *Entrance hall.* One of the three sections of the main building of the Temple. The entrance hall led to the Sanctuary (הֵיכָל). (See plan of the Temple, p. 277; see also בֵּית הַחֲלִיפוֹת).

אוּמָּן   *An artisan.* A professional, highly skilled craftsman. The word אוּמָּן is often used to describe a hired worker, whether a day-laborer or a person who takes it upon himself to perform a complete task for his employer. The laws governing these two types of employees differ, and it is necessary to examine the context in order to be certain which type is being discussed. In the Talmud there is a difference of opinion as to whether an artisan has any proprietary interest in the utensils he makes, before he is paid for his labor (אוּמָּן קוֹנֶה בְּשֶׁבַח כְּלִי).

אוֹנָאָה   *Overreaching, deception, fraud.* (1) In civil law this term refers to the prohibition against deceiving or taking unfair advantage of another person in a business transaction (Leviticus 25:14). If either the buyer or the seller takes unfair advantage of the other, the wronged party has the right to be reimbursed according to the true value of the article. According to Rabbinic law this right may be exercised if either party has overcharged

or underpaid to the extent of one-sixth (שְׁתוּת) of the article's true value. If the אוֹנָאָה is greater than one-sixth of the article's true value, the sale is annulled (בִּיטּוּל מֶקַח). (2) See next entry.

אוֹנָאַת דְּבָרִים   *Wronging, deceiving, with words.* The Torah forbids causing distress to another person by making statements that wound, shame, or embarrass him (see Leviticus 25:17 and *Bava Metzia* 58b).

אוֹנֵן   See אֲנִינוּת.

אוֹנֶס   *Unavoidable accident, compulsion, force.* This term is used to refer to actions which a person was compelled to perform or which he performed unknowingly, e.g., while asleep or during a fit of insanity. It can also refer to circumstances over which a person has no control — force majeure. Generally the Torah does not hold a person liable for sins that he was forced to commit. If a person is compelled to commit a sin under threat of death, it is preferable that he commit the sin rather than die. But there are three exceptions — idol-worship, murder, and forbidden sexual relations.
See, however, שָׁמָד; יֵהָרֵג וְאַל יַעֲבוֹר; יִבּוּם; אָדָם מוּעָד לְעוֹלָם.

אוֹנֵס אִשָּׁה   *Rapist.* A man who rapes an unmarried woman who is between three and twelve-and-a-half years old (see קְטַנָּה; נַעֲרָה) is obliged by the Torah to marry her. He is forbidden to divorce her. He is also obligated to pay a fine for the rape, and to pay damages according to the laws of personal injury (Deuteronomy 22:29). The marriage is subject to her consent and that of her father.

אוֹתוֹ וְאֶת בְּנוֹ   *It and its young.* The Torah prohibits the slaughter of a mother animal and its offspring on the same day (Leviticus 22:28). This prohibition applies to all kosher domesticated animals (see בְּהֵמָה טְהוֹרָה).

אוֹתִיּוֹת   *Letters.* (1) In the context of the thirty-nine categories of labor prohibited on the Sabbath, a person who writes or erases a minimum of two letters in any language is liable under the category of writing (כּוֹתֵב), or erasing (מוֹחֵק). (2) In monetary matters, the term אוֹתִיּוֹת refers to legal documents such as promissory notes. How the ownership of these documents is legally transferred is a matter of much Talmudic debate.

אַזְהָרָה   *A warning.* A prohibition of the Torah; an act the Torah "warned" against committing. See also לָאו.

אַזְכָּרָה   Lit., *a mention.* A term used when referring to the names of God written in the Torah. There are specific rules governing the pronouncing and writing of each of God's names, particularly by a scribe when writing a scroll of the Torah. See also שֵׁם, שֵׁמוֹת and כִּינּוּיִים.

אָחוֹת   *Sister.* The relationship to one's sister is Halakhically significant in the following contexts: (1) Forbidden relationships (עֲרָיוֹת). A person is forbidden under penalty of excision (כָּרֵת) to engage in sexual relations with his paternal or maternal sister (Leviticus 18:9). This applies even if he or she (or both) was (were) born of a forbidden relationship. (2) Priests. They are forbidden to become ritually impure by contact with dead bodies. An exception is made in the case of a paternal sister who was an unmarried virgin — a priest is permitted to take part in her funeral rites (Leviticus 21:3). (3) Mourning. A person is required to observe mourning rites (see אֲבֵילוּת) for a sister, whether paternal or maternal, whether single or married.

אֲחוֹת אִשָּׁה   *The sister of one's wife.* The Torah forbids a man under penalty of excision (כָּרֵת) from marrying his wife's sister or having sexual relations with her as long as his wife is alive (Leviticus 18:18). This prohibition applies even if he has divorced his wife. He is permitted, however, to marry the sister of his deceased wife.

אָחִיו שֶׁלֹּא הָיָה בְּעוֹלָמוֹ   Lit., *his brother who was not in his world.* A brother who was not alive at the same time as his deceased brother. A concept in the laws of יִבּוּם — levirate marriage. If a man dies without children, his surviving brother must either marry his deceased brother's widow or set her free through the act of חֲלִיצָה. This obligation only applies to brothers who lived concurrently with the deceased. If a brother is born after the childless brother's death, he is not obliged to fulfill either יִבּוּם or חֲלִיצָה with the widow, because he did not live "in his brother's world," and she is forbidden to him as his brother's wife (see אֵשֶׁת אָח).

אַחֲרָיוּת   *Responsibility, surety.* A clause included in a loan or a bill of sale, which states that the debtor or the seller guarantees the transaction stated in the document, and pledges his immovable property (נְכָסִים שֶׁיֵּשׁ לָהֶם אַחֲרָיוּת, מְקַרְקְעֵי) as security for the repayment of the loan or the fulfillment of the terms of the sale. In the case of a loan, if the debtor is unable to repay it, the creditor may seize the debtor's property to the value of the loan. In the case of a sale, if the seller's creditors seize the land bought from the seller by the purchaser, the purchaser may then recover the value of the property from the seller's other property, which is mortgaged to him to protect him against such a possibility. Both in the case of a loan and in the case of a sale, the mortgage creates a lien on the debtor's or seller's property, and if this property is later sold by the debtor or the seller to a third party, the creditor or the buyer can expropriate it. (See next entry.)

אַחֲרָיוּת טָעוּת סוֹפֵר   *The omission of the clause accepting responsibility is considered a scribal error.* A Talmudic principle which maintains that it is taken for granted that in the case of a loan the debtor pledges his land as security for the repayment of the loan, and that in the case of a sale the seller pledges his other land as security in the event that a creditor should seize the land he is now selling to the purchaser. If the clause mentioning acceptance of responsibility is omitted from the loan document or the deed of sale, that omission is attributed to a scribal error, and it is considered as if the clause was explicitly mentioned in the document. If the debtor, or the seller, does not wish to accept this responsibility, an explicit provision to that effect must be included in the document.

אֵיבָר מִן הַחַי   *A limb from a living animal.* The prohibition

against eating flesh taken from a living animal; one of the seven commandments that apply to Jews and non-Jews alike. (See שֶׁבַע מִצְווֹת בְּנֵי נֹחַ).

אֵיבָרִים   *Limbs.* (1) Concerning ritual impurity, it refers to a part of the human body containing bone, flesh, and sinews. (2) Concerning sacrificial offerings, it refers to the limbs of the burnt-offering (עוֹלָה), all of which (except the skin and the sciatic nerve) were consumed on the altar. (See רָאשֵׁי אֵיבָרִים).

אַיְילוֹנִית   *A sexually underdeveloped woman,* incapable of bearing children. The male counterpart is סָרִיס. This term is a general definition for women who have some basic flaw in their reproductive system. An אַיְילוֹנִית is exempt from levirate marriage (יִבּוּם) and from the ceremony of חֲלִיצָה.

אַיִל   *Ram.* A male sheep, between the ages of one year and thirty-one days and two years. The guilt-offering (אָשָׁם), the Nazirite's of-fering (אֵיל נָזִיר) and certain of the musaf offerings (מוּסָף) require the sacrifice of an אַיִל.

אֵיל נָזִיר   *A Nazirite's ram.* A peace-offering (see שְׁלָמִים) included among the sacrifices brought by the Nazirite (see נְזִירוּת) on the day he completes his period as a Nazirite. The Nazirite's ram differs in certain respects from other peace offerings: A special portion, the cooked shoulder (זְרוֹעַ בְּשֵׁלָה), is given to the priest. Also, the sacrifice may be eaten only on the day it was offered and the following night. See Numbers 6:14–21.

אֵימוּרִים   *The portions of sin-* (חַטָּאת), *guilt-* (אָשָׁם), *and peace-offerings* (שְׁלָמִים) *that are consumed on the altar [the fats, the kidneys, the fat-tail, etc.].* Occasionally, the limbs of the burnt-offering (עוֹלָה) are also included in this expression. See אֵיבָרִים.

אֵין אִיסוּר חָל עַל אִיסוּר   *One prohibition does not take effect where another prohibition already exists.* A general principle applying to the Torah's prohibitions. If an object or action is already prohibited, additional prohibitions cannot apply to it. For example, a High Priest (כֹּהֵן גָּדוֹל) is forbidden to have sexual relations with a divorcee or a widow. If he did have sexual relations with a woman whose first marriage had ended in divorce and whose second husband had died, he would be liable on one count only — for relations with a divorcee — and not on the second count — for relations with a widow. There are, however, numerous exceptions to this principle. See אִיסוּר בַּת אַחַת; אִיסוּר כּוֹלֵל; אִיסוּר מוֹסִיף.

אֵין בּוֹ דַּעַת לְהִשָּׁאֵל   *One who does not know to be asked.* Generally, if there is a doubt as to whether a person has contracted ritual impurity or not, he is considered ritually impure. However, if such a doubt arises with regard to a person who is not intellectually mature or to an inanimate object, that person or object remains ritually pure.

אֵין בֵּית דִּין שָׁקוּל   *A court may not be composed of an even number of judges.* An even number of judges is never appointed to decide a case, lest they become divided into two equal groups and thus fail to reach a decision.

אֵין יְשִׁיבָה בָּעֲזָרָה   *It is prohibited to sit within the Temple Courtyard.* This prohibition applied to the Temple area from the Israelites' courtyard (עֶזְרַת יִשְׂרָאֵל) and within, including the Temple building itself. The prohibition did not extend to the Gate of Nicanor (שַׁעַר נִיקָנוֹר) and the women's courtyard (עֶזְרַת נָשִׁים). (See plan of the Temple, p. 277.) There is one exception to this principle: kings of the House of David were permitted to sit in the עֶזְרַת יִשְׂרָאֵל.

אֵין שָׁלִיחַ לִדְבַר עֲבֵירָה   *There is no agent for transgression.* If a person is instructed by someone else to commit a sin, he himself bears the responsibility for his actions and not the person who gave him the instructions. The following cases are exceptions to this rule: (1) The unlawful use of sacred objects (מְעִילָה). (2) The slaughter or sale of a stolen animal (טְבִיחָה וּמְכִירָה). (3) Damage caused by an agent who cannot be held responsible for his deeds — a חֵרֵשׁ (deaf-mute), a שׁוֹטֶה (imbecile), and a קָטָן (minor). Some authorities hold that anyone who orders someone else to kill a person is himself guilty — at least morally (see דִּינֵי שָׁמַיִם) — of murder.

אִיסוּר בַּת אַחַת   *Lit., a prohibition [taking effect] at the same time.* An exception to the rule that one prohibition cannot be added to another (see אֵין אִיסוּר חָל עַל אִיסוּר). If two prohibitions come into effect at the same time, a person transgressing them is liable on both counts. For example, a woman is forbidden to the son of the man she marries, both because of the prohibition against relations with a married woman (see אֵשֶׁת אִישׁ) and because of the prohibition against relations with one's father's wife (see אֵשֶׁת אָב), since both prohibitions came into effect simultaneously.

אִיסוּר כּוֹלֵל   *A more inclusive prohibition.* An exception to the rule that one prohibition cannot be added to another (see אֵין אִיסוּר חָל עַל אִיסוּר). The second prohibition takes effect if it is more comprehensive than the first. For example, a person who eats of a trefah animal (טְרֵפָה) on Yom Kippur (יוֹם הַכִּיפּוּרִים) has violated two prohibitions. Such meat is prohibited at all times, but eating it on that day is also a violation of an additional prohibition — eating on Yom Kippur. The latter prohibition takes effect because it is more comprehensive — it includes all foodstuffs, not only trefah meat.

אִיסוּר מוֹסִיף   *A prohibition that adds.* An exception to the rule that one prohibition cannot be added to another (see אֵין אִיסוּר חָל עַל אִיסוּר). The second prohibition takes effect because it applies either to additional individuals, or for a longer period of time, or with greater severity than the first. For example, a man is prohibited from engaging in sexual relations with his wife's sister. If that sister marries, she becomes forbidden to him because of the additional prohibition against relations with a married woman. Since the second prohibition applies to all men, it also applies to the man to whom this woman was already forbidden — her sister's husband.

אִיסוּר מִצְוָה   *Lit., a prohibition resulting from a com-*

mandment. In addition to those sexual relationships that are forbidden on the basis of Torah prohibitions (see עֲרָיוֹת), there are additional relationships that are forbidden by Rabbinic law (שְׁנִיּוֹת). These are called אִיסוּר מִצְוָה — because the basis for their being Rabbinically forbidden is the Torah commandment not to deviate from the words of the Sages (see Deuteronomy 17:11).

אִיסוּר עֲשֵׂה   *A prohibition not stated in the Torah in the form of a negative commandment, but inferred from a positive commandment.* For example, the eating of the Passover offering (see פֶּסַח) is forbidden during the daytime. This is inferred from the positive commandment (Exodus 12:8) to eat the Passover offering at night. See עֲשֵׂה; לָאו הַבָּא מִכְּלַל עֲשֵׂה.

אִיסוּר קְדוּשָׁה   *Lit., a prohibition [stemming from] holiness.* A marriage that is prohibited not because of the family relationship between the parties but because of the more elevated level of holiness of one of the marriage partners. For example, the prohibition against the marriage of a native-born Israelite to a mamzer (see מַמְזֵר); of a priest to a divorcee (see גְרוּשָׁה); or of a High Priest to a widow (see אַלְמָנָה לְכֹהֵן גָּדוֹל; לְכֹהֵן).

אִיסוּרֵי הֲנָאָה   *Things from which benefit is forbidden.* Things from which one is forbidden to derive any kind of benefit or profit, not only by eating them but also by any other use, including selling them, even to a non-Jew. Some אִיסוּרֵי הֲנָאָה are prohibited by Torah law, others only by Rabbinic decree. Some must be disposed of by burning, others by burial. Idols and pagan sacrifices; the male first-born of an ass, before it has been redeemed and after its neck has been broken (see פֶּטֶר חֲמוֹר); an animal that has been sentenced to stoning (see שׁוֹר הַנִּסְקָל); a heifer whose neck has been broken (עֶגְלָה עֲרוּפָה) — all these are among the things that are covered by this prohibition. Today the prohibition applies specifically to wine used for idolatrous purposes (יֵין נֶסֶךְ), meat of kosher domesticated animals (not undomesticated animals or birds) which has been cooked in milk (בָּשָׂר בְּחָלָב), and leaven (חָמֵץ) on Pesaḥ.

אֵירוּסִין   *Betrothal.* The first stage of the marriage process (see נִישּׂוּאִין regarding the second stage, and קִידּוּשִׁין for a description of the ways whereby אֵירוּסִין is effected). The bond created by אֵירוּסִין is so strong that, after betrothal, a woman requires a divorce before she can marry another man. Similarly, sexual relations with other men are considered adulterous and are punishable by death. At this stage the betrothed couple may not yet live together as man and wife, and most of the couple's mutual obligations do not yet apply. See נַעֲרָה הַמְאוֹרָסָה.

אֲכִילָה גַסָּה   *Excessive eating.* Forcing oneself to eat when one is already satiated and has no desire for more. With reference to commandments requiring or forbidding the eating of certain items of food, אֲכִילָה גַסָּה is not considered an act of eating, either to fulfill a positive commandment or to transgress a negative commandment.

אֲכִילָה עַל יְדֵי הַדְּחָק   *Food that is barely fit to be eaten.* Food of a much poorer quality than that normally consumed by the person or animal in question. The act of ingesting such food is generally deemed to come under the category of eating. For

example, if an animal trespassed onto private property and ate produce that was not fit for it to eat, its owner would have to recompense the owner of the produce for willful, unusual, damage (see קֶרֶן) to the amount of fifty percent of the value of the produce. If, however, the animal ate produce that came under the category of אֲכִילָה עַל יְדֵי הַדְּחָק, the owner would be liable for the full amount, as the consuming of such produce is deemed to come under the category of normal eating (see שֵׁן).

אֲכִילַת עֲרַאי *Casual, incidental eating.* Food eaten casually, a snack, in contrast to a regular or set meal. Among the specific applications of this concept are: (1) With reference to tithes (מַעַשְׂרוֹת). If the harvest has not been fully completed, "casual eating" of the produce is permitted before it has been tithed. (See טֶבֶל.) (2) With reference to the laws of Sukkot, "casual eating" is permitted outside a sukkah during the Sukkot Festival.

אַכְסַדְרָה *A structure [from the Greek ἐξέδρα, "exedra"] resembling an open porch adjacent to a building.* An אַכְסַדְרָה possesses a roof, but lacks four walls. Specific regulations apply to it with regard to the laws of carrying on the Sabbath (see הוֹצָאָה), affixing a mezuzah, and constructing a sukkah.

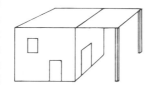

אַלָּם *A strong [violent] man.* A powerful person who illegally and forcibly exerts his influence for his own benefit. The Halakhah includes certain provisions that take this factor into consideration, and thus enable an opposing litigant to have his case tried fairly.

אַלְמָנָה לְכֹהֵן גָּדוֹל *The marriage of a widow to a High Priest.* The Torah forbids a High Priest from marrying a widow (Leviticus 21:14). This prohibition applies even if the widow is a virgin. If, however, he was betrothed to a widow (see אֵירוּסִין) before being appointed High Priest, he may marry her (see נִישּׂוּאִין) after assuming that position.

אַלְמְנַת עִסָּה *A widow from a family of questionable lineage.* Although no definite prohibition exists to prevent a priest from marrying a widow whose first husband came from a family of questionable lineage (see חָלָל), the priests took upon themselves the restriction of not marrying such a woman. (See *Eduyyot* 8:3.)

אֵם אִשְׁתּוֹ *One's wife's mother.* The Torah prohibits relations with one's wife's mother (even after the death of one's wife). The punishment for violation of this prohibition is death by burning (Leviticus 20:14). See שְׂרֵיפָה.

אִם עָלוּ לֹא יֵרְדוּ Lit., *if they ascended, they shall not descend.* A principle applying to sacrificial offerings. An offering which while within the confines of the Temple Courtyard became unfit for sacrifice (see פָּסוּל), but was subsequently brought to the altar for sacrifice, could not be removed from the altar (see *Zevaḥim* 9:2).

אַמָּה (1) *A cubit.* A measure of length based on the distance from the elbow to the tip of the middle finger. There are various estimates as to its length, from forty-five to sixty centimeters (18–24 inches). (See p. 281.) (2) *An irrigation canal.* This name was chosen because these channels were usually one cubit deep. (3) *A euphemism for the male sexual organ.*

אַמָּה טְרַקְסִין *The one-cubit partition.* In the First Temple there was a wall a cubit thick separating the Sanctuary (הֵיכָל) from the Holy of Holies (קֹדֶשׁ הַקֳּדָשִׁים). When constructing the Second Temple, the Sages were unable to build a wall one cubit thick separating the Sanctuary from the Holy of Holies because of the greater height of the planned building. They were also unsure whether the space occupied by this wall in the First Temple had the sanctity of the Sanctuary or of the Holy of Holies. Hence, they left a space of one cubit between the Sanctuary and the Holy of Holies and hung curtains at each side of the space (see פָּרוֹכֶת).

אָמָה עִבְרִיָּה *A Hebrew maidservant.* A girl below the age of twelve who was sold as a maidservant by her father. In many cases the Hebrew maidservant was designated (see יִעוּד) to become the wife of the purchaser or his son. If he or his son did not marry her, the Hebrew maidservant became free either when she attained majority, or after working six years, or upon her purchaser's death, or upon the advent of the Jubilee Year (יוֹבֵל), whichever happened first.

אֲמוֹרִים See אֵימוּרִים

אֲמִירָתוֹ לַגָּבוֹהַּ כִּמְסִירָתוֹ לְהֶדְיוֹט *One's declaration to the Most High [God] is equal to transferring property to a common person.* A basic principle applying to objects dedicated to the Temple (see הֶקְדֵּשׁ). The legal transfer of ownership of an article by one person to another is carried out in various ways (see קִנְיָן), and the article becomes the legal property of its new owner. By contrast, once a person verbally pledges to give or to sell an article to the Temple service, the object is considered to have left his ownership at once and to have become the legal property of the Temple.

אֲמַרְכָּל Lit., *overseer.* The name given to the seven trustees of the Temple. Their duties principally involved supervision of the Temple treasury.

אֲמַתְלָא *A plausible reason.* In certain instances the Sages allowed a person to retract a previous (untrue) statement, if he could provide a convincing reason for having made that statement and could explain why he was retracting it now.

אַנְדְּרוֹגִינוֹס *Male and female.* (From ἀνδρόγυνος, "androgynos.") A person (or animal) with both male and female reproductive organs. The Sages debated whether such a person was to be given the status of a man or of a woman or was to be considered as a separate, intermediate category (see *Bikkurim*, chapter 4). See also טוּמְטוּם.

אֲנִינוּת *Acute mourning.* The period of acute mourning on the day of the death of a close relative (see קָרוֹב). The mourner (אוֹנֵן) is exempt from all positive commandments from the time of the death of the close relative until after the burial. At that point the mourner's status changes from that of an אוֹנֵן to that of an אָבֵל (see אֲבֵילוּת). In Temple times an אוֹנֵן was forbidden to eat מַעֲשֵׂר שֵׁנִי (the second tithe), בִּיכּוּרִים (the first-fruit offerings), and קָדָשִׁים (sacrificial food). If he was a priest he could not take part in the Temple service; this prohibition did not, however, apply to the High Priest (כֹּהֵן גָּדוֹל).

אָסוּפִי *A foundling.* A young child found abandoned in the street, the identity of whose parents is unknown. The legal status of such a child is that of a doubtful mamzer (see מַמְזֵר). See also שְׁתוּקִי.

אָסוּר See אִיסוּר.

אֲסִימוֹן *Uncoined metal, a coin without an official imprint.* Even though the value of the metal in such a coin may be commonly recognized, it cannot be used as money for certain practices — for example, the redemption of the second tithe (מַעֲשֵׂר שֵׁנִי).

אַסְמַכְתָּא Lit., *surety.* An obligation undertaken by a person which he does not expect to be called upon to fulfill. For example, a seller's acceptance of exaggerated fines for failure to deliver merchandise by a certain time. The Sages disagreed whether such a commitment is binding or not. (See אַסְמַכְתָּא in the section on Talmudic terminology for another meaning of the word.)

אַפּוֹטְרוֹפּוֹס *A guardian or trustee.* (From ἐπίτροπος, "epitropos.") A person appointed to administer property belonging to others. This term generally refers to an individual appointed by a Bet Din or by the family to supervise an estate where the heirs are incapable of managing it themselves. If a woman, usually the widow of the deceased, is appointed guardian of the estate, she is called the אַפּוֹטְרוֹפִּיָּא ("administratrix"). See also יְתוֹמִים.

אַפּוֹתֵיקִי *Pledge, mortgage.* (From ὑποθήκη, "hypotheke.") Interpreted by the Sages as meaning: "Claim your loan from here." Land that was stipulated in a legal contract to serve as security for repayment of a loan or the fulfillment of any other financial obligation. See אַחֲרָיוּת.

אֶפִּיקוֹרוֹס *A person who does not accept the fundamental principles of the Torah.* That is the meaning of the term in Rabbinical literature. Possibly it is derived from the name of the Greek philosopher Epicurus (or from the Hebrew word הֶפְקֵר). In particular the term is used of someone who does not accept the authority of the Sages or acts disrespectfully toward them.

אֶפְשָׁר לְצַמְצֵם *The possibility of exact measurement.* The Halakhic question, on which the Sages differ, as to whether it is possible to create two measures of exactly equal size or know whether two events occurred at exactly the same moment. See פָּרוּץ כְּעוֹמֵד.

אַרְבַּע כּוֹסוֹת Lit., *four cups.* The obligation, based on a

Rabbinic enactment, to drink four cups of wine at the Seder service on the first two nights of the Passover Festival (in Israel, on the first night). Every Jew, even a poor man or one who has difficulty drinking wine, is enjoined to fulfill this precept.

אַרְבַּע מִיתוֹת בֵּית דִּין Lit., *the four deaths of the Bet Din.* The four forms of capital punishment prescribed by the Torah and administered by a Bet Din of twenty-three members (see סַנְהֶדְרִי קְטַנָּה). They are (in diminishing order of severity): סְקִילָה — stoning; שְׂרֵיפָה — burning; הֶרֶג (see סַיִף) — decapitation; and חֶנֶק — strangulation.

אַרְבַּע מַתָּנוֹת Lit., *the four presentations.* This refers to the sprinkling of blood on the altar (see הַזָּאָה) as part of the rites of all sin-offerings (חַטָּאת), including those musaf offerings (מוּסָף) brought as sin-offerings (see שְׂעִיר רֹאשׁ חוֹדֶשׁ; שְׂעִירֵי הָרְגָלִים). In the case of a חַטָּאת the priest would dip his finger into a vessel containing the blood of the sacrificial animal and sprinkle it on each of the four corners of the altar (קַרְנוֹת הַמִּזְבֵּחַ).

אַרְבַּע עֲבוֹדוֹת Lit., *the four services.* The four indispensable actions in the offering of sacrifices: שְׁחִיטָה — slaughter; קַבָּלָה — receiving the blood; הוֹלָכָה — carrying it to the altar; זְרִיקָה — sprinkling it on the altar.

אַרְבַּע פָּרָשִׁיּוֹת Lit., *the four Scriptural passages.* Four passages from the Torah, read in addition to the regular Torah readings on four Sabbaths each year (one passage on each Sabbath) during the period from before Purim until before Pesaḥ. The four passages are: (1) פָּרָשַׁת שְׁקָלִים — the obligation to bring a half-shekel (מַחֲצִית הַשֶּׁקֶל) for the communal offerings in the Temple (Exodus 30:11–16); read on the Sabbath preceding the month of Adar (or on Rosh Ḥodesh Adar, if that day falls on a Sabbath). (2) פָּרָשַׁת זָכוֹר — the commandment to remember Amalek (Deuteronomy 25:17–19); read on the Sabbath before Purim. (3) פָּרָשַׁת פָּרָה — the purification process of the פָּרָה אֲדוּמָּה, Red Heifer (Numbers 19:1–22); read on the Sabbath after Purim immediately before the Sabbath of פָּרָשַׁת הַחוֹדֶשׁ (4) פָּרָשַׁת הַחוֹדֶשׁ — the laws governing the Paschal sacrifice (Exodus 12:1–20); read on the last Sabbath of Adar (or on Rosh Ḥodesh Nisan, if that day falls on a Sabbath). In a leap year (see עִיבּוּר הַשָּׁנָה) these readings take place during אֲדָר שֵׁנִי, the second month of Adar.

אַרְבָּעָה וַחֲמִישָׁה Lit., *four and five.* A person who steals and then sells or slaughters an ox is obligated to reimburse its owner five times the value of the stolen animal. If the stolen animal is a sheep, the restitution required is four times the animal's worth (Exodus 21:37). See also כֶּפֶל; טְבִיחָה וּמְכִירָה.

אַרְבָּעָה מִינִים *The four species.* The four plants which are ceremonially taken and held together in order to fulfill the commandment of "taking the Lulav" (נְטִילַת לוּלָב) on the Festival of Sukkot (Leviticus 23:40). They are: (1) לוּלָב — the palm branch; (2) הֲדַס — the myrtle; (3) עֲרָבָה — the willow (these three are bound together and held in one hand); (4) אֶתְרוֹג — the citron, which is held in the other

hand. These "four species" are "taken" on each of the seven days of Sukkot (except on the Sabbath).

אֵרוּסִין *See* אֵירוּסִין.

אָרִיס *A sharecropper.* A person who works a field for its owner and in return receives a portion of its produce (see קַבְּלָן; חוֹכֵר). The laws concerning an אָרִיס are discussed in detail in the ninth chapter of *Bava Metzia*.

אֲרִיסֵי בָּתֵּי אָבוֹת *Family sharecroppers.* Families of sharecroppers who, for generations, on the basis of a long-standing agreement, worked the fields belonging to a particular family.

אֶרֶץ הָעַמִּים Lit., *the land of the nations.* Any territory outside Eretz Israel. The Sages decreed that all land outside Eretz Israel is to be considered ritually impure. Contact with the land or its air space makes one ritually impure.

אֶרֶץ יִשְׂרָאֵל *Eretz Israel, the Land of Israel.* Eretz Israel has particular sanctity, and there are commandments which apply only there. Almost all the commandments connected with land and with agriculture, such as the prohibitions of the Sabbatical Year (see שְׁבִיעִית) and of sowing mixed seeds (see כִּלְאֵי זְרָעִים; כִּלְאֵי הַכֶּרֶם), as well as the setting aside of the priest's portion of the crop (תְּרוּמָה) and tithes (מַעַשְׂרוֹת), apply only there. The cities of Eretz Israel have special regulations and sanctity. The ordination of Sages was performed only in Eretz Israel. In Eretz Israel the second days of Pilgrim Festivals (שָׁלֹשׁ רְגָלִים) are not celebrated, whereas they are in the Diaspora (see יוֹם טוֹב שֵׁנִי שֶׁל גָּלוּיוֹת). Over the generations, with the development of the Torah center of Babylonia, differences in law and custom also developed between Eretz Israel and the Diaspora. The borders of Eretz Israel are defined in various ways, each of which has its own Halakhic significance. See אֶרֶץ הָעַמִּים; סוּרְיָה; תְּחוּם עוֹלֵי בָּבֶל.

אֵשׁ *Fire.* One of the primary categories of damage (see אֲבוֹת נְזִיקִין). It is Halakhically defined as "a person's property that is carried by the wind and does damage at a distance from where it was originally placed." For example, a fire, inadequately contained or guarded, which is spread by the wind; or a knife, blown by the wind off one's roof, which injures a passerby. See טָמוּן בָּאֵשׁ.

אַשְׁבּוֹרֶן Lit., *a collection of water.* Water used for immersion (in a מִקְוֶה, ritual bath, or natural reservoir) which is collected in one place and which does not flow, in contrast to flowing water such as a sea, river, stream, or spring (see זוֹחֲלִין; מַעְיָן). Immersion in rainwater or water from melted snow or ice for the purpose of ritual purification is valid only if the water is collected in one place.

אִשָּׁה *Woman.* Apart from those Halakhic differences deriving from the biological dissimilarities between men and women, different laws apply to women in various areas. In general, women are not required to perform most of the positive commandments related to a specific time (מִצְוַת עֲשֵׂה שֶׁהַזְּמַן גְּרָמָא). Notable exceptions are kiddush on Shabbat, the eating of

matzah on Pesaḥ, the joyous celebration of Festivals, attendance at the Temple for the royal ingathering (see הַקְהֵל), and prayer. Women are normally obligated to perform those positive commandments which are not dependent on a specific time, a notable exception being the obligation to study Torah. All the negative commandments apply to them, except for the prohibitions against shaving the sides of the head and disfiguring the beard, and the priests' prohibition against contact with a dead body. There is no difference between a woman and a man in civil law, nor is there any difference between them regarding punishment for transgressions, except in the case of a designated maidservant (שִׁפְחָה חֲרוּפָה) and the married daughter of a priest (see בַּת כֹּהֵן). Women are not permitted to testify in court except in special circumstances, nor are they permitted to serve as judges or to be appointed to public office. There are also certain differences between men and women regarding vows (see הֲפָרַת נְדָרִים) and Nazirite vows, and also regarding other regulations, mainly for reasons of modesty. See אַנְדְּרוֹגִינוֹס; טוּמְטוּם.

אָשָׁם *Guilt-offering.* One of the categories of sacrifices. There are six sub-categories of the אָשָׁם sacrifice: (1) אָשָׁם גְּזֵילוֹת — a sacrifice brought by a person who denied a debt, swore a false oath that he was not liable, and later admitted that he was liable and that he had sworn falsely. (2) אָשָׁם מְעִילוֹת — a sacrifice brought as atonement for מְעִילָה, the misuse of sacred articles. (3) אָשָׁם שִׁפְחָה חֲרוּפָה — a sacrifice brought as atonement for relations with a partially non-Jewish maidservant designated to be the wife of a Hebrew slave (see שִׁפְחָה חֲרוּפָה). (4) אָשָׁם נָזִיר — a sacrifice brought as part of the purification process of a Nazirite who had become ritually impure (see נְזִירוּת). (5) אָשָׁם מְצוֹרָע — a sacrifice brought as part of the purification process of a leper (see צָרַעַת). (6) אָשָׁם תָּלוּי — a sacrifice brought as atonement in a case where a person is unsure whether or not he committed a sin which requires the bringing of a sin-offering (חַטָּאת). An אָשָׁם is one of the קָדְשֵׁי קָדָשִׁים — sacrifices of the most sacred order — and may only be eaten by priests and only on the day it is offered and the following night. The laws of its slaughter (שְׁחִיטָה), the sprinkling of its blood on the altar (זְרִיקָה), and the offering of its fats (הֶקְטֵר חֲלָבִים) are like those governing the peace-offering (שְׁלָמִים). A ram (אַיִל) is the only animal used for an אָשָׁם.

אָשָׁם גְּזֵילוֹת *A guilt-offering for robbery.* This offering is required when a person has denied that he owes someone money, has taken a false oath to support his claim, and later admitted his guilt. To atone for his misdeed, he must return the money, pay the injured party an additional fifth of the sum (חוֹמֶשׁ), and offer this sacrifice.

אָשָׁם מְעִילוֹת *A guilt-offering for misuse of sacred articles.* A person who unwittingly takes an article or an animal consecrated to the Temple or set aside as a sacrifice and uses it for secular purposes, must restore the value of the article to the Temple, pay an additional fifth of its value (חוֹמֶשׁ), and bring this offering.

אָשָׁם תָּלוּי *A doubtful guilt-offering.* A sacrifice brought by a person who is uncertain as to whether he committed a sin that requires a sin-offering (חַטָּאת). In *Keritot* (17b–18a) the Sages debated the precise definition of the doubt which requires the penalty of this sacrifice. In the Second Temple period, it was even offered by individuals who had no real doubt, but merely a slight suspicion that they had committed a sin. Hence it was also called אָשָׁם חֲסִידִים — "the guilt-offering of the pious."

אַשְׁמוֹרוֹת   *Watches.* The divisions of the night. The Sages differed as to whether the night is divided into three watches or four. The times for such matters as the recitation of the *Shema* (קְרִיאַת שְׁמַע), and the beginning of the daily Temple service (see תְּרוּמַת הַדֶּשֶׁן), are determined according to the watches.

אֲשֵׁרָה   *A tree worshipped as part of idolatrous rites.* The Torah commands that such trees be burned and entirely destroyed (Deuteronomy 12:13). In particular, there are two types of such trees which must be destroyed: (1) A tree which was itself worshipped (אֲשֵׁרָה דְמֹשֶׁה). (2) A tree planted next to an idol to beautify it or to be used in some way in its service. It is forbidden to derive benefit from an אֲשֵׁרָה, which is Halakhically considered to be burnt and non-existent even before it is actually destroyed.

אֵשֶׁת אָב   *One's father's wife.* The Torah prohibits sexual relations with one's father's wife (Leviticus 20:11) (see also עֲרָיוֹת). This prohibition applies even though: (1) the woman is not his mother; (2) she was only betrothed to his father (see אֵירוּסִין) and had not undergone the rites of marriage (see נִישׂוּאִין); (3) his father is no longer alive. Some Talmudic opinions also include within the scope of this prohibition an unmarried woman seduced or raped by his father. Transgression of this prohibition carries the death penalty of stoning (סְקִילָה).

אֵשֶׁת אָח   *One's brother's wife.* The Torah prohibits sexual relations with one's brother's wife (Leviticus 20:11). (See also עֲרָיוֹת.) Trangression of this prohibition carries the punishment of excision (כָּרֵת). The prohibition applies to the wife of both a paternal and a maternal brother, and remains in force even after the brother's death. The only exception to the prohibition is a יְבָמָה, the widow of a brother who died childless (see יִבּוּם).

אֵשֶׁת אִישׁ   *A man's wife.* The Ten Commandments specifically prohibit adultery, and the Torah elsewhere states that the sin of sexual relations with another man's wife is punishable by death (Leviticus 20:10). The prohibition applies both to a

betrothed (see אֵירוּסִין) and to a married woman (see נִישׂוּאִין). Both parties to the adultery are subject to the penalty of death by חֶנֶק (strangulation), and if the female partner is a betrothed virgin between the ages of twelve and twelve-and-a-half (see נַעֲרָה and נַעֲרָה הַמְאוֹרָסָה) the penalty for both parties is סְקִילָה (stoning). A married woman becomes frcc to marry another man only through divorce (see גֵּט) or her husband's death. See also מֵיאוּן.

אִשְׁתּוֹ כְּגוּפוֹ   *One's wife is as oneself.* A principle applying particularly in the laws of evidence. A man's wife is considered to be legally identical with him; hence, if a man is disqualified from testifying for or against a certain relative, he is also disqualified from testifying for or against that relative's wife or husband.

אֶתְנַן זוֹנָה   *The present given to a prostitute.* The Torah forbids the offering as a sacrifice in the Temple of an animal given in payment to a prostitute (Deuteronomy 23:19). See also מְחִיר כֶּלֶב.

אֶתְרוֹג   *Citron.* (1) The citron is one of the four species (אַרְבָּעָה מִינִים) over which a blessing is recited on the Sukkot Festival. The Sages maintained the tradition that the expression פְּרִי עֵץ הָדָר — "the fruit of goodly trees" (Leviticus 23:40) — refers to the citron. Since the Torah specifically refers to the beauty of the fruit, one is commanded to make certain that the citron used on Sukkot is perfect in form, and any outer flaw or unusual appearance makes the citron invalid for use in fulfilling the

commandment. Any citron which is at least partially ripe and which is larger than the size of an egg (see בֵּיצָה) is valid for performing the commandment. A fruit produced by grafting a citron onto another kind of citrus tree is not valid for performing the commandment. (2) With regard to tithes (מַעֲשְׂרוֹת). Since the citron tree produces fruit over a prolonged period (as opposed to a single season), it may at any one time have fruit at different stages of maturity. It also demands artificial irrrigation. Because of these special features, terumah (תְּרוּמָה) and tithes regarding the citron are similar to those governing vegetables rather than those governing other fruit trees.

בָּא בַּמַּחְתֶּרֶת   *One who comes and breaks [lit. tunnels] in.* A thief who breaks into a person's house. The Torah views such a thief as a potential murderer. Therefore, unless the homeowner is sure that the thief has no intention of harming him, he is

permitted not only to defend himself against the thief but even to kill him. (See Exodus 22:1; *Sanhedrin*, chapter 8).

בִּגְדֵי זָהָב   *The golden garments.* The eight garments (שְׁמוֹנָה

(בְּגָדִים) which the High Priest (כֹּהֵן גָּדוֹל) wore every day. They consisted of the four garments worn by all priests in the Temple and an additional four garments worn only by the High Priest. These latter garments contained gold in their manufacture, and thus the eight garments were given the title בִּגְדֵי זָהָב — "the golden garments." See next entry.

בִּגְדֵי לָבָן   *The white garments.* The four garments which the High Priest (כֹּהֵן גָּדוֹל) wore when he entered the Holy of Holies (קֹדֶשׁ הַקֳּדָשִׁים) on the Day of Atonement (יוֹם הַכִּיפּוּרִים). They were: (1) כְּתוֹנֶת, "tunic"; (2) מִכְנָסַיִם, "trousers"; (3) מִצְנֶפֶת, "miter"; (4) אַבְנֵט, "sash" or "girdle." These garments were made entirely of white linen. They were like those worn by a common priest (כֹּהֵן הֶדְיוֹט) throughout the year, except that the אַבְנֵט worn by a common priest was made of a combination of wool and linen. See Leviticus 16:4, and previous entry.

בְּדִיקַת חָמֵץ   *The search for leaven.* The search of one's house that one is obliged to make before the Passover Festival to see whether any חָמֵץ — leaven — still remains in hidden places. (See בִּיעוּר חָמֵץ about the removal of the leaven.)

בְּהֵמָה   *An animal* — more specifically, a domestic mammal. (בְּהֵמָה גַּסָּה; בְּהֵמָה דַּקָּה; בְּהֵמָה טְהוֹרָה; כּוֹי.) Certain Halakhic distinctions are made between a בְּהֵמָה and a non-domesticated animal (חַיָּה). (See כִּיסוּי הַדָּם; חֵלֶב; בָּשָׂר בְּחָלָב; אוֹתוֹ וְאֶת בְּנוֹ.)

בְּהֵמָה גַּסָּה   *A large domestic animal.* Large animals raised for labor or food. Kosher animals included in this category are cattle; among non-kosher animals in this category are horses, camels, and donkeys.

בְּהֵמָה דַּקָּה   *A small domestic animal.* Smaller domestic animals (in contrast to בְּהֵמָה גַּסָּה — large domestic animals). Kosher animals included in this category are goats and sheep; among non-kosher animals in this category are pigs.

בְּהֵמָה טְהוֹרָה   *A clean [kosher] animal.* In general, a species of kosher animal which walks on four legs and nurses its young. In order to be classified as kosher it must have a cloven hoof and must also chew the cud. More specifically, the term is used to refer to cattle, sheep, and goats, in contrast to kosher non-domesticated animals (חַיָּה טְהוֹרָה). There is no obligation to cover the blood of a בְּהֵמָה טְהוֹרָה after its slaughter (see כִּיסוּי הַדָּם), and parts of its fat (see חֵלֶב) may not be eaten.

בַּהֶרֶת   *One of the four skin blemishes that are a sign of* צָרַעַת, leprosy. (See נְגָעִים.) בַּהֶרֶת refers to an extremely bright white blemish (see Leviticus 13:4). In a more general sense the term refers to all four skin blemishes that are signs of צָרַעַת.

בּוֹגֶרֶת   *An adult woman.* When a girl reaches puberty, generally at the age of twelve, she is legally considered a נַעֲרָה — "a young girl," to distinguish her from a קְטַנָּה — "a minor." After a further six months, she is legally considered a בּוֹגֶרֶת — "an adult woman." From this time onward she is considered an independent adult, and her father no longer has authority to make decisions on her behalf.

בּוֹעֵל אֲרַמִית   *One who has sexual relations with a non-Jewess.* Although the Torah prohibits marriage between Jews and non-Jews (Deuteronomy 7:3), there is no explicit Torah prohibition against sexual relations with a non-Jewess out of wedlock. Such relations are, however, prohibited by Rabbinic law, and are subject to the usual penalty for the violation of Rabbinic prohibitions: מַכַּת מַרְדּוּת — "lashes administered for disobedience." Moreover, such an act was viewed so severely that permission was granted to "the zealous" (קַנָּאִים) to kill a person caught committing it in public (see Numbers 25:1–15 and קַנָּאִים פּוֹגְעִים בּוֹ). If the בּוֹעֵל אֲרַמִית was not lashed by order of the Rabbinical Court, he was liable to the divine punishment of excision (כָּרֵת). (See Malachi 2:11–12.)

בּוֹעֵל נִדָּה   *One who has sexual relations with a woman who is ritually impure because of menstruation.* Such an act is a sin requiring the sacrifice of a sin-offering if committed inadvertently (see חַיָּיב חַטָּאת). The man becomes ritually impure for seven days. His status is that of an אַב הַטּוּמְאָה (see אֲבוֹת הַטּוּמְאוֹת), and he conveys ritual impurity to others, whether he engaged in this act willfully or inadvertently. See נִדָּה.

בּוֹר   *A pit.* One of the primary categories of injury (see אֲבוֹת נְזִיקִין). The term is given expanded meaning beyond that of a hole in the ground and includes any obstruction a person may create in a public domain — for example, an obstacle placed in the path of others or a change made in the terrain. This obstruction need not be permanently fixed in one place. On the contrary, we find references to a בּוֹר מִתְגַּלְגֵּל — "a moving pit," i.e., a rolling stone, or a stone kicked from one place to another — which becomes a cause of damage where it lands. The creator of the בּוֹר is liable for the injuries (including death) it causes to animals, and for the injuries (excluding death) it causes to people.

בּוֹשֶׁת   *Shame.* One of the five headings (חֲמִישָׁה דְּבָרִים) under which a person may have to pay damages for an injury he caused another person. If the injured person has been shamed in the process, the person who caused the injury is obligated to compensate his victim for the shame he has caused him. The amount of the payment for בּוֹשֶׁת is evaluated according to the social standing both of the person who suffered the shame and of the person who caused it. Payment is required under the heading of בּוֹשֶׁת even if no physical injury was inflicted, provided that the shame was caused by a physical act; a person who verbally puts another to shame has no financial obligation to him under the heading of בּוֹשֶׁת.
See אוֹנָאַת דְּבָרִים; חוֹבֵל; מְבַזֶּה תַּלְמִיד חָכָם.

בָּזִיכִין   *Vessels, dishes.* The two bowls of frankincense (לְבוֹנָה) which were placed on (or next to) the two arrangements of the shewbread (לֶחֶם הַפָּנִים) on the sacred table (שׁוּלְחַן הַפָּנִים) in the Temple.

בִּטּוּל   See בִּיטוּל.

בָּטְלָה דַּעְתּוֹ אֵצֶל כָּל אָדָם   Lit., *his opinion is cancelled out by the opinions of all other men.* An individual's behavior which runs counter to the accepted norms of behavior of most people, is not considered Halakhically significant and is not used as a basis for Halakhic rulings. For example, if a person ate food in a manner not used by the vast majority of people, and the food itself was Halakhically forbidden, he would not have committed a transgression, because his behavior is cancelled out by the practice of the majority.

בִּיאָה   *Sexual intercourse.* One of the ways in which betrothal is effected (see קִידּוּשִׁין), and the only way in which a levirate marriage (יִבּוּם) is fully consummated. In all forbidden sexual relationships, whatever their degree of prohibition, one is punished only for having actual sexual intercourse, although all forms of sexual contact are forbidden (see הַעֲרָאָה). With regard to almost all the commandments of the Torah there is no difference between vaginal intercourse (בִּיאָה כְּדַרְכָּהּ) and anal intercourse (בִּיאָה שֶׁלֹּא כְּדַרְכָּהּ), though there are some differences in the cases of a "designated" maidservant (שִׁפְחָה חֲרוּפָה) and in the punishment for the rape of a betrothed girl between twelve and twelve-and-a-half years of age (נַעֲרָה הַמְאוֹרָסָה). Any other physical contact, even if its intent is unquestionably sexual, does not come under the category of בִּיאָה.

בִּיאָה בְּמִקְצָת   *Partial entry.* The entry of part of a person's body into a certain place. In connection with certain laws the problem arises as to whether the entry of part of a person's body into a place is considered as if the person's entire body has entered that place. This question is significant with regard to a person's presence in a ritually impure place, such as the case of a priest entering a house containing a dead body, entry into a house affected by leprosy (בַּיִת הַמְנוּגָּע), a Nazirite (see נְזִירוּת) entering a cemetery, etc., and it specifically applies to the entry of a ritually impure person into the Temple area.

בִּיזּוּי אוֹכְלִים   *Disrespect towards food.* It is forbidden to treat food fit for human consumption in a disrespectful manner. Thus it is forbidden to throw food if it will thereby become spoiled. Food that has fallen to the ground must be picked up, and it may only be used for purposes other than those for which it was intended if it is not thereby spoiled.

בִּיטּוּל אִיסּוּרִים   Lit., *the nullification of prohibitions.* The neutralization of the prohibition on a forbidden item when it becomes mixed with other entities; for example, when forbidden food is mixed with permitted food. When a prohibited item is mixed together with other items and can no longer be singled out as an individual unit, the mixture may sometimes be permitted for use. The circumstances under which the mixture containing the prohibited item becomes permitted depend upon the nature of the prohibition and the nature of the mixture. Some prohibited items become permitted in a mixture: (1) where there is a simple majority of permitted substances; or (2) where the taste of the forbidden substance is no longer discernible; or (3) where the permitted substances are sixty times the quantity of the prohibited substance; or (4) where the permitted substances are one hundred times the quantity of the prohibited; or (5) where the permitted substances are two hundred times the quantity of the prohibited. Certain prohibited items or substances can never be neutralized, however much the permitted substances are greater than the prohibited (e.g., ḥametz on Pesaḥ). The neutralization of a prohibited item when mixed with a permitted item can only take effect if the mixture was accidentally created — one may not intentionally effect such a neutralization. A prohibited item can also be neutralized when it loses its importance. For example, a forbidden food may become permitted when it is no longer fit for consumption.

בִּיטּוּל מִקָּח   *The nullification of a transaction.* If unfair advantage (see אוֹנָאָה) was taken of one of the parties to a business transaction and the other party made a profit greater than one-sixth (see שְׁתוּת) of the article's market value, the transaction may be nullified, and the wronged party (according to some authorities: either party) may demand the return of the article or the amount paid.

בִּיטּוּל עֲבוֹדָה זָרָה   *The nullification of idolatry.* It is forbidden to derive any benefit from an idol. If, however, the idol was owned by a non-Jew and he shows, by intentionally damaging the idol or by acting disrespectfully towards it, that he no longer regards it as holy, he has thereby "nullified the idolatry" and a Jew may then use it for his own needs. Idols owned by Jews cannot be "nullified." See also עֲבוֹדָה זָרָה.

בִּיטּוּל רְשׁוּת   *The renunciation of authority over one's property.* A concept applying to the establishment of an eruv (see עֵירוּב חֲצֵירוֹת). If the resident of one of the homes opening onto a common courtyard does not participate in an eruv, none of the residents of the courtyard may carry from their homes into the courtyard or vice versa on the Sabbath. But if the resident who did not participate in the eruv renounces his rights to his property in favor of his neighbors (for that Sabbath), he is thereby considered as a guest and not as the owner of the property. The eruv becomes valid, and the other residents are permitted to carry from their homes into the courtyard and vice versa.

בַּיְיתוֹסִים   *Boethusians.* See צָדוֹקִים וּבַיְיתוֹסִים.

בִּיכּוּרִים   *The first-fruits of the new harvest which were given to the priests.* (See Deuteronomy 26:1 ff.) In Temple times, a farmer would select the first-fruits (according to Rabbinic decree, at least one-sixtieth of the harvest) of the seven types of fruit with which Eretz Israel is specially favored (Deuteronomy 8:8). He would bring them to the Temple in a basket, place them before the altar, and recite prayers of thanks to God. Afterwards the fruit was given to the priests and eaten under the same provisions that govern תְּרוּמָה. The first-fruits were brought to the Temple between the Festivals of Shavuot and Sukkot. If they were not brought within this period, an extension was granted until Ḥanukkah. An entire tractate of the Mishnah, *Bikkurim,* is devoted to the laws and practices governing this commandment.

בֵּין הָאוּלָם וְלַמִּזְבֵּחַ   *Between the entrance hall and the altar.* The area of the Temple Courtyard between the altar (מִזְבֵּחַ) and the entrance (אוּלָם) to the Sanctuary (הֵיכָל) (see plan of the Temple, p. 277). This area possessed a higher level of holiness than the rest of the Temple Courtyard; only priests fit to serve in the Temple (in contrast to priests with physical defects or non-priests) were allowed to enter it. The washbasin or laver (כִּיּוֹר) was also located in this section of the Temple Courtyard.

בֵּין הַבַּדִּים   Lit., *between the staves*. The ark (אֲרוֹן הַבְּרִית) was originally carried by lifting two staves (בַּדִּים) set in rings on either side of it. Even after the ark was permanently placed in the Holy of Holies (קֹדֶשׁ הַקֳּדָשִׁים) in the First Temple, the staves remained in place, and the blood of the bull and the goat that were sacrificed on the Day of Atonement (יוֹם הַכִּיפּוּרִים) had to be sprinkled between these staves (see פַּר יוֹם הַכִּיפּוּרִים; שְׂעִיר יוֹם הַכִּיפּוּרִים). Since there was no ark in the Second Temple, the blood of these offerings was sprinkled where the staves would have been.

בֵּין הַשְּׁמָשׁוֹת   *The twilight period between the end of the day and the beginning of the night.* Usually understood as the period between sunset (שְׁקִיעָה) and the time the stars come out (יְצִאַת הַכּוֹכָבִים). This period is treated as of doubtful status. There is a debate among the Sages concerning its length and when it begins and ends.

בֵּינוֹנִית   *Intermediate quality.* See עִידִית.

בִּיעוּר חָמֵץ   *The removal of leaven.* The obligation to remove any חָמֵץ — leaven — remaining in one's possession before the onset of Passover (or during Passover, if חָמֵץ is discovered then). According to Rabbinic decree, all חָמֵץ must have been removed by the beginning of the sixth hour after daybreak on the morning of the day before Passover. It is customary to burn this חָמֵץ, but it may be disposed of in other ways.

בִּיעוּר מַעַשְׂרוֹת   *The removal of tithes.* The obligation once in three years to complete the giving of all agricultural dues (see מַעַשְׂרוֹת and תְּרוּמָה) by the day before Passover in the fourth and seventh years of the seven-year agricultural cycle (see שְׁבִיעִית). In Temple times, on the afternoon of the seventh day of Passover in these years, a special recital of verses of thanksgiving and praise (see וִידּוּי מַעֲשֵׂר) took place (see Deuteronomy 26:12–15).

בֵּיצָה   *Egg, an egg's bulk.* A Halakhic unit of dry and liquid measurement. This measurement is the minimum unit with regard to the ritual impurity of food, i.e., a smaller quantity of food than this does not convey ritual impurity (nor, according to certain authorities, does it contract ritual impurity). The בֵּיצָה measurement is also used in many other contexts. The volume of a בֵּיצָה is reckoned as being between 2 and 3.5 fluid ounces, 50–100 cc. (but see section on weights and measures, p.287).

בִּירָה   *God's chosen place of residence.* A term referring to the Temple Mount (see הַר הַבַּיִת). There is a debate among the Amoraim whether the term refers to the whole Temple Mount or to one particular section of it where certain disqualified sacrifices were burned (see *Zevaḥim* 104b).

בִּישּׁוּלֵי נָכְרִים   *Food cooked by non-Jews.* The Sages prohibited food cooked by non-Jews even when there was no problem about the kashrut of the food. This prohibition applies to foods that are only eaten cooked (not to foods that are eaten both cooked and raw), and also to important foods ("food fit to be served on a king's table," see *Avodah Zarah* 38a).

בַּיִת   *A house.* Generally, this term refers to a sturdy structure used as a permanent dwelling, with a minimum area of four cubits by four cubits (see אַמָּה) and a minimum height of ten handbreadths (see טֶפַח). However, more specific and restricted definitions are given to a בַּיִת in certain Halakhic contexts.

בֵּית אָב   *An extended paternal family.* A term used mainly with reference to the priestly families. The priests were divided into twenty-four watches, each watch serving in the Temple twice a year for one week at a time. The watches themselves were each divided into six (or, according to another opinion, seven) families. Each family served in the Temple for one day of the week. See מִשְׁמָר.

בֵּית דִּין   *Court, tribunal.* This is a general term for any judicial body in the area of Halakhah. In fact there are a number of levels of Jewish courts, beginning with the highest, the Supreme Court (see סַנְהֶדְרִין גְּדוֹלָה), which consisted of seventy-one members (see also בֵּית דִּין שֶׁל שִׁבְעִים וְאֶחָד). Below that were the courts consisting of twenty-three members (see סַנְהֶדְרִי קְטַנָּה and בֵּית דִּין שֶׁל עֶשְׂרִים וּשְׁלֹשָׁה), and the court of three experts (מוּמְחִים). This latter court was authorized to judge all civil cases, both suits brought in business disputes and cases involving fines. This court could also deal with other transgressions and was permitted to impose corporal punishment, but not the death sentence. There was also a tribunal of three laymen (see הֶדְיוֹט), men without ordination (see סְמִיכַת זְקֵנִים), and they could judge regular civil matters, but not cases involving fines. Nor were they permitted to impose lashes (מַלְקוֹת) as stipulated by the Torah. After ordination was suspended (and in many places outside Eretz Israel even when there were still ordained courts), all Rabbinical Courts came to be regarded as lay courts. They could rule on all Torah matters, and they had the right to impose various punishments in order to reform the community (לְשֵׁם תַּקָּנַת הַצִּיבּוּר). Although by right a single ordained Sage was permitted to pass judgment, he did not constitute a court, and it was considered preferable that two other judges join him. For special kinds of cases the בֵּית דִּין took other forms. In the case of the heifer whose neck was to be broken (עֶגְלָה עֲרוּפָה) there was a five-member tribunal. For the intercalation of the year (עִיבּוּר הַשָּׁנָה), when this was done by a tribunal, there had to be seven judges. For the valuation (see עֲרָכִין) of immovable property or persons, a court of ten was necessary, of whom one had to be a priest. A בֵּית דִּין is not merely a judicial body, but it is also responsible for all community matters, and it must be concerned with the needs of the commuity over which it is appointed (or see to the appointment of people and bodies to carry out that function). It must act so that all the commandments incumbent upon the community, both those between man and his Creator and those between man and his fellowman (the needs of the poor, education, etc.), are indeed carried out properly.

בֵּית דִּין שֶׁל עֶשְׂרִים וּשְׁלֹשָׁה   *A court of twenty-three.* The court that was entitled to judge capital cases (see דִּינֵי נְפָשׁוֹת). See also סַנְהֶדְרִי קְטַנָּה.

בֵּית דִּין שֶׁל שִׁבְעִים וְאֶחָד   *The court of seventy-one.* Ancient Israel's Supreme Court and highest religious body. This court was vested with the power to decide matters that affected the entire nation, such as permission to go to war (see מִלְחֶמֶת הָרְשׁוּת) and the destruction of an idolatrous city (see עִיר הַנִּדַּחַת). It also judged cases involving the king (see מֶלֶךְ), the High Priest (see כֹּהֵן גָּדוֹל), or false prophets (see נְבִיא שֶׁקֶר). Its enactments were binding on the entire nation. It decided cases left undecided by the the lower courts, and was the final authority on Halakhah. See סַנְהֶדְרִין גְּדוֹלָה.

בֵּית הַדֶּשֶׁן   *The place of the ashes.* A place outside Jerusalem where the ashes from the altar were deposited. The sin-offerings of the Day of Atonement (see פַּר יוֹם הַכִּיפּוּרִים; שְׂעִיר יוֹם הַכִּיפּוּרִים) and other public sin-offerings which were not eaten (see פָּרִים הַנִּשְׂרָפִים; שְׂעִירִים הַנִּשְׂרָפִים) were burned there.

בֵּית הַחֲלִיפוֹת   *The chamber of knives.* A chamber in the entrance hall (see אוּלָם) of the Temple (see plan of the Temple, p. 277). It contained apertures in which the priestly watches (see מִשְׁמָר) kept their slaughtering knives.

בֵּית הַכְּנֶסֶת   *A synagogue.* A place where communal prayers are held. Synagogues were also frequently used as meeting-halls for important matters of public concern, as schools, and as houses of study (see בֵּית הַמִּדְרָשׁ.) There is no fixed layout for a synagogue, but it generally includes the following: (1) An ark for the Torah scrolls (in Talmudic times, the ark was often a movable structure which could be taken out of the synagogue after prayer and moved to another room). (2) A raised platform in the center of the synagogue on which the Torah is read. (3) A separate area for women. A synagogue is considered a מִקְדָּשׁ מְעַט (a "Temple in miniature"), and is thus endowed with a certain measure of holiness. Accordingly, it is forbidden to act disrespectfully within it. A synagogue may only be destroyed or sold under certain circumstances.

בֵּית הַמִּדְרָשׁ   *A house of study.* A place designated for the study of Torah. The sanctity of the בֵּית הַמִּדְרָשׁ exceeds that of a synagogue (בֵּית הַכְּנֶסֶת.) Nevertheless, those who study there are allowed to eat and sleep there. These leniencies were granted in order not to force the students to leave the בֵּית הַמִּדְרָשׁ. In practice, most synagogues are built so that they will also serve as houses of study.

בֵּית הַמּוֹקֵד   *The chamber of the hearth.* A square, domed chamber at the side of the Temple Courtyard (see plan of the Temple, p. 277). It contained a large fire, before which the priests would warm themselves, and which was used when necessary for lighting the fire on the altar (מִזְבֵּחַ). The priests mainly used the בֵּית הַמּוֹקֵד as a place to wait and rest during their periods of service in the Temple. It also served as their sleeping quarters, and honor guards of priests were stationed there. At each of the four corners of the בֵּית הַמּוֹקֵד, there was a smaller chamber which served a specific function in the Temple.

בֵּית הַמְנוּגָּע   *A house in which signs of leprosy [*צָרַעַת*] were detected.* (See Leviticus 14.) With respect to these laws any structure of four walls, built of stone, wood, or mud, is considered a house. If a leprous blemish was detected within a house, the house was quarantined for a certain period of time (see נִגְעֵי בָּתִּים). If the blemishes spread, the blemished stones were removed. If the blemishes returned, the entire house had to be destroyed. Any person, or article, that entered the house during the quarantine period became ritually impure.

בֵּית הַמִּקְדָּשׁ   *The Temple.* The edifice in Jerusalem which was the only place where sacrifices were permitted to be brought. The most important religious center of the Jewish people. The Temple replaced the Tabernacle in the desert and also the permanent Tabernacle that was in Shilo. It was erected "in the place which the Lord shall choose" (Deuteronomy 12), on Mount Moriah in Jerusalem. The location of the Temple was determined by prophetic inspiration, and certain points within it (the altar, the Holy of Holies) are fixed forever and will never change. Despite certain differences between the First Temple, built by King Solomon, the Second Temple, built by the exiles returning from Babylonia and restored and changed by King Herod, and the plan of the Third Temple, which will be built in the future (as described in the prophecies of Ezekiel, chapter 40 ff.), it is essentially built according to a single plan. While we have a detailed and precise account only of the measurements of the Second Temple (in tractate *Middot* of the Mishnah, and in many other sources), its general plan combines features of both the First and the Third Temples. The Temple was built on the Temple Mount (Mount Moriah, see הַר הַבַּיִת), which was surrounded by its own wall, and which had a special degree of holiness (parallel to מַחֲנֵה לְוִיָּה, the Camp of the Levites, where the Tribe of the Levites dwelled in the desert), greater than the sanctity of the city of Jerusalem. On the Temple Mount, outside the Courtyard (עֲזָרָה) of the Temple, there was a synagogue where public prayers were held (for in the Temple itself the sacrificial service was performed, and individuals would pray there by themselves). The Temple Mount and the Temple itself were built on various levels, each of which had its own degree of sanctity. Between the various parts were stairways, partitions and gates. The Temple was surrounded by a wall, and most of its area consisted of the courtyards: the women's courtyard, עֶזְרַת נָשִׁים; the Israelites' courtyard, עֶזְרַת יִשְׂרָאֵל; and the priests' courtyard, עֶזְרַת כֹּהֲנִים. These courtyards had no roofs, and within them were offices (לְשָׁכוֹת), large rooms, each of which was used for a special purpose. To the west of the courtyards was the great altar (מִזְבֵּחַ), and to the west of that was the area between the entrance hall to the Sanctuary (אוּלָם) and the altar (see בֵּין הָאוּלָם וְלַמִּזְבֵּחַ). The entrance hall was a wide rectangular building used as an entrance to the Sanctuary (הֵיכָל), which was a tall building (100 cubits in height) containing the golden altar (מִזְבַּח הַזָּהָב), the Menorah (מְנוֹרָה), and the table containing the shewbread (לֶחֶם הַפָּנִים). To the west of the Sanctuary was the Holy of Holies (קֹדֶשׁ הַקֳּדָשִׁים). In the First Temple the Holy of Holies contained the Ark of the Covenant, but in the Second Temple the room was entirely empty, containing only a rock (אֶבֶן שְׁתִיָּה, the foundation stone), on which the Ark of the Covenant had previously rested. The sanctity of the Temple Mount was such that entry to it was forbidden to people rendered ritually impure by gonorrheal or uterine discharges (see זָב and זָבָה), menstrual blood (see נִדָּה), or childbirth (see יוֹלֶדֶת) and who had not yet been ritually purified. The rampart (חֵיל) within the Temple Mount was of a higher degree of sanctity, so that non-Jews and those ritually impure by contact with a corpse (see טֻמְאַת מֵת) were forbidden to enter it. The women's courtyard, which was within the Temple itself, could not be entered by someone who had immersed himself in a mikveh (מִקְוֶה) to regain his ritual purity but who remained impure till the evening (see טְבוּל יוֹם). The Israelites' courtyard was even forbidden to someone who had completed all the other stages of regaining his ritual purity and who only needed to bring a sacrifice to complete his purification (see מְחוּסַר כַּפָּרָה). Anyone who entered it while ritually impure had to bring a sin-offering. The priests' courtyard had a higher degree of holiness, and Israelites could only enter it in order to bring a sacrifice. The area between the altar and the Sanctuary had an even higher degree of holiness, and priests who were blemished (see מוּמִים) were forbidden to enter it. The Sanctuary could only be entered by priests who had washed their hands and feet in the basin (כִּיּוֹר). As for the Holy of Holies, no one at all could enter it except the High Priest (כֹּהֵן גָּדוֹל) on the Day of Atonement (יוֹם הַכִּפּוּרִים), and he could only do so in order to perform the service. Although there are many descriptions of the Second Temple, they are not entirely complete, and over the generations there were Sages who possessed conflicting traditions regarding certain details. From all these traditions it is clear that the Temple was a very splendid building, and the entire Jewish people, wherever they lived in the world, used to contribute to maintaining its splendor. The Temple service was performed by twenty-four watches (see מִשְׁמָר) of priests, who came to perform the service for periods of weeks during the year. Aside from these, there was a permanent staff in the Temple, which included not only the High Priest and his assistant (סְגַן הַכֹּהֲנִים) but also the permanent clerks and workers of the Temple. These officials (a detailed account of them is found in tractate *Shekalim)* were responsible both for the Temple funds and also for the execution of regular tasks, such as the preparation of the shewbread, the incense, and the priestly garments. The vast numbers of visitors to the Temple, especially on the Pilgrim ·Festivals and on Pesaḥ in particular, made it necessary to maintain a well-organized staff of professional workers to see to the various needs of the pilgrims. In addition to the Temple's role as the ceremonial and cultural center of the Jewish people, it also served as a center for all the needs of Jerusalem, since some of the money left over from the Temple expenditure was used for the construction of Jerusalem and its fortification. Another important function filled by the Temple was that it was the center of the nation's spiritual leadership. Several courts sat permanently in the Temple, including the most important of them, the Great Sanhedrin (סַנְהֶדְרִין גְּדוֹלָה) which convened in the Chamber of Hewn Stone (לִשְׁכַּת הַגָּזִית). See plan of the Temple, p. 277.

בֵּית הַסְּתָרִים   *The concealed parts of the body,* i.e., the parts of the body which would not normally be seen even when a person is naked (such as the cavity of the mouth and the throat). This term is frequently used with reference to laws of ritual impurity: (1) If a source of ritual impurity touches a person in any one of these concealed parts of the body, he does not become ritually impure. (2) With reference to the laws of immersion in a mikveh (see טְבִילָה) the water does not need to reach these parts of the body in order to effect ritual purity. (3) With reference to the laws of sprinkling (הַזָּאָה) with the water

of the ashes of the Red Heifer (פָּרָה אֲדוּמָה), if the water touches only one of these parts of the body of the ritually impure person, he does not thereby become ritually pure.

בֵּית הַפְּרָס   *An area in which a doubt exists concerning the location of a grave or a corpse.* Among the examples of a בֵּית הַפְּרָס are: (1) שָׂדֶה שֶׁנֶּחְרַשׁ בָּהּ קֶבֶר — a field containing a grave which was accidentally ploughed over and the bones from which may have been strewn throughout the field; (2) שָׂדֶה שֶׁנֶּאֱבַד בָּהּ קֶבֶר — a field containing a grave the location of which is not known. If a person enters such an area, his ritual purity is in doubt. The Sages discuss methods of clarifying the status of a בֵּית הַפְּרָס and ways of entering it without contracting ritual impurity.

בֵּית חוֹנְיוֹ   *The temple of Onias.* A temple built in Egypt by Onias, one of the High Priests, who fled there during the Second Temple period (possibly around the middle of the second century B.C.E.). The temple of Onias was identical in structure and in ritual to the Temple in Jerusalem. But since it was built outside Jerusalem, all the sacrifices offered in it were forbidden (see שְׁחוּטֵי חוּץ), and all the priests who served within it were prohibited from serving in the Temple. This temple is discussed at the end of tractate *Zevaḥim.*

בֵּית שַׁעַר   *A gatehouse.* A small structure placed at the entrance gate to a courtyard, or at the entrance to a house. Often a guard was positioned there. There are specific laws governing a gatehouse with regard to the mezuzah (מְזוּזָה), the boundaries within which one may carry on the Sabbath (see עֵירוּב חֲצֵירוֹת), and other matters.

בְּכוֹר   *A firstborn male.* The four most common applications of this concept are with reference to: (1) The redemption of a firstborn male child (see בְּכוֹר אָדָם; פִּדְיוֹן הַבֵּן). (2) The double share given to a firstborn male child when an inheritance is divided (see בְּכוֹר לְנַחֲלָה). (3) The sanctity of a firstborn "clean" (kosher) animal (see בְּכוֹר בְּהֵמָה טְהוֹרָה). (4) The redemption of a firstborn donkey (see פֶּטֶר חֲמוֹר).

בְּכוֹר אָדָם   *A woman's firstborn son.* The Torah states: "Sanctify to Me every firstborn, whatever opens the womb... both of man and beast, it is mine" (Exodus 13:2). In practical terms, the sanctity of a firstborn son is limited to the obligation (Exodus 13:13) to redeem him from the priest (Numbers 18:15–16) for five pieces of silver (סְלָעִים, see p. 291; see also פִּדְיוֹן הַבֵּן). It is also customary for firstborn sons to fast on the day before the Passover Festival.

בְּכוֹר בְּהֵמָה טְהוֹרָה   *The male firstborn of a clean [kosher] animal,* i.e., the male firstborn of cattle, sheep or goats belonging to a Jew. Such an animal was holy from birth and had to be given to a priest to be offered on the altar in the Temple, and its flesh was eaten by the priests and their families (Numbers 18:17–18). If a firstborn animal acquired a physical blemish (see מוּמִים) which disqualified it from being offered as a sacrifice (see

(פְּסוּלֵי הַמּוּקְדָּשִׁין), it could be slaughtered and eaten like any other nonsacred kosher animal (see חֻלִּין). Nevertheless, it still had to be given to a priest. It is forbidden to inflict a disqualifying blemish intentionally on a בְּכוֹר. A בְּכוֹר may not be used for any mundane purpose even if it is blemished. It is forbidden to work the animal, and its fleece may not be used. Since the destruction of the Second Temple, a בְּכוֹר has continued to be considered sacred. However, since there is no Temple in which to sacrifice it, and since it may only be slaughtered if it has a marked disqualifying blemish, various Halakhic devices are employed to restrict the classification of animals as בְּכוֹר and to permit their slaughter (as nonsacred animals) after they have acquired disqualifying blemishes.

בְּכוֹר לְנַחֲלָה   *A firstborn in regard to inheritance.* A father's firstborn son is given a double share in the inheritance (Deuteronomy 21:17). This privilege is granted even if he is not the mother's firstborn son and even if he is illegitimate (see מַמְזֵר). The firstborn son receives a share twice as great as that received by each of the other sons. This double share is, however, only given from property actually possessed by the estate at the time of the father's death and not from property accruing to the estate later (see רָאוּי וּמוּחְזָק). The latter property is divided equally among the heirs.

בִּכּוּרִים   See בִּכּוּרִים.

בַּל יַחֵל   *The prohibition against breaking a vow [*נֶדֶר*] or oath [*שְׁבוּעָה*] that one has taken.* (Numbers 30:3.) A person who commits an act in violation of a vow or an oath is liable to the punishment of lashes (מַלְקוּת).

בַּל יֵרָאֶה וּבַל יִמָּצֵא   *The prohibition against* חָמֵץ *[leaven] being seen or found.* During Pesaḥ, Jews are forbidden to own חָמֵץ, and חָמֵץ owned by a Jew during Pesaḥ is forbidden, by the Torah or by Rabbinical decree, after the Festival as well (חָמֵץ שֶׁעָבַר עָלָיו הַפֶּסַח). This prohibition only applies to חָמֵץ which was legally owned by a Jew during Pesaḥ, but if it belonged to a non-Jew during the Festival, it is not subject to this prohibition. This Halakhic distinction is the basis for the practice of selling one's חָמֵץ to a non-Jew before Pesaḥ.

בַּל תְּאַחֵר   *The prohibition against delaying the offering of sacrifices one has pledged.* (Deuteronomy 23:22. See also נֶדֶר; נְדָבָה.) This prohibition is transgressed when one fails to bring a sacrifice within three Pilgrim Festivals (see שָׁלֹשׁ רְגָלִים) after the time it was pledged. The prohibition of בַּל תְּאַחֵר also applies to all obligatory sacrifices, tithes (see תְּרוּמָה; מַעַשְׂרוֹת), obligatory gifts (see מַתְּנוֹת עֲנִיִּים), and pledges to the Temple treasury (see קָדְשֵׁי בֶּדֶק הַבַּיִת). Moreover, this prohibition is extended to cover pledges to charity and the like, which must also be honored within this period of time.

בַּל תִּגְרַע   See בַּל תּוֹסִיף.

בַּל תּוֹסִיף   *The prohibition against adding to the mitzvot of the Torah.* (Deuteronomy 13:1.) There are several ways in which this transgression may be committed, of which the following are examples: (1) If a person adds a new detail to the performance of a mitzvah which prevents it from being fulfilled correctly, e.g., if a priest adds a fourth blessing to the three that constitute the Priestly Benediction (see בִּרְכַּת כֹּהֲנִים), he transgresses the prohibition of בַּל תּוֹסִיף. This prohibition has a counterpart in the prohibition בַּל תִּגְרַע, which forbids *taking away* any elements in the performance of a mitzvah. (2) If a person performs a mitzvah which he is not obliged to perform, e.g., if a person sits in a sukkah in Israel on the eighth day of Sukkot (see שְׁמִינִי עֲצֶרֶת), or on the ninth day of Sukkot outside Israel, with the intention of fulfilling the mitzvah of dwelling in the sukkah, he transgresses the prohibition of בַּל תּוֹסִיף. (3) If a person invents a new mitzvah, he transgresses the prohibition of בַּל תּוֹסִיף.

בַּל תָּלִין   *The prohibition against delaying payment of a hired worker's wages after he has completed his period of work.* (Deuteronomy 24:14.) Payment may not be delayed by more than twelve hours from the moment it becomes due. Slightly different rules apply to a craftsman (אוּמָן) or a contractor (קַבְּלָן) who is employed to complete a specific assignment and is not paid by the day or by the hour. Nevertheless, once he has handed his work to the person who engaged him, he must be paid.

בַּל תַּשְׁחִית   (1) *The prohibition against destroying things of value.* Its Biblical source is Deuteronomy 20:19, which forbids cutting down fruit trees when besieging a city. The Sages explained that the scope of this prohibition extends to forbidding the wanton destruction of any article of value. (2) *The prohibition against shaving the corners of one's beard with a razor.* (Leviticus 19:27.) See פֵּאָה.

בַּל תְּשַׁקְּצוּ   Lit., *you shall not make yourselves abominable.* The prohibition against eating the flesh of animals classified by the Torah as unclean. It applies especially to short-legged mammals such as rodents, and to reptiles, insects and the like (Leviticus 11:43, 20:25; see also שֶׁרֶץ). The Sages extended this prohibition to other deeds that cause self-defilement, e.g., the consumption of any food that is repugnant even though it is otherwise kosher.

בָּמָה   *An improvised altar.* Before the First Temple was built, there were periods when sacrifices were allowed to be offered on these altars; after the Temple was built, sacrifices on these altars were forbidden. (The Bible relates, however, that throughout the First Temple period people continued to offer sacrifices on them.) These altars were of two kinds: בָּמָה גְּדוֹלָה ("a great altar") and בָּמָה קְטַנָּה ("a small [private] altar"). The בָּמָה גְּדוֹלָה was the altar used for communal and personal sacrifices during those periods between the entry of the Children of Israel into Eretz Israel and the building of the First Temple when the Ark of the Covenant was not in the Sanctuary. The three places in which the בָּמָה גְּדוֹלָה was used were Gilgal, Nov, and Givon. A בָּמָה קְטַנָּה was a private altar built by an individual to offer up voluntary private sacrifices. Any person (not only priests) could offer sacrifices on a בָּמָה קְטַנָּה.

בֶּן נֹחַ   Lit., *a descendant of Noah.* Any non-Jew. According to Jewish law all non-Jews are obligated to fulfill seven universal laws referred to as שֶׁבַע מִצְווֹת בְּנֵי נֹחַ — "the seven mitzvot of

Noah's descendants" — and Jews are obligated to influence non-Jews to fulfill these commandments.

בֶּן סוֹרֵר וּמוֹרֶה   *A stubborn and rebellious son.* The Torah (Deuteronomy 21:18–21) and the Mishnah (*Sanhedrin*, chapter 8) describe the punishment given to a son between the age of thirteen and thirteen and three months who steals money from his parents to eat a gluttonous meal of meat and wine in the company of worthless men. If his parents bring him to court for this act, he is exhorted to desist and is punished by lashes. If he repeats the same misdeed and is again brought to court by his parents within this same three-month period, he is liable to the death penalty. Nevertheless, the Halakhic limitations surrounding such a case are so severe that some of the Sages said that the execution of a בֶּן סוֹרֵר וּמוֹרֶה never in fact took place.

בֶּן פְּקוּעָה   *The offspring of a kosher animal removed from its mother's womb after the mother has been slaughtered in the manner required by Jewish law.* (See שְׁחִיטָה.) Even if this offspring continues to live, it is considered as having already been slaughtered. It does not, therefore, need to undergo שְׁחִיטָה in order to be made fit to eat, and it is not subject to the law prohibiting "a limb from a living animal" (אֵיבָר מִן הַחַי).

בֶּן שְׁמוֹנָה חֳדָשִׁים   Lit., *A child of eight months.* A human baby or the offspring of a domestic animal (בְּהֵמָה גַּסָּה) born after a pregnancy of only eight months. Such an offspring is not considered viable.

בֶּן תֵּשַׁע שָׁנִים   *A nine-year-old boy.* A boy who has reached this age is considered sufficiently sexually mature for intercourse with him to be Halakhically significant. If such a child engages in sexual relations with a woman who is forbidden to him (see עֲרָיוֹת), she is punished as if he were already an adult. The child himself, however, is not punished, since he is a minor (קָטָן) and is not legally responsible for his actions.

בָּסִיס לְדָבָר הָאָסוּר   *A base for a forbidden article.* Certain categories of objects are forbidden to be moved during the Sabbath and Festivals (see מוּקְצֶה). If such an object is placed on another object before the commencement of the Sabbath or Festival, the second object, which serves as its base or support, also becomes מוּקְצֶה and may not be moved on that day even if the original מוּקְצֶה article resting on it has been removed.

בְּעוּר   See בִּיעוּר.

בְּעִילַת זְנוּת   *Illicit sexual relations.* Sexual relations that take place outside the framework of a marital relationship. The Halakhah presumes that a person will not readily engage in sexual relations for licentious reasons. Thus, in certain situations where it is possible to interpret sexual relations as an act of marriage, this presumption is made, since the act of cohabitation (בִּיאָה) is one of the methods of effecting a valid betrothal (see קִדּוּשִׁין). See also זוֹנָה.

בַּעַל חוֹב   *A creditor.* The narrow meaning of this term is someone who has lent money to someone else. However, in a broader sense, anyone towards whom someone else has a

defined financial obligation (including a litigant whose opponent has been ordered by the court to make payment to him, or someone who has completed a contract to make a sale) is defined as a בַּעַל חוֹב. This status has Halakhic significance from several points of view, both with regard to the cancellation of debts during the Sabbatical Year (see שְׁבִיעִית), and also with regard to the fact that obligations towards a creditor are personal obligations of the debtor (שִׁיעְבּוּד הַגּוּף), and they cannot in every case be transferred to third parties. There are various ways in which a creditor can guarantee the collection of his debts by placing liens on the debtor's property.

בַּעַל מוּם   *A person or an animal with a physical defect.* See מוּמִים.

בַּעַל קֶרִי   *A person who emitted semen, whether involuntarily, intentionally, or during sexual relations.* Such a person becomes ritually impure. To purify himself, he must immerse himself in a mikveh (מִקְוֶה), and after nightfall on the day of his immersion he again becomes ritually pure (see Leviticus 15:16–18).

בְּפָנַי נִכְתַּב וּבְפָנַי נֶחְתַּם   *In my presence it was written, and in my presence it was signed.* A declaration made by an agent appointed to deliver a bill of divorce (גֵּט) written outside Eretz Israel and Babylonia when he delivers the גֵּט in a Rabbinical Court. In order to enable the woman to remarry, the agent must testify that the bill of divorce was written and signed in his presence and that there is no doubt about its validity.

בַּר מֵצְרָא   *A person whose field borders on the field of his neighbor.* When a person wishes to sell a field, the neighbors whose fields border on his have the first option to buy it before others. This right is based on the verse in the Torah: "And you shall do that which is right and good" (Deuteronomy 6:18).

בָּרִי   *A sure [certain] claim.* A concept often applied in civil law (see דִּינֵי מָמוֹנוֹת). When one litigant makes a claim about which he is certain (בָּרִי) and the other makes a claim about which he is in doubt (שֶׁמָּא), greater weight is usually attached by the court to the claim based on certainty.

בְּרִיָּה   *A creature.* A whole creature, however small, in its original form. Among the Halakhic applications of this concept one finds: (1) According to Torah law, the punishment for eating a forbidden בְּרִיָּה is lashes, even though the בְּרִיָּה is smaller than an olive's bulk (see זַיִת) in size. (2) According to Rabbinic ordinance, the presence of a בְּרִיָּה can never be neutralized in any mixture, even when the permitted substances are more than a thousand times its size (see בִּיטּוּל אִיסּוּרִים).

בְּרֵירָה   *Retroactive designation.* The principle (about which the Sages differed) that an object which was not explicitly designated initially for a certain purpose may retroactively be considered as if it had been designated for that purpose from the outset. For example, if a person declares that the tithe from his granary will consist of the last tenth remaining after the rest of the produce has been consumed. If the principle of בְּרֵירָה is accepted, his separation of the tithe is valid, for although the tithe he designated did not exist as a distinct and separate entity when he made his statement, retroactively it *was* that remaining tenth from the outset. There is a debate among the Sages whether to accept the principle of בְּרֵירָה or not. In practice, the principle is generally accepted with regard to questions of Rabbinic law, but not with regard to matters of Torah law.

בְּרָכָה אַחֲרוֹנָה   *The blessing recited after eating food or drinking a beverage.*

The minimum quantity of food requiring such a blessing is an olive's bulk (see זַיִת). The minimum quantity of drink requiring such a blessing is a רְבִיעִית.
See also בְּרָכָה מֵעֵין שָׁלֹשׁ; בִּרְכַּת הַמָּזוֹן.

בְּרָכָה מֵעֵין שָׁלֹשׁ   Lit., *the blessing like [i.e., summarizing] the three [blessings].*

The blessing recited after partaking of food or drink (with the exception of bread) made from any of the seven fruits with which Eretz Israel is specially favored (see Deuteronomy 8:8). The blessing is given this name — בְּרָכָה מֵעֵין שָׁלֹשׁ — because it consists of a shortened version of the contents of the three blessings of the regular Grace after Meals (see בִּרְכַּת הַמָּזוֹן). (See *Berakhot,* chapter 6.)

בִּרְכוֹת הַנֶּהֱנִין   Lit., *blessings of enjoyments.*

Blessings recited in appreciation of physical enjoyment. Included in this category are the various blessings recited over food and drink, and those recited over pleasant fragrances.

בִּרְכוֹת הָרְאִיָּה   *Blessings recited for things seen.*

Blessings which a person recites when he sees certain people, things, or events. These blessings are of various types. They may express praise for beautiful manifestations of nature or for wonders which transcend normal experience, including the commemoration of miracles performed for the Jewish people or for individuals in specific places. They are recited in memory of tragic and catastrophic events which occurred in specific places. Most of these blessings are enumerated in *Berakhot,* chapter 9.

בִּרְכַּת הַמָּזוֹן   *Grace after Meals.*

The blessing ordained in the Torah (Deuteronomy 8:10) to be recited after eating food. The Torah obligation to recite a blessing after food applies only to a meal that satisfies one's hunger, but the Sages require a person to say בִּרְכַּת הַמָּזוֹן after eating more than an olive's bulk (see זַיִת) of bread. The original structure of בִּרְכַּת הַמָּזוֹן contained three blessings — הַזָּן, "for sustenance"; הָאָרֶץ, "for the Land of Israel"; and בּוֹנֵה יְרוּשָׁלַיִם, "for the rebuilding of Jerusalem" — and a fourth one — הַטּוֹב וְהַמֵּטִיב, "for God's being good and beneficent" — was added later. It is not certain whether women are required by Torah law to recite בִּרְכַּת הַמָּזוֹן, but they are certainly required to do so by Rabbinic ordinance. When three men have eaten together, בִּרְכַּת הַמָּזוֹן is preceded by זִמּוּן — an invitation to the participants in the meal to join together to recite בִּרְכַּת הַמָּזוֹן. Verses in praise of Shabbat, the Festivals and other special occasions are added to בִּרְכַּת הַמָּזוֹן, as well as petitionary prayers (such as הָרַחֲמָן) according to local custom.

בִּרְכַּת הַמִּצְווֹת   *The blessing recited before performing a positive commandment.*

There are two standard forms for these blessings: (1) "...who has sanctified us with His commandments and commanded us *to*..."; — אֲשֶׁר קִדְּשָׁנוּ בְּמִצְווֹתָיו וְצִוָּנוּ לְ... (2) "who has sanctified us with His commandments and commanded us — אֲשֶׁר קִדְּשָׁנוּ בְּמִצְווֹתָיו וְצִוָּנוּ עַל...

with His commandments and commanded us *concerning*...." Halakhic authorities, both early and modern, have attempted to establish general criteria determining when the one, rather than the other, form of blessing is to be used. The blessing must normally be recited immediately before the performance of the mitzvah. But in three cases — the washing of hands (נְטִילַת יָדַיִם), the immersion to attain ritual purity, and the immersion of a convert (see טְבִילָה) — the blessing is recited *after* the mitzvah is performed. In all cases, the effectiveness of the performance of the mitzvah is not dependent on whether or not the blessing is recited. There are also many positive commandments (for instance, giving charity and visiting the sick) for which no blessing is recited.

בִּרְכַּת חֲתָנִים   *The blessing of bridegrooms.*

The seven blessings of the bride and groom recited under the wedding canopy and after grace at each of the wedding meals during the first week after the wedding. These blessings are only recited in full in the presence of at least ten men, including one or preferably two who have not previously participated in the wedding celebrations (see פָּנִים חֲדָשׁוֹת). The bridegroom is included among the ten men needed.

בִּרְכַּת כֹּהֲנִים   *The Priestly Benediction.*

The three verses of blessing (Numbers 6:24–26) with which the priests bless the congregation in the synagogue. The Priestly Benediction is recited between the blessings of מוֹדִים and שִׂים שָׁלוֹם in the repetition of the Amidah prayer (see שְׁמוֹנֶה עֶשְׂרֵה). As the priests turn to face the congregation to recite the Priestly Benediction, they first recite a blessing acknowledging the holiness of the priestly line and their responsibility to bless the people in a spirit of love. While reciting the Priestly Benediction, the priests lift their hands according to a traditional rite (known as נְשִׂיאַת כַּפַּיִם). In Eretz Israel the Priestly Benediction is recited by the priests at every shaharit and musaf service. In the Diaspora, however, there is a long established Ashkenazi practice of reciting it only during the musaf service on Festivals.

בָּשָׂר בְּחָלָב   Lit., *meat in milk.*

The Torah mentions the prohibition against "boiling a kid in its mother's milk" three times (Exodus 23:19, 34:26; Deuteronomy 14:21). The first is explained by the Sages as referring to the prohibition against cooking a mixture of meat and milk; the second refers to the prohibition against eating such a mixture; and the third refers to the prohibition against deriving benefit from it. By Torah law, these prohibitions only apply to mixtures of milk and meat of kosher domesticated animals (בְּהֵמָה טְהוֹרָה). The Sages, however, also forbade the eating of mixtures of milk and kosher fowl or kosher non-domesticated animals (חַיָּה טְהוֹרָה), but it is permissible to benefit from such mixtures. Similarly, though the Torah prohibition only refers to an actual mixture cooked together, the Sages extended the prohibition and forbade eating milk products until a significant period of time has passed since the eating of meat (six hours, according to the common custom).

בָּשָׂר שֶׁנִּתְעַלֵּם מִן הָעַיִן   *[Kosher] meat which has been left unobserved.*

Some of the Sages forbade the consumption of meat which had remained for a period of time without supervision and could have been exchanged for non-kosher meat, unless there was a clearly visible mark on it identifying it as the original kosher piece of meat.

בְּשַׂר תַּאֲוָה   *Meat eaten to satisfy the appetite.* An expression, based on Deuteronomy 12:20, used by the Sages to describe nonsacrificial meat, in contrast to the meat of the sacrifices.

בַּת כֹּהֵן   *The daughter of a priest.* There are two unique laws applying exclusively to a priest's daughter: (1) With regard to adultery. A priest's daughter who commits adultery is subject to the penalty of death by burning (שְׂרֵיפָה) (see Leviticus 21:9), whereas an Israelite woman who commits adultery is subject to the (lesser) penalty of death by strangulation (חֶנֶק). The man who engaged in adultery with a priest's daughter is subject to the penalty of death by strangulation. (2) With regard to the consumption of terumah (תְּרוּמָה), the priest's portion of the crop. A priest's daughter is allowed to eat terumah (and, similarly, certain sacrificial offerings) as long as she is not married. If she marries a non-priest (a Levite, לֵוִי, or an Israelite, יִשְׂרָאֵל), she is forbidden to partake of these sacred foods. If she is widowed or divorced and has no living descendants by her Levite or Israelite husband, she resumes her previous status and is permitted to eat terumah once more (but not sacrificial offerings). If she does have living descendants from her husband, the prohibition against her partaking of all these foods remains in effect after her divorce or the death of her husband.

בְּתוּלָה   *A virgin.* This term is used in a number of Halakhic contexts, among them: (1) Marriage laws: (a) A High Priest (כֹּהֵן גָּדוֹל) may only marry a virgin (Leviticus 21:13). (b) The severe punishment prescribed by the Torah for the adultery of a betrothed maiden (see נַעֲרָה הַמְאוֹרָסָה) only applies if she is a virgin (see Deuteronomy 22:23–24). (c) The sum specified in the marriage contract (כְּתוּבָּה) of a virgin must be at least 200 dinarim (see p. 291), double the minimum to which a non-virgin is entitled. (2) The laws of נִדָּה, a menstruating woman. The term בְּתוּלַת דָּמִים — "a virgin in regard to blood" — refers to a girl who has not yet experienced menstrual bleeding. (3) The laws of ritual impurity. The term בְּתוּלַת קַרְקַע — "virgin soil" — refers to land which has never been worked. If the possibility exists that a grave has been ploughed over and it is necessary to dig in search of the remains of the corpse, once the searchers reach "virgin soil" they need not search there any further. (4) Commercial law. The term בְּתוּלַת שִׁקְמָה — "a virgin sycamore" — refers to a sycamore tree that has never been trimmed.

בָּתֵּי עָרֵי חוֹמָה   *Houses of walled cities.* Houses constructed within a walled city in Eretz Israel. The general rule that property returns to its original owner in the יוֹבֵל — "the Jubilee Year" — does not apply to such houses. Furthermore, an owner is given only one year to redeem such a home if he sells it. Otherwise it becomes the permanent possession of the purchaser (Leviticus 25:29–30).

גְּבוּלִין   *Outlying areas* (lit., "boundaries"). Any area outside the Temple (in some cases any area outside Jerusalem). In addition to the laws of sacrifices, there are many other areas of Halakhah where there are differences between what took place in the Temple and in Jerusalem, and what was done in the towns and villages in the rest of Eretz Israel (גְּבוּלִין). For example, the shofar (שׁוֹפָר) was sounded on the Sabbath in the Temple (according to some authorities, in all Jerusalem), but not in the גְּבוּלִין. The lulav (לוּלָב) was "taken" for seven days in the Temple, but not in the גְּבוּלִין. See מְדִינָה.

גְּבוּרוֹת   *Mighty deeds.* The second blessing of the Amidah prayer (see שְׁמוֹנֶה עֶשְׂרֵה), enumerating God's powers in the physical world. It begins with the words אַתָּה גִבּוֹר — "You are mighty" — and ends with the words מְחַיֵּה הַמֵּתִים — "Blessed are You... who restores the dead to life."

גָּדוֹל   *An adult.* A person who has reached maturity and is considered competent and responsible for his actions. In general, to be considered an adult, one must have reached sexual maturity (women at twelve, men at thirteen), but for

certain purposes a girl must wait an additional half year, and then she becomes a "grown woman" (בּוֹגֶרֶת). Maturity is measured by physical development and by age, and depending on the rate of development a child can remain legally immature until the age of twenty or even thirty-five. See אַיְילוֹנִית; בּוֹגֶרֶת; בֵּן סוֹרֵר וּמוֹרֶה; סָרִיס; קָטָן; קְטַנָּה.

גָּדוֹל בְּחָכְמָה וּבְמִנְיָן   *Greater in wisdom and in number.* One Rabbinical Court cannot nullify the ordinances and enactments of another unless it is greater than the other in wisdom and in number (see *Rambam, Sefer Shofetim, Hilkhot Mamrim* 2, 1–2). According to most commentators, בְּמִנְיָן — "in number" — refers to the number of students attending the court.

גּוֹאֵל הַדָּם   *The avenger [lit., redeemer] of blood.* A relative of a person who was killed, who takes it upon himself to avenge his relative's death. A person who unintentionally but negligently killed another was exiled to a city of refuge (עִיר מִקְלָט, see also גָּלוּת). If he left that city during the lifetime of the current High Priest (כֹּהֵן גָּדוֹל) the גּוֹאֵל הַדָּם was not held liable if he killed him. (See Numbers 35.) If the relative's death was the result of murder, the גּוֹאֵל הַדָּם acted as the executioner of the convicted murderer. But if the deceased did not have a relative to act as executioner, the court would appoint someone else to serve in that capacity.

גּוֹד אֲחֵית מְחִיצָתָא   Lit., *pull down, lower the partition*. A Halakhic principle regarding a partition, in some cases a beam or even a rope, suspended above the ground. It is "pulled down" and viewed as though it reached the ground. Among the contexts in which this concept is used are the boundaries within which one is permitted to walk and carry on the Sabbath (see עֵירוּב חֲצֵירוֹת), and the construction of a sukkah (סוּכָּה•; see next entry).

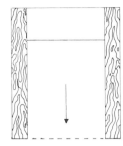

גּוֹד אַסֵּיק מְחִיצָתָא   *Extend and raise the partition*. A wall or partition of a Halakhically significant height (in most cases, a minimum height of ten handbreadths) is considered for Halakhic purposes as if it was extended and continued upwards to an unlimited height. This concept is used with regard to the boundaries within which one is permitted to walk and carry on the Sabbath (see עֵירוּב חֲצֵירוֹת), and with regard to the construction of a sukkah (סוּכָּה•).

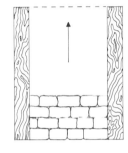

גּוֹנֵב נֶפֶשׁ   *A kidnapper*. The Sages understood the prohibition "Do not steal" in the Ten Commandments (Exodus 20:15; Deuteronomy 5:19) as referring to the crime of kidnapping. If a person kidnapped a fellow-Jew and enslaved him, and then sold him to another, he was subject to the death penalty (Deuteronomy 24:7).

גּוֹסֵס   *A dying person*. Halakhically, such a person is considered alive, and nothing may be done to hasten his death. Evidence of his death based only on his having been seen by witnesses in such a condition is not accepted by a Rabbinical Court as sufficient to permit his wife to remarry.

גִּזְבָּר   *Treasurer*. Officials subordinate to the trustees (see אֲמַרְכָּל) and charged with important financial tasks in the Temple. The minimum number of treasurers was three (according to other opinions, thirteen) and they were responsible for the articles consecrated to the Temple. They decided whether each article could be used in the Temple itself or whether it should be sold and the proceeds used for the Temple's needs.

גְּזֵירָה   *Decree*. A regulation, generally a prohibition, imposed by the Sages regarding something which is essentially permitted, whose purpose is to keep people from sinning. Usually such decrees were enacted in connection with matters which might ultimately lead to serious transgressions. However, occasionally the purpose of a decree is to establish consistent standards (לְהַשְׁווֹת אֶת הַמִּדּוֹת); for example, if people are permitted to do a certain thing, they may mistakenly believe that similar but

forbidden things are permitted. Some decrees were also instituted by the Sages because of an incident that occurred (מַעֲשֶׂה שֶׁהָיָה), in which the danger of transgression, either actual or potential, arose, and they passed a decree about it for all later generations.

גֵּזֶל   *Robbery*. The act of taking an article from its owner by force, openly, and without payment. A robber (גַּזְלָן), and likewise a thief (גַּנָּב•), is obliged to return the article as it was when he took possession of it. If its appearance, or the use that can be made of it, has been changed since the robbery, the robber must reimburse its owner for its value at the time of the robbery. Unlike a thief, a convicted robber does not repay the owner double the value of the article (see כֶּפֶל). But if the robber denies the crime on oath and later confesses, he must pay the owner an additional fifth of the article's value and bring a guilt-offering (אָשָׁם גְּזֵילוֹת•). If a person robs a convert (גֵּר צֶדֶק•) and denies the crime on oath, and if the convert then dies without heirs and the robber confesses to his crime, the robber must then give the object, or its value, and an additional fifth of its value to the priests.

גֵּט   *"Get"; a bill of divorce*. Though the term *get* is sometimes applied to all legal documents, it is generally used to refer specifically to a bill of divorce. The basic text of a גֵּט includes the declaration of the husband that he (identified by name and his father's name) divorces his wife (her name and her father's name must also be mentioned) and that she is permitted to marry any other man. The גֵּט must contain the date it was written and the signatures of two witnesses. In Talmudic times a גֵּט could be written privately by a scribe at the request of the husband. In later generations, it became customary for a גֵּט to be written in a Rabbinical Court with expertise in this field, so that no Halakhic difficulties would arise that might lead to the invalidation of the document.

גֵּט יָשָׁן   *An old bill of divorce*. If after a גֵּט• was written but before it was delivered to the wife, the husband and wife spent time together in private (see יִחוּד), the Sages invalidated the גֵּט on the assumption that the couple had renewed their marriage bonds while together and therefore the date on the גֵּט was incorrect.

גֵּט מְקוּשָׁר   *A folded and sewn up document*. Most commonly a bill of divorce used by priests. In contrast to a regular document (גֵּט פָּשׁוּט), a גֵּט מְקוּשָׁר was folded a number of times and sewn at the folds. At least three witnesses were required for such a גֵּט and one witness had to sign on the outer side of each fold. The original purpose of this elaborate procedure was to delay a hasty decision by a priest to divorce his wife and to allow him time to reconsider before making an irreversible decision, since a priest who divorces his wife is not permitted to remarry her.

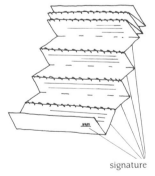

signature

גֵּט קֵרֵחַ   Lit., *a bald bill of divorce*. A גֵּט מְקוּשָׁר (see previous entry) that was invalidated because it lacked a sufficient number of witnesses. This could occur when one of the folds of the bill of divorce was not signed by one of the witnesses.

גִּיד הַנָּשֶׁה   *The sciatic nerve [nervus ischiadicus, running down the back of the hind leg of an animal].* One of the parts of kosher domestic (בְּהֵמָה טְהוֹרָה») and non-domestic (חַיָּה טְהוֹרָה») animals which is forbidden by Torah law to be eaten (Genesis 32:33). In addition to the nerve itself, it is customary not to eat any of its branches or the fat that encloses it.

גִּידּוּלֵי גִידּוּלִים   Lit., *the growths of growths.* Produce that grew from terumah (גִּידּוּלֵי תְּרוּמָה») is given the status of terumah (תְּרוּמָה») by Rabbinic decree. But this ruling is not extended to include גִּידּוּלֵי גִידּוּלִים, produce that grew from the seeds of produce that grew from terumah.

גִּידּוּלֵי תְּרוּמָה   *Produce that grew from terumah. Seeds or fruits set aside as terumah* (תְּרוּמָה») that were not eaten but planted, producing a new crop. By Rabbinic decree this new crop has the status of terumah. See previous entry.

גִּילּוּי   Lit., *uncovering.* Leaving something uncovered. This term is used to refer to wine, water, or other liquids (and certain foods) that were left exposed and unattended. The Sages feared that a poisonous snake might drink from the liquids and deposit venom in them. Because of this danger, they forbade the drinking of such liquids. Wine or water that was left exposed and unattended was forbidden to be used as a libation on the Temple altar (see נִיסּוּךְ הַמַּיִם and נְסָכִים).

גִּילּוּי מִילְתָא   Lit., *the uncovering of a matter.* There are instances of legal procedure in which the formal testimony of two valid witnesses is not required, and in which all that is necessary is גִּילּוּי מִילְתָא, knowledge of the situation in question. In such circumstances, testimony of witnesses who would usually be considered unacceptable may be accepted by the court. See also עֵדוּת אִשָּׁה.

גִּילּוּי עֲרָיוֹת   Lit., *uncovering of nakedness.* A collective term for adulterous or incestuous sexual relations forbidden by the Torah upon pain of severe punishment (see Leviticus 18 and 20; see also עֲרָיוֹת). גִּילּוּי עֲרָיוֹת is one of the three categories of prohibitions which one is forbidden to violate even in order to save oneself from certain death (see יֵהָרֵג וְאַל יַעֲבוֹר).

גִּלְגּוּל שְׁבוּעָה   *The attaching [lit., rolling] of an oath; the adding of one oath to another.* When a defendant is obliged to take an oath in order to free himself of a liability, the plaintiff can require him to extend the oath to include a denial of other claims by the plaintiff, which of themselves would not require the defendant to take an oath. This extension of the oath is called גִּלְגּוּל שְׁבוּעָה.

גָּלוּת   *Exile.* The punishment which the Torah prescribes for a

person who unintentionally but negligently kills another (Numbers 35). The killer was exiled to a city of refuge (עִיר מִקְלָט») and had to remain there until the death of the High Priest (כֹּהֵן גָּדוֹל»). If the killer left the city of refuge, the גּוֹאֵל הַדָּם» (a relative of the dead person who took upon himself the mission of avenging his relative's death) was permitted to kill him.

גְּמִילוּת חֲסָדִים   *Acts of charity, kindness.* A general category of mitzvot which involve personally giving physical or spiritual assistance or both to another person. Among these mitzvot are: giving loans, visiting the sick, and escorting the dead to burial.

גְּמִירַת דַּעַת   Lit., *concluding an opinion.* An inner decision, a firm resolution. This concept is important when doubt arises as to the legal validity of actions and obligations. In such cases it is important to know whether the person who did the deed or undertook the obligation had made an inner decision to do so, i.e., that he had resolved to take the action or the obligation upon himself. An outer action without an inner decision is usually legally ineffective.

גְּמַר דִּין   Lit., *the conclusion of judgment.* The delivery of the verdict by the judges, pronouncing: "You, So-and-so, are חַיָּיב [liable, guilty]," or: "You, So-and-so, are זַכַּאי [free of liability, not guilty]."

גְּמַר מְלָאכָה   *The completion of work.* (1) With regard to the laws of tithes (מַעַשְׂרוֹת»), there is no obligation to tithe produce until its harvesting and ingathering is completed. (2) With regard to the laws of ritual impurity (טוּמְאָה»), an object does not become susceptible to ritual impurity until it is a finished product. (3) With regard to the laws of the Sabbath, see מַכֶּה בְּפַטִּישׁ.

גַּנָּב   *A thief.* Someone who takes someone else's property without the victim's knowledge. The thief violates a negative commandment (Leviticus 19:11) but is not punished by lashes (מַלְקוֹת») for his misdeed, because the Torah created a method of reparation, namely the positive commandment of returning a stolen object (see לָאו הַנִּיתָּק לַעֲשֵׂה). The court can force the thief to return what he has stolen, or, if he no longer has it, to pay for it. He can even be sold as a slave to repay what he has stolen. If there are witnesses to the theft, the thief must repay double the value of the object stolen (see אַרְבָּעָה וַחֲמִשָּׁה; כֶּפֶל). See also גּוֹנֵב נֶפֶשׁ.

גְּנֵיבָה   *Theft.* A person who, without permission, takes something from his fellow in order to acquire it for himself is a thief, and when he is caught and conclusive evidence is brought against him, he must repay double the value of what he has stolen (see כֶּפֶל). If he is unable to pay, he is sold as a slave (see עֶבֶד עִבְרִי) in order to pay for what he has stolen. Someone who steals a sheep or an ox and kills or sells it must repay four or five times the value of the original theft (see אַרְבָּעָה וַחֲמִשָּׁה). The additional amount is a fine (קְנָס»), and it is therefore not imposed except in times when the laws of fines are in force (i.e., when there is Rabbinical ordination, see סְמִיכַת זְקֵנִים), and it is not collected when the thief of his own free will restores what he has stolen. A thief who denies the theft under oath and later confesses must bring a guilt-offering (see גְּזֵילוֹת אָשָׁם) and repay a fifth (חוֹמֶשׁ) more than the amount he has stolen. In various instances the Halakhah differentiates between a thief (גַּנָּב) and a robber (גַּזְלָן, see גֵּזֶל). The latter robs by force and is not frightened whether the owner knows who has taken the object from him. He is not obliged to repay double the value of the object taken. The armed robber (לִיסְטִים מְזוּיָּן), who illegally takes property by force but who hides from people, falls into an intermediate category: in some instances he is judged as a thief and in others as a robber.

גֵּר צֶדֶק   *A righteous convert.* A non-Jew who accepts Judaism. After circumcision (מִילָה), immersion (טְבִילָה) in a mikveh (מִקְוֶה) for the sake of conversion, and acceptance of the mitzvot of the Torah in the presence of a Bet Din, he is considered as a Jew in all respects. In Temple times conversion was not completed until the convert brought an animal or two birds as a burnt offering (עוֹלָה). Even if the convert later returns to his previous faith, his conversion to Judaism is still considered to be in effect and he is viewed as an apostate Jew. The Torah specifically commands Jews to show a convert love, not to cause him distress by reminding him of his past, and to support him in all his needs. According to Torah law, "a convert is like a newborn child." He is considered to have no ties to his natural parents or relatives. Nevertheless, the Sages forbade a convert from marrying relatives of his who had themselves converted. They allowed a convert to inherit his gentile father's estate.

גֵּר תּוֹשָׁב   *A resident alien who has accepted some of the laws of Judaism.* A non-Jew who wishes to live permanently in Eretz Israel must accept certain mitzvot. There are a number of opinions regarding the extent of the commitment he is required to make. Some Sages require only an acceptance of the prohibition against idol worship (עֲבוֹדָה זָרָה). Others require him to observe almost all the negative commandments except for those forbidding the eating of certain foods. Most opinions require him to observe the seven mitzvot of Noah's descendants (שֶׁבַע מִצְווֹת בְּנֵי נֹחַ).

גְּרוֹגֶרֶת   *A dried fig.* A Halakhic measurement of size, particularly with regard to the Sabbath laws. For example, if a person transfers foodstuffs from private property to the public domain on the Sabbath, he is liable only if the amount transferred is the size of a גְּרוֹגֶרֶת or greater.

גְּרוּשָׁה לְכֹהֵן   Lit., *a divorcee [is forbidden] to a priest.* The Torah forbids a priest (כֹּהֵן) to marry a divorcee (Leviticus 21:7). A child born from such a marriage is called a חָלָל (pl. חֲלָלִים) and does not possess the holiness of priesthood. A female חֲלָלָה may not marry a priest. חֲלָלִים may, however, marry freely among non-priests, and are considered their fathers' children in all respects apart from their loss of priestly status. The marriage between a priest and a divorcee is binding, despite the prohibition against it. Nevertheless, a Bet Din would force the priest to divorce her and would deny her the right of a כְּתוּבָה ("marriage settlement").

גְּרַם כִּיבּוּי   *The indirect putting out of a fire.* It is forbidden to extinguish a fire on the Sabbath. If, however, there is a danger that it will spread (and only in that instance), a person may perform an act which will indirectly cause the fire to be extinguished, such as placing utensils filled with water in the path of the fire.

דָּבָר הָאָבֵד   Lit., *something perishable.* Something which, if appropriate action is not taken at the right time to safeguard it, will suffer serious loss. The Sages were lenient in their application of the Halakhah in the following instances of דָּבָר הָאָבֵד among others: (1) With reference to the laws of חוֹל הַמּוֹעֵד, the intermediate days of a Festival. Though certain categories of work are generally forbidden on these days, an exception is made in order to protect a דָּבָר הָאָבֵד. (2) With reference to the laws of mourning. During the first seven days of mourning (שִׁבְעָה), the mourner's place of business must generally be closed. In a case of דָּבָר הָאָבֵד, however, work may be carried out for him by others.

דָּבָר חָשׁוּב   Lit., *an important thing.* There are two applications of this concept: (1) With reference to the laws of nullification of prohibitions (בִּיטּוּל אִיסוּרִים) there are several categories of דָּבָר חָשׁוּב: (a) An item of food that is sold separately and not by weight (דָּבָר שֶׁבְּמִנְיָן). (b) A piece of meat fit to serve guests (חֲתִיכָה הָרְאוּיָה לְהִתְכַּבֵּד). (c) A whole creature, however small (בְּרִיָּה). If such an object is or becomes Halakhically unfit for consumption and is mixed with permitted foods, it can never be neutralized even though it be mixed with any quantity of kosher substances, however great. (2) With reference to the laws of evidence. A witness who has been disqualified from giving testimony because he is suspected of taking money illegally can regain his credibility in court by returning to its rightful owner a lost article which is of substantial value (דָּבָר חָשׁוּב) to the disqualified witness.

דָּבָר שֶׁאֵינוֹ מִתְכַּוֵּן   *An act done unintentionally.* A prohibited act committed unintentionally while performing a permitted act. (1) With reference to the Sabbath prohibitions, a person is not liable if he unintentionally carries out a forbidden act of labor while performing a permitted act, except where the permitted act is such that it must of necessity bring about a violation of the Sabbath laws (see פְּסִיק רֵישֵׁיהּ). (2) With reference to other prohibitions, there is no punishment for their unintentional violation while performing a permitted act.

דָּבָר שֶׁבְּמִנְיָן   *Something which is counted.* Something which, because of its importance or value, is sold in individual units rather than by weight or volume. דָּבָר שֶׁבְּמִנְיָן is considered a ‏דָּבָר חָשׁוּב, and thus a non-kosher דָּבָר שֶׁבְּמִנְיָן can never be neutralized even though it be mixed with any quantity of kosher substances, however great (see בִּיטוּל אִיסוּרִים).

דָּבָר שֶׁזַּרְעוֹ כָּלֶה   *A plant whose seed ceases to exist as the plant grows from it.* For example, wheat. Certain authorities allow the use of ‏יְגִידּוּלֵי תְּרוּמָה (the produce of seeds contributed to the priests as terumah) by non-priests in the case of these kinds of plants.

דָּבָר שֶׁיֵּשׁ לוֹ מַתִּירִין   *An object that is prohibited but whose prohibition can or will lapse at some future time.* For example, an egg laid on the Sabbath (see נוֹלָד), which may not be moved on that day (see מוּקְצֶה), will become permitted to be moved once the Sabbath is over. Similarly, food which may not be eaten at present because of a vow may become permitted by having the vow annulled. Since the prohibition in these and many other cases can or will ultimately lapse, it is treated with greater stringency while it is in effect. Thus, if such an object is mixed with kosher substances, it cannot be neutralized, however great the amount of kosher substance involved (see בִּיטוּל אִיסוּרִים), as long as the prohibition remains in effect.

דָּבָר שֶׁלֹּא בָּא לָעוֹלָם   Lit., *something that has not yet come into the world.* This concept has two meanings: (1) Something that has not yet come into existence — for example, a child that has not yet been born or fruit that has not yet grown. (2) Something which, though in existence, is not yet in a person's possession. Generally, a transaction (or transfer of property) involving a דָּבָר שֶׁלֹּא בָּא לָעוֹלָם has no legal validity. It is legally impossible to sell something that has not yet come into existence or has not yet come into the seller's possession, and it is impossible to sell or give something to someone who has not yet been born. Only in certain pressing circumstances did the Sages grant legal validity to such transactions.

דִּבְרֵי סוֹפְרִים   *The words of the Sages.* The enactments, ordinances, and commandments instituted by the Sages (see גְּזֵירָה). In certain respects (for example, in situations of doubt), less stringent rules apply to Rabbinic prohibitions than to those of the Torah itself, but in other respects Rabbinic decrees may be more severe than Torah commandments.

דּוּכָן   *Platform.* A raised section in the Temple Courtyard on which the Levites stood and sang songs of praise to accompany the sacrifices. This name is also sometimes given to the elevated section in the Temple where the priests recited the Priestly Benediction (יְבִּרְכַּת כֹּהֲנִים). See plan of the Temple, p. 277.

דּוֹפֶן עֲקוּמָה   *A curved wall.* A legal concept unique to the laws of a sukkah. Among the Halakhot transmitted to Moses on Mount Sinai but not specifically mentioned in the Torah (הֲלָכָה לְמֹשֶׁה מִסִּינַי), is the law that a sukkah is still considered valid even though it contains up to 4 cubits (about 6 feet) of invalid סְכָךְ — roofing material (see סוּכָּה) — provided that this סְכָךְ is adjacent to one of the walls of the sukkah. The invalid סְכָךְ is considered an extension of the adjacent wall (i.e., the wall is considered to be curved — דּוֹפֶן עֲקוּמָה), and thus the entire sukkah is not disqualified.

דִּיחוּי   *Rejection.* A concept used with reference to an article or an animal which was dedicated for a sacred purpose in the Temple service or for use in the performance of a mitzvah and was then rejected as unfit for use for that purpose. (1) With reference to animals dedicated for sacrificial purposes: If an animal was at one stage fit for sacrifice but was afterwards rejected as unfit, and later became fit once more, there is a debate among the Sages as to whether the rejection is final or whether the animal can still be used as a sacrifice. (2) With reference to other mitzvot: There is a debate among the Sages as to whether the concept דִּיחוּי applies to objects consecrated for use in the performance of other mitzvot.

דִּימוּעַ   *A mixture of terumah [‏תְּרוּמָה] with non-sacred [‏חוּלִין] or untithed [‏טֶבֶל] produce.* If the amount of terumah in the mixture was not neutralized in relation to the rest of the mixture as required (one part terumah to a hundred parts of non-terumah), the mixture was forbidden to be eaten by Israelites. Hence, it was sold to priests for their personal use.

דִּינָא דְּגַרְמֵי   Lit., *a case of indirect damage.* An action which causes only minimal direct damage, but indirectly brings about a greater loss. For example, a person who destroys someone else's promissory note. Though physically the latter has merely lost a piece of paper, that loss will ultimately result in his being unable to collect a debt. Though the matter is a subject of debate between the Sages, the Halakhah generally obligates the person who caused the initial damage for the total loss suffered by the other person. See הֶיזֵּק שֶׁאֵינוֹ נִיכָּר.

דִּינָא דְּמַלְכוּתָא דִּינָא   Lit., *the law of the kingdom is the law.* The Halakhic principle that Jews must obey the laws of the state in which they live. The laws and regulations of the state are considered valid in Jewish law as well. This obligation applies mainly in civil law, and not in matters of ritual law.

דִּינֵי מָמוֹנוֹת   *Laws governing monetary cases.* The laws governing financial disputes, as distinct from דִּינֵי נְפָשׁוֹת — the laws governing capital cases (see next entry). The nature of the judicial process in monetary matters differs both from that governing cases concerning ritual and ceremonial law (אִיסּוּר וְהֶיתֵּר) and from cases involving the possibility of capital punishment. There are three judicial frameworks in which דִּינֵי מָמוֹנוֹת can be adjudicated: (1) A Bet Din composed of three judges expert in Jewish law. (2) In many cases, דִּינֵי מָמוֹנוֹת are brought before a lay tribunal composed of three lay judges or arbitrators (בֵּית דִּין שֶׁל שְׁלֹשָׁה הֶדְיוֹטוֹת). (3) In some circumstances even a single judge may hear the case if he is sufficiently qualified. The Sages relaxed the rules of evidence and the rules governing the examination of the witnesses (יְדִרִישָׁה וַחֲקִירָה) in many aspects of דִּינֵי מָמוֹנוֹת by comparison with the requirements in capital cases. These differences in procedure are dealt with in *Sanhedrin*, chapter 4.

דִּינֵי נְפָשׁוֹת   *Laws governing capital cases,* i.e., cases involving the possibility of capital punishment. These cases were judged by a court of twenty-three judges (see בֵּית דִּין שֶׁל עֶשְׂרִים וּשְׁלֹשָׁה; סַנְהֶדְרִי קְטַנָּה) and involved extensive and detailed examination of the witnesses (יְדִרִישָׁה וַחֲקִירָה). The court had to consist of ordained judges (see סְמִיכַת זְקֵנִים). Capital cases could only be tried during the period in which the Great Sanhedrin (see בֵּית דִּין שֶׁל שִׁבְעִים וְאֶחָד; סַנְהֶדְרִין גְּדוֹלָה) met in the Chamber of Hewn Stone (יְלִשְׁכַּת הַגָּזִית) in the Temple Courtyard (see plan of the Temple, p. 277). In practice, even before the end of the Second Temple period, capital cases were no longer tried, except in certain instances involving the good of the entire people — for example, the trial of informers to the non-Jewish authorities.

דִּינֵי שָׁמַיִם   Lit., *judgments, laws, of Heaven.* A legal obligation which a human court of law is unable to enforce. There are many instances in Jewish law where a person is exempt according to the laws of man but guilty according to the "laws of Heaven." In such cases there is a moral obligation to conduct oneself in such a way as to satisfy even the laws of Heaven.

דַּלּוּת וְדַלֵּי דַלּוּת   Lit., *poverty and extreme poverty.* With reference to certain sacrificial obligations, the Torah prescribed a varying scale of possible offerings, depending on the person's financial situation. For example, a poor person may in certain cases bring a pair of doves as a sin-offering (see קָרְבָּן עוֹלֶה וְיוֹרֵד), called "a sacrifice of poverty" (דַּלּוּת), where a rich person must bring a female lamb or goat. If the person is extremely poor, he need only bring a meal-offering (see מִנְחַת חוֹטֵא), called a "sacrifice of extreme poverty" (דַּלֵּי דַלּוּת). (See Leviticus 5:1–13.)

דָּם   *Blood.* (1) The Torah prohibits the eating of blood (Leviticus 7:26). This applies to the blood of kosher domestic animals (יְבְּהֵמָה טְהוֹרָה), non-domestic animals (יְחַיָּה טְהוֹרָה), and birds (יְעוֹף טָהוֹר), and to the blood of non-kosher animals and birds. A person who willfully consumes blood is subject to the punishment of יכָּרֵת — the divine punishment of excision. If he does so inadvertently, he must bring a sin-offering (יְחַטָּאת). Meat requires salting before being cooked, in order to remove its blood. See also דַּם הָאֵיבָרִים; דַּם הַנֶּפֶשׁ; דַּם הַתַּמְצִית. (2) One is obligated to cover the blood of a kosher bird or non-domestic animal that has been slaughtered (see דָּם מִן הַחַי). (3) יְכִּסּוּי הַדָּם — "blood from a living animal." Blood extracted from a living animal is forbidden and this prohibition is in addition to the general prohibition against eating blood. (4) Blood is one of the seven liquids that render foodstuffs susceptible to ritual impurity (see הֶכְשֵׁר). (5) The blood of a deceased person conveys ritual

impurity (see דַּם תְּבוּסָה). (6) Regarding menstrual blood, see נִדָּה.

דַּם הָאֵיבָרִים   *The blood of the limbs.* Blood that remains within the limbs of an animal after it has been slaughtered. According to Torah law, there is no prohibition against this blood as long as it remains in its place. Nevertheless, the Sages required the salting of meat lest the blood within the limbs of the animal change position during the cooking process.

דַּם הַנֶּפֶשׁ   *The blood of the soul.* The blood that spurts out from an animal as it is being slaughtered. (1) The punishment of excision (יכָּרֵת) for partaking of blood applies specifically to this blood. (2) Only this blood is fit to be presented (see זְרִיקָה) on the altar when an animal is offered as a sacrifice.

דַּם הַתַּמְצִית   *Blood that flows from an animal after slaughter once the initial spurt of blood has ceased.* Most of the Sages maintain that the punishment of excision (יכָּרֵת) for partaking of blood does not apply to דַּם הַתַּמְצִית, and that it is forbidden under the category of a Torah prohibition.

דַּם טוֹהַר   *Blood of purity.* Vaginal bleeding experienced by a woman from eight to forty days after giving birth to a boy and from fifteen to eighty days after giving birth to a girl. The Torah differentiates between this blood and other menstrual bleeding and states that it does not render a woman ritually impure (Leviticus 12). Nevertheless, according to the Halakhic practice of today, such bleeding does render a woman ritually impure.

דַּם תְּבוּסָה   *Blood which flows from a person at the time of his death or afterwards.* דַּם תְּבוּסָה is considered to be of the same status as the corpse itself and is thus in the severest category of ritual impurity (see יְאֲבִי אֲבוֹת הַטּוּמְאָה), even though it is possible that some of the blood left the body before the person's death.

דְּמַאי   *Produce [or food made from produce] which was purchased from a person who may not have separated the various tithes [יְמַעַשְׂרוֹת] as required by law.* (See עַם הָאָרֶץ.) The literal meaning of the word דְּמַאי is "suspicion," i.e., produce about which there is a suspicion that tithes were not properly taken from it. In the Second Temple period, the Sages decreed that such produce should be considered as of doubtful status, even though the owner claimed that he had separated the tithes, and that the buyer of such produce must tithe it himself (see טֶבֶל). Nevertheless, since it was probable that the produce was in fact tithed, certain leniency was permitted concerning the eating and making use of דְּמַאי.

דְּמֵי וְלָדוֹת   Lit., *payment for the offspring.* If a man, by an inadvertent blow, causes a woman to miscarry, he must compensate her husband for her loss (Exodus 21:22), and this compensation is called דְּמֵי וְלָדוֹת.

דְּרוּסָה   *A clawed animal.* A kosher animal or bird that has been hurt by the claws of a predatory animal or bird. The signs of such an attack upon a kosher animal render it trefah (יְטְרֵפָה) and incapable of being rendered fit to eat through יְשְׁחִיטָה, ritual slaughter.

דְּרִישָׁה וַחֲקִירָה   *The thorough examination of witnesses in a court of law.* A Bet Din is obliged by Torah law to subject the evidence of witnesses to searching scrutiny (Deuteronomy 13:15). The process of examination (by questioning and comparing the testimony of the witnesses) is particularly rigorous in cases involving the possibility of capital punishment (see שֶׁבַע חֲקִירוֹת).

דֶּרֶךְ אֶרֶץ   Lit., *the way of the earth.* (1) Good manners, not specifically required by the Halakhah, but which everyone, particularly Torah scholars, should adopt. Although frequently mentioned in the Talmud, this topic is considered mainly in the minor tractates of דֶּרֶךְ אֶרֶץ זוּטָא and דֶּרֶךְ אֶרֶץ רַבָּה (see p. 47). (2) In a broader sense דֶּרֶךְ אֶרֶץ means the normal course of life, with particular reference to the need to earn a living. (3) Occasionally, the term is a euphemism for sexual relations.

דֶּרֶךְ הַמֶּלֶךְ   *The king's highway.* A king is entitled to expropriate private property in order to build a road (דֶּרֶךְ הַמֶּלֶךְ) for the passage of his troops or for other projects of public benefit. No limit is placed on the width or on the length of such a road.

דֶּרֶךְ הָרַבִּים   *A public thoroughfare.* An important thoroughfare used for communal traffic. Such a public thoroughfare was generally 16 cubits wide (see אַמָּה). It was forbidden to place obstructions there. If a public thoroughfare passed through a person's private property, he was forbidden to prevent passage along it.

דַּרְכֵי הָאֱמוֹרִי   *The customs of the Amorites.* A general term referring to superstitious rites practiced by non-Jews. Jews are forbidden to emulate them lest such behavior lead to idol worship itself. Many of these practices are enumerated in Tosefta, *Shabbat,* chapters 7 and 8.

דַּרְכֵי נוֹעַם   Lit., *ways of pleasantness,* referring to the Biblical verse, "Her ways [the ways of the Torah] are ways of pleasantness, and all her paths are peace" (Proverbs 3:17). A Halakhic principle invoked when there is a doubt as to the intention of a Torah commandment. The Sages seek to interpret the commandment in such a way that it does not conflict with "the ways of pleasantness and peace."

דַּרְכֵי שָׁלוֹם   *The ways of peace.* A general term referring to many Rabbinic enactments instituted to foster peace and to prevent strife and controversy. (1) With reference to monetary matters (דִּינֵי מָמוֹנוֹת): In certain instances, the Sages forbade taking property from a person even though he did not possess full formal legal ownership. (2) With reference to matters of precedence: For example, the Sages instituted a set of procedures to prevent arguments from arising about who should be called up first to the reading of the Torah (קְרִיאַת הַתּוֹרָה) in the synagogue. (3) With reference to relations with common people (see עַם הָאָרֶץ): The Sages permitted certain lenient practices in dealings with עַמֵּי הָאָרֶץ, in order to prevent divisions arising between the Torah community and the common people. (4) With reference to relations with non-Jews: The Sages instructed that charity be given to the non-Jewish poor together with the poor of Israel. Similarly, they instituted other practices to reduce friction between communities and nations.

דְּרָרָא דְּמָמוֹנָא   Lit., *something which leads to money.* A concept used in monetary law (דִּינֵי מָמוֹנוֹת). Some commentators interpret the term as referring to a situation involving a definite financial loss to one of the parties to a dispute. Others interpret it as a doubt arising from the objective facts of the case, independent of the claims of the individual litigants.

דַּת יְהוּדִית   Lit., *Jewish custom.* The practices of modesty appropriate for a married Jewish woman, as distinct from דַּת מֹשֶׁה — "Mosaic law" — which refers to those practices strictly required by the laws of the Torah. According to Rabbinic law, a man has the right to divorce his wife without paying the provisions of her marriage contract (כְּתוּבָּה) if she violates the practices of דַּת יְהוּדִית.

הַבְדָּלָה   Lit., *separation, distinction.* The blessings recited at the conclusion of a Sabbath or Festival to emphasize the sacred nature of these days and the distinction between them and weekdays. At the conclusion of the Sabbath, a blessing is recited over a cup of wine, additional blessings are recited over spices and a lighted candle, and these are followed by the havdalah blessing, the blessing of "separation" ("Blessed are You... Who distinguishes between the holy and the secular"). At the conclusion of Yom Kippur, the same practice is followed, except that the blessing over the spices is omitted. At the conclusion of a Festival, the blessing over the flame is also omitted. See also יקנה"ז for a description of the blessings recited when a Festival commences at the conclusion of the Sabbath. The term הַבְדָּלָה is also used to describe the additional paragraph inserted in the fourth blessing of the Amidah (see שְׁמוֹנֶה עֶשְׂרֵה) during the evening service immediately following a Sabbath or Festival.

הַבְחָנָה   *Differentiation.* The Sages explained that it is possible for a woman to be unaware that she is carrying a baby during the first three months of pregnancy, or for her to conceal the fact that she is pregnant during this three-month period. Accordingly, they obligate a woman to wait at least three months after being widowed or divorced before she may remarry. Thus, it is possible to determine whether her baby's father was her previous husband or her present one. This rule applies to all widows and divorcees, even in cases where there is no possibility of them being pregnant. A female convert must wait a similar three-month period before marriage to determine whether any child she may bear was conceived before her conversion or afterwards.

הַגְבָּהָה   *Lifting up.* One of the formal modes of acquiring ownership of movable property (see קִנְיָן). When the purchaser lifts up the article, it becomes his property. All movable property (מִטַּלְטְלִין•) can be acquired through this procedure. However, in practice it is limited to smaller articles. Objects that cannot be easily lifted are usually acquired by other, related methods. See הַנְהָגָה; מְשִׁיכָה.

הַגְעָלָה   Lit., *scouring, rinsing.* Ritual cleansing of utensils in boiling water. A process of making cooking or eating utensils fit for use according to the requirements of Jewish law. A utensil or dish used to cook or serve forbidden food while hot may absorb a residue of that food. This residue is removed by placing the utensil in boiling water. Most wood and metal utensils may be rendered fit for use in this manner.

הַגְרָמָה   Lit., *deflecting.* A defect in the act of ritual slaughter (שְׁחִיטָה•), in which the throat was cut outside the specified area for שְׁחִיטָה. Such an animal is not kosher and may not be eaten.

הַגָּשָׁה   Lit., *bringing near.* A particular ritual involved in the offering of certain of the meal-offerings (מְנָחוֹת•) in the Temple. The priests were required to carry the offering in their hands and bring it close to the altar.

הֶדְיוֹט   *A common person.* The following are among the frequent applications of the term, which is of Greek origin: (1) כֹּהֵן הֶדְיוֹט• — "a common priest," as distinct from the High Priest (כֹּהֵן גָּדוֹל•). (2) With reference to judges, it is used to describe those who were not ordained or specifically trained to serve in that capacity. (3) With reference to the prohibition of work during חֹל הַמּוֹעֵד•, the intermediate days of the Festivals of Pesaḥ and Sukkot, tasks that can be performed by an untrained person (מַעֲשֵׂה הֶדְיוֹט) are permitted, in contrast to those requiring professional skill (מַעֲשֵׂה אוּמָּן), which are forbidden.

הֲדַס   *A myrtle.* One of the four species of plants (אַרְבָּעָה מִינִים•) required in the mitzvah of "taking the lulav" on the Sukkot Festival. The Torah describes this species as "boughs of thick-leaved trees" (Leviticus 23:40). A הֲדַס is only kosher if its leaves grow in groups of (at least) three, with each group of three growing from the stalk at the same height. If this condition is not met, the branch is described as a הֲדַס שׁוֹטֶה ("wild myrtle") and may not be used for the mitzvah. Three myrtle branches are bound to the lulav. In certain places,

however, it is customary to add additional branches in order to beautify the mitzvah.

הוֹאִיל   Lit., *since.* A Halakhic rationale: Since a particular situation may arise in the future, though at present no such situation has arisen, it is proper to take such a possibility into account. For example, according to some Amoraim, it is impossible to prohibit a person from cooking food on יוֹם טוֹב• (a Festival), even if he intends to use that food on the weekdays that follow, since the possibility exists that additional guests may visit him on the Festival, and in that case he will need this food for them.

הוֹדָאָה שֶׁלֹּא מִמִּין הַטַּעֲנָה   *An admission of debt concerning a different species from that claimed.* This concept describes the situation where a plaintiff demands a certain amount of something from a defendant, who acknowledges that he is in debt to the plaintiff, but claims that his debt consists of another kind of object. Such an admission does not obligate the defendant to take "the judicial oath" (שְׁבוּעַת הַדַּיָּינִים•). In certain cases there is a difference of opinion among the Sages as to whether two objects differ in kind.

הוֹדָאַת בַּעַל דִּין   *The admission of a litigant.* In monetary matters (see דִּינֵי מָמוֹנוֹת•), a litigant's admission, in court or before witnesses, that he owes someone money, is considered a definite statement of liability "equal to the testimony of a hundred witnesses," and no further proof is required (see עֵדִים•). With reference to cases involving corporal punishment (see מַלְקוֹת•) or capital punishment (see דִּינֵי נְפָשׁוֹת•), a person's admission of guilt is not acceptable, and it is not recognized by the court either as conclusive proof or even as evidence.

הוֹלָכָה   *Carrying the blood of a sacrifice to the altar.* One of the four services (אַרְבַּע עֲבוֹדוֹת•) involved in the offering of sacrifices. הוֹלָכָה is specifically defined as the carrying of the blood of a sacrifice to the altar (מִזְבֵּחַ•) in a bowl (מִזְרָק•) from the place where it was received after the animal's slaughter. The term is also used with reference to the bringing of meal-offerings (מְנָחוֹת•) to the altar. Some Tannaim did not think that an improperly performed הוֹלָכָה could invalidate a sacrifice, but the prevailing opinion is that if הוֹלָכָה were performed improperly it would invalidate the sacrifice.

הוֹצָאָה   Lit., *carrying out.* One of the thirty-nine major categories of work (אֲבוֹת מְלָאכוֹת•) prohibited on the Sabbath. הוֹצָאָה is defined as the transfer of an article of significant size from a private domain (רְשׁוּת הַיָּחִיד•) to the public domain (רְשׁוּת הָרַבִּים•). More specifically it involves the uprooting of an object from its position of rest in a private domain (עֲקִירָה•), and the placing of it to rest in the public domain (הַנָּחָה•). (See עֲקִירָה וְהַנָּחָה.) Similarly, transferring an article from the public domain into a private domain (הַכְנָסָה•) and carrying an object 4 cubits in the public domain are included in the category of הוֹצָאָה. (See רְשׁוּיוֹת הַשַּׁבָּת•.) In contrast to other categories of work, הוֹצָאָה does not involve the creation of a new entity. Hence it is considered מְלָאכָה גְּרוּעָה — "lesser work" than the others. Considerable portions of the tractates of *Shabbat* and *Eruvin* are devoted to a detailed analysis of this category of labor and to determining the minimum amounts of different substances which may not be transferred on the Sabbath.

הוּתַּר מִכְּלָלוֹ   *The relaxation of a Torah prohibition because of certain special circumstances.* For example, though priests are generally forbidden to come in contact with dead bodies, the Torah relaxes that prohibition in the instance of a priest's immediate family (Leviticus 21:2). A prohibition that is occasionally relaxed in this manner is considered less severe than one which is not.

הַזָּאָה   Lit., *sprinkling.* (1) The sprinkling of the blood of certain sacrificial offerings (see חַטָּאוֹת הַפְּנִימִיּוֹת). In these cases, instead of the blood being cast against the outer altar (see זְרִיקָה), the priest used a finger to sprinkle a few drops of it on certain designated places, such as the curtain (ʏפָּרוֹכֶת) dividing the Sanctuary (ʏהֵיכָל) from the Holy of Holies (ʏקֹדֶשׁ הַקֳּדָשִׁים). (2) The sprinkling of a mixture of the ashes of the Red Heifer (ʏפָּרָה אֲדוּמָה) with special water (see מֵי חַטָּאת), to purify a person from impurity resulting from contact with a dead body.

הֲזָמָה   See עֵדִים זוֹמְמִים.

הֲטָבַת הַנֵּרוֹת   *The preparation of the lights of the* מְנוֹרָה, *the seven-branched candelabrum in the Temple.* This was one of the regular activities in the Temple, in which the מְנוֹרָה was prepared to be kindled (see Exodus 30:7). It involved the removal of the soot and ash remaining from the previous night and the preparation of the wicks. This service was carried out early in the morning, when most of the lights of the מְנוֹרָה had already burnt out.

הַטּוֹב וְהַמֵּטִיב   Lit., *He who is good and does good.* (1) A blessing of thanksgiving recited by a person when he receives a benefit that will also aid others — for example, rainfall. If the benefit is received by a single individual, such a person recites the blessing שֶׁהֶחֱיָנוּ (see זְמַן). (2) The fourth blessing of Grace after Meals (ʏבִּרְכַּת הַמָּזוֹן) added by the Sages to the original three blessings after the fall of Betar and the burial of its dead at the end of the Bar Kokhba revolt (135 C.E.).

הֶיזֵּק רְאִיָּה   Lit., *damage caused by sight.* Damage or discomfort suffered by a person because he is exposed to the gaze of others while he is in his private domain. In certain instances, a court may force the offending party to prevent such a situation from arising. For example, a person may be required to remove a window which overlooks his neighbor's courtyard.

הֶיזֵּק שֶׁאֵינוֹ נִכָּר   Lit., *damage that is not evident.* A reduction in the value of an article caused by a change in its Halakhic status, even though there is no change in its physical state. For example, if a person imparts ritual impurity to terumah (ʏתְּרוּמָה) belonging to another person, though outwardly the produce remains the same, it is no longer permitted to be eaten, and thus its value is drastically reduced. A person is morally obligated (see דִּינֵי שָׁמַיִם) to pay for such damage. In certain instances, there is a legal obligation to pay based on the principle of indirect damage (see דִּינָא דְּגַרְמֵי).

הֵיכָל   *The Sanctuary, the inner section of the Temple.* The Sanctuary was a roofed building, 100 cubits high, to the west of the Temple Courtyard (עֲזָרָה). It contained the ʏמְנוֹרָה, the seven-branched candelabrum, the gold table for the shewbread (ʏשׁוּלְחַן הַזָּהָב), and the incense altar (ʏמִזְבַּח הַזָּהָב — the golden altar). Next to it, on its western side, was the Holy of Holies (ʏקֹדֶשׁ הַקֳּדָשִׁים). (See plan of the Temple, p. 277.) The term הֵיכָל is sometimes used for the entire building, and sometimes only for the section between the entrance-hall (ʏאוּלָם) and the Holy of Holies.

הֶיסַּח הַדַּעַת   Lit., *the diversion of attention.* (1) This concept is frequently applied in regard to the laws of ritual impurity. In certain situations, an article to which continuous attention was not paid, care not having been taken to prevent it from coming into contact with ritual impurity, may be considered ritually impure because of the doubt created by this lack of attention. (2) With reference to the laws of blessings and prayers: In certain cases, if a person's attention is distracted in the middle of prayers or while eating or performing a mitzvah after having recited the appropriate blessing, the connection with his previous words of prayer or blessing is considered severed, and he may have to repeat the prayer or blessing.

הֶיסֵּט   Lit., *movement, shaking.* A manner in which ritual impurity may be imparted by a ʏזָב — a man suffering from a gonorrheal discharge; a ʏזָבָה — a woman who has a menstrual-type flow of blood when she is not menstruating; a ʏנִדָּה — a menstruating woman; or a ʏיוֹלֶדֶת — a woman after childbirth. Whenever such a person causes an object to move from its place, even though he or she does not actually touch it, such as when it is moved by means of a lever, the article becomes ritually impure.

הֶישֵּׂג יָד   Lit., *[within one's] reach.* The term concerns a person's ability to meet his financial obligations. Certain monetary pledges to the Temple are evaluated by the priest according to the ability to pay of the person making the pledge (see Leviticus 27). If a person is indigent, he is often allowed to fulfill his obligation by paying a minimal sum. Similarly, certain sacrificial obligations are adjusted according to the financial capacity of the person bringing the offering (see דַּלּוּת וְדַלֵּי דַלּוּת).

הַכְחָשָׁה   Lit., *contradiction.* When a pair of witnesses contradicts testimony given previously by other witnesses, the testimony of both pairs of witnesses is nullified and the evidence of neither pair is accepted. No greater weight is attached to the evidence of several witnesses than to that of two. In contrast to a case of עֵדִים זוֹמְמִים (see entry), in a case of הַכְחָשָׁה the later witnesses contradict the earlier witnesses' description of the facts of the case and do not focus on the first pair of witnesses' presence at the scene.

הַכְמָנַת עֵדִים   *The concealing of witnesses.* (1) In monetary disputes (see דִּינֵי מָמוֹנוֹת) the testimony of witnesses whose presence was unknown to one of the litigants at the time of the transaction is not acceptable in court. (2) In cases involving capital punishment (see דִּינֵי נְפָשׁוֹת), the testimony of concealed witnesses is not usually acceptable. Only in the case of a person suspected of incitement to idolatry (מֵסִית וּמַדִּיחַ) does the court intentionally hide witnesses in order to apprehend the offender.

הֶכְשֵׁר   *Making an object liable to contract ritual impurity.* Food or produce cannot contract ritual impurity until (1) it has been severed from its place of growth; and (2) it has come into contact with a liquid, either directly through the action of its owner, or without his direct intervention but nevertheless with his approval. (See Leviticus 11:34–38.) There are seven liquids that make foodstuffs liable to contract ritual impurity: water, wine, honey, olive oil, milk, dew, and blood. Because of the special sanctity of the Temple and its sacrifices, the Sages decreed that sacrifices offered on the altar could contract ritual impurity even though they had had no contact with a liquid.

הַכָּתוּב מְסָרוֹ לַחֲכָמִים   *The Torah placed the matter at the discretion of the Sages.* There are certain Halakhic questions which are not sufficiently explained in the Torah, and for which the general principles that would facilitate their definition are not provided. According to some Rishonim, the Torah left these questions to the discretion of the Sages, allowing them to decide what is permitted and what is forbidden — for example, the categories of work permitted or forbidden during the intermediate days of the Pesaḥ and Sukkot Festivals (see חוֹל הַמּוֹעֵד).

הַלְוָיַת הַמֵּת   Lit., *escorting the dead [to burial].* One of the commandments in the category of גְּמִילוּת חֲסָדִים, acts of charity. Taking part in a funeral is considered an act of respect both to the departed and to the bereaved family. In principle, anyone who sees a funeral procession must participate in it at least for a short time.

הֲלָכָה (or הִלְכְתָא)   *Conclusive law.* Often used in the following ways: (1) A ruling at the end of a Talmudic dispute, usually in the form הִלְכְתָא כְּרִ׳ פְּלוֹנִי — "The Halakhah follows the opinion of Rabbi X." These rulings were generally inserted when the Talmud was finally edited. (2) It is occasionally used in the sense of "a theoretical ruling," as opposed to הֲלָכָה לְמַעֲשֶׂה — "a practical ruling." If a decision was actually carried out in practice, it has far greater legal weight than a decision that was merely issued in theory. (3) In Talmudic language, the word הֲלָכָה is sometimes used as a short form of הֲלָכָה לְמֹשֶׁה מִסִּינַי — "a law of Moses from Sinai," i.e., a law that has no Scriptural basis but, according to tradition, was given by God to Moses orally at the same time as the written Torah. Such laws have the same authority as Scriptural laws.

הִלְכוֹת מְדִינָה   *Local practices.* Practices that were not ordained by the Torah or the Sages, but accepted as local custom. These practices are generally acknowledged as binding in monetary matters.

הַלֵּל   Lit., *praise.* In particular, a reference to Psalms 113–118. These Psalms are recited on the first night(s) of Pesaḥ (and during the offering of the Passover sacrifice, see פֶּסַח), on the first day(s) of Pesaḥ, on Shavuot, on all the days of Sukkot, Shemini Atzeret, Simḥat Torah, and on all eight days of Ḥanukkah. The reciting of הַלֵּל on these days was ordained by the Prophets and Sages and a blessing is said before and after it. In addition, it is customary to recite an abridged version of Hallel on Rosh Ḥodesh and on the intermediate and final days of Pesaḥ. There are different customs in various communities with regard to whether blessings are recited in the case of the abridged הַלֵּל.

הַמּוֹצִיא מֵחֲבֵירוֹ עָלָיו הָרְאָיָה   *The burden of proof rests upon the claimant* (lit., "the person seeking to take [an article] from someone else, upon him is the [burden of] proof"). A general principle applied in monetary disputes (see דִּינֵי מָמוֹנוֹת), placing the burden of proof upon the plaintiff when he claims property in the possession of the defendant. If the plaintiff cannot provide such proof, the article remains in the hands of the defendant even if he, too, is unable to prove ownership. It is only in unusual circumstances that this principle is not applied.

הַנְהָגָה   Lit., *driving.* This term refers to one of the legal methods of formalizing the acquisition (קִנְיָן) of large animals. Since it is impractical to lift up these animals (see הַגְבָּהָה), the purchaser may formalize their acquisition by driving or leading them for a short distance. See מְשִׁיכָה.

הֶנְפֵּק   *A legal endorsement.* The endorsement of a legal document by the court certifying that it has examined the document and the signatures of the witnesses and found everything satisfactory. A promissory note with such an endorsement may be presented for collection and does not require any further substantiation.

הָנֵץ הַחַמָּה   Lit., *the sparkling forth of the [rising] sun.* The moment when the sun's sphere begins to appear on the horizon. In certain contexts this moment is considered as the beginning of the day. The pious (וָתִיקִין) customarily recite the morning service early and reach the Amidah prayer (see שְׁמוֹנֶה עֶשְׂרֵה) at the moment of הָנֵץ הַחַמָּה.

הֶסְפֵּד   *Eulogy.* It is customary to eulogize a person after his death. A eulogy contains praise of the departed (it is permitted to exaggerate slightly) and words of Torah are recited describing his qualities. Eulogies are not recited on Festivals.

הֶעְלֵם אֶחָד   *A single period of unawareness.* In Temple times, if a person inadvertently or unknowingly violated a prohibition whose willful violation carried the penalty of excision (כָּרֵת), he was obligated to bring a sin-offering (חַטָּאת). If he repeated the transgression before realizing that he had sinned ("in a single period of unawareness"), he was usually only obligated to bring one offering. However, if he realized his sin before repeating the act, he was obligated to bring a separate offering for each transgression. Thus it is Halakhically significant to know whether sins were committed in the same "period of unawareness."

הֶעְלֵם טוּמְאָה   Lit., *an unawareness of impurity.* The Torah forbids eating consecrated food while in a state of ritual impurity (Leviticus 7:19–20), and prohibits entering the Temple while ritually impure (Numbers 19:20). If a person commits either of these transgressions while he is unaware of his ritual impurity, he is obligated to bring a sacrifice as atonement. (see קָרְבָּן עוֹלֶה וְיוֹרֵד).

הֶעְלֵם מִקְדָּשׁ   Lit., *an unawareness of the Temple*. This refers to a person who enters the Temple while ritually impure (see הֶעְלֵם טוּמְאָה), aware that he is ritually impure, but without realizing that he has entered the Temple. He is obligated to bring a sacrifice as atonement (see קָרְבָּן עוֹלֶה וְיוֹרֵד).

הַעֲרָאָה   *The first stage of sexual intercourse.* Its exact definition is a matter of Talmudic debate (see *Yevamot* 55b). In most of the cases where the Torah mentions sexual intercourse, either as something forbidden or as the fulfillment of a mitzvah, no differentiation is made between הַעֲרָאָה and the completion of the sexual act (see בִּיאָה). One exception concerns sexual relations with a half-free non-Jewish handmaid designated in marriage to a Jewish slave (see שִׁפְחָה חֲרוּפָה). In such a case הַעֲרָאָה is excluded from punishment (see Leviticus 19:20).

הֶעֱרֵב שֶׁמֶשׁ   Lit., *sunset*. This concept is specifically linked to the laws of ritual impurity. If someone who was ritually impure has immersed himself in a ritual bath (מִקְוֶה, see also טְבִילָה) he remains ritually impure with regard to the eating of תְּרוּמָה until the sun has set and the stars have come out (see צֵאת הַכּוֹכָבִים in the evening following his immersion. After צֵאת הַכּוֹכָבִים he may eat תְּרוּמָה. However, certain categories of people who were ritually impure and who immersed themselves in a ritual bath were prohibited from entering the Temple or coming into contact with sacrifices until they brought expiatory offerings on the day after their immersion. (See טְבוּל יוֹם; מְחוּסַּר כַּפָּרָה.)

הַעֲרָמָה   Lit., *Circumvention*. Circumventing the law in such a way that a person performs a forbidden act (or avoids an obligation) while appearing to be unaware of the consequences of his action. In certain situations the Sages were very strict and levied heavy fines on people who circumvented the law. But in some instances circumvention was permitted to certain people (such as scholars), in order to prevent more serious Halakhic difficulties from arising.

הַפֶּה שֶׁאָסַר הוּא הַפֶּה שֶׁהִתִּיר   Lit., *the mouth that prohibited is the mouth that permitted.* A principle applied in all areas of Halakhah that a person who tells us something we would not have known had he not made his statement, is to be believed if he then says something that cancels out the consequences of the first part of his statement. For example, if a woman comes to a community from a foreign country and claims to have been married, but widowed, her complete statement is accepted and she is allowed to marry freely. Since her listeners have no previous knowledge about her situation, her word is accepted. Since it is her statement ("mouth") that created her married status, her statement can also remove that status.

הַפְטָרָה   *A portion from the Books of the Prophets read following the Torah reading on Sabbaths and Festivals.* Generally, the haftarah follows a theme contained in the Torah reading or is connected with the occasion (the Festival or the special Sabbath) on which it is read. A number of the haftarot are specifically mentioned in the Talmud and others are referred to in tractate *Soferim*. The haftarot for certain Torah portions vary according to local custom. Before reciting the haftarah, the person given that honor recites the closing verses of the Torah reading. Blessings are recited before and after the haftarah. The Halakhah allows a minor to recite the haftarah.

הֶפְקֵר   *Ownerless property, or the nullification of a person's ownership of an article or property.* When declaring something הֶפְקֵר, a person must totally renounce his ownership of the property in question. He may not cede ownership in favor of certain people, thus allowing them to acquire it, while denying others the opportunity of doing so. According to some authorities it is necessary to renounce one's ownership of property in the presence of at least three people. Other authorities maintain that even a private statement is sufficient. Certain property is declared ownerless by the Torah's decree — for example, produce that grows in the Sabbatical Year (שְׁבִיעִית). The property belonging to a convert (גֵּר צֶדֶק) who dies without leaving heirs is also הֶפְקֵר. There is no obligation to tithe (see מַעַשְׂרוֹת) produce that is ownerless.

הֶפְקֵר בֵּית דִּין הֶפְקֵר   Lit., *[property declared] ownerless by the court is ownerless.* The court has the power to cancel a person's ownership of his property, either partially or totally. This step is sometimes taken by the court in order to punish offenders, and on other occasions it is taken to prevent undesirable Halakhic ramifications of certain property transfers.

הֲפָרַת נְדָרִים   *The nullification of vows.* The Torah (Numbers 30) authorizes a father to nullify the vows of his daughter before she either attains majority (see בּוֹגֶרֶת) or marries (see נִישּׂוּאִין). Similarly, a husband is entitled to nullify any vows made by his wife. If a girl is betrothed before she attains majority (see נַעֲרָה הַמְאוֹרָסָה), her vows may be nullified by her husband and father acting together. The vow must be nullified on the same day on which the father or husband heard of it. A husband is only empowered to nullify those vows which either directly or indirectly affect the personal relationship between him and his wife. According to many opinions, this restriction applies to the father as well. See also הַתָּרַת נְדָרִים.

הֶקְדֵּשׁ   *Consecrated property.* Any property that a person consecrates for use in the Temple or as a sacrifice. Property pledged to הֶקְדֵּשׁ becomes consecrated as soon as the pledge is uttered, and from that time on it is no longer considered the private property of the donor (see אֲמִירָתוֹ לַגָּבוֹהַּ כִּמְסִירָתוֹ לְהֶדְיוֹט). The use of הֶקְדֵּשׁ for purposes other than those for which it is pledged is forbidden (see מְעִילָה). See also קָדְשֵׁי בֶּדֶק הַבַּיִת; קָדְשֵׁי מִזְבֵּחַ.

הֶקְדֵּשׁ טָעוּת   *The erroneous or accidental consecration of property.* This can occur through miscalculation, through being unaware of the nature of a particular situation, through forgetfulness, or through a slip of the tongue. The Halakhah does not consider such property as consecrated.

הֶקְדֵּשׁ עִילּוּי   *Consecration by valuation.* A pledge made by a person to consecrate an article which is already sacred — for example, a pledge made to consecrate an animal that was already designated as a sacrifice. In such an instance, the person is obligated to pay the amount a person would be willing to pay in order to offer such a sacrifice, but not necessarily the full worth of the animal.

הַקְהֵל   Lit., *assembly*. The Torah (Deuteronomy 31:10–13) commands the Jewish people to assemble in the Temple Courtyard once every seven years to hear the public reading of the Book of Deuteronomy. The assembly was held during the Festival of Sukkot in the year following the Sabbatical Year (see שְׁבִיעִית). The entire nation — men, women, and children — attended, and the king read the Book of Deuteronomy to them.

הֶקְטֵר חֲלָבִים   Lit., *the burning of fats*. The fat portions of a sacrificial animal had to be burned on the altar (see אֵימוּרִים). While the sacrifice itself had to be offered during the day, the burning of the fats could be carried out during the following night, if necessary.

הַקְטָרָה   *The burning of incense*. One of the daily offerings, brought morning and evening, in the Temple (see Exodus 30). Coals were taken from the outer altar (מִזְבֵּחַ), brought into the Sanctuary (הֵיכָל), and placed on the the golden altar (מִזְבַּח הַזָּהָב). The incense was then poured slowly upon them. In addition to the incense offering brought each day, one of the unique aspects of the Yom Kippur service was the incense offering brought by the High Priest (כֹּהֵן גָּדוֹל) into the Holy of Holies (קֹדֶשׁ הַקֳּדָשִׁים; see also Leviticus 15:12–13). The incense offering was a highly revered service and considered an omen of wealth. Therefore, the priest who brought the incense offering was chosen by lot from among those who had never brought an incense offering before.

הַר הַבַּיִת   *The Temple Mount*. The walled area surrounding the Temple. The status of the Temple Mount paralleled that of the camp of the Levites in the wilderness. It was endowed with a special degree of sanctity; women who were menstrually

impure (see נִדָּה) and זָבִים (see זָב) were forbidden to enter it. The Temple Mount contained a number of auxiliary buildings serving the Temple, and a synagogue.

הֶרֶג   *Execution by decapitation*. One of the four methods of capital punishment (אַרְבַּע מִיתוֹת בֵּית דִּין). See also סַיִף.

הַשָּׁקָה   Lit., *causing contact [of liquids]*. One of the ways of purifying water that has become ritually impure is by placing it in a container and submerging the container in a מִקְוֶה (ritual bath) so that the water of the מִקְוֶה comes into contact with the impure water. This procedure can also by used to supplement the reservoir of an existing מִקְוֶה with water that would otherwise be unfit for use in a מִקְוֶה (see מַיִם שְׁאוּבִים). Many of the ritual baths used today employ this principle.

הַתְרָאָה   *Warning*. A formal warning given to a person who is about to perform a transgression. The warning must state that the act is forbidden and describe the punishment a violator would receive. Capital and corporal punishment cannot be administered unless such a warning was given beforehand and acknowledged by the transgressor. In only a few instances (e.g., מֵסִית — one who incites to idol worship; and עֵדִים זוֹמְמִים — false conspiratorial witnesses) is punishment administered even though no warning was given. See also כִּיפָּה.

הַתָּרַת נְדָרִים   *The dissolution of vows*. Dispensation granted by a Sage nullifying a vow. A person who makes a vow or takes an oath regarding his future behavior and later regrets having made the vow or oath may present the case to a Sage. In certain instances, the Sage has the power to "dissolve" the vow, nullifying it retroactively. There are certain vows that are automatically nullified and do not require release. Others can only be released under specific conditions. See שְׁאֵלָה לְחָכָם.

וִידּוּי   *Confession*. This is an essential part of the process of repentance (תְּשׁוּבָה). The Torah obligates a person who has sinned to confess his sin (see Numbers 5:6–7). This confession, in which the sinner acknowledges and expresses regret for his sin, is made by him alone in private. In certain circumstances, however, where the sin involved has become public knowledge, a public confession is required. In many communities, the confessional prayer אָשַׁמְנוּ is recited every weekday. The Yom Kippur service includes many prayers and petitions for forgiveness, and the extended confessional prayer עַל חֵטְא is recited several times during the course of the day. וִידּוּי was also recited by a person bringing a sin-offering (חַטָּאת), a guilt-offering (אָשָׁם), or a free-will burnt-offering (עוֹלַת נְדָבָה, see

עוֹלָה) at the time he placed his hands on the head of the sacrifice (see סְמִיכָה).

וִידּוּי מַעֲשֵׂר   *The declaration made on the last day of Pesaḥ in the fourth and seventh year of the Sabbatical cycle, stating that one's agricultural obligations regarding tithes [מַעַשְׂרוֹת] had been properly fulfilled*. (See also בִּיעוּר מַעַשְׂרוֹת.) The text of this declaration is found in Deuteronomy 26:13–15. During the Second Temple period, Yoḥanan the High Priest is said to have discontinued the recitation of this declaration out of fear that the agricultural laws were not being properly observed and that the statements being made would therefore be false.

וְלַד הַטּוּמְאָה   Lit., *offspring of impurity*. An object that has become ritually impure from contact with an אַב הַטּוּמְאָה — a primary source of ritual impurity (see אֲבוֹת הַטּוּמְאוֹת). Such an object becomes ritually impure and may impart ritual impurity to foods or liquids with which it comes into contact. But it does not have the power to impart ritual impurity to people or to utensils. A וְלַד הַטּוּמְאָה is also referred to as רִאשׁוֹן לְטוּמְאָה — the first degree of ritual impurity below that of אַב הַטּוּמְאָה.

וַלְדוֹת קָדָשִׁים   *Offspring of consecrated animals.* The young that are born to an animal which has already been consecrated as a sacrifice. Such offspring may not be used for secular purposes. The offspring of animals consecrated as peace-offerings (שְׁלָמִים*) are given as a voluntary-offering (נְדָבָה*). The offspring of animals consecrated as sin-offerings (חַטָּאת*) may not be sacrificed on the altar. Instead they are confined in an enclosure until they die (see חַטָּאוֹת הַמֵּתוֹת).

וֶסֶת   *A set pattern, recurring regularly at a fixed time.* This term is most frequently used in reference to a woman's menstrual cycle. There are many differences in the laws governing a woman with a fixed menstrual cycle (וֶסֶת קָבוּעַ) and

those governing a woman with an irregular menstrual cycle (וֶסֶת שֶׁאֵינוֹ קָבוּעַ), who has to take into account the possibility that she may become ritually impure at any time.

"וְעָשִׂיתָ הַיָּשָׁר וְהַטּוֹב"   *"And you shall do that which is right and good."* (Deuteronomy 6:18.) This moral instruction also implies a specific Halakhic obligation. Wherever possible (and particularly in the case of a publicly respected person, אָדָם חָשׁוּב*, from whom an especially high standard of behavior is expected) a person should go beyond the strict requirements of the law (see לִפְנִים מִשּׁוּרַת הַדִּין) in matters between one person and another, and should even forgo money to which he is legally entitled, as a "right and good" action. In certain cases where no financial loss is involved, the courts can compel a person to behave in a "right and good" fashion (see בַּר מְצָרָא).

וָתִיקִין   Lit., *pious men*. Men who lived in former days and who were extremely scrupulous in the observance of the mitzvot. The custom of the וָתִיקִין of reciting the morning prayers each day at sunrise (הָנֵץ הַחַמָּה*) is well known, and is practiced by many observant Jews to this day.

זָב   *A man suffering from gonorrhea.* The laws relating to the severe ritual impurity caused by this condition are laid down in Leviticus 15 and in the Talmudic tractate *Zavim*. The זָב becomes ritually impure as a result of the secretion of a white, pus-like discharge from his penis. A man who has such a discharge on one occasion becomes ritually impure for one day, like one who has emitted semen (בַּעַל קֶרִי*). If he experiences a second discharge on the same or the following day (or a prolonged initial discharge), he contracts the more severe ritual impurity, lasting seven days, of a זָב. A third discharge experienced within the next twenty-four hours obligates him to bring a sacrifice as part of his purification process (see רְאִיּוֹת הַזָּב; טָהֳרַת הַזָּב). Not only does the person himself become ritually impure, but he imparts ritual impurity by touching articles or persons (טוּמְאַת מַגָּע*); by being moved by them (טוּמְאַת מַשָּׂא*); by moving them (טוּמְאָה הֶיסֵּט*); by lying or sitting on them (מִשְׁכָּב מוֹשָׁב וּמֶרְכָּב*); or through the medium of a large stone (אֶבֶן מְסָמָא*) over them. The fluids he secretes — his spittle, urine and semen — impart ritual impurity, and the article on which he sits or lies becomes an אַב הַטּוּמְאָה (see אֲבוֹת הַטּוּמְאוֹת) and can itself impart ritual impurity to other articles.

זָבָה   *A woman who experiences a flow of menstrual-type blood on three consecutive days during a time of the month when she does not expect to experience menstrual bleeding.* The first secretion makes her ritually impure, but until the third secretion

her status is that of a שׁוֹמֶרֶת יוֹם כְּנֶגֶד יוֹם*, and she is not governed by all the Halakhic rulings of a זָבָה. After experiencing such bleeding on a third day, the woman is considered a זָבָה and is obligated to bring a sacrifice as part of her purification process. A זָבָה imparts ritual impurity in the same way as a זָב. In addition, a man who engages in sexual relations with her becomes an אַב הַטּוּמְאָה (see אֲבוֹת הַטּוּמְאוֹת) and imparts ritual impurity to others. See also בּוֹעֵל נִדָּה; טָהֳרַת הַזָּב.

זוֹחֲלִין   *Moving water.* Ritually impure people and objects can be purified through immersion in a מִקְוֶה* ("ritual bath"), i.e., a body of rainwater. However, a מִקְוֶה only purifies those immersing in it if the water is stationary and of a fixed minimum quantity (see אַשְׁבּוֹרֶן). By contrast, bodies of naturally flowing water such as rivers and springs (see מַעְיָן), and, according to some opinions, seawater as well, purify those immersing in them even though the water is moving (זוֹחֲלִין), and there is no fixed minimum quantity of such water for the purpose of effective immersion.

זוֹנָה   Lit., *a prostitute*. Halakhically, this term refers to a woman who has had sexual relations with a man forbidden to her by the Torah and with whom she cannot establish a marriage bond (for example, relations are forbidden between a married woman and a man who is not her husband, or between a brother and a sister, or between a Jewish woman and a non-Jew). Every female convert is included in this category, regardless of the age at which she converted and regardless of her past history. A woman is placed in the category of a זוֹנָה whether she engaged in these forbidden relations voluntarily or against her will. In either case, she is forbidden thereafter to marry a priest or remain married to one (Leviticus 21:7). Thus, there is no connection between the Halakhic definition of this term and its everyday usage in Biblical and modern Hebrew.

זִיבּוּרִית   *Land of the poorest quality.* See עִידִּית.

זִילוּתָא דְּבֵי דִּינָא   *Disrespect for the court.* Sometimes, when there is a possibility that the reputation and dignity of the court may be brought into disrepute in a particular situation, the court employs additional measures to enforce its decisions and to uphold previous rulings which it might otherwise have overturned. The extent to which the concept of זִילוּתָא דְּבֵי דִּינָא is invoked is the subject of disagreement among the Sages.

זִיקָה   *The levirate bond.* The relationship between a *שׁוֹמֶרֶת יָבָם* (a woman whose husband died without children) and her deceased husband's brothers during the period after the husband's death, before one of the brothers (known as a יָבָם) performs the levirate marriage (*יִבּוּם*) or the ceremony of *חֲלִיצָה* with the widow. The precise nature of the relationship between the יָבָם and the *שׁוֹמֶרֶת יָבָם* during this period is the subject of much Talmudic debate. In certain respects, for instance if the question arises whether the יָבָם may marry a close relative of the *שׁוֹמֶרֶת יָבָם*, they are considered as betrothed from the time of the husband's death. The זִיקָה is either transformed into marriage by יִבּוּם, or nullified and severed by חֲלִיצָה.

זַיִת   *An olive.* The size of an olive is a frequently employed Halakhic measure. It is the minimum quantity for which one may be guilty of eating forbidden food, and also the minimum that one must consume in order to fulfill mitzvot connected with eating — e.g., the eating of matzah (מַצָּה) on the first night of Pesah. This measure is also used in other contexts. (See also in section on weights and measures p. 288.)

זָכִין לְאָדָם שֶׁלֹּא בְּפָנָיו   *One may act in a person's interest in his absence.* A Halakhic principle that allows something which is to a person's benefit, e.g., a present, to be acquired for him by another person without his having knowledge of it, without him being present, and without him having explicitly appointed the other person to act on his behalf. Any person can act as an agent for the person receiving the benefit. This principle only applies if the transaction involves an outright benefit for the person. If both benefits and disadvantages are involved, and it is debatable whether the benefits outweigh the disadvantages, the principle is not applied.

זִכְרוֹנוֹת   *Lit., remembrances.* The name given to the second of the three special blessings added to the Amidah prayer (see שְׁמוֹנֶה עֶשְׂרֵה) in the musaf service (*מוּסָף*) on Rosh HaShanah. See also מַלְכוּיּוֹת; שׁוֹפָרוֹת.

זְמַן (בִּרְכַּת הַזְּמַן)   *Lit., time (the blessing for time).* The

בָּרוּךְ... שֶׁהֶחֱיָנוּ וְקִיְּמָנוּ וְהִגִּיעָנוּ לַזְּמַן הַזֶּה blessing praising God: שֶׁהֶחֱיָנוּ — "Blessed are You... who has granted us life, sustained us, and allowed us to reach this time." There are two main categories of situation in which this blessing is recited: (1) Upon the performance of a mitzvah for the first time, or upon the performance of a mitzvah which is fulfilled at regular, infrequent intervals (e.g., the celebration of the Festivals), or a mitzvah which is not a usual occurrence (e.g., the redemption of a firstborn). (2) When eating certain fruits for the first time in their season, and, in general, upon experiencing any unusual benefit or joy. See הַטּוֹב וְהַמֵּטִיב.

זָקֵן מַמְרֵא   *Rebellious elder.* This refers to a Sage who was duly ordained and fit to serve in the Sanhedrin (see סַנְהֶדְרִין גְּדוֹלָה), but who himself followed a practice or instructed others to follow a practice that contradicted the opinion of the majority of the Sages of his generation. Whenever there was a major debate among Sages as to how a Halakhic practice should be fulfilled, the matter was brought to the Sanhedrin for clarification and decision. The decision reached by that body was binding upon the entire nation. A Sage could disagree with that decision, but he was obliged to follow the majority opinion and to instruct others to do likewise. If he gave contrary instructions or violated the decision himself, he was a זָקֵן מַמְרֵא and liable to be executed by strangulation (*חֶנֶק*), provided that the question in dispute was of a high degree of importance. The execution of a זָקֵן מַמְרֵא was to be carried out during one of the three Pilgrim Festivals (*שָׁלֹשׁ רְגָלִים*) when many people were assembled in Jerusalem, for then it would be most effective as a deterrent, in accordance with the verse: "All the people shall hear, and fear, and do no more presumptuously" (Deuteronomy 17:13). (See also *Sanhedrin* 89a.)

זָר   Lit., *a stranger.* Specifically: a non-priest. The Torah (Numbers 18:7) forbids a non-priest from taking part in the priestly service, on pain of death by the hand of God (*מִיתָה בִּידֵי שָׁמַיִם*).

זְרוֹעַ, לְחָיַיִם, וְקֵיבָה   *The foreleg, the jaw, and the maw.* The Torah commands that these portions be given to a priest when nonsacrificial animals (cattle, sheep, and goats) are slaughtered for food (Deuteronomy 18:3). No sacred quality is attached to these gifts, and once they have been given to a priest he may give or sell them to a non-priest.

זְרִיקָה   *Throwing, sprinkling.* This term refers to the presentation of sacrificial blood on the altar (*מִזְבֵּחַ*). It is one of the four essential actions (*אַרְבַּע עֲבוֹדוֹת*) in the offering of every animal sacrifice in the Temple. The manner in which the blood was presented on the altar varied according to the nature of the particular sacrifice (see הַזָּאָה; שְׁתַּיִם שֶׁהֵן אַרְבַּע). The presentation of blood on the altar was the essential element necessary for a sacrifice to bring about atonement. Accordingly, as soon as the blood was presented as required on the altar, the person who brought the sacrifice received atonement, even if the later services connected with the sacrifice were not completed in the required manner.

חֲבוּרָה   Lit., *a company.* In particular, a group of people who arranged to partake together of a single Paschal sacrifice (see פֶּסַח). Until the sacrifice was slaughtered, a person could change from one company to another. Afterwards, however, one was not allowed to change groups.

חֲבִיתִין   *A meal-offering [see* מְנָחוֹת*], one-tenth of an Ephah, prepared in a manner resembling a wafer.* The High Priest (כֹּהֵן גָּדוֹל) would bring this offering each day, half in the morning and half in the evening. (See Leviticus 6:12–15.) Every priest would bring a similar offering, called מִנְחַת חִינוּךְ, on the first day of his service in the Temple.

חָבֵר (pl. חֲבֵרִים)   Lit., *an associate, a colleague.* In the Talmudic period, this referred to a person who became a member of a group dedicated to the precise observance of mitzvot. A person who wished to enter such a society had formally to accept its practices in the presence of three other members. The main stress of these groups was the strict observance of the laws of terumah (תְּרוּמָה) and tithes (מַעַשְׂרוֹת) and careful adherence to ritual purity, so much so that they would eat even nonsacrificial food (חוּלִין) in a state of ritual purity. In practice, all Torah scholars were חֲבֵרִים. However, many of the common people (see עַם הָאָרֶץ) and even some Samaritans (see כּוּתִי) were included in this category. Acceptance as a חָבֵר removed an individual from the category of an עַם הָאָרֶץ and his statements regarding tithes and ritual purity were accepted as true and were relied upon. In later generations, the term חָבֵר took on a more restricted meaning and was used to refer only to important scholars.

חֲגִיגָה   *Festival-offering.* A peace-offering (שְׁלָמִים) that was sacrificed in honor of the three Pilgrim Festivals (שָׁלֹשׁ רְגָלִים). Every person required to make the pilgrimage to Jerusalem for the Festival was obligated to bring this sacrifice. The sacrifice was to be offered on the first day of the Festival. However, if one did not do so, it could be offered during חוֹל הַמּוֹעֵד, the intermediate days of the Pesaḥ and Sukkot Festivals, on the last day of Pesaḥ or Shemini Atzeret (שְׁמִינִי עֲצֶרֶת), or during the six days following the Festival of Shavuot. (See Deuteronomy 16:15–16 and commentaries.)

חֲגִיגַת אַרְבָּעָה עָשָׂר   Lit., *the Festival-offering of the fourteenth.* The special peace-offering (שְׁלָמִים) sacrificed on the fourteenth of Nisan to accompany the Paschal sacrifice (see פֶּסַח). Often, the number of people in a group (חֲבוּרָה) designated to partake of a particular Paschal sacrifice was too great to allow each individual to receive a portion large enough to satisfy him. Accordingly, the additional Festival sacrifice, חֲגִיגַת אַרְבָּעָה עָשָׂר, was offered to supplement that portion. It was only offered when Pesaḥ Eve fell on a weekday, and was governed by the laws

pertaining to a peace-offering, in that it could be brought from male or female cattle or sheep.

חָדָשׁ   Lit., *new.* This term refers to new grain ripening in the period before Pesaḥ. The Torah forbids harvesting and eating this produce until after the offering of the Omer sacrifice (see עוֹמֶר) on the 16th of Nisan (Leviticus 23:14).

חוֹבֵל   Lit., *injuring, wounding.* A person who performs a deed that directly injures someone. He may be obligated to reimburse him under the following five headings (see respective entries): נֶזֶק — injury; צַעַר — pain; רִיפּוּי — healing (i.e. medical costs); שֶׁבֶת — loss of livelihood; and בּוֹשֶׁת — humiliation.

חוּט הַסִּיקְרָא   Lit., *the red thread.* A line painted in red encircling the Temple altar (מִזְבֵּחַ) at precisely half its height. This marking was necessary because the blood of animal sin-offerings (see חַטָּאת) and birds brought as burnt-offerings (see עוֹלַת הָעוֹף) had to be spilled on the upper portion of the altar, above the חוּט הַסִּיקְרָא, whereas the blood of all other sacrifices had to be spilled on the lower portion, below the חוּט הַסִּיקְרָא.

חוֹכֵר   *A tenant farmer.* A person who leases a field from its owner, paying the owner rent in the form of a fixed quantity of the produce harvested, irrespective of the total amount of the harvest. See אָרִיס; קַבְּלָן.

חוֹל הַמּוֹעֵד   *The intermediate days of a Festival.* The days between the first and last days of Pesaḥ and Sukkot. They are not considered full holidays, but they are not ordinary weekdays either, and with certain exceptions it is forbidden to work on חוֹל הַמּוֹעֵד. The exceptions include דָּבָר הָאָבֵד, a task which will cause an irretrievable loss if not performed, and צוֹרֶךְ הַמּוֹעֵד, a task whose purpose is to enhance the Festival celebrations. It is also forbidden to perform weddings on חוֹל הַמּוֹעֵד, so that the rejoicing associated with the wedding not be mixed with that related to the Festival. The tractate of *Moed Katan* deals extensively with the laws pertaining to חוֹל הַמּוֹעֵד. See also הֶדְיוֹט.

חוּלִין   *Secular.* That which does not belong to the Temple or its consecrated objects. In certain contexts, produce that has already been, or does not need to be, tithed. Several prohibitions (see מְעִילָה) and regulations apply only to consecrated things (the laws of sacrifices and the like). There is also a difference between the way secular and consecrated things are acquired, and certain regulations apply only to secular things (the obligation to bring offerings and tithes from produce, the prohibition of interest).

חוּלִין בָּעֲזָרָה   Lit., *a nonsacrificial animal in the Temple Courtyard.* It is forbidden to bring, and, even more so, to slaughter, unconsecrated animals in the Temple Courtyard. There is a dispute among the Sages as to whether this is a specific Torah prohibition (see לָאו), but all agree that it is prohibited.

חוֹלֵק עַל הַגּוֹרֶן Lit., *he receives his portion at the granary*. A priest is entitled to go to a person's granary and to receive there the terumah (תְּרוּמָה) to which he is entitled. Though a priest's slaves and wives were entitled to partake of terumah, they would generally not collect it at the granaries.

חוֹמֶשׁ Lit., *a fifth*. An additional fifth of the value of an article added to its price as a punishment or fine, or in order to emphasize its importance. חוֹמֶשׁ occurs in the following contexts: (1) The secular use of consecrated things (מְעִילָה). If a person inadvertently uses a consecrated animal or article for his own secular purposes, he must add an extra fifth of its value when reimbursing the Temple. (2) Terumah (תְּרוּמָה). A non-priest (זָר) who inadvertently partakes of תְּרוּמָה must pay a priest the value of the תְּרוּמָה plus an additional fifth. (3) Compensation for robbery (גֵּזֶל). When a person is obligated to bring a guilt-offering for robbery (אֲשַׁם גְּזֵילוֹת), he must also add a fifth to the value of the property when reimbursing its owner for its loss (Leviticus 5:24). (4) The redemption of the second tithe (פִּדְיוֹן מַעֲשֵׂר שֵׁנִי). When a person redeems his own second tithe (Leviticus 27: 31), he must add an extra fifth of its value. The same law applies to the redemption of the produce of the fourth year (see נֶטַע רְבָעִי). (5) The redemption of sacred property (פִּדְיוֹן הֶקְדֵּשׁ). A person who redeems property that he himself dedicated to the Temple or animals which he himself consecrated as sacrifices and which were found to be unfit to be sacrificed must add a fifth of their value.

חוּפָּה *Wedding canopy*. A symbolic home, which a bridegroom enters together with his bride. The structure of the חוּפָּה depends on local custom. However, in most places it is currently accepted as a canopy without walls. Entry into the חוּפָּה marks the transition from betrothal (אֵירוּסִין) to marriage (נִישּׂוּאִין), and the marriage blessings (בִּרְכַּת חֲתָנִים) are recited then. Nowadays, the ceremony of אֵירוּסִין is immediately followed by that of נִישּׂוּאִין, and it is customary to perform them both under the חוּפָּה.

חוּץ לָאָרֶץ *Outside the Land of Israel*. Anywhere that is outside the boundary of Eretz Israel (אֶרֶץ יִשְׂרָאֵל). Because of the special sanctity of the Land of Israel, the Halakhah distinguishes between the Land of Israel and areas outside it. Even during the period when sacrifice was permitted outside the Temple (see בָּמָה), it was nevertheless forbidden outside the Land of Israel. חוּץ לָאָרֶץ was considered by Rabbinical law to be ritually impure (see אֶרֶץ הָעַמִּים), and because of that impurity the laws of the Nazirite (see נְזִירוּת) were only practiced in the Land of Israel. Because Rabbinical ordination (סְמִיכַת זְקֵנִים) can only be practiced within the Land of Israel, once that institution ceased to be in effect there, it could not be maintained abroad; therefore, all Rabbinical courts outside אֶרֶץ יִשְׂרָאֵל are considered lay courts (בָּתֵּי דִין שֶׁל הֶדְיוֹטוֹת). Another difference involves the calendar: since the intercalation of months (עִיבּוּר הַחֹדֶשׁ) took place in the Land of Israel, the dates of the Festivals had to be announced to the communities abroad. Because doubts arose as to the correct date, it was declared that Festivals abroad should be

celebrated on two days, and this still holds true today, though we have a fixed calendar (see יוֹם טוֹב שֵׁנִי שֶׁל גָּלוּיוֹת). Yet another difference is that an agent delivering a bill of divorce (גֵּט) outside אֶרֶץ יִשְׂרָאֵל to חוּץ לָאָרֶץ or from אֶרֶץ יִשְׂרָאֵל must make a special declaration when handing over the גֵּט (see בְּפָנַי נִכְתַּב וּבְפָנַי נֶחְתַּם). According to ancient tradition or by Rabbinical decree, in some foreign territories close to the Land of Israel the laws of the Land of Israel are applied, such as those of the Sabbatical Year (שְׁבִיעִית), priestly dues (see תְּרוּמָה) and tithes (מַעֲשְׂרוֹת; see also סוּרְיָה). The Halakhah also distinguishes between Babylonia and other places outside the Land of Israel in some respects.

חוּץ לִזְמַנּוֹ Lit., *outside its appointed time*. The sprinkling of the blood of a sacrifice on the altar (זְרִיקָה), or the burning of its fats (see אֵימוּרִים) on the altar, or the partaking of its meat, after the time designated for that particular service. Such an action is invalid. If the sacrifice was slaughtered with the intention that one of these services would be performed after its designated time, the entire sacrifice was disqualified (see פִּיגּוּל), even if the services themselves were performed correctly and at the right time. See also next entry.

חוּץ לִמְקוֹמוֹ Lit., *outside its [proper] place*. The performance of one of the services associated with a sacrifice — the sprinkling of its blood (זְרִיקָה), the burning of its fats (see אֵימוּרִים), or the partaking of its meat — outside the area designated for that function. See also פָּסוּל; פִּיגּוּל; חוּץ לִזְמַנּוֹ.

חוֹצֵץ מִפְּנֵי הַטּוּמְאָה *An object located within or above a cavity containing ritual impurity, preventing ritual impurity from spreading to objects located on its other side.* For an object to prevent ritual impurity from spreading in this way, it must not itself be able to become ritually impure due to its size, the material from which it is made, or its position. See אֹהֶל הַמֵּת; פּוֹתֵחַ טֶפַח; צָמִיד פָּתִיל.

חַזָּן Lit., *officer, superintendent*. In Talmudic times this term referred to an attendant charged with maintaining order, particularly in synagogues. At times such an attendant would also supervise the children studying there. The use of the term to refer to the leader of communal prayer (see שְׁלִיחַ צִיבּוּר) came much later in Jewish history.

חֲזָקָה *Possession, taking possession, presumption*. A term frequently used in Halakhah with different meanings depending on the context: (1) In general, חֲזָקָה means a presumption based on facts, or circumstances, or an accepted custom, or on the behavioral tendencies of man, which we accept as true. For example, among the accepted חֲזָקוֹת are the presumptions that "an agent carries out the mission with which he was charged," and that "children who are treated as family members are, in fact, their parents' offspring." Unless the facts prove otherwise, these presumptions are accepted as true, and even corporal punishment is meted out because of them. (2) With reference to legal claims, חֲזָקָה means possession of property. If a person has been physically in possession of an object for a period of time (the period varies according to the nature of the object; e.g., immovable property, מְקַרְקְעֵי, requires three years), this serves as proof that the person in possession is in fact, as he claims, the legal owner. A person who is able to prove uninterrupted possession for the necessary period is no longer required to produce documentary evidence of his legal title to the object. The חֲזָקָה is proof enough. (See חֲזָקָה; הַמּוֹצִיא מֵחֲבֵירוֹ עָלָיו הָרְאָיָה.) (3) With reference to the transfer of ownership of immovable property, חֲזָקָה means demonstrating one's ownership by performing an act denoting ownership. The performance of such an act represents a קִנְיָן, in which one person formally acquires property received as a gift or purchased from another person. (4) With reference to the use of property (easement), חֲזָקָה means the privilege to use property, even though it inconveniences another party. For example, if one person's window overlooks someone else's courtyard, this represents an invasion of privacy. Nevertheless, if the owner of the courtyard has allowed the window to be used for a certain period of time, the owner of the window has acquired a חֲזָקָה and the owner of the courtyard cannot sue to have the window removed. See הֶיזֵק רְאִיָה.

חֲזָקָה שֶׁאֵין עִמָּהּ טַעֲנָה   *Possession that is not accompanied by a claim.*

A person in possession of property is presumed to be its owner unless proved otherwise. However, this presumption is only made when he claims that he legally acquired the property in question — i.e., that he bought it, received it as a gift, or inherited it. If he does not make such a claim, his possession is not in itself proof of ownership, regardless of the period of time the property has been in his possession.

חַטָּאוֹת הַמֵּתוֹת   *Sin-offerings left to die.*

Sin-offerings (see חַטָּאת) that have become disqualified and, hence, can no longer be sacrificed on the altar. Such animals are confined in an enclosure until they die. According to some authorities, there are five animals placed in this category: (1) The offspring of a sin-offering (see וַלְדוֹת קֳדָשִׁים). (2) An animal substituted (see תְּמוּרָה) for a sin-offering. (3) A sin-offering whose owners have died. (4) A sin-offering whose owners have already gained atonement through another offering. (5) A sin-offering (of sheep or goats) which is more than a year old. Other authorities do not accept this classification in its entirety. See יִרְעֶה עַד שֶׁיִּסְתָּאֵב.

חַטָּאוֹת הַפְּנִימִיּוֹת   Lit., *inner sin-offerings.*

Sacrifices whose blood is sprinkled in the Sanctuary (הֵיכָל) or in the Holy of Holies (קֹדֶשׁ הַקֳּדָשִׁים), including the Yom Kippur bullock (פַּר) and goat (שְׂעִיר יוֹם הַכִּיפּוּרִים), whose blood is sprinkled between the staves of the ark (see בֵּין הַבַּדִּים), on the curtain (פָּרוֹכֶת) and on the golden altar (מִזְבַּח הַזָּהָב). Other such sacrifices are the bullock for unwitting communal sin (פַּר הֶעְלֵם דָּבָר), the bullock of the Anointed Priest (פַּר כֹּהֵן מָשִׁיחַ), and the goats of idol worship (שְׂעִירֵי עֲבוֹדָה זָרָה), whose blood is sprinkled on the curtain and on the golden altar. In all these cases, unlike other sacrifices, any omission in the ceremony of sprinkling the blood invalidates them. The remaining blood is poured on the western base of the outer altar, and the meat of these sacrifices is not eaten but burned in the place where the ashes are deposited (see בֵּית הַדֶּשֶׁן), after being cut into pieces, with all its inner parts and excreta. Ordinary sin-offerings are occasionally called "outer sin-offerings" (חַטָּאוֹת חִיצוֹנִיּוֹת) in contrast to these "inner" ones.

חַטָּאוֹת הַצִּיבּוּר   *Communal sin-offerings.*

Sin-offerings brought on behalf of the community, in contrast to those brought by private individuals (see חַטָּאת). Some of these sacrifices were offered as part of the musaf (מוּסָף) offerings on Festivals and the New Moon (רֹאשׁ חוֹדֶשׁ). See שְׂעִיר רֹאשׁ חוֹדֶשׁ; שְׂעִירֵי הָרְגָלִים. See also פַּר הֶעְלֵם דָּבָר; שְׂעִיר יוֹם הַכִּיפּוּרִים.

חַטָּאת   *Sin-offering.*

A person who inadvertently committed a sin punishable by excision (כָּרֵת) must bring a sin-offering as atonement (see חַיָּיב חַטָּאת). Such a sin-offering brought by a private individual must be a female lamb or goat less than one year old. It must be slaughtered in the northern section of the Temple Courtyard and its blood received there (see קַבָּלָה). The blood is sprinkled on each of the four corners of the altar (see אַרְבַּע מַתָּנוֹת). The fats (אֵימוּרִים) of the sin-offering are burned on the altar, and its meat is eaten by the priests. Other sin-offerings are brought in certain cases as part of the purification ceremonies at the end of a period of ritual impurity (see טָהֳרַת הַזָּב; טָהֳרַת הַמְצוֹרָע). There are other sin-offerings to atone for the community (see חַטָּאוֹת הַצִּיבּוּר) and special sin-offerings are brought by the leaders of the people to atone for transgression (see שְׂעִיר נָשִׂיא). See also קָרְבָּן עוֹלֶה וְיוֹרֵד.

חַטַּאת הָעוֹף   *A bird sacrificed as a sin-offering.*

A sin-offering brought by poor people (see דַּלּוּת וְדַלֵּי דַלּוּת), in the case of a "sliding-scale" sacrifice (see קָרְבָּן עוֹלֶה וְיוֹרֵד). A bird is also brought as a sin-offering by a woman who has given birth (יוֹלֶדֶת), by a זָב and a זָבָה, and by a poor leper (מְצוֹרָע), at the end of their period of ritual impurity (see מְחוּסַר כַּפָּרָה), as well as by a Nazirite who became ritually impure. All cases of חַטַּאת הָעוֹף are accompanied by a bird sacrificed as a burnt-offering (see עוֹלַת הָעוֹף). The חַטַּאת הָעוֹף is killed by the priest with his fingernail (see מְלִיקָה), and its blood is sprinkled on the lower half of the altar in the southwestern corner, beneath the red dividing line (see חוּט הַסִּיקְרָא), so that all its blood drains to the foot of the altar. Birds sacrificed as sin-offerings belong entirely to the priests, and they alone are entitled to eat them. A non-priest (see זָר) who eats חַטַּאת הָעוֹף is guilty not only of eating forbidden sacrificial meat, but also of eating the meat of a bird that has not been ritually slaughtered (see שְׁחִיטָה). He thus receives two sets of lashes (see מַלְקוּת).

חַי נוֹשֵׂא אֶת עַצְמוֹ   Lit., *a living being carries itself.*

A principle relevant to the prohibition of carrying (הוֹצָאָה) on the Sabbath. A living being, especially a human being, "carries itself" and does not make itself a burden for a person carrying it. Accordingly, carrying a human being is not considered as an act of labor prohibited on the Sabbath by Torah law.

חִיבַּת הַקּוֹדֶשׁ   *The respect in which sacred objects are held.*

An object that has been consecrated for use as part of the sacrificial services in the Temple becomes capable of contracting ritual impurity like an item of food by the very fact of its consecration (חִיבַּת הַקּוֹדֶשׁ), even if, otherwise, it would not contract such impurity. Thus, items that are not food (such as the wood for the altar, or the incense), or items of food that have not been rendered capable of contracting ritual impurity by contact with water or other liquids (see הֶכְשֵׁר), once they are consecrated for use in the sacrificial services automatically become capable of contracting ritual impurity.

חַיָּה *An undomesticated mammal.* In contrast to the term בְּהֵמָה,• which refers to domesticated mammals, the term חַיָּה usually applies to mammals that are not normally raised by man — e.g., deer. There are some instances where the term חַיָּה is subsumed under the term בְּהֵמָה, and others where the reverse is the case. See also חַיָּה טְהוֹרָה.

חַיָּה טְהוֹרָה Lit., *a clean [kosher] undomesticated mammal.* An undomesticated mammal that chews the cud (מַעֲלָה גֵרָה) and has a cloven hoof (מַפְרִיס פַּרְסָה). The Torah (Deuteronomy 14:5) mentions seven species of kosher undomesticated mammals. However, the precise definition of some of the species remains unclear. There are two major differences between the laws governing a kosher domesticated mammal (בְּהֵמָה טְהוֹרָה•) and those governing a kosher undomesticated mammal, חַיָּה טְהוֹרָה: (1) The fat (חֵלֶב•) of a חַיָּה טְהוֹרָה may be eaten. (2) The blood of a חַיָּה טְהוֹרָה must be covered after slaughter (see כִּסּוּי הַדָּם). In all other respects the laws regarding a בְּהֵמָה טְהוֹרָה and a חַיָּה טְהוֹרָה are the same. See כּוֹי.

חַיָּיב חַטָּאת *Obligated to bring a sin-offering.* If a person inadvertently commits a transgression for which he would be liable to the penalty of excision (כָּרֵת•) had he committed it intentionally, he must bring a sin-offering (חַטָּאת•). Furthermore, the transgressor must have remained unaware of the sin until after committing the act (see הֶעְלֵם אֶחָד). The obligation to bring a sin-offering does not apply if the person was forced to commit the transgression (see אוֹנֶס). When the term חַיָּיב alone is used in the context of Sabbath prohibitions, the implication is חַיָּיב חַטָּאת, one is obligated to bring a sin-offering.

חֵיל *A low wall surrounding the Temple Courtyard and the buildings within it.* The חֵיל and the area within it was on a higher level of sanctity than the area of the Temple Mount outside it, and non-Jews and those ritually impure because of contact with a dead body were forbidden to enter there.

חִילּוּל (1) *Desecration.* Generally, a pejorative term applying to the profanation of something holy. For example: חִילּוּל הַשֵּׁם — the desecration of God's name; חִילּוּל שַׁבָּת — the desecration of the Sabbath. (2) *Redemption, secularization.* The term חִילּוּל also refers to the transfer of sanctity from consecrated articles to money or other objects, so that the previously consecrated object loses its sanctity. For example, the second tithe (מַעֲשֵׂר שֵׁנִי•) and the produce of fruit trees and vines in the fourth year after their planting (see נֶטַע רְבָעִי) are endowed with a certain degree of sanctity and must be eaten within Jerusalem. However, if it is impossible to bring that produce to Jerusalem, it may be exchanged for money, and its sanctity is transferred to those coins (see Deuteronomy 14:24–25).

חָכָם Lit., *wise man.* In the Talmud, a reference to a Sage learned in the Torah, Mishnah and Gemara. More particularly the term referred to a Sage who had been ordained (received סְמִיכַת זְקֵנִים•), while a scholar lacking that distinction was called a תַּלְמִיד• — a student. In later generations, scholars saw themselves as תַּלְמִידֵי חֲכָמִים — the students of the חֲכָמִים — and are referred to in this way (see תַּלְמִיד חָכָם).

חֲכָמִים עָשׂוּ חִיזּוּק לְדִבְרֵיהֶם Lit., *the Sages reinforced their words.* A Halakhic argument. In many instances, the Sages reinforced the prohibitions and practices they instituted so that they would not be treated lightly. In certain cases, Rabbinic enactments were given the same or even greater severity than Torah law.

חֵלֶב Lit., *fat.* Animal fats prohibited by Torah law (in contrast to שׁוּמָן, which refers to permitted fats). Intentionally eating such fat of kosher domesticated mammals (see בְּהֵמָה טְהוֹרָה•) is punishable by excision (כָּרֵת•). (Leviticus 7:22–25.) A sin-offering (חַטָּאת•) must be brought for partaking of it inadvertently. The fat of undomesticated kosher mammals (see חַיָּה טְהוֹרָה•) and of kosher birds (see עוֹף טָהוֹר) may be eaten. Among the signs differentiating חֵלֶב from שׁוּמָן is the fact that חֵלֶב lies above the meat and is not intertwined with it. It is enclosed by a thin membrane and is easily peeled away from the meat. Most of the חֵלֶב of a sacrificial animal was offered on the altar (see אֵימוּרִים). However, the terms אֵימוּרִים and חֵלֶב are not synonymous. Some forbidden fats were not consumed on the altar and the אֵימוּרִים consisted of other elements in addition to forbidden fats.

חֲלָדָה Lit., *thrusting underneath, concealing.* A defect in the act of ritual slaughter (שְׁחִיטָה•) of an animal or a bird, which renders the slaughter invalid and causes the animal or the bird to be forbidden to be eaten (see נְבֵלָה). Instead of the esophagus and the windpipe being severed from above, חֲלָדָה involves inserting the slaughtering knife into the animal's neck between the esophagus and the windpipe and severing one of these organs from below.

חַלָּה Lit., *cake, loaf.* The Torah commands the giving of a portion of dough to the priests (Numbers 15:20). This portion is called חַלָּה and is governed by all the rules pertaining to תְּרוּמָה•, the priests' portion of the crop. The Torah does not specify a measure for חַלָּה. The Sages required a private person to give one twenty-fourth of his dough, and a commercial baker one forty-eighth. חַלָּה must be taken from all dough made from any one of the five types of grain (חֲמִישָׁה מִינֵי דָגָן•), provided that the quantity of flour is at least a tenth of an אֵיפָה in volume (see section on weights and measures, p. 288). If חַלָּה is not taken, the dough is considered untithed produce (טֶבֶל•), and may not be eaten. Nowadays, since all Jews have the status of being ritually impure, חַלָּה is governed by the same laws as ritually impure תְּרוּמָה and must be burned. Accordingly, the measures mentioned above no longer apply — only a small portion is separated from the dough and burned, and the rest of the dough may then be used. A blessing is recited for the separation of חַלָּה. חַלָּה is considered one of the mitzvot practiced particularly by women, who are familiar with its observance. The laws governing this mitzvah are discussed comprehensively in tractate Ḥallah.

חֲלוּצָה *A woman, whose husband died without children, who has undergone the ceremony of חֲלִיצָה• with a brother of the deceased.* After חֲלִיצָה she is permitted to remarry, but she may not marry any one of her deceased husband's brothers; according to Rabbinic law a חֲלִיצָה has the same legal status as a divorcee and may not marry a priest.

חֲלִיפִין   Lit., *exchange*. A legal act of acquisition (see קִנְיָן) formalizing the transfer of ownership of an article. Once two parties agree on the barter of one article for another, the acquisition by one party of one of the articles through a recognized mode of acquisition (for example, by מְשִׁיכָה) automatically causes the second article to become the legal property of the other party. This principle is also the basis for the transfer of ownership by means of קִנְיָן אַגַּב סוּדָר, a symbolic form of barter that extends the principle of חֲלִיפִין to many formal legal acts of acquisition. There are differing views in the Talmud as to whether money and other things are able to be acquired by means of חֲלִיפִין or not.

חֲלִיצָה   Lit., *removal*. The ceremony that frees the widow of a man who died without children (see שׁוֹמֶרֶת יָבָם) from the obligation to marry one of her deceased husband's brothers (see יִבּוּם) and allows her to remarry (see Deuteronomy 25:7-10). The name חֲלִיצָה is derived from the central element of this ceremony, which involves the removal by the widow of a special sandal from the foot of one of her deceased husband's brothers. חֲלִיצָה must be performed before a Rabbinical Court. The laws governing this ceremony are discussed in detail in tractate *Yevamot*.

חָלָל   *A person rendered unfit for priesthood.* A son born to a priest and a woman whom the priest is forbidden to marry (a divorcee, a זוֹנָה, or a חֲלָלָה in the case of a common priest [כֹּהֵן הֶדְיוֹט], and also a widow in the case of a High Priest [כֹּהֵן גָּדוֹל]). Even though the priest is considered the father of the חָלָל, the חָלָל does not have the legal status of a priest but that of an Israelite. A daughter born of such a forbidden relationship is called a חֲלָלָה and may not marry a priest. Similarly, the daughter of a חָלָל and the widow of a חָלָל may not marry a priest.

חֲלַל חֶרֶב   Lit., *one that is slain with a sword* (Numbers 19:16). A term referring to metal articles that contracted ritual impurity from a dead body (אֲבִי אֲבוֹת הַטּוּמְאָה). Although objects that come into contact with a source of ritual impurity generally contract a lesser degree of ritual impurity than the source itself, this principle does not apply to metal objects. These contract the same degree of ritual impurity as the source with which they have come into contact. According to some authorities, this regulation applies to other utensils too (with the exception of earthenware vessels; see כְּלֵי חֶרֶס).

חֲלָלָה   *A woman disqualified from marrying a priest.* There are four kinds of חֲלָלָה: (1) A woman, forbidden to marry a priest, who nevertheless engages in sexual relations with him — e.g., a divorcee with a common priest (see גְּרוּשָׁה לְכֹהֵן), or a widow with a High Priest (see אַלְמָנָה לְכֹהֵן גָּדוֹל). (2) The daughter born of such a union. (3) The wife of the son born of such a union. (4) The daughter of the son born of such a union. See also חָלָל.

חֲמִשָּׁה דְּבָרִים   Lit., *five things*. The five general categories

of damages for which a person who injures another person (see חוֹבֵל) must reimburse him: נֶזֶק — injury; צַעַר — pain; בּוֹשֶׁת — humiliation; רִיפּוּי — medical costs; שֶׁבֶת — loss of livelihood. (See *Bava Kamma* 83b.)

חֲמִשָּׁה מִינֵי דָגָן   Lit., *the five types of grain*. Wheat, barley, spelt, oats, and rye. Only bread made from these types of grain requires the recitation of the blessing over bread (בִּרְכַּת הַמּוֹצִיא). A person who eats food — other than bread — made from these grains recites the blessing בּוֹרֵא מִינֵי מְזוֹנוֹת. It is only from products of these grains that חַלָּה is separated. These are the only grains that can be used for matzah, and they are also the only grains that can become חָמֵץ (leaven).

חֲמִשָּׁה סְלָעִים   *Five Sela'im*. The amount of money designated by the Torah to be given to a priest for the redemption of a firstborn male Israelite (see פִּדְיוֹן הַבֵּן; see also Numbers 18:15-16). Silver coins or their equivalent in goods (מְטַלְטְלִין) must be given for this sum. Immovable property (מְקַרְקְעֵי) may not be used for this purpose.

חָמָס   Lit., *violence*. The seizure of an object from its owner against his will, even though reimbursement was made.

חָמֵץ   *Grain that has become leavened*. (1) With reference to the Festival of Pesaḥ. It is forbidden to eat, benefit from or possess חָמֵץ throughout the Pesaḥ Festival. Eating חָמֵץ during Pesaḥ is punishable by excision (כָּרֵת). (See Exodus 12:19, 13:17; see also בַּל יֵרָאֶה וּבַל יִמָּצֵא.) (2) With reference to the meal-offerings (מְנָחוֹת). With the exception of the two loaves (שְׁתֵּי הַלֶּחֶם) offered on Shavuot and some of the loaves of the thanks-offering (תּוֹדָה), all the meal-offerings were unleavened. If they became leavened, they were invalid. This prohibition applied even to those portions of the meal-offerings eaten by the priests after the handful (קוֹמֶץ, see קְמִיצָה) of the meal-offering taken by the priest had been offered on the altar (Leviticus 2:11). (3) With reference to sacrifices burned on the altar. חָמֵץ may not be burned on the altar. The violation of this prohibition is punishable by lashes (Leviticus 2:11).

חָמֵץ נוּקְשֶׁה   Lit., *hardened leaven*. Leaven that is not suitable for consumption, e.g., glue made from flour. According to some opinions חָמֵץ נוּקְשֶׁה is only prohibited on Pesaḥ by Rabbinic decree, but all agree that it is forbidden under a lesser degree of severity than regular חָמֵץ.

חֲנוּכָּה   *Hanukkah*. A festival established by the Sages in commemoration of the purification and rededication of the Temple after the defeat of the Greeks (Hellenized Syrians) by the Maccabees (c. 165 B.C.E.), and in commemoration of the miracle that took place in kindling the lights in the Temple at that time. Ḥanukkah begins on the 25th of Kislev and lasts eight days. Candles are lit every evening after the reciting of special blessings. The accepted custom is to light a single candle on the first night, adding another candle on each successive night. הַלֵּל is recited each morning, and the prayer עַל הַנִּיסִים is added to Grace after Meals (בִּרְכַּת הַמָּזוֹן) and to the Amidah prayer (see שְׁמוֹנֶה עֶשְׂרֵה). Special readings from the Torah (see קְרִיאַת הַתּוֹרָה) and from the Books of the Prophets (see הַפְטָרָה) are also added.

There is no essential prohibition against doing work on Ḥanukkah, but it is customary to refrain from work for a certain time each evening while the candles are burning. During Ḥanukkah it is forbidden to fast or to deliver eulogies at funerals.

חֵנֶק   *Strangulation.* The least severe of the four types of capital punishment administered by the court (see **סַנְהֶדְרֵי קְטַנָּה**). Strangulation was performed by wrapping a scarf around the violator's neck and then pulling simultaneously at both ends till he expired. The following transgressors were to be executed by strangulation: a person who struck his father or mother (**•מַכֵּה אָבִיו וְאִמּוֹ**); a kidnapper (**•גּוֹנֵב נֶפֶשׁ**); a rebellious elder (**•זָקֵן מַמְרֵא**); a false prophet (**•נְבִיא שֶׁקֶר**); adulterers (see **אֵשֶׁת אִישׁ**); and a man who committed adultery with a priest's daughter (see **בַּת כֹּהֵן**).

חַסִימָה   *Muzzling.* It is forbidden to use an animal in any labor associated with food, such as threshing, and prevent it from eating the food. The violation of this prohibition is punishable by lashes (Deuteronomy 25:4).

חֲפִינָה   Lit., *taking a handful.* One of the labors performed by the High Priest (**•כֹּהֵן גָּדוֹל**) on Yom Kippur (**•יוֹם הַכִּפּוּרִים**). In performing **חֲפִינָה** he places his hands together and fills them with incense to be burned in the Holy of Holies (**•קֹדֶשׁ הַקֳּדָשִׁים**). (See Leviticus 16:12.) **חֲפִינָה** was considered one of the most difficult Temple services, because while the High Priest was gathering the incense, he also had to hold the receptacle in which the incense was to be placed.

חֲצִי נֶזֶק   *Half the damage.* The Sages explained that the owner of an ox (or any other animal) which had no history of causing malicious damage (see **תָּם** and **מוּעָד**) is only required to pay one-half of such damage maliciously caused by his animal to other animals or to human beings (see Exodus 21:35). The Sages debated whether the reason for the half damages was that the owner should really have been obligated to pay the entire sum and the Torah reduced his liability, or that no payment should really have been required at all and the Torah obligated him to pay this amount as a fine (**•קְנָס**). The owner of an animal which indirectly damaged property by causing clods of dirt or pebbles to fly while walking in its usual way (see **צְרוֹרוֹת**) must also pay half of the damage caused. This is an oral law transmitted to Moses at Sinai (**הֲלָכָה לְמֹשֶׁה מִסִּינַי**), and all agree that it is a case of reduced liability and not a fine.

חֲצִי שִׁיעוּר   Lit., *half the [legal] quantity.* Many of the Torah's prohibitions involve a specific measure of activity that may not be performed or quantity of food that may not be consumed. According to Torah law no punishment is administered if that measure or quantity is lacking. The Amoraim debated whether performing or consuming less than the required measure is prohibited by the Torah or is only forbidden by Rabbinic decree in order to prevent a person from transgressing the prohibition itself. In this context the term "half" is not meant to be taken literally, and implies any fraction of the forbidden measure or quantity.

חֶצְיוֹ עֶבֶד וְחֶצְיוֹ בֶּן חוֹרִין   Lit., *half of him is a slave and half of him is a free man.* A non-Jewish slave who was owned jointly by two or more Jewish masters and who was set free by one of them. The status of such an individual raises problems in many areas of Jewish law. Accordingly, the Sages decreed that the other owner(s) should be forced to free the slave and that the slave must reimburse him (them) for the financial loss incurred. See **שִׁפְחָה חֲרוּפָה**.

חֲצִיצָה   Lit., *intervening object.* This concept is applied, *inter alia:* (1) With reference to immersion in a **•מִקְוֶה** (ritual bath; see also **טְבִילָה**). Neither a person nor a utensil being immersed in a **מִקְוֶה** may have any object or substance (on the person or on the utensil) intervening between the person or the utensil and the water of the **מִקְוֶה**. If such an object does intervene, the immersion is invalid. Various measures are given in the Halakhic sources regarding the extent to which a substance must prevent contact between the person or object and the water according to Torah and Rabbinic law for the immersion to be ineffective. (2) With reference to the priestly service in the Temple. The service of a priest is rendered invalid if there are any foreign substances intervening between his person and the priestly garments he is wearing, or between his feet and the floor of the Temple, or between his hands and the vessels he holds during the offering of the sacrifices. (3) With reference to ritual impurity. See **חוֹצֵץ מִפְּנֵי הַטּוּמְאָה**.

חָצֵר   *Courtyard.* A courtyard or other area not built on, belonging to one or several owners. This concept is significant in several areas of the Halakhah. (1) With reference to the laws of acquisition (see **קִנְיָן**). A person's courtyard acquires for him. That is to say, an unowned object which is found in a person's courtyard enters the ownership of the owner of the courtyard without his having to perform any other formal act of acquisition. The manner of acquisition through a courtyard is unique, and occasionally the Sages also extend the principle governing it to places or objects that are not literally courtyards. The laws of acquisition distinguish between a guarded courtyard (**חָצֵר הַמִּשְׁתַּמֶּרֶת**) and an unguarded one. The former type is fenced and well locked, and it has a strong power of acquisition for its owner, whereas the latter type has less power to acquire for its owner. Similarly, there is a difference between a courtyard purposely guarded by its owner and one which is not purposely guarded. (2) With reference to the use of jointly owned property. This refers to a fenced courtyard, generally the area in front of a building where a number of families live. There are many detailed laws regarding the division of a courtyard among a number of heirs. Essentially a courtyard is divided according to the number of doors and each door is accorded a certain area for the purpose of entering and transferring goods. There are also many laws regarding the right to use various items within a courtyard, as well as the apportioning of a courtyard too small to be divided. These laws have ramifications in the case of vows (see **נֶדֶר** sworn by joint owners. (3) With reference to the Sabbath laws. Although a fenced courtyard in front of a house is considered a private domain (**רְשׁוּת הַיָּחִיד**), one may not carry things on the Sabbath from the houses to the courtyard or vice versa if it is shared by a number of residents. To overcome this difficulty, a "merging of courtyards" (**•עֵירוּב חֲצֵירוֹת**) can be arranged, making it permissible to carry within it and from the courtyard to the various houses. There is a difference in the Halakhah between a front courtyard through which people pass regularly and which is in constant use and a back courtyard (קַרְפֵּף•), which is mainly used for storage.

חֲקִירָה וּדְרִישָׁה   See שֶׁבַע חֲקִירוֹת; דְּרִישָׁה וַחֲקִירָה.

חֲרִישָׁה בְּשׁוֹר וּבַחֲמוֹר   Lit., *ploughing with an ox and an ass*. It is forbidden to work a team of animals comprising different species (Deuteronomy 22:10). The violation of this prohibition is punishable by lashes. See also כִּלְאֵי בְהֵמָה•.

חֵרֶם   *Ban, excommunication.* The partial or complete removal of a person from the community of the Jewish people as a punishment or as a means of exerting pressure upon him to change his behavior. There are degrees of severity in the imposition of a ban (see נִידּוּי•; שַׁמְתָּא). In its precise meaning, חֵרֶם refers to the most severe of these bans — excommunication from the Jewish people as a whole. A person in such a situation is no longer considered a member of the community. He is not included in a מִנְיָן• — a quorum for prayer — or any other religious activities. It is forbidden to stand within 4 cubits of him, or to have commercial dealings with him. The term חֵרֶם is also used with reference to the consecration of articles for Temple or priestly use (Leviticus 27:28–29). See חֶרְמֵי גָבוֹהַּ; חֶרְמֵי כֹהֲנִים.

חֶרְמֵי גָבוֹהַּ   *Articles consecrated for use in the Temple.* In this context the term חֵרֶם refers to a declaration that an article or property was consecrated for use in the Temple. Property

consecrated in this manner has the status of קָדְשֵׁי בֶדֶק הַבַּיִת•. See also עֲרָכִין•.

חֶרְמֵי כֹהֲנִים   *Articles or property consecrated for use by the priests.* Such consecration could come about in two ways: (1) A person could specifically consecrate his property for use by the priests. (2) Immovable property consecrated to the Temple and not redeemed in the Jubilee Year (יוֹבֵל•) would become the priests' property (see Leviticus 27:20–21; Numbers 18:14).

חֵרֵשׁ   *A deaf-mute.* The Halakhic definiton of a חֵרֵשׁ is a person who cannot speak and cannot hear. The legal status of such a person is limited. He is not obliged to perform any mitzvot, nor is he responsible for any damage he may cause or financial obligations he may incur. A female deaf-mute is governed by the same laws as a male. The Sages ordained that a deaf-mute may marry, and they accepted as Rabbinically valid a marriage between two deaf-mutes or between a deaf-mute and a normal person. These marriages present many Halakhic difficulties, particularly with reference to levirate marriage (יִבּוּם•).

חֵרֵשׁ, שׁוֹטֶה, וְקָטָן   *A deaf-mute, imbecile, or minor.* Members of these three categories are frequently grouped together because of their limited intellectual capacity and/or their inability to act responsibly. They are not obliged to perform mitzvot, nor are they held responsible for damage they may cause. They also lack the legal capacity to act as agents (see שְׁלִיחוּת•). Though all three are often considered as one category, there are many differences between the laws governing each of them (see their individual entries).

טְבוּל יוֹם   Lit., *one who has immersed himself during the day.* There are many instances of ritual impurity whose nullification requires two steps: (1) Immersion in a מִקְוֶה• (ritual bath). See טְבִילָה•. (2) The conclusion of the day on which the ritually impure person must immerse himself — i.e., nightfall. See הֶעֱרֵב שֶׁמֶשׁ•. During the period between immersion and nightfall, a certain measure of impurity remains. Thus, a טְבוּל יוֹם remains forbidden to eat sacrifices or terumah (תְּרוּמָה•) if he is a priest, but is permitted to eat nonconsecrated food and the second tithe (מַעֲשֵׂר שֵׁנִי•).

טְבִיחָה וּמְכִירָה   Lit., *slaughter and sale.* If a person stole an ox or a sheep and subsequently slaughtered or sold the animal, he has to reimburse its owner five times the value of the ox and four times the value of the sheep (Exodus 21:37; see also אַרְבָּעָה וַחֲמִשָּׁה•). The thief is obliged to pay this fine even if he did not personally sell or slaughter the animal, but merely instructed another person to do so. This is one of the few instances where

the Torah holds a person responsible for transgressions committed by his agent. See אֵין שָׁלִיחַ לִדְבַר עֲבֵירָה•.

טְבִילָה   *Immersion.* This term generally refers to the immersion of a person or an article in the waters of a מִקְוֶה• (ritual bath). This concept is applied, *inter alia:* (1) With reference to ritual purity. Immersion in a מִקְוֶה is the usual means whereby a person or article regains ritual purity after having been impure. The purification process for all forms of ritual impurity involves immersion in a מִקְוֶה, but in certain instances other ceremonies of purification are also required. (2) With reference to conversion to Judaism (גִּיּוּר•). Immersion in a מִקְוֶה is one of the fundamental acts in the conversion process for both men and women. Only after immersion is the convert considered a Jew. (3) With reference to the acquisition of non-Jewish slaves (see עֶבֶד כְּנַעֲנִי•). When a Jew purchased a non-Jew (man or woman) as a slave, the slave had to be immersed in a מִקְוֶה in order to acquire the new status of עֶבֶד כְּנַעֲנִי. Once an עֶבֶד כְּנַעֲנִי had undergone immersion in a מִקְוֶה he was obliged to observe all the Torah's prohibitions and to fulfill all those positive commandments that have no specific time for their performance. (4) With reference to the acquisition of utensils used in the preparation and eating of food. Such utensils acquired by a Jew from a non-Jew must be immersed in a מִקְוֶה before use.

טְבִיעוּת עַיִן   *Recognizing something by sight.* The ability to recognize or identify something even though it does not have any particular or distinguishing identifying marks (i.e., the ability to recognize an article or a person by its or his general appearance). The Sages also speak about טְבִיעוּת עֵינָא דְּקָלָא — recognizing a person by his voice. See סִימָן.

טֶבֶל   *Produce from which the priestly dues [see* תְּרוּמָה*] and the other tithes [*מַעַשְׂרוֹת*] have not been separated, or dough from which* חַלָּה *has not been separated.* The Torah prohibits the consumption of טֶבֶל. But once the tithes have been set aside, even though they have not yet been given to those for whom they are designated, the produce is no longer טֶבֶל and may be eaten.

טַבָּעוֹת   Lit., *rings.* Specifically this term is used to refer to an area in the Temple Courtyard in which twenty-four metal rings were fixed in the marble floor to secure the sacrificial animals while they were slaughtered. Each of the twenty-four priestly watches (see מִשְׁמָר) had a ring specifically designated for its use. (See plan of the Temple, p. 277.)

טָהֳרַת הַזָּב   *The purification of a* זָב *[someone suffering from gonorrhea].* The Torah (Leviticus 15:13-15) describes the purification process by which a זָב (and, similarly, a זָבָה) regains ritual purity. First, he (or she) must count "seven clean days" (שִׁבְעָה נְקִיִּים) in which no trace of the secretion is seen. Afterwards, he must immerse himself in spring water (מַיִם חַיִּים). (In this respect there is a difference between a זָב and a זָבָה. A זָבָה need not immerse herself in מַיִם חַיִּים to attain ritual purity. A מִקְוֶה [ritual bath] is sufficient.) After nightfall of the day of his immersion (see הֶעֱרֵב שֶׁמֶשׁ; טְבוּל יוֹם) he becomes ritually pure. But he may not enter the Temple or eat sacrificial food until he has brought a special purification sacrifice: a pair of doves (see קֵן), one for a sin-offering (see חַטַּאת הָעוֹף) and one for a burnt-offering (see עוֹלַת הָעוֹף).

טָהֳרַת הַמְצוֹרָע   *The purification of the leper* (מְצוֹרָע). The Torah (Leviticus 14) prescribes the following process by which a person previously afflicted with leprosy (צָרַעַת) regains ritual purity. After the priest has definitely established that the affliction has healed, he takes two kosher birds (see צִיפּוֹרֵי מְצוֹרָע), a piece of cedar wood, a hyssop branch, and a length of scarlet wool. One bird is slaughtered over a vessel filled with מַיִם חַיִּים (spring water). Afterwards, the live bird, together with the other articles, is dipped into the mixture of water and blood and this mixture is sprinkled seven times on the person seeking purification. His entire body is then shaved (see תִּגְלַחַת) and he immerses himself in a מִקְוֶה — ritual bath. (See also טְבִילָה.) This completes the first stage of the purification process. The leper then waits six days. On the seventh day, his entire body is again shaved and he then immerses himself in the מִקְוֶה a second time.

On the following day, he comes to the Temple and brings one male lamb as a guilt-offering (אָשָׁם), one female lamb as a sin-offering (חַטָּאת) and another male lamb as a burnt-offering (עוֹלָה), in addition to a meal-offering (see מְנָחוֹת) and a לוֹג — measure of oil. (If the person is poor, the value of the offering is reduced, and he can bring two birds in place of the two latter lambs.) The oil and the blood of the guilt-offering are then placed on certain parts of his body. This completes his purification process.

טָהֳרַת הַקּוֹדֶשׁ   *The purity applying to sacrificial foods.* Stricter rules governed the ritual purity of sacrificial foods than that of תְּרוּמָה — the portion of the crop given to the priest — or nonsacred foods (חוּלִין). Only sacrificial foods can become impure in the fourth degree (רְבִיעִי לְטוּמְאָה). Many of the pious would take upon themselves the practice of eating *all* foods with all the stringencies that applied to sacred foods (עַל טָהֳרַת הַקּוֹדֶשׁ).

טוֹבַת הֲנָאָה   *The value a person attaches to his right to distribute obligatory dues [e.g., the priestly and Levitical dues] to persons of his own choice.* See מַעַשְׂרוֹת and תְּרוּמָה. A person is not considered the full owner of the priestly and Levitical tithes he separates from his produce, since the Torah obliges him to give them to the priests and Levites. Nevertheless, he has the right to give the produce to the priest or Levite of his choice. Furthermore, there may be a financial advantage (טוֹבַת הֲנָאָה) attached to this right. Though a priest is forbidden to pay someone to give him תְּרוּמָה, another party may stipulate as part of a business agreement that תְּרוּמָה be given to a specific priest. The Sages debated whether the money value of טוֹבַת הֲנָאָה amounts to a kind of ownership and whether it can be used to acquire goods or money.

טוּמְאָה   *Ritual impurity.* One of the fundamental concepts in the Halakhah. An entire order of the Mishnah (טָהֳרוֹת), and many passages throughout the Talmud are devoted to this subject. טוּמְאָה is a unique Torah concept, unrelated to hygiene or utility, and it is placed in the category of חוּקִים — laws of the Torah which have no explanation. Usually טוּמְאָה is connected with death — of a person or an animal — or with illness. According to Torah law the impurity of a living person applies only to Jews. A ritually impure object is not in itself forbidden to be eaten or touched (see, however, בְּהֵמָה טְמֵאָה, where the term is used in an entirely different sense). Ritual impurity is the antithesis of holiness. A ritually impure person may not touch a holy object or eat it, or enter the Temple. Moreover, a priest and a Nazirite (see נְזִירוּת) are forbidden to become ritually impure through contact with a dead body, although they are not forbidden to become ritually impure by other means. There are various degrees of טוּמְאָה, depending on the nature of the source from which the impurity was contracted. A human corpse (אֲבִי אֲבוֹת הַטוּמְאָה) is the most severe category of ritual impurity. Not only does a person coming into contact with it become ritually impure, but he also has the potential to render others ritually impure. Similarly, other sources of ritual impurity are described under the heading אֲבוֹת הַטּוּמְאוֹת — i.e., ritual impurity one degree less than אֲבִי אֲבוֹת הַטּוּמְאָה. An object that comes into contact with an אַב טוּמְאָה is called רִאשׁוֹן לְטוּמְאָה — "an article of the first degree of ritual

impurity." An object that comes into contact with a רִאשׁוֹן
לְטוּמְאָה is referred to as שֵׁנִי לְטוּמְאָה• — "an article of the second
degree of ritual impurity." There is also a "third" (שְׁלִישִׁי לְטוּמְאָה•)
and a "fourth" (רְבִיעִי לְטוּמְאָה) degree of ritual impurity. A
nonsacred item of food (see חוּלִּין) can only contract ritual
impurity to the second degree, תְּרוּמָה can contract ritual
impurity to the third degree, and sacrificial foods (קָדָשִׁים) can
contract ritual impurity to the fourth degree. An article which
itself becomes ritually impure but which does not impart ritual
impurity is referred to as פָּסוּל•.

טוּמְאָה בְּחִיבּוּרִים   *Ritual impurity acquired through a*
chain of contact. For example, if people were holding on to each
other in a chain and one of them came into contact with a dead
body, they would all be considered ritually impure, regardless of
how many people were involved. This law is a Rabbinic decree.

טוּמְאָה דְּחוּיָה בְּצִיבּוּר   Lit., *ritual impurity is suspended*
for a community. If the majority of the people or the majority of
the priests are ritually impure, the Temple service continues to
be performed despite this ritual impurity. This lenient provision
applies only to communal sacrifices and to the Paschal sacrifice.
Individual sacrifices may not be offered in such circumstances.

טוּמְאָה יְשָׁנָה   *Previous [lit., old] ritual impurity.* The
fragments of an article that was ritually impure and was broken
or destroyed are no longer considered ritually impure.
Nevertheless, the Sages decreed that the fragments of a ritually
impure metal utensil would retain their previous ritual impurity
if they were later fashioned into another utensil. Certain Sages
maintained that this only applied to articles that had become
ritually impure as a result of contact with a dead body.

טוּמְאָה רְצוּצָה   Lit., *pressed ritual impurity.* A dead body (or
part of a dead body) located under a roof or a covering (see אֹהֶל
הַמֵּת) only imparts ritual impurity to objects under that covering;
anything above the covering remains ritually pure. This only
applies, however, if there is a handbreadth (טֶפַח•) of space
between the dead body and the roof or covering. If there is no
such space, the dead body is considered "pressed" (רְצוּצָה), as it
were, against the roof, and the ritual impurity passes through the
roof and rises upwards indefinitely.

טוּמְאַת אוֹכְלִין   *Ritual impurity of foods.* Foods, depending
on their level of sanctity, can contract different levels of ritual
impurity, from אֲבוֹת• — רִאשׁוֹן לְטוּמְאָה — the first degree, after
הַטּוּמְאוֹת — רְבִיעִי לְטוּמְאָה — to, in the case of sacrificial food,
the fourth degree. Food can never become an אַב הַטּוּמְאָה — a
primary source of ritual impurity. Thus, a person or a utensil can
impart ritual impurity to foods, but foods cannot impart ritual
impurity to a person, unless he eats them. Similarly, foods cannot
impart ritual impurity to other foods, but they can impart ritual
impurity to liquids. An item of food cannot impart ritual impurity
unless it is at least the size of an egg (see בֵּיצָה). Certain
authorities maintain that it also cannot contract ritual impurity
unless it is at least that size.

טוּמְאַת הַתְּהוֹם   *Ritual impurity imparted by a grave that is*
deep in the ground. A special principle applied to a grave

discovered in a place where people had no previous knowledge
of its existence. If a Nazirite (see נְזִירוּת) passes over such a grave
unknowingly and becomes aware of its existence only after his
Nazirite vow is completed, he is not considered to have
contracted ritual impurity. The same principle applies if a person
bringing a Paschal sacrifice (פֶּסַח•) passes over such a grave and
becomes aware of it only after offering his sacrifice. It is an oral
law transmitted to Moses at Sinai (הֲלָכָה לְמֹשֶׁה מִסִּינַי) that the
צִיץ•, the front plate worn by the High Priest on his forehead,
atones for this inadvertent transgression.

טוּמְאַת יָדַיִם   *Ritual impurity of hands.* A Rabbinic decree
declaring that a person's hands are presumed to be שֵׁנִי
לְטוּמְאָה• — on the second level of ritual impurity — if (1) he was not
careful to preserve their ritual purity; (2) they came into contact
with any article that would make terumah (תְּרוּמָה•) unfit to be
eaten; or (3) he touched scrolls of the Bible. Hands that have
contracted ritual impurity can regain ritual purity through נְטִילַת
יָדַיִם• — the ritual washing of hands.

טוּמְאַת מַגָּע   *Ritual impurity imparted by contact.* Physical
contact with a source of ritual impurity can transfer this impurity
from one article to another. Almost all forms of ritual impurity
can be transferred in this manner. For certain types of ritual
impurity, this is the only means whereby the impurity can be
transferred.

טוּמְאַת מִדְרָס   Lit., *ritual impurity [imparted] by treading.* A
form of ritual impurity imparted by a זָב• — a man suffering from
gonorrhea; a זָבָה• — a woman suffering from a menstrual-type
flow of blood when not menstruating; a יוֹלֶדֶת• — a woman after
childbirth; and a נִדָּה• — a menstruating woman. The זָב (and the
others mentioned above) renders objects on which he stands,
sits, lies, or leans ritually impure. Such an object is called מִדְרָס
הַזָּב, and is of the same category of אַב הַטּוּמְאָה — "a primary
source of ritual impurity" — as the זָב himself (see אֲבוֹת הַטּוּמְאוֹת).
It imparts ritual impurity to people (or objects) who carry it or
touch it (see טוּמְאַת מַגָּע, טוּמְאַת מַשָּׂא). Only objects which are
specifically intended for sitting or lying upon can become a מִדְרָס
הַזָּב; other objects upon which a זָב stands or sits become ritually
impure, but are only considered to be רִאשׁוֹן לְטוּמְאָה• — "impure
in the first degree."

טוּמְאַת מִקְדָּשׁ וְקָדָשָׁיו   *Ritual impurity with regard to the*
Sanctuary and its sacred articles. The Torah forbids a person who
is ritually impure to eat consecrated food (Leviticus 7:19-20),
and prohibits a person from entering the Temple while ritually
impure (Numbers 19:20). If a person deliberately commits either
of these transgressions, he is liable to excision (כָּרֵת•). If he
transgresses these commandments inadvertently, he must bring
a sacrifice as atonement. The nature of this sacrifice depends on
the financial state of the person bringing it (see קָרְבָּן עוֹלֶה וְיוֹרֵד•).
There is a unique aspect of the inadvertent transgression of
these commandments. To be obligated to bring a sacrifice a
person must first, before committing the transgression, have
been aware both of his personal state and of the sanctity of the
Temple or of the consecrated foods involved. He must then have
forgotten one of the factors while committing the transgression,
and must have remembered it afterwards. If he was unaware of

both of them before committing the transgression, even if he became aware of them afterwards, he does not bring a sacrifice. See הֶעְלֵם אֶחָד; הֶעְלֵם טוּמְאָה; הֶעְלֵם מִקְדָּשׁ.

טוּמְאַת מַשָּׂא *Ritual impurity imparted by carrying.* There are certain primary sources of ritual impurity (אֲבוֹת הַטּוּמְאוֹת) that impart this impurity when a person carries them, even though he does not touch them directly. The אֲבוֹת הַטּוּמְאוֹת that impart ritual impurity in this manner are: (1) the carcass of an animal (see טוּמְאַת נְבֵלָה); (2) an article on which a זָב sat or lay (see טוּמְאַת מִדְרָס); (3) a זָב himself; (4) a person afflicted with leprosy (see צָרַעַת); (5) a number of the אֲבוֹת הַטּוּמְאוֹת associated with a human corpse.

טוּמְאַת מֵת *Ritual impurity imparted by a corpse.* Corpses are the ultimate primary source of ritual impurity (אֲבִי אֲבוֹת הַטּוּמְאָה), and a person or object rendered ritually impure by a corpse becomes a primary source of ritual impurity (אַב הַטּוּמְאָה, see אֲבוֹת הַטּוּמְאוֹת) and imparts that ritual impurity to people and garments for a period of seven days. A corpse imparts ritual impurity by contact and by being carried, and also, uniquely, by what is known as "tent impurity" (see אֹהֶל הַמֵּת). This ritual impurity is caused not only by a whole corpse but also by parts of a dead body, though there are many complex rules and regulations regarding the parts of a body considered important enough to impart this form of ritual impurity. Many authorities argue, and this is also the conclusion of the Halakhah, that only Jewish corpses cause "tent impurity." Another peculiarity regarding the ritual impurity caused by corpses is that a metal utensil or vessel that comes into direct contact with a corpse takes on the status of the corpse itself and causes anyone who touches it or comes under the same roof as it to become ritually impure in the category of an אַב הַטּוּמְאָה. The laws of the ritual impurity of a corpse are mainly presented in tractate *Ohalot.*

טוּמְאַת נְבֵלָה *Ritual impurity imparted by the carcass of an animal.* The carcass (or a portion of a carcass the size of an olive, כְּזַיִת) of any non-kosher or kosher animal (if the latter was not ritually slaughtered) imparts ritual impurity to a person or to utensils if touched (see טוּמְאַת מַגָּע), and to a person if carried (see טוּמְאַת מַשָּׂא). The clothes of the person touching or carrying the carcass also become ritually impure. The ritual impurity imparted by a נְבֵלָה lasts for one day (see טוּמְאַת עֶרֶב). The concept of טוּמְאַת נְבֵלָה applies to the carcasses of domesticated (בְּהֵמָה) and undomesticated (חַיָּה) mammals only. Different rules apply to the carcasses of kosher birds (see נִבְלַת עוֹף טָהוֹר) and to certain reptiles and rodents (see שְׁמוֹנָה שְׁרָצִים). All other animal carcasses, e.g., non-kosher birds, fish, insects, and most reptiles do not impart ritual impurity. A person who contracts this ritual impurity can regain ritual purity by טְבִילָה, immersing himself in a מִקְוֶה (ritual bath). His ritual purity is restored at nightfall following his immersion.

טוּמְאַת עֲבוֹדָה זָרָה *Ritual impurity imparted by idol worship.* The Sages decreed that a person contracts ritual impurity by touching an idol or statue that is the object of idol worship. The Tannaim debated whether the idol imparts ritual impurity in the same manner as a נִדָּה — a menstruating woman — or as a שֶׁרֶץ — a ritually impure reptile or rodent. (See שְׁמוֹנָה

שְׁרָצִים.) Similarly, articles used in idol worship, the remains of idolatrous sacrifices, and the remains of idolatrous libations also impart ritual impurity.

טוּמְאַת עֶרֶב *Ritual impurity that lasts only until the evening.* Certain types of ritual impurity last for the duration of one day. A person who contracts such ritual impurity immerses himself in a ritual bath (מִקְוֶה, see also טְבִילָה), and waits until the day has passed (see הֶעֱרֵב שֶׁמֶשׁ). He regains his ritual purity at nightfall following the day on which he became impure. טוּמְאַת עֶרֶב is a mild form of ritual impurity. See טוּמְאַת שִׁבְעָה.

טוּמְאַת שִׁבְעָה *Ritual impurity that lasts for seven days.* A person who contracts a severe form of ritual impurity, for example, a person who has sexual relations with a נִדָּה — a menstruating woman — or a person who contracts ritual impurity from a human corpse (see טוּמְאַת מֵת), must wait at least seven days before he can regain ritual purity.

טוּמְטוּם Lit., *covered, hidden.* A person (or an animal) whose sexual organs from birth are concealed or are so undeveloped that it is impossible to determine whether the person is male or female. See אַנְדְּרוֹגִינוֹס.

טוֹפֶס *A formula, the blank part of a document.* The section of a legal document that contains the standard phraseology appropriate to that document, but which has not yet been filled in with the required information (exact names, date, etc.), called the תּוֹרֶף.

טִירְפָּא *A document giving the right to seize the property a debtor sold after taking a loan.* If a borrower has mortgaged his property to a lender as security for a loan and has formalized the mortgage in a contract, the lender may seize the property in lieu of payment, even if the property was subsequently sold to another person, provided that the borrower has no other resources with which to repay the debt. A טִירְפָּא is the document issued by the court giving the lender the right to seize such property. In such an instance, the purchaser of the property from the borrower can seek reimbursement only from the borrower who sold it to him. See אַדְרַכְתָּא.

טָמוּן בָּאֵשׁ *A hidden article damaged by fire.* A person who starts a fire is not responsible for articles destroyed by the fire, if such articles would not normally be placed in the place where the fire occurred. For example, if a wallet containing money is buried in a pile of agricultural produce, a person who destroys the produce by fire is liable for the value of the produce, but not for the money buried there.

טְעִינָה Lit., *loading.* The Torah requires a person who sees an animal that has fallen under its load to help its master reload it (Exodus 23:5). See also פְּרִיקָה.

טַעֲנַת בְּתוּלִים Lit., *a claim concerning virginity.* The claim made by a man who married a woman under the assumption that she was a virgin and composed her marriage contract (כְּתוּבָּה) accordingly, but discovered when consummating the marriage that she was not a virgin. The husband may make this claim in order to reduce the financial obligation he accepted in the marriage contract, or his purpose may be to nullify the marriage as having been entered into under false premises (see מֶקַח טָעוּת). This subject is discussed in tractate *Ketubot*, chapter 1.

טֶפַח (pl. טְפָחִים) *A handbreadth.* One of the measures of length frequently used in the Talmud. According to some modern Halakhic opinions the length of a טֶפַח is 3.78 inches/9.6 centimeters, and according to others 3.15 inches/8 centimeters. This measure is applied, *inter alia*: (1) With reference to ritual impurity. An opening the size of a cubic טֶפַח is of fundamental importance in many laws concerning ritual impurity imparted by a human corpse (see פּוֹתֵחַ טֶפַח). (2) With reference to the concept לָבוּד°. Two solid surfaces are considered to be connected if there is a gap of less than 3 טְפָחִים between them. The concept לָבוּד is found with reference to the construction of the walls of a sukkah (סוּכָּה°). (3) In determining what constitutes a "significant area" (מָקוֹם חָשׁוּב). Four טְפָחִים square is the minimum area to have this status. (4) With reference to height, the

Halakhah recognizes 10 טְפָחִים as the minimum for a partition (מְחִיצָה°), a house (בַּיִת°), or a pit (בּוֹר°).

טְרֵפָה *An animal torn by a beast of prey, or afflicted with a severe organic disease or congenital defect.* Halakhically, a live kosher animal or bird suffering from a wound or illness that will cause it to die within twelve months. Such an animal is forbidden to be eaten (see Exodus 22:30) even after proper ritual slaughter (שְׁחִיטָה°). The Sages described in detail the possible illnesses and defects that could render an animal טְרֵפָה. In most cases they do not require that the organs of a properly slaughtered animal be checked for these defects. A notable exception is the lungs. Since lesions and adhesions are common in the lungs, they are customarily checked. The concept of טְרֵפָה is also applied to human beings suffering from a fatal wound or defect. In certain circumstances, for instance, in the laws of murder and the laws of testimony (see *Sanhedrin* 78a), different rules may be applied to such individuals from those applied to healthy people.

יֵאוּשׁ Lit., *despair.* יֵאוּשׁ refers to the owner's despair of recovering an article that was lost or stolen. A lost article whose owner has given up hope of its recovery is considered ownerless (הֶפְקֵר°) and may be acquired by the finder. If an article is lost in a natural disaster, e.g., a flood, it is considered as if the owner despaired of its recovery immediately. With reference to stolen property, the owner's despair of the article's return removes his ownership over the property and allows it to be acquired by the person to whom it is given or sold by the thief. In such a case, the article itself need not be returned to its original owner. However, the thief himself is required to return the object if he has it, or to reimburse the owner for its value. (See שִׁינּוּי°.)

יֵאוּשׁ שֶׁלֹּא מִדַּעַת Lit., *unknowing despair.* The Sages debated whether an article lost by a person, which he could never hope to recover, is immediately considered as ownerless (הֶפְקֵר°), even though the owner has not yet become aware of his loss. Some Sages maintain that as soon as the article is lost, it may be acquired by another person. The Halakhah, however, is that until the owner discovers (and despairs of) his loss, the article remains his property.

יִבּוּם *Levirate marriage.* A man whose brother died without children is obliged by Torah law to marry his deceased brother's widow or grant her *ḥalitzah* (חֲלִיצָה°; see Deuteronomy 25:5–10). As long as neither יִבּוּם nor חֲלִיצָה has taken place, she is forbidden to marry another person (see זִיקָה°; שׁוֹמֶרֶת יָבָם). According to the Torah, יִבּוּם is effected by the act of sexual intercourse (בִּיאָה°). The Sages, however, instituted the practice

of *ma'amar* (מַאֲמָר°), in which the deceased husband's brother, the יָבָם, betroths the widow (see אֵירוּסִין; קִידּוּשִׁין°), even though this betrothal is not effective by Torah law without intercourse. Sexual relations consummate the marriage between the deceased's brother and the widow and she is thereafter considered his wife in all respects. A גֵּט° (bill of divorce) is necessary to formalize their divorce. Today, in most Jewish communities the יָבָם is required to free his brother's widow of her obligation through חֲלִיצָה, and he is not permitted to marry her through יִבּוּם.

יָבָם See יִבּוּם.

יָד Lit., *hand.* (1) With reference to the laws of acquisition, יָד describes something in a person's possession that is considered a legal extension of the person himself. Objects that are transferred to a person's יָד are considered as if they have been physically handed over to the person himself. This extension of the concept of יָד does not apply to everybody, and it is uncertain whether a person who lacks a complete legal personality can acquire property through the institution of יָד. A person acting on another's behalf may be considered as the latter's יָד. Thus charitable overseers and a Rabbinical Court are called יְדֵי עֲנִיִּים — "the hands of the poor." Despite the similarity between the concepts of יָד and חָצֵר° ("courtyard"), there are certain Halakhic differences between them. (2) With reference to the laws of ritual impurity, יָד means something by means of which something else is held. It is considered like the object held and contracts ritual impurity together with it. See also יָדוֹת אוֹכְלִין.

יָדוֹת   Lit., *hands*. An expression describing a form of words used by a person conveying a certain intention that can be understood from the context or from the general subject of the words said, but which is not clearly and explicitly expressed. In certain areas of the Halakhah, such as the laws of the Nazirite (see נְזִירוּת), vows (see נֶדֶר), marriage, divorce, and others, the Sages inquire whether יָדוֹת should be regarded as explicit statements.

יָדוֹת אוֹכָלִין   Lit., *handles of food*. Something that is itself inedible but is used to hold on to the edible part of food. In certain instances, these inedible parts are considered as part of the food and may thus contract ritual impurity. In other cases they may even serve to increase the food's volume to the minimum size liable to contract ritual impurity (see טוּמְאַת אוֹכָלִין). This subject is discussed primarily in the tractate *Uktzin*.

יָדַיִם עַסְקָנִיּוֹת הֵן   Lit., *hands are busy*. The Halakhic principle explaining the requirement for washing hands even though one is not sure whether they have contracted ritual impurity or come in contact with dirt. Since a person constantly handles and touches things without necessarily paying attention to what he is doing, it is presumed inevitable that his hands have become dirty or ritually impure.

יְדִיעָה לַחֲצִי שִׁיעוּר   Lit., *knowledge [coming after] half the quantity*. A person is liable to bring a sin-offering (חַטָּאת) for the inadvertent violation of a serious transgression (see כָּרֵת) if he completes that particular, forbidden, activity or consumes a minimum amount of that particular, forbidden, food. The concept יְדִיעָה לַחֲצִי שִׁיעוּר revolves around the following question: Must a person bring such a sacrifice if he became aware of the transgression before consuming the minimum amount of food or completing the minimum activity for which the sin-offering is required? In such a situation, some Sages free the person of the obligation to bring a sacrifice, even if he subsequently again forgot the nature of the sin and inadvertently completed the transgression.

יְדִיעוֹת הַטּוּמְאָה   Lit., *the knowledge of impurity*. A person is not obligated to bring a sacrifice for inadvertently entering the Temple or eating consecrated foods when ritually impure, unless he was aware both of his state of ritual impurity and of the sanctity of the Temple or the consecrated food before and after the inadvertent transgression, but forgot one or the other while committing the transgression.
See הֶעְלֵם טוּמְאָה; טוּמְאַת מִקְדָּשׁ וְקָדָשָׁיו.

יֵהָרֵג וְאַל יַעֲבוֹר   Lit., *let him be killed, and let him not transgress*. A term that expresses a Jew's obligation to sacrifice his life to sanctify God's name rather than violate certain commandments. Generally, if forced to commit a sin on pain of death, a Jew need not (and according to certain opinions, must not) sacrifice his life rather than commit the sin. Similar principles permit a person to violate Torah laws because of life-threatening illness. However, there are certain exceptions: (1) With regard to idol worship (עֲבוֹדָה זָרָה), murder (שְׁפִיכוּת דָּמִים) and forbidden sexual relations (גִּילּוּי עֲרָיוֹת); in these cases a Jew must be prepared to sacrifice his life rather than commit the

transgression. (2) Instances in which the transgression is to be performed in public and the person threatening to kill the Jew seeks no personal benefit by forcing him to sin, but rather his intent is to cause the Jew to abandon his faith. (3) In times of mass persecution when Jews are forced to abandon their faith (see שְׁמָד), a Jew is obligated to sacrifice his life rather than transgress even minor commandments or Jewish customs.

יוֹבֵל   *The Jubilee Year*. The fiftieth year, the one following seven Sabbatical cycles of seven years, has a unique status. All the agricultural laws that are followed in the Sabbatical Year (שְׁבִיעִית) must also be observed in the Jubilee Year. In addition, all Jewish slaves (including those who agreed to continue in servitude beyond their initial obligation) are freed, and fields that have been sold are returned to their original owners (see Leviticus 25). The freeing of the slaves and the return of the fields take place after Yom Kippur (יוֹם הַכִּיפּוּרִים). On Yom Kippur of that year, special prayers are recited and the shofar is sounded in a manner similar to that practiced on Rosh HaShanah. The יוֹבֵל is only observed when the majority of the Jewish people are living in Israel. Hence, its observance was discontinued during the First Temple period and was never renewed.

יוֹלֶדֶת   *A woman who gave birth*. The Torah describes various regulations governing a woman who gave birth naturally (as opposed to Caesarean section). She is considered ritually impure for seven days if she gave birth to a boy, and for fourteen days if she gave birth to a girl. Later, after immersion in a מִקְוֶה (ritual bath; see also טְבִילָה), she is ritually pure for the next thirty-three and sixty-six days, respectively, even if she discovers uterine bleeding (see דַּם טוֹהַר). Nevertheless, during this period of forty days for a boy and eighty days for a girl, she is forbidden to enter the Temple and to partake of the meat of sacrifices. From the fortieth (or eightieth) day after the birth, she must offer a purification sacrifice in the Temple. This sacrifice consists of a lamb less than one year old for a burnt-offering (עוֹלָה), and a young pigeon or turtledove for a sin-offering (חַטָּאת). If she cannot afford the cost of a lamb for the burnt-offering, she can bring two turtledoves or two young pigeons, one for a burnt-offering and the other for a sin-offering. She may then enter the Temple and partake of sacrificial foods. (See Leviticus 12:1-8.)

יוֹלִיךְ לְיַם הַמֶּלַח   *Let him cast it into the Dead Sea*. A figurative expression for the disposal of articles from which a person is forbidden to benefit (see אִיסּוּרֵי הֲנָאָה), particularly things associated with idol worship (see עֲבוֹדָה זָרָה). If they could not be burned (see נִשְׂרָפִין) or buried (see נִקְבָּרִין), they would be cast into the sea. Any sea, not only the Dead Sea, could be used for this purpose.

יוֹם הַכִּיפּוּרִים   *The Day of Atonement, Yom Kippur*. The Torah describes the unique service carried out in the Temple on the 10th of Tishri (Yom Kippur) and establishes it as a day of fasting and atonement (Leviticus 16). All the acts of work prohibited on the Sabbath are also forbidden on Yom Kippur. However, the punishment for the violation of these laws is different: The violation of the Sabbath laws is punishable by execution by an earthly court, while the violation of the Yom

Kippur laws is punishable by excision (*כָּרֵת*). In addition to the prohibition against work on Yom Kippur, it is forbidden to eat or drink, to wear leather shoes, to wash, to anoint oneself with oil, or to engage in sexual relations. (See *תַּעֲנִית צִיבּוּר*.) On Yom Kippur, God forgives the Jewish people, both for not fulfilling positive commandments and for transgressing negative commandments, whether deliberately or inadvertently. However, Yom Kippur does not provide atonement for sins against one's fellowman, unless there is prior reconciliation between the parties. There are five prayer services on Yom Kippur, including a special concluding service (*נְעִילָה*). *וִידּוּי* — the confessional prayer — is recited in each of these services. The Temple service on Yom Kippur was conducted exclusively by the High Priest (*כֹּהֵן גָּדוֹל*). It contained many unique elements and was distinguished by a number of special sacrifices. (See *שָׂעִיר הַמִּשְׁתַּלֵּחַ*; *שָׂעִיר יוֹם הַכִּיפּוּרִים*; *פַּר יוֹם הַכִּיפּוּרִים*.) During some of these special parts of the Temple service the High Priest would enter the Holy of Holies (*קֹדֶשׁ הַקֳּדָשִׁים*) dressed in special white garments (*בִּגְדֵי לָבָן*). The laws and practices of Yom Kippur are discussed in great detail in tractate *Yoma*.

יוֹם הַכְּנִיסָה Lit., *the day of gathering*. Monday and Thursday, the days on which people living in villages would gather in larger towns. The Torah was read in the synagogue on these days, which were fixed as the days when the courts would hold their sessions. Accordingly, the weddings of virgin brides were held on Wednesdays, in case the groom should lodge a complaint against his bride (see *טַעֲנַת בְּתוּלִים*). It was customary to read the *Megillah* (the Scroll of Esther) on these days before Purim for the benefit of those villagers who would otherwise not be present at its reading. Today, most of the special practices associated with יוֹם הַכְּנִיסָה are no longer followed. Only the Torah reading and the recitation of a longer form of *Taḥanun* (*תַּחֲנוּן*).

יוֹם הֶנֶף Lit., *the day of waving [the omer]*. The 16th of Nisan, the day the omer (*עוֹמֶר*), the first offering of barley, was brought to the Temple. Only after this offering had been brought was it permitted to eat *חָדָשׁ*, the new produce recently harvested. After the destruction of the Second Temple, the prohibition was extended to the whole day on the 16th of Nisan. Thus, it is forbidden to eat such produce until the 17th of Nisan.

יוֹם טְבוֹחַ Lit., *a day of slaughtering*. If the Festival of Shavuot fell on a Sabbath, the burnt-offerings (see *עוֹלַת רְאִיָּה*) and peace-offerings (*שַׁלְמֵי חֲגִיגָה*) required to be brought to the Temple on the Festival by a pilgrim were sacrificed on the following day, יוֹם טְבוֹחַ.

יוֹם טוֹב A Festival [mentioned in the Torah]. This term specifically refers to the following Festivals: Pesaḥ (the first and seventh days), Shavuot, Rosh HaShanah, and Sukkot (the first and eighth days). In certain contexts, the term is also applied to Yom Kippur. Though each Festival has unique aspects and laws of its own, they all share the same general status and certain laws apply to all of them. Among these are: (1) The prohibition of all acts of work forbidden on the Sabbath, with the exception of those associated with preparing food (e.g., cooking) or transferring articles from one domain to another. The violation of this prohibition is punishable by lashes. (2) The obligation to

rejoice together with one's family. (3) The sacrifice of special additional Festival-offerings in the Temple and the recitation of special musaf prayers (see *מוּסָף*). The laws concerning Festivals are discussed mainly in tractate *Betzah*.

יוֹם טוֹב שֵׁנִי שֶׁל גָּלוּיּוֹת The second day of a Festival, observed in the Diaspora. Originally, the Hebrew calendar was fixed in accordance with the testimony of witnesses who had seen the new moon. This information could not always be communicated to the Jews living in the Diaspora in time for them to know the proper day on which to celebrate the Festivals. Accordingly, the Sages instituted that the observance of each Festival be extended to two days in the Diaspora because of this doubt. Even after a fixed calendar was instituted, the observance of the second day in the Diaspora was continued. The second day of יוֹם טוֹב is observed in exactly the same manner as the first except with regard to burial of the dead, and the Torah and Haftarah readings in the synagogue (see also *שְׁמִינִי עֲצֶרֶת*). Because of the practical difficulties involved in fasting for two days, the Sages did not institute an additional day of Yom Kippur.

יוֹצֵא Lit., *[one that has] gone out*. A sacrificial animal (or a portion of one) that was taken outside the limits within which it was permitted to be eaten. Taking the sacrifice out caused it to be forbidden to be eaten and made it necessary to burn it. If only a portion of the sacrifice was taken outside those limits, that portion had to be cut off and burned, and the remainder of the sacrifice was permitted.

יוֹצֵא דוֹפֶן Lit., *[an infant] that goes out [through the] wall [of the abdomen]*, i.e., a child born by Caesarean section. Such a child is subject to different rules from those applying to one born naturally. Among the differences are the following: (1) he is not considered a firstborn (*בְּכוֹר*), and (2) the mother of such a child is not subject to those laws of ritual purity that apply to a woman who gave birth naturally (see *יוֹלֶדֶת*).

יִחוּד Lit., *being alone together*. A man and a woman between whom sexual relations are forbidden may not be alone together behind closed doors. According to tradition, in the era of King David this prohibition was extended to forbid a man from being alone with an unmarried woman. Exceptions to these rules include a father and daughter and a mother and son. A man is also forbidden to be alone together with two women.

יֵין נֶסֶךְ Wine poured as a libation. In its strict sense this term refers to wine used in idol worship. It is forbidden to drink or benefit from such wine (see Deuteronomy 32:38). The Sages extended the scope of this prohibition and forbade drinking any wine touched by non-Jews even though it was not used, or intended, for idol worship (*סְתָם יֵינָם*).

יְסוֹד הַמִּזְבֵּחַ The base of the altar. The bottom level of the altar (*מִזְבֵּחַ*), 1 cubit high with a ledge 1 cubit wide. (See diagram, p. 276.) After the appropriate ritual sprinkling of sacrificial blood on the altar, the remaining blood was poured out on this base, in some cases on the southern side and in other cases on the western side. The base did not surround the altar on all four sides. It was missing at the southeastern corner, and, according to most opinions, on almost the entire southern and eastern sides.

יְעוּד Lit., *designation*. The right granted by the Torah to the purchaser of a Hebrew maidservant (אָמָה עִבְרִיָּה) to designate her, at any time after her purchase and before her release, as a bride for himself or for his son (Exodus 21:8–9). In such an instance, the purchaser is not required to give anything further to effect the betrothal (קִידּוּשִׁין). The money which he originally paid to purchase her as a maidservant is considered as having been given for that purpose, and from the moment of יְעוּד she has the status of a married woman (see אֵשֶׁת אִישׁ).

יְפַת תּוֹאַר Lit., *a woman of beautiful appearance*. A non-Jewish female prisoner of war (see Deuteronomy 21:10–14). According to some authorities, a soldier was allowed to engage in sexual relations with such a woman in wartime. Afterwards, if he desired to take her as a wife, she had to shave her head, let her nails grow and undergo a month-long period of mourning in his home. When that period was over, if she decided to convert to Judaism, they could marry. According to other authorities, sexual relations with a captive during wartime were forbidden, but the soldier had the right to convert his captive and marry her after the mourning period was concluded. According to both opinions, these rights were granted to the soldier as "a concession to the evil inclination."

יקנה"ז An acronym indicating the order of the kiddush blessings to be recited when a Festival falls on Saturday night. יַיִן — the blessing over wine; קִידּוּשׁ — the blessing inaugurating and honoring the Festival; נֵר — the blessing (בּוֹרֵא מְאוֹרֵי הָאֵשׁ) over a lighted candle; הַבְדָּלָה — the blessing marking the conclusion of the Sabbath; זְמַן — the blessing (שֶׁהֶחֱיָנוּ) thanking God for having allowed us to reach this joyous time. The הַבְדָּלָה blessing differs from the usual text and concludes הַמַּבְדִּיל בֵּין קוֹדֶשׁ לְקוֹדֶשׁ — "He who differentiates between holiness and holiness" (i.e. between the greater holiness of the Sabbath and the lesser holiness of the Festivals).

יְרוּשָׁה *Inheritance.* The right of a relative to inherit the property of his deceased kin. The basic laws of inheritance are stated in the Torah (Numbers 27:8–11). The main points are as follows: A father's property is inherited by his sons, with the firstborn son receiving a double share. If the deceased had no sons, or if his sons have died and left no heirs, his daughters receive the inheritance. If he has no offspring at all, the inheritance passes to his father, and then to his father's heirs. The process continues generation by generation, moving back through the paternal family. In this matter the Sages laid down the general principle that, in matters of inheritance, a father takes precedence over all his offspring (see אָב קוֹדֶם לְכָל יוֹצְאֵי חֲלָצָיו). With regard to inheritance, there is no difference between a legitimate child and a mamzer (מַמְזֵר), or a child born of a forbidden marriage or out of wedlock, if he can prove the father's paternity. Exceptions to this are children born to non-Jewish women or to non-Jewish maidservants. Such

children are not considered related to the father. The right to inherit is immediate and not dependent on a will, and in most cases the heirs may not forgo their share before receiving it. (See יְרוּשַׁת הַבַּעַל; יְתוֹמִים.)

יְרוּשַׁת הַבַּעַל *The husband's inheritance.* A husband's right to inherit his wife's property. There is a difference of opinion among the Sages as to whether the husband inherits his wife's property by Torah law or by Rabbinic decree. However, unlike other cases, the husband may forgo this inheritance. Regulations introduced over the generations modified the conditions of the marriage contract (כְּתוּבָּה) and somewhat limited the husband's right to inherit his wife's property.

יִרְעֶה עַד שֶׁיִּסְתָּאֵב Lit., *it shall graze until it becomes unfit [for sacrifice]*. Sometimes an animal designated as an offering in the Temple became disqualified for sacrifice, e.g., because its owner had died or because he had received atonement through a different sacrifice, or because the animal originally designated as a sacrifice had been lost and was later found. Such an animal was disqualified for sacrifice but was forbidden to be used for secular purposes. In such an instance, the animal was sent out to pasture until it received a blemish that in itself disqualified it for sacrifice. Once it had received such a blemish, it could be redeemed and used for secular purposes. The money with which it was redeemed could then be used to purchase another sacrifice. See, however, חַטָּאוֹת הַמֵּתוֹת; פְּסוּלֵי הַמוּקְדָּשִׁין.

יִשְׂרָאֵל *An Israelite.* (1) A Jew, as opposed to a non-Jew. (2) An Israelite, one of the genealogical categories of the Jewish people. An Israelite is neither a priest (כֹּהֵן) nor a Levite (לֵוִי), but is descended from one of the other tribes. The precise meaning of the term in the context of lineage is that of an Israelite of unblemished descent, as opposed to slaves and people of blemished lineage of all kinds. The latter are forbidden, depending on the severity of the blemish in their lineage, to marry priests, Levites, or Israelites.

יְתוֹמִים Lit., *orphans*. This term is used to refer to heirs, generally minors, who inherited their father's estate. The Sages instituted certain provisions to protect them against people who might seek to take advantage of their youth and inexperience, or their lack of knowledge of their father's affairs. Among the provisions applying to all orphans, adult or minor, are the following: Money can only be collected from an orphan's inheritance after the taking of an oath; orphans or their guardian (אַפּוֹטְרוֹפּוֹס) can free themselves from certain claims by stating that they know nothing about them; minor orphans cannot be compelled to pay any debt of their father's estate until they reach majority.

יָתֵר כְּנָטוּל דָּמֵי Lit., *an extra [organ] is considered as if [the organ itself] was removed*. A principle applying to the laws of kashrut. An animal is considered טְרֵפָה — unfit to be eaten — if one of its vital organs is missing. It is similarly considered טְרֵפָה if it was born with two such organs instead of one. (See *Ḥullin* 58b.)

כָּאן נִמְצָא כָּאן הָיָה   Lit., *here it was found. Here it was.* A principle applied in many aspects of Jewish law. An article discovered in a particular place is presumed to have previously been in that place and not to have been moved there from somewhere else. Similarly, the discovery of a forbidden article in one place does not arouse suspicion that similar articles are to be found in other places. Rather, we presume that the prohibited article was the only one of its kind, and was only found in the place it was discovered.

כָּבוֹד   *Honor.* The commandment or the social requirement to behave with respect towards certain people and places. The commandment of honoring applies not only to God but also to a king, parents, Sages, and holy places. The social requirement of behaving with respect towards certain people is a ground for Halakhic decisions in certain areas. For example, it is permitted to break off in the middle of saying prayers in order to pay respect to a distinguished person, and certain people are exempt from the observance of various commandments, such as returning a lost object, because to perform them would be an infringement of their honor.

כִּבּוּד אָב וָאֵם   *Honoring one's father and mother.* One of the Ten Commandments in the Torah, related to another commandment, "You shall fear each man his mother and his father" (Leviticus 19:3), known as מוֹרָא אָב. The essential element of this commandment is that a person must behave with respect towards his father and mother, and he must satisfy their needs. Although the Halakhic conclusion is that a person is not required to spend money to perform this commandment, nevertheless when a parent cannot afford his own upkeep, his child has a particular obligation to support him as an act of charity that takes precedence over other charitable causes. According to the Torah and to the oral tradition, honoring one's father and mother applies also to a stepparent and older siblings.

כְּבוֹד הַבְּרִיּוֹת   *Respect for people.* This is a ground for Halakhic decisions in a number of areas: (1) With regard to the burial of someone who had no relatives to have him buried (see מֵת מִצְוָה), and, more generally, with regard to treating corpses with respect. (2) With regard to relaxing certain Rabbinic restrictions, in circumstances where their fulfillment would cause an infringement of a person's dignity.

כְּבוֹד חֲכָמִים   *Respect for Sages.* A Torah commandment (based on "you shall honor the face of the old man," Leviticus 19:32) to honor Torah scholars. In addition to standing in their presence and honoring them in other ways, one is commanded to try to stay close to them and help them in every way. The honor owed by a disciple to his Rabbi is special, being modelled

upon the honor owed by a child to a parent, and even taking precedence over it in certain situations. Thus, many of the laws of mourning for a deceased parent apply equally in the case of one's deceased teacher. See רַב.

כֶּבֶשׁ   *Ramp.* This term refers to the ramp that was used by the priests to ascend to the altar in the Temple. The portions of the sacrifices to be burned on the altar were laid on the ramp, and from there they were taken up to the altar. See מִזְבֵּחַ.

כֶּבֶשׁ פָּרָה   *The ramp for the Red Heifer.* A ramp supported on arches on which the Red Heifer (פָּרָה אֲדוּמָה) was led from the Temple to the place where it would be slaughtered and burned on the Mount of Olives.

כִּבְשֵׂי עֲצֶרֶת   *The lambs sacrificed on Shavuot.* The Torah (Leviticus 23:17–20) requires that two male lambs be sacrificed as peace-offerings (see שַׁלְמֵי צִיבּוּר) to accompany the two loaves of bread (שְׁתֵּי הַלֶּחֶם) offered in the Temple on Shavuot. The loaves and the sheep were waved together in a special ceremony (תְּנוּפָה) before the altar.

כֹּהֵן, כֹּהֲנִים   *Priest(s).* The descendants of Aaron, the priest, who serve in the Temple. Particular commandments apply to them, and they have unique rights. Apart from the Temple service, most of which is limited to priests and prohibited to non-priests, other special commandments also apply to them. Priests are forbidden to contract ritual impurity through proximity with a corpse, except at the funeral of certain of their closest relatives. A priest may not marry a divorcee, a *zonah* (זוֹנָה), or a woman of blemished lineage (חֲלָלָה). The priests are commanded to recite the Priestly Benediction (בִּרְכַּת כֹּהֲנִים), and they alone are permitted to decide whether a leper (מְצוֹרָע) is ritually impure or not. The priests are entitled to twenty-four different kinds of contributions (see מַתְּנוֹת כְּהוּנָה), some of which are from sacrifices brought to the Temple, while others are from agricultural produce (see תְּרוּמָה; חַלָּה), from animals (see זְרוֹעַ, לְחָיַיִם וְקֵיבָה; חֶרְמֵי כֹּהֲנִים), and from land (see רֵאשִׁית הַגֵּז). In Temple times there was also a Priestly Court, and the priests followed certain special rules regarding their family status in marriage contracts and other areas. A regular priest, as opposed to one occupying a special post, is called a כֹּהֵן הֶדְיוֹט — "a common priest."

כֹּהֵן גָּדוֹל   *High Priest.* Certain duties in the Temple could be fulfilled only by the High Priest. Only the High Priest could perform the Yom Kippur service (see חֲפִינָה; שָׂעִיר הַמִּשְׁתַּלֵּחַ; שָׂעִיר פַּר יוֹם הַכִּיפּוּרִים; יוֹם הַכִּיפּוּרִים). During the rest of the year, he was entitled to perform any service he chose, without waiting for his turn like the regular priests. Twice daily he brought a special meal-offering (see חֲבִיתִּין). The High Priest was subject to special regulations. He wore four special garments in addition to the four garments worn by all priests (see שְׁמוֹנָה בְּגָדִים). Unlike other priests, he was permitted to serve even on the day of death of a close relative (see אֲנִינוּת). If he committed certain grave sins, he brought a bull as a sin-offering (see פַּר כֹּהֵן מָשִׁיחַ). Each Sabbath, when the shewbread (לֶחֶם הַפָּנִים•) was distributed among the priests, the High Priest was awarded half the loaves. Even outside the Temple, the High Priest had a unique status. In addition to the regular laws governing all priests, he was forbidden to marry a widow and commanded to marry a virgin. He was forbidden to come in contact with any dead body, even that of a close relative (except in the case of a מֵת מִצְוָה•). People exiled to the cities of refuge (see עִיר מִקְלָט•) as a penalty for having committed unintentional but negligent manslaughter (see גָּלוּת) were allowed to return home upon the death of the High Priest. See also מְרוּבֵּה בְגָדִים; מָשׁוּחַ בְּשֶׁמֶן הַמִּשְׁחָה; מְשׁוּחַ מִלְחָמָה.

כֹּהֲנִים זְרִיזִים הֵם   *The priests are zealous, diligent.* It was assumed that the priests serving in the Temple were zealous and diligent, and therefore scrupulous about even the most detailed aspects of the Temple service. Accordingly, many Halakhic restrictions applied by the Sages to the Jewish people at large were not instituted in the Temple out of consideration for the priests' zeal.

כַּוָּונָה   *Intent.* (1) This concept has two meanings with regard to commandments in general. The first meaning is being aware that the action being performed is a Divine command. For the question of whether this intent is absolutely required, see מִצְווֹת צְרִיכוֹת כַּוָּונָה. The second meaning is appreciation of the spiritual significance of a commandment. This form of intent is strongly encouraged, though it is not absolutely required for most commandments, with a few exceptions, notably the recitation of the *Shema* (see קְרִיאַת שְׁמַע) and the Amidah (see שְׁמוֹנָה עֶשְׂרֵה). (2) A priest offering a sacrifice is required to have in mind the type of sacrifice being brought, the identity of the person offering it, and many other details (see פִּיגּוּל; פָּסוּל). (3) Regarding intent in the laws of ritual impurity, see מַחֲשָׁבָה. (4) Regarding intent in ritual and criminal law, see שׁוֹגֵג.

כּוֹי   *A kosher animal with characteristics of both a* בְּהֵמָה• — *a domesticated animal — and a* חַיָּה• — *an undomesticated [wild] animal.* The Sages were in doubt as to whether it should be classed in an independent, intermediate category between a בְּהֵמָה and a חַיָּה, or whether it should be considered as one or the other. Since the Sages were unable to determine this, they applied the more stringent laws governing both categories to it (see *Bikkurim* 2:8–11).

כּוֹס שֶׁל בְּרָכָה   Lit., *a cup of blessing.* The cup of wine on which blessings, e.g., kiddush, Grace after Meals (בִּרְכַּת הַמָּזוֹן•) or the marriage blessings (בִּרְכַּת חֲתָנִים•) are recited. This cup must contain at least a רְבִיעִית• (3 or 5 oz.) of wine. Among the regulations applying to this cup are that it must be rinsed before use and that it must be full. It is customary for those present to drink from this wine after the blessings have been recited.

כּוֹפִין אוֹתוֹ עַד שֶׁיֹּאמַר רוֹצֶה אֲנִי   Lit., *they force him*

until he says "I want to...." Some actions, e.g., the offering of certain sacrifices, or the giving of a גֵּט• (bill of divorce), can be effective only if they are performed with the consent of the person on whose behalf they are being carried out. If the person does not consent to these actions, the court will, in certain instances, apply pressure and at times even physical coercion to force him to consent.

כּוֹפֶר   *Ransom, indemnity.* Specifically used to describe the fine which the Torah imposes on a man whose ox or other animal killed a fellow Jew (Exodus 21:30). This fine is only imposed if the animal has already perpetrated a series of malicious attacks (see מוּעָד) and hence precautions should have been taken by its owner to restrain it. The verse describes the fine as "ransom of his life." The Sages debated whether it refers to the value of the life of the owner or the value of the life of the victim.

כּוּתִי   *Cuthean.* A term used to describe the Samaritans, the non-Jews who settled in Samaria and the surrounding territory after the exile of the ten tribes. Though they converted to Judaism, they had ulterior motives for so doing (see II Kings 17), and were not scrupulous in their observance of the mitzvot. Accordingly, it was a matter of debate among the Sages whether or not they were to be considered as Jews. In the Mishnah the Samaritans are given an intermediate status between Jews and non-Jews. In later generations they totally abandoned Jewish practices and the Sages decreed that they should be treated as non-Jews.

כַּזַּיִת   See זַיִת.

כִּי יוּתַּן   Lit., *"if [water] be put [on seeds]...."* An abbreviated quotation from Leviticus 11:38. In order for agricultural produce to become capable of contracting ritual impurity, it must be detached from the earth and then come into contact with water or certain other liquids (see הֶכְשֵׁר). The expression כִּי יוּתַּן implies that the owner of the produce must be satisfied with the fact that the produce became wet. If the owner was not pleased, the produce still cannot contract ritual impurity. The Talmud contains many discussions about specific instances in which it is not certain whether the conditions of כִּי יוּתַּן have been fulfilled.

כִּיּוֹר   *Basin.* A large bronze basin of water in the Temple Courtyard, placed between the altar (מִזְבֵּחַ•) and the Sanctuary (הֵיכָל•; see Exodus 30:18–21). This basin had twelve taps from which the priests would wash their hands and feet before beginning their service in the Temple (see קִידּוּשׁ יָדַיִם וְרַגְלַיִם).

כִּנּוּיֵי הַשֵּׁם   *Substitute names for God.* The Tetragrammaton, called שֵׁם הַמְפוֹרָשׁ, and other names of God appearing in the Bible, such as א-ל, ש-ד-י, are the names by which God is called. Other expressions used to refer to God, e.g., "the Holy One, Blessed be He" (הַקָּדוֹשׁ בָּרוּךְ הוּא) are called כִּנּוּיִים — substitute names. In certain matters (see, for example, מְקַלֵּל אָבִיו וְאִמּוֹ), it is Halakhically significant whether God's name or a כִּנּוּי was used.

כִּנּוּיֵי נְדָרִים *Terms used as substitutes for the language of vows.* The Torah uses three terms to refer to vows and oaths: שְׁבוּעָה ,נֶדֶר and חֵרֶם (see entries). The common people, and, at times, the Sages, would use other equivalent terms. The alternative terms were referred to as כִּנּוּיֵי נְדָרִים. If a person made a declaration using one of these terms and it was obvious that he intended his statement to be a vow, his words had that status and he was bound by what he said.

כִּנּוּיֵי נְזִירוּת *Terms used as substitutes for the language of Nazirite vows.* A Nazirite vow in which euphemisms such as נָזִיק or פָּזִיחַ or נָזִיחַ were substituted for נָזִיר. See כִּנּוּיֵי נְדָרִים.

כִּנּוּיִים *Substituted names.* Often, in addition to the name by which he is commonly called, a person may have other names by which he is called. In certain instances, such as the writing of a גֵט (a bill of divorce), these secondary names are Halakhically significant. A גֵט written without these names being included is considered invalid.

כִּסּוּי הַדָּם Lit., *the covering of the blood.* A person who slaughters a kosher bird or a kosher undomesticated animal (see עוֹף טָהוֹר ;חַיָּה טְהוֹרָה) must cover its blood with earth (see Leviticus 17:13). Ashes and several other powdery substances may also be used for this purpose. A blessing is recited before fulfilling this mitzvah.

כִּיפָּה *A narrow, vaulted chamber in which certain serious criminals were imprisoned for life.* The כִּיפָּה punishment is not mentioned in the Torah, but was instituted by the Sages in fulfillment of the Biblical expression: "And you shall put the evil away from your midst." (See Deuteronomy 13:6, 17:7, 19:19, etc.) This punishment was reserved for known murderers who could not be executed because of legal technicalities, and for a person who had on three occasions committed a sin punishable by excision (כָּרֵת) and had been punished three times by lashes (מַלְקוֹת).

כָּל דְּאַלִּים גָּבֵר Lit., *whoever is stronger wins.* A legal solution sometimes applied in civil disputes, where neither litigant has convincing evidence to support his claim. The court refuses to judge the case and leaves the claimants to settle the matter themselves, in the hope that the true owner will exert himself and win. This solution is applied only in certain rigorously defined situations. See also שׁוּדָא דְּדַיָּנֵי.

כָּל הַחוֹזֵר בּוֹ יָדוֹ עַל הַתַּחְתּוֹנָה *Whoever reneges on a commitment is at a disadvantage.* When two parties enter into an agreement and one party reneges on his commitment, the second party can either force the first party to carry out the original agreement or receive a favorable settlement if he agrees to nullify it.

כָּל הַמְשַׁנֶּה יָדוֹ עַל הַתַּחְתּוֹנָה *Whoever changes the terms of an agreement is at a disadvantage.* If a person does not abide by a contract, he is at a disadvantage in negotiating a settlement. For example, if a craftsman makes major changes in the work for which he was contracted, the person who contracted him is not obligated to pay him what he originally promised. Instead, he is given the right to pay either the value of the article he receives or the craftsman's expenses, whichever is less.

כָּל הָרָאוּי לְבִילָה אֵין בִּילָה מְעַכֶּבֶת בּוֹ Lit., *whatever [meal-offering] is fit to be mixed, [the fact that it has not been] mixed does not invalidate it.* Many meal-offerings have to be mixed with oil (see Leviticus 2:2–7). However, as long as there is nothing to prevent the two substances from being mixed, the fact that they have not been mixed does not invalidate the offering. This principle was also extended to certain other Halakhic areas, in which the Sages stated that certain acts need not be carried out if the potential for their performance exists.

כִּלְאַחַר יָד *In an unusual manner* (lit., "as if with the back of the hand"). A person is not liable for punishment for violating the Sabbath laws if he performed a forbidden act of work in an unusual manner (כִּלְאַחַר יָד). For example, if instead of picking up something normally he did so with the back of his hand, or if instead of writing normally he did so in an unusual or awkward way. In situations of special need, the Sages sometimes even permitted a person to perform forbidden labors in this manner. See שִׁינּוּי.

כִּלְאֵי בְגָדִים See שַׁעַטְנֵז.

כִּלְאֵי בְהֵמָה *The forbidden crossbreeding of livestock.* The Torah prohibits crossbreeding different species of animals (Leviticus 19:19). This transgression is punishable by lashes. However, it is permitted to make use of the offspring of such crossbreeding, e.g., a mule, which is the offspring of an ass and a horse. The laws governing this prohibition are discussed in tractate *Kilayim.* See חֲרִישָׁה בְּשׁוֹר וּבַחֲמוֹר.

כִּלְאֵי הַכֶּרֶם *Food crops [such as wheat] in a vineyard.* It is prohibited to plant or maintain other crops in a vineyard (Deuteronomy 22:9). In contrast to the prohibition of כִּלְאֵי זְרָעִים, the forbidden crop grown in a vineyard may not be eaten or used, and it causes the entire vineyard to be likewise forbidden. All the produce must be burned. This prohibition is discussed in tractate *Kilayim.*

כִּלְאֵי זְרָעִים *A forbidden mixture of seeds.* It is forbidden to plant different species of crops in one area of the same field or graft different species of trees onto one another (Leviticus 19:19). This prohibition is discussed in tractate *Kilayim.* See כִּלְאֵי הַכֶּרֶם.

כִּלְאַיִם Lit., *diverse kinds.* The general term referring to all types of forbidden mixtures: כִּלְאֵי בְהֵמָה ,כִּלְאֵי זְרָעִים ,כִּלְאֵי הַכֶּרֶם and כִּלְאֵי בְגָדִים. In a more restricted sense this term refers to the crossbreeding of a goat and a sheep. Though such crossbreeding is forbidden, the offspring is governed by all the rules applying to a kosher domestic animal (בְּהֵמָה טְהוֹרָה) with one exception — it may not be offered as a sacrifice in the Temple.

כְּלֵי זְכוּכִית *Glass utensils.* There are two special Halakhic principles applying to these utensils. (1) With reference to ritual purity. According to Torah law glass utensils do not contract ritual impurity. Nevertheless, according to Rabbinic decree the laws of ritual purity and impurity do apply to them, and they are rendered ritually pure by immersion in a mikveh (מִקְוֶה•). (2) With reference to the laws of kashrut. The nature of glass utensils raises questions regarding the extent to which they absorb substances and their ability to discharge the substances they absorb. These issues are significant in determining whether such utensils can ever become prohibited for use because they have absorbed a forbidden mixture of food, and, conversely, if they have become forbidden, whether they can become permitted for use afterwards. Some authorities maintain that they can never become forbidden for use; others maintain that they can become prohibited, and, once in that condition, can never become permitted again; and others maintain that glass utensils can become prohibited and can become permitted for use afterwards.

כְּלֵי חֶרֶס   *Earthenware utensils or vessels.* (1) With reference to ritual purity. A number of unique laws apply to earthenware vessels (see Leviticus 11:33 and Rashi's commentary). Among them are the following: (a) They only become ritually impure from their inner side. Nevertheless, the source of ritual impurity need not touch their inner side. As soon as it enters their inner cavity, they become ritually impure. (b) Only concave earthenware utensils can contract ritual impurity. Flat utensils cannot. (c) An earthenware utensil cannot regain ritual purity through immersion (טְבִילָה•) in a mikveh (מִקְוֶה•). It can only regain ritual purity if a hole is made in its underside large enough to render it useless as a receptacle. This causes it to become ritually pure. If the hole is repaired afterwards, the utensil remains ritually pure. (2) With reference to the laws of kashrut. An earthenware vessel which has become forbidden for use because it has absorbed non-kosher food cannot be made fit for use through purging in boiling water (הַגְעָלָה•). The only effective method is to place it in an oven or furnace hot enough to fire pottery.

כְּלֵי מַתֶּכֶת   *Metal utensils or vessels.* (1) With reference to ritual purity. In contrast to wooden or earthenware utensils, all metal utensils can become ritually impure (see חֲלַל חֶרֶב). They can regain their ritual purity through immersion (טְבִילָה•) in a mikveh (מִקְוֶה•). Similarly, if they are broken, their ritual impurity ends. Nevertheless, if they are later repaired, that impurity returns (see טוּמְאָה יְשָׁנָה). (2) With reference to the laws of kashrut. A metal vessel that became forbidden for use may be restored to use according to the principle כְּבוֹלְעוֹ כָּךְ פּוֹלְטוֹ — "As it absorbed the forbidden substance, so it discharges it." Thus, if it has been used for cold forbidden foods, it becomes permitted by being washed with cold water. If forbidden foods have been boiled in it, it becomes permitted through purging in boiling water (הַגְעָלָה•). If forbidden foods have been roasted in it, it becomes permitted through exposure to fire (לִיבּוּן•).

כְּלֵי עֵץ   *Wooden utensils or vessels.* (1) With reference to ritual purity. Only concave wooden utensils can contract ritual impurity. Flat wooden vessels cannot (but see פְּשׁוּטֵי כְּלֵי עֵץ•). Furthermore, extremely large wooden vessels — those with a capacity of more than 40 סְאָה (see p. 288) — cannot contract ritual impurity. A ritually impure wooden article can regain ritual

purity through immersion (טְבִילָה•) in a mikveh (מִקְוֶה•). (2) With reference to the laws of kashrut. A wooden utensil that has absorbed non-kosher substances can become permitted for use through purging in boiling water (הַגְעָלָה•).

כְּלֵי שָׁרֵת   *A vessel or utensil used in the Temple service.* With the exception of the blades used on the knives and axes, which were of iron, every effort was made to use precious metals for the כְּלֵי שָׁרֵת. There is a debate among the Sages whether musical instruments used by the Levites were included in the category of כְּלֵי שָׁרֵת.

כְּלֵי שָׁרֵת מְקַדֵּשׁ מִדַּעַת   Lit., *sacred vessels render holy [only] intentionally.* According to one opinion, sacrificial offerings placed in a sacred vessel attain their complete holy status only if they were placed there with the intention that they thereby become holy. Others maintain that the intention is immaterial.

כֵּלִים   *Utensils.* Any manmade movable object designed to be used purposefully. This includes clothing, boxes, tools, mats, etc. It does not include food, plants, animals, rocks, etc., nor does it include buildings. Utensils have Halakhic significance in several contexts. Among them: (1) Under certain circumstances, placing an object in a person's utensils can be a valid method of formally transferring ownership to him (see קִנְיָן•). (2) Utensils can be acquired by any method valid for movable objects (מִטַּלְטְלִין•), including חֲלִיפִין•. (3) The laws of ritual impurity. Some utensils are always susceptible to ritual impurity, some are never susceptible, and some are susceptible sometimes, depending on the circumstances. The detailed and complicated laws of ritual impurity of utensils are discussed primarily in tractate *Kelim*. In general, unfinished utensils (גּוֹלְמֵי כֵלִים), utensils fixed to the ground, utensils too large to be moved, utensils that are used only by animals, and utensils made of stone or dung or the remains of marine animals are never susceptible to ritual impurity. The laws for other utensils vary. In most cases, utensils that become ritually impure can be purified by immersion in a ritual bath (מִקְוֶה•). See כְּלֵי זְכוּכִית; כְּלֵי חֶרֶס; כְּלֵי עֵץ; כְּלֵי מַתֶּכֶת.

כְּנִיסָה   Lit., *entering.* In the context of marital relationships this term refers to a bride's "entry" into the groom's home or domain. This is accomplished through the נִישׂוּאִין ceremony, and is normally performed under a חוּפָּה• (wedding canopy). Through this rite the bride and groom become fully married to each other.

כֶּסֶף   *Money.* To acquire legal ownership of an object it is necessary to perform a formal act of acquisition (קִנְיָן•). In many cases, the payment of money is itself a valid קִנְיָן, particularly in the following transactions: (1) To acquire landed property or real estate (see מְקַרְקְעֵי; נְכָסִים שֶׁיֵּשׁ לָהֶם אַחֲרָיוּת). (2) To acquire Hebrew slaves (see עֶבֶד עִבְרִי) and Canaanite slaves (see עֶבֶד כְּנַעֲנִי). (3) To sell an article of any kind to the Temple treasury (see הֶקְדֵּשׁ). (4) To betroth a woman (see קִידּוּשִׁין). (5) To redeem second tithe produce (see פִּדְיוֹן מַעֲשֵׂר שֵׁנִי); to redeem dedicated articles (see פִּדְיוֹן הֶקְדֵּשׁ); to redeem a firstborn son (see חֲמִישָׁה סְלָעִים; פִּדְיוֹן הַבֵּן); etc. The payment of money is not a valid קִנְיָן to purchase movable property (מִטַּלְטְלִין•). Even after the seller has been paid, the object remains his until a valid קִנְיָן is performed — usually a form of physical transfer (see הַגְבָּהָה; מְשִׁיכָה). There is an Amoraic dispute whether this regulation is a Torah law or a Rabbinic decree, and the Halakhah follows the former opinion. For most purposes, any article of value (שָׁוֶה כֶּסֶף) can serve as a substitute for money. A notable exception is the redemption of second tithe produce, which can only be performed with minted coins.

כְּפִיַּת הַמִּטָּה   *Overturning the bed.* An ancient mourning practice during the first seven days of mourning (שִׁבְעָה•). All the beds in a mourner's house had to be overturned. The mourner would only sleep on them if they were arranged in that fashion. Though this custom was prevalent in Talmudic times, it is no longer observed.

כֶּפֶל   Lit., *double.* A thief must repay twice the value of a stolen article (Exodus 22:3), i.e., he must restore the article itself to its legal owner and must make an additional payment equal to the value of the article. This obligation is considered a fine (קְנָס•). Accordingly, a thief is only required to make this payment if he is apprehended by others. If he voluntarily admits his wrongdoing and desires to restore the stolen article or its value, he does not make the additional payment. Similarly, a person who swears that something placed in his care was stolen, is himself obligated to pay כֶּפֶל if the object is found to be still in his possession. See אַרְבָּעָה וַחֲמִשָׁה.

כְּרַכִּים מוּקָפִים חוֹמָה   *Cities surrounded by walls.* A city in Eretz Israel that was surrounded by a wall at the time of Joshua's conquest of the country. The inhabitants of these cities are required to read the *Megillah* (the Scroll of Esther) and fulfill the other Purim mitzvot on the 15th of Adar and not on the 14th. Nowadays, Jerusalem is the only city definitely placed in this category. There is a doubt concerning other ancient cities in Eretz Israel, and their inhabitants fulfill the Purim mitzvot on both the 14th and the 15th of Adar.

כֶּרֶם רְבָעִי   Lit., *vineyard of the fourth [year].* A law applying to grapes of a vine in the fourth year after its planting. The grapes are permitted to be eaten, but only in the manner analogous to the second tithe (מַעֲשֵׂר שֵׁנִי•). They must be brought to Jerusalem and eaten in a state of ritual purity, or they must be redeemed and the money used to buy other food in Jerusalem. There is a dispute in the Talmud whether a similar law (נֶטַע רְבָעִי•) applies to other fruits apart from grapes.

כַּרְמְלִית   *An intermediate category of domain established by the Sages between a private domain* (רְשׁוּת הַיָּחִיד) *and a public domain* (רְשׁוּת הָרַבִּים). (See רְשׁוּיוֹת הַשַּׁבָּת.) The Sages extended the prohibition against carrying on the Sabbath from a private domain to a public domain or carrying within the public domain to include certain areas which resemble a public domain. Any open area larger than 4 handbreadths square which is not a public thoroughfare is placed in the category of a כַּרְמְלִית. Thus it includes fields, seas, rivers, alleys, and lanes. On the Sabbath it is forbidden to carry an article 4 cubits within a כַּרְמְלִית or to transfer an article from a private or a public domain to a כַּרְמְלִית or vice versa.

כָּרֵת   *Excision, premature death.* A divine punishment for serious transgressions. The precise definition of the term is a matter of debate among the commentators. Among the characteristics of כָּרֵת mentioned are: (1) premature or sudden death; (2) barrenness and the death of the sinner's children; (3) the soul's being "cut off" in the World to Come. The tractate *Keritot* mentions thirty-six transgressions punishable by כָּרֵת. With the exception of two — failing to bring the Paschal sacrifice (see פֶּסַח) and failing to perform circumcision (מִילָה•) — all the others are violations of negative commandments. כָּרֵת only applies to a person who intentionally commits a transgression. In certain instances, if the transgression was committed in the presence of witnesses, the transgressor is liable to execution by an earthly court, or to the penalty of lashes (מַלְקוֹת•). Anyone who inadvertently transgresses one of the negative commandments punishable by כָּרֵת must bring a sin-offering (חַטָּאת•) as atonement.

כִּתְבֵי הַקּוֹדֶשׁ   Lit., *holy writings.* A reference to the twenty-four books of the Bible. Among the Halakhic regulations applying to these books are: (1) With reference to their sanctity. All handwritten Bible texts and the parchment on which they are written are considered sacred articles and have to be treated with respect. If they become worn, they may not be thrown away, but must be buried in a respectful manner. (2) With reference to ritual purity. The Sages decreed that a person's hands become ritually impure (see טוּמְאַת יָדַיִם•) if he touches handwritten Bible texts. This enactment was instituted lest food be placed within or close to the sacred texts and in order to prevent unnecessary handling of them.

כְּתוּבָּה   *Ketubah [lit., a written document], a marriage contract.* A legal document given by a husband to his wife on their marriage, stating his obligations towards her during and after their marriage. The כְּתוּבָּה includes a lien on the husband's estate (the minimum amount being 200 dinarim [see דִּינָר, p. 291] for a virgin bride and 100 dinarim for other brides) payable upon divorce or widowhood. The general guidelines for a כְּתוּבָּה are provided by the Talmud. However, its particular provisions are often based on local custom. In addition, the כְּתוּבָּה may include individual stipulations agreed to by the husband and wife. The כְּתוּבָּה gives a marriage Halakhic legitimacy. Without one, the couple's relationship is considered licentious.

כְּתוֹנֶת   *The tunic.* One of the four priestly garments worn by all priests. The כְּתוֹנֶת was made entirely of linen. It had to be woven entirely in one piece, without seams. The sleeves were woven separately, also in one piece, and then attached. The כְּתוֹנֶת had to fit the priest perfectly and cover his entire body down to his ankles.

כְּתָמִים   *Stains.* A woman who discovers a bloodstain on a part of her clothing where it may be attributed to uterine bleeding must consider herself ritually impure. However, since this state of impurity is a matter of doubt, the Rabbis allowed certain leniencies. For example, if the stain can be attributed to an external source such as a wound or a bite, or if it was discovered on that part of the garment where uterine blood is unlikely to be found, the woman is not considered ritually impure.

לֹא עָלָה לַבְּעָלִים *The owners of the sacrifice are not credited with having fulfilled their obligation.* Sometimes a mistake is made in the process of offering a sacrifice (e.g., if a sacrifice intended for one purpose is offered up with the intention that it serve for another purpose). Though the error does not disqualify the offering entirely, it is significant enough that its owner may not be considered to have fulfilled his obligation and may be required to bring another offering in its place.

לֹא קָרֵב הַמַּתִּיר כְּמִצְוָתוֹ *The portion of the sacrifice that renders the sacrifice permitted for consumption was not offered according to law.* Certain portions of each sacrifice (e.g., the blood, the אֵימוּרִים, the קוֹמֶץ [see קְמִיצָה] of the meal-offering) must be offered on the altar. The sprinkling of the blood and the offering up of the קוֹמֶץ render the remainder of the respective sacrifices permitted to be eaten. If at any stage of the sacrificial ceremony the priest has in mind to sprinkle the blood, or offer up the אֵימוּרִים, or eat the offering at a time later than that permitted for the particular sacrifice, he renders the sacrifice invalid (פִּיגוּל). This disqualification takes place only if in all other respects the ceremony was carried out correctly. If, however, the other aspects of the sacrifice were not carried out correctly (לֹא קָרֵב הַמַּתִּיר כְּמִצְוָתוֹ) and the sacrifice was disqualified as a result, the concept of פִּיגוּל with its severe consequences is not applicable. (See *Zevaḥim* 2:3–4.)

לֹא רָאִינוּ אֵינוֹ רְאָיָה *Statements by people that they did not witness a particular act is no proof that it did not occur.* Generally, the fact that witnesses did not observe an act is not considered significant in court and cannot be adduced as proof that the act did not take place. Nevertheless, there are certain exceptions where lack of witnesses is considered significant. If, for example, witnesses cannot be found to testify that events that regularly occur in public did in fact take place, such negative evidence is sometimes given weight.

לָאו *A prohibition.* The name regularly given in the Talmud to a prohibition (מִצְוַת לֹא תַּעֲשֶׂה) of the Torah. The punishment for violating a prohibition is greater than for omitting to perform a positive commandment, for the transgressor is generally condemned to lashes. There are, however, many exceptions to this rule (see לָאו הַנִּיתָק לַעֲשֵׂה; לָאו שֶׁאֵין בּוֹ מַעֲשֶׂה; לָאו שֶׁבִּכְלָלוֹת). When the observance of a positive commandment necessitates the violation of a prohibition, the obligation to fulfill the positive commandment generally takes precedence over avoiding transgressing the prohibition. Traditionally the Torah is said to contain 365 prohibitions.

לָאו הַבָּא מִכְּלַל עֲשֵׂה *A prohibition that stems from a positive commandment.* An act forbidden implicitly by the Torah, but which the Torah itself does not explicitly mention. Rather, it states a positive commandment and the prohibition is derived from it. For example, Exodus 12:8 states: "And they shall eat the meat [of the Paschal sacrifice] *in that night*." This positive statement is interpreted by the Sages as a prohibition against the eating of the Paschal sacrifice during the day. (See *Pesaḥim* 41b.) The violation of an implicit prohibition is considered as the violation of a positive commandment. Accordingly, an earthly court will not administer any punishment for its violation.

לָאו הַנִּיתָק לַעֲשֵׂה *A prohibition whose violation can be rectified by the fulfillment of a positive commandment.* For example, the prohibition, "You shall not take the mother bird with the young" (Deuteronomy 22:6), can be rectified by fulfilling the positive commandment, "You shall surely let the mother go" (ibid., 7). Lashes are not administered for the violation of such a prohibition, unless it can never be rectified.

לָאו שֶׁאֵין בּוֹ מַעֲשֶׂה Lit., *a prohibition that does not involve an action.* A prohibition of the Torah which is transgressed by thought or speech but which does not involve a physical act. For example, the prohibition against hating one's fellowman or bearing a grudge against him (Leviticus 19:17–18). Generally, punishment is not administered for violating such a prohibition. There are, however, exceptions: One who curses another or himself using the name of God (מְקַלֵּל); witnesses guilty of conspiracy (עֵדִים זוֹמְמִים); one who swears falsely (see שְׁבוּעַת שָׁוְא); and one who attempts to substitute another animal for a sacrificial animal (see תְּמוּרָה).

לָאו שֶׁאֵינוֹ שָׁוֶה בַּכֹּל *A prohibition that is not equally applicable to all.* For example, prohibitions that apply only to priests. In certain respects, such prohibitions are considered less severe than those applicable to all Jews.

לָאו שֶׁבִּכְלָלוֹת *A prohibition stated in general terms.* A prohibition of the Torah containing several particular prohibitions of different kinds. For example: "You shall not eat anything with the blood" (Leviticus 19:26) contains several prohibitions, among them the prohibition against eating an animal before it is completely dead; the prohibition against eating a sacrificial animal before its blood has been sprinkled on the altar; and the prohibition forbidding judges who have condemned a man to death from eating food on the day of his execution. (See *Pesaḥim* 24a, *Sanhedrin* 63a.) No punishment is administered by an earthly court for the violation of such a prohibition, even if one violates all the individual prohibitions at once.

לָאו שֶׁנִּיתָּן לְאַזְהָרַת מִיתַת בֵּית דִּין Lit., *a prohibition that serves as a warning of death at the hands of the Bet Din.* A prohibition which, if all the necessary conditions are fulfilled, is punishable by execution by an earthly court, and not merely by the penalty of lashes like most prohibitions. A person who violates such a prohibition is not given the punishment of lashes even if certain factors prevent the court from administering the death penalty.

לָבוּד   *Joined, connected.* A law given to Moses at Sinai but not specifically mentioned in the Torah (הֲלָכָה לְמֹשֶׁה מִסִּינַי), stating that two solid surfaces are considered as connected if there is a gap of less than 3 handbreadths (see טֶפַח) between them. The law of לָבוּד is used in reference to the laws of Sabbath boundaries and the laws of the construction of a sukkah.

לְבוֹנָה   *Frankincense.* An aromatic spice used in various Temple services. (1) One of the main ingredients of the incense (קְטֹרֶת). (2) One of the ingredients of the anointing oil (שֶׁמֶן הַמִּשְׁחָה). (3) An addition to most of the meal-offerings, except for the sinner's meal-offering (מִנְחַת חוֹטֵא) and the "jealousy meal-offering" (מִנְחַת קְנָאוֹת). It was offered on the altar together with the קוֹמֶץ — "the handful of meal." (See קְמִיצָה.) (4) Two handfuls of it (see בָּזִיכִין) were placed alongside the shewbread (לֶחֶם הַפָּנִים).

לוֹג (pl. לוּגִּים)   *Log.* A frequently used liquid measure equal to the volume of six eggs. Most sacrificial offerings of wine and oil were measured in whole numbers of לוּגִּים. In fact, there was a special measuring vessel of that volume in the Temple. There was also a dry measure equal to the volume of six eggs, called a רוֹבַע. A רְבִיעִית, one of the most common Halakhic liquid measures until today, is one-fourth of a לוֹג. (See also p. 287.)

לֵוִי   *A Levite.* A direct male descendant of Levi, the son of Jacob. He has certain special rights and duties. (1) In the Temple. When the Children of Israel were in the wilderness, the Levites transported the Tabernacle and its holy vessels. After the building of the Temple, this function ceased to exist (see I Chronicles 23:25–32), but the Levites continued to assist in the Temple service. They were divided, by family, into singers and musicians (מְשׁוֹרְרִים) who offered musical accompaniment to the sacrificial services, and watchmen (שׁוֹעֲרִים) who locked and unlocked the gates of the Temple and stood guard over it. (2) With reference to tithes. Levites are entitled to receive the first tithe (מַעֲשֵׂר רִאשׁוֹן). This is purely a property right. The tithe has no sanctity and may be eaten by anyone to whom the Levite cares to give it. Ezra punished the Levites by decreeing that, in at least some cases, the tithe should be given to the priests instead. (3) With reference to the public reading of the Torah (קְרִיאַת הַתּוֹרָה). When a priest is present, he is called up to read the first portion, and a Levite is called up to read the second portion. (4) The firstborn son of a Levite and the firstborn son of the daughter of a Levite are exempt from the requirement that they be redeemed by paying a sum of money to the priest (see חֲמִשָּׁה סְלָעִים; פִּדְיוֹן הַבֵּן).

לוּלָב   *Lulav, palm branch.* Referred to in the Torah as "branches of palm trees" (Leviticus 23:40). The lulav is required to be held in the hand together with three other plants (אֶתְרוֹג, הֲדַס, עֲרָבָה) on the Festival of Sukkot (see אַרְבָּעָה מִינִים). This

לוּלָב is a young branch of a date palm, with the leaves still pressed tightly against the branch. All four plants must be of high quality. Therefore the לוּלָב may not be crooked, nor may its top be damaged or broken. It must be at least 4 handbreadths (about 35 cm.) long.

לֶחִי   *A narrow pole at least 10 handbreadths high that serves as a symbolic partition.* This concept is applied in two areas of Halakhah: (1) The laws of extending borders with regard to carrying and walking on the Sabbath. Affixing a לֶחִי at the entrance to an alley which ends in a dead end makes it permissible to carry within the alley (see עֵירוּב; שִׁיתּוּפֵי מְבוֹאוֹת; חֲצֵירוֹת).(2) The laws of constructing a sukkah (סוּכָּה). A לֶחִי can be used to complete one of the walls of a sukkah.

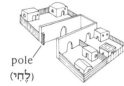

pole (לֶחִי)

לֶחֶם הַפָּנִים   *The shewbread.* The Torah (Leviticus 24:5–9) describes the offering of the twelve shewbreads that were placed on the sacred table (שׁוּלְחַן הַפָּנִים) in the Sanctuary (הֵיכָל) each Sabbath. The bread of the previous week was divided among the priests and eaten by them. The shewbread was unleavened and placed on the table in two arrangements of six loaves each. Two bowls (בָּזִיכִין) of frankincense (לְבוֹנָה) were placed between them (or on top of them, according to other opinions).

לִיבּוּן   Lit., *whitening.* (1) In the sense of bleaching or laundering, one of the thirty-nine primary categories of labor prohibited on the Sabbath (see אֲבוֹת מְלָאכוֹת). (2) With reference to the laws governing menstruating women (see נִדָּה), יְמֵי לִיבּוּן — "the days of whitening" — are a period of time after menstruation when the woman wears white undergarments to enable her to be certain that all traces of the flow have ceased. During this period she remains ritually impure. (3) With reference to the regulations for koshering utensils that were used with non-kosher food while it was in direct contact with fire (e.g., roasting spits). Such utensils can only be made kosher by subjecting them also to direct contact with fire. In some cases the vessels must be heated until they are white hot, and this process is called לִיבּוּן.

לִיסְטִים(ס) מְזוּיָּן   *An armed bandit.* From the Greek λῃστής, meaning "robber." There is a Halakhic question whether the לִיסְטִים has the status of a robber (see גֶּזֶל), because he uses force, or that of a thief (see גַּנָּב), because he flees and hides. The laws concerning robbers and thieves differ with regard to the application of the double payment (כֶּפֶל).

לִיקּוּט עֲצָמוֹת   Lit., *the gathering of bones.* A burial practice in Talmudic times. First, a corpse would be buried in the ground. After the flesh had decomposed, the bones would be dug up, placed in a coffin, and buried in a vault.

לְמַפְרֵעַ   *Not in the correct order, retroactively.* A person who reads the *Shema* (see קְרִיאַת שְׁמַע) or the *Megillah* (the Scroll of Esther) in an incorrect order, reading a later verse before an earlier one, is not considered to have fulfilled his obligation. This principle applies to most cases where there is an obligation to recite a specific passage of the Bible as part of the fulfillment of a commandment. In other contexts, this term refers to an action or development that may have a retroactive effect. If, for example, a witness is convicted of perjury, all his previous testimony, from the moment he gave the perjured testimony until the moment of his conviction, is retroactively (לְמַפְרֵעַ) rendered invalid (*Sanhedrin* 27a). (See also בְּרֵירָה.)

לִפְנֵי עִוֵּר לֹא תִתֵּן מִכְשֹׁל *"You shall not put a stumbling block before the blind"* (Leviticus 19:14). In addition to its literal meaning, this Torah prohibition forbids causing a person who is morally blind (and does not appreciate the seriousness of a sin) or conceptually blind (and does not realize the negative implication of his behavior) to stumble. A particular aspect of this prohibition is that any person who assists another in committing a sin violates this prohibition. However, according to Torah law, a person only violates this prohibition if it would have been impossible for the transgressor to have committed the sin without his assistance.

לִפְנִים מִשּׁוּרַת הַדִּין Lit., *inside the line of justice.* The forgoing of a legal right. This concept is applied in civil law (see דִּינֵי מָמוֹנוֹת), when the letter of the law would grant a litigant certain rights, but he forgoes them as an act of generosity to the other person. Though the Sages could not always compel someone to go לִפְנִים מִשּׁוּרַת הַדִּין — "beyond the requirements of the law" — they strongly advised it. Indeed, the Talmud says that Jerusalem was destroyed only because its inhabitants conducted their affairs according to the strict rules of the law (*Bava Metzia* 30b).

לֶקֶט *Gleanings.* One of the obligatory agricultural gifts given to the poor (see מַתְּנוֹת עֲנִיִּים). The Torah prohibits the owner of a field from gleaning individual stalks that have fallen during the harvest (Leviticus 19:9). Less than three stalks that have fallen in one place are deemed לֶקֶט and considered the property of the poor. The owner of the field is forbidden to take them for his own use.

לָשׁוֹן שֶׁל זְהוֹרִית Lit., *a strip of crimson.* A tongue-shaped strip of wool dyed with a special crimson dye (תּוֹלַעַת שָׁנִי). A strip of this wool was employed in the performance of several mitzvot: (1) The sacrifice of the Red Heifer (פָּרָה אֲדוּמָּה; Numbers 19:6). (2) The purification ritual of a person previously afflicted with leprosy (צָרַעַת; see also טָהֳרַת מְצוֹרָע and Leviticus 14:4–6). (3) The Yom Kippur offerings. It was customary to tie such a crimson strip around the neck of the goat offered as a sin-offering (see שְׂעִיר יוֹם הַכִּיפּוּרִים) and between the horns of the goat sent to Azazel (see שָׂעִיר הַמִּשְׁתַּלֵּחַ).

לָשׁוֹן הָרָע Lit., *evil speech.* The Torah severely prohibits

לָשׁוֹן הָרָע — adverse criticism and gossip (Leviticus 19:16). It is forbidden to mention disparaging things in conversation about another person, even if they are true. *False* disparaging remarks are considered an even more serious sin, מוֹצִיא שֵׁם רַע. Under certain conditions, it may be permitted to mention matters that are already public knowledge. The Sages extended the scope of this prohibition and forbade many other forms of gossip, referring to them as אֲבַק לָשׁוֹן הָרָע (see אֲבַק). Included in this category are statements that are not themselves harmful to the person mentioned, but might prompt others to make disparaging remarks. The Sages frequently mentioned the severity of this prohibition, declaring that it is equivalent to the most serious sins, such as murder and adultery.

לְשָׁכוֹת Lit., *chambers.* Halls and storerooms in the Temple. They were built at the sides of the Temple courtyards or near or above their gates, and served many purposes, including storage and preparation of the offerings. They were also used as rooms where the priests could rest. Those chambers that opened into the Temple courtyards had the same sanctity as the courtyards themselves. Those that opened into the area outside the courtyards were not granted that status. (See plan of the Temple, p. 277.)

לִשְׁכַּת הַגָּזִית Lit., *the Chamber of Hewn Stone.* The chamber in the Temple that served as the seat of the Great Sanhedrin (see בֵּית דִּין שֶׁל שִׁבְעִים וְאֶחָד; סַנְהֶדְרִין גְּדוֹלָה). About forty years before the destruction of the Temple, the Sanhedrin was prevented from continuing to hold sessions in this chamber. From that time onward, no Rabbinical Courts were empowered to administer capital punishment (דִּינֵי נְפָשׁוֹת).

לִשְׁמוֹ וְלִשְׁמָהּ Lit., *for his name and for her name.* The Torah requires that a bill of divorce (גֵּט) be written with the specific intention of effecting a divorce between the two marriage partners. It must be written specifically for the husband and specifically for his wife (לִשְׁמוֹ וְלִשְׁמָהּ). A bill of divorce that is not written with this intention, even though it contains the correct names of the husband and the wife (e.g., a bill of divorce written for another couple bearing the same names), cannot be used in divorce proceedings and is without effect.

לִתְלוֹת Lit., *to leave pending.* A concept used in connection with terumah (תְּרוּמָה), the portion of the crop given to the priests. If a doubt arises concerning the ritual purity of terumah (or if terumah contracts one of the forms of ritual impurity instituted by Rabbinic decree alone), the terumah cannot be eaten, for it may be ritually impure. Nor may it be burned as impure terumah, for it may be ritually pure, in which case it is forbidden to be destroyed. Hence, it is "left pending," i.e., it is left in its place until it is no longer fit to be used, at which point it may be disposed of.

מַאֲכִיל בִּתְרוּמָה   Lit., *feeds terumah*. According to Torah law, people who are not priests are usually not permitted to eat terumah (יתְרוּמָה), the agricultural levy given to the priests. However, in certain cases, relations (or dependants) of priests may eat terumah, even though they themselves are not priests. Thus, a male adult priest "feeds terumah" (i.e., "confers the right to eat terumah") to his wife, sons, daughters, slaves and animals. The widow of a priest (even if she herself is not the daughter of a priest) is permitted to eat terumah if she has children (or grandchildren) from her deceased husband. Indeed, the surviving descendants of a priest enable not only their mother but also slaves whom she inherited to continue to eat terumah.

מַאֲכַל בֶּן דְּרוֹסַאי   Lit., *the food of Ben Drosai*. Food that has already been partially cooked before the Sabbath may be left on the fire on the Sabbath, provided that it was at least somewhat edible before the Sabbath. Such barely edible food is called "the food of Ben Drosai." Ben Drosai was a robber who lived during the Talmudic period and did not have time to cook his food properly (since he was always hurrying to escape). Food that has been cooked half (according to some opinions, one-third) as much as it would normally be cooked is considered to be מַאֲכַל בֶּן דְּרוֹסַאי.

מַאֲמָר   Lit., *statement*. If a married man dies without leaving any children, his brother must either marry the deceased husband's widow (this is called יבּוּם — levirate marriage) or perform חֲלִיצָה — "loosening of the shoe." According to Torah law, levirate marriage can only be effected by conjugal relations (יבִּיאָה), in contrast to ordinary marriage (יקִדּוּשִׁין), where betrothal can also be effected by a document or by a transfer of money. The Sages, however, decreed that, even in cases of levirate marriage, betrothal should first take place by means of a document or a transfer of money, accompanied by a verbal declaration of betrothal, even though such an act of betrothal is not binding according to Torah law. This verbal declaration of betrothal is called מַאֲמָר.

מָבוֹי   *Alley, narrow lane, not frequented by the general public.* Two types of alley are discussed in the Talmud: (1) מָבוֹי מְפוּלָשׁ — "an open alley," i.e., an alley or narrow lane that is enclosed by two walls and opens onto a public domain (ירְשׁוּת הָרַבִּים) at both ends. (2) מָבוֹי סָתוּם — "closed alley," i.e., an alley or a narrow lane that is enclosed by three walls and open to a public domain on the fourth side only. Usually, the courtyards around which people's homes were located opened onto these alleys. Carrying inside an alley is permitted on the Sabbath only if two conditions are fulfilled: (1) All the residents of the מָבוֹי contribute a certain quantity of food and put all the contributions together in a specially designated place (see שִׁיתּוּפֵי מְבוֹאוֹת). (2) Certain

minimum physical alterations are made in the structure of the alley. Specifically, a "closed alley" must at least have a pole (ילְחִי) erected next to one side of the entrance to the public domain, or a beam (יקוֹרָה) placed across the top of this entrance. An open alley must at least have a צוּרַת הַפֶּתַח — "form of a door," i.e., two parallel upright posts with a beam or string or wire stretched across them, erected at one of the entrances to the public domain — and a pole or beam (see above) erected at the other entrance.

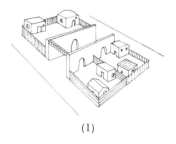
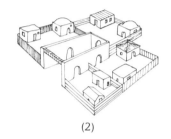

(1)   (2)

מְבַזֶּה תַּלְמִיד חָכָם   *One who despises, insults a scholar.* Showing contempt towards a scholar is considered tantamount to acting contemptuously towards the Torah itself. In Talmudic literature a person who acts in this way is occasionally termed an יאֶפִּיקוֹרוֹס (lit., "heretic"). In Talmudic times, a person who acted contemptuously towards a scholar was subject to excommunication and/or a monetary fine (according to the Jerusalem Talmud, "a litra [pound] of gold"). In later periods, however, such fines were not imposed.

מֵבִיא אֶת הַטּוּמְאָה   *Transmits ritual impurity.* By Torah law, a dead body imparts ritual impurity not only to items that come into contact with it, but even to items located near it under the same "tent" (see אֹהֶל הַמֵּת). This "tent" can be any object that is at least 1 cubic handbreadth (יטֶפַח) in volume. Such a tent is said to "transmit ritual impurity" (מֵבִיא אֶת הַטּוּמְאָה) to anyone under it. See פּוֹתֵחַ טֶפַח.

מְגַדֵּף   *Blasphemer.* Blasphemy is defined as cursing God when referring to Him by His four-letter name in Hebrew. This offense is punishable by stoning (Leviticus 24:15–16; Numbers 15:30–31). Some scholars maintain that the "blasphemy" mentioned in the source in Numbers refers to other sins that entail profanation of God's name.

מְדוֹר הַגּוֹיִים   *Gentile dwelling-place.* By Rabbinic decree a dwelling-place where non-Jews lived was considered ritually impure, and rendered objects inside it likewise ritually impure, because the Sages were afraid that an aborted fetus (which imparts ritual impurity) might have been buried there.

מְדִינָה　Lit., *country*. In certain contexts this term means any place outside the Temple (or, according to some opinions, outside Jerusalem; see *Rosh HaShanah* 29b). With regard to many Halakhot there is a difference between what was done in the Temple and what was done outside it. See גְּבוּלִין.

מַדָּף לְטוּמְאָה　*Indirect contact for [= conferring] ritual impurity*. Certain types of ritual impurity according to Rabbinic decree (but not according to Torah law). This term is specifically used with reference to objects *above* a zav (זָב — a person suffering from gonorrhea) to which he imparts ritual impurity of the first degree (רִאשׁוֹן לְטוּמְאָה), as distinct from objects upon which a *zav* sits, lies or stands (see טוּמְאַת מִדְרָס), to which he imparts ritual impurity of the primary category like his own (see אֲבוֹת הַטּוּמְאוֹת).

מִדְרַס הַזָּב　See טוּמְאַת מִדְרָס.

מַה לִי לְשַׁקֵּר　*Why should I lie?* See מִיגוֹ.

מוֹדֶה בְּמִקְצָת　*One who admits to part*. If a person claims that another owes him money, and this second person admits that he owes part of the sum, then the defendant must take an oath that he owes no additional money. He is then exempt from paying more than the amount he admitted. If he refuses to take the oath, he must pay the full amount of the debt claimed.

מוֹדָעָה　Lit., *declaration*. If one of the parties to an agreement is about to be compelled to sign under duress, he can nullify the agreement by serving advance notice before witnesses that the contract or agreement is being signed under duress. Such a declaration is called a מוֹדָעָה. The witnesses must have direct personal knowledge of the nature of the duress that makes it necessary for him to sign the contract. Later, he may nullify the agreement by revealing the fact that he had previously made the מוֹדָעָה.

מוּדָּר הֲנָאָה　*One who is forbidden by a vow from having enjoyment*. If one person takes a vow (יִדֹּר) not to derive any enjoyment or benefit from another person, or if one person (A) takes a vow prohibiting another (B) from deriving any enjoyment or benefit from his (A's) property, the person forbidden to derive benefit is called a מוּדָּר הֲנָאָה. A מוּדָּר הֲנָאָה may receive nothing from the property included in the vow that confers a benefit, neither food nor anything else having monetary value. However, a מוּדָּר הֲנָאָה may make use of such property to perform a mitzvah, because a mitzvah is Halakhically considered as something from which one does not derive "benefit" or "enjoyment" (הֲנָאָה). The precise details of what is considered הֲנָאָה in this context are set forth in tractate *Nedarim*.

מוֹכֵר בְּעַיִן יָפָה מוֹכֵר　*One who sells, sells generously*. Sometimes it is not clear from an agreement made between a buyer and a seller whether or not a certain item was included in the sale. In such cases, certain authorities maintain that "the seller sells generously," and hence the questionable item is assumed to have been included in the sale (other authorities, however, disagree). According to all opinions, one who gives a gift to another person or dedicates property to the Temple is assumed to have done so "generously," and hence, in cases of doubt, the item belongs to the recipient.

מוּכַּת עֵץ　Lit., *a woman wounded by a piece of wood*, i.e., a woman whose hymen was torn accidentally, and not through sexual intercourse. Such a woman receives the כְּתוּבָּה ("marriage settlement") of a widow or divorcee, and is not permitted to marry a High Priest (כֹּהֵן גָּדוֹל; see Leviticus 21:13).

מוֹלֶךְ　*Molekh*. A type of idol. Molekh worship is punishable by stoning (see Leviticus 20:2–5). Specifically, the Molekh was worshipped by passing one's children through a fire in honor of the idol. The laws pertaining to Molekh worship are discussed in detail in tractate *Sanhedrin*. According to most opinions, the children need not be burned in the fire for this prohibition to be violated.

מוּם עוֹבֵר　*A temporary blemish*. Blemished animals may not be offered as sacrifices (Leviticus 22:20) and are normally redeemed. However, animals with "temporary blemishes" that will eventually heal may be neither sacrificed nor redeemed. Blemished priests may not take part in the Temple service (Leviticus 21:17), and priests suffering from "temporary blemishes" are also specifically forbidden to do so. Once the temporary blemish has healed, the priest is again permitted to take part in the Temple service.

מוּמְחֶה לְבֵית דִּין　Lit., *an expert for the court*. A scholar who has been granted permission by the Nasi (נָשִׂיא) or Exilarch (רֵישׁ גָּלוּתָא) to rule on specific Halakhic questions as an expert. If such an "expert judge" rules incorrectly, and one of the parties in the case incurs a financial loss because of his decision, the judge is generally exempt from reimbursing him, since he had been granted permission to adjudicate the matter.

מוּמִים　*Blemishes*. (1) With reference to the laws of sacrifices. Certain types of blemishes render an animal unfit to be sacrificed and render a priest unfit to serve in the Temple. The laws of these blemishes are discussed in tractate *Bekhorot*. Some blemishes are bodily imperfections such as blindness, and others are deformities making the blemished animal unlike others of its species. Many of the blemishes that render animals unfit as sacrifices render priests unfit for Temple service, although there are blemishes that only apply to animals and others that only apply to priests. Blemishes do not render birds unfit for sacrifice (see, however, מְחוּסַּר אֵיבָר). (2) With reference to the laws of marriage. If a man marries a woman with physical defects (generally similar to those that render a priest unfit for Temple service), which were unknown to him before the marriage, he can divorce her and not pay her כְּתוּבָּה (marriage settlement) by claiming that he entered into the marriage under false pretenses. Only blemishes that the husband was unable to find out about before the marriage are grounds for divorce without payment of the כְּתוּבָּה.

מוּסָף　Lit., *addition*. (1) The additional public sacrifices offered on Sabbaths, New Moons, and Festivals. They could be brought at any time during the day, but usually they were brought immediately after the morning daily offering (תָּמִיד שֶׁל שַׁחַר). See

211

Numbers 28-29. (2) The fourth service (containing the Amidah prayer), in addition to the three regular daily services, recited on those days on which in Temple times a מוּסָף sacrifice was brought. Normally מוּסָף is recited immediately after the morning service (שַׁחֲרִית). It consists of seven blessings. The first three and the last three are the blessings that open and close the daily Amidah prayer (see שְׁמוֹנֶה עֶשְׂרֵה), whereas the middle blessing (קְדוּשַּׁת הַיּוֹם) consists of a brief description of the significance of the day, including the sacrifices brought in the Temple. On Rosh HaShanah, the מוּסָף prayer contains nine blessings. See also מַלְכוּיּוֹת; זִכְרוֹנוֹת; שׁוֹפָרוֹת.

מוּעָד   Lit., *forewarned*. (1) In its more limited sense, this expression is used to refer to a שׁוֹר מוּעָד — "an ox whose owner has been forewarned," i.e., an ox that has gored three times. If an ox causes damage by goring, or, in general, any animal causes *malicious* damage (see קֶרֶן), the first three times that it gores, the owner is liable for only half of the resulting damage (see חֲצִי נֶזֶק; תָּם). If, however, the ox gores a fourth time, and the owner was officially notified that it had gored three times previously, the animal is considered a שׁוֹר מוּעָד, and the owner must pay in full for the resulting damage. (2) The term מוּעָד may also be used in the broader sense of any type of damage for which the person responsible must pay full indemnity (נֶזֶק שָׁלֵם), e.g., damage caused by an animal eating or treading on other people's property. See אָדָם מוּעָד לְעוֹלָם; רֶגֶל; שֵׁן.

מוּפְלָא הַסָּמוּךְ לְאִישׁ   Lit., *a doubtful person close to manhood,* i.e., a child one year before he or she reaches maturity (thus a girl becomes מוּפְלָא הַסָּמוּךְ לְאִישׁ at the age of eleven, and a boy at the age of twelve). The vow of such a child is binding, if it can be shown that the child understood the nature of the vow. This law is based on a Rabbinic interpretation of the Biblical verse (Numbers 6:2).

מוּפְלָא שֶׁבְּבֵית דִּין   Lit., *the distinguished [member] of the court,* i.e., the most learned member of the Great Sanhedrin (סַנְהֶדְרִין גְּדוֹלָה). Certain types of Halakhic ruling were not binding without the presence of the מוּפְלָא שֶׁבְּבֵית דִּין. It would appear that this scholar was not always a member of the court (e.g., if he was too old to serve there). If an erroneous Halakhic ruling was issued in his absence, and people followed this ruling, the Sanhedrin was not required to bring a פַּר הֶעְלֵם דָּבָר (a type of expiatory offering).

מוֹצִיא שֵׁם רַע   *Slanderer*. (1) A man who falsely maintains that his wife was not a virgin when she married him, and who brings false witnesses who testify that she committed adultery while betrothed to him, is called a מוֹצִיא שֵׁם רַע (Deuteronomy 22:13-19). The מוֹצִיא שֵׁם רַע is fined 100 shekels (paid to his wife's father) and flogged (see מַלְקוֹת), and he is permanently forbidden to divorce his wife. The witnesses are punishable by death, if it can be proved that they lied (see עֵדִים זוֹמְמִים). (2) In a more general sense, מוֹצִיא שֵׁם רַע refers to anyone guilty of slander.

מוּקְצֶה   Lit., *set aside*. (1) An item that is forbidden to be picked up and handled on Shabbat and Festivals, because its normal use involves an activity that is not permitted on these days. Among the different types of מוּקְצֶה are: (a) מוּקְצֶה מֵחֲמַת גוּפוֹ — lit., "מוּקְצֶה because of itself" — raw materials that were not prepared for use before Shabbat, e.g., dirt and stones; (b) כְּלִי שֶׁמְּלַאכְתּוֹ לְאִיסּוּר — "a utensil whose function is prohibited," i.e., an item, such as a pen, that is ordinarily used for work forbidden on Shabbat; (c) מוּקְצֶה — "מוּקְצֶה מֵחֲמַת מִיאוּס because of repulsiveness," i.e., an item that is dirty and repellent and hence not usually handled; (d) מוּקְצֶה — מוּקְצֶה מֵחֲמַת חֶסְרוֹן כִּיס because of monetary loss," i.e., a valuable object or an item that is intended for sale, and hence is not intended for everyday use; (e) מוּקְצֶה בְּיָדַיִם — lit., "מוּקְצֶה with the hands," i.e., an item that one had specifically designated not to be used on Shabbat (e.g., wet clothing that was washed before Shabbat, which one did not expect would be dry enough to be worn on Shabbat). According to some Tannaim and Amoraim, certain types of מוּקְצֶה may be handled on Shabbat and Festivals. (See בָּסִיס לְדָבָר הָאָסוּר.) (2) With reference to the laws of sacrifices. An animal that has been designated for idolatrous purposes. Such an animal is unfit to be sacrificed.

מוֹרָא מִקְדָּשׁ   Lit., *fear of the Sanctuary*. The commandment to behave with great respect towards the Temple (Leviticus 19:30). One may not enter the Temple area if one is wearing shoes or carrying money-bags. One may not spit there or otherwise behave disrespectfully. Even outside the Temple, one must show it respect, e.g., when one is facing in its direction. One must treat a "miniature Temple," i.e., the synagogue, similarly and not behave disrespectfully inside it.

מוֹרֶדֶת   *A rebellious woman*. A woman who refuses to fulfill her obligations towards her husband (particularly, a woman who refuses to have conjugal relations with her husband). Such a woman may be fined by having money deducted from her כְּתוּבָּה (marriage settlement), and her husband may force her to accept a divorce. A husband who "rebels" against his wife may also be subject to monetary fines that increase the amount of his wife's כְּתוּבָּה.

מִזְבֵּחַ   *Altar*. The altar usually mentioned in Talmudic literature, also known as the מִזְבֵּחַ הַחִיצוֹן — "the outer altar" — was situated next to the עֶזְרַת כֹּהֲנִים — the priests' section of the Temple Courtyard. (See diagram, p. 277.) It was a large, square, stepped structure (see יְסוֹד הַמִּזְבֵּחַ; סוֹבֵב), 32 cubits by 32 cubits at the bottom, and 10 cubits high at its uppermost corners (see קַרְנוֹת הַמִּזְבֵּחַ). The altar was constructed from a mixture of lime, sand, and smooth river pebbles. It was then coated with plaster to make it completely smooth on the outside. The top of the altar was connected to the ground by a ramp 32 cubits long, up which the priests carried the sacrificial portions to be burned on the altar. The blood of the sacrifices was sprinkled on the altar (see הַזָּאָה; זְרִיקָה), and libations of wine and oil were poured over it (see נְסָכִים). The burnt-offerings (see עוֹלָה), the קוֹמֶץ ("handful," see קְמִיצָה) from meal-offerings (see מְנָחוֹת), and the fat from other sacrifices (see אֵימוּרִים; חֵלֶב) were burned on the altar. The fire on the altar was constantly kept alive, and efforts were made to ensure that at least one sacrifice was being offered there at all times when the Temple service was in progress, from the time of the *Tamid*-offering (see תָּמִיד and קַיץ הַמִּזְבֵּחַ) each morning until the time of the *Tamid*-offering each evening.

מִזְבַּח הַזָּהָב *The golden altar.* Also known as the מִזְבֵּחַ הַפְּנִימִי — "the inner altar" — or the מִזְבֵּחַ הַקְּטֹרֶת — "the altar of incense." This altar stood in the middle of the Sanctuary (יְהֵיכָל, see plan of the Temple, p. 277), and it was 1 cubit long by 1 cubit wide, and 2 cubits high. This altar was overlaid with gold, and it had four protruding horns (see קַרְנוֹת הַמִּזְבֵּחַ), one on each corner. Incense was offered every day on the inner altar, and on Yom Kippur the blood of the special Yom Kippur offerings (see פַּר יוֹם הַכִּפּוּרִים; שְׂעִיר יוֹם הַכִּפּוּרִים) was sprinkled on top of it and on its horns. See also חַטָּאוֹת הַפְּנִימִיּוֹת.

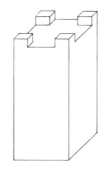

מְזוּזָה *Mezuzah* (lit., "doorpost"). A piece of parchment on which two passages of the Torah (שְׁמַע, Deuteronomy 6:4–9, and וְהָיָה אִם שָׁמֹעַ, ibid., 11:13–21; see also תְּפִילִין) have been written by a scribe. The Torah commands us (ibid., 6:9 and 11:20) to affix mezuzot on the doorposts of our homes. The mezuzah is usually enclosed in a case, to protect it, and is placed on the right-hand doorpost of each room. All rooms where people live and sleep must have mezuzot; likewise, mezuzot must be affixed to the gates of courtyards and cities (i.e., walled cities). Rooms where people do not live or sleep do not need mezuzot; rooms used for functions not in keeping with the sanctity of the mezuzah (e.g., bathrooms), do not have mezuzot.

מִזְרָק *Bowl.* One of the sacred utensils used in the Temple service (see כְּלֵי שָׁרֵת). The blood from the sacrifices was collected in the מִזְרָק, and from there it was sprinkled on the altar. The מִזְרָק was designed not to stand upright on its own, in order to prevent people from putting it down and thereby allowing the blood in it to congeal.

מְחוּסַּר אֵיבָר *Lacking a limb.* An animal lacking a limb (e.g., a foot) is unfit to be sacrificed. Even birds, which are usually not rendered unfit by blemishes (מוּמִים), may not be offered if they are lacking limbs.

מְחוּסַּר בְּגָדִים *Lacking priestly garments.* A priest who performs the Temple service without wearing all the priestly garments (see בִּגְדֵי זָהָב; בִּגְדֵי לָבָן) renders the sacrifices he offers unfit, and is punishable by death inflicted by Heaven (מִיתָה בִּידֵי שָׁמַיִם). (See Exodus 29: 9 and *Zevaḥim* 17b.)

מְחוּסַּר זְמַן Lit., *lacking time.* A sacrifice that cannot be offered because its time to be offered has not yet arrived, is termed מְחוּסַּר זְמַן. Usually this term is applied to an animal that is less that eight days old. Likewise, a peace-offering (see שְׁלָמִים) offered before the Temple gates were opened, was considered מְחוּסַּר זְמַן.

מְחוּסַּר כַּפָּרָה *Lacking atonement.* Certain categories of people who are ritually impure — a woman who has recently given birth (יוֹלֶדֶת), a man healed after suffering from gonorrhea (זָב), a woman who experienced a menstrual-type flow of blood when it was not the time of her period (see זָבָה), and a healed leper (מְצוֹרָע, see צָרַעַת) — must bring sacrifices in order to complete their purification process. Before they have brought these sacrifices, they are considered מְחוּסְּרֵי כַּפָּרָה, and they are not permitted to enter the Temple or to partake of sacrificial foods.

מִחְיָה Lit., *healthy flesh.* A concept in the laws of leprosy (צָרַעַת). If healthy looking flesh (מִחְיָה) appears within leprous spots on the skin, the leper is immediately declared ritually impure, and there is no need to quarantine him in order to determine whether or not he is suffering from leprosy. See מְצוֹרָע מוּחְלָט; מְצוֹרָע מוּסְגָּר.

מְחִיר כֶּלֶב (מְחִיר) Lit., *the price of a dog.* By Torah law (Deuteronomy 23:19), any kosher animal received in exchange for the sale of a dog may not be offered as a sacrifice (*Temurah* 6:3). See אֶתְנַן זוֹנָה.

מַחְמִיר עַל עַצְמוֹ *One who is strict with himself.* In certain matters it is permitted to be stricter than the Halakhah requires. But the conduct of people who are stricter with themselves than the Halakhah requires cannot be used as proof of what the Halakhah is.

מְחַמֵּר *One who drives a laden animal.* It is prohibited to drive a donkey (or any other animal) carrying a burden on Shabbat. A person who does so violates the positive commandment "that your ox and your ass may rest" (Exodus 23: 12), but is not required to bring a sin-offering (חַטָּאת), as is ordinarily the case with Sabbath violators.

מַחֲנֵה יִשְׂרָאֵל *The Camp of Israel.* The area within which the Tribes of Israel encamped during their journeys in the wilderness. This area was invested with a limited degree of sanctity. During later periods, walled cities in Eretz Israel and in particular Jerusalem outside the Temple Mount were considered the מַחֲנֵה יִשְׂרָאֵל. A leper (מְצוֹרָע, see צָרַעַת) was not permitted to enter the מַחֲנֵה יִשְׂרָאֵל, because of its sanctity. See מַחֲנֵה לְוִיָה; מַחֲנֵה שְׁכִינָה.

מַחֲנֵה לְוִיָה *The Camp of the Levites.* The area where the Levites encamped during the journeys of the Tribes of Israel in the wilderness. During later periods in Eretz Israel the Temple Mount as far as the Gate of Nicanor (שַׁעַר נִיקָנוֹר) was considered the מַחֲנֵה לְוִיָה. Men suffering from gonorrhea (see זָב), women ritually impure because of menstrual or other bleeding (see זָבָה; נִדָּה), or because they had recently given birth (see יוֹלֶדֶת), were not permitted to enter the מַחֲנֵה לְוִיָה because of its sanctity. See מַחֲנֵה יִשְׂרָאֵל; מַחֲנֵה שְׁכִינָה.

מַחֲנֵה שְׁכִינָה *The Camp of the Divine Presence.* The area within the courtyard of the Tent of Meeting in the wilderness. During later periods in Eretz Israel, the inner courtyard of the Temple from the Gate of Nicanor (שַׁעַר נִיקָנוֹר), including the Sanctuary itself, was considered the מַחֲנֵה שְׁכִינָה. All ritually impure people were forbidden to enter the מַחֲנֵה שְׁכִינָה (see טוּמְאַת מִקְדָּשׁ וְקָדָשָׁיו), and a ritually impure person who entered this area unintentionally was required to bring an expiatory sacrifice. See מַחֲנֶה לְוִיָּה; מַחֲנֶה יִשְׂרָאֵל.

מַחֲצִית הַשֶּׁקֶל   *Half-shekel.*

An annual contribution to the Temple. All male Jews were annually required to contribute half a shekel to the Temple before the first day of the month of Nisan, which was the first day of the New Year in the Temple. This money was used to cover the expenses of the Temple (which included buying communal sacrifices and paying for repairs), and to maintain and repair the walls of Jerusalem. From the beginning of the month of Adar, notice was served to the public that the half-shekel contributions would soon be due. The exact value of the half-shekel changed several times in the course of the generations. Nowadays, towards the end of the Fast of Esther on the 13th of Adar, before the beginning of the Festival of Purim, people contribute to charity "in memory of the half-shekel." The laws of the half-shekel contributions made to the Temple are discussed in tractate *Shekalim*. See קַלְבּוֹן.

מַחֲשָׁבָה   *Thought, intention.*

(1) With reference to the laws of sacrifices. The intention of the priest offering a particular sacrifice. Incorrect intentions (e.g., if the priest intends to eat the sacrifice in the wrong place, or after the permitted time) may render a sacrifice unfit. According to some authorities, such an intention has to be expressed aloud in order to be Halakhically binding (see פִּיגּוּל; פָּסוּל). (2) With reference to the laws of ritual purity, "intention" has two primary ramifications: (a) Only a finished utensil is susceptible to ritual impurity. The criterion for determining whether or not a utensil is finished is "intention," i.e., whether or not one intends to use the utensil in its present form. (b) Solid foods are susceptible to ritual impurity only if certain liquids fall on them "intentionally" (see הֶכְשֵׁר; כִּי יֻתַּן; מְטַמֵּא לְרָצוֹן). Among the principles governing the laws of intention are: חֵרֵשׁ שׁוֹטֶה וְקָטָן אֵין לָהֶם מַחֲשָׁבָה אֲבָל יֵשׁ לָהֶם מַעֲשֶׂה — "A deaf-mute, an imbecile, and a minor have no intention, but they do have action," i.e., their intentions have no Halakhic significance, but their actions do (see *Ḥullin* 13a); and כָּל הַכֵּלִים יוֹרְדִין לִידֵי טוּמְאָתָן בְּמַחֲשָׁבָה וְאֵינָן עוֹלִים (*Kelim* 25:9) מִידֵי טוּמְאָתָן אֶלָּא בְּשִׁנּוּי מַעֲשֶׂה — "All utensils become susceptible to ritual impurity through intention, but they only lose their susceptibility to ritual impurity through change brought about by action," i.e., once a utensil has become susceptible to ritual impurity, the only way to alter its status is by physically changing it; mere intention can no longer affect its status.

מַחְתָּה   *Coal-pan.*

One of the sacred utensils used for the Temple service (see כְּלִי שָׁרֵת). The מַחְתָּה was used for carrying the coals used to burn the incense on the inner altar (see מִזְבַּח הַזָּהָב). On Yom Kippur, the High Priest (כֹּהֵן גָּדוֹל) used a special מַחְתָּה.

מְטַהֵר בְּזוֹחֲלִין   See זוֹחֲלִין.

מְטַלְטְלִין   *Movable property.*

This differs Halakhically from immovable property (מְקַרְקְעֵי), i.e., real estate, in many ways. Certain modes of acquisition are effective only with regard to movable property (e.g., pulling [מְשִׁיכָה], or lifting [הַגְבָּהָה] the

item being purchased), and not with regard to real estate. Similarly, the modes of acquisition that are effective with regard to real estate are generally ineffective with regard to מְטַלְטְלִין. In a lawsuit, the litigants cannot be required to take an oath unless the property in dispute is a movable object. According to Talmudic law, movable property may not be collected in payment for debts against the borrower's will (see נְכָסִים שֶׁיֵּשׁ לָהֶם אַחֲרָיוּת; אַחֲרָיוּת), although a Geonic ruling, based on certain Talmudic precedents, permitted collecting payment from the heirs of the borrower even from movable property. The laws of overcharging (אוֹנָאָה) apply only to movable property. With regard to certain laws, the Halakhic status of documents (see שְׁטָר) and slaves (see עֶבֶד כְּנַעֲנִי) is the same as that of land, even though they are in fact movable objects. This is so because of special Biblical rulings (גְּזֵירַת הַכָּתוּב) or because of the nature of the Halakhot under discussion.

מְטַמֵּא לְרָצוֹן   *Confers susceptibility to ritual impurity with intention.*

Solid foods become susceptible to ritual impurity only after they have come in contact with the "seven liquids" (water, oil, wine, etc., see הֶכְשֵׁר; שִׁבְעָה מַשְׁקִין). Foods that have not been touched by any of these liquids cannot become ritually impure, even if they touch something impure. The seven liquids confer susceptibility to ritual impurity only if they are poured on the food or moved from their original location to the satisfaction of the owner of the food. However, if one of the liquids is itself ritually impure, it confers susceptibility to ritual impurity even if it is not intentionally moved from its original location and even if it falls on the food unintentionally.

מֵי חַטָּאת   Lit., *water of a purification offering,*

i.e., water mixed with the ashes of the Red Heifer (פָּרָה אֲדוּמָּה), which was used to purify people and objects that had contracted ritual impurity by contact with a dead body (see טוּמְאַת מֵת). Specifically, naturally flowing water (מַיִם חַיִּים) was placed in a container, and a small amount of ashes from the Red Heifer was added. The resulting mixture, called מֵי חַטָּאת (or מֵי נִדָּה), was sprinkled on the people or objects to be purified. The process of mixing the ashes with water is called קִידּוּשׁ מֵי חַטָּאת — "sanctification of the purifying water" — and may be performed by anyone except a deaf-mute, an imbecile, or a minor (see חֵרֵשׁ שׁוֹטֶה וְקָטָן). Even though מֵי חַטָּאת purifies those who are ritually impure, if a person who is ritually pure touches or carries מֵי חַטָּאת, he becomes ritually impure for one day (see טוּמְאַת עֶרֶב), unless he was carrying or touching the מֵי חַטָּאת while participating in the purification process. The ceremony of purification involves taking a bundle of three branches of hyssop (אֵזוֹב) and using it to sprinkle the מֵי חַטָּאת on the ritually impure person on the third and the seventh day after he became ritually impure.

מִי שֶׁפָּרַע   Lit., *He who exacted payment.*

Short for the formula: "He who exacted payment from the generation of the flood and the generation of the Tower of Babel will exact payment from whoever does not stand by his word." If payment has been made for merchandise, and before the formal act of acquisition the buyer or the seller retracts, the court cannot force the two sides to complete the transaction. The person who retracted is, however, censured by the court (according to some opinions, cursed) with the formula: "He who exacted payment," etc. In other words, this formula is a kind of moral censure administered by the court against a person breaking an unenforceable contract.

מֵיאוּן   Lit., *refusal.* A girl under the age of twelve can be married off by her father. If, however, her father is no longer alive, then according to Torah law she cannot get married while still a minor. Nevertheless, the Sages decreed that her mother or brothers may marry her off with her consent. The girl may terminate this marriage before she reaches the age of twelve by performing מֵיאוּן, or "refusing," i.e., declaring that she does not want the marriage. In such cases, no bill of divorce (*גֵּט*) is necessary. When a girl performs מֵיאוּן, the marriage is nullified retroactively, and she is considered never to have been married at all. Most of the laws of מֵיאוּן are discussed in tractate *Yevamot.*

מִיגּוֹ   Lit., *from the midst of, since.* An important legal argument, used to support the claim of one of the parties in a dispute. If one of the litigants could have made a claim more advantageous to his cause than he actually did, we assume he was telling the truth. The מִיגּוֹ argument may be expressed in the following way: "Since he could have made a better claim (for had he wanted to lie, he would presumably have put forward a claim more advantageous to himself), we assume that he must be telling the truth." For he could say: מַה לִּי לְשַׁקֵּר — "What reason do I have to lie?" There are, however, certain limitations governing the application of this principle; for example, אֵין מִיגּוֹ בִּמְקוֹם עֵדִים — "There is no מִיגּוֹ where there are witnesses." In other words, מִיגּוֹ is not effective where witnesses contradict the litigant's claim. The principle of מִיגּוֹ is the subject of profound legal analysis in the Talmud and its commentaries.

מִדַּת סְדוֹם   Lit., *behavior characteristic of Sodom,* i.e., malicious selfishness. If a person denies someone use of his possessions, even though he would incur no loss or damage by granting this person use of the property, his conduct is considered to be מִדַּת סְדוֹם. The courts may sometimes for the sake of equity compel a person displaying מִדַּת סְדוֹם to waive his legal rights (כּוֹפִין עַל מִדַּת סְדוֹם — "We compel in an instance of מִדַּת סְדוֹם").

מִיטַּלְטֵל מָלֵא וְרֵיקָן   *Can be moved when full or when empty.* A wooden utensil or container is only susceptible to ritual impurity if it "can be moved whether empty or full." If it is so large that its cubic capacity is more than 40 *se'ah* (about 90 gallons or 330 liters), it is not susceptible to ritual impurity.

מִילָה   *Circumcision.* By Torah law (Genesis 17:10 ff.), it is obligatory to circumcise all male Jews. This obligation devolves on the father of a son eight days after birth. If the child is weak or ill, the circumcision is postponed until the baby is healthy. If the father is unavailable on the eighth day after birth, the Rabbinical Court sees to it that the child is circumcised. If, for whatever reason, the child is still not circumcised, then he is obligated to have himself circumcised when he reaches the age of thirteen. A boy who reaches maturity and is not circumcised

violates a positive commandment and is subject to כָּרֵת — "excision" (ibid., verse 14). If a child was born without a foreskin, he must have a drop of blood let in lieu of actual circumcision; this is called הַטָּפַת דַּם בְּרִית (lit., "dripping of the blood of the covenant"). Generally, circumcisions may be performed on Shabbat, if that happens to be the eighth day, but if the circumcision is postponed, it may only be performed on a weekday. It is customary to celebrate a circumcision with a festive meal, and this meal is deemed a סְעוּדַת מִצְוָה — "a meal at a religious ceremony." Circumcision is also necessary for men who wish to convert to Judaism. The potential convert must be circumcised and must then immerse himself in a *מִקְוֶה* (ritual bath) as part of the conversion process.

מַיִם אַחֲרוֹנִים   Lit., *last water.* The water used for washing one's hands after a meal, before *בִּרְכַּת הַמָּזוֹן* — Grace after Meals. This obligation was imposed primarily for health reasons, and in later generations the practice was not universally observed.

מַיִם חַיִּים   *Fresh, running water from a spring that is fit to drink.* מַיִם חַיִּים is needed in the purification from ritual impurity of three categories of ritually impure persons: (1) Men who have been suffering from gonorrhea (see זָב) and have recovered must undergo purification in order to be restored to ritual purity. They must immerse themselves in מַיִם חַיִּים; immersion in a *מִקְוֶה* — a ritual bath — is insufficient. (2) Only מַיִם חַיִּים can be used to prepare *מֵי חַטָּאת* — the water used to purify those suffering from ritual impurity caused by contact with a dead body. There is a complicated procedure to ensure that water in a container remains מַיִם חַיִּים. (3) מַיִם חַיִּים is also used in the purification process of a leper (see טָהֳרַת הַמְצוֹרָע; מְצוֹרָע מוּחְלָט; מְצוֹרָע מוּסְגָּר). One of the two birds brought as a sacrifice by a leper must be sacrificed over a vessel containing מַיִם חַיִּים, and the other must be dipped in the vessel containing blood of this sacrifice and the מַיִם חַיִּים. (See Leviticus 14:4–7.)

מַיִם מוּכִּין   Lit., *afflicted water.* Flowing water is suitable for preparing *מֵי חַטָּאת* — "purification water," i.e., water used for purifying those suffering from ritual impurity caused by contact with a dead body — only if it is drinkable. Salty water and warm water from hot springs are considered "afflicted water" and may not be used to prepare מֵי חַטָּאת.

מַיִם רִאשׁוֹנִים   Lit., *first water.* The water used to wash one's hands before a meal. See נְטִילַת יָדַיִם.

מַיִם שְׁאוּבִים   Lit., *drawn water.* Water taken from a container, as opposed to springwater or rainwater. If a *מִקְוֶה* — a ritual bath — has less than the minimum required amount of water in it (i.e., less than 40 *se'ah,* about 90 gallons or 330 litres), and three *lugin* (about a quart or a liter, see לוֹג) of drawn water are added to it, all the water in the מִקְוֶה becomes unfit for use. Clearly a מִקְוֶה filled completely with drawn water is not suitable for ritual immersion. If a מִקְוֶה already contains the required 40 *se'ah* of rainwater, no additional quantity of מַיִם שְׁאוּבִים can render it unfit.

מַיִם שֶׁאֵין לָהֶם סוֹף   Lit., *[a body of] water without an end.* A body of water so large that the further shore cannot be seen. If witnesses testify that a person fell into such a body of water, and he was not seen to emerge, we do not automatically assume that he drowned (and that his wife is a widow and should therefore be allowed to remarry), since he might have come out of the water in a place where the witnesses could not see him. See עֲגוּנָה.

מִין בְּשֶׁאֵינוֹ מִינוֹ   Lit., *one type [of food] in another type.* An accidental mixing of one type of food, which is non-kosher, with another type of food, which is kosher (e.g., a mixture of pig fat and kosher fish). Such a mixture is kosher only if the taste of the non-kosher food is no longer noticeable. The kosher food is said to "neutralize" (מְבַטֵּל) the non-kosher food. Where tasting is impractical the Sages ordained that such a combination requires that the kosher food must be sixty times the quantity of the non-kosher food for the neutralization to be effective. A different law applies to mixtures of מִין בְּמִינוֹ ("one type in the same type"), i.e., the accidental mixing of kosher and non-kosher foods of the same type (e.g., a mixture of prohibited animal fat [חֵלֶב] and the permitted fat [שׁוּמָן] taken from the same animal, which both taste the same). In such cases there is a dispute among the Sages. Some say that the mixture is not kosher, no matter what the proportions are. Others say that according to Torah law the mixture is kosher if the kosher food exceeds the non-kosher food in quantity, but that by Rabbinic decree the kosher food must be sixty times the quantity of the non-kosher food for the neutralization to be effective.

מֵיפַּךְ שְׁבוּעָה   *Reversing, transferring an oath.* In a case where the defendant completely denies the plaintiff's claim, the Sages imposed an oath on the defendant, called "שְׁבוּעַת הֶיסֵת — "an oath of inducement." The defendant can "transfer the oath" (מֵיפַּךְ שְׁבוּעָה) to the plaintiff, and if the latter takes the oath he receives payment in full. See *Shevuot* 41a.

מִיצּוּי   Lit., *wringing out.* A term used in the laws of sacrifices of birds. Blood is wrung out of such sacrifices as follows: When a bird is sacrificed, after its neck has been pinched (see מְלִיקָה) and (in the case of a sin-offering) its blood sprinkled on the altar (see הַזָּאָה), the priest wrings its blood out on the sides of the altar. In the case of a חַטָּאת — a sin-offering; see חַטַּאת הָעוֹף — the priest lets its blood flow down from below the middle of the height of the altar (see חוּט הַסִּיקְרָא) to the יְסוֹד הַמִּזְבֵּחַ — "base of the altar." To wring out the blood of an עוֹלָה — a burnt-offering — the head and body of the bird are pressed against the side of the altar from above the חוּט הַסִּיקְרָא (see עוֹלַת הָעוֹף).

מִיתָה בִּידֵי שָׁמַיִם   *Death at the hands of Heaven.* This punishment is divinely meted out. It is similar to "כָּרֵת — "excision" — but is slightly less severe. People who willfully take part in the Temple service, although forbidden to do so (e.g., non-priests [see זָר], or priests while not wearing the priestly garments [see מְחוּסַּר בְּגָדִים], and non-priests who eat תְּרוּמָה, among others, are subject to מִיתָה בִּידֵי שָׁמַיִם.

מַכֶּה אָבִיו וְאִמּוֹ   *One who strikes his father or mother.* It is prohibited by Torah law (Exodus 21:15) to strike one's father or mother. One who violates this prohibition is subject to the death penalty by strangulation (see חֶנֶק). If a child strikes one of his parents, leaving a wound or a bruise, he has violated this prohibition and is liable to the death penalty.

מַכֶּה בַּפַּטִּישׁ   Lit., *striking with a hammer.* Putting the finishing touches to an object (or to other work). This is one of the thirty-nine categories of work prohibited on Shabbat (see אֲבוֹת מְלָאכוֹת; גְּמַר מְלָאכָה). The Talmud offers no clear definition of this type of labor, nor a precise description of the extent of the repairs that must be made in order for an act to be considered מַכֶּה בַּפַּטִּישׁ. Each action must be judged individually to determine its final stage.

מִכְוָה   *A burn.* Special laws (Leviticus 13:24–28) apply to spots of leprosy (צָרַעַת) appearing in burns (מִכְוָה) already existing on the skin. They differ from the laws applying to spots of leprosy appearing on normal skin. See שְׁחִין.

מַכּוֹת הָרְאוּיוֹת לְהִשְׁתַּלֵּשׁ   Lit., *lashes that can be divided by three,* i.e., administered in a number that is a multiple of three. According to Torah law (Deuteronomy 25:2–3), a person receiving lashes (מַלְקוֹת) was whipped thirty-nine times. If he was incapable, for health reasons, of bearing the normal number of lashes, he was given the number he was capable of receiving. However, that number had to be a multiple of three, since for each stripe given to the offender on the front of his body, two were given on his back.

מַכְשִׁירֵי אוֹכֶל נֶפֶשׁ   *Acts that precede and facilitate the preparation of food.* Work directly necessary for the preparation of food, e.g., cooking and baking, is permitted on Festivals. Such work is called מְלֶאכֶת אוֹכֶל נֶפֶשׁ — "work for food." However, work that does not involve food but merely facilitates its preparation, such as sharpening a knife for cutting or slaughtering, is called מַכְשִׁירֵי אוֹכֶל נֶפֶשׁ. There is a dispute among the Tannaim as to whether or not such work is permitted. See *Betzah* 28a/b, *Megillah* 7b.

מַכְשִׁירֵי מִצְוָה   *Items facilitating the performance of a mitzvah.* Certain mitzvot (e.g., circumcision) override the prohibition against performing work on Shabbat and Festivals. There is, however, a Tannaitic controversy as to whether the preparation of utensils that is not in itself part of the mitzvah but facilitates the performance of a mitzvah, e.g., preparing a knife for circumcision on Shabbat, also overrides Shabbat prohibitions. See *Shabbat* 130a/132b.

מַכַּת מְדִינָה   *A regional disaster,* i.e., a natural disaster befalling an entire region and not just a specific, limited area. With reference to certain Halakhot there is a difference between a disaster affecting a single field and one affecting an entire area. For example, if someone leases a field and agrees to pay the owner a fixed amount of produce in return (see חוֹכֵר), and the field is subsequently damaged, the lessee may deduct a certain part of the payment (depending on how much damage was done to the field) if the damage was caused by a מַכַּת מְדִינָה — "a regional disaster."

מַכַּת מַרְדּוּת   Lit., *a lashing for rebelliousness,* i.e., lashes administered by Rabbinic decree, rather than by Torah law. A disciplinary measure imposed to prevent or restrict social licence. In certain cases מַכַּת מַרְדּוּת was a set punishment imposed on anyone who violated specific Rabbinical prohibitions. מַכַּת מַרְדּוּת was also imposed on people who were disobedient or disrespectful towards a Rabbinical Court. Similarly, people who refuse to fulfill positive Torah commandments (see עֲשֵׂה) may be given lashes, a type of מַכַּת מַרְדּוּת. The number of stripes administered is not fixed. The judges can increase or moderate the punishment, depending on the specific case (by contrast, when flogging is administered by Torah law, no more than thirty-nine lashes may be given). Even after Rabbinical Courts ceased imposing the penalty of Torah-ordained lashes, they continued to administer מַכַּת מַרְדּוּת, both in Eretz Israel and in the Diaspora.

מְלָאכָה שָׁאֵינָה צְרִיכָה לְגוּפָה   Work that is not necessary for its own sake,

i.e., prohibited work performed on Shabbat for a purpose differing from that for which such work was performed in the Sanctuary. For example, extinguishing a fire to save fuel, rather than to produce coals (the purpose for which "extinguishing" was performed in the Sanctuary) is considered a מְלָאכָה שָׁאֵינָה צְרִיכָה לְגוּפָה. According to other opinions, מְלָאכָה שָׁאֵינָה צְרִיכָה לְגוּפָה means work performed for a "negative" purpose — in the previous case, for example, extinguishing a fire to avoid using the fuel, rather than to create something new (i.e., coals). There is a controversy among the Tannaim and also among later Halakhic authorities as to whether מְלָאכָה שָׁאֵינָה צְרִיכָה לְגוּפָה is prohibited by Torah law or only by Rabbinic injunction. See מְלֶאכֶת מַחֲשֶׁבֶת; פְּסִיק רֵישֵׁיהּ.

מְלֶאכֶת מַחֲשֶׁבֶת   Lit., planned, thoughtful, creative work.

Work on Shabbat is only prohibited by Torah law if it is מְלֶאכֶת מַחֲשֶׁבֶת — i.e., creative, purposeful work intentionally performed. Work that is not מְלֶאכֶת מַחֲשֶׁבֶת is prohibited only by Rabbinic decree. All the thirty-nine main categories of labor prohibited on Shabbat (see אֲבוֹת מְלָאכוֹת) are derived from the various activities involved in the construction of the Sanctuary (מִשְׁכָּן) in the wilderness. This construction work is termed מְלֶאכֶת מַחֲשֶׁבֶת (see Exodus 35:33), and thus all categories of work prohibited by Torah law on Shabbat must contain this element of creative work.

מִלְחֶמֶת מִצְוָה   Mandatory war (lit., "a war [that is] a mitzvah"),

a war that the Jewish people is obliged to wage. A מִלְחֶמֶת מִצְוָה may be waged without prior permission from the Sanhedrin, and all Jews are required to participate in such a war, even those who are exempted by the Torah (Deuteronomy 20:5-8). The category of מִלְחֶמֶת מִצְוָה includes: (1) war against Amalek, (2) war for the conquest of Eretz Israel from the Canaanites, and (3) war in self-defense. See also מִלְחֶמֶת רְשׁוּת. Many authorities place the third category in a higher category than the others and call it מִלְחֶמֶת חוֹבָה — "an obligatory war."

מִלְחֶמֶת רְשׁוּת   Optional war (in contrast to mandatory war;

see previous entry). A war waged by a Jewish King to enlarge the boundaries of Eretz Israel, or for some other reason that does not come under the category of מִלְחֶמֶת מִצְוָה. Such a war may only be undertaken with permission of the Sanhedrin

(see בֵּית דִּין שֶׁל שִׁבְעִים וְאֶחָד). Certain people are exempt from participating in a מִלְחֶמֶת רְשׁוּת, such as (1) a newlywed husband during the first year of his marriage (Deuteronomy 24:5); (2) one who has built a new house (ibid. 20:5) or planted a vineyard (ibid. 6) and has not yet benefitted from them; (3) one who has betrothed a woman and has not yet married her (ibid. 7); (4) one who is cowardly or fainthearted (ibid. 8). Before setting out to battle, the Jews are assembled and addressed by the מְשׁוּחַ מִלְחָמָה — "the priest anointed for war" — and the שׁוֹטְרִים — "officers" — who announce that those who are exempt may return home, though all except for category (1) had to assist in the war effort.

מְלִיחָה   Salting.

The salting of food to make it fit for consumption or sacrifice. (1) In order to make the meat of domesticated and non-domesticated animals (see חַיָּה טְהוֹרָה; בְּהֵמָה טְהוֹרָה) and of poultry (see עוֹף טָהוֹר) fit for eating, the meat must be salted before being cooked, so that the salt will absorb the blood found in the meat. After salting, the meat is rinsed. (2) With reference to sacrifices, any offering placed on the altar must have some salt added to it, so as to fulfill the Torah commandment, "With all your offerings you shall offer salt" (Leviticus 2:13).

מְלִיקָה   Lit., pinching, nipping.

Turtledoves and young pigeons offered as sacrifices in the Temple were not killed like other sacrifices by ritual slaughter with a knife, but rather by "pinching" their necks. This was considered an especially difficult activity to perform. The priest would hold the bird in his left hand with its legs and wings between his fingers, and the back of its neck stretched out and facing upwards. With his right fingernail, which he grew especially long for this purpose, the priest would cut the bird's neck and spine from the back until he reached and severed its windpipe and gullet. If the bird was to be offered as a burnt-offering (עוֹלַת הָעוֹף), the priest would completely sever its head. If it was to be offered as a sin-offering (חַטַּאת הָעוֹף), he would leave the head unsevered. A bird killed by מְלִיקָה that was not intended for sacrificial use was considered a נְבֵלָה and was not permitted to be eaten. But a bird killed by מְלִיקָה and offered as a sin-offering (חַטַּאת הָעוֹף) was permitted to be eaten by the priests. Only a priest was permitted to perform מְלִיקָה, whereas animals intended as sacrifices in the Temple could be slaughtered by a non-priest.

מֶלֶךְ   King.

By Torah law (Deuteronomy 17:14-20), the Jewish people are permitted to select a king to rule over them, if they so desire. This king must be of Jewish birth, and he may not be the offspring of converts. A number of special positive and negative commandments apply to such a king. He must have a special Torah scroll written for himself. He may not marry more than eighteen women, nor may he "multiply horses or money" (ibid.), i.e., possess more horses or money than he needs for his personal use and for that of the kingdom. All are obligated to honor and respect the king, and no one is allowed to treat him disrespectfully (including the king himself). A king who unintentionally committed a sin (Leviticus 4:22ff.) must bring a special sin-offering (a male goat, see שְׂעִיר נָשִׂיא). The king is authorized to appoint officials over the people and to impose his will on the people. He may collect taxes, appoint judges, and institute laws for the benefit of the people. The king is considered the leader of his people, and even takes precedence over a High Priest (כֹּהֵן גָּדוֹל) and a prophet (נָבִיא). One who sees a king must recite a special blessing. See also מַלְכֵי בֵּית דָּוִד; מַלְכֵי יִשְׂרָאֵל.

מַלְכֻיּוֹת Lit., *kingdoms, majesties.* The first of the three special blessings added to the musaf (מוּסָף) prayer on Rosh HaShanah. This blessing includes many Biblical verses on the theme of God as King of the universe. See זִכְרוֹנוֹת; שׁוֹפָרוֹת.

מַלְכֵי בֵּית דָּוִד *The Kings of the House of David.* The Kings of the Davidic dynasty were assured (II Samuel 7:16) that they would rule over the Jewish people forever. Since these Kings observed the laws of the Torah, they were permitted to serve as judges, could appear as defendants (but not as witnesses), and witnesses could testify against them (see מַלְכֵי יִשְׂרָאֵל). Only Kings of the House of David were permitted to sit in the Temple Courtyard (עֲזָרָה). See מֶלֶךְ.

מַלְכֵי יִשְׂרָאֵל *Kings of Israel.* Jewish Kings not of Davidic descent, in particular those who ruled during the Hasmonean era. Since these Kings did not follow the laws of the Torah, the Sages decreed that they could not participate in the judicial process either as judges, defendants or witnesses. See מֶלֶךְ; מַלְכֵי בֵּית דָּוִד.

מַלְקוֹת *Lashes.* A form of punishment. The victim is tied to a post in a leaning position and whipped on his back and his chest. The Sages interpreted the verse, "Forty stripes he may give him and not exceed" (Deuteronomy 25:3), to mean that the number of lashes administered per transgression is thirty-nine. But if the victim cannot survive that number of lashes, he receives the number he can bear (see מַכּוֹת הָרְאוּיוֹת לְהִשְׁתַּלֵּשׁ). Negative commandments (see לָאו) are usually punishable by lashes. However, there are a number of exceptions, notably: (1) a commandment that is violated without action (לָאו שֶׁאֵין בּוֹ מַעֲשֶׂה), (2) a transgression for which the Torah provided a means of reparation (לָאו הַנִּיתָּק לַעֲשֵׂה), (3) a collective prohibition that includes several different laws (לָאו שֶׁבִּכְלָלוֹת), and (4) a transgression that under certain circumstances could be subject to the death penalty (לָאו שֶׁנִּיתָּן לְאַזְהָרַת מִיתַת בֵּית דִּין). Lashes are not administered unless there are two witnesses to the transgression, and unless the sinner was warned immediately before his transgression. According to the Halakhah, a court of three is required in order to administer lashes.

מָמוֹן הַמּוּטָל בְּסָפֵק Lit., *money lying in doubt.* Property of doubtful ownership. For example, where two litigants each claim that a certain item is theirs, and neither can prove his claim. Usually the Halakhic principle that applies in such cases is הַמּוֹצִיא מֵחֲבֵירוֹ עָלָיו הָרְאָיָה — "the burden of proof rests upon the one who wishes to extract something from his fellow," i.e., if someone claims that he is entitled to property at present in the possession of another, the burden of proof rests upon the claimant. There are, however, certain cases in which other rules are followed.

מָמוֹנָא מֵאִיסּוּרָא לָא יָלְפִינַן *We do not learn monetary matters from ritual matters.* Since civil law, דִּינֵי מָמוֹנוֹת, which concerns the relationship between man and man, and ritual law,

אִיסּוּר וְהֶיתֵּר, which concerns the relationship between man and God, constitute two distinct legal spheres, conclusions regarding ritual matters may not be drawn from civil law, and vice versa.

מָמוֹנָא מִקְנָסָא לָא יָלְפִינַן Lit., *we do not learn monetary matters from fines.* The Halakhah distinguishes between two types of payments, namely: (1) מָמוֹנָא — lit., "money," i.e., payments resulting from contractual obligations, or compensation for damages equal in value to the amount of damage caused; and (2) קְנָסָא (or קְנָס*) — "fines," i.e., fixed indemnities, or indemnities not equal to the value of the damage caused. Even though both are monetary payments, each type has certain distinctive characteristics, and conclusions may not be drawn from one type and applied to the other.

מְמוּנֶּה Lit., *appointed person.* A high official in the Temple; in particular, the High Priest's deputy. There was a מְמוּנֶּה in charge of the guards on the Temple Mount, and one in charge of the lots used for assigning the priests their duties in the Temple service (see פַּיִס). See also *Shekalim* 5:1.

מַמְזֵר, מַמְזֶרֶת *A child born from an incestuous or adulterous relationship,* i.e., a child born from relations between a married woman and a man other than her husband, or between relatives who are forbidden to marry by Torah law, where the participants in such a relationship are subject to כָּרֵת ("excision"). An exception to this rule is a menstruating woman (נִדָּה), with whom sexual relations are forbidden under penalty of כָּרֵת, but whose offspring is not a מַמְזֵר. The offspring of an unmarried couple is not a מַמְזֵר. A מַמְזֵר inherits from his natural father and is Halakhically considered his father's son in all respects. A מַמְזֵר may only marry a מַמְזֶרֶת (a female mamzer) or a convert to Judaism. Likewise, a מַמְזֶרֶת may only marry a מַמְזֵר or a convert. The offspring of such a union is a מַמְזֵר.

מִן הַצַּד Lit., *from the side.* Usually, in court cases about civil or ritual matters, the most learned and experienced judge would open the discussion, and the other judges would follow, beginning with the next most learned judge and proceeding to the least experienced member of the court. In capital cases, however, the discussion was begun "from the side," i.e., by the youngest judges, seated furthest away from the presiding judge, to make sure that they would have full opportunity to express their views freely. Only later did the more senior members of the court proceed to express their views. It is related (*Sanhedrin* 36a) that all discussions in the court of Rabbi Yehudah HaNasi began "from the side," as it was assumed that no one would dare to take issue with Rabbi Yehudah.

מִנְהַג הַמְּדִינָה *Regional custom.* In many types of civil disputes, the rule followed is הַכֹּל כְּמִנְהַג הַמְּדִינָה — "everything follows the local custom." Specifically, we assume that buyer and seller, or employer and employee, are legally bound by the conditions of purchase or employment ordinarily followed in a given locality, unless they explicitly specified otherwise. See *Bava Metzia* 7:1.

מָנוּי Lit., *registered person.* By Torah law (see Exodus 12:4 and commentators), the Paschal lamb (קָרְבָּן פֶּסַח, see פֶּסַח) was only to be eaten by people who had arranged in advance to eat it together. Such people are called מְנוּיִים — "registered people." If the Paschal lamb was sacrificed for the sake of people who had not arranged in advance to eat it, it is deemed unfit (פָּסוּל), and may not be eaten.

מְנוֹרָה *Candelabrum.* One of the sacred utensils in the Temple. The מְנוֹרָה was made out of gold, and stood on the south side of the Sanctuary (הֵיכָל). It had seven decorated branches, on top of which were נֵרוֹת, containers for oil into which wicks were inserted. The מְנוֹרָה was lit in the evening, and fueled with sufficient oil so that it would burn until the morning, no matter how long the night lasted (see נֵר מַעֲרָבִי). The מְנוֹרָה was 18 *tefahim* high (a little less than 2 meters), and in front of it was a small platform with three steps for the priest who lit and cleaned it. In times of emergency it was permitted to make the מְנוֹרָה out of metals other than gold, but it still had to have seven branches.

Detail of Tiberian mosaic showing the menorah

מִנְחָה (1) *Afternoon prayer.* One of the three fixed daily prayers. מִנְחָה is recited during the time when the daily afternoon burnt-offering (תָּמִיד שֶׁל בֵּין הָעַרְבַּיִם) was offered in the Temple, i.e., from half an hour after midday until sunset. The principal component of the מִנְחָה service is the שְׁמוֹנֶה עֶשְׂרֵה* — "the eighteen benedictions" — which is preceded by אַשְׁרֵי — *Ashrei* (Psalm 145) — and followed by *Taḥanun* (תַּחֲנוּן) and the *Alenu* prayer. (2) *Meal-offering.* See מְנָחוֹת.

מִנְחָה גְדוֹלָה, מִנְחָה קְטַנָה Lit., *greater [i.e., early] minḥah, lesser [i.e., later] minḥah.* The daily afternoon burnt-offering (תָּמִיד שֶׁל בֵּין הָעַרְבַּיִם) was usually offered three-and-a-half (seasonal) hours after midday, although it was actually permissible to offer this sacrifice as early as half an hour after midday. (A "seasonal hour" is one-twelfth of the period from sunrise to sunset [according to other opinions, from dawn until three stars appear].) The three-hour period beginning half an hour after midday is called מִנְחָה גְדוֹלָה. The period from three-and-a-half (seasonal) hours after midday until sunset, which was the latest possible time that the daily afternoon burnt-offering could be offered, is called מִנְחָה קְטַנָה. See מִנְחָה.

מְנָחוֹת *Meal-offerings.* מְנָחוֹת include all offerings of flour or bread brought in the Temple. Among the מְנָחוֹת are the two loaves of bread brought on Shavuot (שְׁתֵּי הַלֶּחֶם); the Temple shewbread (לֶחֶם הַפָּנִים); the various kinds of voluntary meal-offerings (מְנָחוֹת נְדָבָה); the sinner's meal-offering (מִנְחַת חוֹטֵא); the loaves of bread accompanying a thanks-offering (לַחְמֵי תּוֹדָה, see תּוֹדָה); the meal-offerings that accompany libations (מְנָחוֹת נְסָכִים); the meal-offering of a suspected adulteress (מִנְחַת קְנָאוֹת, see סוֹטָה); and the omer-offering (מִנְחַת הָעוֹמֶר, see עוֹמֶר). Numerous complex laws apply to these meal-offerings, and most of tractate *Menaḥot* is devoted to a detailed discussion of them. Most of the מְנָחוֹת are brought from unleavened wheat flour. Likewise, most of these offerings require קְמִיצָה* — "taking a fistful" (of the offering) — which is an essential element in the

sacrificial ceremony. Many types of meal-offering have oil mixed with them, or incense added to them, at some stage of their preparation (see, however, כָּל הָרָאוּי לְבִילָה אֵין בִּילָה מְעַכֶּבֶת בּוֹ). The laws of meal-offerings parallel the laws of animal sacrifices in numerous respects, and many of the acts that render animal sacrifices unfit also render meal-offerings unfit.

מִנְחַת הָעוֹמֶר See עוֹמֶר.

מִנְחַת חֲבִיתִין See חֲבִיתִין.

מִנְחַת חוֹטֵא *Sinner's meal-offering.* A meal-offering (no less than one-tenth of an ephah of fine wheat flour) brought by people who had committed certain types of sins (entering the Temple while ritually impure [see טוּמְאַת מִקְדָּשׁ וְקָדָשָׁיו], and swearing certain types of false oaths [see שְׁבוּעַת בִּיטוּי; שְׁבוּעַת הָעֵדוּת]). See Leviticus 5:1–13. A person guilty of such transgressions who cannot afford to bring an animal sacrifice may bring a meal-offering instead (ibid., 11–13, see also קָרְבָּן עוֹלֶה וְיוֹרֵד), and this meal-offering is called a מִנְחַת חוֹטֵא. No oil or incense is added to this meal-offering. The priest removes a fistful of the flour (see קְמִיצָה), and then burns it on the altar. The rest of the offering is eaten by the priests. In many respects, the laws of the sinner's meal-offering parallel those of animal sin-offerings, e.g., the same types of incorrect intention (see מַחֲשָׁבָה) which render animal sin-offerings unfit also render these meal-offerings unfit.

מִנְחַת כֹּהֲנִים *Priests' meal-offering.* Any meal-offering, contributed and brought by a priest, whether voluntarily (מִנְחַת נְדָבָה) or as a sin-offering (מִנְחַת חוֹטֵא). The same laws apply to meal-offerings of priests as apply to other meal-offerings, with one exception: a priest's meal-offering is not eaten. The entire offering is burned on the altar (see Leviticus 6:16).

מִנְחַת מַחֲבַת A *meal-offering prepared in a pan.* A type of meal-offering, fried on a flat pan. Such an offering can be voluntary (see מְנָחוֹת). It is also offered daily by the High Priest, as well as by every priest on his first day of service in the Temple (see חֲבִיתִין).

מִנְחַת מַרְחֶשֶׁת A *meal-offering prepared in a deep container.* A type of meal-offering, fried in a deep container full of oil. Such an offering is voluntary (see מְנָחוֹת) and has no parallel among the obligatory or communal offerings.

מִנְחַת נְסָכִים A *meal-offering accompanying libations.* A meal-offering (see מְנָחוֹת) brought together with all burnt-offerings of animals (see עוֹלָה) and all peace-offerings (שְׁלָמִים), both individual and communal. This meal-offering is accompanied by a libation offering of wine (see נְסָכִים). Oil is added to the מִנְחַת נְסָכִים, although incense is not. No fistful of flour (קוֹמֶץ, see קְמִיצָה) is removed from the מִנְחַת נְסָכִים, nor is it "waved" (see תְּנוּפָה) or "brought close" (see הַגָּשָׁה) to the altar (מִזְבֵּחַ), as are other types of meal-offerings. The entire מִנְחַת נְסָכִים is burned on the altar, and none of it is eaten by the priests. The quantities of flour brought for מִנְחוֹת נְסָכִים are fixed by the Torah: three עֶשְׂרוֹנִים for a bull, two עֶשְׂרוֹנִים for a ram, and one עִשָּׂרוֹן for a lamb (an עִשָּׂרוֹן, a tenth of an אֵיפָה, is approximately 3 liters). The animal sacrifices accompanied by a מִנְחַת נְסָכִים are not rendered unfit if the meal-offering was not offered; likewise, while the מִנְחַת נְסָכִים is supposed to be offered together with the animal sacrifice, it remains acceptable even if it was offered later.

מִנְחַת סוֹטָה   See מִנְחַת קְנָאוֹת.

מִנְחַת קְנָאוֹת   Lit., *a meal-offering of jealousy.* The meal-offering (see מְנָחוֹת) brought by a suspected adulteress (סוֹטָה, see Numbers 5:11–31). A suspected adulteress, whose husband brings her to the Temple to undergo the Biblical procedure to test her faithfulness to him, is required to bring a meal-offering of barley flour (unlike most meal-offerings, which are brought from wheat flour). No oil or incense is added to it (ibid., 15). A fistful of flour is removed from this offering (see קְמִיצָה), and the remainder of it is eaten by the priests (ibid., 25–26). The same categories of incorrect intention that render a sinner's meal-offering unfit (see מִנְחַת חוֹטֵא), also render a מִנְחַת קְנָאוֹת unfit.

מִנְיָן   *Quorum* (lit., "number"). Usually, the quorum needed to constitute a "congregation" (עֵדָה) — ten adult Jewish males. This quorum is required in order to perform any ritual considered especially holy (דְּבָרִים שֶׁבִּקְדוּשָׁה), such as congregational prayer, recitation of the kaddish (קַדִּיש), etc. When a מִנְיָן eats together, the name of God is added to the invitation to Grace after Meals. Certain of the blessings recited at wedding ceremonies require a מִנְיָן, as do the blessings recited when consoling mourners.

מְסַדְּרִים   Lit., *we arrange, arranging.* A rule governing debt-collection. If someone owes money to somebody else, or to the Temple, and he does not have enough money to repay his debt, all his property may be taken in payment for the debt except objects necessary for day-to-day living, such as personal effects and work tools. This procedure of leaving such items in the borrower's possession is called סִידּוּר, "exempting from seizure."

מֵסִיחַ לְפִי תוּמוֹ   *An incidental, unconsidered remark* (lit., "speaks innocently"). Someone who describes something that he witnessed, without having the intention of giving formal testimony. In certain cases, a remark of this kind is acceptable as testimony. For example, a child's innocent description of events he saw is acceptable proof that a woman who was kidnapped was not raped. In certain cases, remarks made by people whose testimony is not normally accepted are believed if they are speaking without being aware that their words have consequence. For example, a non-Jew's unconsidered description of how he saw a man die is acceptable proof that the man is dead, and his wife is consequently free to remarry.

מְסִירָה   Lit., *handing over.* One of the modes of acquisition through which movable property is acquired (see חֲלִיפִין; מְשִׁיכָה; הַגְבָּהָה). מְסִירָה entails having the seller (or donor of a gift) hand over the item being sold (or given) to the buyer (or recipient). In the case of מְסִירָה, the article must be too heavy to be easily lifted or even pulled, and the transfer is only effective in a public domain or in a private domain not that of the seller or the buyer.

Once the buyer or recipient has taken hold of the article the ownership passes to him and (in the case of sale) he owes the seller the value of the article. See קִנְיָן.

מֵסִית וּמַדִּיחַ   *One who incites and leads astray.* A person who incites others to worship idols. A מֵסִית incites an individual to worship idols, whereas a מַדִּיחַ incites a community to do so. Since incitement to idolatry is such a serious offense, attacking the very foundations of Judaism, the Torah ordains that "your eye shall not pity nor shall you spare [the inciter]" (Deuteronomy 13:9). The Sages therefore deprived מֵסִית and מַדִּיחַ of certain legal benefits ordinarily conferred on suspects in capital cases. For example, it is permissible to conceal witnesses to observe the suspect מֵסִית and even to trick him into committing his crime in the presence of witnesses (see הַכְמָנַת עֵדִים). Similarly, no special attempt is made in the trial of a מֵסִית to find exonerating considerations. The punishment for incitement to idol-worship is stoning (see סְקִילָה).

מְעוֹרָב שֶׁמֶשׁ   See הֶעֱרֵב שֶׁמֶשׁ.

מְעִילָה   Lit., *trespass.* The unlawful use of consecrated property (הֶקְדֵּשׁ). Anyone who benefits from consecrated property or damages it through use is guilty of מְעִילָה. Intentional מְעִילָה is punishable by death at the hand of Heaven (מִיתָה בִּידֵי שָׁמַיִם), according to some authorities, and by lashes (מַלְקוּת), according to others. One who commits מְעִילָה unintentionally, or even under duress, must repay the Temple for the loss he caused or the benefit he gained, plus a fine of one-fifth (see חוֹמֶשׁ) of the value of the loss or of the benefit he gained. He must also bring a special sacrifice, אֲשַׁם מְעִילוֹת — a "guilt-offering for trespass." (See Leviticus 5:15–16.) The laws of מְעִילָה apply to all types of consecrated property, whether sacrifices or money or objects donated to the Temple. מְעִילָה is a special case in that the principle of אֵין שָׁלִיחַ לִדְבַר עֲבֵירָה — "there is no agency for crime" — does not apply to it. If someone commits a crime at the behest of someone else, only the person who actually committed the crime is usually liable to punishment, and not the person who sent him. In the case of מְעִילָה, however, if an agent was sent by someone else to make use of consecrated property (הֶקְדֵּשׁ), the sender is the one who transgressed. See קָדְשֵׁי קָדָשִׁים; קָדָשִׁים קַלִּים.

מַעְיָן   *Foundation, spring.* Spring water purifies from ritual impurity those immersing in it, as stated in the Torah (Leviticus 11:36). It may be used for immersion even though the water is moving (see אַשְׁבּוֹרֶן; זוֹחֲלִין), which is not so in the case of a מִקְוֶה (ritual bath). Moreover, immersion in spring water purifies all types of people suffering from bodily discharge, whereas a מִקְוֶה does not. A מַעְיָן is kosher for immersion no matter what quantity of water it contains; a מִקְוֶה, by contrast, requires a minimum of 40 *se'ah.* If the waters of a מַעְיָן are drinkable and constantly flowing, it is considered מַיִם חַיִּים.

מְעַכֵּב   Lit., *detains, prevents,* i.e., is indispensable. A concept encountered in many areas of the Halakhah, particularly with reference to sacrificial law. There is often a particular, proper way of performing a מִצְוָה, but one who does not perform the מִצְוָה in this fashion has still fulfilled his obligation. Regarding other

מִצְוֹת, however, the failure to carry out certain details may render the מִצְוָה unacceptable. These details are deemed "indispensable" (מְעַכֵּב). The distinction between elements in the performance of a מִצְוָה that are required only *ab initio* (לְמִצְוָה), and details that are deemed "indispensable" (לְעַכֵּב), is encountered primarily in the laws of sacrifices. See next entry.

מְעַכְּבִים זֶה אֶת זֶה   Lit., *prevent each other,* i.e., are mutually indispensable. This applies when a mitzvah is composed of several parts, and the omission of one of the parts renders the entire mitzvah valueless. In such cases, each part of the mitzvah is considered "indispensable." For example, the Torah commands us to put צִיצִית — "fringes" — on each corner of four-cornered garments. If fringes are not put on one of the corners, the mitzvah of צִיצִית has not been even partially fulfilled. By contrast, there are other mitzvot that have more than one part, but omission of one part does not render the other part(s) worthless (though ideally all should be performed together). For example, a man who wears only head תְּפִילִין (phylacteries) and not hand תְּפִילִין, or vice versa, still fulfills that part of the mitzvah that he has performed.

מַעֲלֶה אֶת הַמִּקְוֶה   Lit., *raises the mikveh,* i.e., renders a mikveh kosher. A מִקְוֶה (ritual bath) containing less than 40 סְאָה of rainwater is not kosher. But certain substances other than rainwater may be added to such a מִקְוֶה to complete the required 40 סְאָה (e.g., snow). These substances are said to "raise the mikveh."

מַעֲמָד pl., (מַעֲמָדוֹת)   Lit., *post, division.* Sacrifices in the Temple were offered by twenty-four groups of priests known as מִשְׁמָרוֹת — "watches" (see מִשְׁמָר). Each group in turn was responsible for offering the sacrifices for a week. They were called upon to perform this service twice a year on average. Corresponding to each of these "watches" was a group of non-priests, called a מַעֲמָד. The entire Jewish people in Eretz Israel was divided into twenty-four מַעֲמָדוֹת, and each time a מִשְׁמָר went to Jerusalem to offer sacrifices, part of the corresponding מַעֲמָד would go there as well. The remainder of the מַעֲמָד would remain at home, and during that week would fast each day (from Monday to Thursday), read special portions from the Torah and say special prayers.

מַעֲמָד וּמוֹשָׁב   *Standing up and sitting down.* A mourning custom observed during the Mishnaic and Talmudic period. At a funeral service, one of the people present would make the following request: "Sit down, dear people, sit down," and would deliver a eulogy. This would be followed by: "Stand up, dear people, stand up," and another eulogy. This formula was recited several times as a sign of mourning. Today, this custom is no longer practiced.

מַעֲמִיד   *Binder, ingredient that curdles, supporter.* (1) Ordinarily, if a minute quantity of non-kosher food is mixed with kosher food, the resulting mixture is kosher, since the non-kosher food is בָּטֵל — "neutralized" — by the kosher food. If, however, the non-kosher food serves as a curdling agent and gives the kosher food consistency (e.g., if non-kosher rennet was used in the making of cheese), then the resulting mixture is not kosher,

no matter how small the quantity of the מַעֲמִיד. (2) Those parts of the sukkah walls that support the covering (סְכָךְ) of the sukkah. (See סוּכָּה.) According to some opinions, this "supporting part" of the sukkah may not be made of material that is susceptible to ritual impurity.

מַעֲקֶה   *Guard-rail.* It is a positive commandment (Deuteronomy 22:8) to erect a guardrail around the flat roof of a house or any other building. This commandment is interpreted as forbidding a person from keeping any object in his possession that might endanger other people (e.g., a vicious dog, or an unsafe ladder), as it is written: "You shall not bring blood upon your house" (ibid.).

מַעֲרָכָה   Lit., *arrangement,* i.e., the pile of wood on the altar (מִזְבֵּחַ). Three piles of wood were placed on the altar each day: the מַעֲרָכָה גְדוֹלָה — "great pile of wood" — on which burnt-offerings (see עוֹלָה) and the sacrificial portions of other offerings (see אֵימוּרִים) were burned; a second pile, from which coals were taken for burning the incense (קְטוֹרֶת) on the inner altar (מִזְבַּח הַזָּהָב); and a third pile, which was left burning constantly, in fulfillment of the commandment (Leviticus 6:5) to leave a fire burning on the altar at all times (אֵשׁ תָּמִיד). On Yom Kippur (יוֹם הַכִּיפּוּרִים), an extra pile of wood was added, from which the coals used for burning the incense in the קוֹדֶשׁ הַקֳּדָשִׁים ("Holy of Holies") were taken. See diagram on p. 276.

מַעֲשֵׂר בְּהֵמָה   *Animal tithe.* On three occasions each year, the owner of a herd of kosher animals was required to gather all the animals born during the preceding period into an enclosure, and to let them out one by one. These animals were passed "under the shepherd's rod" (see Leviticus 27:32), and every tenth animal was marked with red paint, to indicate that it was holy. These animals are called מַעֲשֵׂר בְּהֵמָה. The מַעֲשֵׂר בְּהֵמָה was brought to the Temple, if it was fit to be sacrificed, and it was offered in a manner similar to that of a peace-offering (שְׁלָמִים). Its blood was sprinkled on the altar, and its meat was eaten by its owner (but not by the priests). The details of the laws of מַעֲשֵׂר בְּהֵמָה are set out in tractate *Bekhorot.*

מַעֲשֵׂר עָנִי   *Poor man's tithe.* A special tithe set aside from agricultural produce and distributed to the poor. During the third and sixth years of the Sabbatical cycle (see שְׁבִיעִית), after the priests' share of the produce (see תְּרוּמָה) and the first tithe (מַעֲשֵׂר רִאשׁוֹן) have been set aside, one-tenth of the remaining produce is distributed to the poor. This tithe is called מַעֲשֵׂר עָנִי. During the other years of the Sabbatical cycle, מַעֲשֵׂר שֵׁנִי — the second tithe — is set aside instead of מַעֲשֵׂר עָנִי. מַעֲשֵׂר עָנִי is not holy, but until it has been set aside the produce is deemed טֶבֶל — "untithed produce" — and may not be eaten. מַעֲשֵׂר עָנִי is separated from דְּמַאי — "doubtfully tithed produce" — but it is not given to the poor, since the principle of הַמּוֹצִיא מֵחֲבֵירוֹ עָלָיו הָרְאָיָה — "the burden of proof rests upon the person wishing to extract something from another" — applies here. Therefore a poor person who laid claim to מַעֲשֵׂר עָנִי in such a case had to prove that this tithe had not already been separated from this produce. See מַעַשְׂרוֹת.

מַעֲשֵׂר רִאשׁוֹן   *First tithe.* One-tenth of agricultural produce remaining after terumah (תְּרוּמָה), the portion of the crop given to the priests, has been set aside, is distributed to the Levites. This produce is called מַעֲשֵׂר רִאשׁוֹן — "first tithe." The owner was permitted to give מַעֲשֵׂר רִאשׁוֹן to any Levite he wished. A Levite who received מַעֲשֵׂר רִאשׁוֹן had in turn to set aside one-tenth of this tithe as תְּרוּמַת מַעֲשֵׂר — "terumah of the tithe" — and give it to a priest. The rest of the מַעֲשֵׂר רִאשׁוֹן, after the Levite set aside the תְּרוּמַת מַעֲשֵׂר, remained the Levite's property. It had no sanctity, and could be eaten by anyone. Produce from which מַעֲשֵׂר רִאשׁוֹן has not been set aside is in the category of טֶבֶל — "untithed produce" — and may not be eaten. Since not everyone was conscientious about setting aside מַעֲשֵׂר רִאשׁוֹן, the Sages ordained that this tithe had to be set aside from דְּמַאי — "doubtfully tithed produce." However, it was not given to a Levite.

מַעֲשֵׂר שֵׁנִי Second tithe.
A tithe set aside after the priestly dues (תְּרוּמָה) had been given to the priests and the first tithe (מַעֲשֵׂר רִאשׁוֹן) had been given to the Levites. מַעֲשֵׂר שֵׁנִי was given during the first, second, fourth, and fifth years of the Sabbatical cycle (see שְׁבִיעִית). After מַעֲשֵׂר שֵׁנִי was set aside, it was brought to Jerusalem to be eaten there by its owner. If the journey to Jerusalem was too long, so that it would be difficult to carry all the מַעֲשֵׂר שֵׁנִי there, or if the produce became ritually impure, it could be redeemed for an equivalent sum of money (if the owner redeemed his own produce, he had to add one-fifth of its value). This redemption money (פִּדְיוֹן מַעֲשֵׂר שֵׁנִי) was brought to Jerusalem, where it was spent on food. מַעֲשֵׂר שֵׁנִי could only be redeemed with coins bearing an impression; unstamped coins and promissory notes could not be used. Today, מַעֲשֵׂר שֵׁנִי is still redeemed, but only for a nominal sum, since in the absence of the Temple it is no longer brought to Jerusalem. The laws of מַעֲשֵׂר שֵׁנִי are discussed in tractate *Ma'aser Sheni*. See also next entry.

מַעַשְׂרוֹת Tithes.
Certain portions of agricultural produce designated by Torah law for special purposes (see previous entries). According to most opinions, only grain, wine, and olive oil are required by Torah law to be tithed. By Rabbinic decree, however, any food that grows from the ground must be tithed. There are three main types of tithes: מַעֲשֵׂר רִאשׁוֹן — "first tithe"; מַעֲשֵׂר שֵׁנִי — "second tithe"; and מַעֲשַׂר עָנִי — "poor man's tithe." (See respective entries.) These tithes are set aside from foods after they have ripened and been brought into the house. Ownerless food is exempt from tithes, and hence no tithes are taken during the Sabbatical Year (see שְׁבִיעִית), when all food growing from the ground is deemed ownerless. Similarly, food eaten in the course of an אֲכִילַת עֲרַאי — "an incidental meal" (e.g., fruit eaten straight from the tree) — need not be tithed. Most of the laws of tithes are described in tractate *Ma'aserot*. See also מַעְשַׂר בְּהֵמָה.

מְפַתֶּה Seducer.
A man who persuades an unmarried girl between twelve and twelve-and-a-half years of age to have sexual relations with him is called a מְפַתֶּה (see Exodus 22:16). He must reimburse the girl's father for the humiliation he has caused, and pay a fine equivalent in value to "the virgins' dowry" (מוֹהַר הַבְּתוּלוֹת, i.e., 200 *zuz*). The seduction of a girl under the age of twelve is considered rape, since the consent expressed by a minor is not legally valid. See אוֹנֵס אִשָׁה.

מִצְוָה הַבָּאָה בַּעֲבֵירָה
Lit., *a commandment that comes through a transgression*. A commandment whose performance was made possible through a transgression, e.g., use of a stolen lulav on Sukkot (see אַרְבָּעָה מִינִים and *Sukkah* 30a). A commandment performed in such a way is considered Halakhically valueless.

מִצְווֹת צְרִיכוֹת כַּוָּונָה
Commandments require intention. There is a controversy among the Rabbis in the Talmud as to whether or not "commandments require intention," i.e., whether a person fulfills a commandment if he does not have the specific intention of fulfilling his obligation when he performs it. All, however, agree that a commandment performed under duress or without awareness of one's actions (see מִתְעַסֵּק) is invalid.

מְצוֹרָע See צָרַעַת.

מְצוֹרָע מוּחְלָט A confirmed leper.
A leper (see צָרַעַת) who has been declared conclusively ritually impure by a priest. All the laws applying to a suspected leper (see מְצוֹרָע מוּסְגָּר) apply to a מְצוֹרָע מוּחְלָט. A confirmed leper must grow his hair long and rend his garments (see פְּרִיעָה וּפְרִימָה). To purify himself when healed (see טָהֳרַת מְצוֹרָע), he must shave all his hair (see תִּגְלַחַת) and bring a special purification offering (אֲשַׁם מְצוֹרָע).

מְצוֹרָע מוּסְגָּר
Lit., *a locked-up leper*, i.e., a suspected leper who has not yet been declared conclusively impure by a priest. Such a leper must be isolated for a period of up to two weeks until the priest determines conclusively whether or not he is suffering from leprosy (צָרַעַת). A מְצוֹרָע מוּסְגָּר is ritually impure, and most of the laws applying to a leper apply to him, e.g., exclusion from the Israelite Camp (see מַחֲנֵה יִשְׂרָאֵל). A מְצוֹרָע מוּסְגָּר who is subsequently declared pure by the priest must immerse himself in a ritual bath (מִקְוֶה) in order to purify himself. If, however, the priest decides that the leper is in fact suffering from צָרַעַת, he becomes a מְצוֹרָע מוּחְלָט — "a confirmed leper" (see previous entry).

מִצְוַת עֲשֵׂה שֶׁהַזְּמַן גְּרָמָא
Lit., *a positive commandment caused by time*, i.e., a positive commandment that can only be performed at a certain time of day, or during the day rather than during the night, or on certain days of the year. Generally, women and slaves are exempt from such commandments, although there are some time-related positive commandments which women are required to perform, e.g., remembering the Sabbath day to keep it holy (see קִידּוּשׁ הַיּוֹם), eating matzah (מַצָּה) on Passover (פֶּסַח) night, "public assembly" (הַקְהֵל), and prayer (תְּפִילָה). Women and slaves are required to perform those positive commandments that are not restricted to a particular time for their performance, e.g., contributing to charity, affixing a mezuzah (מְזוּזָה), etc., although here too there are certain exceptions (such as Torah study) from which women and slaves are exempt.

מַצִּילִין אוֹתוֹ בְּנַפְשׁוֹ
Lit., *we save him by his soul*, i.e., by taking his life. Someone who is about to commit an exceptionally grave crime may be killed, if necessary, to prevent him from committing the crime. The Talmud describes this as "saving the potential criminal from sin by his soul," i.e., even at the cost of

his life. Specifically, it is permitted to kill someone about to commit murder, homosexual rape, rape of a betrothed girl between the ages of twelve and twelve-and-a-half (נַעֲרָה הַמְאוֹרָסָה), or rape of any of the women (עֲרָיוֹת) with whom sexual relations are forbidden under penalty of death or excision (כָּרֵת), if there is no other way to prevent him from committing these crimes. See רוֹדֵף.

מִצְרִי   *Egyptian.* A proselyte of Egyptian extraction, whether male or female, may not marry a Jew by birth for two generations (although he may marry another proselyte). An Egyptian proselyte who marries a Jew violates a positive commandment. The Sages ruled, however, that since the destruction of Samaria in First Temple times and the attendant upheaval and mass migrations of populations, this law no longer applies. See אֲדוֹמִי; עַמּוֹנִי וּמוֹאָבִי.

מִקְוֶה   *Ritual bath.* A body of stationary water used for ritual purification. By Torah law, a ritually impure person or object can be purified only through immersion in naturally flowing water (e.g., a spring) or in a מִקְוֶה. A מִקְוֶה must contain at least 40 *se'ah* (see p. 288) of water accumulated naturally, rather than through human effort (see מַיִם שְׁאוּבִים). Usually, the mikveh is filled with rainwater. Many natural bodies of water qualify as מִקְוָאוֹת (e.g., certain rivers, ponds, the sea). See מַיִם חַיִּים; מַעְיָן; אַשְׁבּוֹרֶן. Some are effective only when stationary, others when moving.

מְקוֹם פְּטוֹר   *Neutral domain* (lit., "exempt place"). A concept in the laws of carrying on Shabbat (see רְשׁוּיוֹת הַשַּׁבָּת; הוֹצָאָה). A neutral domain is an area of less than 4 *tefaḥim* (see p. 283) by 4 *tefaḥim* in area that is set apart from the surrounding area by a wall or a height difference of at least 3 *tefaḥim*. The entire air space above 10 *tefaḥim* in height in a public domain (רְשׁוּת הָרַבִּים) or a quasi-public domain (כַּרְמְלִית) is also considered a neutral domain. It is permitted to carry things into or out of a neutral domain from (or to) any of the other Shabbat domains; but one may not use it to transfer things from one domain to another.

מִקַּח טָעוּת   *A transaction made by mistake.* A transaction in which one of the participants was under a false impression regarding its terms. Such a transaction is considered a mistake and the injured party can invalidate it. For example, if someone buys an animal and discovers it to be diseased, he can invalidate the sale. A related concept is בִּיטּוּל מֶקַח — "the invalidation of a transaction." If an object is overpriced or underpriced by more than one-sixth, the sale is invalid and either party can retract (see אוֹנָאָה; שְׁתוּת). Similarly, if a man marries a woman and subsequently discovers that she has serious physical defects of which he was unaware at the time of the marriage, he can divorce her and not pay her marriage settlement (כְּתוּבָּה).

מְקַלֵּל   *One who curses another Jew.* It is prohibited by Torah law to curse any law-abiding Jew, even if the person being cursed does not know it, e.g., because he is deaf. (Leviticus 19:14.) One who curses another Jew using God's name is subject to lashes (מַלְקוּת) by Torah law (Deuteronomy 28:58-9).

מְקַלֵּל אָבִיו וְאִמּוֹ   *One who curses his father or mother.* One who curses his father or mother using God's name, whether while they are alive or after they have died, is subject to death by stoning (Leviticus 20:9).

מִקְצָת הַיּוֹם כְּכוּלּוֹ   *Part of the day is like all of it.* A principle applied in many different areas of the Halakhah (e.g., laws of mourning, ritual impurity, and Nazirite vows). For example, a mourner is required to observe seven days of mourning (see שִׁבְעָה וּשְׁלֹשִׁים), but the day of the funeral is counted as a full day, even if only a small part of the day remains after the funeral. The mourner is then only required to observe five more full days plus part of the seventh, which is again considered as a full day because of the same principle.

מְקַרְקְעֵי   *Real estate.* Land and buildings. There are various differences between the laws applying to real estate and those applying to movable property (מִטַּלְטְלִין). For example, litigants are not required to take an oath regarding the truth of their claims, if the disputed property is land. The laws against overcharging (אוֹנָאָה) do not apply to land (unless the land was measured incorrectly). Land is not purchased through the same modes of acquisition as movable property, but rather through other modes such as חֲזָקָה — "taking possession" (see חֲזָקָה, subsection 3). Land may be used as security for the repayment of loans and other outstanding debts. See נְכָסִים שֶׁיֵּשׁ לָהֶם אַחֲרָיוּת.

מַרְאִית עַיִן   Lit., *appearance.* Sometimes, permissible actions, which might be mistaken for prohibited conduct by an observer, were prohibited by the Rabbis, both to prevent people from unjustifiably suspecting others of misconduct, and to prevent people from incorrectly inferring that forbidden actions are permissible. Most authorities maintain that actions prohibited because of מַרְאִית עַיִן are forbidden even in private.

מְרוּבֶּה בְּגָדִים   Lit., *one with many garments.* During the Second Temple period, when the שֶׁמֶן הַמִּשְׁחָה — "oil of installation" — was no longer available for anointing High Priests (see מָשׁוּחַ בְּשֶׁמֶן הַמִּשְׁחָה), the High Priest (כֹּהֵן גָּדוֹל) was consecrated by wearing the eight garments (שְׁמוֹנָה בְּגָדִים) worn only by High Priests. A High Priest consecrated in this fashion was called a מְרוּבֶּה בְּגָדִים, and all the laws applying to High Priests applied to him, with one exception. He did not bring the special sacrifice of a bullock, which was brought under certain circumstances by an anointed High Priest guilty of unintentional sin (see פַּר כֹּהֵן מָשִׁיחַ), but instead brought a young female lamb or a goat, like a private individual.

מָרוֹר   *Bitter herbs.* By Torah law, the Paschal sacrifice (פֶּסַח) that was eaten on the first night of Pesaḥ had to be eaten together with matzah and bitter herbs (Exodus 12:8). Now that the Passover sacrifice is no longer offered, the requirement to eat bitter herbs on Pesaḥ night is only of Rabbinic authority. There are several vegetables that can serve as מָרוֹר. In general, any edible vegetable from which a white juice can be extracted and is bitter will serve. The recommended vegetable is a type of lettuce.

מַרְחֶשֶׁת   *Deep, covered frying pan.* See מִנְחַת מַרְחֶשֶׁת.

מְרִיקָה וּשְׁטִיפָה *Scouring and rinsing.* A utensil in which the meat of sacrifices was cooked or roasted had to be cleansed by washing it with hot water (מְרִיקָה), and then with cold water (שְׁטִיפָה), in order to remove the food it had absorbed. This washing and rinsing took place after the end of the period of time during which the sacrifice was permitted to be eaten.

מַשֶּׁהוּ Lit., *something,* i.e., a very small, undefined, quantity. Certain mitzvot can be fulfilled, or transgressions committed, by consuming (or performing some other action with) an extremely minute quantity of material; such a minute quantity of material is called a מַשֶּׁהוּ. Although מַשֶּׁהוּ is very small, it is nevertheless a finite amount, and it is possible for a quantity to be so small that it is not even מַשֶּׁהוּ.

מָשׁוּחַ בְּשֶׁמֶן הַמִּשְׁחָה *A High Priest anointed with the oil of anointing.* During the First Temple period, the High Priests were consecrated not only with the "eight garments" (שְׁמוֹנָה בְּגָדִים) unique to the High Priest (כֹּהֵן גָּדוֹל), but also with special oil that was spread on their heads in the shape of an "X." All the laws of the High Priesthood applied only to a priest consecrated in this fashion, in contrast to a מְרוּבֵּה בְּגָדִים.

מָשׁוּחַ מִלְחָמָה *A priest anointed for war.* Before the Jews set out to war, a special priest was appointed to perform certain duties in connection with the war. This priest, who was anointed with שֶׁמֶן הַמִּשְׁחָה — "anointing oil" — was called the מָשׁוּחַ מִלְחָמָה. He was responsible for reminding those exempt from fighting to return home (see מִלְחֶמֶת רְשׁוּת), and for encouraging the other soldiers to go out and fight, as stated in the Torah (Deuteronomy 20:2ff). The אוּרִים וְתוּמִים ("oracular stones") in the breastplate that he wore would be consulted before the army went out to battle. The same prohibitions that apply to a High Priest applied to the מָשׁוּחַ מִלְחָמָה, although he did not bring the sacrifices brought by a High Priest, and his special status was not inherited by his sons. The institution of מָשׁוּחַ מִלְחָמָה ceased to exist as far back as the beginning of the Second Temple period.

מָשׁוּחַ שֶׁעָבַר *An anointed High Priest who left the High Priesthood.* A priest who ceased to serve as High Priest (even if he had not been anointed [see מָשׁוּחַ בְּשֶׁמֶן הַמִּשְׁחָה], but had been consecrated with the שְׁמוֹנָה בְּגָדִים — "the eight garments"). All the prohibitions applying to a regular High Priest apply to a former High Priest. He may bring all the sacrifices brought by a High Priest, except the bullock offered on Yom Kippur (פַּר יוֹם הַכִּיפּוּרִים) and the tenth of an אֵיפָה meal-offering offered daily (see חֲבִיתִּין).

מְשִׁיכָה *Pulling.* One of the modes of acquisition of movable property. Specifically, the purchaser of an object too heavy to be lifted (see הַגְבָּהָה), or the recipient, if the object is given as a gift, must pull it in the presence of the seller (or donor) in order to acquire it. According to the Halakhah, the transfer of ownership of movable property is not effected through the transfer of money that usually accompanies מְשִׁיכָה, but only through the actual, physical transfer of the object. See קִנְיָן.

מִשְׁכָּב מוֹשָׁב וּמֶרְכָּב *Something upon which a person lies,* sits or rides. A זָב, a man suffering from gonorrhea, renders objects designed for lying, sitting or riding upon ritually impure by placing his weight on them in any way (sitting, standing, lying, leaning). Such objects are considered to be a primary source of ritual impurity (see אֲבוֹת הַטּוּמְאוֹת). They render anyone who touches or carries them ritually impure (see רִאשׁוֹן לְטוּמְאָה). Not only a זָב transmits ritual impurity in this way. Similar rules apply to a זָבָה, a woman suffering from a menstrual-type flow of blood when she is not menstruating, to a נִדָּה, a menstruating woman, to a יוֹלֶדֶת, a woman who has recently given birth, and (partially) to a leper (see צָרַעַת).

מִשְׁכָּב תַּחְתּוֹן כְּעֶלְיוֹן Lit., *the lower* מִשְׁכָּב *like the upper one.* Certain types of ritually impure people (e.g., בּוֹעֵל נִדָּה — a man who has sexual intercourse with a menstruating woman) render the objects upon which they lie (מִשְׁכָּב) ritually impure. The lower מִשְׁכָּב of a בּוֹעֵל נִדָּה conveys the same level of ritual impurity as the cover (עֶלְיוֹן) over a man suffering from gonorrhea (זָב), and hence it renders food and drinks ritually impure, but not people or utensils.

מַשְׁכּוֹן *Security, pledge.* An item taken by a creditor from a borrower to ensure payment of a loan. Utensils used for the preparation of food may not be taken as security. Other utensils essential to the borrower must be returned to him when he needs them. Thus, clothing worn during the day which is taken as a pledge, must be returned to the borrower by morning; and clothing worn at night, must be returned by nightfall. It is forbidden to take any pledge from a widow, however wealthy. Debts due to a creditor who retains a מַשְׁכּוֹן are not cancelled in the Sabbatical Year (see שְׁבִיעִית).

מַשְׁכַּנְתָּא דְּסוּרָא *A mortgage according to the custom in Sura [a town in Babylonia].* A form of mortgage in which the borrower temporarily transfers land to the creditor, and permits him to till it and deduct a fixed amount each year as repayment of the debt until it is repaid in full. Such a transaction is not prohibited as usury (see רִיבִּית).

מַשְׁמִיעַ קוֹל *Something that makes a noise.* (1) With regard to the laws of Shabbat: By Rabbinic decree, it is prohibited to make musical sounds on any musical instrument on Shabbat (according to some authorities, it is forbidden to make non-musical noises as well). (2) With regard to the laws of ritual impurity: A utensil used for making noise is susceptible to ritual impurity, even if it serves no other function (see מְשַׁמְּשֵׁי אָדָם).

מִשְׁמָר *Watch.* The priests who served in the Temple were divided into twenty-four groups, called "watches." Each watch served for one week at a time. Thus each watch performed the Temple service for approximately two weeks every year. During the Pilgrim Festivals, all the watches went to the Temple and performed the Temple service together. Each watch received the מַתְּנוֹת כְּהוּנָה — the priestly gifts, which were contributed to the Temple during their week of Temple service. The watches were divided into בָּתֵּי אָב — "families." Corresponding to each watch there was a מַעֲמָד — "post" or "division" — a group of non-priests, who accompanied the members of the watch to Jerusalem. The priests were originally divided into watches in the time of King David. During the Second Temple period, when many of the Jews who had been exiled to Babylonia after the destruction of the First Temple returned to Eretz Israel, some of the watches remained in Babylonia. Those priests who did return to Eretz Israel had to be divided once again into twenty-four watches.

מְשַׁמְּשֵׁי אָדָם   Lit., *Things that serve a person's needs.* A utensil is only susceptible to ritual impurity if it serves a person's needs. Depending on the nature of the utensil and the material from which it is made, distinctions are sometimes made between utensils that directly serve a person (מְשַׁמְּשֵׁי אָדָם) and utensils that serve animals or other utensils.

מִשְׁנֶה מִמַּטְבֵּעַ שֶׁטָּבְעוּ חֲכָמִים   *Deviating from the formula coined by the Sages.* (1) With regard to prayers and blessings: It is forbidden to alter the wording of the prayers and blessings as fixed by the Sages. However, if someone deviates only slightly from the wording of the prayers while retaining their basic ideas, he still fulfills his obligation to pray. (2) With regard to a *גֵּט* — "bill of divorce": According to one opinion, any deviation from the standard wording of the גֵּט fixed by the Sages renders the גֵּט invalid for use.

מַשְׁקֵה בֵּית מַטְבְּחַיָּא   Lit., *liquid of [the Temple] abattoir.* A unique Halakhah states that the blood of animals slaughtered in the abattoir in the Temple Courtyard and the water used there (and possibly the wine and oil as well) do not render foods susceptible to ritual impurity (see הֶכְשֵׁר), and do not become ritually impure themselves.

מַשְׁקֵה הַזָּב   *The liquid of a person suffering from gonorrhea* (זָב), i.e., his spittle, urine, semen, or gonorrheal discharge. These liquids are considered an אַב הַטּוּמְאָה — "a primary source of ritual impurity" (see אֲבוֹת הַטּוּמְאוֹת). However, other liquids coming from a person with gonorrhea, such as his blood or tears, are considered a וְלַד הַטּוּמְאָה — "a secondary source of ritual impurity" — and have the same status as other liquids that came in contact with him. Still others, such as sweat, are completely ritually pure.

מַשְׁקִין טְמֵאִים   *Ritually impure liquids.* Liquids fit to drink that became ritually impure. By Rabbinic decree, all ritually impure liquids have the status of רִאשׁוֹן לְטוּמְאָה — "first-degree ritual impurity" — and render any food that comes in contact with them ritually impure. See הֶכְשֵׁר for a list of the seven liquids included in this classification.

מֵת מִצְוָה   Lit., *a mitzvah-corpse.* A dead body with no one available to bury it. It is an important religious obligation to take part in the burial of a dead person. If the deceased had no friends or relatives to bury him, everyone is obligated to assist in his burial. According to the Halakhah, a מֵת מִצְוָה "acquires his place," i.e., the body must be interred where it was found (provided that this is an honorable location; otherwise, the body must be buried in the nearest cemetery). This religious duty is so important that even priests and Nazirites, who are ordinarily forbidden to come in contact with a dead body, may bury a deserted corpse if there is no one else available to do so.

Similarly, the obligation to bury a מֵת מִצְוָה takes precedence over nearly all other religious obligations.

מַתִּיר   *The permitting factor,* i.e., that portion of a sacrifice that must be offered in order to discharge the sacrificial obligation. In animal sacrifices the blood is considered the permitting factor, while in meal offerings (מְנָחוֹת) it is the קוֹמֶץ — "handful" of flour (see קְמִיצָה). A sacrifice whose מַתִּיר was not offered as required by the Halakhah is not rendered unfit by improper intention (see לֹא קָרַב הַמַּתִּיר כְּמִצְוָתוֹ; מַחֲשָׁבָה). The מַתִּיר itself cannot become פִּיגּוּל — "unfit through intention to offer the sacrifice after the proper time." There is a controversy regarding sacrifices that have more than one מַתִּיר, as to whether both must be offered in order to render the sacrificial ceremony complete, and as to the relation between them.

מַתְּנָה עַל מַה שֶּׁכָּתוּב בַּתּוֹרָה   *Making a condition that runs counter to what is written in the Torah,* i.e., stipulating that an obligation laid down in the Torah should not apply to a particular transaction (e.g., a creditor stipulates that the Sabbatical Year should not cancel a certain debt). According to some authorities, such stipulations are binding if made in connection with monetary dealings. All, however, agree that conditions that run counter to a commandment of the Torah regarding other matters, such as obligations between man and wife, are null and void.

מַתְּנוֹת כְּהוּנָּה   *Gifts of the priesthood.* A general term used to refer to all the various gifts to which the priests are entitled. The Talmud lists twenty-four such gifts, among them the various sacrifices (or parts of sacrifices) given to the priests; תְּרוּמָה — the agricultural levy given to the priests; רֵאשִׁית הַגֵּז — "the first-shearing" (of sheep's wool); זְרוֹעַ לְחָיַיִם וְקֵיבָה — "the shoulder, two cheeks, and maw" (of a non-sacrificial animal that was slaughtered); פִּדְיוֹן הַבֵּן — "the redemption of the firstborn son"; פִּדְיוֹן פֶּטֶר חֲמוֹר — "the redemption of a firstborn donkey" (see פֶּטֶר חֲמוֹר); שְׂדֵה אֲחוּזָה — "the inherited field" (if donated to the Temple and not redeemed until the Jubilee Year); שְׂדֵה הַחֵרֶם — "the consecrated field" (see חֶרְמֵי כֹהֲנִים); גֵּזֶל הַגֵּר — "robbery from a proselyte" (who died without leaving heirs to whom the object or its value could be returned). Some of these gifts are holy, and may only be eaten by male priests in the עֲזָרָה — "Temple Courtyard"; others are less holy, and may be eaten anywhere in Jerusalem, both by priests and by members of their households; still others may be eaten anywhere by priests and their households; others have no sanctity whatsoever.

מַתְּנוֹת עֲנִיִּים   *Gifts to the poor.* Apart from the general obligation to give charity to the poor, the Torah stipulates that certain portions of the crop be donated to the poor (some of these have fixed quantities, while others do not), namely: מַעְשַׂר עָנִי — "poor man's tithe"; לֶקֶט — "gleanings"; שִׁכְחָה — "forgotten sheaves"; פֵּאָה — "corner of the field"; פֶּרֶט — "single grapes that fell during the harvest"; עוֹלֵלוֹת — "small, loosely packed bunches of grapes."

מַתְּנַת שְׁכִיב מְרַע   *A gift of a person on his deathbed.* By Rabbinic decree, gifts given by a person on his deathbed differ in several ways from those given by ordinary people. For example, the gift of a person on his deathbed is valid even if no act of acquisition (קִנְיָן) was performed, as long as the donor expressed his intention in words. Likewise, a mortally ill person may retract his gift as many times as he wishes, provided that he is of sound mind when doing so. All gifts given by a person on his deathbed are invalidated if he recovers.

מִתְעַסֵּק   *Acting unawares,* i.e., a person who performed an act by accident without having any intention of doing so. Not to be confused with שׁוֹגֵג* — "acting unwittingly" — when a person

performs an act by mistake, because of lack of information. (1) With regard to prohibitions: There is no need for sacrificial atonement for transgressions committed while unaware, unless the transgression entailed physical pleasure, such as eating prohibited food or engaging in prohibited sexual relations. (2) With regard to positive commandments: According to some authorities, one who performs a mitzvah while unaware does not fulfill his obligation, even according to those who maintain that mitzvot can be fulfilled without the express intention of doing so (see מִצְוֹת צְרִיכוֹת כַּוָּנָה).

נֶאֱכָלִין לְיוֹם וָלַיְלָה   *Sacrifices that may be eaten for one day and one night.* All those קָדְשֵׁי קָדָשִׁים — "sacrifices of the highest degree of sanctity" — that are permitted to be eaten, and some קָדָשִׁים קַלִּים — "sacrifices of a lesser degree of sanctity" (the תּוֹדָה* — "the thanks-offering"; and אֵיל נָזִיר* — "the ram of the Nazirite") — may be eaten on the day they were sacrificed and during the following night (until midnight). After this time, these sacrifices are considered נוֹתָר* — "left over" — and they may no longer be eaten. קָדָשִׁים קַלִּים may usually be eaten for "two days and one night," i.e., on the day they were sacrificed, the night following, and the following day (until nightfall).

נֶאֱמָנוּת   *Trust, belief, credibility.* Belief in things that a person says about himself or about others. In some cases this belief is commanded by the Torah (one takes a father's word as to whom he has had his daughter married), whereas in other cases נֶאֱמָנוּת is a matter of Rabbinic decree, both in civil cases and in other matters. There are many factors determining trust (such as מַה הַפֶּה שֶׁאָסַר הוּא* — and מִיגוֹ* [see — "Why should I lie?" — לִי לְשַׁקֵּר הַפֶּה שֶׁהִתִּיר — "The mouth that prohibited is the mouth that permitted"), and there are other considerations regarding whether one should give credence to certain claims.

נְבִיא שֶׁקֶר   *A false prophet.* Someone who claims to be a divinely inspired prophet is tested to determine whether he is telling the truth. If his optimistic prophecies are not fulfilled, or if he tells others to violate the Torah's commandments, he is deemed a false prophet and is tried by a court of seventy-one judges (בֵּית דִּין שֶׁל שִׁבְעִים וְאֶחָד*). If found guilty, he is subject to the death penalty by strangulation (see חֶנֶק).

נְבֵלָה   *The carcass of an animal.* Not all carcasses of animals come within the Halakhic definition of נְבֵלָה. Specifically, it includes the carcasses of large mammals, whether or not they are kosher animals. Among kosher animals a נְבֵלָה is an animal that (1) died of natural causes or (2) died as a result of an improperly carried out act of ritual slaughter (שְׁחִיטָה*). A נְבֵלָה is forbidden to be eaten, and is "a primary source of ritual impurity"

(see אֲבוֹת הַטּוּמְאוֹת). It renders those who touch or carry it ritually impure until nightfall (see טוּמְאַת עֶרֶב). Although the נְבֵלָה of a kosher animal may not be eaten, one may derive financial benefit from it. Certain types of severe anatomical defects (e.g., a completely broken neck) render an animal a נְבֵלָה even while it is still alive. Special rules of ritual impurity apply to the נְבֵלָה of kosher birds (see next entry).

נִבְלַת עוֹף טָהוֹר   *The carcass of a clean [i.e., kosher] bird.* One who eats the carcass of a kosher bird becomes ritually impure, as does the clothing he is wearing, even though the carcass does not render those who touch it ritually impure. "Eating" here is defined as swallowing at least an olive's bulk (כַּזַּיִת*) of the carcass.

נִגְעֵי בְגָדִים   *Leprosy [lit., plagues] of clothing.* By Torah law, if bright red or green spots appear on clothing, the clothing must be brought to a priest to determine whether or not the spots are "leprosy of clothing" (see Leviticus 13:47–59). The affected garment is then set aside for a week, after which it is reexamined by the priest. If the spots have spread, the clothing is immediately declared ritually impure by the priest and burned. If, however, the spots have not spread, the clothing is laundered and then set aside for another week, after which the priest reexamines it. If the spots have disappeared or become darker, the clothing is laundered and immersed in a ritual bath (מִקְוֶה), after which it is considered clean; otherwise, the affected part, and sometimes the entire cloth, must be burned. A leprous garment may not be used, and it renders people and things that come in contact with it ritually impure, exactly as a leprous person does (see צָרַעַת). The laws of "leprosy of clothing" apply only to undyed leather, wool, and linen garments.

נִגְעֵי בָתִּים   *House leprosy* (lit., "plagues"). By Torah law (Leviticus 14:33–57), if leprous spots appear in a house, all the objects in the house must be removed in order to prevent them from becoming ritually impure, after which a priest is brought to examine the house. If the priest confirms that there is evidence of leprosy, the house is left uninhabited for a week, after which it is reexamined by the priest. If the leprous spots have darkened or disappeared, the house is declared ritually pure. If the spots are unchanged, the house is isolated for a second week. If the spots have then darkened, the house is declared ritually pure after the purification process described below. But if the spots are unchanged or have spread, the affected parts of the house are removed and replaced with new material, after which the house is isolated a third time. If the spots reappear, the entire house must be destroyed, and its stones are disposed of in a ritually impure place. A leprous house renders people who enter it and objects (except those in hermetically sealed earthenware containers) that are located inside it ritually impure. If, however, the house is declared free of leprosy, it must be purified by a process involving birds, cedar wood, and red thread, in the same way as a leprous person is purified (see צִיפּוֹרֵי; מְצוֹרָע מוּחְלָט; מְצוֹרָע). There are many Halakhic limitations on the applicability of the laws pertaining to leprous houses.

נְגָעִים   Lit., *plagues.* Symptoms of leprosy (צָרַעַת). In the Halakhic sense of this term it refers to spots and various changes of color appearing in a person's skin or hair, in his clothes, or in the walls of houses (see נִגְעֵי בְגָדִים; נִגְעֵי בָתִּים). The נְגָעִים that cause ritual impurity are those of leprosy, but there are also נְגָעִים, some of which are mentioned in the Torah, that do not cause ritual impurity, although they may be painful and disfigure the person suffering from them.

נְדָבָה   *Free-will offering.* (1) Sometimes this expression is used in the general sense of any voluntary religious contribution, whether to charity or for other religious purposes. Someone who undertakes to give such a contribution and fails to keep his word within the statutory time violates the commandment: "You shall not delay [fulfilling your obligation]" (Deuteronomy 23:22). (2) With regard to the laws of sacrifices: A sacrifice that a person offers to bring of his own free will by saying, "I undertake to bring *this* animal," is called a נְדָבָה. In such cases, the person's obligation applies only to the specific animal. Hence, if this animal is lost or dies, there is no obligation to bring another offering in its place. See נֶדֶר.

נִדָּה   *A menstruating woman.* (1) With regard to the laws of ritual purity: By Torah law, a woman is ritually impure for seven days after she begins to have menstrual bleeding; on the eve of the eighth day, she immerses herself in a spring (מַעְיָן) or ritual bath (מִקְוֶה) to purify herself. According to Torah law, a נִדָּה may purify herself on the eighth day, even if she had been bleeding for the entire seven-day period. The Talmud, however, states that women are stricter with themselves, and thus any woman who has uterine bleeding is required to wait seven days without any bleeding before immersing in the מִקְוֶה. While a woman is a נִדָּה (i.e., from the beginning of her period, until she immerses herself), she renders both people and objects that come in contact with her or carry her ritually impure. Similarly, a man who has sexual intercourse with her (see בּוֹעֵל נִדָּה) becomes ritually impure for seven days. (2) With regard to the laws of forbidden sexual relations: It is prohibited to have sexual relations with a נִדָּה until she has purified herself, and anyone who intentionally engages in sexual intercourse with her is subject to excision (כָּרֵת).

However, unlike other types of relationships prohibited by Torah law (i.e., adulterous or incestuous relationships), קִידּוּשִׁין — betrothal — with a נִדָּה is valid, and if she became pregnant as the result of sexual intercourse while she was a נִדָּה her offspring is not considered a מַמְזֵר — "an illegitimate child." For this reason, the child of a נִדָּה is permitted to marry other Jews.

נֶדֶר   *Vow.* (1) A personal vow, i.e., a voluntary obligation to refrain from doing something (or benefiting from someone). Such a vow is, in effect, a type of "reverse consecration." Instead of consecrating the object, the person taking the vow pledges himself to regard the object he wishes to deny himself (or the person from whom he wishes not to benefit) as though it were consecrated to the Temple. Any object can be forsworn, and one who fails to fulfill his vow violates the commandment: "He shall not break his word" (Numbers 30:3). It is also possible to forbid one's own property to another by means of a נֶדֶר. The other person must then regard such property as being consecrated. It is not possible to forbid another person's property to anyone other than oneself. The vows of a young girl (a קְטַנָּה or a נַעֲרָה) or of a wife may be annulled by the father or husband, respectively (see הֲפָרַת נְדָרִים). Other people can also be released from their vows (see הַתָּרַת נְדָרִים) by a Torah scholar (or a Rabbinical Court), if it can be shown that their vows were not made with full knowledge and intent. The Talmudic Rabbis were very strongly opposed to the taking of vows (hence the practice of saying בְּלִי נֶדֶר — "without a vow" — before undertaking certain obligations), and they encouraged people who had taken vows to have them dissolved. If a person makes a statement, using the form of a vow, but it is evident that he did not mean to utter a vow but rather to express an exaggeration or a superlative, such a "vow" is not considered binding. (2) With regard to the laws of sacrifices: A sacrifice that a person offers to bring by saying, "I undertake to bring an animal," is called a נֶדֶר. In such cases, the person does not obligate himself to bring a specific animal. Hence, if the animal that he has designated as a sacrifice is lost or dies, the owner must bring another offering in its place. See נְדָבָה.

נֶדֶר שֶׁהוּתַר מִקְצָתוֹ   *A vow, part of which was dissolved.* If a person took a vow relating to a number of people or objects, and then part of the vow was dissolved (or shown to be invalid), the entire vow is not binding.

נִדְרֵי זֵירוּזִין   Lit., *vows of urging.* A vow taken to encourage someone to perform a particular action. For example, a vow taken by the seller of an object to influence a potential buyer to buy it (or vice versa): "If I agree to sell this object for less than such-and-such an amount, may this object be forbidden to me." It is assumed that people who express themselves in such a fashion do not really intend to take a vow, and are not speaking seriously. Hence, such "vows" are invalid, and need not be dissolved. See נֶדֶר.

נִדְרֵי עִינּוּי נֶפֶשׁ   Lit., *vows of afflicting the soul.* A husband is only allowed to annul his wife's vows if they affect their marital relations, or if they cause the wife discomfort (e.g., if she vows not to eat fruit or meat); the latter category of vows is called נִדְרֵי עִינּוּי נֶפֶשׁ (see Numbers 30:14). See also הֲפָרַת נְדָרִים.

נֶהֱנֶה שֶׁלֹּא פָּגַם *One who has benefit without causing depreciation.* One who derives benefit from Temple property without causing it to depreciate in value (e.g., by riding on an animal that had been consecrated to the Temple) is nevertheless guilty of מְעִילָה* — "trespass, misappropriation of property dedicated to the Temple."

נוֹלָד Lit., *born.* (1) With regard to the laws of Shabbat and Festivals: An object that came into being or assumed its present form on Shabbat or a Festival (e.g., an egg that was laid, or a utensil that was broken on Shabbat or a Festival). This is one of the types of מוּקְצֶה* — "objects that may not be moved" — and such an object is not handled on Shabbat or Festivals. (2) With regard to the dissolution of vows (see נֶדֶר; הַתָּרַת נְדָרִים): A new situation. Ordinarily, vows can be dissolved if it is shown that they were not made with full intent and knowledge. But a vow may not be dissolved on grounds of lack of intent if the person who vowed failed to anticipate an unpredictable situation in which he would not have taken such a vow. For example, if someone vowed not to derive any benefit from a certain person, and that person later became a distinguished scholar, the vow cannot be dissolved on the grounds that at the time he vowed he did not realize that the person would become a distinguished scholar.

נוֹשֵׂא שָׂכָר See שׁוֹמֵר שָׂכָר.

נוֹתֵן טַעַם *Something that gives taste.* Usually, when non-kosher food is mixed with kosher food, and the taste of the non-kosher food can no longer be detected, the mixture is permitted. Such a mixture may be given to a non-Jewish cook to determine whether or not the taste of the non-kosher ingredients is noticeable. If this is not possible, the mixture is presumed to be kosher, if it contains at least sixty times as much kosher food as non-kosher food. See next entry and also בִּיטוּל אִיסּוּרִים.

נוֹתֵן טַעַם לִפְגָם *Something that gives a bad taste.* If non-kosher food is mixed with kosher food, the resulting mixture is generally permitted if the non-kosher ingredient gave it a bad taste. Similarly, non-kosher food absorbed by a utensil that was subsequently not used for cooking for twenty-four hours is ordinarily assumed to "give a bad taste," and hence such a utensil does not render other foods subsequently cooked in it non-kosher. The utensil itself must, of course, be koshered (see הַגְעָלָה).

נוֹתָר Lit. *left over.* Part of a sacrifice left over after the time permitted for it to be eaten. One who eats נוֹתָר is subject to כָּרֵת* — excision. The Sages decreed that נוֹתָר should be considered ritually impure, so that the priests be prompt and meticulous in its removal. See עִיבּוּר צוּרָה.

נָזִיר לְעוֹלָם *A Nazirite forever.* A person who vowed to be a Nazirite for an extremely long period of time (whether through a single Nazirite vow or through a number of consecutive Nazirite vows). Practically speaking, such a person remains a Nazirite for the rest of his life. All the laws of a regular Nazirite apply to him and he may shave at the end of his period of being

a Nazirite, if he lives long enough (or at the end of each of the consecutive periods of his Nazirite vows, if he vowed that way). See נְזִיר עוֹלָם; נְזִיר שִׁמְשׁוֹן.

נְזִיר עוֹלָם *A permanent Nazirite.* A person who vowed to be a Nazirite for his entire life. Unlike other Nazirites, a נְזִיר עוֹלָם may cut his hair and bring the sacrifices of a Nazirite whenever his hair grows too long, although he must resume his Nazirite observances immediately thereafter. See נָזִיר לְעוֹלָם; נְזִיר שִׁמְשׁוֹן.

נְזִיר שִׁמְשׁוֹן *A Nazirite like Samson.* A person who vowed to be a Nazirite like Samson. According to some authorities, such a person is not a Nazirite at all (since Samson himself did not take a Nazirite vow); others, however, set norms for a נְזִיר שִׁמְשׁוֹן, permitting him to become ritually impure by coming in contact with dead bodies (thereby freeing him from the obligation to bring the special Nazirite sacrifices if he becomes ritually impure), but forbidding him from cutting his hair or drinking wine. Such a Nazirite vow is permanent, and cannot be annulled (see נְזִירוּת).

נְזִירוּת *Naziriteship.* The status conferred on a person by his taking Nazirite vows, as laid down in the Torah (Numbers 6:1-21). A Nazirite must refrain from eating (or drinking) anything derived from the vine (especially wine). He must avoid becoming ritually impure by contact with dead bodies, and must refrain from cutting his hair. A Nazirite who violates any of these prohibitions is subject to lashes (מַלְקוֹת*). A person can vow to be a Nazirite for any period of time that he wishes, but the minimum period is thirty days. One who does not specify how long he wishes to be a Nazirite assumes Nazirite obligations for thirty days. If a Nazirite becomes ritually impure by contact with a dead body, whether intentionally or not, he must first purify himself and then bring two pigeons to the Temple as sacrifices (one as a sin-offering and the other as a burnt-offering), as well as a lamb as a guilt-offering; after this, he must start his period of being a Nazirite over again. When the Nazirite completes the period of his vow, he must bring two lambs as sacrifices (one female as a sin-offering and one male as a burnt-offering) and a ram as a peace-offering (אֵיל נָזִיר*—"Nazirite's ram"). He must shave off his hair, and burn it beneath the pot in which the ram offered as a peace-offering is cooked. After these sacrifices have been offered, the period of being a Nazirite ends, and the former Nazirite is no different from anyone else. The laws of the Nazirite are discussed in the Talmudic tractate *Nazir.*

נֶזֶק Lit., *damage.* One of the five types of indemnity (see חֲמִישָׁה דְּבָרִים) that are paid by someone who injures another person. Specifically, נֶזֶק is the value of the damage caused to the person injured (i.e., the decrease in this person's value). נֶזֶק is assessed by determining how much the injured person would have been worth on the slave market before his injury, taking into consideration his professional qualifications, compared with what he is now worth. (See בּוֹשֶׁת; צַעַר; רִיפּוּי; שֶׁבֶת.) Payment for the injury done to a raped woman (see פְּגָם) is a form of payment for damage.

נְחִירָה Lit. *stabbing,* i.e., killing an animal, rather than ritually slaughtering it according to the Halakhah. Killing kosher animals by methods other than יִשְׁחִיטָה does not have the same Halakhic consequences as ritually slaughtering them. Hence it is permissible to ritually slaughter the offspring of an animal that had been killed by another method that day (it is prohibited to ritually slaughter an animal and its offspring on the same day; see אוֹתוֹ וְאֶת בְּנוֹ). Similarly, one who kills kosher birds or kosher undomesticated animals (see חַיָּה טְהוֹרָה) by a method other than שְׁחִיטָה need not cover the blood. One who ritually slaughters such animals, by contrast, must cover the blood (see יכִּסּוּי הַדָּם).

נְטִילַת יָדַיִם   *Washing the hands.*

A mitzvah instituted by the Sages for purposes of cleanliness and purity. (1) Before eating: By Rabbinic decree, unwashed hands are considered in the category of יִשֵׁנִי לְטוּמְאָה — "defiled with second-degree ritual impurity"; therefore, one who wishes to purify his hands must either wash them with a *revi'it* (יְרְבִיעִית) of water (see entry and also p. 287), poured from a vessel, or immerse his hands in a spring or a ritual bath (יִמִקְוֶה). Originally, only people eating יתְּרוּמָה, the priest's dues from the crops, were required to wash their hands before eating, but later the Rabbis extended this obligation to anyone who eats bread. (2) Before praying: The Sages ruled that people must wash their hands before praying. No minimum quantity of water is required. If a person wishes to pray, but has no water, he may wipe his hands on anything that will clean them. (3) After using the toilet, one must wash one's hands and recite the blessing אֲשֶׁר יָצַר — "Blessed are You, Who has formed us with wisdom...." (4) One must wash one's hands on waking up in the morning. This mitzvah was not only instituted for reasons of cleanliness, but also to remove the "evil spirit" that rests on the hands after a night's sleep. (5) Regarding washing hands after eating, see מַיִם אַחֲרוֹנִים.

נֶטַע רְבָעִי   *Fourth-year produce.*

Fruit of a tree during the fourth year after the tree was planted. Fruit growing on a tree during the first three years after it was planted is called יעָרְלָה — *orlah* — and may not be eaten (nor may any other benefit be derived from it). The fruit that grows during the following year is treated like יִמַעֲשֵׂר שֵׁנִי — the "second tithe." It must be brought to Jerusalem and eaten there. If it cannot be brought to Jerusalem, it is redeemed and the redemption money is brought to Jerusalem, where it is spent on food and drink. As long as the Temple was standing, the Sages ordained that anyone who lived a single day's journey from Jerusalem was not allowed to redeem his grapes of יכֶּרֶם רְבָעִי, but had to bring them to Jerusalem in order to "adorn the streets of Jerusalem with fruit" (*Betzah* 5a). Nowadays, נֶטַע רְבָעִי is still redeemed, albeit for a nominal sum (rather than for its real value), since the redemption money is not brought to Jerusalem and spent there.

נִידּוּי   *Ostracism, isolation.*

A person who violates certain laws may be subjected to ostracism, either as a punishment or in order to compel him to submit to the law. The Talmud specifies twenty-four transgressions that are punishable by ostracism, and any Jew is authorized to pronounce נִידּוּי upon a person guilty of these offenses. A person who has been ostracized may not wear leather shoes or cut his hair, and other people must keep at least four cubits' distance from him. But it is permissible to do business with him, to study with him or to teach him. If a person was ostracized and did not mend his ways to have himself released from the ban, he may be subjected to an even more severe punishment — excommunication (יחֵרֶם). See שַׁמְתָּא.

נִיסּוּךְ הַמַּיִם   *Water libation.*

During the Festival of Sukkot, in addition to the other special sacrifices offered in the Temple, a water libation was poured over the altar. This libation is not mentioned explicitly in the Torah, its source being an oral tradition transmitted to Moses on Mount Sinai הֲלָכָה לְמֹשֶׁה מִסִּינַי). The water libation was accompanied by great festivity and ceremony, from the time that the water was drawn from the Siloam Spring until it was poured over the altar. The water libation was offered on all seven days of Sukkot, including Shabbat, even though it was not permitted to draw water for this offering on Shabbat. See שִׂמְחַת בֵּית הַשּׁוֹאֵבָה.

נִיצּוֹק   *An uninterrupted flow of liquid,*

i.e., liquid that is poured from one container to another. With regard to certain laws, the contents of the upper container may be treated as if they were connected to those in the lower container by the fact of being poured from the one into the other. For example, thick liquids, such as honey, connect the contents of different containers with regard to the laws of ritual impurity, and the impurity is passed from one container into the other by the flow. According to some authorities, liquid flow can connect different containers with regard to the laws of יַיִן נֶסֶךְ — "libation wine" (i.e., wine handled by a non-Jew).

נִישׂוּאִין   *Marriage.*

The second stage of the marriage process, following יאֵירוּסִין — "betrothal." Marriage is effected by having the bride and groom come under the bridal canopy (יחוּפָּה), and it immediately confers both the privileges and responsibilities associated with marriage upon the newlywed couple. After marriage, if one spouse dies, all the laws of mourning for a close blood relation apply to the surviving spouse. If the wife of a priest dies, he is permitted to make himself ritually impure to bury her. All the monetary rights and obligations applying to married couples take effect after נִישׂוּאִין. A married woman is permitted to eat יתְּרוּמָה — the priests' dues from the crop — if her husband is a priest.

נִיתּוּחַ   *Cutting, dissection.*

The cutting up of the limbs of a burnt-offering (יעוֹלָה) and of those sin-offerings יחַטָּאוֹת הַפְּנִימִיּוֹת) whose blood was sprinkled in the Sanctuary (יהֵיכָל) or the Holy of Holies (קֹדֶשׁ הַקֳּדָשִׁים). Such cutting up was done in a special manner after the removal of the animal's skin (in the case of an יעוֹלָה). The limbs would then be carried to the altar by the priests and burned there. The נִיתּוּחַ of חַטָּאוֹת הַפְּנִימִיּוֹת was done before they were burned in the יבֵּית הַדֶּשֶׁן.

נִיתָּנִים לְמַטָּה   Lit., *placed below.*

The altar in the Temple was divided by a red line (יחוּט הַסִּיקְרָא) between its upper and lower parts. Certain sacrifices (viz., animals brought as sin-offerings [יחַטָּאת] and birds brought as burnt-offerings [יעוֹלַת הָעוֹף]) had their blood sprinkled on the upper part of the altar, whereas the other sacrifices had their blood "placed below," i.e., sprinkled on the lower part of the altar. If the blood to be sprinkled on the upper part of the altar and the blood to be sprinkled on the lower part of the altar became intermingled, the mixture had to be poured down a special channel in the Temple and the sacrifices were invalid. But if the mixture was sprinkled on both the upper and the lower parts of the altar, then the sacrifices were acceptable *de facto*.

נִכְסֵי דְּלָא נַיְידֵי   *Immovable property.* See מְקַרְקְעֵי.

נִכְסֵי מְלוֹג   Lit., *property of plucking.* Usufruct property, a wife's personal property from which her husband is entitled to benefit. A married woman's property is divided into two categories, נִכְסֵי צֹאן בַּרְזֶל and נִכְסֵי מְלוֹג (see next entry). נִכְסֵי מְלוֹג is the property that a wife brings to the marriage from her father's home and which is not included in her marriage settlement (כְּתוּבָּה), and property that she inherits or receives as a gift after her marriage. All this property remains hers even after she is married, and her husband is not permitted to sell it, although he is entitled to benefit from its פֵּירוֹת — "fruits" (profits). The husband must take care of this property, although he is not responsible if it decreases in value, provided that the loss was not intentionally caused by him. The property is returned to the wife if the husband dies or divorces her, and any increase or decrease in its value at that time by comparison with its value at the beginning of the marriage is *her* profit or loss. If she dies during the lifetime of her husband, he inherits the property. Before marriage, a couple may make any agreement they wish regarding נִכְסֵי מְלוֹג.

נִכְסֵי צֹאן בַּרְזֶל   Lit., *property of iron sheep.* This is the property that a wife brings into her marriage as a dowry and which is recorded in her כְּתוּבָּה — "marriage settlement." The husband may make use of this property as he sees fit. Any profit or loss accruing from his use of it belongs to him. He bears full responsibility, however, for the value of the property, and if he dies or divorces his wife, it must be returned to her at its full, original value. See also previous entry.

נְכָסִים שֶׁיֵּשׁ לָהֶם אַחֲרָיוּת   Lit., *property with responsibility,* i.e., mortgagable property, real estate, immovable property, land; usually real estate, which can be mortgaged to guarantee a loan, and from which debts may ultimately be paid. Written contracts normally establish a lien on all of a person's *landed* property (the Geonim subsequently decreed that debts may be collected from *movable* property as well). Special modes of acquisition (קִנְיָן) must be used to purchase land, although one who purchases land can, at the same time, acquire movable property together with the land. One who purchases land can acquire separate lots located in different areas, or even in different countries, simultaneously. A פְּרוֹזְבּוֹל — a special document of release, permitting loans to be collected after the Sabbatical Year — may only be written if the debtor owns land. However, since all Jews are Halakhically assumed to own at least 4 cubits by 4 cubits of land in Eretz Israel, this land may be used either for the establishing of liens or for writing a פְּרוֹזְבּוֹל.

נִלְקַח בְּכֶסֶף מַעֲשֵׂר   *It may be purchased with second-tithe money.* When a person redeems the second tithe (מַעֲשֵׂר שֵׁנִי) instead of bringing it to the Temple, the money must be taken to Jerusalem, where it may only be used to buy certain specific things, mainly food and drink, and not land or other articles of general use. There is a difference of opinion among the Sages as to exactly what may be bought. Food and drink bought with this redemption money may be eaten only inside the Jerusalem city limits, and may not be removed from Jerusalem.

נַנָּסִין   *Small columns.* There were eight small stone columns in the Temple abattoir, upon which certain animals used for sacrifices were hung before they were flayed.

נְסָכִים   *Libations,* i.e., the wine offered on the altar. Wine libations were offered together with burnt-offerings of animals (see עוֹלָה) and with peace-offerings (שְׁלָמִים), as well as with the sin- and guilt-offerings of the leper. Different quantities of wine were offered, depending on the animal that was sacrificed: a fourth of a hin (i.e., 3 *lugin*) was offered for any sheep other than a ram, a third of a hin (4 *lugin*) was offered for a ram, and half a hin (6 *lugin*) was offered for a bullock. Libations of wine could also be brought as independent, voluntary offerings. See לוֹג.

נְעִילָה   *Closing service.* The special closing service, including recitation of the שְׁמוֹנֶה עֶשְׂרֵה — "eighteen blessings" — recited at the conclusion of certain fast days after the afternoon service (מִנְחָה), towards evening. During Talmudic times, נְעִילָה was recited during major public fasts and on Yom Kippur; today, however, this prayer is recited only on Yom Kippur.

נַעֲרָה   Lit., *a young girl.* A young woman between twelve and twelve-and-a-half years old, who has reached puberty (as evidenced by her having grown at least two pubic hairs), but not full Halakhic maturity. During this period, special laws apply to her. She is no longer considered a minor, nor is she yet an adult. Accordingly, her father retains certain authority over her. See בּוֹגֶרֶת; קְטַנָּה.

נַעֲרָה הַמְאוֹרָסָה   *A girl aged between twelve and twelve-and-a-half, who is betrothed but not yet married.* (See נַעֲרָה.) With regard to many laws, she must also still be a virgin. (1) With regard to the laws of vows (see נֶדֶר): The vows of a נַעֲרָה הַמְאוֹרָסָה can only be annulled by her father and betrothed husband together; neither can annul her vows on his own. (2) Adultery with a נַעֲרָה הַמְאוֹרָסָה is punishable by stoning.

נֶפֶשׁ הַמֵּת   *A special structure erected over a dead person's grave (somewhat like a tombstone).* Such a structure may not be used for any other purpose (like any other object designated for a dead person's use). The Rabbis noted that "we do not erect memorials for the righteous, as their deeds are their memorial."

נִקְבָּרִין   *Items that are buried.* Among those things from which a person is forbidden to benefit (see אִיסּוּרֵי הֲנָאָה), some must be disposed of by burial. For example, a sacrificial animal that died; the aborted fetus of a sacrificial animal; a שׁוֹר הַנִּסְקָל — "an ox that had to be stoned"; an עֶגְלָה עֲרוּפָה — "a heifer whose neck was broken"; the birds offered as a sacrifice by a leper צִיפּוֹרֵי מְצוֹרָע); the hair of a ritually impure Nazirite; a פֶּטֶר חֲמוֹר — "an unredeemed firstborn ass"; mixtures of meat and milk; and animals other than sacrifices that were slaughtered in the Temple Courtyard (see חוּלִּין בָּעֲזָרָה). Other אִיסּוּרֵי הֲנָאָה are disposed of by burning (see נִשְׂרָפִין) or by being cast into the Dead Sea (see יוֹלִיךְ לְיָם הַמֶּלַח). Items that are to be disposed of by burial may not be burned, and items that are to be disposed of by burning may not be buried. If something that was supposed to be buried was burnt instead, it is forbidden to benefit from its ashes, and they too must be buried.

נִקְרָא וְלֹא מִיתַּרְגֵּם   *Read but not translated.* In the Talmudic period, the Torah was translated into Aramaic during the public Torah reading, for the benefit of those who did not know Hebrew. Certain passages in the Torah, however, were read only in the original Hebrew and were not translated, either because they might reflect negatively on the forefathers of the Jewish people, or because they could be misunderstood and lead to heresy. Nowadays, however, all of these passages appear in the written Targum, the Aramaic translation of the Torah.

נֵר לְאֶחָד נֵר לְמֵאָה   Lit., *a candle for one [person] is a candle for a hundred.* Sometimes a Jew is permitted to benefit from work performed by a non-Jew for his own purposes on Shabbat, if the non-Jew did not have to perform any additional labor on account of the Jew. For example, if a non-Jew lit a candle on Shabbat, the Jew may benefit from its light, since the candle provides illumination for the general public and not just for the individual who lit it for himself.

נֵר מַעֲרָבִי   *Western light.* The westernmost light (according to other opinions, the second from the eastern end) on the Temple candelabrum (see מְנוֹרָה), according to the view that the Temple candelabrum was aligned from east to west, or the central light, according to the view that the candelabrum was aligned from north to south. This light served as the נֵר תָּמִיד — "the perpetual light" — in the Temple and was filled with oil in the morning, so that it could burn during the day and not just during the night.

נִשְׁבָּע וְנוֹטֵל   *One who swears and takes.* Usually the function of an oath in a monetary dispute is to deny the plaintiff's claim and absolve the defendant from the obligation to pay. In certain cases, however, the oath is "reversed" (see מִיפָּךְ שְׁבוּעָה), and the *claimant* must swear that the defendant owes him money, after which the claimant may collect. Such an oath is taken by a worker whose employer claims that he has already paid him, and by a storekeeper who paid his customer's workers on behalf of his customer and comes to claim the money back.

נשג"ז   *An acronym for* נִדָּה, שִׁפְחָה, גּוֹיָה, זוֹנָה — *menstruating woman, slave, non-Jewess, zonah.* Although the Torah does not

explicitly forbid Jews to have sexual intercourse with non-Jewish women outside marriage *(see* בּוֹעֵל אֲרַמִּית), it is clear that this is considered a very serious offense, since Pineḥas was permitted to kill Zimri, who had relations with a Midianite woman (Numbers 25:6–15). By Rabbinic decree such a transgression was placed in the category of other severely prohibited sexual relations, and it is considered as if the offender had intercourse with a menstruating woman, a slave, a non-Jewess and a *zonah*.

נָשִׂיא   Lit., *exalted.* In Biblical language this refers to the head of a tribe. It is also sometimes used to refer to a king — for example, with regard to the male goat brought by a king as a sin-offering (see שְׂעִיר נָשִׂיא). In the Talmud, the term is used to refer to the president of the Great Sanhedrin (see אַב בֵּית דִּין).

נְשִׂיאַת כַּפַּיִם   See בִּרְכַּת כֹּהֲנִים.

נִשְׂרָפִין   *Items which are burned.* Among those things from which a person is forbidden to benefit (see אִיסּוּרֵי הֲנָאָה), some must be disposed of by burning. These include the hair of a ritually pure Nazirite (נָזִיר); ritually impure terumah (תְּרוּמָה); fruit that grew during the first three years after a tree was planted (עָרְלָה); mixed plants that grew in a vineyard (כִּלְאֵי הַכֶּרֶם); and sacrifices that were offered after the permissible time limit or outside the Temple (see חוּץ לִזְמַנּוֹ; שְׁחוּטֵי חוּץ). It is permissible to benefit from the ashes of such items after they have been burned. Other אִיסּוּרֵי הֲנָאָה are disposed of by burial (see נִקְבָּרִין) or by being cast into the Dead Sea (see יוֹלִיךְ לְיָם הַמֶּלַח). Items that are to be disposed of by burial may not be burned, and items that are to be disposed of by burning may not be buried.

נָתִין   *A Natin.* A descendant of the Gibeonites, one of the ten categories of lineage within the Jewish people (see עֲשָׂרָה יוֹחֲסִין). According to most authorities, by Torah law, the Gibeonites could have been treated as ordinary proselytes, but first Joshua and then King David decreed that they should be treated as מַמְזֵרִים (see מַמְזֵר), and hence Jews were forbidden to marry them. There were hardly any נְתִינִים during the Talmudic period, and subsequently they completely disappeared.

נֶתֶק   *A type of leprous spot that appears where hair grows on the head or on the beard.* The symptom of a נֶתֶק, a fine yellow hair, differs from other symptoms of skin leprosy (see צָרַעַת; בַּהֶרֶת), and the rules for its treatment are different (Leviticus 13:29–37). The Torah also states (ibid. 13:40–44) that bald spots on the back or front of the head cannot come under the category of נֶתֶק, but can come under the category of skin blemishes (see מִחְיָה; פִּשְׂיוֹן).

סַבְלוֹנוֹת   *Presents sent by a groom to his bride, either before*   *or after betrothal* (קִידּוּשִׁין). The Sages debated whether the giving of such presents could be considered as a method of betrothal or as evidence that a betrothal had taken place.

סְגָן ,סְגַן הַכֹּהֲנִים   *The deputy of the High Priest.* This priest would serve in the Temple in place of the High Priest when necessary (see *Yoma* 39a). He was responsible for the supervision of the daily service and took a leading role in the Temple administration. See כֹּהֵן גָּדוֹל.

סוֹבֵב   *Surrounding ledge.* Part of the altar in the Temple (see מִזְבֵּחַ). The סוֹבֵב was a ledge, raised 5 cubits from the altar's base (see יְסוֹד הַמִּזְבֵּחַ), 6 cubits from the ground. It was 1 cubit wide on all sides, surrounding the altar. The priests would walk on this ledge while performing certain sacrificial functions. (See diagram, p. 276).

סוֹטָה   *A woman suspected by her husband of having been unfaithful.* The Torah describes the procedure governing such a woman (Numbers 5:11-31): First, her husband warns her in the presence of witnesses (see קִינּוּי) against being alone (see יִחוּד) with a specific man about whom he is suspicious. If she disobeys this warning and is observed alone with that man (even though there is no concrete evidence that she actually committed adultery), she and her husband can no longer live together as man and wife until she has undergone the following test to determine whether she has committed adultery. The woman (accompanied by her husband and two scholars) is taken to the Temple in Jerusalem and forced by the priests to stand in a public place while holding the special meal-offering she is required to bring (מִנְחַת קְנָאוֹת). There she is again questioned about her behavior. If she continues to protest her fidelity and takes an oath to that effect, a scroll is brought and the curses of the סוֹטָה mentioned in the Torah passage cited above are written on it. If she does not admit that she has committed adultery, the scroll is submerged in a clay vessel filled with water taken from the Temple basin (כִּיּוֹר) and some earth from the floor of the Temple, and the scroll's writing is dissolved in the water. She is then forced to drink that water. If the husband's allegation is true, in the words of the Torah, "her belly shall swell and her thigh shall fall away" (ibid. 5:27), until ultimately she will die from the water's curse. If she is innocent, the water will bring her blessing and she is permitted to resume normal marital relations with her husband.

סוּכָּה   *Booth, hut, tabernacle.* The term סוּכָּה generally refers to the temporary structure in which a Jew is commanded to dwell for seven days during the Sukkot Festival (Leviticus 23:42–43). A sukkah must have a minimum length and breadth of 7 handbreadths and a minimum height of 10 handbreadths. Its maximum height is 20 cubits. It must have at least three walls, one of which need not be complete. The sukkah must be roofed with material (known as סְכָךְ) that grew from the earth but has been severed (such as cut branches, leaves, etc.), and which is not susceptible to ritual impurity. Fulfillment of the commandment to live in a

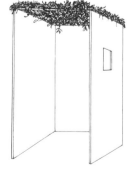

sukkah for the seven days of the Sukkot Festival involves living in the sukkah in the same manner as one lives in one's home. Thus, one must eat and sleep in the sukkah. It is permitted, however, to eat a casual meal (see אֲכִילַת עֲרַאי) outside the sukkah. Women, the sick, those involved in the performance of other mitzvot, and those who suffer undue discomfort while living in a sukkah are absolved from observing the commandment.

סוֹפְרֵי הַדַּיָּנִים   *The judges' scribes.* (1) In general, the scribes responsible for keeping the records of the verdicts decided by the court and for the writing of other legal documents. (2) In particular, three scribes, each with a specific function, were assigned to a court of twenty-three judges (בֵּית דִּין שֶׁל עֶשְׂרִים וּשְׁלֹשָׁה). One scribe would record the statements of those judges inclining to condemn the defendant; the second would record the statements in favor of the defendant; the third would record all the judges' statements. These records were necessary, for there are times when a judge is not allowed to retract a previously stated opinion. This procedure also made it possible, when necessary, to compare the different positions adopted by the judges.

סוּרְיָה   *Syria.* The land located to the north of Eretz Israel extending to the Euphrates River. King David conquered most of Syria. Since this conquest was carried out before the full conquest of Eretz Israel proper, Syria was not incorporated as part of Eretz Israel. Nevertheless, the Sages decreed that, in certain respects (for example, with regard to first-fruits, בִּיכּוּרִים), Syria was to be considered as Eretz Israel, and in other specific matters (such as כִּלְאֵי הַכֶּרֶם and עָרְלָה), it was to be given an intermediate status between Eretz Israel and the Diaspora.

סִידּוּר   See מְסַדְּרִים.

סִימָן (סִימָנִים)   Lit., *mark, sign.* An identification mark. (1) With regard to the return of lost objects, סִימָנִים are means by which an article may be identified. Generally, a person who finds a lost object possessing marks that allow for its identification must announce its discovery. When the owner comes to claim the article, he demonstrates his ownership by mentioning these סִימָנִים. There is a debate among the Sages as to whether the identification of an article through סִימָנִים is a Torah law or a Rabbinic ordinance. Nevertheless, all agree that identification based on an extremely specific sign (סִימָן מוּבְהָק) has the strength of Torah law. In contrast, if someone finds a lost object that lacks identifying marks, in many cases he is allowed to keep the article and need make no effort to locate the owner. (2) With regard to the identification of a dead body. The accurate determination of a dead body's identity is extremely important in order to grant a widow permission to remarry and to give heirs the right to inherit property. If the face of the dead person is not recognizable (see טְבִיעוּת עַיִן), only specific signs (סִימָן מוּבְהָק) are considered as acceptable evidence in these matters. (3) With regard to ritual slaughter (שְׁחִיטָה). The ritual slaughter of any kosher animal involves cutting its windpipe and esophagus. The ritual slaughter of a bird involves cutting either of these organs. These organs are frequently referred to as סִימָנִים. (4) With regard to determining the kashrut of an animal. The Torah mentions characteristics that determine whether animals, birds, fish, and locusts are kosher or not. These characteristics are called סִימָנִים. (5) Signs of puberty. See שְׁתֵּי שְׂעָרוֹת.

סַיִף Lit., *a sword*. Decapitation by the sword, one of the four methods of capital punishment mentioned in the Torah (see Deuteronomy 13:16 and also אַרְבַּע מִיתוֹת בֵּית דִּין). This form of punishment is also called הֶרֶג. A murderer and the inhabitants of an idolatrous city (עִיר הַנִּדַּחַת) are punished in this manner. This same punishment is also administered to those rebelling against a king.

סִיקָרִיקִין *Violent men [from the Latin* sicarii = *murderers, robbers] who would seize fields from their owners with the support of the Roman government in the period of unrest following the destruction of the Second Temple.* The Sages enacted a number of rulings to limit the sale of such property and protect the rights of the original owners.

סֵירוּגִין Lit., *at intervals*. An activity that is not carried out continuously, but rather with interruptions or pauses. A number of commandments that require continuous activity, for example, the reading of the *Shema* (see קְרִיאַת שְׁמַע) or the *Megillah* (the Scroll of Esther), may be performed with limited pauses between passages. The term סֵירוּגִין is also used in connection with the menstrual patterns of women (see וֶסֶת) and the goring patterns of oxen (see מוּעָד), to refer to an interrupted cyclic pattern.

סֵירוּס *Castration*. The Torah prohibits the castration of human beings and animals. The violation of this prohibition is punishable by lashes (Leviticus 22:24). (See also סָרִיס.)

סָמוּךְ מִיעוּטָא לַחֲזָקָה Lit., *join the minority to the presumption*. A Halakhic principle regarding the concept of חֲזָקָה (see entry, subsection 1). A חֲזָקָה, in this sense, is a presumption that is accepted as true and has legal force until new facts prove it to be incorrect (e.g., a מִקְוֶה that has been found to be valid is assumed to have remained valid unless proven otherwise). Nevertheless, there are certain factors that can negate a חֲזָקָה, among them, רוֹב — "the accepted practice of the majority." When the general rule, רוֹב, runs contrary to a חֲזָקָה, the חֲזָקָה is no longer accepted. There are, however, circumstances where the practice of the minority (מִיעוּטָא) is considered of sufficient importance that when the strength of the חֲזָקָה and the מִיעוּטָא are combined, they balance the רוֹב. (See *Yevamot* 119b, *Kiddushin* 80a.)

סְמִיכָה *Placing hands on the head of a sacrifice*. (1) All sacrifices brought to the Temple by an individual (except בְּכוֹר; מַעֲשֵׂר בְּהֵמָה; פֶּסַח (בְּהֵמָה טְהוֹרָה require the person bringing the sacrifice to perform סְמִיכָה, to press both of his hands down with all his strength on the head of the animal to be offered (between its horns), before it is slaughtered. No communal sacrifices require this ceremony except the שָׂעִיר and פַּר הֶעְלֵם דָּבָר הַמִּשְׁתַּלֵּחַ. When performing this ritual for a sin-offering (חַטָּאת), a guilt-offering (אָשָׁם), or a free-will burnt-offering (עוֹלַת נְדָבָה), the person bringing the sacrifice also recites וִידּוּי — a confessional prayer. A sacrifice requiring סְמִיכָה is not invalidated if this ceremony is not performed. Women are not obligated to perform סְמִיכָה. However, according to some opinions, they may

perform a similar ceremony if they so desire. (2) The term סְמִיכָה is also used to refer to the ordination of Rabbis (see סְמִיכַת זְקֵנִים).

סְמִיכַת זְקֵנִים *The ordination of Sages, also referred to as* סְמִיכָה. In Biblical and Talmudic times, when a Torah scholar was considered qualified to decide Halakhic questions, he was formally ordained by his teachers. This ordination had to be conferred by three Sages, one of them himself ordained, who were given the authority to ordain others by the נָשִׂיא, the president of the Sanhedrin. By tradition, the chain of Rabbinic ordination stretched back to Moses himself. This סְמִיכָה was conferred verbally and did not require the physical "laying on of hands." סְמִיכָה could only be conferred in Eretz Israel. A Sage who was given סְמִיכָה was called Rabbi (רַבִּי). Only ordained Sages could serve as members of a סַנְהֶדְרִי קְטַנָּה or the סַנְהֶדְרִין גְּדוֹלָה, and only they had the authority to judge capital cases (דִּינֵי נְפָשׁוֹת) and cases involving fines (see קְנָס). Approximately 400 years after the destruction of the Second Temple, the practice of סְמִיכָה ceased, and the Rabbinical ordination conveyed upon Sages was of a different nature and of lesser authority. In subsequent generations, attempts have been made to renew the practice of סְמִיכָה.

סִמְפוֹן *The cancellation or undermining of an agreement*. This term (possibly of Greek origin) was used by the Sages to refer to a condition or postscript attached to a legal document, nullifying the power of that document or business transaction. For example, a receipt that cancels a promissory note, or a physical deformity discovered in a woman after marriage, which is grounds for divorce and the forfeiture of her ketubah (כְּתוּבָה).

סַנְהֶדְרִי קְטַנָּה Lit., *a small, lesser Sanhedrin*. Also referred to as בֵּית דִּין שֶׁל עֶשְׂרִים וּשְׁלֹשָׁה — "a court of twenty-three judges." These were the lowest courts that had the authority to judge offenses for which the death penalty could be imposed. Some capital cases, however, were outside their authority, such as the case of a man accused of being a false prophet (נָבִיא שֶׁקֶר) or a High Priest (כֹּהֵן גָּדוֹל) who committed a capital offense. Courts of twenty-three judges were convened when necessary in all settlements of 120 men or more. In addition, there were district courts of twenty-three judges in every region in Israel. Furthermore, there appear to have been special courts of this size in Jerusalem, charged with reviewing appeals against decisions made by courts throughout Eretz Israel.

סַנְהֶדְרִין גְּדוֹלָה *The Great Sanhedrin*. Also referred to as בֵּית דִּין שֶׁל שִׁבְעִים וְאֶחָד — "the court of seventy-one judges." The סַנְהֶדְרִין גְּדוֹלָה was ancient Israel's supreme legislative and religious body. It met in the Chamber of Hewn Stone (לִשְׁכַּת הַגָּזִית) in the Temple Courtyard and was vested with the power to decide all matters of national importance. Its enactments were binding on the entire nation, and it promulgated both permanent decrees and temporary regulations. It decided cases left undecided by the lower courts, and was the final authority on Halakhah. The term סַנְהֶדְרִין, when used without an adjective, usually refers to the סַנְהֶדְרִין גְּדוֹלָה.

סְעוּדַת הַבְרָאָה *Meal of comfort*. The first meal served to mourners on their return from a funeral. This meal must be prepared by friends or neighbors from food that does not belong to the mourners. Certain foods, such as eggs and lentils, are customarily served at this meal.

סְפִיחִים   *Plants that grew in the Sabbatical Year [see שְׁבִיעִית] without being purposely planted, as an aftergrowth of the plants of the previous year.* By Torah law, this produce may be eaten in the Sabbatical Year by those who find it in the fields. Nevertheless, the Sages in most cases forbade eating it, lest people plant crops in the Sabbatical Year and sell the produce under the pretense that they are merely סְפִיחִים.

סְפִירַת הָעוֹמֶר   *The counting of the omer.* The positive commandment to count seven weeks beginning on the night following the first day of Passover, the night preceding the day on which the omer of barley (the beginning of the barley harvest) was brought as a wave-offering in the Temple (Leviticus 23:15). The commandment involves counting each night both the days and the weeks that have passed. After forty-nine days have been counted, on the fiftieth day the festival of Shavuot is celebrated. The commandment to count the omer remains in effect to this day. See also עוֹמֶר.

סָפֵק   *Doubt.* Something that is not clear to us, either because the facts cannot be definitely established or because no clear Halakhic decision has emerged. In doubtful cases, the general principle is this: In relation to commandments from the Torah (סְפֵיקָא דְּאוֹרָיְיתָא), one leans towards severity; whereas in Rabbinical rulings (סְפֵיקָא דְּרַבָּנָן) one leans towards leniency. In cases of doubt in monetary disputes, one generally follows the rule that whoever is in possession of the disputed sum or object may keep it. See הַמּוֹצִיא מֵחֲבֵירוֹ עָלָיו הָרְאָיָה.

סְפֵק הִינּוּחַ   *There is a doubt whether it has been left deliberately.* A concept in the laws of lost property. If there is a doubt whether something was purposely left by its owner where it was later found, or whether it was inadvertently lost there, it is forbidden to pick up the article even if one's intention is to announce its discovery. Nevertheless, if someone finds and takes such an article, he is only required to announce its discovery if it has a distinguishing mark (סִימָן) by which it can be identified. Otherwise, he may, according to some authorities, keep it as his own. According to others, he must look after it indefinitely.

סְפֵק טוּמְאָה בִּרְשׁוּת הָרַבִּים   *A doubt concerning ritual impurity in a public domain.* By Torah law, if a doubt arises concerning the ritual purity of a person or an object, and the person or object is in a public domain, they are considered to be ritually pure. If the situation arose in a private domain, they are considered to be ritually impure. Whether a place is a public or private domain, in this context, depends on its accessibility to the general public.

סְפֵיק סְפֵיקָא   *A double doubt.* A case with two independent doubtful aspects. Generally, even in cases where one rules

severely with regard to one doubt, one may rule leniently with regard to two. For example, it is forbidden to tithe untithed produce on the Sabbath. Moreover, even if one is in doubt whether the Sabbath has begun, one may not tithe it. Even produce about which one is in doubt as to whether it has been tithed, may not be tithed on the Sabbath. However, if one was in doubt both about whether the Sabbath had begun and about whether the produce had been tithed, the tithing is permitted.

סְפָר   *An area near the border of a country.* (1) Greater stress is placed on the defense of border cities than of others. If such a city is attacked, even if the raider only intends to plunder (and not destroy) it, all Jews are obligated to come to the city's defense. The Sabbath laws may be violated for this purpose. (2) Such a city cannot be judged as an עִיר הַנִּדַּחַת — an idolatrous city. Rather, its accused inhabitants are judged as individuals, and the city may not be destroyed, in order not to impair the defense of the country's borders.

סְפָרִים   *Scrolls, books.* This term is often used to refer to all sacred Biblical texts (see כִּתְבֵי הַקּוֹדֶשׁ). In the Talmud, it is generally used specifically to refer to handwritten Torah scrolls. A סֵפֶר תּוֹרָה — Torah scroll — must be written on parchment, with special ink, as a scroll. It may only be written in Hebrew, using unique calligraphy. No vowels or punctuation marks may be included. It is a positive Torah commandment for each Jew to write (or participate in the writing of) a Torah scroll (see Deuteronomy 31:19). In the absence of the Temple, Torah scrolls have the highest degree of sanctity, surpassing that of a synagogue, an ark, or holy books. If a Torah scroll becomes worn with use, it is buried. Similarly, the articles associated with the Torah scroll, e.g., the ark, the mantle and the crown, have the title תַּשְׁמִישֵׁי קְדוּשָׁה — "utensils used for a sacred purpose" — and are treated with great respect.

סְקִילָה   *Stoning to death.* One of the four methods of execution mentioned in the Torah (see also אַרְבַּע מִיתוֹת בֵּית דִּין). סְקִילָה is considered the severest of the death penalties, and many of the prohibitions that carry the death penalty are punishable by סְקִילָה. Among these prohibitions are incest with one's mother; incest with one's father's wife; incest with one's son's wife; sexual relations between males; sexual relations between a human and an animal; cursing God; worshipping idols; worshipping Molekh; necromancy; the desecration of the Sabbath; cursing one's parents; adultery with a betrothed girl (see נַעֲרָה הַמְאוֹרָסָה); solicitation to worship idols (see מֵסִית וּמַדִּיחַ); witchcraft; acting as a "stubborn and rebellious son" (בֵּן סוֹרֵר וּמוֹרֶה). סְקִילָה was carried out in the following way: The person to be executed was pushed to the ground from a height of 8 cubits (about 4 meters). If he did not die on hitting the ground, the witnesses whose testimony caused him to be convicted had to cast a heavy stone upon him. If he was still alive after this, the entire populace had to continue stoning him until he died. In cases of cursing God and worshipping idols, the bodies of men stoned to death were afterwards hanged.

סָרִיס   *A sexually impotent or castrated male.* There are two categories of such individuals: סְרִיס חַמָּה — a person who, from birth, was entirely lacking in sexual capacity; and סְרִיס אָדָם — a person who was castrated. A סְרִיס חַמָּה is considered to have reached majority at the age of twenty if he has manifested signs of his disability before that age. If he does not show such signs, he is not considered to have reached majority until the age of thirty-five. A סְרִיס אָדָם is forbidden to marry a native-born Jewess (Deuteronomy 23, 2; see also פְּצוּעַ דַּכָּא). However, if he violates this prohibition and marries, the marriage is valid. No restrictions are placed on the marriage of a סְרִיס חַמָּה. With regard to levirate marriage (יִבּוּם) and חֲלִיצָה, special rules apply to the סָרִיס: A סְרִיס אָדָם must give חֲלִיצָה to his brother's childless widow and חֲלִיצָה must be given to his childless widow. A סְרִיס חַמָּה may not perform חֲלִיצָה, and neither יבום nor חֲלִיצָה is necessary to grant his childless widow the opportunity to remarry.

סְתִירָה   *Hiding, tearing down.* (1) With regard to the laws of

a סְתִירָה, סוֹטָה is the term used to describe a situation where a married woman is alone in private with a man whom her husband suspects of adultery with her, and with whom her husband has warned her not to be alone (see קִינוּי). If they remain together long enough to engage in sexual relations, she is considered a סוֹטָה and is forbidden to him until she has undergone the ordeal of a סוֹטָה. There is a debate among the Sages as to whether the woman must be seen with the man by witnesses to subject her to the ordeal, or whether the husband's testimony is sufficient. All agree that the husband's testimony is sufficient to forbid them from living together, and if the ordeal is not applicable, he must divorce her. (2) With regard to the laws of Shabbat, סְתִירָה refers to the destruction, "tearing down," of a building. Destruction of a structure or building is not considered a "creative" act and is thus in principle not forbidden on Shabbat. But destruction of a building in order to build something else in its place *is* considered a creative act and is thus forbidden on Shabbat (see מְלָאכֶת מַחֲשֶׁבֶת).

עֶבֶד כְּנַעֲנִי   Lit., *a Canaanite slave.* A non-Jewish slave purchased by a Jew. (See Leviticus 25:44-46.) A female non-Jewish slave is called a שִׁפְחָה כְּנַעֲנִית. A non-Jewish slave purchased by a Jew must be immersed in a מִקְוֶה (ritual bath), and, if male, circumcised. These acts signify a change in the slave's status. Though not yet a Jew in all respects, a Canaanite slave must observe all the Torah's prohibitions and must fulfill all the positive commandments that are not dependent on a specific time for their performance (see מִצְוַת עֲשֵׂה שֶׁהַזְּמַן גְּרָמָא). In many respects Canaanite slaves are their masters' property and may be sold and purchased like other possessions. Generally, the laws governing slaves resemble those governing real estate (מְקַרְקְעֵי). For example, they are acquired by the same legal procedures as real estate, and they are treated as such with regard to the laws of אוֹנָאָה — overreaching. A Canaanite slave must serve his master for life and is inherited by his master's heirs. His master can free him by giving him a deed of emancipation (גֵּט שִׁחְרוּר), resembling a bill of divorce. But it is a positive commandment not to free a Canaanite slave without compelling reasons. There is one exception to the above principle. A master must set his slave free if he blinds him, knocks out his tooth, or destroys any one of 24 other limbs (רָאשֵׁי אֵיבָרִים). This applies regardless of whether the master caused the damage intentionally. (See Exodus 21:26-27.) If a master severely beats his slave, and the slave dies within twenty-four hours of the beating, the master is executed as a murderer (Exodus 21:20-21). A Canaanite slave may not marry into the Jewish people. If he violates this prohibition and engages in relations with a Jewish woman, any child born of such a union is considered solely as the mother's. A child born to a female

Canaanite slave becomes a slave from birth. Slaves are considered to have no connection to their natural father even when his identity is known. If a master sells his Canaanite slave to a non-Jew, or if a master living in Eretz Israel sells his slave to a Jew living outside Eretz Israel, or if an adult Canaanite slave flees to Eretz Israel or is declared ownerless (הֶפְקֵר) by his master, his master must give him a deed of emancipation and free him. A Canaanite slave owned by a priest may partake of תְּרוּמָה — the agricultural dues given to the priests.

עֶבֶד מְשׁוּחְרָר   *A freed slave.* A male or female Canaanite slave freed by his or her Jewish master. To obtain his freedom, the slave must receive a deed of emancipation (called a גֵּט שִׁחְרוּר) from his master. Alternatively, another person can buy the slave's freedom from the master for money. After obtaining his freedom, the slave has all the obligations and privileges of a Jew and has the status of a convert. However, the Sages required him to immerse himself in a mikveh (מִקְוֶה) like all regular converts.

עֶבֶד עִבְרִי   *A Hebrew slave.* An adult male Jew who becomes the slave of another Jew. There are two ways a Jew can enter such servitude: (1) The court may sell a thief into slavery if he does not have the means to make restitution for his theft (Exodus 22:2). (2) If a Jew becomes impoverished, he may sell himself because of his poverty (Leviticus 25:39). A Hebrew slave sold by the court receives his freedom after serving his master for six years (Exodus 21:2). A person who sells himself as a slave may sell himself for six years or for a longer period. In the event of his master's death, a Hebrew slave is required to continue serving his son until the end of the period for which he was originally sold. But if the master did not leave any sons, the slave is not obligated to continue serving other heirs. In the Jubilee Year (יוֹבֵל), all Hebrew slaves are freed irrespective of how long they have served (Leviticus 25:40). When a Hebrew slave attains his freedom in one of these ways, his master (or heirs) must give him a severance gift (Deuteronomy 15:13-14). A Hebrew slave may also attain his freedom by paying his master the value of the remainder of the term for which he was sold. If a Hebrew slave has a wife and children, his master is obligated to provide for their livelihood as well. According to some authorities, they, in turn, are obligated to render the master the same services that they would render their husband and father. If a slave becomes ill or incapacitated, his master must care for him, and the period of his illness counts towards his years of service, up to a maximum of three years. When a Hebrew slave who is married and has children is sold by the court, his master is entitled to give him a Canaanite maidservant as a wife. If she bears children, they become the property of the master and have no legal connection with their natural father (Exodus 21:4). In all other respects, the Hebrew slave has all the obligations of a free Israelite and is bound by all other positive and negative commandments. Should the Hebrew slave sold by the court desire to remain with his wife (the Canaanite maidservant) and children after the six years of his servitude are concluded, he must go through a ceremonial rite (רְצִיעָה) involving the piercing of his ear (Exodus 21:5-6). Afterwards he remains a slave until the Jubilee Year (יוֹבֵל) or until the death of his master. It is the slave's right to insist on undergoing the ceremony of רְצִיעָה, but it is strongly discouraged. It is forbidden to give a Hebrew slave humiliating work, even if some free men would be willing to accept such tasks. Nor is it permitted to overwork him (see Leviticus 25:39-43). In all matters (e.g., food and sleeping quarters), the Hebrew slave and his family must be treated as the master himself. See אָמָה עִבְרִיָה.

עֲבוֹדָה זָרָה   *Idolatry.*

The prohibition against idolatry is one of the most severe in the Torah (see Exodus 20:3-5), and is punishable by stoning (סְקִילָה; see Deuteronomy 17:2-7). It is one of the three commandments which a Jew must keep even if he is threatened with death for doing so (see יֵיהָרֵג וְאַל יַעֲבוֹר). The scope of the prohibition includes accepting another deity as a god (even together with God) or worshipping another deity. Idol worship may involve: (1) Serving the god in the manner in which other idolators worship it. (2) Serving the false god in the same manner in which God is worshipped; e.g., through sacrifice or libation, or by bowing down to it. (3) Accepting it as one's god. Other signs of veneration (such as kissing an idol or embracing it), are forbidden, but are not punishable by death. The term עֲבוֹדָה זָרָה is also used to refer not only to the act of idolatry, but to the idols, pictures or images worshipped. Benefit may not be derived from them, nor from sacrifices offered to them, nor from buildings constructed for their worship, if they were planted or fashioned or constructed by human hands for idolatrous purposes. They must be utterly destroyed (see יוֹלִיךְ לְיַם הַמֶּלַח). But benefit may be derived from עֲבוֹדָה זָרָה that has been broken and has ceased to be used for idolatry. Any natural spring, mountain, animal, or tree planted for the purpose of providing fruit, does not become prohibited if idolatrously

worshipped. The above only applies to עֲבוֹדָה זָרָה belonging to a gentile. עֲבוֹדָה זָרָה belonging to a Jew can never have its status as an object of idolatrous worship altered and remains forbidden forever. The Sages decreed that עֲבוֹדָה זָרָה imparts ritual impurity as an אַב הַטּוּמְאָה (see טוּמְאַת עֲבוֹדָה זָרָה, see also יֵין נֶסֶךְ; תִּקְרוֹבֶת עֲבוֹדָה זָרָה).

עִבּוּר   See עִיבּוּר.

עֵבֶר הַיַּרְדֵּן   *Transjordan.*

The part of Eretz Israel on the east bank of the Jordan conquered by Moses (the area allocated to the tribes of Reuben, Gad, and half of the tribe of Menasheh). With regard to most of the commandments of the Torah, Transjordan is considered as the Land of Israel, and it is listed together with Judea and Galilee as one of the three major parts (אֲרָצוֹת) of the country. There were three cities of refuge (see עִיר מִקְלָט) in Transjordan, in addition to those on the west bank of the Jordan. In certain contexts, the neighboring lands of Edom, Ammon and Moab, which were not conquered by Moses and not given to the Jewish people as an inheritance, are sometimes referred to as Transjordan.

עֲגוּנָה   *A deserted [lit., tied] wife.*

A woman whose husband has deserted her, or whose husband has disappeared and may no longer be alive. Since a Jewish marriage can be dissolved only by establishing that the husband has died or by a bill of divorce granted willingly by the husband, the status of an עֲגוּנָה can only be resolved by her obtaining a bill of divorce or by her presenting acceptable testimony that her husband has died. The Halakhic tradition is to be as lenient as possible in these matters. Many leniencies were instituted in accepting evidence of death (see עֵדוּת אִשָׁה) and in validating bills of divorce, to save a wife from the fate of remaining an עֲגוּנָה.

עֶגְלָה עֲרוּפָה   Lit., *a heifer whose neck is broken.*

When a murdered person's body is found outside a town and it is not known who caused his death, the following procedure takes place (see Deuteronomy 21:1-9). First, judges from the Great Sanhedrin (סַנְהֶדְרִין גְדוֹלָה) come to measure the distance between the corpse and the nearest town, to determine which town must perform the rite of the עֶגְלָה עֲרוּפָה. This measurement is carried out even if it is clear beyond any doubt which town is closest to the corpse. Afterwards, the elders of that town must bring a heifer that has never been used for any work and break its neck in a riverbed that is not tilled. The elders wash their hands and make a statement absolving themselves from guilt. If the murderer is discovered before the heifer has been killed, the rite of עֶגְלָה עֲרוּפָה is not performed.

עֵד אֶחָד   *One witness.*

The Torah states: "One witness shall not rise up against a man" (Deuteronomy 19:15). Thus, in most instances, the testimony of a single witness has no legal standing. Indeed, in certain cases, he is forbidden to testify, lest he damage the defendant's reputation. Nevertheless, there are a few instances where credence is given to the testimony of a single witness: (1) In monetary matters (דִינֵי מָמוֹנוֹת), if a witness corroborates a claimant's statements, his testimony is not sufficient to obligate the defendant to pay. But his testimony forces the defendant to take an oath to support his own statements. (2) With regard to matters involving ritual prohibitions, the testimony of a single witness that a particular item is prohibited by Torah law is sufficient to render that article forbidden. Likewise, in most cases, testimony by one witness that the item is permitted is also sufficient. (3) With regard to the laws of a wife suspected of infidelity (סוֹטָה), the testimony of a single witness that a woman who had secluded herself with the man against whom she had been warned committed adultery with him is sufficient to require her husband to divorce her. (4) With regard to testimony concerning the death of a married man, see עֵדוּת אִשָּׁה.

עַד וָעַד בִּכְלָל   *Up to and including.* The question of whether or not the word עַד — "until, up to" — includes the target date is important in any instance where oral or written obligations are at issue. In the case of vows, for example, if a person agreed or vowed to continue performing a particular task until (עַד) Passover: Did he intend to include Passover in his vow (עַד בִּכְלָל — i.e., the final point is included) or did he mean until Passover, but not including Passover itself (וְלֹא עַד בִּכְלָל — the final point is not included)? If possible this question is determined by looking at the logical implications of the statement, according to the normal way in which people use language. But the Sages were not able to establish an all-inclusive rule.

עַד מִפִּי עַד   *Testimony given by a witness, based on the statements of another witness,* i.e., hearsay evidence. Generally, such testimony is not accepted. A notable exception to this rule is עֵדוּת אִשָּׁה — testimony concerning the death of a married man that will allow his widow to remarry.

עַד נַעֲשָׂה דַיָּין   *Can a witness become a judge?* The Sages questioned whether a witness to an event can also serve as a judge to decide the matter, or whether these two functions must be performed by two separate individuals. Though in many areas the subject remained a matter of debate, with regard to evidence in capital cases (specifically, cases of murder), all authorities would forbid a witness to serve as a judge. The assumption is that once a person has witnessed what seems to be a murder, there is no way that he can possibly appreciate any extenuating arguments. He cannot, therefore, serve as a judge in the case.

עַד שֶׁיָּבוֹא אֵלִיָּהוּ   *Until Elijah comes.* In monetary matters that cannot be resolved (for example, a lost object that no one claims or an object that is claimed by two people), the court may rule that the object remain in the hands of the court or of a third party currently in possession of it, "until Elijah comes," i.e., for an indefinite period, until the question can be resolved through prophetic vision. (See Ezra 2:63 for a similar statement.)

עֵדוּת אִשָּׁה   *Testimony concerning a woman.* Testimony attesting to the death of a married man. Although a husband is missing and presumed dead, until his death is established by the court his wife is not considered a widow and may not remarry. In this situation, many exceptional leniencies regarding the testimony of witnesses were granted, so that the woman should not be forced to remain alone for the rest of her life (see עֲגוּנָה). The consequences for the future of the woman and her children, should she remarry while her first husband is still alive, are very

severe. Hence we assume that she would not seek permission to remarry unless she was sure that her first husband had, in fact, died. For these reasons the court accepts testimony from the following individuals, although generally such testimony is unacceptable: (1) A single witness. (2) Women. (3) Relatives. Even the wife herself can testify to her husband's death. (4) Witnesses disqualified by Rabbinic decree. (5) Someone who did not witness the event himself, but testifies on the basis of another person's statements (עַד מִפִּי עַד). (6) A non-Jew who makes incidental statements in the course of conversation while unaware of their legal significance (see מֵסִיחַ לְפִי תוּמּוֹ).

עֵדֵי חֲתִימָה   *Witnesses whose signatures appear on a legal document.* With regard to many legal documents, the authenticated signatures of two qualified witnesses are all that is needed to establish the legal validity of the document. All other forms of verification are of secondary importance. See next entry.

עֵדֵי מְסִירָה   *Witnesses who observe the delivery of a legal document.* Specifically, with reference to the witnesses to the delivery of a גֵּט (bill of divorce), there is a difference of opinion among the Sages whether these witnesses or the witnesses whose signatures appear on the גֵּט (עֵדֵי חֲתִימָה) are the witnesses who make the document effective.

עֵדִים   *Witnesses.* The Torah states: "According to the testimony of two witnesses ... shall a matter be established" (Deuteronomy 19:15). Thus, the authenticated testimony of two witnesses is generally needed in order to establish the truth about an event or the validity of a claim (see עֵד אֶחָד). Testimony authenticated by a court is the highest form of proof and is almost impossible to refute. Even a subsequent retraction by the witnesses or a confession of perjury is insufficient to contradict it. There is no difference between the legal force of the testimony of two witnesses and that of 100 witnesses. Generally, only male adult Jews, who are not related to the litigants or to each other, and who have no personal interest in the case, are acceptable as witnesses (see פְּסוּלֵי עֵדוּת; קָרוֹב; עֵדוּת אִשָּׁה). Witnesses who are known to have given false testimony (see עֵדִים זוֹמְמִים) are disqualified from serving as witnesses in the future and are considered to be wicked, even where, because of some technicality, they are not punished. Witnesses in civil cases must testify in the presence of both litigants, and, in criminal cases, in the presence of the accused. Each witness testifies separately. In capital and in certain other cases the witnesses are subjected to a lengthy process of examination (see דְּרִישָׁה וַחֲקִירָה), and they must have witnessed the crime together. Witnesses serve three primary functions that are occasionally interrelated: (1) To verify what happened in a particular instance or circumstance. (2) To publicize a legal act. For example, with regard to contracts and acts of legal transfer (see קִנְיָן), the participation of witnesses is a sign that the transaction has become public knowledge. (3) In certain instances, e.g., קִידּוּשִׁין, the participation of the witnesses is indispensable in order to give the act legal validity. If witnesses were not present, the marriage is not valid, even if both parties to the marriage acknowledge that the act of קִידּוּשִׁין took place.

עֵדִים זוֹמְמִים   *False conspiring witnesses.* Witnesses who are proved to have perjured themselves to make someone lose a monetary dispute or to cause him to be punished by the court. There are two ways in which the testimony of witnesses can be invalidated: (1) If two other witnesses testify that something did not happen as described by the first pair of witnesses (see הַכְחָשָׁה*). In such a case, the testimony of neither pair is accepted, and the matter is left undecided. (2) If two witnesses testify that the first pair of witnesses, whose testimony condemned the defendant, were elsewhere (with the second pair of witnesses) when the incident transpired, and could not have witnessed the events about which they testified. The second pair of witnesses are not contradicting the evidence of the first pair (which may indeed be true). They are testifying that the first pair were not present and therefore were not in a position to know. In such a case, the testimony of the second pair of witnesses is accepted, and the testimony of the first pair of witnesses is rejected. Furthermore, the first pair of witnesses, the עֵדִים זוֹמְמִים, pay the penalty they sought to inflict by their testimony on the defendant (see Deuteronomy 19:16-19). Thus, if their testimony would have resulted in having the defendant killed, they are both killed. If their testimony would have resulted in his receiving lashes, they are both lashed. If their testimony would have resulted in a penalty that cannot be applied to them (if, for example, their evidence would have disqualified the defendant from the priesthood), they are given lashes. The acceptance of the testimony of the second pair of witnesses is a חִידוּשׁ, a unique law not necessarily following from existing Torah principles. Accordingly, many limitations are placed on its application. Among them: (1) *Both* the first pair of witnesses (or *all* the witnesses, if there are more than two) must be proven to be conspiring witnesses before the retaliatory punishment is carried out on any of them. (2) עֵדִים זוֹמְמִים are not punished unless the defendant has already been convicted on the basis of their testimony. (3) In capital cases, the death penalty is only administered to the witnesses if it has *not* been administered to the defendant. If, however, the defendant *has* already been executed, the witnesses are not executed.

עוֹבָּר יֶרֶךְ אִמּוֹ   Lit., *a fetus is [considered as] the thigh of its mother*, i.e., it is like a limb of the mother, and is not a separate entity. Thus, if a mother animal was forbidden to be eaten because of injury or disease (see טְרֵיפָה*), the fetus too is forbidden to be eaten. If the mother animal is dedicated as a sacrifice, the fetus is also considered as dedicated. If the mother is ritually slaughtered (see שְׁחִיטָה*), the fetus is fit, by Torah law, to be eaten without itself being ritually slaughtered (see בֶּן פְּקוּעָה*). However, by Rabbinic decree it is in many cases forbidden. Although in principle the concept עוֹבָּר יֶרֶךְ אִמּוֹ does not apply to human beings, there are a number of laws that, in practice, treat a human fetus as less than a fully independent human being. Thus, if a pregnant non-Jewish woman becomes a convert to Judaism, her child is born Jewish. A fetus cannot inherit property until it is born.

עוֹלָה   *An offering that is totally consumed on the altar in the Temple.* This is generally referred to as a "burnt-offering" (see Leviticus, chapter 1). A burnt-offering may be brought from male cattle, sheep, or goats, or from doves (see עוֹלַת הָעוֹף*). Private individuals generally bring this sacrifice as a voluntary offering (נְדָבָה*). However, there are times when it is offered to atone for

the willful non-fulfillment of a positive commandment or for immoral or idolatrous thoughts, and there are certain situations where individuals are required to bring a burnt-offering together with other sacrifices (see, for example, יוֹלֶדֶת and טָהֲרַת מְצוֹרָע). Many of the communal offerings, e.g., the daily offering (תָּמִיד*) and many of the additional offerings (see מוּסָף*) brought on Sabbaths and Festivals, are burnt-offerings (see Numbers, chapters 28-29). The burnt-offerings are considered as קָדְשֵׁי* קָדָשִׁים — "sacrifices of the most sacred order." They must be slaughtered in the northern portion of the Temple Courtyard and their blood is sprinkled (see זְרִיקָה*) at the two opposite (northeastern and southwestern) corners of the altar, so that it touches all four sides (see שְׁתַּיִם שֶׁהֵן אַרְבַּע*). Afterwards, the animal's hide is removed (it becomes the property of the priests) and its limbs are separated (see נִיתּוּחַ*). The remainder of the blood (שִׁירַיִים*) is then poured out at the base of the altar (יְסוֹד* הַמִּזְבֵּחַ), and the limbs are offered on the altar. Certain burnt-offerings that were sacrificed as atonement depended on a person's wealth. Thus a wealthy leper would bring a lamb and a poor leper a dove as a burnt-offering. In certain cases a poor person would bring inexpensive burnt- and sin-offerings, whereas a rich man would bring an expensive sin-offering and no burnt-offering at all (see קָרְבָּן עוֹלֶה וְיוֹרֵד).

עוֹלְלוֹת   *Small, incompletely formed clusters of grapes.* Clusters of grapes lacking a central stalk, or ones in which the grapes do not hang down one upon the other. The Torah prohibits gathering such incompletely formed clusters of grapes (Leviticus 19:20; see also Deuteronomy 24:21). They must be left for the poor (see מַתְּנוֹת עֲנִיִּים*). The Sages differed as to whether this law applies if a person's entire vineyard grew in this manner.

עוֹלַת הָעוֹף   *A bird sacrificed as a burnt-offering.* Turtledoves (תּוֹרִים*) and young pigeons (בְּנֵי יוֹנָה*) are the only species of bird used for this and all other sacrifices of birds in the Temple. The priest kills the bird by cutting through the back of its neck with his fingernail (see מְלִיקָה*). After the blood of the bird's body and head has been squeezed out on the altar (see מִיצּוּי*), the bird's excrement is removed and the entire bird is burned on the altar. This is a sacrifice from which the priests derive no benefit (הֲנָאָה*) whatsoever. Certain individuals, for example, a זָב* upon purification (see Leviticus 15:14), bring a קֵן* — a pair of birds, one as a burnt-offering (עוֹלָה*) and one as a sin-offering (חַטָּאת*). A convert (גֵּר צֶדֶק*) also brings a pair of birds (or a male animal) as a burnt-offering. See זָבָה; טָהֲרַת מְצוֹרָע; יוֹלֶדֶת; קָרְבָּן עוֹלֶה וְיוֹרֵד.

עוֹלַת רְאִיָּה   Lit., *a burnt-offering of appearance [in the Temple].* The burnt-offering brought to the Temple by pilgrims on the three Pilgrim Festivals (שָׁלֹשׁ רְגָלִים*). The Torah prohibits a pilgrim from coming to the Temple on these Festivals "empty-handed" (Deuteronomy 16:16-17). See also חֲגִיגָה and רְאִיָּה.

עוֹמֶר   *Omer.* A measure of grain, one-tenth of an אֵיפָה (see section on weights and measures, p. 288). This term is used to refer to the measure of barley offered in the Temple on the sixteenth of Nisan, the day following the first day of Pesaḥ. The sacrifice was brought irrespective of whether the 16th of Nisan was a Sabbath or a weekday. The עוֹמֶר was harvested on the night following the first day of Pesaḥ from the newly ripe grain and was prepared as roasted flour. A handful was burned on the altar, the rest was eaten by the priests. In addition to the עוֹמֶר of barley, a male sheep was sacrificed as a burnt-offering (עוֹלָה•), together with a wine libation and two-tenths of an אֵיפָה of wheat flour as a meal-offering (מִנְחָה•). Once the עוֹמֶר had been offered, grain from the new harvest (חָדָשׁ•) could be eaten. It is a Torah obligation to count the days from the 16th of Nisan until the Festival of Shavuot (see סְפִירַת הָעוֹמֶר•).

עוֹנָה   *A period, a set interval of time.* This term applies Halakhically, *inter alia*: (1) With regard to the laws governing a menstruating woman (נִדָּה•) and other regulations governing ritual purity. עוֹנָה in this context refers to half a daily cycle, either the daytime or the nighttime. Occasionally עוֹנָה is also used to refer to a woman's monthly cycle. For example, עוֹנָה בֵּינוֹנִית — "an average interval" — refers to the monthly menstrual cycle experienced by most women. (2) With regard to marriage, עוֹנָה refers to the husband's obligation to engage in sexual relations with his wife at regular intervals. Though the matter depends on the mutual agreement of the two partners, the Sages mentioned a number of guidelines based on the nature of the work performed by the husband and the amount of time he is usually at home. This obligation is stipulated in the Torah (Exodus 21·10) and is specifically mentioned in the marriage contract (כְּתוּבָּה•). See also מוֹרֶדֶת and שְׁאֵר כְּסוּת וְעוֹנָה.

עוֹנַת הַמַּעַשְׂרוֹת   Lit., *the season of tithes.* The stage at which produce is ripe enough to eat. From this time onwards, tithes must be separated from the produce. Fruit on trees that has reached this stage of development may not be destroyed in the Sabbatical Year (שְׁבִיעִית•).

עוֹף טָהוֹר   *A pure [kosher] bird,* i.e., a species of bird that may be eaten if slaughtered in a kosher manner. In contrast to the signs distinguishing kosher animals and fish, the Torah does not mention specific signs that distinguish birds as kosher. Rather, Leviticus 11:13-19 and Deuteronomy 14:12-19 list the names of the non-kosher birds. Nevertheless, the Sages gave three signs by which to identify a kosher bird: (1) One of its toes must be much longer than the others. (2) It must have a discernible crop. (3) Its craw (thick muscular stomach) must be easily peeled. Moreover, it must not be a bird of prey. Similarly, there is a sign by which to identify the eggs of kosher birds: One end of the egg must be somewhat pointed, the other rounded. Despite these signs, the Sages declared that a species of bird should only be considered kosher if there is an accepted tradition to that effect. The blood of a bird must be covered after slaughter (see כִּיסּוּי הַדָּם•; see also נִבְלַת עוֹף טָהוֹר•).

עוֹרוֹ כִּבְשָׂרוֹ   Lit., *its skin is considered like its flesh.* A principle applying to the laws of ritual impurity. Certain animals have an outer skin that is so soft as to be considered part of their flesh. In this category are human beings, certain crawling animals (see שֶׁרֶץ•) and the soft edible skin of young animals. This skin is considered as flesh with regard to the laws of ritual impurity (see Mishnah *Ḥullin* 9:2).

עֶזְרַת יִשְׂרָאֵל   *The Courtyard of the Israelites.* Part of the Temple (see plan of the Temple, p. 277), separated by steps from the עֶזְרַת כֹּהֲנִים•, the priests' courtyard, on one side, and from the עֶזְרַת נָשִׁים•, the women's courtyard, on the other. The עֶזְרַת יִשְׂרָאֵל was an area 135 cubits long and 11 cubits wide, extending across the width of the Temple. Generally it was reserved for men, but women passed through it when they had to enter the עֶזְרַת כֹּהֲנִים to bring a sacrifice. This part of the Temple was of a higher degree of holiness than the עֶזְרַת נָשִׁים. A person whose period of ritual impurity had ended but who had not yet brought the sacrifice to complete the process of purification (see מְחוּסַּר כַּפָּרָה•) was not allowed to enter the עֶזְרַת יִשְׂרָאֵל. A ritually impure person who entered it inadvertently had to bring a sin-offering (חַטָּאת•).

עֶזְרַת כֹּהֲנִים   *The courtyard of the priests.* Part of the Temple, in which only the priests were generally permitted to be. Non-priests could only enter it for specific limited parts of the sacrificial service (see סְמִיכָה•). The עֶזְרַת כֹּהֲנִים was next to the עֶזְרַת יִשְׂרָאֵל• (see plan of the Temple, p. 277), at a height of 2.5 cubits above it. Between the two was a platform (דּוּכָן•) on which the Levites stood to sing. This platform was built in the form of a series of steps, each half a cubit in height. The עֶזְרַת כֹּהֲנִים was 11 cubits wide and extended across the entire width of the Temple. On the same level as the עֶזְרַת כֹּהֲנִים and nearer to the Sanctuary (הֵיכָל•) was the altar (מִזְבֵּחַ•). It and the area around it were of a higher level of sanctity than the עֶזְרַת כֹּהֲנִים itself. See בֵּית הַמִּקְדָּשׁ; עֶזְרַת נָשִׁים.

עֶזְרַת נָשִׁים   *The women's courtyard.* The largest courtyard in the Temple (see plan of the Temple, p. 277), separated from the עֶזְרַת יִשְׂרָאֵל by the Gate of Nicanor (שַׁעַר נִיקָנוֹר•). It was square, measuring 135 cubits by 135 cubits. Most people visiting the Temple, both men and women, stood in the עֶזְרַת נָשִׁים. It was of a higher degree of holiness than the חֵיל• (the wall surrounding the Temple Courtyard) and the הַר הַבַּיִת• (the Temple Mount). Ritually impure people who had immersed themselves, but who would not regain ritual purity until the evening (see טְבוּל יוֹם•), were not allowed to enter it. On the Festival of Sukkot the celebrations of שִׂמְחַת בֵּית הַשּׁוֹאֵבָה• were held in the עֶזְרַת נָשִׁים. Special lighting was installed, and balconies were set up from which the women watched the festivities.

עִיבּוּר הַחוֹדֶשׁ   *The addition of an extra day to a month.* The moon's monthly cycle is slightly more than twenty-nine-and-a-half days. In the Talmud, unless stated otherwise, a month is understood as having twenty-nine days. But it was, of course, frequently necessary to add an additional day to the month. During the long period in antiquity when the Hebrew calendar was established by the Bet Din according to the testimony of witnesses who had seen the New Moon (see קִידּוּשׁ הַחוֹדֶשׁ•), the addition of an extra day to a month was determined by their testimony. If the moon was sighted on the night after the twenty-ninth day of the month, the next day was the first day of the following month. If, however, the moon was not sighted that night, or if witnesses to the New Moon did not appear in Jerusalem to testify the following day, an extra day was added to the previous month, giving it thirty days. Both the thirtieth and the thirty-first day would be treated as רֹאשׁ חוֹדֶשׁ. Since the fourth century C.E., the Jewish calendar has operated on a fixed astronomical system in which, generally, months of twenty-nine days alternate with those of thirty days.

עִיבּוּר הַשָּׁנָה   *The addition of an extra month to the year.* The annual Jewish calendar follows a lunar cycle of twelve months of twenty-nine or thirty days. But it is also related to the solar calendar because the Festivals must be held in the appropriate seasons. In particular, Pesaḥ must be at the time of the barley harvest, and Sukkot at the time of the autumn equinox. The solar year is slightly more than eleven days longer than the lunar year. To compensate for this difference, a thirteenth lunar month is occasionally added after the month of Adar, and is referred to as Adar Sheni ("Second Adar"). See אֲדָר רִאשׁוֹן וַאֲדָר שֵׁנִי. During the period when the calendar was still set every year by the Sanhedrin, the question of whether to add an extra month required a unique decision-making process. First, the matter was considered by three judges selected from the Sanhedrin. If they thought an additional month was necessary, two more judges were asked to join the deliberations. If this body also agreed, two more judges were added, bringing the total to seven. These judges would make the final decision. Among the factors the judges would consider, in addition to the need for the Festivals to fall in their appropriate seasons, were the climatic conditions and whether the crops had ripened sufficiently. Since the fourth century C.E., the Jewish calendar has operated on a fixed astronomical system using a nineteen-year cycle, correlating the lunar and solar calendars. Months are added in the 3rd, 6th, 8th, 11th, 14th, 17th, and 19th years of each cycle.

עִיבּוּר צוּרָה   Lit., *the decay of its form.* A sacrifice may sometimes become disqualified from being eaten, but the disqualification may not be sufficiently serious as to require the sacrifice to be burned at once. In such a case, the sacrifice is left until it becomes forbidden as נוֹתָר, at which time it can be burned. This period of delay is called עִיבּוּר צוּרָה, indicating that the status of the sacrifice has changed beyond recall.

עִיבּוּרָה שֶׁל עִיר   *The outskirts of a city, the city limits.* A term used in connection with the laws forbidding walking long distances from one's place of residence on the Sabbath (see תְּחוּם שַׁבָּת, עֵירוּב תְּחוּמִים). Although a person is forbidden to walk more than 2,000 cubits from his home on the Sabbath, the entire city or town in which he lives is considered as his place of residence. Within the city a person may walk even for miles, and the restriction of 2,000 cubits begins from the city's outer limits (עִיבּוּרָה שֶׁל עִיר). The outskirts of a city are defined as the area where houses are still located close to each other. Any house that is on the edge of a city and is within a little more than 70 cubits from one of the other houses of the city, is considered as included within the city and extends its limits accordingly.

עִידִית   *Land of the highest quality.* Landed property may be of three qualities: עִידִית — the highest; בֵּינוֹנִית — the intermediate; and זִיבּוּרִית — the lowest. If the law requires a person to make a payment of money, and he does not have it, his land may be confiscated as payment. In such circumstances the following rules apply: Compensation for damage must be paid from the עִידִית; debts must be paid at least from the בֵּינוֹנִית; and a person's obligations to his wife resulting from her כְּתוּבָּה — marriage contract — may be paid from the זִיבּוּרִית.

עַיִן יָפָה   Lit., *[with a] good eye,* i.e., in a spirit of generosity A term used frequently with regard to business transactions and dedications to the Temple (see מוֹכֵר בְּעַיִן יָפָה מוֹכֵר). The term עַיִן יָפָה has a specific meaning with regard to תְּרוּמָה, the agricultural levy given to the priests. Though the Torah did not lay down a minimum amount of תְּרוּמָה to which the priest was entitled, the Sages set the following standards: An average gift (בְּעַיִן בֵּינוֹנִית — "with an average eye") would be one-fiftieth of one's crop; a miserly gift (בְּעַיִן רָעָה — "with a bad eye") would be one-sixtieth; and a generous gift (בְּעַיִן יָפָה — "with a good eye") would be one-fortieth.

עִיקּוּר   Lit., *tearing loose.* One of the ways in which the ritual slaughter of an animal may be rendered invalid (see הַגְרָמָה; חֲלָדָה). In order to perform a valid שְׁחִיטָה — ritual slaughter — it is necessary to sever the animal's windpipe and esophagus. If, instead of severing these organs, the slaughterer tears them loose, the slaughter is invalidated and the animal may not be eaten (see נְבֵלָה).

עִיר מִקְלָט   *A city of refuge.* Numbers 35:10–34, and Deuteronomy 19:1–13 describe the commandment to establish cities of refuge to protect someone who committed inadvertent manslaughter through negligence. The Sages explain that anyone who has caused another person's death must flee to a city of refuge. From there, he is taken to his trial. If he is convicted of intentional murder, he is executed. If the other person's death was a complete accident, he is released. If, however, the court decides that he is guilty of negligent manslaughter, he must return to the city of refuge and remain there during the lifetime of the High Priest. If, for any reason, he leaves the עִיר מִקְלָט, he may be killed by his victim's avenger (see גּוֹאֵל הַדָּם). After the death of the High Priest, he may return to his own city. The Torah mentions the establishment of six cities of refuge, three in the area of Eretz Israel west of the Jordan River and three in the area east of the Jordan. All six cities were among the forty-eight cities given to the Levites. The Sages explained, however, that the other forty-two cities given to the Levites (Numbers 35:2–8) also served as cities of refuge.

עִיר הַנִּדַּחַת   *An entire city a majority of whose inhabitants committed idolatry* (Deuteronomy 13:13–19). Such a city is judged by the Great Sanhedrin of seventy-one members (בֵּית דִּין שֶׁל שִׁבְעִים וְאֶחָד). The Sanhedrin has the authority to send an army to subdue the city. Afterwards, courts are convened and each of the city's adult inhabitants is judged. Those found guilty of idol worship are beheaded (rather than stoned, the usual penalty for idolatry). The innocent are not slain. All the property in the city (including that of the righteous) is destroyed, and all its buildings are razed to the ground. It must remain a ruin forever. See also סְפָר.

עֵירוּב חֲצֵירוֹת   Lit., *the joining of courtyards.* The Sages established restrictions against carrying between the private domains of different people on the Sabbath, even though Torah law permits carrying between private domains. Together with these restrictions, however, the Sages also provided Halakhic devices that make it permissible to carry in these areas on the Sabbath. The Sages forbade carrying on the Sabbath in property that is owned or rented by more than one individual. Thus, if two or more houses share a common courtyard, none of the inhabitants is, in principle, allowed to carry between the houses that share it. But the Sages also ordained that if the inhabitants of all these homes put food in one communal place before the Sabbath, they are considered as one extended household and may carry within the courtyard. This placing of food in one shared place is called עֵירוּב חֲצֵרוֹת. A blessing, עַל מִצְוַת עֵירוּב, is recited when placing the עֵירוּב חֲצֵרוֹת. There are many specific laws governing the definition of a courtyard and the kind of enclosure necessary. They are described in detail in tractate *Eruvin*. It is possible to include within an עֵירוּב not only a particular courtyard, but entire towns and villages, by constructing various types of Halakhically recognized walls and partitions, and thus to permit carrying on the Sabbath within the whole town.

עירוב תַּבְשִׁילִין   Lit., *the joining of cooked food*.

It is forbidden to prepare food on a Festival for the following day. This prohibition creates difficulty if a Sabbath, when it is forbidden to cook, follows directly after the Festival. In such circumstances, the Sages allowed the preparation of food on the Festival for the Sabbath under the following conditions: Before the Festival begins, one sets aside bread and one cooked dish as the עֵירוּב תַּבְשִׁילִין to be eaten on the Sabbath. These are considered the primary elements of one's Sabbath meal, and it is permitted to add to them, if necessary, by cooking on the Festival. A blessing, עַל מִצְוַת עֵירוּב, is recited when preparing an עֵירוּב תַּבְשִׁילִין. The detailed laws governing this subject are found in tractate *Betzah*.

עירוב תְּחוּמִין   Lit., *the joining of Sabbath borders*.

A person is forbidden to walk more than 2,000 cubits from his home on the Sabbath (see תְּחוּם שַׁבָּת). Nevertheless, the entire city in which he lives is considered as his "place of residence" and the 2,000 cubits are counted from its limits (see עִיבּוּרָהּ שֶׁל עִיר). Since this prohibition (or its major aspects) is Rabbinic in origin, the Sages also offered a way to extend the limit of 2,000 cubits. By placing before the Sabbath enough food for a small meal somewhere within one's 2,000 cubit limit (even at its furthest edge), one establishes the location of that food as one's "place of residence" for the Sabbath, and the 2,000 cubits are counted from there. This placing of food to extend the distance one is permitted to walk on the Sabbath is called עֵירוּב תְּחוּמִין, and the detailed laws governing the subject are to be found in tractate *Eruvin*. A blessing, עַל מִצְוַת עֵירוּב, is recited when placing an עֵירוּב תְּחוּמִין.

עישׂוּר נְכָסִים   A tenth of one's estate.

It was an accepted practice for a father to give his daughter a dowry. If a man passes away leaving unmarried daughters, a certain proportion of his estate is set aside as a dowry for each of them. The size of the dowry is determined according to the dowry he gave to his other daughters in his lifetime. If it is impossible to make such a determination, one-tenth of the remaining estate (עִישׂוּר נְכָסִים) is designated for each daughter in succession (i.e., one-tenth for the first, nine-hundredths for the second, etc.).

עם הָאָרֶץ   A common, uneducated person

(lit., "the people of the land"). A term specifically used in the Mishnaic period to refer to an ignorant person who is not scrupulous in his observance of the commandments. At times the term was used to refer only to those who were far from Torah practice, but it also referred, on occasion, to those who maintained a certain level of religious observance. The opposite of an עם הָאָרֶץ is a "colleague" (חָבֵר). There were many restrictions governing relations between "colleagues" and "common people" (עַמֵּי הָאָרֶץ), particularly in the areas of ritual purity and tithes (מַעַשְׂרוֹת). For example, an עם הָאָרֶץ and his clothes were considered ritually impure, and contact with him imparted ritual impurity. Similarly, with regard to tithes and certain other prohibitions, the word of an עם הָאָרֶץ was not accepted. These restrictions were relaxed during the Festival seasons. Towards the end of the Mishnaic period most of the restrictions governing the עם הָאָרֶץ were rescinded, partly out of fear of causing division within the Jewish people and partly because there was a significant improvement in the religious observance of the masses. Thus, though colloquial usage of the term עם הָאָרֶץ remains, it no longer has Halakhic significance.

עמוּד הַשַּׁחַר   Dawn, the first light of the sun before sunrise

[הָנֵץ הַחַמָּה]. With regard to many Halakhot, such as the eating of sacrifices at night, the reciting of the *Shema* at night, and the permissibility of eating before a fast, עמוּד הַשַּׁחַר is considered the time when night ends. The definition of the precise time of עמוּד הַשַּׁחַר is uncertain. Nowadays it is generally accepted that in Eretz Israel עמוּד הַשַּׁחַר occurs approximately one-and-a-quarter hours before sunrise.

עמונִי וּמוֹאָבִי   An Ammonite and a Moabite.

The Torah prohibits a convert from these two nations or his descendants from ever marrying freely among the Jewish people (Deuteronomy 23:4). This prohibition only applies to male converts (and their male descendants). Female converts from Ammon and Moab (the most noted example being Ruth, the Moabitess) may marry freely immediately upon conversion. An Ammonite or Moabite male convert may not marry a native-born Jewess of pure lineage, but he may marry a female convert (from any nation) or a mamzeret (see מַמְזֵר) or other Jewess of blemished lineage. Sennacherib, the Assyrian king who exiled the ten tribes of Israel in the eighth century B.C.E., conquered most of the area around Eretz Israel. In order to suppress possible revolutions, he engaged in a policy of mass population transfer that obliterated the national identity of most of Israel's neighbors. Thus, from that time onwards, there was no prohibition against marrying converts from the lands of Ammon and Moab.

עסקָא   Lit., business.

A partnership arrangement allowing a person to benefit from the investment of his money without violating the prohibition against taking interest. In such an arrangement, one party agrees to invest money and the other to manage the investment. The potential profit and loss from the investment must *not* be allocated equally between the parties; the party investing the money must agree to accept a greater share of the possible loss. An arrangement based on this principle, referred to as a הֶיתֵּר עִסְקָא, is frequently employed by banks and individuals to avoid violating the prohibition against taking interest.

עֵצָה טוֹבָה קָא מַשְׁמַע לַן   *He is giving us good advice.* The Gemara sometimes uses this expression to explain that a certain statement in the Bible, the Mishnah or the Talmud does not prescribe a particular practice as binding Halakhah. Rather, it suggests it as a proper course of behavior, but one is not *required* to follow this suggestion.

עֲצֶרֶת   Lit., *assembly.* The term generally used by the Talmud to refer to the Festival of Shavuot. See שְׁמִינִי עֲצֶרֶת.

עֲקִירָה וְהַנָחָה   Lit., *uprooting and putting down.* A fundamental concept applying to the prohibition against transferring an article from one domain to another on the Sabbath (הוֹצָאָה*) and against carrying in the public domain (רְשׁוּת הָרַבִּים; see also רְשׁוּיוֹת הַשַּׁבָּת). The violation of this prohibition involves: (1) עֲקִירָה — the lifting up of an object from its position of rest in one domain; and (2) הַנָחָה — putting it down to rest in another domain. A person does not transgress the prohibition of הוֹצָאָה unless he performs both actions, עֲקִירָה and הַנָחָה. If two people join in transferring the article, one lifting it from its place, and the other putting it down, neither is liable according to Torah law. Nevertheless, the Sages forbade transferring articles in this fashion.

עָרֵב   *A guarantor, a surety.* A person who accepts responsibility for someone else's financial obligation. There are two types of עָרֵב: (1) An עָרֵב סְתָם — a regular guarantor — who is responsible for someone else's obligation only after the funds have been demanded from the latter and he has proved unable to pay. (2) An עָרֵב קַבְּלָן — a contracting guarantor — from whom payment can be demanded even before the borrower is asked to meet his obligation.

עָרֵב הַיוֹצֵא לְאַחַר חִיתּוּם שְׁטָרוֹת   *A guarantor who made his commitment after the promissory note had been signed,* i.e., who wrote the guarantee clause at the bottom of the document, below the signatures of the witnesses. Since the agreement has already been concluded, the commitment made by the guarantor is a separate agreement not covered by the regulations normally applying to promissory notes. The creditor has no lien on the guarantor's property, and can only collect from the guarantor's available assets.

עֲרָבָה   *Willow.* This species of tree is used for three particular rituals in connection with the Sukkot Festival: (1) As part of the commandment of lulav (לוּלָב*) and etrog (אֶתְרוֹג*; see also אַרְבָּעָה מִינִים), two willow branches are bound to the lulav. Leviticus 23:40, the source for this commandment, mentions "willows of the river." Nevertheless, many species of willow may be used. Willow branches that have dried out, or from which the tops have been cut off, are invalid. (2) In the Temple, on Sukkot, it was customary to adorn the altar with willow branches. (3) On Hoshanah Rabbah, the seventh day of Sukkot, the prophets instituted a custom of taking one or more willow branches (separate from the lulav) and beating them on the ground. This custom is still practiced today. The custom today is to take five willow branches.

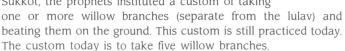

עֵרוּב   See עֵירוּב.

עָרֵי הַלְוִיִּים   *The cities of the Levites.* Since the Levites were not given a tribal inheritance in Eretz Israel, they were granted forty-eight cities (and some land surrounding them) as their own (Numbers 35:2–8). These cities became their property in perpetuity, and could, if sold, be redeemed at any time. Like fields that were the ancestral property of Israelites (see שָׂדֶה אֲחוּזָּה), the cities of the Levites would, if sold, return to them in the Jubilee (יוֹבֵל*) Year (see Leviticus 25:33). The laws restricting the return of homes in walled cities (see בָּתֵּי עָרֵי חוֹמָה) in the Jubilee did not apply to the cities of the Levites (see Leviticus 25:29–34). The cities of the Levites also served as cities of refuge (see עִיר מִקְלָט).

עֲרָיוֹת   *Forbidden sexual relations, whether incestuous or adulterous.* Leviticus (chapters 18 and 20) lists these severely prohibited forbidden relationships. Indeed, they are among the three categories of sins that a person is commanded to sacrifice his life rather than commit (see יֵהָרֵג וְאַל יַעֲבוֹר). Among the עֲרָיוֹת are: One's mother, one's father's wife, one's father's sister, one's mother's sister, one's own sister, one's daughter, one's daughter-in-law, one's brother's wife (see, however, יִבּוּם), one's wife's sister (during one's wife's lifetime), one's wife's mother, and any married woman. In some contexts, a menstruating woman (נִדָּה*) is also included in this category. Some of these prohibitions are punishable by execution by the court, and all are punishable by כָּרֵת — excision. These prohibitions apply equally to the man and the woman involved, and both are punished equally.

עָרִים הַמּוּקָּפוֹת חוֹמָה (עָרֵי חוֹמָה)   *Cities surrounded by a wall.* Cities walled from the time of Joshua's conquest of Eretz Israel are equivalent to the מַחֲנֵה יִשְׂרָאֵל* — the Camp of Israel — in the desert. Hence, a person afflicted with leprosy (צָרַעַת*) may not enter them (see Leviticus 13:46). Similarly, there are certain restrictions concerning burial within these cities. No person from outside the city can be buried within it without the consent of its inhabitants. See also בָּתֵּי עָרֵי חוֹמָה. The Book of Esther was read in such cities on the 15th of Adar (Shushan Purim). Today the only city that certainly falls within this category is Jerusalem.

עֲרָכִין   *Valuations, assessments.* Leviticus, chapter 27, describes vows made using the expressions, "I promise to pay the value [עֶרֶךְ] of so and so," or "I promise to pay my value." The sum to be paid is not calculated according to the presumed market value of the particular person if he were sold as a slave, but is established according to specific values set by the Torah. These values depend only on the sex and age of the person whose value was promised, and apply to all Jews over one month old. Vows in the form of "assessments" are like all other vows to the Temple, and the money involved goes to the Temple treasury (see קָדְשֵׁי בֶּדֶק הַבַּיִת). If the person making the vow is unable to pay the full value set by the Torah, a priest evaluates his ability to pay and reduces his obligation accordingly. Nevertheless, he is always required to pay a minimum of one סֶלַע (see section on weights and measures, p. 291).

עָרֵל   *An uncircumcised person.* A Jewish male must be circumcised when he is eight days old, and if for any reason the circumcision is deferred the obligation remains. If a child reaches the age of majority without having been circumcised he becomes liable to the punishment of כָּרֵת — excision. The obligation of circumcision does not apply if the operation would cause danger to the person's life. An uncircumcised adult may not serve in the Temple or partake of the sacrifices, and this restriction applies irrespective of the reason why he has not been circumcised.

עָרְלָה   *The fruit that grows in the first three years after a tree has been planted.* It is forbidden to eat this fruit or to derive benefit (הֲנָאָה) from it (see Leviticus 19:23). This prohibition applies only to the fruit but not to the other parts of the tree, nor does it apply to trees planted not for fruit but rather as a fence for property or as a windbreak. See נֶטַע רְבָעִי.

עִרְעוּר   *Contesting [lit., upsetting] the legality of something.* An attempt to overturn a decision of a court by casting doubt upon its legal validity. For example, the validity of a bill of divorce (גֵּט) may be disputed by claiming that it was forged or that it was composed improperly. The participation of witnesses or judges in a particular case may be challenged by allegations of family ties to one of the litigants or disqualifying factors in their personal history.

עֲשֵׂה   *A positive commandment.* There are 248 positive commandments in the Torah. They fall into a number of categories, such as those positive commandments that are dependent on a specific time for their performance (see מִצְוַת עֲשֵׂה שֶׁהַזְּמַן גְּרָמָא) and those which are not; positive commandments that involve action, and those that do not. A commandment is considered positive if the language used by the Torah to describe it is positive. Thus the commandment not to eat on Yom Kippur is positive because it is phrased: "You shall afflict your souls" (Leviticus 23:27). Generally, the failure to perform a positive commandment does not make a person liable for punishment or require a sacrifice to be brought as atonement. Nevertheless, it was customary to bring a burnt-offering (עוֹלָה) to atone for failure to observe such a commandment. There are, however, two positive commandments for which a person is liable to the punishment of כָּרֵת — excision — if he does not observe them: circumcision (מִילָה) and the Paschal sacrifice (פֶּסַח). Furthermore, according to Rabbinic law the Sages have the right to administer lashes (see מַכַּת מַרְדּוּת) to a person to compel him to perform a positive commandment. If the performance of a positive commandment involves the negation

of a Torah prohibition, the performance of the positive commandment generally takes precedence. (See next entry.)

עֲשֵׂה וְלֹא תַעֲשֶׂה   *A positive and a negative commandment.* A commandment that is stated in the Torah both positively and negatively. Certain commandments have positive and negative components. Sometimes the positive commandment is merely the positive expression of the negative commandment; for example, the positive commandment to rest on the Sabbath and Festivals complements the prohibition forbidding work on those days. The fact that a commandment is stated both positively and negatively has Halakhic significance: although the performance of a positive commandment supersedes a negative commandment (see עֲשֵׂה), this rule does not apply if the negative commandment is itself reinforced by a positive commandment.

עֲשָׂרָה בַּטְלָנִים   Lit, *ten idle persons.* Ten men who have no fixed occupation, and are always available for the needs of the city, such as forming the necessary quorum for synagogue services. A place that lacks ten such men is not considered a city with regard to reading the *Megillah* (the Scroll of Esther) or the establishment of courts of law (see סַנְהֶדְרֵי קְטַנָּה). The עֲשָׂרָה בַּטְלָנִים are also charged with certain aspects of the management of the city's affairs.

עֲשָׂרָה יוֹחָסִין   *The ten categories of lineage within the Jewish people.* They are: (1) כֹּהֲנִים — priests. (2) לְוִיִּים — Levites. (3) יִשְׂרְאֵלִים — Israelites. (4) חֲלָלִים — children of priests disqualified from the priesthood. (5) גֵּרִים — converts. (6) עֲבָדִים מְשׁוּחְרָרִים — freed slaves (see also עֶבֶד כְּנַעֲנִי). (7) מַמְזֵרִים — illegitimate offspring (8) נְתִינִים — Gibeonites. (9) שְׁתוּקִים — children whose father's identity is unknown. (10) אֲסוּפִים — foundlings. The first three categories may marry freely among themselves. Levites, Israelites, חֲלָלִים, converts, and freed slaves may marry freely among themselves. Similarly, categories (5) to (8) may marry freely among themselves. Categories (9) and (10) cannot even marry people in their own category. They may marry people in categories (5), (6), and (8). (See *Kiddushin* 4:1.)

עִתִּים חָלִים עִתִּים שׁוֹטֶה   *At times sane, at times insane.* A mentally unstable person who has periods of sanity and insanity. In monetary matters, all business transactions in which such a person engages while sane are legally binding. However, during his periods of insanity, he is not considered responsible for his behavior, and all of his transactions then are without effect.

פֵּאָה   *Corner.* This term is used, *inter alia*, for: (1) Part of the agricultural produce that a farmer is commanded by the Torah

to leave for the poor (see מַתְּנוֹת עֲנִיִּים). פֵּאָה is the portion of the crop left standing "in the corner of the field" to be harvested and kept by the poor (see Leviticus 19:9). The Torah did not specify a minimum amount that should be left as פֵּאָה. But the Sages stipulated that it must be at least one-sixtieth of the crop. פֵּאָה is set aside only from crops that have ripened at one time and are harvested at one time. The poor are allowed to use their own initiative to reap the פֵּאָה left in the fields. But the owner of an orchard must see that each of the poor gets a fixed share of the פֵּאָה from places that are difficult to reach. The poor come to collect פֵּאָה three times a day. The laws of פֵּאָה are discussed in detail in tractate *Pe'ah*. (2) With regard to the shaving of hair (בַּל תַּקִּיף). The Torah prohibits men from shaving the hair at the side of the head, i.e., the hair on the temples (Leviticus 19:27). (3) With regard to shaving the beard (see בַּל תַּשְׁחִית). The Torah prohibits men from shaving the five "corners" of the beard (Leviticus 19:27). Shaving even one of them is a violation of this prohibition.

פְּגַם   *Blemish, deterioration.* One of the categories of reimbursement that a man who seduces or rapes a girl must pay. פְּגַם is assessed according to the reduction in the girl's value, caused by the loss of her virginity, if she were to be sold as a handmaiden. See also אוֹנֵס אִשָּׁה; מְפַתֶּה.

פְּגַם מִשְׁפָּחָה   Lit., *a blemish to a family.* A situation that would embarrass a family. Sometimes a person may be legally entitled to certain property, but the court will obligate him to transfer it to others. For example, according to Jewish law, unless a will states otherwise, a husband inherits all his wife's property. If, however, her possessions include certain property to which her family has a sentimental attachment, such as a family burial plot, her widower may be obligated to sell it to her family. The term פְּגַם מִשְׁפָּחָה is also used to refer to flaws in a person's lineage. Occasionally it may refer to allegations of blemished lineage that embarrass (or discredit) an entire family.

פִּדְיוֹן הַבֵּן   *The redemption of the firstborn.* The Torah requires that all firstborn sons must be redeemed from a priest (Exodus 13:12–13). This positive commandment applies to a woman's firstborn son, provided that she is not the daughter of a priest or Levite or that the father of the child is not a priest or Levite. Only children born by natural birth are redeemed; those born by Caesarean section are excluded.
See חֲמִשָּׁה סְלָעִים; בְּכוֹר אָדָם.

פִּדְיוֹן הֶקְדֵּשׁ   *Redemption of consecrated things.* Items that have been consecrated to the Temple (such as gifts for its upkeep, see קָדְשֵׁי בֶּדֶק הַבַּיִת) and sacrificial animals that have become blemished (see מוּמִים) can be redeemed from the Temple treasury. In such a case, the consecrated object loses its sacred character (מִתְחַלֵּל) and the money takes on the sacred character of the item that was consecrated. When the owners themselves redeem the article, they must add a fifth (חוֹמֶשׁ) to its value. Unblemished sacrificial animals may not be redeemed.

פִּדְיוֹן מַעֲשֵׂר שֵׁנִי   *The redemption of the second tithe* (מַעֲשֵׂר שֵׁנִי). The Torah says (Deuteronomy 14:25) that if it is difficult to bring the second tithe itself to Jerusalem, one may redeem (מְחַלְּלִים) it with money (minted coins only, not paper money, bullion, or any other commodity), and then the produce

itself is no longer consecrated. The money, however, takes on the sanctity of the second tithe, and it must be brought up to Jerusalem, where it must be used to buy food and drink. The money then loses its sanctity, and the purchased food becomes consecrated as though it itself was second tithe produce, and it must be eaten in Jerusalem. When the owner is the one who redeems the tithed produce, he must add a fifth (חוֹמֶשׁ) to its price.

פִּדְיוֹן שְׁבוּיִים   *The ransom of prisoners.* It is a positive commandment to redeem Jewish prisoners, including slaves. This commandment is very important and takes precedence over other commandments regarding charity. In the ransom of prisoners, women take priority over men. One of the clauses of a marriage contract (כְּתוּבָּה) is that a husband takes it upon himself to redeem his wife from captivity. The Sages ruled that one must not redeem prisoners for more than their value, so as not to encourage the taking of Jewish prisoners for ransom. See שְׁבוּיָה.

פּוֹגֶמֶת כְּתוּבָּתָה   Lit., *she damages her marriage settlement.* A term used to refer to a situation where a woman's statement raises questions about the validity of her claim to her marriage settlement (כְּתוּבָּה). If a divorced or widowed woman acknowledges having already received a certain portion of the money due her in payment of her כְּתוּבָּה and demands that the remainder be paid, her husband, or his heirs, have the right to require her to take an oath that she is not demanding more than she is entitled to. This oath resembles the one taken by someone who makes a partial admission of a claim (מוֹדֶה בְּמִקְצָת). See *Ketubot* 9, 7–8.

פּוֹעֵל   *A worker who is paid according to the time he works, i.e., by the hour or day.* A worker must be paid a short time after he has finished his work (see בַּל תָּלִין). To prevent interfering with his work, a worker is permitted to shorten the Grace after Meals. While they are working, workers are entitled to eat from the produce that they are harvesting.

פּוֹתֵחַ טֶפַח   Lit., *opening a handbreadth.* A concept in the laws of ritual purity. An enclosed covered cavity at least a cubic handbreadth (טֶפַח) in size. If it contains a corpse (or portion of a corpse larger than a זַיִת), it becomes an אֹהֶל הַמֵּת and imparts ritual impurity to any person or article within it. The outer side of its wall does not become ritually impure.

פֶּטֶר חֲמוֹר   *The firstling of an ass.* The Torah requires that all firstborn male asses must be redeemed by giving a lamb in exchange for them to a priest. If the ass is not redeemed in this way, its neck must be broken (Exodus 13:13).

פִּיגוּל   *An offering disqualified by improper intention.* A disqualifying intention in the offering of a sacrifice, whether an animal, a bird, or a meal-offering. If, while engaged in bringing a sacrifice, a priest expresses the intention of sprinkling the blood of the sacrifice (see זְרִיקָה), or burning it on the altar (see הֶקְטֵר חֲלָבִים), or eating it *after the appropriate time,* this intention disqualifies the sacrifice and renders it פִּיגוּל. An offering that has become פִּיגוּל may not be sacrificed, and the person bringing it has not fulfilled his obligation. Anyone willfully eating from such a sacrifice is liable to the penalty of כָּרֵת — excision. The Sages also decreed that such a sacrifice imparts ritual impurity. The intention of the priest offering the sacrifice and *not* that of the person bringing it determines whether it becomes פִּיגוּל or not. See לֹא קָרֵב הַמַּתִּיר כְּמִצְוָתוֹ; פָּסוּל.

פַּיִס   *Allocation, balloting.* The manner in which the priests were chosen daily to participate in four parts of the Temple service: the cleaning of the altar (תְּרוּמַת הַמִּזְבֵּחַ), bringing the daily sacrifice (תָּמִיד), bringing the incense offering (הַקְטָרָה), and bringing the limbs of the sacrifice from the ramp to the altar (see אֵימוּרִים). The priests who wished to take part in these services gathered in the Chamber of Hewn Stone (לִשְׁכַּת הַגָּזִית). They stood in a circle and each extended a finger. The priest who assigned the services would take hold of the miter of one of the priests to indicate that the balloting would begin from him. He would arbitrarily choose a number and count the fingers until that number was reached. The priest at whose finger the count ended was selected for the service.

פִּיקוּחַ נֶפֶשׁ   *The saving of life.* The effort to save a human life supersedes all the commandments of the Torah, both positive and negative, with the exception of idolatry, murder, and forbidden sexual relations. When a person's life is in danger, time should not be wasted in lengthy deliberations; rather, an attempt should be made immediately to save the life. When it is necessary to transgress a prohibition in order to save a life, it is proper that Rabbinic scholars and other prominent people take part, to show that there is no question about its permissibility. Even fairly remote dangers are considered פִּיקוּחַ נֶפֶשׁ.

פֵּירוֹת   *Fruits, usufruct.* By extension this term applies not only to agricultural produce but to all profits, including the proceeds of business investments. See (2) קֶרֶן.

פַּלְגִּינַן דִּיבּוּרָא   *We divide the statement.* A person's self-incriminating testimony is not accepted by the court as valid evidence. But if he makes a statement that includes both self-incriminating testimony and other information, the court "divides his statement," accepting as evidence only that information that is not self-incriminating. For example, if a person testifies that he has killed someone, his statements regarding his own guilt are *not* accepted as evidence. But his testimony about the victim's death *is* accepted, and the widow may remarry. See also עֵדוּת אִשָּׁה.

פַּלְגָּס   *A young ram at an intermediate age when it is unfit to be used as a sacrifice.* Certain offerings require a lamb (כֶּבֶשׂ), a male sheep no more than one year old. Other offerings require a ram (אַיִל), a male sheep at least one-year-and-one-month old. Between the ages of one year and one-year-and-a-month, the sheep is referred to as a פַּלְגָּס and may not be offered as a sacrifice.

פָּנִים חֲדָשׁוֹת   Lit., *new faces.* Guests who have not previously participated in a particular event. Among the applications of this concept are: (1) During the week after a wedding, it is customary to host the bride and groom at meals in their honor. In order to recite the special blessings in honor of the bride and groom (called בִּרְכַּת חֲתָנִים or שֶׁבַע בְּרָכוֹת), one or preferably two guests should be פָּנִים חֲדָשׁוֹת, guests who have not attended any previous celebrations for this couple. (2) The expression פָּנִים חֲדָשׁוֹת is also used to mean a "new entity." If a utensil is destroyed and then remanufactured, it is "a new entity" and not the original utensil. This has Halakhic significance for the laws of theft and robbery (see *Bava Kamma* 96b).

פָּסוּל   Lit., *disqualified, invalid.* This general concept applies in these cases, among others: (1) With regard to sacrificial offerings. If a person, during the sacrificial ritual, states his intention of performing one of the services associated with the sacrifice — for example, offering it, sprinkling its blood or eating it — in a place inappropriate for that service, the sacrifice is disqualified. This concept resembles that of פִּיגוּל, except that, unlike פִּיגוּל, eating a disqualified sacrifice is not punishable by כָּרֵת — excision. (2) With regard to the laws of ritual impurity, the term פָּסוּל refers to something that has become ritually impure itself, but does not impart that impurity to other things. For example, nonsacramental food (חוּלִין) that came into contact with a רִאשׁוֹן לְטוּמְאָה — an object that had itself contracted ritual impurity from a primary source of ritual impurity (see אֲבוֹת הַטּוּמְאוֹת) — is called שֵׁנִי לְטוּמְאָה. It becomes ritually impure itself, but cannot impart ritual impurity to other things.

פְּסוּלֵי הַמּוּקְדָּשִׁין   *Consecrated animals that have been disqualified for sacrifice.* In a restricted sense, this term is used to refer to sacrifices that were disqualified after slaughtering (see פְּסוּלָן בַּקּוֹדֶשׁ). In a more general sense, it may also be used to refer to animals that were disqualified at an earlier stage because of a blemish or the death of the animal's owner, or some other reason. In most cases, such an animal must be redeemed and the money used to buy other sacrifices, but in some cases the animal cannot be redeemed and must be destroyed (see חַטָּאוֹת הַמֵּתוֹת; יִרְעֶה עַד שֶׁיִּסְתָּאֵב). Once disqualified, an animal is no longer considered consecrated. Nevertheless, to a certain extent, it must be treated as sacred. It is forbidden to use it for work or to use its wool. In certain cases, the meat from these animals should not be sold publicly like other, nonsacred meat.

פְּסוּלֵי עֵדוּת   *People disqualified from serving as witnesses.* Among those in this category are: (1) Those disqualified because of family ties to the accused (in a criminal case) or to the litigants (in a civil case). (See קָרוֹב.) They are forbidden to testify either on their relative's behalf or against him. Similarly, two relatives cannot serve as witnesses in the same case. (2) Those disqualified because of a transgression. Any person known to have violated a severe commandment of the Torah, whether between man and man or between man and God. Such a person is disqualified until it is known that he has repented. (3) Those disqualified because they have a vested interest in the case being judged. (4) Those disqualified by Rabbinic decree, such as persons who have transgressed Rabbinic prohibitions; idle people who derive their livelihood from morally improper occupations; and people who behave in public without dignity or self-respect.

פְּסוּלָן בַּקּוֹדֶשׁ   *Sacrifices disqualified within the Temple Courtyard,* i.e., from the time they were slaughtered and the sacrificial ritual had already begun (see פְּסוּלֵי הַמּוּקְדָּשִׁין). For example, an animal that was not sacrificed with the proper intentions (פִּיגּוּל; "פָּסוּל; "שֶׁלֹּא לִשְׁמוֹ). These disqualified sacrifices are in a special category: If a disqualified sacrifice of this kind was brought to the altar in error, it was burned there. (See *Zevaḥim,* chapter 9, for a detailed discussion of this subject.

פֶּסַח   *Pesaḥ, Passover.* This term is used to refer both to the Passover sacrifice and to the Festival of the same name. (1) The Paschal sacrifice. The Torah commands that all adult Jews bring a sacrifice to the Temple on the afternoon of the 14th of Nisan to be eaten that evening after nightfall. The sacrifice may be a male lamb or goat less than a year old. (Exodus 12; Deuteronomy 16:2 ff.) The Paschal sacrifice is considered "קָדָשִׁים קַלִּים, a sacrifice of lesser sanctity. It may be slaughtered anywhere within the Temple Courtyard. Its blood is poured above the base of the altar. It is brought by groups of individuals acting in partnership (see חֲבוּרָה), and certain of its laws resemble those of the communal offerings. Thus, it can be offered on the Sabbath or when the majority of the community is in a state of ritual impurity (see טוּמְאָה דְּחוּיָה בְּצִיבּוּר). If the offering is sacrificed without the proper intention (שֶׁלֹּא לִשְׁמוֹ") or not for the sake of the people specifically designated in advance to partake of it, it is invalid. An animal which was designated for sacrifice as a Paschal offering, and which, for whatever reason, was not sacrificed at the appointed time, is sacrificed later as a peace-offering (שְׁלָמִים"). The Paschal sacrifice may only be eaten by people who, before it is sacrificed, have already registered to eat it in a group. It must be eaten in one place, and it must be eaten with matzah and bitter herbs. It is forbidden to break any of its bones (Exodus 12:46). It may be eaten only until midnight (according to some authorities, by Torah law, according to others, by Rabbinic decree) on the first night of Pesaḥ, and no other food should be eaten after it that night. Those offering the Paschal sacrifice in the Temple are divided into three groups. While each group is offering its sacrifices in the Temple Courtyard, the Levites recite the Hallel (הַלֵּל"). Similarly, Hallel is recited by the participants when eating the sacrifice. Usually, an additional sacrifice (חֲגִיגַת אַרְבָּעָה עָשָׂר") is offered at the same time. The positive commandment concerning the Paschal sacrifice is one of two whose deliberate violation is punishable by כָּרֵת — excision. However, if a person did not bring the sacrifice, he can compensate by offering a sacrifice on the fourteenth day of the following month (פֶּסַח שֵׁנִי"). (2) The Passover Festival, also referred to as the "Festival of Matzot" (Leviticus 23:6). In Eretz Israel it lasts seven days. The first and the last days are holy days (see יוֹם טוֹב), while the intermediate days are referred to as חֹל הַמּוֹעֵד". In the Diaspora the first two days are Festivals (יוֹם טוֹב; see יוֹם טוֹב שֵׁנִי שֶׁל גָּלֻיּוֹת), the next four days are חֹל הַמּוֹעֵד, and an additional day is added after the seventh day, the seventh and eighth days being Festivals (יוֹם טוֹב). The first night of Pesaḥ is distinguished by a number of commandments: The eating of the Paschal sacrifice, of matzah (on the Seder night, there is a positive commandment to eat matzah; during the remaining days of Pesaḥ the eating of matzah is optional), of bitter herbs (מָרוֹר"), and the recital of the Haggadah describing the Exodus from Egypt. During the entire Festival of Pesaḥ, it is forbidden to eat, derive benefit from, or possess חָמֵץ"

(leaven). The complete Hallel is recited on the first night of Pesaḥ and on the following day (in the Diaspora, on the first two nights and days). On the remaining days, an abbreviated version of the Hallel is recited.

פֶּסַח שֵׁנִי   *The second Pesaḥ.* A person who was ritually impure or on a distant journey (see Numbers 9:9ff) or who failed to bring the Paschal sacrifice at its proper time on the 14th of Nisan, may compensate by bringing the offering on the 14th of Iyar. There is a Tannaitic dispute as to whether a person who was not obligated to bring a Paschal sacrifice need bring a second Pesaḥ on the 14th of Iyar. All the laws applying to the offering of the first Paschal sacrifice apply to the second, with one exception: There is no prohibition against eating or possessing חָמֵץ" on that day. חָמֵץ may not, however, be eaten together with the second Paschal sacrifice itself. There is a difference of opinion among the Sages as to whether women are obligated or even allowed to bring this sacrifice.

פַּסֵּי בֵירָאוֹת   *Symbolic barriers erected to allow Festival pilgrims to use wells in the public thoroughfare on the Sabbath.* The well itself is considered a רְשׁוּת הַיָּחִיד — a private domain (see רְשׁוּיוֹת הַשַּׁבָּת). In contrast, the public thoroughfare is a רְשׁוּת הָרַבִּים — a public domain — and transfer from one to the other is forbidden on the Sabbath. To allow the pilgrims to use such a well, a symbolic fence was built around it, so that the area around the well would be considered רְשׁוּת הַיָּחִיד. Pillars were erected at the four corners of a rectangle with dividers around them. The dividers were only positioned at the corners and did not enclose the entire area. This would not be considered an enclosure for other purposes, but in this specific instance special leniency was shown.

פְּסִיק רֵישֵׁיהּ   Lit., *cut off its head.* A shortened form of the rhetorical question: "If its head is cut off, will it not die?" This expression is used to describe the *inevitable consequence* of an action. In many instances, particularly with regard to the Sabbath laws, a person is not liable for the forbidden, but unintended, results of certain actions. This exemption from liability applies, however, only if the forbidden result is possible, not inevitable. If the result is inevitable, one cannot claim that it was unintentional, just as one cannot claim that one merely wanted to cut off an animal's head, but had no intention of killing it. See דָּבָר שֶׁאֵינוֹ מִתְכַּוֵּון.

פָּעוֹטוֹת   *Young children.* This term is used to refer to children approximately six or seven years old. If they are able to understand the significance of a business transaction, their purchase or sale of goods (מִטַּלְטְלִין", movable property) is valid. However, the purchase or sale of landed property (מְקַרְקְעֵי") is not valid unless the participants in the transaction are adults.

פְּצוּעַ דַּכָּא   *A man with crushed testicles or with other wounds to his genitals.* The Torah prohibits such a man from marrying a woman who was born Jewish (Deuteronomy 23:2), and the transgression is punishable by lashes. Nevertheless, he is permitted to marry a convert.

פַּר הַבָּא עַל כָּל הַמִּצְווֹת   See כֹּהֵן מָשִׁיחַ".

פַּר הֶעְלֵם דָּבָר *A bull sacrificed because of an unwitting trangression committed by the community as a whole.* A communal sin-offering brought because of the active unwitting transgression of a commandment by the Jewish people, as a result of an erroneous Halakhic decision handed down by the Great Sanhedrin (סַנְהֶדְרִין גְּדוֹלָה). Members of the Sanhedrin would perform סְמִיכָה on the bull. As in the case of the the פַּר כֹּהֵן מָשִׁיחַ, the blood of this sacrifice is sprinkled against the פָּרוֹכֶת — (the curtain dividing the Sanctuary from the Holy of Holies) — and on the Temple's inner altar (מִזְבֵּח הַזָּהָב). The אֵימוּרִים are burned on the outer altar, and the rest of the meat and the skin are burned outside Jerusalem in the בֵּית הַדֶּשֶׁן. See חַטָּאוֹת הַפְּנִימִיּוֹת.

פַּר יוֹם הַכִּפּוּרִים *The bull sacrificed on Yom Kippur.* On Yom Kippur the High Priest sacrifices a bull as a sin-offering for himself, his family, and all the members of the priesthood (see Leviticus 16). The bull's slaughter, the burning of its flesh and the sprinkling of its blood resemble the procedures of the פָּרִים (פַּר הֶעְלֵם דָּבָר; פַּר כֹּהֵן מָשִׁיחַ; חַטָּאוֹת הַפְּנִימִיּוֹת see הַנִּשְׂרָפִים). However, its blood is also sprinkled between the staves (see בֵּין הַבַּדִּים) of the holy ark in the Holy of Holies (see קֹדֶשׁ הַקֳּדָשִׁים). The blood of this bull is first sprinkled separately, and is afterwards mixed with the blood of the goat offered as a sin-offering for the entire people (see שְׂעִיר יוֹם הַכִּפּוּרִים), and the mixture is sprinkled on the inner altar (מִזְבַּח הַזָּהָב).

פַּר כֹּהֵן מָשִׁיחַ *The bull brought as a sin-offering by an anointed High Priest.* If a High Priest (כֹּהֵן גָּדוֹל) unwittingly made an erroneous Halakhic decision, and ruled that he was *permitted* to commit a transgression requiring a mandatory sin-offering if committed unwittingly, and if he also *acted* according to his mistaken ruling, he must offer a bull as a sacrifice. The blood of this sacrifice is sprinkled against the פָּרוֹכֶת — the curtain dividing the Sanctuary (הֵיכָל) from the Holy of Holies (קֹדֶשׁ הַקֳּדָשִׁים) — and on the Temple's inner altar (מִזְבַּח הַזָּהָב). The אֵימוּרִים are burned on the outer altar, and the rest of the meat and the skin are burned outside Jerusalem in the בֵּית הַדֶּשֶׁן. See חַטָּאוֹת הַפְּנִימִיּוֹת

פָּרָה אֲדֻמָּה *The Red Heifer.* In order to remove the ritual impurity resulting from contact with a human corpse, purification by means of water mixed with the ashes of a Red Heifer is necessary (see Numbers 19). This heifer and all its hairs must be entirely red. Even one black hair disqualifies it. Similarly, it may not have any blemishes, nor may it have been used for any work. The Red Heifer was slaughtered on the Mount of Olives outside Jerusalem (see כֶּבֶשׁ הַפָּרָה), and its blood was sprinkled seven times opposite the entrance of the Temple. Its body was then burned on a special pyre, onto which were tossed cedarwood, hyssop, and scarlet wool (Numbers 19:6). The ashes from this pyre were then gathered and used for the purification ceremonies. The offering of the Red Heifer was an extremely infrequent event. According to tradition, from the time of the construction of the Sanctuary in the wilderness until the destruction of the Second Temple, only nine Red Heifers were offered. The Sages disagreed with the Sadducees as to whether a טְבוּל יוֹם could participate in the offering of the Red Heifer. The Sages maintained that it was permitted, and to

emphasize their point all those involved in the offering of the Red Heifer were טְבוּלֵי יוֹם. The same disagreement between the Sages and the Sadducees existed regarding the sprinkling of the water mixed with the heifer's ashes (מֵי חַטָּאת), and here too all those involved in the ceremony of purification by מֵי חַטָּאת were טְבוּלֵי יוֹם. Nevertheless, in order to emphasize the importance of the Red Heifer, the Sages placed many restrictions on the ritual purity associated with its ashes and the water with which they were mixed. These restrictions are more severe than those associated with the sacrifices. For example, children were raised where it was certain that they would never become ritually defiled by a corpse, and they were the ones who drew the water for the מֵי חַטָּאת. All the priests involved with the offering of the Red Heifer became ritually impure until the evening. The Red Heifer could have been offered by any priest, but it was customarily offered by the High Priest (כֹּהֵן גָּדוֹל).

פְּרוֹזְבּוֹל *Prosbul.* A Rabbinic enactment allowing for loans to be collected after the Sabbatical Year (see שְׁבִיעִית). The Torah requires all loans to be cancelled at the end of the seventh year of the seven-year cycle (see Deuteronomy 15:1–11). If, however, the loan contract has been given to the court for collection, the loan is not cancelled. When Hillel the Elder saw that many people were refusing to lend money in the years preceding the seventh year because they were afraid that they would not get their money back, he instituted a process whereby the lender authorizes the court to collect all his debts. In this way no debts are cancelled by the Sabbatical Year. Hillel's innovation lay in making this arrangement, which had existed before his day, public by means of the פְּרוֹזְבּוֹל, a document formalizing the transfer of authority to the court. Even today, it is customary to draw up a פְּרוֹזְבּוֹל to allow for the collection of loans after the Sabbatical Year.

פָּרוֹכֶת *Curtain.* The curtain (in the Second Temple — two curtains, see אַמָּה טְרַקְסִין) dividing the Sanctuary (הֵיכָל) from the Holy of Holies (קֹדֶשׁ הַקֳּדָשִׁים). The blood of the פָּרִים הַנִּשְׂרָפִים and of the שְׂעִירִים הַנִּשְׂרָפִים, as well as of the sacrifices offered by the High Priest on Yom Kippur (see שְׂעִיר יוֹם הַכִּפּוּרִים; פַּר יוֹם הַכִּפּוּרִים), was sprinkled on this curtain. The term פָּרוֹכֶת also refers to other curtains hung over certain gates in the Temple complex.

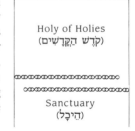

Holy of Holies (קֹדֶשׁ הַקֳּדָשִׁים)

Sanctuary (הֵיכָל)

פְּרוּעֵי רֹאשׁ Lit., *with wild, neglected hair.* Priests were not permitted to participate in the Temple services if their hair was overgrown (see Leviticus 10:6; Ezekiel 44:20). Services performed by priests in this state were invalid.

פָּרוּץ כְּעוֹמֵד Lit., *the breached [portion] is equal to the standing [portion].* A problem in the laws governing enclosures. Sometimes a (notionally) enclosed area is in fact partially open, because there are gaps in the fence enclosing it. If more than half of its fence is standing, the area is considered totally enclosed. Conversely, if less than half of the fence enclosing the area is standing, the area is considered open. If, however, the open and closed portions of the fence are equal, the Sages questioned how to judge the issue (see *Eruvin* 15b).

פֶּרֶט   *Single grapes.* The owner of a vineyard is forbidden to collect individual fallen grapes at the time of the harvest. Such grapes must be left for the poor (see עוֹלְלוֹת; פֵּאָה; מַתְּנוֹת עֲנִיִּים).

פָּרִים הַנִּשְׂרָפִים   Lit., *the bulls that are burned.* Generally, the meat of the sin-offerings (see חַטָּאת) is eaten by the priests. There are, however, certain exceptions to this principle: The פָּרִים הַנִּשְׂרָפִים and the שְׂעִירִים הַנִּשְׂרָפִים, whose meat was not eaten but was burnt outside Jerusalem in the בֵּית הַדֶּשֶׁן. There are two categories of פָּרִים הַנִּשְׂרָפִים: the פַּר כֹּהֵן מָשִׁיחַ and the פַּר הֶעְלֵם דָּבָר (see חַטָּאוֹת הַפְּנִימִיּוֹת).

פְּרִיעָה   Lit., *uncovering.* In the laws of circumcision, this term refers to the folding back of the thin membrane that lies under the thick foreskin. This is a fundamental element of circumcision. If it is not performed, the circumcision is invalid.

פְּרִיעָה וּפְרִימָה   *Letting the hair grow and rending garments.* A person afflicted by leprosy (צָרַעַת) whose status has been confirmed by a priest (see מְצוֹרָע מוּחְלָט) must let his hair grow long and rend his clothes (see Leviticus 13:45).

פְּרִיקָה   *Unloading.* The positive commandment to help another person unload an animal that has fallen under its load (see Exodus 23:5; see also טְעִינָה). This commandment is considered an act of kindness (גְּמִילוּת חֲסָדִים) to the other person and also an observance of the prohibition against cruelty to animals (צַעַר בַּעֲלֵי חַיִּים). Though this commandment applies to animals belonging to anyone, the abovementioned verse refers to "the ass of him that hates you," for it is a greater mitzvah to overcome one's natural impulse and show this act of kindness to an enemy.

פָּרָשַׁת הַמֶּלֶךְ   *The portion pertaining to the king.* The passage from Deuteronomy (17:14–20) recited publicly by the king at the הַקְהֵל ceremony during the Sukkot Festival in the year following the Sabbatical Year (see שְׁבִיעִית). See also *Sotah* 7,8.

פָּרַת חַטָּאת   *A term used in the Mishnah to refer to the Red Heifer, the* פָּרָה אֲדוּמָּה.

פְּשׁוּטֵי כְּלֵי עֵץ   *Flat wooden utensils.* Only those wooden utensils that are hollow receptacles can contract ritual impurity

according to Torah law. Nevertheless, the Sages decreed that certain flat wooden vessels can contract ritual impurity if articles are ordinarily placed upon them and in that respect they resemble those that are hollow.

פִּשְׂיוֹן   *Spreading.* With regard to the laws of leprosy (צָרַעַת), whether leprosy of a person, or of garments, or of houses (see נִגְעֵי בְגָדִים; נִגְעֵי בָתִּים), the spreading (פִּשְׂיוֹן) of a blemish is considered a definite indication of disease (see מְצוֹרָע מוּחְלָט).

פְּשִׁיעָה   *Negligence.* The most common application of this concept is in connection with שׁוֹמְרִים, bailees, with whom things have been deposited. Though there are four different categories of שׁוֹמְרִים, each with different obligations (see שׁוֹמֵר; שׁוֹכֵר; שׁוֹאֵל; שָׂכָר; שׁוֹמֵר חִנָּם), all are liable if *because of their negligence* an article was lost, broken, or stolen. The Sages debated the extent of a שׁוֹמֵר's liability in a situation where he was initially negligent in the care of the article entrusted to him, and it was subsequently destroyed by forces beyond his control (see אוֹנֶס) and unconnected with his negligence.

פַּת גּוֹיִים   *Bread of non-Jews.* The Sages forbade eating bread baked by non-Jews, in order to prevent unnecessary contact with them, even when there was no question of forbidden substances having been included in the baking of the bread. This decree was issued very early in Jewish history. Indeed, allusions to it are found in the Book of Daniel. Over the generations, however, certain leniencies were granted. In general, whenever there is a possibility of obtaining bread baked by Jews, it is prohibited to eat the same type baked by non-Jews.

פֶּתַח הָאוּלָם   *The gateway to the entrance-hall.* The אוּלָם was the antechamber to the main Temple building. (See plan of the Temple, p. 277.) Its gateway was the largest in the entire Temple complex, being 40 cubits high and 20 cubits wide. It was also the only entrance without gates. Accordingly, the expression פִּתְחוֹ שֶׁל אוּלָם is sometimes used to refer to any large opening.

פֶּתַח פָּתוּחַ   Lit., *an open entrance.* A euphemism for "without hymen." An allegation made by a bridegroom who married on the presumption that his bride was a virgin and, when consummating the marriage, found "an open entrance," i.e., no hymen. At times this allegation is made with the intent of reducing the obligations of the bridegroom under the terms of the marriage contract (see כְּתוּבָּה), and at times the intent is to enable him to divorce her immediately without a כְּתוּבָּה at all.

צֹאן בַּרְזֶל   Lit., *iron sheep.* A form of investment in which the investor not only receives profits, but also stipulates that his

investment must be secure from any loss. Such an arrangement is considered a form of usury (see רִיבִּית), and is therefore forbidden. For example: *B* agrees to tend *A*'s flock of sheep for one year, and both agree to share equally in the profits from the flock's offspring, milk, and wool, but *A* stipulates that if any of the sheep are lost, die, or decrease in value because of injury, *B* is fully responsible for any loss incurred. This form of investment is forbidden, because *A* is protected against all losses, and has, as it were, lent the animals to *B*, and his (*A*'s) profits are interest on the loan. See נְכְסֵי צֹאן בַּרְזֶל and עִסְקָא.

צֵאת הַכּוֹכָבִים Lit., *when the stars come out*. The time, shortly after sunset, when the stars begin to appear. It marks the beginning of the night. It also (except with regard to the laws of sacrifices) marks the start of a new day, since according to the Halakhah each new day begins at night. צֵאת הַכּוֹכָבִים is defined as the time when three average-sized stars can be seen. There are considerable differences of opinion among the authorities as to precisely when this takes place.

צְדוֹקִים וּבַיְיתּוֹסִים *Sadducees and Boethusians.* Heterodox sects during the Second Temple period. These sects did not accept the Oral Law at all, and they interpreted the Written Torah in their own way. A number of customs were introduced during the Second Temple period in order to show the Sadducees the error of their ways (לְהוֹצִיא מִלִּבָּם שֶׁל צָדוֹקִים), i.e., to bring out the differences between correct practice and their viewpoint, and to show that the Halakhah ignores their opinions (see פָּרָה אֲדוּמָה). Among these innovations were: Making the High Priest take an oath before entering the Holy of Holies, and the need to bring witnesses to testify to the reliability of the witnesses to the New Moon. In the matter of the joining of Sabbath domains (עֵירוּבֵי חֲצֵירוֹת), since a Sadducee does not admit the validity of these enactments, he cannot take part in the עֵירוּב or even symbolically forgo his rights to his property (see בִּיטוּל רְשׁוּת), and he is regarded as a non-Jew from whom property must be formally rented.

צוּרַת הַפֶּתַח Lit., *the form of a door*. A structure, often symbolic, that closes off an opening by means of two doorposts and a lintel above them. Where the צוּרַת הַפֶּתַח is placed, the opening is considered sealed, as though the opening was a wall with an open door in it. This has Halakhic implications in several areas. Among them: Laws of partitions (מְחִיצוֹת) as applied to Sabbath domains (see עֵירוּבֵי חֲצֵירוֹת); diverse kinds (כִּלְאַיִם); and sukkot. Only those openings in houses that have a proper צוּרַת הַפֶּתַח require a mezuzah (מְזוּזָה) to be placed on them.

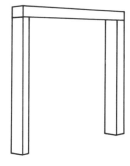

צִיפּוֹרֵי מְצוֹרָע Lit., *the birds [used in the purification] of a leper* (see צָרַעַת). The Torah prescribes the use of two birds in the purification ceremony undergone by a cured leper (מְצוֹרָע) or a previously leprous house (בַּיִת הַמְנוּגָע; see also Leviticus 14:4–7; 14:49–53). Both these birds have to be alive, whole, undomesticated, and from a kosher species. The general practice was to use a species of bird known as דְּרוֹר, a kind of sparrow. One of the birds is slaughtered over an earthenware vessel filled with springwater (מַיִם חַיִּים) and its blood is drained into the

water in this vessel. This mixture is sprinkled on the cured leper or house. The other bird is dipped in the mixture of blood and water and set free. The second bird is not considered holy. If it is captured after being set free, it may be slaughtered and eaten, or used for any other purpose. See טָהֳרַת מְצוֹרָע.

צִיץ *The plate worn by the High Priest* (כֹּהֵן גָּדוֹל) *across his forehead* (see Exodus 28:36–38). This was one of the eight vestments (see שְׁמוֹנָה בְּגָדִים) that the High Priest was required to wear. It was made of gold, and extended across the High Priest's forehead from one ear to the other. It was held in place by threads. On the plate was written קֹדֶשׁ לַה' — "Holy to the Lord." There is a difference of opinion among the Tannaim as to how these words were written on the צִיץ. The צִיץ atoned for ritual impurity contracted by sacrifices in the Temple without the knowledge of those offering them. See טוּמְאַת הַתְּהוֹם.

צִיצִית Lit., *fringe*. The positive commandment of the Torah to place fringes on the four corners of garments (Numbers 15:37–41). They are only put on a garment with four or more corners. The garment must be large enough to enable a person to wrap it around himself (לְהִתְעַטֵּף בָּה). Each צִיצִית is made up of four threads, generally of wool. The threads are folded over, bringing their number to eight. The upper part of the צִיצִית (called the גְּדִיל) is knotted in a prescribed manner, and from it hang the eight half-threads. There are different customs as to how precisely to knot the צִיצִית. Originally a צִיצִית was made up of three white threads and one thread dyed blue (פְּתִיל תְּכֵלֶת; see תְּכֵלֶת). There is no obligation for a person to wear צִיצִית unless he is wearing a garment that requires them, and one is not obligated to wear such a garment. Nevertheless, it is customary to wear a large four-cornered garment (טַלִּית) during the morning prayer service and a smaller four-cornered garment (טַלִּית קָטָן) throughout the day. The obligation of צִיצִית applies during the daytime but not at night. Its fulfilment is incumbent upon men but not upon women.

small four-cornered garment (טַלִּית קָטָן)

fringe — (צִיצִית)

צָמִיד פָּתִיל *A covering bound tightly over the opening of a vessel*, i.e., an airtight lid. The outside surface of earthenware vessels (כְּלִי חֶרֶס) does not contract or impart ritual impurity. Only the space within an earthenware vessel can impart ritual impurity. If such a vessel has an airtight lid it does not contract ritual impurity when found in a tent or building containing a dead body (see אֹהֶל הַמֵּת), or in a leprous house (see נִגְעֵי בָתִּים). Thus anything contained within such a vessel remains ritually pure.

צַעַר *Pain*. One of five categories of compensation for damage that are made by a person who injured another (see חֹבֶל; חֲמִשָּׁה דְבָרִים). The injured person must be reimbursed for the pain he has suffered. At times, compensation under the category of צַעַר is paid together with other types of compensation (see בּוֹשֶׁת; נֶזֶק; שֶׁבֶת; רִיפּוּי), but sometimes the court rules that it is the only compensation to be paid.

צַעַר בַּעֲלֵי חַיִּים   *Pain caused to animals.* The prohibition against inflicting unnecessary pain on animals. According to the accepted Halakhah, this prohibition is of Torah authority. The Sages emphasized the need to bear it constantly in mind both in its own right and also as a reason for leniency in certain Halakhic issues, such as the laws of Shabbat, and in other contexts.

צְרוֹרוֹת   Lit., *pebbles, stones.* A term used for indirect damage caused by an animal — for example, if it kicks up stones or clods of earth while walking, and these cause damage (see רֶגֶל). It is an established Halakhic rule (הֲלָכָה לְמֹשֶׁה מִסִּינַי) that the owner of the animal must pay compensation for only half the damage caused by צְרוֹרוֹת (see חֲצִי נֶזֶק).

צָרַעַת   *Leprosy.* Traditionally rendered as "leprosy," צָרַעַת is not necessarily to be identified medically with that illness. צָרַעַת refers to symptoms that convey serious ritual impurity. The laws governing these symptoms are given at length in Leviticus, chapters 13–15, and in the Mishnah, tractate *Negaim.* There can be leprosy of the skin, of the hair, of articles of clothing, and of houses (see נִגְעֵי בְגָדִים; נִגְעֵי בָתִּים). When a symptom appears, it is examined by a priest, and only a priest may determine whether to quarantine the affected person for a certain period (see מְצֹרָע מוּסְגָּר) or to declare immediately that the symptom is or is not leprosy. Leprosy is a primary source of ritual impurity (see אֲבוֹת הַטּוּמְאוֹת), and it is particularly severe in that it imparts ritual impurity to objects found in the same enclosure with it, like the contamination caused by corpses (see אֹהֶל הַמֵּת).

A person afflicted with leprosy is sent out of the Camp of Israel (מַחֲנֵה יִשְׂרָאֵל) and must live alone until his affliction is cured. A garment affected by leprosy is burned, and a contaminated house is entirely destroyed, and its rubble is thrown into a ritually impure place. A cured leper undergoes a special ceremony outside the city (see טָהֳרַת מְצֹרָע; צִיפּוֹרֵי מְצֹרָע), and a special purification ceremony in the Temple itself, and he must bring special sacrifices as part of his purification.

צָרַת עֶרְוָה   *A co-wife of a forbidden relation.* If a man who has two (or more) wives dies childless, his surviving brother is obliged either to marry one of the widows (see יִבּוּם) or to free both the widows of their obligation through חֲלִיצָה with one of them. But if one of the widows is unable to marry this brother-in-law, because their family relationship makes marriage between them forbidden (for example, if the widow is his wife's sister), both she and all the other wives of the deceased are exempt from both יִבּוּם and חֲלִיצָה. In other words, the exemption of the one widow exempts all her co-wives (צָרַת עֶרְוָה), even though any of the others could have married this surviving brother had it not been for their co-wife. Moreover, if the deceased brother left another surviving brother, and one of the other widows married this other brother and he too died childless, the widow of this brother, who was originally forbidden to marry the other surviving brother because her co-wife was forbidden to him, is now forbidden to him again because of her status as צָרַת עֶרְוָה, "a co-wife of a forbidden relation." Not only is she exempt from יִבּוּם and חֲלִיצָה, but she also exempts all the other wives (צָרַת צָרָה) of her deceased second husband.

קַבָּלָה   Lit., *receiving.* The act of receiving the blood that spurts from the neck of a sacrificial animal when it is slaughtered. The blood is received in one of the holy vessels (see מִזְרָק) used in the Temple. קַבָּלָה was one of the four services essential in the sacrifice of an animal (see אַרְבַּע עֲבוֹדוֹת). It could only be performed by a priest.

קַבְּלָן   *A contractor.* A worker who is paid for a whole job, in contrast to a laborer paid on an hourly or daily basis (see פּוֹעֵל). Different laws from those applying to a laborer apply to a contractor with regard to the prohibition against delaying payment (see בַּל תָּלִין).

קְדוּשָׁה   Lit., *holiness.* Beyond its general meaning, this is the name given to the responsive prayer of praise (based on three Biblical verses: Isaiah 6:3, Ezekiel 3:12, and Psalms 146:10) recited during the repetition of the Amidah prayer (see שְׁמוֹנֶה עֶשְׂרֵה). This prayer is recited alternately by the prayer leader (שְׁלִיחַ צִבּוּר) and the congregation, after the second blessing of

the Amidah prayer. It is recited standing, and only when ten men or more are present (see מִנְיָן). A shortened version of קְדוּשָׁה, called קְדוּשַׁת יוֹצֵר (in which the verse from Psalms 146:10 is omitted), is to be found in every morning service (שַׁחֲרִית), in the blessing יוֹצֵר אוֹר. The verses from Isaiah and Ezekiel, together with a verse from Exodus (15:18) replacing the verse from Psalms, are recited in the prayer וּבָא לְצִיּוֹן towards the end of the weekday morning service (שַׁחֲרִית), and at the beginning of the afternoon service (מִנְחָה) on Sabbaths and Festivals. Each of the verses is followed by a translation of it into Aramaic, and this קְדוּשָׁה is given the title קְדוּשָׁה דְּסִדְרָא.

קְדוּשַׁת הַיּוֹם   Lit., *the holiness of the day.* The name given to the fourth blessing in the Amidah prayer (see שְׁמוֹנֶה עֶשְׂרֵה) recited on Sabbaths and Festivals. During the morning, afternoon and evening services (and in neilah [נְעִילָה] on Yom Kippur) this prayer is devoted to a general appreciation of the significance of the day. The musaf (מוּסָף) version includes a brief description of the additional sacrifices offered on the particular day, and a prayer for the speedy restoration of the sacrificial service.

קָדִישׁ   *Kaddish,* lit., "holy" in Aramaic. A responsive prayer of praise, composed in Aramaic. It is recited after communal study, by mourners at a funeral and during their period of mourning, and on various other occasions. Different forms of the kaddish are recited by the prayer leader (שְׁלִיחַ צִיבּוּר°) during the daily prayers. Mourners recite the kaddish in order to elevate the soul of a deceased relative (this custom is first mentioned in tractate *Kallah*). Kaddish is only recited when ten or more men are present (see מִנְיָן°).

קֹדֶשׁ הַקֳּדָשִׁים   *The Holy of Holies.* The innermost and holiest part of the Temple (בֵּית הַמִּקְדָּשׁ°), separated from the Sanctuary (הֵיכָל°) by a curtain (פָּרוֹכֶת°). During the First Temple period the Ark of the Covenant was kept in the Holy of Holies. Entry to the קֹדֶשׁ הַקֳּדָשִׁים was forbidden to all — including priests. The High Priest (כֹּהֵן גָּדוֹל°) entered this area once a year on the Day of Atonement (see יוֹם הַכִּיפּוּרִים°). See plan of the Temple, p. 277.

קְדֵשָׁה   *A prostitute.* The Torah forbids the presence of a קְדֵשָׁה among the Jewish people (Deuteronomy 23:18). The Sages and commentators differed as to the interpretation of this verse. Some interpret the verse as a prohibition against all prostitution. Others explain that the term קְדֵשָׁה refers to a woman who has intercourse with a man with whom she cannot establish a legal marriage bond, e.g., a slave.

קָדְשֵׁי בֶּדֶק הַבַּיִת   *Objects consecrated for maintaining the Temple.* This term includes objects dedicated for the repair and upkeep of the Temple itself and for all the needs of the Temple, except for items fit to be used in sacrifices (see קָדְשֵׁי מִזְבֵּחַ°). Money or goods could be donated for this purpose, and once consecrated, they could no longer be used for other purposes. To do so would transgress the prohibition against misappropriation of consecrated objects (מְעִילָה°). If the Temple treasurer (גִּזְבָּר°) sells the consecrated object, it loses its sacred status. It is forbidden to consecrate for the maintenance of the Temple a kosher animal that is unblemished and fit for sacrifice. If a person does so, the animal must be offered as a sacrifice.

קָדְשֵׁי מִזְבֵּחַ   *Consecrated for the altar.* Unblemished animals or wine, oil, flour, and wood consecrated for sacrifice on the altar (Leviticus 22:20). Such items may not be sold or exchanged, neither by the owner nor by the Temple treasurer (גִּזְבָּר°). If a person attempts to substitute another animal for one designated for this purpose (see תְּמוּרָה°), both are considered consecrated. If the animal "consecrated for the altar" acquires a blemish, it becomes disqualified for sacrifice (see פְּסוּלֵי הַמּוּקְדָּשִׁים°).

קָדְשֵׁי קָדָשִׁים   *The holiest sacrifices.* In this category are עוֹלוֹת° (burnt-offerings), חַטָּאוֹת° (sin-offerings), אֲשָׁמוֹת° offerings), and שַׁלְמֵי צִיבּוּר° (communal peace-offerings). The following regulations apply specifically to these sacrifices: (1) They are slaughtered only in the northern section of the Temple Courtyard. (2) Those sacrifices that are eaten may only be eaten on the day the animal is sacrificed and the night following that day. (3) They may only be eaten by male priests and only within the Temple Courtyard. (4) The prohibition against misappropriating Temple property (מְעִילָה°), applies to קָדְשֵׁי קָדָשִׁים as soon as they are consecrated. Once their blood has been sprinkled on the altar, the prohibition against misappropriation continues to apply to the portions that must be burned on the altar (אֵימוּרִים°), but not to the portions of the sacrifice that are to be eaten.

קָדָשִׁים קַלִּים   *Sacrifices of lesser holiness.* In this category are the various types of individual peace-offerings (שְׁלָמִים°), the thanks-offering (תּוֹדָה°), the Nazirite's ram (אַיִל נָזִיר°), the firstborn (בְּכוֹר°), the animal tithes (מַעֲשַׂר בְּהֵמָה°), and the Paschal sacrifice (פֶּסַח°). These sacrifices may be slaughtered anywhere in the Temple Courtyard. With the exception of the thanks-offering, the Nazirite's ram, and the Paschal sacrifice, they may be eaten during a period of two days and the intervening night from the time they were sacrificed. They may be eaten by the priests, their wives, children, servants, and, with the exception of the firstborn, by the people bringing the sacrifices and any ritually pure, circumcised person they invite. There is no need to consume them within the Temple premises, but they must be eaten within the walls of Jerusalem. The prohibition against misappropriation (מְעִילָה°) applies only to those portions to be burned on the altar (אֵימוּרִים°) and only after the blood has been sprinkled on the altar (see זְרִיקָה°).

קוּלֵי בֵּית שַׁמַּאי וְחוּמְרֵי בֵּית הִלֵּל   *Leniencies of Bet Shammai and stringencies of Bet Hillel.* Generally the School of Shammai took a more stringent attitude on Halakhic questions than did the School of Hillel, and most ambiguous differences of opinion between them are usually interpreted to conform with this principle. Nevertheless there are a number of exceptional cases, where the School of Shammai is lenient and the School of Hillel is strict. Most of them are mentioned at the beginning of tractate *Eduyyot.*

קוּם עֲשֵׂה   Lit., *get up and do.* A mitzvah or positive act whose fulfillment requires a specific deed. This term often refers to the performance of a positive commandment correcting or reversing the effect of a previous transgression of a negative commandment. See לָאו הַנִּיתָּק לַעֲשֵׂה; שֵׁב וְאַל תַּעֲשֶׂה.

קוֹמֶץ   See קְמִיצָה.

קוֹנָם   *Konam.* A type of vow (נֶדֶר°). A קוֹנָם is a specific type of vow whereby a person forbids himself to eat something or derive benefit from something or someone by saying: "That person is to me a קוֹנָם." The word קוֹנָם is a substitute for the word קָרְבָּן — "sacrifice" — and is used in order to avoid using the word קָרְבָּן itself.

קוֹרָה   Lit., *beam.* An alley ending in a cul-de-sac may be enclosed, for the purpose of permitting carrying on the Sabbath and Festivals, by placing a beam across its entrance. This beam must be at least a handbreadth (טֶפַח°) wide and must be placed at a height no lower than 10

beam
(קוֹרָה)

handbreadths nor higher than 20 cubits from the ground. This beam serves as a reminder that carrying beyond it is not permitted.

קְטוֹרֶת   *Incense.* A mixture of ingredients that was placed on the golden altar (מִזְבַּח הַזָּהָב) in the Temple and burned each morning and evening. The incense contained eleven ingredients in fixed proportions. As with all other sacrifices, some salt was added to the incense. A kind of herb was also added, which would smolder and emit a column of smoke that rose straight up. Generally the incense would be prepared in sufficient quantity for an entire solar year, including the amounts needed daily and the additional requirements for the Yom Kippur service. It was severely prohibited, under pain of excision (כָּרֵת), to prepare incense according to the Temple recipe for use outside the Temple. See הַקְטָרָה.

קָטָן   *A minor.* Someone who has not reached maturity. A minor is not considered legally competent (see also חֵרֵשׁ שׁוֹטֶה וְקָטָן). He bears no criminal responsibility for his acts, and he is exempt from the obligation to perform mitzvot. Nevertheless a number of regulations and customs were introduced to educate minors for adult life. Certain educational commandments are incumbent upon the child's father and mother, or upon the court as the child's guardian, in order to train the child to perform the commandments. One begins with commandments that a minor can become accustomed to performing properly. A minor boy may read from the Torah (see קְרִיאַת הַתּוֹרָה), and he is entitled to be called up to read the additional portion from the Prophets (הַפְטָרָה). The Sages were divided as to whether one is obliged to prevent a minor from transgressing a prohibition from which he may derive enjoyment — for example, eating non-kosher food. Many of the commandments pertaining to a minor are actually the father's responsibility — for example, circumcision (מִילָה) and the redemption of the firstborn (פִּדְיוֹן הַבֵּן). See also בֶּן תֵּשַׁע שָׁנִים; שְׁתֵּי שְׂעָרוֹת.

קְטַנָּה   *A female minor.* A girl before puberty (Halakhically, the appearance of two pubic hairs, שְׁתֵּי שְׂעָרוֹת), generally until the age of twelve. A קְטַנָּה (like a male minor, see קָטָן) is not considered a responsible person in the full juridical sense, and a number of particular laws apply to her. As long as she is a minor, her father may sell her to be a Hebrew handmaiden (אָמָה עִבְרִיָּה); he may have her married, even without her consent (even while she is a נַעֲרָה), and such a marriage is entirely valid in every respect. The father may also receive his minor daughter's marriage settlement and he alone has the right to accept her bill of divorce on her behalf. The father's rights over his daughter cease once she is fully married (see נִישׂוּאִין), even though she may still be a minor. The Sages decreed that the relatives (the mother or brothers) of a minor girl whose father has died may have her married, with her consent, but such a marriage is not entirely valid, and the minor girl may sever the bond by refusing to remain married (see מֵיאוּן). Sexual intercourse with a girl under three years old is not considered Halakhically to be true intercourse for any legal purpose, but sexual intercourse with a minor girl above that age is considered Halakhically significant. Thus, a man who commits incest with a minor girl over the age of three is punishable, though the girl herself is not punished

since she is not yet legally responsible for her acts. Intercourse with a girl over the age of three is a legally effective method of betrothal (קִידוּשִׁין). The seduction (פִּיתּוּי) of a minor girl is not considered as seduction but as rape.

קִידוּשׁ הַחוֹדֶשׁ   *Sanctification of the month.* The judicial discussion and the declaration issued by the authorized Rabbinical Court announcing the beginning of a new month. In ancient times, when the new month was announced on the basis of the testimony of witnesses, people who had seen the new moon appeared before a central court (in Temple times, in Jerusalem) to testify that they had seen it. Their testimony was examined and if it was found correct by the court, the new month would be announced and sanctified. This announcement is referred to as קִידוּשׁ הַחוֹדֶשׁ. Opinions are divided among the Tannaim as to whether only a new moon following a month of twenty-nine days (חוֹדֶשׁ חָסֵר) had to be legally sanctified on the thirtieth day, or whether the new moon following a month of thirty days (חוֹדֶשׁ מְעוּבָּר) also had to be sanctified on the thirty-first day.

קִידוּשׁ הַיּוֹם   Lit., *the sanctification of the day.* Also known simply as kiddush. The blessing recited at the beginning of Sabbaths and Festivals, acknowledging the sacred nature of the day. This blessing is always recited over a cup of wine (or over bread). While the text of the kiddush is Rabbinic in origin, the recitation of kiddush is the fulfillment of the Torah commandment: "Remember the Sabbath day to keep it holy" (Exodus 20:8). However, there is a difference of opinion as to whether this mitzvah is fulfilled by reciting the fourth blessing of the Friday evening Amidah prayer (קְדוּשַׁת הַיּוֹם) or only when reciting kiddush over a cup of wine.

קִידוּשׁ הַשֵּׁם   Lit., *sanctification of the Name.* In general, this refers to the obligation to show the utmost respect for God and the Torah. Included in this category are: (1) The obligation to give one's life, under certain circumstances, rather than violate the Torah (see יֵהָרֵג וְאַל יַעֲבוֹר). (2) The obligation to show outstanding devotion to one or more particular mitzvot. (3) The obligation of a well-known religious figure to behave in an exemplary manner that does honor to the principles he represents. The opposite of קִידוּשׁ הַשֵּׁם is חִילוּל הַשֵּׁם — "desecration of the Name."

קִידוּשׁ יָדַיִם וְרַגְלַיִם   *The sanctification of hands and feet.* Before the priests begin their service in the Temple, they are required to wash (sanctify) their hands and feet (see Exodus 30:18–21). If a priest serves in the Temple without washing his hands beforehand, his service is disqualified and he is liable to the penalty of death at God's hand (מִיתָה בִּידֵי שָׁמַיִם). The priests would lay right hand on right foot and left hand on left foot and would wash both hands and feet at the same time from special faucets in the washbasin (כִּיוֹר) of the Temple.

קִידוּשׁ מֵי חַטָּאת   Lit., *the sanctification of the waters of the sin-offering.* The mixing of the ashes of the Red Heifer (פָּרָה אֲדוּמָה) with water from a flowing stream (see מַיִם חַיִּים. מֵי חַטָּאת) were used to purify people who had touched a corpse or had been in the same building with one (see אֹהֶל הַמֵּת). קִידוּשׁ מֵי

חַטָּאת is subject to several procedural regulations, and may only be performed by a legally competent person (see חֵרֵשׁ שׁוֹטֶה וְקָטָן).

קִדּוּשִׁין   *Betrothal* (lit., "consecrations"). The act by which a woman becomes betrothed to a man. In principle there are three ways of betrothing a woman: (1) With money (כֶּסֶף) or with something worth money, such as a ring, which the bridegroom gives to the bride. (2) With a document (שְׁטָר) in which he attests that he is betrothing the woman. (3) By sexual intercourse (בִּיאָה). The third method, though legal, was forbidden by the Sages to prevent licentiousness. All three methods require that the act of betrothal be performed willingly by both the man and the woman (if she is a minor, her father must approve), and that there be two proper witnesses to the act. After the couple have become betrothed, the woman is forbidden (as an אֵשֶׁת אִישׁ, a married woman) to have sexual relations with any other man. Moreover, her mother, daughter and other close relatives become permanently forbidden to her husband; likewise, his father, son, and other close relatives become permanently forbidden to her. The betrothed couple may not live together until the נִישׂוּאִין — the marriage ceremony when they enter the wedding canopy (חוּפָּה) and the marriage blessings (בִּרְכַּת חֲתָנִים) are recited. For many generations betrothal and marriage have been performed together on the same occasion, in order to prevent many Halakhic and practical difficulties.

קִיּוּם שְׁטָרוֹת   *The ratification of legal documents.* The process by which the court verifies the authenticity of the witnesses' signatures. Once their signatures have been authenticated, the court issues an order (see הָנְפֵּק) for the document's terms to be executed.

קִם לֵיהּ בִּדְרַבָּה מִנֵּיהּ   Lit., *he is sure of the greater than it.* A general rule regarding legal penalties. A person who has committed two or more transgressions with a single act is exempt from punishment for the less severe crime. Thus, if a person committed an act entailing the death penalty and the payment of monetary compensation, the more severe penalty (death) is imposed on him, and he is exempt from the monetary payment.

קִנּוּי   Lit., *jealousy.* The warning given by a husband to a wife suspected of adultery (סוֹטָה). If a husband suspects that his wife may be committing adultery, he must declare himself "jealous," and warn her that he does not wish her to be alone with the man he suspects. According to some authorities the warning must be given in the presence of two witnesses. See סְתִירָה.

קֵיץ הַמִּזְבֵּחַ   Lit., *the summer fruits of the altar.* When there are no individual or communal sacrifices being offered on the altar, animal burnt-offerings (עוֹלוֹת בְּהֵמָה) are sacrificed so that the altar not be empty. This period is called קֵיץ הַמִּזְבֵּחַ. These sacrifices were purchased from special consecrated funds (see תְּרוּמַת הַלִּשְׁכָּה).

קַלְבּוֹן   *Agio, premium.* A term used in connection with the payment of the half-shekel Temple dues (מַחֲצִית הַשֶּׁקֶל). Someone who pays the half-shekel for himself and for someone else and uses a whole shekel to do so must add a small sum,

referred to as a קַלְבּוֹן, to pay for exchanging the shekel for two halves. On certain occasions it was not necessary to pay the קַלְבּוֹן. For example, when a person paid a half-shekel for himself and a half-shekel as a gift for a poor person.

קָלוּט   *Not cloven-hoofed.* (1) A non-kosher animal with a solid hoof, such as a donkey. (2) An animal of a kosher species, but whose hoof is not cloven. Since this animal was born of a kosher animal, even though it would appear to lack one of the signs of being kosher, it is nevertheless considered kosher by virtue of its birth.

קָלוּטָה כְּמִי שֶׁהוּנְחָה   Lit., *[something] intercepted is [considered] laid down.* A principle referring to an object that has passed through a certain air space, such as through a private domain with regard to the Sabbath laws, or through an individual's courtyard, with regard to establishing ownership. Some Sages hold that an object's having been as it were intercepted in the air of a certain domain is equivalent to its having come to rest in that domain and then picked up and taken out of it. However, other Sages disagree. The principle works in the following ways: (1) With regard to the laws of the Sabbath. If a person threw an article from a public domain through a private domain, and out again, he would be considered to have violated the prohibition against transferring an article from one domain to another. See הוֹצָאָה; עֲקִירָה וְהַנָּחָה; רְשׁוּיוֹת הַשַּׁבָּת. (2) With regard to the acquisition of an ownerless (הֶפְקֵר) object. If such an object passes over a person's property, he is considered to have the potential of acquiring it without having physically to take possession of it.

קְלָעִים   *Hangings.* The curtains that enclosed the area surrounding the Sanctuary in the wilderness. This area corresponds to the Temple Courtyard (עֲזָרָה). The most sacred sacrifices (קָדְשֵׁי קָדָשִׁים) had to be eaten within this area. If they were taken outside its confines, the sacrifice became disqualified.

קַלְפֵּי   *A receptacle in which lots were placed.* In the Temple such a receptacle was used for the lots to select which goat would be sacrificed in the Temple on Yom Kippur and which would be sent to Azazel. See שָׂעִיר הַמִּשְׁתַּלֵּחַ; שָׂעִיר יוֹם הַכִּיפּוּרִים.

קְמִיצָה   Lit., *handful.* The scooping out of a handful of flour from the meal-offering (see מְנָחוֹת) in order to burn it on the altar. Most meal-offerings required קְמִיצָה (e.g., Leviticus 2:2). This service, which paralleled the slaughtering of an animal sacrifice, could only be performed by a priest. According to many authorities, the priest would scoop the flour out with the three middle fingers of his right hand, using his thumb and little finger to remove any surplus flour. He would then place the flour in a sacred vessel used in the Temple service (כְּלִי שָׁרֵת) to  consecrate it. Since the priest had to scoop out an exact handful of flour, no more and no less, קְמִיצָה was one of the more difficult services in the Temple.

קֵן   Lit., *a nest*. A pair of doves (either turtledoves or pigeons). Generally one dove was brought as a burnt-offering (see עוֹלַת הָעוֹף) and the other as a sin-offering (see חַטַּאת הָעוֹף) by a woman after she gave birth (see יוֹלֶדֶת), or as part of the purification process of a woman who had suffered from an unusual discharge of uterine blood (see זָבָה). (Leviticus 12:6, 15:29.) There are other cases, however, where both doves were brought as burnt-offerings. Some of the issues regarding this sacrifice (e.g., what happens if the birds are accidentally switched) are discussed in the tractate *Kinnim*.

קֵן מְפוֹרֶשֶׁת   *A specified pair of doves*. This term is used to refer to a pair of doves (see קֵן) whose owner has specified which is to be offered as a sin-offering (see חַטַּאת הָעוֹף) and which as a burnt-offering (see עוֹלַת הָעוֹף). The term קֵן מְפוֹרֶשֶׁת is used in contrast to the term קֵן סְתוּמָה, whose owner has not specified the particular offering for which each bird is to be used.

קַנָּאִים פּוֹגְעִים בּוֹ   Lit., *the zealous may attack him*. There are a number of transgressions for which Torah law does not require that capital punishment be administered by a court of law. Nevertheless, if a "zealous person" (קַנַּאי) apprehends an individual committing one of these transgressions, he may kill him. These transgressions are: the theft of sacred utensils (see כְּלֵי שָׁרֵת); cursing God by using the name of a false god; public sexual relations with a non-Jewish woman (see בּוֹעֵל אֲרַמִית); and serving in the Temple while ritually impure. If a "zealous person" witnessed one of these transgressions and then went to ask advice of a court, the court could not advise him to slay the offender. Permission to do so was only granted if the "zealous person" acted while the offender was actually committing the transgression.

קְנוּנְיָא   *Collusion, conspiracy*. Sometimes contracts of loan or sale are not upheld in court because of a suspicion that the parties involved were conspiring to deceive an innocent third party. For example, a loan contract might be predated. This is significant, because property sold by the borrower after the loan was contracted is subject to a lien to guarantee the loan. If a debtor defaults, any property he owned at the time of the loan may be seized for payment, even though it may have been sold to a third party. The third party may seek restitution from the seller. Thus, if a loan contract is predated, the borrower might have conspired with the lender to claim bankruptcy and pay his debt from property that had actually been sold before the loan was made. Although the borrower would eventually have to repay the purchaser, he would benefit from the delay during the process of collection.

קִנְיָן   *Acquisition, mode of acquisition*. A formal procedure to render an agreement legally binding. Usually קִנְיָן refers to a mode of acquisition. After the act of קִנְיָן has taken place, the object is legally the property of the buyer. Neither party can go back on the agreement, regardless of any change in market values, or any unanticipated change in the article itself. Even if the object were to be destroyed while still in the physical possession of the seller, the buyer would not be entitled to get his money back. Various modes of acquisition confer ownership, depending on the nature of the object, such as מְשִׁיכָה• — pulling the article; מְסִירָה• —

transfer; חֲזָקָה• — performing an act of taking possession; הַגְבָּהָה• — lifting up the article; חֲלִיפִין• — exchange or barter. The word קִנְיָן when used alone without further definition usually refers to קִנְיָן סוּדָר (see next entry). On occasion, more than one action may be involved in the acquisition of an object. For example, money may be paid and the object may then be physically picked up. The Sages discussed the question of which act is the legal קִנְיָן. In general, money is not a valid קִנְיָן for acquiring movable property (see כֶּסֶף; מְטַלְטְלִין). The word קִנְיָן may also refer to taking possession of abandoned property (see הֶפְקֵר•) or to the precise moment when a forbidden action, such as theft or robbery, is said to have taken place. The term קִנְיָן also applies to the conclusion and ratification of an action not directly connected to purchase and sale, such as performing a קִנְיָן to confirm one's acceptance of responsibility with regard to a future action or actions. See also קִנְיָן (אַגַּב) סוּדָר.

קִנְיָן (אַגַּב) סוּדָר   *The transfer of ownership by means of a kerchief*. An extension of the principle of חֲלִיפִין• — barter. When two articles are exchanged for one another, the formal acquisition of one of the articles automatically transfers ownership of the second article as well. Since there is no formal requirement for the objects exchanged in this way to be of equal value, the symbolic transfer of a handkerchief or some other small article from one party to another formalizes any agreements made between them. See also קִנְיָן. Normally, in the case of קִנְיָן סוּדָר, the seller simply takes the buyer's handkerchief in his hand and then returns it to him.

קְנָס   *A fine*. A sum that a person must pay as a punishment. In various laws the Torah stipulates that a transgressor must pay a fine; for example, a rapist (see אוֹנֵס אִשָּׁה•) or seducer (see מְפַתֶּה•) — fifty pieces of silver; a thief — double the value of the object (כֶּפֶל•) or four or five times its value (אַרְבָּעָה וַחֲמִשָּׁה•); compensation for another person's Canaanite slave (see עֶבֶד כְּנַעֲנִי•) killed by one's animal; half the damage (חֲצִי נֶזֶק•) in certain cases of damage caused by animals; and so on. A fine can be distinguished from normal compensation for damage (מָמוֹן) in that the sum involved is either more than would be required to compensate (e.g., double the value) or is a fixed sum unrelated to the damage (e.g., in the case of rape). The regulations concerning fines differ from those of normal compensation in several respects. For example, only a court of fully ordained Rabbis (see סְמִיכַת זְקֵנִים•), not of ordinary Rabbis or laymen, may impose a fine. Furthermore, a person who admits his transgression before he is convicted in court is not liable to a fine, though he must pay compensation for any damage caused. Because of the law requiring fully ordained Rabbis, fines could not be imposed in Babylonia during Talmudic times, and cannot be imposed today.

קָרְבָּן עוֹלֶה וְיוֹרֵד   *A sliding-scale sacrifice*. There are three sins where the financial situation of the sinner is taken into account in deciding what sin-offering he must bring. The three sins are the following: (1) The violation of an oath (see שְׁבוּעַת בִּיטּוּי•). (2) The taking of a false oath to evade giving testimony (see שְׁבוּעַת הָעֵדוּת•). (3) The entering of the Temple or partaking of sacrifices while ritually impure (see טוּמְאַת מִקְדָּשׁ וְקָדָשָׁיו•). In these three cases the sinner must bring a sin-offering of a female lamb or goat. But if he cannot afford such an animal (see דַּלּוֹת וְדַלֵּי דַלּוֹת) he may instead bring a pair of doves (see קֵן), one as a burnt-offering (עוֹלָה*) and the other as a sin-offering (חַטָּאת*). If he cannot afford this sacrifice, he may instead bring a meal-offering (see מִנְחַת חוֹטֵא).

קָרְבַּן עֵצִים   *A sacrifice of wood.* One of the offerings an individual can make to the Temple. In the early years of the Second Temple, there was not sufficient wood to burn the sacrifices on the altar, and certain families volunteered to supply it. Later, to commemorate their generosity, the days on which those families had brought wood for the altar became a festival for them. On these days, they would bring wood to be offered on the altar (קָרְבַּן עֵצִים) and were forbidden to fast or recite eulogies.

קָרוֹב   *A close relative.* The word קָרוֹב has different definitions in different contexts: (1) With regard to court procedure. Close relatives cannot serve as witnesses or judges in cases involving a family member. Nor can two of the judges or witnesses be related to each other. They are disqualified whether their testimony or judgment is in favor of their relative or against him. In this context, the definition of a close relative is based on the number of generations between the people involved and their common relative. Thus, two brothers are referred to as רִאשׁוֹן בְּרִאשׁוֹן, "first to first"; they have a common father. First cousins are called שֵׁנִי בְּשֵׁנִי, "second to second"; they have a common grandparent. An uncle and nephew are "first to second," and so forth. According to all opinions, שֵׁנִי בְּשֵׁנִי and any closer relatives are unacceptable. Some authorities disqualify even more distant relations. A husband and wife are considered as one (see אִשְׁתּוֹ כְּגוּפוֹ). Thus, relatives who may not testify against one spouse may not testify against the other. (2) With regard to mourning (אֲבֵילוּת*). A person is obligated to mourn the passing of seven types of relative: a wife or husband, a father, mother, son, daughter, brother, or sister. (3) A priest may become ritually impure in mourning for any of the above relatives. However, in the case of a sister, this permission is only granted if she was still a virgin and unmarried.

קֶרִי   *The emission of semen.* A person who emits semen, whether involuntarily or intentionally, during sexual relations or otherwise, becomes ritually impure. To regain ritual purity, he must immerse himself in a ritual bath (מִקְוֶה*) and after nightfall on the day of his immersion he becomes ritually pure again. Semen is one of the primary sources of ritual impurity (אֲבוֹת הַטּוּמְאוֹת*). See also Deuteronomy 23:11–12, and בַּעַל קֶרִי.

קְרִיאַת הַתּוֹרָה   *The reading of the Torah.* From the time of Moses onward, it has been an accepted custom to read the Torah in public on the Sabbath, on Mondays and Thursdays, on Festivals, and on fast days. The number of people called to the reading of the Torah depends on the importance of the day. On Sabbath mornings, seven people are called to the Torah; on Yom Kippur — six; on the Festivals and Rosh HaShanah — five; on the intermediate days of Pesaḥ and Sukkot (חוֹל הַמּוֹעֵד*) and Rosh Ḥodesh — four; and on Mondays, Thursdays, Sabbath afternoons, fast days, Ḥanukkah, Purim and the afternoon (מִנְחָה) service of Yom Kippur — three. The Torah is divided into

portions that are read every Sabbath, so that the entire Torah is read every year. In previous generations, some communities followed a practice of completing the Torah in a three-year cycle. However, at present, the custom is to read the entire Torah in the course of one year. During Shabbat afternoons and on Mondays and Thursdays, the first section of the following Sabbath portion is read. On the Festivals, a Torah reading appropriate to the Festival is chosen. On the Sabbath, during Festivals, and on the Ninth of Av (and in some communities on the afternoon of fast-days), a passage from the Prophets (הַפְטָרָה*) is recited after the conclusion of the Torah reading.

קְרִיאַת שְׁמַע   *Reciting the Shema.* It is a Torah commandment to recite the *Shema* ("Hear, O Israel...") in the morning and evening. This consists of two passages from Deuteronomy (6:4–9 and 11:13–21), to which a third passage was added (Numbers 15:37–41), containing the commandment to wear ritual fringes (צִיצִית*), so as to recall the Exodus from Egypt. In reciting the entire *Shema*, one fulfills one's obligation merely by the act of reciting it, but in reciting the first verse, "Hear, O Israel, the Lord our God, the Lord is one," one is also required to pay specific attention to the meaning of the words (see כַּוָּונָה).

קְרִיעָה   *The rending of garments as a sign of mourning.* Among those required to rend their garments are: (1) A person who hears of the death of a close relative. (2) Someone who is present at the death of any person. (3) A student who hears of the death of his teacher. (4) A person who hears a Jew curse God. (5) A person who sees the Temple site in its state of destruction. The tear must be made on a visible part of the garment. The tear made upon hearing of the death of one's parents or seeing the Temple site in its state of destruction may never be entirely mended. A High Priest is forbidden to rend his garments as a sign of mourning.

קֶרֶן   (1) *An animal's horn.* One of the primary categories of damage (אֲבוֹת נְזִיקִין*). By extension, it refers to all damage caused by animals with the intention of injuring; for example, an ox that gores or a dog that bites. The laws governing the assessment of this form of damage vary depending on whether the animal has previously been known to cause such damage (see מוּעָד) or not (see תָּם). The owner of a מוּעָד animal must pay for all the damage. In contrast, the owner of a תָּם animal is only required to pay for half the damage. (2) *The principal, the initial investment.* Used in contrast to פֵּירוֹת* — the fruits or profits — and in contrast to רִיבִּית* — the interest.

קַרְנוֹת הַמִּזְבֵּחַ   Lit., *the horns of the altar.* Extensions of the corners of the altar. The horns of the outer altar (see מִזְבֵּחַ*) were a cubit high and a cubit wide. They were considered an essential part of its structure, and the blood of the sin-offerings (see חַטָּאת) was sprinkled upon them. The horns of the inner altar (מִזְבֵּחַ הַזָּהָב*) were smaller. The blood of the sin-offerings that was sprinkled on the פָּרוֹכֶת* — the curtain separating the Holy of Holies (קֹדֶשׁ הַקֳּדָשִׁים*) from the Sanctuary (הֵיכָל*) — was sprinkled on it. See also חַטָּאוֹת הַפְּנִימִיּוֹת.

קַרְפֵּף   *Enclosure.* (1) With reference to the laws against transferring articles from one domain to another on the Sabbath see קֶרְפֵּף (הוֹצָאָה), refers to an enclosed storage space behind a house. This enclosure is considered a private domain (רְשׁוּת הַיָּחִיד). Nevertheless, if the קֶרְפֵּף was not enclosed for the purpose of living in it, and if it is larger than the area sufficient to grow two סְאָה of wheat (see בֵּית סָאתַיִם in the section on weights and measures, p. 285), it is considered a semi-private domain (כַּרְמְלִית) even though it possesses walls. (2) With regard to the limit beyond which a person is not permitted to walk on the

Sabbath (see תְּחוּם שַׁבָּת), the קֶרְפֵּף is an area of slightly more than 70 cubits beyond the boundary of a town, that is added to the city limits (see עִיבּוּרָהּ שֶׁל עִיר). If two cities are close to each other, they are both granted a קֶרְפֵּף, and if, through the addition of these 140 cubits, the cities become connected, they are considered as one city.

קְרְקַע   See מְקַרְקְעֵי.

רָאוּי וּמוּחְזָק   Lit., *what is potentially due and what is possessed.* Contrasting terms regarding property, particularly in relation to inheritance. מוּחְזָק refers to property that is actually in a person's possession; רָאוּי refers to property to which he has a right, but does not at present possess. A firstborn receives a double share of the property in his father's possession (מוּחְזָק). He does not receive a double share in property to which his father merely has a right, or which his father may eventually acquire (רָאוּי).

רְאִיָּה, רְאִיּוֹן   Lit., *appearance [in the Temple].* The obligation to appear in the Temple on each of the three Pilgrim Festivals (Deuteronomy 16:16; see שָׁלֹשׁ רְגָלִים). The burnt-offering brought on these pilgrimages was called עוֹלַת רְאִיָּה. It was also sometimes referred to by the term רְאִיּוֹן. A peace-offering was also required (see חֲגִיגָה).

רְאִיּוֹת הַזָּב   Lit., *the sightings of a man suffering from gonorrhea.* In the laws governing gonorrheal secretions (see זָב) it is Halakhically significant how often the secretion occurs. Before definitely attributing a secretion to gonorrhea, an effort is made to attribute it to some other physical or mental condition. Unlike menstrual bleeding, the impurity of a person with gonorrhea depends on the number of secretions within three days.

רֹאשׁ בֵּית אָב   Lit., *the head of a patrilineal family.* Each week different מִשְׁמָרוֹת — "watches" — of priests would serve in the Temple (see מִשְׁמָר). These מִשְׁמָרוֹת were further subdivided into בָּתֵּי אָב, patrilineal families, which performed the Temple service on each day of the week (see בֵּית אָב). The head of each family of priests was in charge of supervising that service. In certain matters of the Temple service, he was next in command following the High Priest's deputy (סְגַן הַכֹּהֲנִים). For example, on Yom Kippur, he would accompany the High Priest in some parts of his service.

רֹאשׁ הַשָּׁנָה   Rosh HaShanah (lit., "the head of the year"). The Festival of the Jewish New Year. (1) Rosh HaShanah occurs on the first two days of the month of Tishri. According to the

Torah, Rosh HaShanah is a single day, but as early as Temple times, because of problems related to testimony regarding the New Moon, it was occasionally required to be celebrated on two days, and this custom became the accepted practice throughout the Jewish world, including Eretz Israel. Rosh HaShanah is a Festival, and the laws applying to it are those of Festivals (see יוֹם טוֹב). The special commandment that applies uniquely to Rosh HaShanah is the sounding of the shofar (שׁוֹפָר), but when Rosh HaShanah falls on Shabbat, the shofar is not sounded except in the Temple or in the place of the Great Sanhedrin (סַנְהֶדְרִין גְּדוֹלָה). Rosh HaShanah has a special additional prayer service (מוּסָף) in which blessings relating to kingship (מַלְכֻיּוֹת), to remembrance (זִכְרוֹנוֹת), and to the shofar (שׁוֹפָרוֹת) are recited. One begins reckoning dates from Rosh HaShanah for promissory notes, and for the Sabbatical and Jubilee Year cycles (see שְׁבִיעִית and יוֹבֵל). (2) For the other days that are called Rosh HaShanah, see רָאשֵׁי שָׁנָה.

רֹאשׁ חוֹדֶשׁ   Lit., *the head of the month.* The New Moon, the first day of the lunar month. At the end of a thirty-day month (חוֹדֶשׁ מְעוּבָּר) two days of the New Moon are celebrated (the thirtieth day of the previous month and the first day of the new month). All work is permitted on the New Moon, but from ancient times women have refrained from carrying out certain tasks on this day, and this is considered a praiseworthy custom. On the New Moon a special section of the Torah is read in the synagogue, and four men are called up to this reading of the Torah. There is a special additional prayer (מוּסָף), the Hallel (הַלֵּל) is read in part, and one adds a special prayer ("יַעֲלֶה וְיָבוֹא") both to Grace after Meals (בִּרְכַּת הַמָּזוֹן) and to the Amidah prayer (see שְׁמוֹנֶה עֶשְׂרֵה).

רִאשׁוֹן לְטוּמְאָה   Lit., *first [category] of ritual impurity.* Any person or object that became ritually impure by contact with a primary source of ritual impurity (אַב הַטּוּמְאָה, see אֲבוֹת הַטּוּמְאוֹת) has the status of רִאשׁוֹן לְטוּמְאָה — "the first degree of ritual impurity" — otherwise known as יֶלֶד הַטּוּמְאָה — "offspring of impurity." Foods that come in contact with a רִאשׁוֹן לְטוּמְאָה acquire the status of שֵׁנִי לְטוּמְאָה — "the second degree of ritual impurity." There is a Rabbinical decree that liquids that have become ritually impure, even if only by contact with a שֵׁנִי לְטוּמְאָה, become themselves a רִאשׁוֹן לְטוּמְאָה.

רָאשֵׁי אֵיבָרִים Lit., *the heads of limbs*. A master who blinds a non-Jewish slave (יֵעָבֶד כְּנַעֲנִי) or knocks out his tooth must set him free (Exodus 21:26–27). Freedom is also granted if any of the following twenty-four רָאשֵׁי אֵיבָרִים are destroyed: the ends of the ten fingers and toes, the ears, the nose, the penis, or a woman's nipples. The term רָאשֵׁי אֵיבָרִים is also used with regard to leprosy (יְצָרַעַת). One of the symptoms of leprosy is יְמִחְיָה. This occurs where the diseased flesh forms a ring round an area of healthy flesh. A leper can only be declared ritually impure if the priest can see a sufficient amount of diseased flesh at once, without shifting his gaze. Thus, if a fingertip is healthy and around its sides there is a ring of leprosy, the priest cannot see the מִחְיָה at once, and must declare the leper ritually pure.

רָאשֵׁי שָׁנָה Lit., *heads of the year*. In addition to the 1st of Tishri (see רֹאשׁ הַשָּׁנָה), there are three other dates that, in different contexts, are regarded as the beginning of the year: (1) The 1st of Nisan — the beginning of the year with regard to Festivals and dating the reign of a Jewish King. In general, the sacrificial year in the Temple also began on the 1st of Nisan. (2) The 1st of Elul — the beginning of the year with regard to the tithing of one's herd (see מַעֲשַׂר בְּהֵמָה). (3) The 15th of Shevat — the beginning of the year with regard to the fruit that grows in the first three years after a tree has been planted (יְעָרְלָה), and to the tithing of fruit from trees (see מַעַשְׂרוֹת).

רֵאשִׁית הַגֵּז *The first shearing*. The obligation to give the priest the first portion of any fleece shorn from a flock of five sheep or more (see Deuteronomy 18:4). This donation must weigh at least five סְלָעִים (see סֶלַע, p. 291), and becomes the personal property of the priest. It is not considered sacred.

רַב *Master, teacher*. (1) The man from whom one has learned Torah is called one's master, one's Rabbi, and it is a Torah commandment that one must greatly honor one's Rabbi, beyond the general respect one owes to Sages, and one must hold him in awe ("the awe of your Rabbi should be like the awe of Heaven"). One must rise in his honor, and one must honor him as he rises and when he walks. Honoring one's Rabbi and the needs of one's Rabbi takes precedence over honoring one's father and his needs. For example, if one is faced with the choice of ransoming one's Rabbi or one's father, one's Rabbi takes precedence. When a Rabbi dies, his disciples rend their garments (see קְרִיעָה). A disciple may not call his Rabbi by name. These laws, in all their severity, apply to one's main teacher, the person from whom one has received most of one's knowledge, but several of them also apply to a Rabbi who is not one's main teacher, but from whom one has learned. Some say that the foremost Rabbi of the generation (גְּדוֹל הַדּוֹר) is to be regarded as one's Rabbi, even if one has not studied under him. (2) The title רַב was applied to Babylonian scholars (Amoraim). The Rabbinical title applied to Palestinian scholars who had received full ordination (see סְמִיכַת זְקֵנִים) was רַבִּי.

רְבִיעָה *Rainy season*. There are three rainy seasons, which follow each other but not at specific dates. The first rainy season is generally reckoned to begin on the 7th of Heshvan. The rainy season is of particular Halakhic significance with regard to the prayer for rain and for vows. If rain has not fallen by a specific date there is a prescribed formula for special prayers and fasts (see תַּעֲנִית צִבּוּר).

רְבִיעִית Lit., *a quarter*. A unit of liquid measurement (see section on weights and measures, p. 287). When unqualified, a רְבִיעִית equals a quarter of a *log* (see לוֹג). The רְבִיעִית is a standard unit of measurement in certain matters. For example, a רְבִיעִית is the minimum amount of wine over which kiddush may be recited; the amount of wine which a Nazirite (see נְזִירוּת) is punished for drinking; and the minimum quantity of certain foods for which one becomes liable for violating the prohibition against transferring objects from one domain to another on the Sabbath. A רְבִיעִית of blood from a corpse conveys ritual impurity.

רֶגֶל Lit., *foot*. (1) The term for one of the primary categories of damage or injury (יְאָבוֹת נְזִיקִין). It refers to damage caused unintentionally by domesticated animals in their normal behavior (for example, accidentally trampling goods or produce). The animal's owner must reimburse the injured party to the full extent of the damage done to his property (נֶזֶק שָׁלֵם). A related, but different category of damage is יְצְרוֹרוֹת — indirect damage (e.g., damage caused by stones kicked by an animal while proceeding on its way). (2) A term used to refer to any one of the three Pilgrim Festivals: Pesaḥ, Shavuot, and Sukkot (see יְשָׁלֹשׁ רְגָלִים).

רוֹב Lit., *a majority*. A fundamental principle in Halakhic decision-making. On the basis of what is written in the Torah (Exodus 23:2), a court decides in accordance with the majority of judges when making a ruling. Similarly, one follows the majority of evidence (the majority of cases, the majority of people) in certain cases where there is doubt regarding the facts. The Halakhah discusses the difference between an evident majority (רוּבָּא דְּאִיתָא קַמָּן) and one based on general statistical information (רוּבָּא דְּלֵיתָא קַמָּן). There are a number of Talmudic discussions as to which Halakhic principle takes precedence when there is a clash between two fundamental principles, for example majority versus proximity, majority versus legal presumption (יְחַזָקָה), etc.

רוֹב בִּנְיָן Lit., *most of the structure*. If part of a corpse is located underneath a covering or structure (see אֹהֶל הַמֵּת), it cannot impart ritual impurity unless *most* of it (רוֹב) is found there. This is determined by the size of the bones (such as the vertebrae and the legs) relative to the entire skeleton, or by their number, 125 or more out of all 248 bones.

רוֹבֵעַ וְנִרְבָּע *An animal used by a man or a woman for sexual relations*. The Torah prohibits sexual relations with animals (Leviticus 20:15–16). For this transgression both the humans and the animals are stoned to death. If the animal was not executed (for example, if valid witnesses were not present when the transgression was committed), it is nevertheless disqualified for use as a sacrifice.

רוֹדֵף *Pursuer* (i.e., assailant). Someone about to commit rape or murder. Any means may be used to prevent such a crime, even to the extent of killing the assailant. The assailant is not liable for any damage he caused while in pursuit of his victim, because he is subject to a more severe penalty than a monetary one (see קִים לֵיהּ בְּדְרַבָּה מִינֵּיהּ). Nor is someone who pursues the assailant to prevent the crime liable for damage he may cause. This regulation was designed so that people would not be deterred from helping others (see תִּיקּוּן הָעוֹלָם).

רוֹעֶה   *A herdsman.* A herdsman is a paid bailee (שׁוֹמֵר שָׂכָר"). But he may entrust the herd to his assistants, since that is customarily agreed upon between the parties in advance. See the next entry (רוֹעֶה צֹאן) about a herdsman's acceptability as a witness.

רוֹעֶה צֹאן   *A shepherd.* Generally, a person who looks after his own sheep is suspected of theft, since shepherds frequently graze their flocks on other people's fields. Hence a shepherd whose honesty has not been proven is regarded as suspect and is disqualified from serving as a witness. This does not apply to a hired shepherd or to men who herd cattle — though, because of their profession, they are considered unlettered and without experience of the complexity of urban life.

רִיבִּית   *Interest.* Any addition made when returning a loan to compensate the lender for the time that the loan was in the borrower's possession. According to the Torah it is forbidden to lend or borrow money at interest (see Exodus 22:24, Leviticus 25:36–37, and Deuteronomy 23:20). This prohibition applies to the borrower, the lender, and any scribe, witness, or guarantor who might take any part in such a transaction. The prohibition against interest applies both to loans of money and to loans in kind, so long as the borrower does not return the specific goods or object but rather money or goods of the same value as the loan. Any addition of any kind is prohibited as interest (see רִיבִּית דְּבָרִים), including arrangements not originally intended as interest, but which subseqently become interest. For example, if one borrows something and promises to return something similar to it, this could in effect be interest, if the value of the article to be returned has increased.

See also רִיבִּית מִצַּד אֶחָד; עִסְקָא; מַשְׁכַּנְתָּא דְּסוּרָא.

רִיבִּית דְּבָרִים   Lit., *verbal interest.* The Sages included in the prohibition of interest (רִיבִּית) intangible benefits that the lender gets in exchange for his loan. These are called רִיבִּית דְּבָרִים. For example, a borrower must not behave in an unusually respectful manner towards a lender, or greet him with excessive ceremony.

רִיבִּית מִצַּד אֶחָד   Lit., *interest from one side,* i.e., an innocent transaction that may ultimately entail interest. Some Sages permitted this, provided that the transaction was a sale and not a loan. Thus, if, instead of borrowing money, a person sells his field with a stipulation that he can buy it back for its original value within a certain period, failure to buy it back within the period makes the transaction an innocent sale. But if he does buy it back, the entire sale was a legal fiction, and the "buyer's" use of the field for the period amounts to interest. The Halakhah follows the opinion that even רִיבִּית מִצַּד אֶחָד is strictly forbidden.

רִיבִּית קְצוּצָה   Lit., *fixed interest.* Whenever the interest to be paid is predetermined and is completely independent of subsequent events — i.e., it is a fixed amount or it is dependent only on the passage of time — it is called רִיבִּית קְצוּצָה. This is the only form of interest forbidden by Torah law. רִיבִּית קְצוּצָה must be returned to the borrower from whom it was extorted. It may not be retained even with the borrower's permission. A person violating this prohibition is disqualified by the Torah from serving as a witness. Other forms of interest, forbidden by Rabbinic decree, are called אֲבַק רִיבִּית (see ...אֲבַק).

רִיפּוּי   Lit., *Medical treatment.* One of the five categories of restitution for damage that must be made by a person who injured another (see חֲמִישָׁה דְּבָרִים; חוֹבֵל). If the injured person requires medical treatment, the person who caused the injury must pay for the treatment. He may not provide free treatment or himself treat the injured person (even if he is a qualified doctor).

רְצִיעָה   *Piercing a Hebrew servant's ear with an awl.* A Hebrew manservant (עֶבֶד עִבְרִי") who does not wish to terminate his servitude may remain with his master until the Jubilee Year (יוֹבֵל") or his master's death. (See Exodus 21:6; Leviticus 25:41–4.) Only a servant who was given a slave as a wife by his master and has children by her may make this request. The master brings the servant to the court, and after they have investigated the matter the servant stands next to a doorpost and an awl or similar metal instrument is driven though his ear. This is only done if there is a strong bond of friendship between the servant and his master. A priest who was sold into slavery may not have his ear pierced, since that act makes him blemished. The ceremony of רְצִיעָה may only be performed on a servant sold by the court and not on one who sold himself into slavery.

רָקִיק   Lit., *wafer.* One of the types of meal-offering (see Leviticus 2:4). This offering resembled matzah and was baked in an oven. Afterwards, oil was spread on it in the shape of an X. Like other meal-offerings brought voluntarily, the רְקִיקִים had to be broken into small pieces and a portion scooped up and burned on the altar (see קְמִיצָה).

רְשׁוּיוֹת הַשַּׁבָּת   Lit., *the domains of Shabbat.* The four categories of place with regard to carrying (הוֹצָאָה") on the Sabbath. A private domain (רְשׁוּת הַיָּחִיד) is an area larger than 4 by 4 handbreadths (see טֶפַח), divided from the surrounding area by a fence at least 10 handbreadths high. It is permitted to carry within the private domain, which is considered to extend upwards to the sky. The public domain (רְשׁוּת הָרַבִּים) is a place at least 16 cubits wide, through which many people pass daily (some authorities say 600,000). The public domain is considered to extend upwards 10 handbreadths. On the Sabbath and Festivals it is forbidden to carry objects a distance of more than 4 cubits in the public domain. It is also forbidden to transfer objects to or from the public domain. The third type of domain is an "exempt place" (מְקוֹם פְּטוֹר"), which is an area less than 4 by 4 handbreadths and is separated from the surrounding area. The Sages added a fourth type of intermediate domain, called a כַּרְמְלִית". The authorities were strict not only with regard to the creation of a כַּרְמְלִית, but also with regard to the restriction of carrying within the private domain. See עֵירוּב חֲצֵירוֹת.

רְשׁוּת הָרַבִּים Lit., *public domain.* (1) With regard to Shabbat, see רְשׁוּיוֹת הַשַּׁבָּת. (2) With regard to ritual impurity, any doubt concerning ritual impurity that arises in a public domain is judged leniently and the object is considered ritually pure. רְשׁוּת הָרַבִּים is defined as any area open to the public. (3) With regard to the acquisition of property (see קִנְיָן), there are special laws governing the modes of acquisition of property in a public domain. (See אַרְבַּע אַמּוֹת.) (4) With regard to damages, everyone has permission to proceed freely within the public domain. No one can sue another person for damage caused when using the public domain in a normal manner. (See בּוֹר.)

שְׁאִילָה בִּבְעָלִים *Borrowing an object and borrowing or hiring its owner with it.* A borrower (שׁוֹאֵל) is responsible for the things that he borrows. However, if the owner of a borrowed animal or object was employed by the borrower at the time it was borrowed, and the animal died or the object was destroyed, the borrower is free of all liability, even if he was negligent. This also applies if the owner was not present when the animal died or the object was destroyed. The basis for the law is found in Exodus 22:14.

שְׁאֵלָה לְחָכָם Lit., *a request [made] to a scholar.* If a person makes a vow (נֶדֶר) or takes an oath (שְׁבוּעָה), or consecrates property (see הֶקְדֵּשׁ), and afterwards regrets having done so, he may go to a scholar and request of him that he release him from his vow. This request is called שְׁאֵלָה לְחָכָם. See הַתָּרַת נְדָרִים.

שְׁאֵלַת גְּשָׁמִים Lit., *the request for rain.* During the season when it normally rains in Eretz Israel a request for rain is added in the Amidah prayer (see שְׁמוֹנֶה עֶשְׂרֵה) in the blessing (בִּרְכַּת הַשָּׁנִים) thanking God for the produce of the fields. In Eretz Israel, this addition is made from the 7th of Ḥeshvan until the Pesaḥ Festival. In the Diaspora, the addition is generally made from the sixtieth day after the autumnal equinox until Pesaḥ. However, in certain countries, if the rainy season falls after Pesaḥ, different laws may apply. שְׁאֵלַת גְּשָׁמִים is not to be confused with הַזְכָּרַת גְּשָׁמִים — "mentioning rain" — which is the term used to describe the phrase — מַשִּׁיב הָרוּחַ וּמוֹרִיד הַגֶּשֶׁם — "who causes the wind to blow and the rain to fall" — that is added to the second blessing of the Amidah prayer (see גְּבוּרוֹת) between Shemini Atzeret (שְׁמִינִי עֲצֶרֶת) and Pesaḥ.

שְׁאֵר כְּסוּת וְעוֹנָה *Food, clothing, and conjugal rights.* In general these are defined as a husband's principal marital obligations. These terms are used in the Torah (Exodus 21:10) with reference to a master who has married a Hebrew maidservant (אָמָה עִבְרִיָּה), though there are differences of opinion regarding their meaning in that context.

שְׂאֵת Lit., *sore.* One of the symptoms of skin leprosy (צָרַעַת) (see Leviticus 13:2). שְׂאֵת is the color of clean, white wool, slightly darker than בַּהֶרֶת, but lighter than normal skin.

שֵׁב וְאַל תַּעֲשֶׂה Lit., *sit and do nothing.* Sometimes used in contrast to קוּם עֲשֵׂה. There are three contexts in which this expression is frequently used: (1) With regard to the Torah's prohibitions, it refers to the commandments that require us to refrain from performing an act. (2) The expression שֵׁב וְאַל תַּעֲשֶׂה is also used to explain refraining from action in any context. In particular, the Sages occasionally overrode a positive Torah commandment in view of other considerations. Thus, the Sages ruled that the shofar should not be sounded on Rosh HaShanah when that day falls on the Sabbath. (3) In cases where various contradictory factors are in force, the Sages often advised: "Sit and do nothing," because the consequences of refraining from action are generally less severe than when a commandment is actively transgressed.

שְׁבוּיָה *A woman taken captive.* A term used in the laws of marriage and lineage. A שְׁבוּיָה is a woman who has been captured or seized, generally by an enemy army. It is assumed that most captive women are raped by those who capture them. Hence a woman released from such captivity is forbidden to marry a priest (see זוֹנָה). Since the prohibition against a priest marrying a שְׁבוּיָה is Rabbinic in origin, the Sages introduced considerable leniency in this matter. For example, the testimony of most witnesses (even, under certain conditions, the woman's young child) that the woman has not been raped is accepted. One of a husband's obligations, mentioned in the marriage contract (כְּתוּבָה), is that he must release his wife from captivity.

שְׁבוּעָה *Oath.* A statement implicitly or explicitly invoking the name of God, in which a person confirms the truth of something or commits himself to do or not to do some act. Although there is a positive commandment in the Torah (Deuteronomy 6:13) to take oaths under certain circumstances, it was said that a person taking an oath must be worthy, and that there must be no suspicion of falsehood, either intentional or unintentional, in an oath. For that reason the Sages almost completely abolished oaths from court procedure and substituted other regulations. The punishment for a false oath is very severe, since it involves the desecration of God's name (חִילוּל הַשֵׁם). Sometimes oaths were reinforced by being sworn on holy objects such as a holy book or a ritual article such as phylacteries (תְּפִילִין).

שְׁבוּעַת בִּיטוּי

Lit., *an oath on a statement*. An oath expressed by a person to reinforce a promise or an obligation or to confirm the veracity of a story. In general, all true oaths that are not connected with testimony in court or with debts are in this category. One who violates such an oath unintentionally must bring a sin-offering (see קָרְבָּן עוֹלֶה וְיוֹרֵד).

שְׁבוּעַת הַדַּיָּינִים

Lit., *the oath of the judges*. An oath taken in a court of law to clear oneself of a claim. Such an oath is taken only where the claim is of a certain minimum amount (two silver *ma'ah*). By Torah law, it is taken only if the defendant admits part of an obligation (מוֹדֶה בְּמִקְצָת), or if one witness has testified against the defendant (see עֵד אֶחָד), or if the defendant claims to have lost an article placed in his care (שְׁבוּעַת הַשׁוֹמְרִים). By Rabbinic decree, there are many other oaths imposed by the court (see שְׁבוּעַת הֵיסֵת).

שְׁבוּעַת הֵיסֵת

Lit., *an oath of inducement*. An oath instituted by the Rabbis in a case where a defendant completely denies a claim. By Torah law a defendant is only required to take an oath if the plaintiff has a partial case against him, if one witness (עֵד אֶחָד) testifies against the defendant, or if he makes a partial admission of liability (see מוֹדֶה בְּמִקְצָת). However, in the time of the Talmud the Sages (according to tradition, Rav Naḥman) decreed that someone who completely denies a claim, if he has no other way of refuting it, must take a שְׁבוּעַת הֵיסֵת to clear himself of suspicion.

שְׁבוּעַת הָעֵדוּת

Lit., *the oath of testimony*. If witnesses have information supporting a plaintiff's claim and he requests them to give evidence on his behalf, and they then deny that they have this information, refuse to testify, and take an oath that they do not have the information, such an oath is called שְׁבוּעַת הָעֵדוּת. They must bring a sin-offering as atonement (see קָרְבָּן עוֹלֶה וְיוֹרֵד, Leviticus 5:1). This law is unusual in that the penalty is the same for both inadvertent and intentional violation.

שְׁבוּעַת הַפִּיקָדוֹן

Lit., *the oath of a deposit*. This refers to an oath taken with the intention of falsely denying a deposit or a debt. A person who owes another money or property and denies his obligation under oath is in this category, whether the false oath was deliberate or the result of an honest mistake. One who falsely swore in this manner must pay his debt and add one-fifth to it (see חוֹמֶשׁ). He must bring a ram as a guilt-offering (see אֲשַׁם גְּזֵילוֹת).

שְׁבוּעַת הַשׁוֹמְרִים

Lit., *the oath of the bailees*. A bailee who seeks to free himself from liability for something entrusted to him that he cannot return (Exodus 22:9) must support his statement with an oath. The bailee must swear that he is not guilty for the loss of the object (each type of bailee according to the area of his responsibility, see שׁוֹמֵר), and that he is not liable to pay. The Sages added that he must swear two more oaths: (1) that the article is no longer in his possession; (2) that he did not use the object for his own benefit.

שְׁבוּעַת שָׁוְא

Lit., *an oath taken in vain*. In the Halakhah there is no difference between a vain oath and a lie. Whenever someone swears to something untrue, it comes into this category (see שְׁבוּעַת בִּיטוּי). However, a vain oath means in particular an oath that is patently untrue, such as where a person takes two contradictory oaths: one of the two is a vain oath. If a person purposely takes a vain oath, he is punishable by lashes (מַלְקוֹת). If he does so unintentionally, there is no punishment, unless the oath also fits into another forbidden category. In addition, if a person takes an oath that a known object is precisely what everyone perceives it to be, e.g., if one swears that a particular man is indeed a man, such an oath comes under the category of שְׁבוּעַת שָׁוְא.

שְׁבוּת

Lit., *rest*. All the restrictions instituted by the Sages on the Sabbath and the Festivals to prevent the violation of Torah prohibitions or to enhance the holiness of the day fall in this category. One example is the prohibition against doing business. Many of the restrictions in this category are very ancient; indeed, some are mentioned in the Bible. Usually, these restrictions were not applied in the Temple (אֵין שְׁבוּת בַּמִּקְדָּשׁ). This was because they would interfere with the Temple service, and because the priests in the Temple were very scrupulous (כֹּהֲנִים זְרִיזִים הֵם) and would not abuse this relaxation in the rules in order to violate other commandments.

שֶׁבַח

Lit., *improvement*. A term used in the laws of purchase and contracts. Improvement comprises added value, the increase in the value of property as a result of labor that has been invested in it. In some cases the relation between the value of the improvement and its cost must be calculated so as to work out the value of the שֶׁבַח. שֶׁבַח is also used to describe windfall profits not brought about by any effort on the investor's part, e.g., a change in market values.

שֶׁבַח בֵּית אָב

Lit., *the honor of one's father's household*. This refers to property to which the family of its previous owner feels a powerful tie. For example, by law a widower inherits all his late wife's possessions. However, if they include ancestral burial plots or servants whose families have served in the wife's family for generations, her family is given the option of buying these possessions from him. See פְּגַם מִשְׁפָּחָה.

שְׁבִיעִית

Lit., *seventh*. The seventh and last year in the Sabbatical cycle. The first such cycle began after the conquest of Canaan by Joshua. It is also known as שְׁמִיטָה — lit., "abandonment," "release." The laws of שְׁבִיעִית are based on Torah law (Leviticus 25:1-7; Deuteronomy 15:1-6), but most authorities maintain that the conditions for the applicability of the Torah commandment to observe שְׁבִיעִית have lapsed, and its present-day observance is based on Rabbinic decree. The particular regulations that apply to this year fall into two main categories: (1) שְׁמִיטַת קַרְקַע — lit., "the release of the soil." All agricultural land must lie fallow. It is prohibited to work the land, except for what is necessary to keep existing crops alive. All produce that does grow is ownerless and must be left unguarded in the fields so that any creature, including wild animals and birds, can have ready access to it. So long as produce can still be found in the fields, it may be eaten, though it may not be bought and sold in the normal manner or used for purposes other than food. After the last of a crop has been removed from the field, that crop may no longer be eaten, unless a "removal ceremony" called בִּיעוּר is promptly performed. Produce that grew from seeds during שְׁבִיעִית, even if it grew by itself (see סְפִיחִים), is forbidden by Rabbinic decree to be consumed (according to a few authorities, by Torah law). (2) שְׁמִיטַת כְּסָפִים — "cancellation of cash debts." All outstanding debts owed by Jews to each other are cancelled on the last day of the seventh year. This does not apply to debts whose payment is not yet due on this day, nor does it apply when collection proceedings have already been initiated in court (see פְּרוֹזְבּוּל).

שְׁבִירַת עֶצֶם
Lit., *the breaking of a bone.* The Torah prohibits breaking any of the bones in the Paschal sacrifice during its preparation and consumption (Exodus 12:46). At times, this prohibition raises difficulties if part of the sacrifice becomes ritually impure or otherwise disqualified for use.

שְׁבִירָתָן הִיא טָהֳרָתָן
Breaking them restores their ritual purity. Most articles that become ritually impure can regain ritual purity through immersion in a מִקְוֶה (ritual bath). Earthenware vessels (כְּלֵי חֶרֶס) are an exception. Once they become ritually impure, the only way they can regain ritual purity is by being broken until they are no longer usable (see Leviticus 11:35). Utensils made of other materials can also regain ritual purity in the same way, but the Sages decreed in some cases that they again become ritually impure if they are reconstructed.

שְׁבִיתַת כֵּלִים
Lit., *the resting of utensils.* According to Bet Shammai, not only a person and his animals, but also all property belonging to him, must rest on the Sabbath. According to this view, even devices that function automatically may not operate on the Sabbath. The Halakhah follows the opposing viewpoint, that of Bet Hillel, which generally permits work by inanimate objects on the Sabbath.

שֶׁבַע חֲקִירוֹת
Lit., *seven examinations.* In the judges' examination of witnesses, seven fundamental questions are asked, six concerning the time the event in question took place, and the seventh concerning the place. They are: (1) In which of the seven Sabbatical Year cycles (see שְׁבִיעִית) of the Jubilee (50-year) cycle (see יוֹבֵל) did the event take place? (2) In which year of the seven-year cycle did the event take place? (3) In which month? (4) On which day of the month? (5) On which day of the week? (6) At what time of the day? (7) Where did the event take place? Testimony is unacceptable if the witnesses contradict each other on these matters or if one of them cannot answer one of these questions. Testimony that does not stipulate the time and place of the act is unacceptable, because it is not capable of being contradicted (see הַזָּמָה). See also דְּרִישָׁה וַחֲקִירָה.

שֶׁבַע מִצְווֹת בְּנֵי נֹחַ
Lit., *the seven commandments [given] to Noah's descendants.* Seven universal laws binding on all mankind. They are: (1) The prohibition against idolatry. (2) The prohibition against murder. (3) The prohibition against incest and adultery (see גִּלּוּי עֲרָיוֹת). (4) The prohibition against robbery (גֶּזֶל) and kidnapping. (5) The prohibition against blasphemy. (6) The prohibition against eating flesh torn from a living animal

(אֵיבָר מִן הַחַי). (7) The obligation to establish courts of law. A non-Jew who disobeys one of these commandments is liable to the death penalty. Although the commonly accepted number for the Noachide laws is seven, some authorities have compiled more extensive lists comprising up to thirty commandments. However, the death penalty applies only to the seven listed above.

שִׁבְעָה, שְׁלשִׁים
Lit., *seven [days], thirty [days].* Different stages in mourning (see אֲבֵילוּת). The first seven days after a close relative's death are days of severe mourning during which the mourner is prohibited (among other things) from leaving his home, performing work, sitting on a chair of normal height, washing himself for pleasure, wearing leather shoes, or engaging in sexual relations. The thirty-day period is one in which eulogies (see הֶסְפֵּד) are recited for important people (see Deuteronomy 34:8). During this period, the mourner is not allowed to wear new clothes, cut his hair, partake in festivities, or marry. Nor may he repair the garment he has torn as a sign of mourning (see קְרִיעָה). After thirty days, all mourning rites are concluded except those observed for the passing of a father or a mother. These mourning rites are not publicly observed on the Sabbath, but the Sabbath is counted as a day of mourning. If a Festival occurs during the seven days of mourning, they come to an end when the Festival begins. Similarly, if a Festival occurs during the period between the end of the seven days of mourning and the end of the thirty days, the thirty-day period ends when the Festival begins.

שִׁבְעָה מַשְׁקִין
Lit., *seven liquids.* Food or produce cannot usually contract ritual impurity until: (1) it is severed from its place of growth; and (2) it comes into contact with one of seven specific types of liquids according to the wish of its owner (see Leviticus 11:34). The article's contact with one of these liquids makes it capable of contracting ritual impurity (see הֶכְשֵׁר). The seven liquids are: water, wine, honey, oil, milk, dew and blood.

שִׁבְעָה נְקִיִּים
Lit., *seven clean [days].* A man suffering from a gonorrheal discharge (see זָב) and a woman experiencing an unusual flow of uterine blood (see זָבָה) must examine themselves and allow seven days to pass without seeing any discharge before they begin their purification process (see Leviticus 15:13,28). Today menstruating women observe the same restrictions after their regular period ends. Hence, before a woman can immerse herself in a מִקְוֶה (ritual bath, see also טְבִילָה) and resume normal marital relations, she must count שִׁבְעָה נְקִיִּים — "seven clean days" — after her period has ended.

שֶׁבֶת
Compensation for loss of time. Reimbursement for the time when one was unable to work because of injury. One of the five categories of damages (see חֲמִשָּׁה דְּבָרִים) that a person may be obligated to pay another as compensation for injury done to him. The compensation for not working is not calculated solely according to the previous salary of the injured party, but also takes into account the fact that the injured party may no longer be able to do difficult work, even after his recovery.

שַׁבָּת
The Sabbath. The seventh day of the week, a day of holiness, rest, and the prohibition of labor. Both positive and negative commandments apply to the Sabbath. Some of these

commandments are written in the Torah, whereas others were ordained by the Sages. In addition to the positive commandment to rest (שְׁבִיתָה) on the Sabbath, the Torah also commands us to sanctify the day. However, unlike the Festivals and other holy days, the sanctity of the Sabbath does not depend in any way upon its being proclaimed by a court or by a private individual. One is commanded to sanctify the Sabbath day by reciting verses and benedictions that recall its sanctity. In addition to mentioning the Sabbath in prayer (see קְדוּשַּׁת הַיּוֹם) one also recites a blessing (see קִידּוּשׁ הַיּוֹם) over wine or bread on the Sabbath Eve, and an additional benediction the following day (קִידּוּשָׁא רַבָּא). According to the Sages (and this is already mentioned by the Prophets) one is commanded to honor the Sabbath day by wearing fine clothes and to make the day a pleasant one by eating special food (three festive meals, שָׁלֹשׁ סְעוּדוֹת) and by enjoying the other physical pleasures permitted on that day. To honor the Sabbath and to add to its pleasure, the Sages ordained the lighting of Sabbath candles and, to honor it further, the ceremony of havdalah (הַבְדָּלָה) after the close of the Sabbath. The Torah forbids us to perform any kind of labor on the Sabbath, according to a special definition of labor for this purpose (see מְלָאכָה), and it is also forbidden to make an animal work on the Sabbath. It is forbidden to go a long distance away from the place where one is staying on the Sabbath (see תְּחוּם שַׁבָּת). In the opinion of most authorities, this is at least partly a Torah prohibition. The Sages added many other prohibitions to keep people from performing forbidden labor on the Sabbath, and most of these are included under the general category of שְׁבוּת — "rest." The Sages forbade doing incomplete work as well as certain acts that cause the performance of forbidden labor. They also prohibited commerce (this, too, is mentioned by the Prophets), efforts to improve one's health (though not treatment of real illness), the playing of musical instruments, and other actions on the Sabbath. They extended the prohibition against the removal of objects from one domain to another on the Sabbath (see רְשֻׁיּוֹת הַשַּׁבָּת) by adding another category of domain, the כַּרְמְלִית, and by forbidding the transfer of an object from one person's private domain to that of another (though this may be made possible by the construction of a Sabbath boundary; see עֵירוּב חֲצֵירוֹת; שִׁיתּוּפֵי מְבוֹאוֹת). They also forbade moving certain objects not needed for the Sabbath (see מוּקְצֶה). The Sages and the Prophets forbade discussion on the Sabbath of things that involved planning for weekdays, and they also forbade asking a non-Jew to perform work for a Jew on the Sabbath. These and other matters are included in the category of weekday activities, and they are forbidden on the Sabbath. During the Temple period, a special additional sacrifice (מוּסָף) was brought on the Sabbath. After the destruction of the Temple, the Sages ordained in place of the sacrifice an additional Sabbath prayer with the same name. Similarly, there is an ancient decree (attributed to Moses) according to which the Torah is read publicly every Sabbath (see קְרִיאַת הַתּוֹרָה).

שָׂדֶה אֲחוּזָה   *An ancestral field.* A field that a person inherits from his ancestors within his family holdings in Eretz Israel. When the Israelites entered and conquered Eretz Israel it was divided up among the tribes and among households within the tribes. Ancestral land cannot be sold forever, but only until the

Jubilee Year (יוֹבֵל), at a price that takes into consideration the number of years remaining from the date of sale until the Jubilee. If the seller of the field obtains some money in the interim, he may buy back his field after two years have passed. If someone consecrates an ancestral field, he may redeem it at a set price (עֶרֶךְ) that takes into account the number of years remaining until the Jubilee. If one has not redeemed one's field, and the Temple treasurers have sold it to someone else, it does not revert to its owner in the Jubilee Year, but to the priests who are on duty when the Jubilee Year begins (Leviticus 27:16–21).

שָׂדֶה מִקְנָה   Lit., *an acquired field.* In contrast to a שָׂדֶה אֲחוּזָה — an ancestral field — a שָׂדֶה מִקְנָה is a field that is not one's ancestral heritage, but was acquired from someone else. Such a field must be returned to its original owner in the Jubilee Year (יוֹבֵל). If it is consecrated, it reverts to its original owner in the Jubilee Year (see Leviticus 27:22–24).

שֶׁהֶחֱיָנוּ   See זְמַן.

שׁוֹאֵל   *A borrower.* A person who receives something from its owner with permission to use it without having to pay for its use. One of the four categories of bailee (שׁוֹמֵר). Since the borrower enjoys the full benefit of the use of the article, the Torah holds him responsible for it, and he must make restitution if it is lost, stolen or destroyed, even as the result of developments beyond his control (see Exodus 22:13–14). There are two exceptions to this rule: (1) When the article was destroyed during normal use by the borrower. (2) When the lender was employed by the borrower at the time the article was borrowed (see שְׁאִילָה בִּבְעָלִים).

שׁוֹבֵר   *A receipt for repayment of a debt or fulfillment of some other obligation.* There is a difference of opinion among the Sages as to whether a lender who has lost the original promissory note can collect his debt and give a receipt, or whether he must return the original promissory note so that the borrower can destroy it. Nevertheless, when the original obligation was not recorded in a written contract, but was a legal obligation imposed by a court (such as a marriage contract [כְּתוּבָּה] in those communities where the כְּתוּבָּה is not written down), all authorities agree that a receipt is sufficient.

שׁוֹגֵג   *An unintentional sinner.* A person who commits a transgression without criminal intent, because of lack of information. An unintentional sinner does not incur the same punishments as one who purposely commits a transgression (מֵזִיד), but he does bear a certain responsibility for what he has done, and he must atone for his transgression by bringing a sacrifice or by another means of atonement. Most cases of שׁוֹגֵג fall into two categories: either the sinner is ignorant of a detail of the law, e.g., he forgot that it is forbidden to light a fire on the Sabbath, or he lacks a crucial piece of factual information, e.g., he was confused as to the day of the week. Regarding a person who was so lacking in Jewish education that he knew nothing of the Sabbath at all, there is a dispute in the Talmud. The Halakhah is that he is considered a שׁוֹגֵג, albeit with a reduced atonement requirement. One is not liable to bring a sacrifice for an unintentional transgression unless the act remains un–

intentional during the entire time it is being committed. If one becomes aware of one's error while committing the transgression, one may no longer bring the sacrifice of an unintentional sinner (see אָשָׁם; אָשָׁם תָּלוּי; חַטָּאת). The term שׁוֹגֵג is defined somewhat differently in connection with the exile (see גָּלוּת) of someone who unintentionally kills a human being. The unintentional sinner is only absolved from criminal responsibility for his action, but he must pay for damages caused by himself or by his property, even if he had no intention of causing damage.

שׁוּדָא דְּדַיָּנֵי   *The discretion of the court.* In certain cases, neither litigant can prove ownership of a disputed object. Then the case is left to the discretion of the court, to the adjudication of the judges, without evidence. Their decision may be based on their subjective impressions, according to their view of what is the just decision, without reference to the claims of the litigants.

שׁוֹטֶה   *An imbecile.* A person so intellectually and emotionally unstable that he is not responsible for his actions. There are three classes of people who are not responsible for their behavior: חֵרֵשׁ — a deaf-mute; שׁוֹטֶה — an imbecile; and קָטָן — a minor. Of the three, a שׁוֹטֶה is considered the most severely incapacitated. He has no religious obligations and no act that he performs has legal validity. The Sages discussed the legal definition of a שׁוֹטֶה. They defined several levels of imbecility or madness, and the extent to which a שׁוֹטֶה is considered criminally responsible for his actions.

שׂוֹכֵר   *A hirer.* A person who pays a fee for the use of an item. The Torah (Exodus 22:14) mentions a hirer, but does not set out his responsibility if the rented article is lost or stolen. The Sages debated whether his responsibilities resemble those of a paid bailee (שׁוֹמֵר שָׂכָר) or an unpaid one (שׁוֹמֵר חִנָּם). In practice, the Halakhah rules that he has the obligations of a paid bailee.

שׁוֹלֵחַ יָד בְּפִיקָדוֹן   *One who wrongfully makes use of, misappropriates, a deposit.* A person who steals something that has been left in his safekeeping. Such a person is a thief in every respect, and he bears full responsibility for his deed from the moment he misappropriates the object, even if he has not transferred it to another domain. The absence of the physical transfer of the object is the major distinction between this kind of theft and others.

שׁוּמָא   *Appraisal of an article's worth.* When property is sold to repay a debt, its worth must be appraised by a Rabbinical Court or by experts. There is a difference of opinion in the Talmud as to whether, after the property has been evaluated, the owner may pay his debt through other means and retain the property, or whether the debtor has already lost possession of the property by the act of appraisal. The Halakhah is that not only may he retain the property, but he may even regain it at any future time if he has the means to buy it back at the originally appraised value.

שׁוֹמֵר   There are two meanings of this term: (1) *A bailee.* A person who has received an item from its owner, and has also accepted the obligation to look after it. There are four categories of bailee: the unpaid bailee (שׁוֹמֵר חִנָּם); the paid bailee (שׁוֹמֵר שָׂכָר); the hirer (שׂוֹכֵר); and the borrower (שׁוֹאֵל). (2) *The protective part of a plant.* With regard to the laws of ritual impurity, a shell, stem, or part of a fruit that is not itself eaten, but is left on the fruit because it protects it and keeps it from becoming spoiled. The שׁוֹמֵר is considered part of the fruit. Thus, if it comes into contact with anything that is ritually impure, the entire fruit becomes ritually impure. The שׁוֹמֵר is also included when determining whether a fruit is of the minimum size required to contract ritual impurity.

שׁוֹמֵר חִנָּם   *An unpaid bailee.* One of the four categories of bailee (שׁוֹמֵר; see also Exodus 22:6–8). A person who accepts an article for safekeeping without remuneration and without permission to use it for his own benefit. An unpaid bailee is not required to recompense the owner of the article if it is lost or stolen from him, or taken away by forces beyond his control. He is only liable if he is criminally negligent or if he takes the article for himself (see שׁוֹלֵחַ יָד בְּפִיקָדוֹן).

שׁוֹמֵר שָׂכָר   *A paid bailee.* One of the four categories of bailee (שׁוֹמֵר; see also Exodus 22:9–12). A person who accepts an article for safekeeping for a fee. In addition to the responsibilities imposed on an unpaid bailee (שׁוֹמֵר חִנָּם), a paid bailee must reimburse the owner of the article if it is lost or stolen. But he is free of liability if the article is taken by robbers or damaged by forces beyond his control.

שׁוֹמֶרֶת יָבָם   Lit., *a woman who waits for her brother-in-law.* A widow whose husband died childless and who is not permitted to marry another man until one of her husband's surviving brothers either marries her (see יִבּוּם) or absolves her of this obligation through the חֲלִיצָה ceremony. See זִיקָה.

שׁוֹמֶרֶת יוֹם כְּנֶגֶד יוֹם   Lit., *a woman who watches a day as against a day.* A woman is only considered to be a זָבָה if she has vaginal bleeding on three consecutive days not during her menstrual period. Nevertheless, as soon as she has even one discharge, she becomes ritually impure and may not engage in sexual relations. According to the letter of the law, she need wait until only one day has passed (יוֹם כְּנֶגֶד יוֹם) without any discharge of blood before she immerses herself in a ritual bath (מִקְוֶה) to regain ritual purity. Today it is customary for women to follow all the laws pertaining to a זָבָה whenever they have even a slight discharge of uterine blood, and they count seven clean days (שִׁבְעָה נְקִיִּים).

שׁוֹפָר   *A trumpet made from the horn of an animal.* The שׁוֹפָר is sounded on Rosh HaShanah (Leviticus 23:24). It is also used to proclaim the Jubilee Year (יוֹבֵל) (Leviticus 25:9), and for other ritual purposes. Only an animal horn that is naturally hollow (such as that of a ram,

a goat, or an antelope) may be used for this purpose. A solid horn and the horn of a cow are unacceptable. In the Temple it was customary to use the horn of a mountain goat. The term שׁוֹפָר is also used to refer to the horn-shaped containers in which donations for the Temple were placed. See תְּקִיעָה and תְּקִיעוֹת בַּמִּקְדָּשׁ.

שׁוֹפָרוֹת One of the three special blessings added during the additional service (מוּסָף) on Rosh HaShanah (רֹאשׁ הַשָּׁנָה). See זִכְרוֹנוֹת; מַלְכוּיוֹת.

שׁוֹר Ox. One of the primary categories of damage (אָבוֹת נְזִיקִין). There is a difference of opinion in the Talmud as to the definition of שׁוֹר. Some authorities maintain that it corresponds to קֶרֶן — "horn" — and refers to malicious damage caused by an animal. Others maintain that שׁוֹר corresponds to רֶגֶל — "foot" — and refers to unintentional damage done by a domesticated animal while behaving normally.

שׁוֹר הַנִּסְקָל Lit., an ox that is stoned. An ox that has killed a person must be stoned to death, regardless of whether the ox had previously behaved maliciously (see מוּעָד; תָּם) or whether the victim was an adult, a child, or a Canaanite slave (עֶבֶד כְּנַעֲנִי). It is forbidden to derive any benefit from an ox that has been stoned, not only after it has been killed, but from the moment the court, a tribunal of twenty-three members, has delivered its verdict. The term שׁוֹר הַנִּסְקָל is used for any domesticated or undomesticated animal (see חַיָּה; בְּהֵמָה) that has killed someone, whether the animal be large or small, or even a bird.

שׁוּרָה Lit., a line. A term used to describe one of the customs of mourning (אֲבֵילוּת). After the funeral, the mourners (or, depending on local custom, those who pay condolences), stand in a line outside the cemetery and the people pass by to comfort them. In addition to the mourners, at least ten people must participate.

שׁוֹשְׁבִין Friend, best man. An attendant to the bride or groom, who helps arrange the wedding feast. He would also give presents to the couple. Being the best man was considered a great honor. When the שׁוֹשְׁבִין himself got married, the groom was obligated to reciprocate and serve in this capacity for him. Today, this practice is no longer followed. However, the term שׁוֹשְׁבִין is used to refer to the people who lead the bride and groom to the wedding canopy (חוּפָּה).

שְׁחוּטֵי חוּץ Sacrifices duly consecrated but slaughtered outside the Temple. This is a severe transgression and is punishable by כָּרֵת — excision — if violated intentionally. It is forbidden to derive benefit (הֲנָאָה) from the slaughtered animal.

שְׁחִיטָה Ritual slaughter. The method by means of which permitted (kosher) animals and birds are killed so that they may be eaten. שְׁחִיטָה involves cutting the animal's throat with a finely sharpened knife that has no notches. The knife is passed over the animal's throat without pressing down or inserting it under the skin or flesh (see הַגְרָמָה; חַלָּדָה; עִיקּוּר). The slaughterer moves the knife back and forth until most of the windpipe and the esophagus are severed (with a fowl, it is only necessary to sever one of the two). Any flaw in the process of slaughter or in the knife invalidates the slaughter and renders the animal forbidden for consumption (see נְבֵלָה). Ritual slaughter is only acceptable if performed by a Jew. It may not be performed by a non-Jew or a machine or an animal. According to the Torah, any person who is responsible for his actions may slaughter an animal. Even a

person who is not responsible for his actions (see חֵרֵשׁ שׁוֹטֶה וְקָטָן) may perform שְׁחִיטָה if he is supervised by someone responsible. In present-day practice, ritual slaughter is only entrusted to men who are thoroughly familiar with its laws. A blessing is recited before the slaughter of an animal. However, the slaughter is valid even if the blessing is not recited. The blood of birds or undomesticated animals (see חַיָּה) that are slaughtered must be covered (see כִּיסּוּי הַדָּם).

שְׁחִיטָה שֶׁאֵינָהּ רְאוּיָה Lit., ineffectual slaughter. An act of ritual slaughter that is technically faultless, but does not permit the animal to be eaten for some other reason, e.g., if the animal was טְרֵפָה. There is a dispute among the Sages as to whether such an act of שְׁחִיטָה is considered valid for the purposes of prohibiting the ritual slaughter of the mother or the offspring of the animal on the same day (see אוֹתוֹ וְאֶת בְּנוֹ), or whether it is equivalent to killing the animal in some other way.

שְׁחִין Inflammation. A term used to describe a symptom of leprosy (צָרַעַת). שְׁחִין refers to skin inflammations resulting from any cause other than fire. The Torah describes symptoms of leprosy that become manifest in such inflammations, and these are treated differently from symptoms of leprosy in otherwise healthy tissue (Leviticus 13:18–23).

שְׁטָר Any document of legal significance, in particular a promissory note. Included in the category of שְׁטָרוֹת are certain documents that themselves effect a legal change, such as bills of divorce (see גֵּט), deeds of marriage (שְׁטָר קִידּוּשִׁין, not to be confused with כְּתוּבָּה) and certain bills of sale, primarily of real estate, which themselves effect a transfer regardless of any question of payment. Another form of שְׁטָר is שְׁטָר רְאָיָה, an evidential שְׁטָר which serves as conclusive proof that a legal transaction has taken place. Included in this category are promissory notes of various kinds, court decisions, documentary proof that certain ceremonies have been performed (e.g., שְׁטָר חֲלִיצָה), and others. In many ways, documents signed by witnesses are more effective than verbal testimony since they are considered to have given the transaction publicity. Thus a loan supported by a properly witnessed promissory note establishes a lien on the debtor's property, while the same loan supported only by witnesses does not. In Jewish law, documents are not signed by both parties. Rather, they must be signed either by the party obligating himself, or by witnesses who sign at his behest, and then formally delivered to the other party. Normally, documents are signed by the contractor, or the witnesses, on the same side of the page as the text of the agreement, immediately below it (שְׁטָר פָּשׁוּט). There also exists a "bound document" (שְׁטָר מְקוּשָּׁר [גֵּט]), which is folded in several places and sewn together, with the signatures appearing on the outside of the document, over the folds.

שְׁטַר אֲמָנָה Lit., a document of trust. An illegal document, attesting to a loan that has not taken place. The borrower plans to borrow the money later on, and writes the promissory note in advance, for reasons of convenience, trusting the lender not to produce the document for collection unless and until he actually lends the money. שְׁטַר אֲמָנָה is by its nature false testimony and hence illegal. The Sages forbade the use of such documents lest the lender's heirs or creditors discover them and present them for collection.

שְׁטַר הַקְנָאָה Lit., *deed of transfer*. In Aramaic a שְׁטַר הַקְנָאָה is referred to as שְׁטַר אַקְנְיָיתָא. A loan contract in which the borrower includes mention of an act of acquisition (יקִנְיַן סוּדָר) in the language of the note. Such a note transfers the right of collection, and establishes a lien on the borrower's property from the time the note is signed, even though the loan has not yet been given.

שְׁטָר מְאוּחָר A *postdated promissory note*. The date of a document containing an obligation by one party to another is significant, because any property that the borrower owns on that date is subject to a lien to cover the debt. Unlike a predated document (שְׁטָר מוּקְדָּם), a postdated one is not disqualified by the Sages, provided that the lender was willing to accept it. Postdating a document presents no opportunity for defrauding other creditors.

שְׁטָר מוּקְדָּם A *predated promissory note*. In contrast to a שְׁטָר מְאוּחָר — a postdated note — the Sages nullified a predated promissory note because it offered the possibility of fraud. In the case of a loan, a lien exists on the borrower's property from the date on which the loan contract is signed. If a borrower sold property before a loan was actually made, but after the date appearing on the promissory note, the property, which was actually free of all liens at the time of the sale, would now appear to be mortgaged to the lender. Hence, the borrower could conspire to declare bankruptcy, allowing the lender to demand the property from its purchaser. For this reason, a predated promissory note does not establish a lien, even from the true date of the loan. It can, however, serve as proof of the loan for the purpose of collecting it from the borrower himself.

שְׁיָירֵי הַלִּשְׁכָּה *Money remaining in the Temple treasury*. Each year, every adult Jewish male was obligated to donate a half shekel (מַחֲצִית הַשֶּׁקֶל) to the Temple. These funds were used to purchase communal sacrifices and provide for certain other needs in the Temple (see תְּרוּמַת הַלִּשְׁכָּה). The money left over, called שְׁיָירֵי הַלִּשְׁכָּה, was used for building and maintaining communal structures in Jerusalem, and for purchasing sacrifices to be offered when no other sacrifices were being offered (see קֵיץ הַמִּזְבֵּחַ).

שְׁיָירֵי מִצְוָה Lit., *the remaining parts of a commandment*. Something not indispensable to the performance of a commandment. In the context of the laws of sacrifices there are many procedures prescribed by the Torah that do not invalidate the entire ceremony if they are omitted (see שְׁיָרַיִם). From here the term שְׁיָירֵי מִצְוָה was borrowed for any part of a commandment whose omission does not invalidate the fulfillment of the commandment. The Sages warned against ignoring such procedures, and urged people to be as scrupulous as possible in performing them.

שִׁילּוּחַ הַקֵּן Lit., *the release of a nest*. There is a positive Torah commandment (Deuteronomy 22:6–7) that if a person finds a bird's nest with the mother sitting on the eggs or the fledglings, he must set the mother free before taking the eggs or the chicks. The Sages explained that this commandment applies only to kosher birds.

שִׁימּוּשׁ בְּבַעֲלֵי חַיִּים *Use of animals*. Animals may not be used on the Sabbath for any kind of work. Among the reasons for the institution of this prohibition are: (1) The commandment to let animals rest on the Sabbath (see Exodus 20:10). (2) The possibility that if one used animals on the Sabbath, one might be led to perform forbidden labors.

שִׁינּוּי Lit., *a change*. (1) With regard to the Sabbath, שִׁינּוּי means performing an action in an unusual and awkward way. Frequently, a person who does some forbidden labor on the Sabbath in an unusual fashion is not liable for punishment, and in certain cases one is even permitted to carry out an action in a different way so as to avoid violating the Torah. See כְּלְאַחַר יָד. (2) With regard to the acquisition of property. One of the ways of manifesting ownership (see חֲזָקָה) of landed property (מְקַרְקְעֵי) is to make a permanent change in the property. This act may serve as a sign of the transfer of ownership of the property. (3) In the case of theft, although a thief is obligated to return a stolen article, if he makes a change in it he is only liable for the return of its value, not the article itself. See שִׁינּוּי הַחוֹזֵר לִבְרִיָּיתוֹ.

שִׁינּוּי הַחוֹזֵר לִבְרִיָּיתוֹ *A change that reverts to its original state*. If a stolen article can easily be changed back to its original state, the change made by the thief has no Halakhic significance. For example, superficial adornments that can easily be removed are not considered a "change," and a thief must return such "changed" stolen goods. See שִׁינּוּי.

שִׁינּוּי שֵׁם Lit., *change of name*. A thief who irreversibly changes a stolen article is only liable for the reimbursement of its value and may keep the article. שִׁינּוּי שֵׁם refers to a change in an object's status, even without a significant change in its physical appearance, e.g., a calf that becomes a cow.

שִׁיעְבּוּד *A lien on a person's property*. When a person takes a loan or accepts a financial obligation, and this loan or obligation is formally recorded in a document (שְׁטָר), all his landed property is regarded as security to cover that obligation. Should he be unable to meet his obligation, his creditor may seize his property in lieu of payment. Furthermore, even if the property has been sold, the creditor may seize it from the purchasers (see טִירְפָּא; נְכָסִים שֶׁיֵּשׁ לָהֶם אַחֲרָיוּת).

שֵׂיעַר פְּקוּדָה Lit., *remaining hair*. A white hair that appears in a leprous spot is a clear sign of leprosy (יצָרַעַת) and obviates the need for quarantine (see מְצוֹרָע מוּחְלָט; מְצוֹרָע מוּסְגָּר). A white hair that grew before the leprous spot appeared is of no significance. A white hair remaining from a previous attack of leprosy is itself unimportant. However, if a new spot appears around it, there is a dispute among the Sages whether to treat it like a white hair growing out of a leprous spot or like a white hair that was present before the spot appeared.

שִׁיקוּל הַדַּעַת Lit., *the weighing of opinions*. If judges have made an error in their decision, in some cases the decision is reversed, and in other cases it stands. If the court erred through ignorance of the Halakhah, the case is retried, but if it erred in its judgment (in its שִׁיקוּל הַדַּעַת), for example, by deciding in a disputed area of the Halakhah against commonly held opinion, the judgment stands. In certain cases, the judges must compensate the claimant who was hurt by their erroneous decision.

שִׁיָרַיִם Lit., *what remains*. Blood of a sacrifice remaining after the ceremony of the sprinkling of blood (זְרִיקָה) on the altar. Generally, the remaining blood was poured out on the base of the altar (יְסוֹד הַמִּזְבֵּחַ). Though pouring this blood was a mitzvah, failure to do so did not invalidate the sacrifice.

שִׁיתּוּפֵי מְבוֹאוֹת Lit. *the merging of alleys*. A means of allowing people to carry in an alleyway on the Sabbath (see עֵירוּב חֲצֵירוֹת). The Sages ordained that if a number of courtyards open onto a common alleyway, the inhabitants of the houses in the courtyards are forbidden to carry within the alleyway. However, there are Halakhic methods whereby they may be permitted to do so. For instance, the inhabitants of each house put food in one place for the duration of the Sabbath. This symbolic act converts the courtyard into one extended household. In addition, a pole (לֶחִי) is placed at the

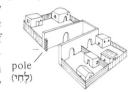

pole (לֶחִי)

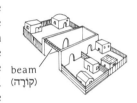

beam (קוֹרָה)

entrance to the alleyway or a beam (קוֹרָה) is placed across it to mark the entrance to the alleyway and to remind people that it is forbidden to carry outside it. See also מָבוֹי.

שִׁיתִין Two drainpipes near the southwest corner of the base *of the outer altar* (מִזְבֵּחַ). Some of the sacrificial blood and most of the wine libations were poured down them. According to some authorities, these pipes extended into the very depths of the earth. Others explain that from these pipes the blood or wine would flow through a drainage channel into the Kidron River.

שִׁכְחָה *Forgotten sheaves*. One of the agricultural gifts to which the poor are entitled (see מַתְּנוֹת עֲנִיִּים). A farmer who has forgotten a sheaf in the field while harvesting his grain may not return to collect it. It must be left instead for the poor (Deuteronomy 24:19). See לֶקֶט; פֵּאָה.

שֶׁלֹּא כְּדַרְכָּה Lit., *in an abnormal way*. Sexual relations carried out in an abnormal manner, i.e., anal intercourse. This form of intercourse is Halakhically equivalent to normal sexual relations in all matters. For example, it is considered intercourse as far as violation of the prohibitions against incest or adultery is concerned, and with regard to levirate marriage (יִבּוּם).

שֶׁלֹּא לִשְׁמוֹ Lit., *not for its name*. A sacrifice that the priest mistakenly declared himself to be offering for a different purpose, during one of the four essential parts of the sacrificial service (see אַרְבַּע עֲבוֹדוֹת). A Paschal lamb (פֶּסַח) and a sin-offering

(חַטָּאת) are invalidated by such false intentions. Other sacrifices are valid, but they do not release their owner from his obligation; hence he must bring another sacrifice.

שָׁלִיחַ לְהוֹלָכָה Lit., *an agent for delivering*. An agent appointed to bring a גֵּט (bill of divorce) from the husband to his wife. This agent is legally the same as the husband. When he gives the גֵּט to the woman, the divorce is effected. The wife can also appoint an agent, called a שָׁלִיחַ לְקַבָּלָה — "an agent for receiving." This agent is legally the same as the wife, and when the גֵּט reaches his hands the divorce takes effect.

שְׁלִיחַ צִיבּוּר Lit., *the agent of the community*. The person who leads a congregation in prayer. He recites certain prayers out loud, in particular the repetition of the Amidah prayer (see שְׁמוֹנֶה עֶשְׂרֵה). In Talmudic times, and similarly in later generations, it was not common to have a fixed שְׁלִיחַ צִיבּוּר. Rather, a leader for each prayer service would be chosen by the congregation. On certain days, such as public fasts (תַּעֲנִית צִיבּוּר), the Sages placed certain conditions on the choice of a prayer leader, among them: that he be righteous, fearful of sin, humble, and beloved by the community. As early as Talmudic times, the Sages criticized the appointment of a cantor whose only virtue was a pleasant voice.

שְׁלִיחוּת *Agency*. The appointment of an agent (שָׁלִיחַ) to perform an act on behalf of the person who appointed him (מְשַׁלֵּחַ). The rule is that the agent of a person is like the person himself (שְׁלוּחוֹ שֶׁל אָדָם כְּמוֹתוֹ). An agent can substitute for his principal in most legal matters. However, an agency to violate commandments of the Torah is legally null and void (see אֵין שָׁלִיחַ לִדְבַר עֲבֵירָה), and any transgressions are the responsibility of the agent. Agency can be effected only with the principal's conscious consent, and the agent must be legally competent (see חֵרֵשׁ שׁוֹטֶה וְקָטָן). An agent can perform all monetary transactions, sacrifices, separation of tithes, betrothal, divorce, and many other things. There is a legal presumption (חֲזָקָה) that an agent performs his assignment as agreed. Thus, when it is impossible to establish the facts, we assume that the mission was fulfilled. An agent cannot fulfill a duty that must be performed by the principal himself. Thus, a שָׁלִיחַ cannot perform חֲלִיצָה on behalf of the יָבָם, nor can a שָׁלִיחַ put on phylacteries (תְּפִילִין) on behalf of someone else.

שָׁלִישׁ *A third party*. A person entrusted with an article or given instructions regarding other people. He may be appointed by a court or by the parties to a transaction to keep certain documents or to serve as an agent to perform some task. The third party must follow the instructions given him and may not act at his own discretion unless explicitly told to do so. The third party guarantees the validity of the documents entrusted to him and the instructions given him.

שְׁלִישִׁי לְטוּמְאָה *The third degree of ritual impurity*. Something that has been made ritually impure by an object of the second degree of ritual impurity (שֵׁנִי לְטוּמְאָה). The rules regarding the third degree of ritual impurity apply only to terumah (תְּרוּמָה) and sacrificial food, but not to nonsacred food (חוּלִין). The third degree of ritual impurity of terumah is called

פָּסוּל ("disqualified"). It is itself ritually impure, but it does not convey ritual impurity to other things except to sacrificial food.

שַׁלְמֵי צִיבּוּר *Peace-offerings of the community.* This term refers to the two lambs that were sacrificed as communal offerings on Shavuot together with the two loaves of bread (*שְׁתֵּי הַלֶּחֶם*) offered at that time (Leviticus 23:19). These lambs are sacrificed in the same manner as the other peace-offerings (*שְׁלָמִים*), except that they are sacrifices of the most sacred order (*קָדְשֵׁי קָדָשִׁים*) and may be eaten only by the priests within the Temple Courtyard on the day they are sacrificed and on the night following.

שְׁלָמִים *Peace-offerings.* Male and female cattle or sheep may be offered for these sacrifices (see Leviticus, chapter 3). They are sacrifices of lesser holiness (*קָדָשִׁים קַלִּים*) and may be sacrificed anywhere within the Temple Courtyard. Their blood is sprinkled on the two opposite corners of the altar in such a manner that it will descend on each of the altar's four sides (see *שְׁתַּיִם שֶׁהֵן אַרְבַּע*). A part of each peace-offering was burned on the altar (see *אֵימוּרִים*), a part was given to the priests (the breast [*חָזֶה*] and the right hind leg [*שׁוֹק*]), and the rest was eaten by the person bringing the sacrifice, with his family, anywhere in the city on the day the animal was sacrificed, on the following day, and during the intervening night. With the exception of the peace-offering brought on Festivals (*חֲגִיגָה*), and a few other cases, the peace-offerings were voluntary gifts (*נְדָבָה*). The word *זֶבַח* — "sacrifice" — used without qualification usually means *שְׁלָמִים* — "a peace-offering."

שָׁלֹשׁ עַל שָׁלֹשׁ *Three fingerbreadths by 3 fingerbreadths.* The minimum size of a woven cloth that can become susceptible to ritual purity.

שָׁלֹשׁ רְגָלִים *The three Pilgrim Festivals.* Pesaḥ, Shavuot, and Sukkot. On these three Festivals Jewish men were obligated to appear in the Temple (Deuteronomy 16:16). All the sacrifices previously pledged to the Temple (see *נְדָבָה; נֶדֶר*) were also brought on these Festivals, so as not to violate the prohibition against delaying sacrifices that one had pledged (see *בַּל תְּאַחֵר*).

שְׁלֹשָׁה מַחֲנוֹת *The three Camps of the Israelites in the wilderness.* They are: the Camp of Israel (*מַחֲנֶה יִשְׂרָאֵל*), and, within it, the Camp of the Levites (*מַחֲנֶה לְוִיָּה*), and, within that, the Camp of the Divine Presence (*מַחֲנֶה שְׁכִינָה*). Certain ritually impure people are only forbidden to enter the Camp of the Divine Presence, others are also barred from the Camp of the Levites, and yet others, such as lepers (see *צָרַעַת*), are banned even from the Camp of Israel. The Temple and its Courtyard (*עֲזָרָה*) correspond to the Camp of the Divine Presence; the Temple Mount corresponds to the Camp of the Levites; and Jerusalem and other walled cities correspond to the Camp of Israel.

שֵׁם; שֵׁמוֹת *Name; names.* The names of God. God's name must be treated with reverence. It may not be uttered in vain or recited in a dirty place or when one is naked. There are seven names of God that may not be erased. Their erasure constitutes the violation of a Torah prohibition (see commentaries to Deuteronomy 12:4). There are many detailed laws governing the writing of these names in a Torah scroll.

שֵׁם לְוַאי *An auxiliary name.* Occasionally the name of a species of animal or plant mentioned in the Torah is differentiated from the name of another species by the addition of an auxiliary name. The second species cannot be used in place of the first for the performance of a mitzvah. For example, the Torah requires that hyssop (*אֵזוֹב*) be used in certain ritual functions. There is a similar plant referred to as *אֵזוֹב כּוֹחֲלִי*, Kohalithian hyssop, which cannot be used where regular hyssop is required.

שֵׁם הַמְפוֹרָשׁ *Lit., the explicit name.* The Divine Name of Four Letters "*י-ה-ו-ה*." This name was never pronounced outside the Temple. Even within the Temple premises, it was only mentioned by the High Priest on Yom Kippur and by common priests while reciting the Priestly Benediction (*בִּרְכַּת כֹּהֲנִים*). Some authorities believe that the *שֵׁם הַמְפוֹרָשׁ* referred to a special appellation with many letters (twelve, forty-two), which was only rarely pronounced.

שֶׁמָּא *Lit., maybe.* An uncertain assertion: "Perhaps it happened this way." Frequently both litigants in a dispute can only make uncertain claims, because they were not present when an act was performed, and in such cases both their claims have equal weight. However, even if one litigant lodges a definite claim (*בָּרִי*) while the other can only make an uncertain claim (*שֶׁמָּא*), the decision is not necessarily made in favor of the definite claim, although it is given greater weight.

שְׁמָד *Apostasy.* A decree issued in times of persecution forcing the Jews to abandon the Torah, in whole or in part. The Sages say that, in the face of such decrees, every Jew is obligated to sacrifice his life rather than transgress even minor commandments or Jewish customs (see *יֵהָרֵג וְאַל יַעֲבוֹר*).

שְׁמוֹנָה בְּגָדִים *The eight garments.* The garments worn by the High Priest (*כֹּהֵן גָּדוֹל*), also referred to as *בִּגְדֵי זָהָב* — "the golden garments." (See Exodus, chapter 28.) Four of them — the breastplate (*חוֹשֶׁן*), the ephod (*אֵפוֹד*), the robe (*מְעִיל*), and the forehead plate (*צִיץ*) — were unique to the High Priest. Four other garments — the trousers (*מִכְנָסַיִם*), the tunic (*כֻּתוֹנֶת*), the sash (*אַבְנֵט*), and the miter (*מִצְנֶפֶת*) — resembled those worn by common priests (*כֹּהֵן הֶדְיוֹט*). There was a debate among the Sages whether the sash worn by the High Priest was identical to that worn by the common priests. It appears that the miters differed, at least in the way they were worn.

שְׁמוֹנָה עָשָׂר דָּבָר *Lit., eighteen matters.* Eighteen ancient rulings delivered at the end of the Second Temple period. Many concern ritual impurity. All the rulings tend to severity, showing the influence of Bet Shammai. The authority of these rulings is unalterable.

שְׁמוֹנֶה עֶשְׂרֵה *Lit., eighteen [blessings].* The Amidah (lit., "standing") prayer, which occupies a central place in all prayer services. The name derives from eighteen blessings originally included in this prayer. After the destruction of the Second

Temple, a nineteenth blessing was added. This prayer must be recited silently, while standing with one's feet together. According to most authorities, women are also obligated to recite this prayer. During congregational prayer (see מִנְיָן), in all but the evening service (עַרְבִית), after the congregation has recited the שְׁמוֹנֶה עֶשְׂרֵה silently, the שְׁלִיחַ צִיבּוּר (prayer leader) repeats the prayer aloud.

שְׁמוֹנָה שְׁרָצִים   *Eight creeping animals.* These are eight creeping animals (small mammals and lizards) whose carcasses convey ritual impurity upon contact (Leviticus 11:29-30). These are the only carcasses of creeping animals that impart ritual impurity upon contact. (See, however, טוּמְאַת נְבֵלָה.) The Rabbis have extensively debated the identification of these eight creatures. The popularly accepted (but doubtful) identifications are: חֹלֶד — weasel; עַכְבָּר — mouse, צָב — toad; אֲנָקָה — hedgehog; כֹּחַ — chameleon; לְטָאָה — lizard; חֹמֶט — snail; תִּנְשֶׁמֶת — mole.

שִׂמְחַת בֵּית הַשּׁוֹאֵבָה   *The celebration of drawing water from the spring.* The festivity that accompanied the drawing of water for the water libation on the Sukkot Festival. This celebration was held at night in the women's courtyard (עֶזְרַת נָשִׁים) on all the intermediate nights of the Festival except the Sabbath. All the different musical instruments in the Temple were played, and the pious and the Sages would sing, dance and celebrate before the people. Large torches were placed on high pillars to illuminate the area. A special wooden balcony was constructed for the women. The ground area was reserved for the men.

שִׂמְחַת תּוֹרָה   See שְׁמִינִי עֲצֶרֶת.

שְׁמִיטָה   See שְׁבִיעִית.

שְׁמִיטַת כְּסָפִים   See שְׁבִיעִית.

שְׁמִינִי עֲצֶרֶת   *The eighth day of assembly.* The eighth day after the beginning of the Sukkot Festival. It follows the seven days of Sukkot (see Leviticus 23:34-36). Though שְׁמִינִי עֲצֶרֶת follows Sukkot, it has certain independent aspects. The two commandments associated with Sukkot, dwelling in the sukkah and waving the lulav and etrog, are not observed on this day. In Temple times, special sacrifices were offered on שְׁמִינִי עֲצֶרֶת; today special prayers and blessings are recited. The annual cycle of the Torah reading is completed on שְׁמִינִי עֲצֶרֶת in Eretz Israel and on the second day of the Festival (שִׂמְחַת תּוֹרָה) in the Diaspora. This is an occasion for special celebration, including bearing the Torah scrolls around the synagogue and dancing with them.

שֶׁמֶן הַמִּשְׁחָה   *The oil used for anointing.* The specially prepared spiced oil used for the anointing of the sacred utensils in the Sanctuary and the Temple, the anointing of the High Priests, and of kings (Exodus 30:23-33). It is forbidden to reproduce this oil or to use it for other purposes. The violation of this prohibition is punishable by כָּרֵת — excision.

שֶׁמֶן שְׂרֵיפָה   *Oil that must be burned.* Terumah (תְּרוּמָה)

from oil that has become ritually impure must be destroyed by burning. Nevertheless, the priests are allowed to derive benefit (הֲנָאָה) from the oil while it is burning (e.g., for light). This oil is not burned on Sabbaths or Festivals.

שַׁמְתָּא   *A severe ban of excommunication.* After a person has been condemned to ostracism (נִידוּי) and has still not changed his behavior, he may be placed under this more severe ban (see also חֵרֶם).

שֵׁן   Lit., *tooth.* One of the primary categories of damage (אָבוֹת נְזִיקִין). It is caused by an animal when acting for its own satisfaction. The most common example of damage under the heading of שֵׁן occurs when an animal grazes in another person's field. This category also includes such incidents as an animal rubbing its back against a wall and damaging it. שֵׁן damage is assumed to be predictable, and the owner is therefore expected to control his animal, and must pay in full for any damage it causes. The owner is liable for שֵׁן damage attributable to his animal in another person's private domain. But he is not liable for such damage if it is caused in the public domain (רְשׁוּת הָרַבִּים), where all are permitted to move freely.

שֵׁנִי לְטוּמְאָה   *The second degree of ritual impurity.* Something that has become ritually impure by contact with an object of the first degree of ritual impurity (רִאשׁוֹן לְטוּמְאָה). Ritually impure food of the second degree is called פָּסוּל — "disqualified." It can confer the third degree of ritual impurity (שְׁלִישִׁי לְטוּמְאָה) to terumah (תְּרוּמָה) and sacrificial food. Any liquids that come in contact with something of the second degree of ritual impurity themselves become ritually impure in the first degree. The Sages decreed that certain things, such as holy books and unwashed hands in general, are in the second degree of ritual impurity.

שְׁנֵי סְדָרִים   Lit., *two orders.* The לֶחֶם הַפָּנִים (shewbread) was arranged on the sacred table in the Temple (שׁוּלְחָן הַפָּנִים) in two piles, each containing six loaves, on shelves placed one upon the other. Two bowls of frankincense were also placed on the table. According to some authorities, one bowl was placed on top of each group of loaves. Other authorities maintain that both bowls were placed between the two groups. See בָּזִיכִין.

שְׁנִיּוֹת   *Secondary relationships.* Relationships forbidden as incestuous by Rabbinic decree. The Torah (Leviticus, chapters 18 and 20) lists many incestuous relationships (עֲרָיוֹת). The Sages expanded this list to include one's maternal and paternal grandmother; the mother of one's maternal and paternal grandfather; the wife of one's maternal and paternal grandfather (even though she is not one's grandmother); the wives of one's father's maternal brothers (his paternal brother's wives are forbidden by Torah law); the wives of one's maternal uncles; one's son's or daughter's daughter-in-law; one's great-granddaughters; one's wife's great-granddaughters from previous marriages; and one's wife's maternal and paternal greatgrandmothers. These prohibited relationships are also referred to as אִיסוּר מִצְוָה in the context of the laws of levirate marriage (יִבּוּם). A man who marries a woman related to him in one of these ways is obligated to divorce her and need not pay her marriage settlement (כְּתוּבָה). Violation of these prohibitions is punished by יַמַכַּת מַרְדּוּת — lashes given for the transgression of a Rabbinic decree. Should one of these women become obligated to perform יִבּוּם — levirate marriage — she must be released from the obligation through the יחֲלִיצָה ceremony.

שַׁעַטְנֵז   *A mixture of wool and linen.* (Leviticus 19:19; Deuteronomy 22:11). It is forbidden to wear a garment in which these two materials have been spun, woven, or sewn together. Certain other combinations are forbidden by Rabbinic decree. According to Torah law it is forbidden to wear שַׁעַטְנֵז. However, one may create, sell, or benefit from such garments. The Sages also prohibited lying on mattresses containing שַׁעַטְנֵז. See אַבְנֵט.

שָׂעִיר הַמִּשְׁתַּלֵּחַ   *The goat sent away.* The Torah requires that on Yom Kippur lots be drawn for two goats, one to be sacrificed as a sin-offering in the Temple (see שָׂעִיר יוֹם הַכִּיפּוּרִים), and one to be sent to Azazel (שָׂעִיר הַמִּשְׁתַּלֵּחַ; see Leviticus, chapter 16). This goat was thrown from a high desert cliff some 12 to 15 kilometers from Jerusalem. Before sending the goat to its death, the High Priest would burden it with all the sins of the Jewish people, their intentional and inadvertent violations. Afterwards, he would send the goat to the desert with a person specifically designated for this task. The service associated with this goat, an essential part of the Yom Kippur ritual, atoned for sins not atoned for by any other sacrifice.

שָׂעִיר יוֹם הַכִּיפּוּרִים   *The goat offered on Yom Kippur.* The Torah (Leviticus, chapter 16) requires that on Yom Kippur lots be drawn for two goats, one to be sacrificed as a sin-offering in the Temple (שָׂעִיר יוֹם הַכִּיפּוּרִים); and one to be sent to Azazel (see שָׂעִיר הַמִּשְׁתַּלֵּחַ). The goat sacrificed as a sin-offering is slaughtered in the northern section of the Temple Courtyard. Afterwards, the High Priest takes its blood into the Holy of Holies (יקֹדֶשׁ הַקֳּדָשִׁים) and sprinkles it between the staves (יבֵּין הַבַּדִּים) of the holy ark (אֲרוֹן הַבְּרִית). Upon leaving the Holy of Holies, he sprinkles its blood on the curtain (יפָּרוֹכֶת) separating the Holy of Holies from the Sanctuary (יהֵיכָל). Afterwards, he mixes the goat's blood with that of the bull sacrificed previously (see פַּר יוֹם הַכִּיפּוּרִים) and sprinkles that mixture on the golden altar (ימִזְבַּח הַזָּהָב). All these acts are necessary for the sacrifice to be valid. The remaining blood is poured at the western base of the outer altar (see יְסוֹד הַמִּזְבֵּחַ). The meat and the hide of this goat are burned in a special place outside Jerusalem (see בֵּית הַדֶּשֶׁן).

שָׂעִיר נָשִׂיא   Lit., *the prince's goat.* If a King of Israel sins in a manner requiring a sin-offering (יחַטָּאת) he does not bring a female goat or lamb, like an ordinary person, but rather a young male goat. In all other respects, this sacrifice follows a procedure identical to that of the regular sin-offering.

שָׂעִיר רֹאשׁ חֹדֶשׁ   *The goat offered on the first day of the month* (Rosh Ḥodesh). The Torah (Numbers 28:15) requires a goat to be sacrificed as a sin-offering on יראֹשׁ חֹדֶשׁ (the New Moon) as a communal sin-offering (see חַטֹּאות הַצִּיבּוּר). Its sacrifice followed the same procedure as that used for sin-offerings of a private individual and it was intended to atone for certain transgressions involving ritual impurity in the Temple service (יטוּמְאַת מִקְדָּשׁ וְקָדָשָׁיו).

שְׂעִירֵי הָרְגָלִים   Lit., *the goats of the Festivals.* The Torah (Numbers, chapter 28) requires a goat to be sacrificed on every day of each Festival, including Rosh Ḥodesh (יראֹשׁ חֹדֶשׁ, see שָׂעִיר רֹאשׁ חֹדֶשׁ). These sacrifices were communal sin-offerings (יחַטָּאות הַצִּיבּוּר). Their sacrifice followed the same procedure as the sin-offerings of a private individual, and they were intended to atone for transgressions involving ritual impurity in the Temple service (יטוּמְאַת מִקְדָּשׁ וְקָדָשָׁיו).

שְׂעִירִים הַנִּשְׂרָפִים   Lit., *goats that are burned.* Goats that are brought by the community (each tribe) for the inadvertent transgression of the prohibition against idol worship (see Numbers 15:22–26). This sacrifice resembles the יפַּר הֶעְלֵם דָּבָר in all its particulars. However, because of the severity of the sin of idol worship, a bull must be brought as a burnt-offering (יעוֹלָה) and a goat as a sin-offering (יחַטָּאת).

שַׁעַר נִיקָנוֹר   *The Gate of Nicanor.* The eastern entrance to the Temple Courtyard (יעֲזָרָה; see plan of the Temple, p. 277). It differed from the other gates in the Second Temple in that it was made of bronze. Healed lepers used to stand at the gate, and it was there that their thumbs were anointed with oil when they were purified.

שִׁפְחָה חֲרוּפָה   *A designated maidservant.* A woman who is half slave and half free and who is betrothed to a Hebrew slave (יעֶבֶד עִבְרִי). Since the woman is not entirely free, her marriage bonds are not complete. Hence, if a man has sexual relations with her, it is not considered as a normal case of adultery. The woman is given lashes and the man is required to bring a guilt-offering (יאָשָׁם). The sacrifice must be brought whether or not the man knew the woman's status at the time he had relations with her. See Leviticus 19:20–22. See also שׁוֹגֵג.

שְׁפִיכָה   Lit., *pouring.* Unlike most sacrifices, the blood of the firstborn offering (יבְּכוֹר), the tithe offering (ימַעְשַׂר בְּהֵמָה), and the Paschal sacrifice (יפֶּסַח) is not sprinkled on the altar. It is poured on the base of the altar (ייְסוֹד הַמִּזְבֵּחַ). The blood that remains from other sacrifices after sprinkling (see שְׁיָרִים) is also poured there. The term שְׁפִיכָה is also used to refer to the pouring of the blood of disqualified sacrifices into the drainage channel in the Temple.

שְׁפִיכוּת דָּמִים   *Bloodshed.* A synonym for murder. A Jew must sacrifice his life rather than commit murder (see יֵהָרֵג וְאַל יַעֲבוֹר).

שְׁקִיעָה, שְׁקִיעַת הַחַמָּה   *Sunset.* The point at which the entire solar disc drops below the horizon. From sunset until the emergence of the stars (יצֵאת הַכּוֹכָבִים) is a doubtful period called יבֵּין הַשְּׁמָשׁוֹת — "twilight." At some point during this period the day ends and the next day begins. The entire period is considered doubtful, and various restrictions are applied to it. Thus for certain purposes sunset is treated as the end of the day, whereas for others צֵאת הַכּוֹכָבִים signifies the end of the day.

שְׁקָלִים   See מַחֲצִית הַשֶּׁקֶל.

שְׂרֵיפָה   *Burning.* (1) In particular this term is used to refer to one of the four forms of capital punishment (אַרְבַּע מִיתוֹת בֵּית דִּין•). The condemned criminal was executed by pouring molten lead down his throat. The crimes punished in this manner were sexual intercourse with both a woman and her mother or grandmother, and adultery committed by the daughter of a priest (בַּת כֹּהֵן•). The adulterer was executed by strangulation (חֶנֶק•). (2) See נִשְׂרָפִין•.

שֶׁרֶץ   Lit., *a creeping animal*. Generally, rodents, lizards, insects or any other small creature that crawls. Ritual impurity is imparted by the carcasses of eight different creeping animals (Leviticus 11:29–37; see שְׁמוֹנָה שְׁרָצִים•). The Talmud often refers to these eight creatures by the term שֶׁרֶץ, without any further description. The Sages stated that the smallest of these eight animals was from birth at least the size of a lentil's bulk (כַּעֲדָשָׁה•). Hence, to contract ritual impurity one must touch a piece no smaller than that size of the carcass of a creeping animal. Moreover, one is liable to lashes (מַלְקוֹת•) for eating a lentil's bulk of such an animal.

שֶׁרֶץ הָעוֹף   *Flying insects*. The Torah (Leviticus 11:20–23) prohibits the eating of all flying insects with the exception of certain species of grasshoppers that can be identified by the following signs: (1) They must have six feet, two of which are extended (called כְּרָעַיִם) and used for hopping. (2) They must have wings that cover the majority of their bodies. (3) They must belong to the species known as חָגָב. Despite the prohibition against eating flying insects, it is permitted to eat honey, since it is not a true secretion of the bee and not part of its body.

שְׁתוּיֵי יַיִן   *Intoxicated with wine*. It is forbidden to enter the Temple Courtyard while drunk, and violation of this prohibition by a priest is a capital offence, though the sentence is meted out by divine retribution (מִיתָה בִּידֵי שָׁמַיִם•) and not by an earthly court. Anyone who drinks a רְבִיעִית• of wine is included in this category. If a priest serves in the Temple while drunk, his service is disqualified.

שְׁתוּקִי   *A child whose mother's identity is known but whose father's identity is not*. With regard to the laws of marriage a שְׁתוּקִי is considered as a possible מַמְזֵר•. See עֲשָׂרָה יוֹחָסִין•; אֲסוּפִי•.

שְׁתוּת   *A sixth*. The Sages ordained that the profit taken by an individual on basic necessities may not exceed this proportion. Similarly, any transaction in which an article is sold for a sixth more than its value is considered fraud (אוֹנָאָה•), and the difference must be returned. The usual reckoning of a שְׁתוּת is in relation to the total amount involved. In other words, twenty percent more than the real value.

שְׁתֵּי הַלֶּחֶם   *The two loaves*. Two loaves brought as a communal offering on the Festival of Shavuot (Leviticus 2:17). In contrast to most of the other meal-offerings (מְנָחוֹת•), these loaves are of leaven. Their shape resembles that of the shewbread (לֶחֶם הַפָּנִים•) which, however, was unleavened. Two lambs were brought as peace-offerings (שְׁלָמִים•) together with these two loaves (שַׁלְמֵי צִיבּוּר•). Both the loaves and the lambs are ceremonially waved. Afterwards, they are divided up among the priests and eaten in the Temple Courtyard (עֲזָרָה•).

שְׁתֵּי שְׂעָרוֹת   *Two pubic hairs*. When girls reach twelve and boys thirteen, and these pubic hairs appear, the Halakhah considers them adults. Both conditions are necessary.

שְׁתַּיִם שֶׁהֵן אַרְבַּע   Lit., *two that constitute four*. The manner in which the blood of burnt-offerings (עוֹלָה•), guilt-offerings (אָשָׁם•), and peace-offerings (שְׁלָמִים•) is presented on the altar. The blood is sprinkled on the two opposite corners of the altar so that it will run down on each of the four sides. The blood is sprinkled on the northeastern and southwestern corners of the altar.

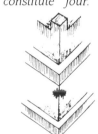

תִּגְלַחַת   *Shaving*. In the following instances, the Torah requires shaving one's head or one's entire body as part of a process of purification and the assumption of a different status: (1) A Nazirite (נָזִיר see נְזִירוּת•) who completes his Nazirite vow (see Numbers 6:18–19). Upon the termination of the period of his vow, a Nazirite shaves his head. This was carried out in a special chamber within the women's courtyard in the Temple (see עֶזְרַת נָשִׁים•). Afterwards, the Nazirite's hair was placed in the fire over which his peace-offering was cooked (see אֵיל נָזִיר•). (2) A Nazirite who has become ritually impure because of contact with a dead body must shave his head on the day he purifies himself. On the following day, he brings the required sacrifices and begins his Nazirite vow anew (see Numbers 6:9). (3) The process of ritual purification (see טָהֳרַת מְצוֹרָע• after צָרַעַת• (leprosy) involves shaving all the hairy portions of one's body including the beard, the armpits, the pubic area and the eyebrows. Afterwards, the healed leper must wait seven days and shave his body again. Then he brings the required sacrifices (see Leviticus 14:8–9). (4) As part of the initiation of the Levites into the service in the Sanctuary in the wilderness, God commanded them to shave their entire bodies (Numbers 8:7).

תָּדִיר   Lit., *frequently, regularly*. A frequent, recurring factor. A mitzvah that occurs more frequently takes precedence over another that occurs less frequently. For example, in the Sabbath kiddush (see קִידוּשׁ הַיוֹם), the blessing over the wine is recited before the blessing for the Sabbath day. Similarly, if a person can afford to perform one out of two mitzvot and must choose between them, תָּדִיר is often a consideration.

תּוֹדָה   *The thanks-offering*. A type of peace-offering (שְׁלָמִים*) brought by a person in appreciation of God's beneficence (see Leviticus 7:12–15). In particular, the following persons are required to bring a תּוֹדָה offering: (1) A person who completed a journey at sea. (2) A person who crossed a desert. (3) A person who was freed from prison. (4) A sick person who recovered from his illness. This sacrifice is of lesser holiness (see קֳדָשִׁים קַלִּים), and resembles a peace-offering. But it may only be eaten on the day on which it was offered and the following night, in contrast to the peace-offering, which may be eaten on the subsequent day as well. In addition to the animal תּוֹדָה sacrifice, forty loaves of bread are brought as a meal-offering. Ten are leavened and thirty are equally divided into three types of unleavened bread: רְבוּכָה and חַלּוֹת, רְקִיקִים. The priest is given four loaves, one from each category. Because of the meal-offering of leavened bread, the thanks-offering may not be brought from Passover Eve until the conclusion of that Festival.

תּוֹךְ כְּדֵי דִיבּוּר   Lit., *within [the time needed for] speaking*. A Halakhic unit of time. The amount of time it takes for someone to say "שָׁלוֹם עָלֶיךָ רַבִּי" — "Greetings to you, my teacher." In almost every area of the Halakhah, תּוֹךְ כְּדֵי דִיבּוּר is regarded as a continuation of the act of speaking, and a person can retract what he first said if he makes the retraction within this short period of time after he has finished speaking. There are certain exceptions to this rule: cursing God (מְגַדֵּף*) or idol worship (עֲבוֹדָה זָרָה*), and certain dedications (see הֶקְדֵּשׁ).

תּוֹכָחָה   *Rebuke, reprimand*. There is a positive Torah commandment (Leviticus 19:17) to admonish a fellow-Jew for behaving improperly. If a person sees his fellow performing a reprehensible act, he must reprimand him for his deed again and again. Several conditions are attached to the act of reprimanding: One should avoid publicly embarrassing the wrongdoer, one must only reprimand someone who will accept the reprimand, and one must not reprimand someone who has vehemently expressed unwillingness to be reprimanded. The Sages disagree over the extent to which one should continue to rebuke such a person. If someone is able to reprimand a wrongdoer and does not do so, he is to some extent considered an accessory to the misdeed.

תּוֹלָדָה, תּוֹלָדוֹת   Lit., *offspring*. Something secondary or derived from something fundamental. Something that is not a primary source but derives from such a source, either as a legal inference or as a factual derivative. (1) In ritual matters, תּוֹלָדוֹת are prohibitions not explicitly mentioned in the Torah. For example, prohibitions derived from the main categories of work (אֲבוֹת מְלָאכוֹת*) forbidden on the Sabbath; prohibitions derived from the main prohibition against taking oaths (see שְׁבוּעָה); and the subsidiary categories derived from the main categories of damage (אֲבוֹת נְזִיקִין*). In certain cases the rules governing these תּוֹלָדוֹת are the same as those governing the main categories, and the only difference between an אָב and a תּוֹלָדָה is in the way they are listed. In other cases, the derived prohibitions are less severe than the principal ones. (2) A factual consequence of a physical act. An object that has become ritually impure by contact with a primary source of ritual impurity (see אֲבוֹת הַטּוּמְאוֹת) is called an offspring of impurity (יְלַד הַטּוּמְאָה*). With regard to the Sabbath laws, something that is not hot in itself but has been heated by a fire or the sun is called the תּוֹלָדָה of the fire or of the sun. There is sometimes a Halakhic difference between a primary source and a derivative.

תּוֹרֶף   *The essential part of a document* (שְׁטָר*). The תּוֹרֶף contains a summary of the transaction recorded in the document: its main conditions, the date, and the names of the parties involved. The rest of the document is known as the טוֹפֶס*, and it contains the standard formulae appropriate to the document.

תְּחוּם עוֹלֵי בָּבֶל   *The territorial limits of Eretz Israel as established by those who returned from the Babylonian exile*. The area settled by the Jews returning from Babylon was considerably smaller than the area of Eretz Israel originally conquered by the Children of Israel (see Numbers 34:1–13). This difference is Halakhically significant. The Babylonian conquest nullified the sanctity of Eretz Israel and the agricultural obligations connected with its produce. When the Jews returned after the exile, this sanctity and the accompanying obligations were renewed. However, they applied only to those portions of Eretz Israel in which those who returned settled. Nevertheless, certain observances were also required in those areas included in the original boundaries but which were not part of the later settlement; e.g., the prohibition against working the land in the Sabbatical Year (שְׁבִיעִית*). The limits of Eretz Israel are also significant with regard to the laws of ritual purity (see אֶרֶץ הָעַמִּים).

תְּחוּם שַׁבָּת   Lit., *the Sabbath limit*. A concept used in laws regarding movement on the Sabbath, essentially the distance that a person is permitted to walk on the Sabbath. The תְּחוּם שַׁבָּת for each person is the area where he is living on the Sabbath. If this is in an isolated place, with no fences or partitions, the תְּחוּם שַׁבָּת is defined as 4 cubits square, and if it is a place surrounded by a fence, the תְּחוּם שַׁבָּת is defined as the area within the enclosure. In a city, it includes the entire area of the city. This area, as well as 2,000 cubits in every direction beyond it, is the תְּחוּם שַׁבָּת for those living in the city. Some authorities hold that, in contrast to this concept, which derives from a Rabbinical ordinance, there is also a תְּחוּם שַׁבָּת stipulated by the Torah, which is approximately 12 miles in every direction.

תֵּיבָה   (1) *Word*. With regard to writing a Torah scroll, there are rules governing how many words may be included in a line, whether a word may be written outside a column, etc. (2) *Ark*. The box or cupboard in which Torah scrolls were placed. In Talmudic times the ark was not a fixed structure. Rather, it was brought into the synagogue during the prayer services and then returned to a locked room. On public fast days (יּתַעֲנִית צִיבּוּר), the ark was taken into the street and prayers were recited there. That custom is no longer practiced.

תִּיקּוּן הָעוֹלָם   Lit., *the improvement of the world*. Certain Rabbinic ordinances were instituted to prevent difficulties for people or to prevent strife and conflict. These ordinances are described as having been instituted מִפְּנֵי תִּיקּוּן הָעוֹלָם — "to make the world a better place."

תְּכֵלֶת   *A sky-blue dye*. A special dye produced from a species of snail. In Talmudic times this dye was already quite rare, and the means of preparing it, including the species of snail used, were eventually forgotten. In recent generations efforts have been made to identify the snail and to resume use of the dye. In the Torah (Numbers 15:38) there is a positive commandment to use wool dyed this color for two purposes: (1) In ritual fringes (יּצִיצִית). One of the eight threads of the fringes must be dyed with this special blue dye, and it is wound around the other threads. However, the commandment to wear fringes does not depend on one of the threads being dyed, and today ritual fringes are made without the dyed thread. (2) In the priest's vestments. Some of these, such as the girdle (יּאַבְנֵט), the entire cloak (מְעִיל), the ephod (אֵפוֹד), and the breastplate (חוֹשֶׁן) have parts that consist of wool dyed with תְּכֵלֶת.

תַּלְמִיד   *Disciple*. With regard to the relationship between a disciple and a teacher, see רַב. With regard to the definition of a Torah scholar, see תַּלְמִיד חָכָם.

תַּלְמִיד חָבֵר   Lit., *a student-colleague*. The student of a Sage who has advanced beyond the level of being the Sage's disciple. In certain respects, such as his breadth of knowledge and intellectual power, he is like a colleague of his teacher. A student-colleague is not required to treat his teacher with the same degree of deference as a disciple, and he is to some extent permitted to behave like his teacher's companion.

תַּלְמִיד חָכָם   *A Torah scholar* (lit., "the disciple of a Sage"). A person who has studied the Bible, the Mishnah, and the Gemara and has been the disciple of Torah scholars. A תַּלְמִיד חָכָם is not merely someone who has intellectually mastered the Torah. He must also be punctilious in the performance of the mitzvot, adopting higher standards than those observed by the people at large. One is required to treat a תַּלְמִיד חָכָם with great honor, to rise in his presence, and to give him special consideration in his efforts to earn a living. Many obligations imposed on the community are not imposed on him. In certain matters, he is given even greater respect than the king or the High Priest. In Talmudic times, it was decreed that anyone who acts contemptuously towards a תַּלְמִיד חָכָם must pay a fine of a pound of gold. However, it has been said that in our generation there are no scholars of the stature to warrant such a fine. The Halakhah offers a definition of a תַּלְמִיד חָכָם: he is not identical with a חָכָם, a Rabbi who teaches Torah, but he must be thoroughly versed in at least one tractate of Talmud.

תָּם   Lit., *innocent*. An animal that is not known to cause damage with the intent to injure (see קֶרֶן). The first three times

an animal causes an injury of this nature, its owner is only required to pay half the damage it has caused (יּחֲצִי נֶזֶק). Afterwards it becomes an attested dangerous animal (see מוּעָד), an animal with a history of causing injury. The owner of a מוּעָד animal is required to pay for all the damage it causes. An animal can be considered a תָּם with regard to certain kinds of damage and a מוּעָד with regard to others. For example, an ox that has a history of goring other oxen is still considered תָּם with regard to goring humans. Similarly, if it is established that the animal causes injury only on certain days, for example, on Sabbaths and Festivals, it may be considered a מוּעָד on those days alone and a תָּם during the rest of the week. An animal that is a מוּעָד can regain the status of תָּם if, on three separate occasions, animals that it was accustomed to attacking passed by and it refrained from attacking them. See שׁוֹר הַנִּסְקָל.

תְּמוּרָה   *Exchange, substitution*. The prohibition against substituting another animal for one designated as a sacrifice (Leviticus 27:33). If a person violates this prohibition, both the original animal and the substitute are considered as consecrated. Substitution only applies to animals brought as sacrifices by private individuals and not to those designated as communal sacrifices. Even an animal that has a blemish that renders it unfit for sacrifice can become consecrated if substituted in this manner. The laws governing this subject are discussed in tractate *Temurah*.

תַּמְחוּי   *A large receptacle for food*. In the Halakhah this term refers to a receptacle for donations of food for the poor. Only those poor who were in serious need of food were allowed to take from this pot.

תָּמִיד   Lit., *constantly, daily*. The daily sacrifice of two lambs, one in the morning and one in the afternoon, offered each day in the Temple. (See Numbers 28:1-8.)

תָּמִים, תְּמִימִים   Lit., *perfect*. Animals without blemishes. Only such animals are fit for sacrifice on the Temple altar (see Leviticus 22:19). The term תָּמִים is used in contrast to the term בַּעַל מוּם — "blemished" (see מוּמִים).

תְּנַאי   *Condition*. A condition is the insertion of a certain reservation in an agreement or juridical act, so that the act or agreement has no force unless the condition is fulfilled. Regarding conditional marriages and divorces, the authorities decreed that, before failure to fulfill the condition can cancel the marriage or divorce, it must be a double condition (יּתְנַאי כָּפוּל). This means that, in the formulation of the conditional clause, the negative side (לָאו), stipulating what constitutes an infraction of the condition, must be stated explicitly, and must be stated after the positive side (הֵן). The condition must be a feasible one. If one of these features is lacking, the condition is void. One does not write a condition into the body of the text of a bill of divorce, and if a condition is inserted in this way, it usually invalidates the bill of divorce. Many Sages hold that conditional business contracts are valid even if all the features mentioned above are not present. The validity of a normal conditional agreement only begins when the condition is fulfilled; until the condition is fulfilled, the agreement is invalid. A normal condition is phrased as "if... but if not..." (אִם... וְאִם...). But if the phrase "in order that" (עַל מְנָת שֶׁ...) or the phrase "from this moment" (מֵעַכְשָׁיו...) is used, then the agreement is in force from the moment it is made, and the fulfillment of the condition makes it retroactively effective.

תְּנַאי בֵּית דִּין   Lit., *a condition of the court*. A Halakhic assumption applicable in many areas, regarding acts, agreements, dedications to the Temple, and the like. The Halakhah assumes that these legal acts have been performed in accordance with a condition stipulated by the court. Even if those who wrote the note or consecrated their property did not state the condition explicitly, they are regarded as if they had done so, because the court has passed this regulation. In some cases, these conditions cannot be waived even by explicit stipulation. Conditions of the court were instituted either to promote the general welfare of society or to solve specific social problems. Such conditions are found in almost every area of the Halakhah.

תְּנַאי בְּנֵי גָד וּבְנֵי רְאוּבֵן   Lit., *the condition of the sons of Gad and the sons of Reuven*. A conditional agreement whose form is modelled after the agreement proposed to Moses by the tribes of Gad and Reuven allowing them to take Transjordan as an ancestral heritage. Since this agreement is mentioned in the Torah (Numbers, chapter 32), it is taken as a model for the language to be used in all other conditional agreements. See תְּנַאי כָּפוּל.

תְּנַאי כָּפוּל   Lit., *a double condition*. A form of contractual obligation. A simple condition merely states the positive side of an obligation: If X, then Y. But a double condition (תְּנַאי כָּפוּל) also states the negative side: If not X, then.... Some authorities maintain that the violation of a simple condition, where the negative side of the case is not stated, does not nullify an agreement.

תַּעֲנִית   *A fast day*. The Halakhah includes various kinds of fasts: individual and public, short and long, lenient and strict. The principal feature of a fast is that one does not eat or drink for a certain time. In severe fasts one is also forbidden to wear leather shoes, to wash, and to have sexual intercourse. A short fast begins at dawn (see עַמּוּד הַשַּׁחַר) on the day of the fast and lasts until the stars come out (יְצִיאַת הַכּוֹכָבִים). A long fast begins the previous evening, at sundown (שְׁקִיעַת הַחַמָּה). Generally one does not fast on Shabbat, and if a fast day falls on Shabbat, it is put off until the following day. Yom Kippur is the exception to this rule. It is also observed on Shabbat, if it falls on that day, because, although it is similar to fast days in the prohibition of pleasures, it is also a fixed Torah Festival. There are fast days fixed by the calendar, and there are fast days decreed in times of trouble and distress. If a person wishes to take upon himself the obligation of observing an individual fast, he does so at the time of afternoon prayers (מִנְחָה) on the day before the proposed fast.

תַּעֲנִית חֲלוֹם   *A fast for a dream*. If a person has had a disturbing dream during the night, he may wish to undo its bad effects by fasting that day. A fast for a dream may even be observed on Shabbat and Festivals. However, someone who fasts on those days must observe an additional fast to atone for fasting on the Sabbath. Today fasts for dreams are seldom observed, except for certain kinds of dreams, and even in these cases the fast is not obligatory but depends on the wish of the person who had the dream.

תַּעֲנִית צִיבּוּר   *A communal fast, for the entire Jewish people or for a certain community*. Such a fast is more severe than an individual fast. This is especially the case with regard to great public fasts, such as those that used to be observed because of drought or other impending dangers. These fasts, which are no longer observed, comprised a series of fasts of increasing severity and were proclaimed by the court. On some of them six blessings were added to the Amidah prayer (see שְׁמוֹנֶה עֶשְׂרֵה) and a closing prayer (נְעִילָה) was recited at the end of the day. Today the only severe public fast is that of the Ninth of Av (תִּשְׁעָה בְּאָב). The other public fasts are not so severe. They begin at dawn (see עַמּוּד הַשַּׁחַר) and one does not refrain from work, etc. These fasts are: the Fast of Gedaliah (on the 3rd of Tishri), the Fast of the Tenth of Tevet, the Fast of Esther before Purim, and the Fast of the Seventeenth of Tammuz.

תַּעֲרוֹבֶת   *Mixture*. Something combined with other things in such a way that it is impossible to recognize it or remove it from the mixture. With regard to a forbidden substance mixed with permitted substances, see בִּיטוּל אִיסּוּרִים — "the nullification of prohibitions." In certain mixtures of forbidden things, not only is the prohibition not nullified, but the prohibition is extended to things mixed with it (חֲתִיכָה נַעֲשֵׂית נְבֵלָה). In some cases the mixture (no matter what its proportions) is regarded as unmixed, and all its components are treated as though separate (e.g., in the throwing of the blood of sacrifices that have become mixed). In other cases, such as the mixture of various liquids in the water of a ritual bath (מִקְוֶה), the classification of the mixture depends on its physical appearance.

תַּעֲשֶׂה וְלֹא מִן הֶעָשׂוּי   Lit., *make it, and not from what has already been made*. A principle applicable to many Halakhot. In certain matters, such as building a sukkah (סוּכָּה) or tying ritual fringes (צִיצִית), the Torah orders us to carry out a certain commandment. If the action involved in fulfilling the commandment has already effectively been performed, and all that remains to be done is to remove some Halakhic constraint, the removal of the constraint is not a fulfillment of the commandment, as it is considered to have been performed "from what has already been made." Thus, if a person were to sew a piece of cloth, with a ritual fringe already attached, onto a piece of clothing, the finished item would not be acceptable as צִיצִית.

תַּפּוּחַ   *The pile of ash on the altar left after the burning of the sacrifices*. Each morning, the ash was swept into a large circular pile in the center of the altar in the Temple. When the pile became extremely large, it was deposited in an area outside Jerusalem (see בֵּית הַדֶּשֶׁן). See also diagram of the altar, p. 276.

תְּפִילָה   Lit., *prayer*. (1) As a general concept this refers to the regular prayers instituted by the men of the Great Assembly (אַנְשֵׁי כְּנֶסֶת הַגְּדוֹלָה) and the Sages who followed them. There are three regular prayer services every day: Morning prayers (שַׁחֲרִית), in the morning hours, until four hours of day have passed (corresponding to the morning יַתְּמִיד — the daily morning sacrifice); afternoon prayers (מִנְחָה; corresponding to the afternoon תְּמִיד); and evening prayers (עַרְבִית). On days when an additional sacrifice (יַמוּסָף) was offered in the Temple (the Sabbath, Festivals, the New Moon, the intermediate days of Festivals), there is an additional (מוּסָף) prayer. On Yom Kippur there is yet another additional closing prayer, יַנְעִילָה. All these prayers include the Amidah prayer (see שְׁמוֹנֶה עֶשְׂרֵה), to which other elements, such as the *Shema* in the mornings and the evenings, and various other prayers, have been added. (2) In a more restricted sense the term תְּפִילָה refers specifically to the Amidah prayer (שְׁמוֹנֶה עֶשְׂרֵה).

תְּפִילִין   *Tefillin, phylacteries.*

There is a Torah commandment that men tie tefillin on their arm and head each day. The תְּפִילִין of the arm and of the head are considered as separate mitzvot, independent of each other. Each תְּפִילָה consists of a cube-shaped leather box containing parchment on which are written four passages from the Torah: (1) שְׁמַע — Deuteronomy 6:4–9; (2) וְהָיָה אִם שָׁמֹעַ — Deuteronomy 11:13–21; (3) קַדֶּשׁ Exodus 13:1–10; (4) וְהָיָה כִּי יְבִאֲךָ — Exodus 13:11–16. In the תְּפִילָה worn on the head, these portions are written on four separate parchments and placed in four separate subcompartments, together forming the cube. In the תְּפִילָה worn on the arm, all four portions are written on the same parchment. There are different opinions (that of Rashi, Rabbenu Tam, etc.) regarding the order in which the portions are written and placed in the containers, and this results in a variety of customs in the wearing of תְּפִילִין today. The תְּפִילִין boxes are each attached to long black leather straps, used to tie them to the head and the arm. The תְּפִילָה of the head is placed in the center of the head at about the beginning of a person's original hairline. The תְּפִילָה of the arm is bound to the area on the muscle above the elbow of the left arm, and is placed facing the heart. A left-handed person places the תְּפִילָה on his right arm. There are varying customs as to how to tie the various knots of the תְּפִילִין and how to wrap the straps around the arm. תְּפִילִין are holy. Therefore, they should not be worn in an unclean place or at a time when a person fears incontinence and cannot maintain his body in a state of cleanliness. In ancient times, תְּפִילִין were worn the entire day. However, nowadays, it is customary to wear them only during the morning service (שַׁחֲרִית). תְּפִילִין are not worn on the Sabbath or on Festivals. There is a difference of opinion among the Halakhic authorities whether they should be worn on the intermediate days of Festivals (יַחוֹל הַמּוֹעֵד). Women and slaves are exempt from the commandment of תְּפִילִין.

תְּקוּפָה   *Season, period.*

The four seasons begin on the following days: The season of Nisan, spring, begins on the spring equinox. The season of Tammuz, summer, begins on the summer solstice. The season of Tishri, autumn, begins on the autumn equinox. The season of Tevet, winter, begins on the winter solstice. Halakhically the autumn equinox is particularly

significant because the Torah commands that it coincide with Sukkot, and it is connected to the daily prayer requesting rain (see שְׁאֵלַת גְּשָׁמִים). In the Diaspora, this prayer is recited from the sixtieth day after the beginning of the תְּקוּפָה of Tishri until Pesaḥ.

תְּקִיעָה   *A shofar blast* (see שׁוֹפָר).

In a general sense this refers to any sound produced by a shofar or by the trumpets (חֲצוֹצְרוֹת) that were used in the Temple. There is a Torah commandment to sound the shofar on Rosh HaShanah, on Yom Kippur in the Jubilee Year (יַיוֹבֵל), as well as on public fast days, and for public sacrifices. The character of the sound produced by the shofar is not defined as needing to be full or thin, so long as it is produced on a kosher shofar. The notes of the shofar have been defined as follows: תְּקִיעָה, a simple, uninterrupted sound; שְׁבָרִים, a broken sound; יַתְּרוּעָה, a series of short blasts, extremely close to each other. Most of the shofar sounds prescribed by the Torah follow a set order: תְּקִיעָה-תְּרוּעָה-תְּקִיעָה. The תְּרוּעָה in the middle may be either a שְׁבָרִים or a תְּרוּעָה, or both together.

תְּקִיעוֹת בַּמִּקְדָּשׁ   *Sounding the shofar or trumpet in the Temple.*

In the Temple, the shofar or trumpet was sounded on different occasions, e.g., when the communal sacrifices were offered, when the gates to the Temple Mount were opened, and to mark the entrance of the Sabbath, twenty-one times in all on an average weekday. However, on Sabbaths and Festivals, that number would rise, reaching as many as forty-eight.

תַּקָּנָה, תַּקָּנוֹת   *Ruling, ordinance.*

These are laws ordained by the Sages to regulate life. Such ordinances came into being to regulate the observance of many commandments and, in particular, civil matters. Some ancient regulations are attributed to Moses (such as the public reading of the Torah and others), to Joshua (regarding the settlement of the Land of Israel and the public and private use of it), to Ezra the Scribe (the convening of courts of law, laws of modesty, and so on. Other ordinances were established by Rabbinic scholars in various communities (such as the ordinances of Speyer, Worms, and Mainz [שו"מ] regarding marriage contracts), enacted by the Committee of the Four Lands, and the like, or established in recent generations. In certain contexts, תַּקָּנוֹת are to be distinguished from יַגְּזֵרוֹת — "decrees" — established by the Rabbis as extensions of Torah laws.

תַּקָּנוֹת אוּשָׁא   *The Rabbinic ordinances instituted in Usha.*

After the destruction of the Second Temple, the seat of the Sanhedrin, Israel's highest court, changed several times. At one point, it was located in the town of Usha. At that time, many significant Rabbinic ordinances were instituted, among them the obligation to support one's children until they reach maturity, and the prohibition against giving more than a fifth of one's property to charity.

תַּקָּנַת הַשָּׁבִים   *A measure instituted for the penitent.*

According to Torah law, a robber is obligated to return any stolen article in his possession, if he has not changed its form. If he stole a beam and implanted it in a building, he would, according to the letter of the law, have to destroy the building and return the beam. Nevertheless, in order to encourage repentance, the Sages were lenient and only required the robber to return the value of the stolen article. The Sages instituted other, similar measures to encourage repentance.

תִּקְרוֹבֶת עֲבוֹדָה זָרָה   *An idolatrous offering.* It is prohibited to derive any benefit (הֲנָאָה) from an animal or article offered for an idolatrous purpose, and it must be destroyed.

תְּרוּמָה, תְּרוּמָה גְדוֹלָה   *Terumah, the great terumah.* Whenever the term תְּרוּמָה appears without qualification, it refers to this offering, תְּרוּמָה גְדוֹלָה. Deuteronomy 18:4 commands that "the first fruit of your corn, of your wine, and of your oil" be given to the priest (see also Numbers 18:12). The Sages extended the scope of this commandment to include all produce. This mitzvah only applies in Eretz Israel. After the בִּיכּוּרִים° — the first fruits — have been set aside, a certain portion of the produce must be set aside for priests. The Torah does not specify the amount of terumah that must be set aside; one may theoretically fulfill one's obligation by giving even a single kernel of grain from an entire crop. The Sages established a measure: one-fortieth for a generous gift, one-fiftieth for an average gift, and one-sixtieth for a miserly gift. A person should not set aside the other tithes (see מַעַשְׂרוֹת°) until he has set aside תְּרוּמָה. תְּרוּמָה is considered holy and may only be eaten by a priest and his household while they are in a state of ritual purity (see Leviticus 22:9–15). To emphasize that state of ritual purity, the Sages obligated the priests to wash their hands before partaking of it. This is the source for the practice of נְטִילַת יָדַיִם°. A ritually impure priest or a non-priest who eats תְּרוּמָה is subject to the penalty of death at the hand of Heaven (מִיתָה בִּידֵי שָׁמַיִם°). If תְּרוּמָה contracts ritual impurity, it may no longer be eaten and must be burned. Nevertheless, it remains the property of the priest and he may benefit from its being burned (see שֶׁמֶן שְׂרֵיפָה). Nowadays, תְּרוּמָה is not given to the priests because they have no definite proof of their priestly lineage. Nevertheless, the obligation to separate

תְּרוּמָה still remains; but only a small portion of the produce is separated.

תְּרוּמַת הַדֶּשֶׁן   *The removal of ashes from the altar.* It is a positive commandment to remove some of the ash from the altar each morning and bring it to the floor of the Courtyard (see Leviticus 6:14). This was the first of the daily services performed in the Temple. In addition, from time to time, when the ashes accumulated, they would be removed from the Temple to a place set aside outside Jerusalem called בֵּית הַדֶּשֶׁן°.

תְּרוּמַת הַלִּשְׁכָּה   Lit., *lifting up [the money stored in] the chamber.* The half-shekels (see מַחֲצִית הַשֶּׁקֶל) donated by the entire people each year were kept in a specific chamber (לִשְׁכָּה) in the Temple complex. Three times a year, a priest would enter this chamber with three containers and lift up (תּוֹרֵם) the money and place it in the containers. The money was used to purchase animals for communal sacrifices and other needs of the Temple. For the use made of the remaining money, see שְׁיָירֵי הַלִּשְׁכָּה.

תְּרוּמַת מַעֲשֵׂר   *The terumah of the tithe.* The Levites are commanded to separate a certain portion of the tithe given to them and to donate it to the priests (Numbers 18:26–32). All the laws applying to תְּרוּמָה° also apply to תְּרוּמַת מַעֲשֵׂר. Even today, תְּרוּמַת מַעֲשֵׂר must be separated from produce, though it is in a state of ritual impurity and cannot therefore be used.

תְּרוּעָה   *Teruah, one of the sounds of the shofar.* A shofar is sounded in a series of calls — תְּקִיעָה-תְּרוּעָה-תְּקִיעָה°. There are differing opinions among the Sages as to the definition of the term תְּרוּעָה. Some defined it as a series of staccato blasts. Others define it as longer blasts, similar to a person's moaning in a broken voice (שְׁבָרִים). A third opinion considers it to be a combination of both of the previous two. To satisfy all these opinions, the shofar is sounded on Rosh HaShanah in three series, each reflecting one of these opinions.

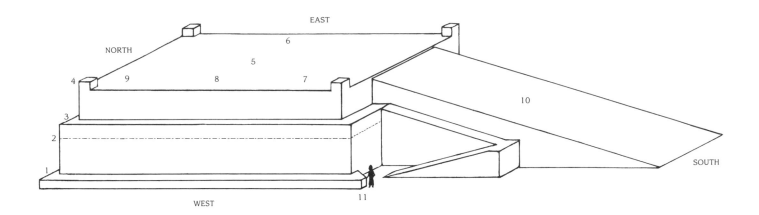

1   יְסוֹד הַמִּזְבֵּחַ* – The base of the altar

2   חוּט הַסִּיקְרָא* – The red line

3   סוֹבֵב* – The surrounding ledge

4   קַרְנוֹת הַמִּזְבֵּחַ* – The altar's horns

5   תַּפּוּחַ* – The pile of ash

6   מַעֲרָכָה גְדוֹלָה* – The large arrangement of wood

7   מַעֲרֶכֶת הַקְּטוֹרֶת – The arrangement for the incense

8   מַעֲרָכָה לְיוֹם הַכִּפּוּרִים – The arrangement for Yom Kippur

9   אֵשׁ תָּמִיד – The perpetual fire

10   כֶּבֶשׁ* – The ramp

11   שִׁיתִּין* – The drain pipes

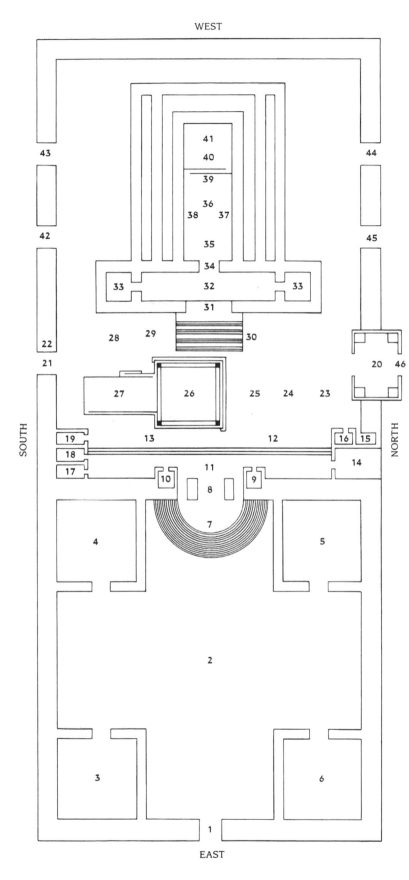

WEST

WEST

SOUTH

NORTH

EAST

1 שַׁעַר עֶזְרַת נָשִׁים – Gate to the women's courtyard

2 *עֶזְרַת נָשִׁים – Women's courtyard

3 לִשְׁכַּת הַנְּזִירִים – Chamber of Nazirites

4 לִשְׁכַּת הַשְּׁמָנִים – Chamber of Oils

5 לִשְׁכַּת הַמְּצוֹרָעִים – Chamber of Lepers

6 לִשְׁכַּת הָעֵצִים – Chamber of Wood

7 מַעֲלוֹת לָעֲזָרָה – Stairs leading to the Israelites' courtyard

8 *שַׁעַר נִיקָנוֹר – Gate of Nicanor

9 לִשְׁכַּת פִּנְחָס הַמַּלְבִּישׁ – Chamber of Pineḥas, Keeper of Vestments

10 לִשְׁכַּת *חֲבִיתִּין – Havitin Chamber

11 *עֶזְרַת יִשְׂרָאֵל – Israelites' courtyard

12 *דּוּכָן – Platform

13 *עֶזְרַת כֹּהֲנִים – Priests' courtyard

14 *לִשְׁכַּת הַגָּזִית – Chamber of Hewn Stone

15 לִשְׁכַּת פַּרְהֶדְרִין – Chamber of the Parhedrin

16 לִשְׁכַּת הַגּוֹלָה – Golah Chamber

17 לִשְׁכַּת הַמֶּלַח – Salt Chamber

18 לִשְׁכַּת הַפַּרְוָה – Parvah Chamber

19 לִשְׁכַּת הַמַּדִּיחִין – Rinsing Chamber

20 *בֵּית הַמּוֹקֵד – Chamber of the Hearth

21 שַׁעַר הַמַּיִם – Water Gate

22 לִשְׁכַּת בֵּית אַבְטִינָס – Chamber of the House of Avtinas

23 *נַנָּסִים – Small columns

24 שֻׁלְחָנוֹת שֶׁל בֵּית הַמִּטְבָּחַיִם – Tables of the slaughterhouse

25 *טַבָּעוֹת – Rings to secure the sacrificial animals for slaughter

26 *מִזְבֵּחַ – Altar

27 *כֶּבֶשׁ – Ramp

28 *כִּיּוֹר – Basin

29 *בֵּין הָאוּלָם וְלַמִּזְבֵּחַ – Between the entrance hall and the altar

30 מַעֲלוֹת בֵּין הָאוּלָם וְלַמִּזְבֵּחַ – Steps leading to the entrance hall

31 פֶּתַח הָאוּלָם – Gateway to the entrance hall

32 *אוּלָם – Entrance hall

33 *בֵּית הַחֲלִיפוֹת – Chamber of Knives

34 *שַׁעַר הַהֵיכָל – Gate of the Sanctuary

35 *הֵיכָל – Sanctuary

36 *מִזְבַּח הַזָּהָב – Golden (incense) altar

37 שֻׁלְחָן – Table

38 *מְנוֹרָה – Candelabrum

39 פָּרוֹכֶת (יאמה טְרַקְסִין) – Curtain

40 *קֹדֶשׁ הַקֳּדָשִׁים – Holy of Holies

41 *אֲרוֹן הַבְּרִית – Ark of the Covenant

42 שַׁעַר הַבְּכוֹרוֹת – Gate of Firstlings

43 שַׁעַר הַדֶּלֶק – Gate of Kindling

44 שַׁעַר הַנִּיצוֹץ – Gate of the Flame

45 שַׁעַר הַקָּרְבָּן – Offering Gate

46 שַׁעַר בֵּית הַמּוֹקֵד – Gate of the Chamber of the Hearth

Talmudic Weights and Measures

An analysis of the weights and measures used in ancient times poses complicated problems. It is not always easy to determine the mutual relationships between the units of weights and measures within any given system, and it is particularly difficult to ascertain their modern-day equivalents. Matters arc further complicated by the fact that units of measurement from different parts of the world were often used simultaneously. Indeed, these problems affected almost all measurement systems until modern times, when the various units of weights and measures were almost universally standardized.

All these problems and many others are encountered in connection with the weights and measures mentioned in the Talmud. These units do not derive from a single historical period. Indeed, their development extends from Biblical times through the entire Talmudic period. Moreover, the values of the different units of measurement changed frequently even during the Talmudic period itself. At various times the rulers of both Eretz Israel and Babylonia introduced their own currencies and their own units of measurement, and different standards of measurement were used simultaneously in different parts of each country. Clearly, therefore, it is difficult to formulate a consistent system of Talmudic weights and measures.

Further difficulties arise when we attempt to determine the relationship between the ancient units of measurement and their modern-day equivalents. It is true that archeological finds and historical literary sources provide us with much helpful material, but they still do not give us sufficient information to ascertain the exact modern equivalents of the weights and measures mentioned in Rabbinic literature and the other sources. Nor is the Halakhic tradition helpful in resolving these problems, since different Halakhic rulings were followed in different places.

Two main viewpoints have been proposed by contemporary Halakhic authorities regarding the value of the basic units of length in the Talmud.

These differ from each other by about 20%, and thus lead to very substantial differences with regard to units of area and volume. In practice both opinions are followed today, the general tendency being to adopt whichever view is stricter, at least in questions of Torah law.

Apart from the standard units of measurement, which have fixed mutual relationships, there are also a great many units of measurement of Biblical origin found in Rabbinic literature. These quantities and measurements are sometimes related to the standard units of measurement, but they are frequently based on measurements taken from objects in nature or from utensils in use at the time.

These quantities and measurements are very numerous (their full extent in every category comes to several hundred individual units of measurement), and regarding many of them we can make only approximate estimates.

In the tables that follow, the basic units of measurement are presented (in descending order), together with some of the most important quantities and measurements used in the Talmud and in Rabbinic literature.

Units of Time   **יוֹבֵל**   *Jubilee.* (1) A period of fifty years (according to some opinions, forty-nine years; see below), the longest unit of time mentioned in the Talmud. (2) The fiftieth year of the fifty-year cycle. The first of these fifty-year cycles began in the fifteenth year after the conquest of the land of Israel in Joshua's time. The year that concludes each Jubilee period is called the יוֹבֵל or שְׁנַת הַיּוֹבֵל (Jubilee Year), and the laws of this special year are laid down in the Torah (Leviticus 25:9 ff.). Observance of the Jubilee Year ceased before the end of the First Temple period, even though the system of counting the fifty-year cycle may still have been kept up. There is a controversy among the Tannaim as to whether the Jubilee Year was reckoned as the first year of the new Sabbatical cycle (in which case, the Jubilee period would last only forty-nine years), or whether the fiftieth year that followed the seventh Sabbatical cycle was a special additional year (in which case the Jubilee period would be fifty years). (See next entry.)

שְׁמִיטָה (also שָׁבוּעַ)   *The seven-year period concluded by the* שְׁנַת הַשְּׁמִיטָה *or* שְׁבִיעִית — *the Sabbatical Year.* Note that the term שָׁבוּעַ, which means "week" in modern Hebrew, in the Talmud usually means "the seven-year period ending with the Sabbatical Year."

שָׁנָה   *Year.* The years mentioned in the Talmud are lunar years, each consisting of twelve lunar months. Generally, there are 354 days in a lunar year, although occasionally the year may be one day longer or shorter. In the Mishnaic period, the variations may have been slightly more pronounced. A regular lunar year was called a שָׁנָה פְּשׁוּטָה — "an ordinary year" — to differentiate it from a leap year — שָׁנָה מְעוּבֶּרֶת. See next entry.

שָׁנָה מְעוּבֶּרֶת   *A leap year, consisting of thirteen lunar months.* There are 384 days in a leap year (plus or minus one day).

שְׁנַת חַמָּה   *A solar year* (sometimes also called שָׁנָה תְּמִימָה — "a full year"), consisting of 365 or, in some contexts, 365 1/4 days.

תְּקוּפָה   Lit., *turn, circuit.* This term can be used in two ways: (1) "Turn" of the sun; thus: תְּקוּפַת נִיסָן — the vernal equinox; תְּקוּפַת תַּמּוּז — the summer solstice; תְּקוּפַת תִּשְׁרֵי — the fall equinox; תְּקוּפַת טֵבֵת — the winter solstice. (2) Sometimes the term תְּקוּפָה refers to a period of a quarter of a solar year, lasting ninety-one days and seven-and-a-half hours (תְּקוּפַת שְׁמוּאֵל) or a little less (תְּקוּפַת רַב אַדָּא).

חוֹדֶשׁ   *Month.* The months in the Talmudic calendar are lunar months, whose length was determined either by actual observation or by astronomical calculation. There are two types of lunar months: חוֹדֶשׁ חָסֵר — a short month, consisting of twenty-nine days;

and חוֹדֶשׁ מָלֵא (also called חוֹדֶשׁ מְעוּבָּר) — a long month, an intercalary month, consisting of thirty days.

שַׁבָּת (also שָׁבוּעַ) (1) *The Sabbath day*. (2) *A week* (particularly, the period from one Shabbat to the next). The term שַׁבָּת (in modern Hebrew, "Shabbat," the Sabbath day) usually means "week" in the Talmud, and the word שָׁבוּעַ (in modern Hebrew, "week") is usually used in the Talmud to describe the seven-year Sabbatical cycle (see שְׁמִיטָה).

יוֹם *Day*. In Hebrew, as in many other languages, this word has two meanings: (1) A unit of time lasting twenty-four hours, and (2) daytime as distinct from nighttime. The Halakhic "day" of twenty-four hours usually begins at nighttime with the appearance of three medium-sized stars (צֵאת הַכּוֹכָבִים); hence, according to the Talmud, the day follows the night rather than the other way round. An exception occurs, however, with regard to the laws of the Temple service. In this case the day is considered to begin in the morning (at dawn or at sunrise), and hence as far as these laws are concerned the night follows the day.

מֵעֵת לְעֵת Lit., *from [one] time to [the next] time. A twenty-four hour period.*

עוֹנָה Lit., *period. A half-day period, either the daytime or the nighttime.*

שָׁעָה *Hour*. This word has two meanings in Rabbinic literature: (1) As a fixed unit of time, an "hour" is defined as one twenty-fourth of a day. This definition is followed with regard to astronomical reckonings and many Halakhic calculations, and corresponds to the modern definition of an "hour." (2) Usually, however, the hours referred to in the Talmud are not fixed in length; these hours, known in more recent Halakhic literature as "relative hours" (שָׁעוֹת זְמַנִיּוֹת), each last one-twelfth of the length of the day, and onetwelfth of the length of the night at any given date, whether the daylight period is long or short. The length of the hour is therefore not constant, but varies from day to day. During the summer the daylight hours are longer and during the winter they are shorter. The twelve daylight hours are measured from sunrise to sunset (according to another opinion, from dawn until the appearance of three medium-sized stars). Thus, three שָׁעוֹת זְמַנִיּוֹת are equal to one-quarter of the length of the day (on the day of the equinox, 6:00–9:00 A.M.), six שָׁעוֹת זְמַנִיּוֹת last from sunrise until noon, etc. It was natural to use these units where time was measured according to the position of the sun (e.g., by a sundial); the times of prayer, *inter alia*, are still fixed according to שָׁעוֹת זְמַנִיּוֹת. Sometimes, however, the expression שָׁעָה in the Talmud does not refer to a fixed time unit, but rather to an unspecified period of time (e.g., שָׁעָה אֲרוּכָּה — "a long time," and שָׁעָה קְצָרָה — "a short time"). The hour is often divided into smaller time units in Rabbinic literature (e.g., half an hour, one-third of an hour). In addition, there are two sets of fixed units into which the hour may be divided: (1) The units used for astronomical calculations, which include the חֵלֶק ("part") = $^1/_{1080}$ of an hour (each חֵלֶק lasts 3 $^1/_3$ seconds), and the רֶגַע ("moment") = $^1/_{76}$ of a חֵלֶק. To this day these units are used to calculate the length of the Hebrew months. (2) The hour can also be divided into 24 "periods" (עוֹנוֹת), each consisting of two-and-a-half minutes; these עוֹנוֹת may in turn be further subdivided into 24 "times" עִתִּים, each consisting of 6 $^1/_4$ seconds, and the עִתִּים may be subdivided into 24 "moments" (רְגָעִים), each lasting approximately one-quarter of a second. Sometimes, however, רֶגַע refers to an undefined, momentary period, rather than to a fixed quantity of time; this usage is found primarily in the context of Aggadic Midrashim. Yet another system of measuring time is found in the Talmud, primarily in astrological contexts (although these measurements occasionally have Halakhic implications as well); these hours are associated with seven celestial bodies: Saturn, Jupiter, Mars, the sun, Venus, Mercury, and the moon (often referred to in the Talmud by their Hebrew acronym: שַׁבְּתַאי, צֶדֶק, מַאֲדִים, חַמָּה, נוֹגַהּ, כּוֹכָב, לְבָנָה — שצ"מ חנכ"ל). The first hour of the day (in the morning) is called "Mercury" (on Sunday), "Jupiter" (on Monday), "Venus" (on Tuesday), "Saturn" (on Wednesday), "Sun" (on Thursday), "Moon" (on Friday), and "Mars" (on Shabbat). This system of measuring time is used to determine the twenty-eight year solar cycle, which always begins on the first Wednesday in the month of Nisan.

Counting the Years. Various systems of counting the years were employed during the Talmudic period, sometimes simultaneously. In Biblical times, and in official documents from later periods as well, events were usually dated from the beginning of the reign of the ruling official, whether Jewish (e.g., a High Priest or king) or gentile. In the Talmud, the writings of the Geonim, and medieval Jewish historical literature, the years were often dated from the beginning of the Seleucid era (312/311 B.C.E. = 3450 years from Creation. In fact, this מִנְיַן הַשְּׁטָרוֹת ("count of the documents"), as it is sometimes called, was used by Yemenite Jews until recently. The Talmud also mentions the practice of dating events from the destruction of the Second Temple. Dating events from Creation, although mentioned in the Talmud, gained acceptance only hundreds of years later.

OTHER MEASUREMENTS CONNECTED TO QUANTITIES OF TIME
The most important of these are:
(1) הִילּוּךְ מִיל   *The time it takes to walk a* מִיל — *2,000 cubits.* Opinions differ as to its length, ranging between 18 and 24 minutes. This unit of time is used in determining whether food has become חָמֵץ (leaven, which is forbidden on Passover), and it also plays a role in connection with certain laws of prayer.

(2) אֲכִילַת פְּרָס   *The amount of time it takes to eat half a loaf of bread* (loaves of bread are assumed to have a fixed size of six eggs in the Halakhah [see בֵּיצָה, p. 287]). The duration of אֲכִילַת פְּרָס is the subject of considerable controversy. Opinions vary between two and nine minutes. This unit of time plays an important role in connection with many laws related to food.

(3) תּוֹךְ כְּדֵי דִיבּוּר   *Speaking time.* The amount of time it takes to say שָׁלוֹם עָלֶיךָ רַבִּי — "Peace unto you, my teacher". According to the Halakhah, certain acts are rendered invalid by an interruption only if the interruption is longer than תּוֹךְ כְּדֵי דִיבּוּר. Moreover, most Halakhically significant statements (blessings, testimony, etc.) may be retracted or altered within this period without penalty.

Units of Length

Serious problems arise in connection with the units of length mentioned in the Talmud. These units are often used inconsistently (see אַמָּה, below). Furthermore, it is necessary to distinguish between two types of measurements: (1) the so-called מִידָה עֲצֵבָה — "sad measurement" — which is slightly less than a full measure, and (2) the מִידָה שׂוֹחֶקֶת — "smiling measurement" — which is slightly more than a full measure. The difference between these two measurements can come to several percent of each unit of length.

אֶצְבַּע (pl. אֶצְבָּעוֹת)   *A fingerbreadth (thumbwidth).* The basic unit of length in the Talmud. Normally this is the smallest measure of length used. As with other measures, it is based on nature: the width of the thumb at its widest point. There is a dispute among contemporary Halakhic authorities concerning the length of the Talmudic fingerbreadth. Opinions range between 1.9 and 2.5 cm. The two most common views are (1) the one known as the "Na'eh" measure — 2 cm. (0.79 in.), and (2) the one known as the "Ḥazon Ish" measure — 2.4 cm. (0.94 in.). These views are named after two great twentieth-century authorities, Rabbi A.H. Na'eh and Rabbi A.I. Karelitz, known as the Ḥazon Ish, who publicized them in their writings. As a result of this difference of opinion, they of course also differ with regard to all the other units of length.

טֶפַח (pl. טְפָחִים)   *A handbreadth*, i.e., the width of a clenched fist. One טֶפַח = four אֶצְבָּעוֹת (fingerbreadths), equivalent to five times the width of the middle finger, or six times the width of the little finger (זֶרֶת). According to the Na'eh measure, it is 8 cm. (3.15 in.) long. According to the Ḥazon Ish measure, it is 9.6 cm. (3.78 in.) long. The טֶפַח is sometimes called טוֹפַח in Biblical Hebrew, and פּוּשְׁכָּא in Aramaic.

אַמָּה (pl. אַמּוֹת)   *A cubit.* A number of different lengths are referred to by this name. The physical origin of the אַמָּה measure is the distance from the elbow to the end of the middle finger (this finger is also called אַמָּה in Hebrew). The common אַמָּה, known as the אַמָּה בֵּינוֹנִית ("standard אַמָּה"), is six טְפָחִים long, 48 cm. (18.9 in.) according to the Na'eh scale, and 57.6 cm. (22.7 in.) according to the Ḥazon Ish scale. However, the Talmud also mentions a "short אַמָּה" (אַמָּה בַּת חֲמִישָּׁה or אַמָּה קְטַנָּה), which is five טְפָחִים long, and in certain rare contexts other אַמּוֹת are used. In addition, there were two other types of אַמּוֹת that were used in the Temple for special measurements, one that was half a fingerbreadth wider than the standard אַמָּה, and the other that was a full fingerbreadth wider.

מִיל   *The Talmudic "mile."* A unit of distance related to (but not identical with) the Roman mile, from which it received its name. One מִיל = 2,000 cubits, 960 m. (1,049 yd.) according to Na'eh, 1,150 m. (1,258 yd.) according to the Ḥazon Ish.

פַּרְסָה   *A parasang* (Persian mile). In the Talmud one parasang = 4 מִיל (see above), 3.84 km. (2.4 mi.) according to Na'eh, 4.6 km. (2.88 mi.) according to the Ḥazon Ish.

These are the standard units of measurement in the Talmud. One does, nevertheless, encounter certain other units in special contexts:

סִיט   *The distance between the index finger and the middle finger, when held as far apart as possible.* The סִיט is generally assumed to be equal in length to one טֶפַח. This unit is used for measuring pieces of fabric.

סִיט כָּפוּל   *Double* sit, i.e., two *sits.* The distance between the thumb and the index finger, when held as far apart as possible. Also used for measuring pieces of fabric.

זֶרֶת   *Little finger* (span). The distance between the thumb and the end of the little finger. This unit is already mentioned in the Bible. Different opinions regarding the length of the זֶרֶת are already found in ancient sources, and it is therefore possible to encounter the different views in different sources in Rabbinic literature. It is genrally accepted that the זֶרֶת is one half of an אַמָּה (= three טְפָחִים), though some opinions maintain that it is two טְפָחִים in length.

קָנֶה   *Reed.* This measurement, too, is mentioned in the Bible, but rarely encountered in the Talmud. The קָנֶה was used for measuring buildings. One קָנֶה = six אַמּוֹת.

רִיס   *A ris.* Apparently borrowed from the Greeks, this unit was very close to the Greek *stadium* in length. The רִיס is 2/15 of a מִיל (which is 266 2/3 אַמּוֹת or between 128 and 153 m. [139–167 yd.]).

מַהֲלַךְ יוֹם   *A day's walk.* Certain distances mentioned in the Talmud are measured by how long it takes to walk them. The Talmud assumes that the average person can walk ten parasangs (i.e. forty מִיל = 38.4 or 46 km. [24 or 28.75 mi.]) in a day, beginning at dawn and ending when it is completely dark. The "day's walk" is used to define other, larger units, such as a "six months' walk," "a year's walk," and astronomical distances such as "a five-hundred years' walk" (approximately 7,500,000 km.).

Small Units of Length

	אֶצְבַּע Fingerbreadth	טֶפַח Handbreadth	אַמָּה Cubit	קָנֶה Reed
אֶצְבַּע Fingerbreadth	1	1/4	1/24	1/144
טֶפַח Handbreadth	4	1	1/6	1/36
אַמָּה Cubit	24	6	1	1/6
קָנֶה Reed	144	36	6	1

Large Units of Length

	אַמָּה Cubit	רִיס Ris	מִיל Mil	פַּרְסָה Parasang
אַמָּה Cubit	1	1/266	1/2000	1/8000
רִיס Ris	266	1	2/15	1/30
מִיל Mil	2000	7 1/2	1	1/4
פַּרְסָה Parasang	8000	30	4	1

Units of Area

Measurements of area in the Talmud are based on two systems which were related to each other in the Talmud itself by means of standard conversion values. The one system is based on squaring the standard units of length. It is subject to the same difference of opinion among modern Halakhic authorities as are measures of length. The other system, used in larger measurements, is based on the amount of space required to plant certain quantities of produce. This system is therefore related to the basic units of volume (see below). There are also units of measurement of Biblical origin found in Rabbinic literature for various measurements of surface area. This is an entirely different system, partially independent and based entirely on objects found in nature.

אֶצְבַּע מְרוּבַּעַת *A square fingerbreadth*. This unit is used primarily to measure small pieces of fabric (in order to decide whether they are susceptible to ritual impurity) and other small items: 4 sq. cm. (0.62 sq. in.) according to Na'eh and 5.76 sq. cm. (0.89 sq. in.) according to Ḥazon Ish.

טֶפַח מְרוּבַּע *A square handbreadth*. Used for measuring larger pieces of fabric, holes and spaces in partitions, etc.: 64 sq. cm. (9.92 sq. in.) or 92.16 sq. cm. (14.28 sq. in.).

אַמָּה מְרוּבַּעַת *A square cubit*. This unit is found in diverse Halakhic contexts. Areas of four אַמוֹת by four אַמוֹת are also frequently mentioned in the Talmud, often abbreviated as "four אַמּוֹת"; 2,304 sq. cm. (357 sq. in.) or 3,318 sq. cm. (514 sq. in.) = one square אַמָּה; 3.69 sq. m. (4.41 sq. yd.) or 5.31 sq. m. (6.35 sq. yd.) = four אַמָּה square.

בֵּית רוֹבַע   *The minimum amount of space required in order to sow one-quarter of a* קַב *of produce* (see below בֵּית קַב and בֵּית סְאָה). This space is 104 ⅙ square אַמּוֹת, 24 sq. m. (28 sq. yd.) according to Na'eh, 35 sq. m. (41 sq. yd.) according to the Ḥazon Ish.

בֵּית קַב   *The minimum amount of space required in order to sow one* קַב *of produce.* This equals 416 ⅔ square אַמּוֹת, 96 sq. m. (115 sq. yd.) according to Na'eh, 138 sq. m. (165 sq. yd.) according to the Ḥazon Ish.

בֵּית סְאָה   *The minimum amount of space required in order to sow one* סְאָה *of produce.* According to the Talmud, one בֵּית סְאָה = 50 אַמּוֹת by 50 אַמּוֹת, i.e., 2,500 square אַמּוֹת, 576 sq. m. (689 sq. yd.) according to Na'eh, 830 sq. m. (992 sq. yd.) according to the Ḥazon Ish.

בֵּית סָאתַיִם   *The amount of space necessary to sow two* סְאָה *of produce.* This unit comprises 50 x 100 אַמּוֹת, and is used for many Halakhic measurements (e.g., the standard courtyard was one בֵּית סָאתַיִם in area; this was also the size of the courtyard of the Tabernacle in the wilderness). In a square with an area of בֵּית סָאתַיִם, each side will be שִׁבְעִים אַמָּה וְשִׁירַיִם ("seventy אַמּוֹת and a remainder" = slightly more than 70 ⅔ אַמּוֹת). בֵּית סָאתַיִם is another unit of measurement frequently found in Halakhic contexts, and is the basis of the conversion formulae from square אַמּוֹת to planting areas.

בֵּית כּוֹר   *The minimum amount of space required in order to sow one* כּוֹר *of produce.* This is 75,000 square אַמּוֹת, 17,280 sq. m. (20,670 sq. yd.) according to Na'eh, 24,900 sq. m. (29,780 sq. yd.) according to the Ḥazon Ish. These are the most frequently encountered units of surface area, although on occasion other units are used. The latter are generated either by using units of length (e.g., one זֶרֶת by one זֶרֶת) or units of volume based on the relationship between a סְאָה and the area sown in a בֵּית סְאָה. In addition to the units mentioned above, there are also other special quantities used for measuring area:

שְׂעָרוֹת   *Hairs* (hairbreadths). The space between two adjacent hairs (whether on the head or on the rest of the body is a matter of dispute) or the space surrounding each hair; one "hair" is approximately equivalent to 9 sq. mm. or 3 mm. sq.

עֲדָשָׁה   *A lentil's area,* i.e., two hairbreadths by two hairbreadths (see previous entry).

גְּרִיס   *A bean's area.* The area of a Cilician bean, thirty six-square hairbreadths.

Small Units of Area

	אֶצְבַּע מְרוּבַּעַת Sq. fingerbreadth	טֶפַח מְרוּבַּע Sq. handbreadth	אַמָּה מְרוּבַּעַת Sq. cubit	סמ"ר Sq. cm.
אֶצְבַּע מְרוּבַּעַת Sq. fingerbreadth	1	¹⁄₁₆	¹⁄₅₇₆	4
טֶפַח מְרוּבַּע Sq. handbreadth	16	1	36	64
אַמָּה מְרוּבַּעַת Sq. cubit	675	30	1	2304

Large Units of Area

	אַמָּה מְרוּבַּעַת Sq. cubit	בֵּית רוֹבַע Bet rova	בֵּית קַב Bet kav	בֵּית סְאָה Bet se'ah	בֵּית כּוֹר Bet kor
אַמָּה מְרוּבַּעַת Sq. cubit	1	$6/625$	$24/652$	$1/2500$	$1/75000$
בֵּית רוֹבַע Bet rova	$104\,1/6$	1	$1/4$	$1/24$	$1/720$
בֵּית קַב Bet kav	$416\,2/3$	4	1	$1/6$	$1/180$
בֵּית סְאָה Bet se'ah	2500	24	6	1	$1/30$
בֵּית כּוֹר Bet kor	75000	720	180	30	1

Units of Volume

Units of volume in the Talmud are among the most complicated units of measurement, because of the existence of several independent systems. Moreover, even though the Talmud does offer a series of formulae to convert between systems, these formulae are themselves unclear and frequently appear to contradict each other. Moreover, there are different measures, and different terms used for the same measure, in the systems used in the Torah and in the Talmud, and various units of volume of Biblical origin found their way into the Rabbinic literature without there being any clear and precise way to convert them to the standard Talmudic units.

Even within the same system, there were different measures used for dry and liquid capacity. This was not simply a matter of nomenclature; different types of containers were used for measuring liquids and solids. When a person bought a measure of a solid, he expected the commodity to be heaped up; needless to say, this was impossible with liquids. As a result, measures that were to hold dry material were designed to permit a 50% overflow, and a person purchasing a סְאָה of grain, for example, would expect to get 50% more than a person purchasing a סְאָה of wine. However, this was important only for business considerations. When assessing volume for Halakhic purposes, only the interior of the measure was considered, and a סְאָה of liquid would be equal to a סְאָה of solid.

An additional complicating element was the fact that most, but not all, of the units of volume were changed systematically at least twice; thus units designated by the same term may have three different sizes, each appropriate to its own period or context.

Volume is frequently measured in מִידוֹת מִדְבָּרִיּוֹת —"wilderness units" — units used by the Jews when they were wandering in the wilderness. Later (apparently during the Second Temple Period), all the units of measurement were increased in size, and these new units were called מִידוֹת יְרוּשַׁלְמִיּוֹת — "Jerusalem units". These מִידוֹת יְרוּשַׁלְמִיּוֹת were 20% larger than the previous מִידוֹת מִדְבָּרִיּוֹת (thus, 5 קַב in מִידוֹת יְרוּשַׁלְמִיּוֹת = 6 קַב in מִידוֹת מִדְבָּרִיּוֹת). These units, too, were changed in the course of time, and yet another system of measurements, מִידוֹת צִיפּוֹרִיּוֹת — "Tzipori units," named after the city of Tzipori — was instituted. The units in this system were 20% larger than the מִידוֹת יְרוּשַׁלְמִיּוֹת. In particular, there are three sizes of eggs, a basic unit of measurement. Occasionally, thorough examination is necessary in order to determine to which system of measurements the Talmud is referring.

MEASUREMENTS FOUND IN THE TALMUD

The Talmudic Rabbis used many of the larger measuring units mentioned in the Bible (see below, p. 288) but they also added many new, smaller units.

בֵּיצָה   *An egg's bulk* (i.e., the bulk of an average egg). In a sense, this unit is one of the most important, as it is used as the basis for calculating all the other measures, both dry and liquid. It is also used as one of the dry measures (see p. 288). The Talmud defined the egg in terms of units of length. The egg used in the "wilderness" system (see introduction), was calculated to have a volume equal to 2 x 2 x 1.8 fingerbreadths (for details, see אַרְבָּעִים סְאָה, p. 288). According to the Na'eh system (see אֶצְבַּע in "Length" section, p. 282) this would give the "wilderness" egg a volume of 4 x 4 x 3.6 = 57.6 cc. (2 fl. oz.), whereas according to the Ḥazon Ish system, its volume would be 4.8 x 4.8 x 4.32 = 99.5 cc. (3.5 fl. oz.). The "Jerusalem" egg was 20% larger than the "wilderness" egg — 69.1 cc. (2.4 fl. oz.) or 119.4 cc. (4.2 fl. oz), and the "Tzipori" egg was 20% larger again — 82.9 cc. (2.9 fl. oz.) or 143.3 cc. (4.9 fl. oz.). Clearly, none of these measures bears much resemblance to the actual size of the present-day chicken egg — about 50 cc. Moreover, the difference between the Ḥazon Ish and Na'eh scales is so great — about 75% — that it appears to be unbridgeable. These questions have exercised the minds of many modern authorities. In the volume measures below, the size of the units will be given in terms of "eggs."

בֵּיצָה   *An egg's bulk.* The smallest dry measure regularly used (see above). One בֵּיצָה = *Dry Measures* ⅓ תּוֹמֶן (= ¹/₂₄ קַב).

עוּכְלָא (or: כְּלָה)   *The equivalent of* ¹/₂₀ קַב *or* 1.2 *eggs.*

תּוֹמֶן   *One-eighth of a* קַב *or* 3 *eggs.* Half a תּוֹמֶן is also mentioned as a unit of measurement.

רוֹבַע   *One-quarter of a* קַב *or* 6 *eggs.*

קַב   This is a basic unit of measurement from which many other small units are derived. *One-sixth of a* סְאָה *or* 24 *eggs.* The expression קַבַּיִים (2 קַב) is frequently used, as is the expression "half a קַב."

תַּרְקַב   *Half a* סְאָה *or* 72 *eggs.* The Rabbis interpreted this word as meaning — תְּרֵי וְקַב "two and a *kav*," i.e., three קַב.

סְאָה   *One-thirtieth of a* כּוֹר *or* 144 *eggs.*

כּוֹר   *Thirty* סְאָה *or* 4,320 *eggs.* The largest measure mentioned by name. In the "wilderness" system, according to Na'eh, 248 liters (7 bushels), according to the Ḥazon Ish, 430 liters (12 bushels).

קוֹרְטוֹב   *One-sixty-fourth of a* לוֹג *or* ³/₃₂ *of an egg.* 5.4 cc. (Na'eh) or 9.3 cc. (Ḥazon Ish).   *Liquid Measures*

רְבִיעִית   *One quarter of a* לוֹג *or* 1.5 *eggs.* (Note that this is not identical to the רוֹבַע, which is a dry measure; see above.) This unit is used very frequently to measure liquids. Half a רְבִיעִית is sometimes called a שְׁמִינִית ("eighth"), or תַּמְנִיתָא in Aramaic.

לוֹג   *Six eggs.* The basic unit of liquid measurement in the Talmud, from which all other larger units of volume are derived (also related to a half, a third, and a quarter of a הִין), as well as a series of smaller measurements, such as half a לוֹג.

הִין   *Twelve* לוֹג *or* 72 *eggs.*

אַרְבָּעִים סְאָה **Forty se'ah**, i.e., the equivalent of 80 הִין or 5,760 eggs. The minimum quantity of water necessary for a מִקְוֶה (ritual bath). A container large enough to hold 40 סְאָה or more is no longer considered to be a utensil, but rather a sort of building. This has ramifications in such areas as the laws of ritual impurity, and the laws of the Sabbath. The 40 סְאָה measure is the basis of all our modern calculations of the various measures of volume. The Talmud tells us that the dimensions of a מִקְוֶה must be 3 אַמּוֹת by 1 אַמָּה, and that its volume must be 40 סְאָה. Thus, according to the Na'eh scale, a מִקְוֶה must contain 332 liters of water (87 U.S. gal.), and, according to the Ḥazon Ish, 573 liters (151 U.S. gal.).

MEASUREMENTS FOUND IN THE BIBLE

Dry Measures

חוֹמֶר **Thirty** סְאָה or 10 אֵיפָה. The largest measure mentioned by name. Equivalent to the Talmudic כּוֹר (see above).

לֶתֶךְ **Half a** כּוֹר.

אֵיפָה **One-twentieth of a** כּוֹר, i.e., 3 סְאָה.

סְאָה **One-third of an** אֵיפָה.

עִשָּׂרוֹן (or: עוֹמֶר*) **One-tenth of an** אֵיפָה.

Liquid Measures

כּוֹר **Kor.** The largest liquid measure, equal in volume to the dry חוֹמֶר (see p. 287).

בַּת **One-tenth of a** כּוֹר. This is equal in volume to one אֵיפָה (= 6 הִין).

הִין **One-sixth of a** בַּת or 1/60 כּוֹר.

לוֹג **One-twelfth of a** הִין.

מְשׂוּרָה **One thirty-sixth of a** log. According to Rabbinic interpretation, this is the smallest measure mentioned in the Bible.

OTHER UNITS OF VOLUME FOUND IN THE HALAKHAH

In addition to the measurements mentioned above, there are several units of volume of crucial importance in various Halakhic contexts. Their size was fixed by the Torah. Most of these units are based on objects found in nature, particularly fruits and vegetables. It is not always possible to convert them easily to the standard Talmudic measurements based on the egg. Among these measurements are:

כְּזַיִת **An olive's bulk.** This is one of the most important Halakhic units of volume. According to Torah law, eating is defined as swallowing one כְּזַיִת, and every Torah law that either commands or prohibits eating is referring to this quantity. The measure is defined in terms of the water displacement of a particular strain of olive, and the precise size of this measurement is not clear. From one Talmudic passage it appears to be almost half the size of an egg, and from another it appears to be less than a third of the size of an egg. Given the wide range of views on the size of the egg (see p. 287), the opinions on the size of the olive range from 15 cc. to 50 cc.

כּוֹתֶבֶת **The volume of a large date.** This unit is larger than a כְּזַיִת, but smaller than a כְּבֵיצָה. Eating on Yom Kippur is liable to divine punishment by excision (כָּרֵת), but only if one eats at least a כּוֹתֶבֶת of food.

גְּרוֹגֶרֶת   *The volume of a dry fig.* This is the standard unit for food on the Sabbath. One who violates the Sabbath unintentionally is only required to bring a sin-offering (חַטָּאת) if the size of the object involved was greater than a statutory amount, the size varying not with the type of work but with the nature of the object itself. The dried fig is the statutory quantity for any form of prohibited work involving food. Thus, a person who bakes less than one fig's volume of bread is not obligated to bring a sin-offering. Likewise, a person who carries food from one domain to another must bring a sin-offering only if he carried a fig's volume of food, etc. A fig is slightly larger than an olive, but smaller than a date. Its precise size is subject to considerable dispute (see also כְּזַיִת, p. 288).

כַּעֲדָשָׁה   *A lentil's bulk.* A dead reptile (of the species mentioned in Leviticus 11:29–30) can render other objects ritually impure if it is at least 1 כַּעֲדָשָׁה in volume (see also עֲדָשָׁה, p. 285).

שְׂעוֹרָה   *The volume of a barleycorn.* A bone from a dead person can render other objects ritually unclean if it is at least 1 barleycorn in volume.

פּוֹל הַלָּבָן   *The volume of a "white bean."* This unit is frequently used to determine whether certain fruits, such as grapes, are large enough to be considered an item of food (e.g., with regard to the laws of tithes).

פּוֹתֵחַ טֶפַח   *One cubic handbreadth* (lit. "the opening of a handbreadth"). The basic measuring unit used for determining whether a given space blocks or transmits corpse impurity (טוּמְאַת אֹהֶל). Another measuring unit encountered in connection with laws of טוּמְאַת אֹהֶל is the אֶגְרוֹף — "fist". This unit, which was approximately the size of an infant's head, was first based on the fist of a giant named Ben Bati'aḥ (see *Kelim* 17:12).

Many other units of volume appear in connection with the various laws of ritual impurity, and some of these units are based on utensils used during the Mishnaic period (e.g., תַּרְוָד — a type of spoon; and מַקְדֵּחַ שֶׁל רוֹפְאִים — "physician's drill").

Large Units

יָבֵשׁ Dry	Liquid	כּוֹר (חוֹמֶר) Kor / כּוֹר Kor	אֵיפָה Ephah / בַּת Bat	סְאָה Se'ah	תַּרְקַב Tarkav / הִין Hin	עִשָּׂרוֹן Isaron	קַב Kav	לוֹג Log / לוֹג Log
כּוֹר Kor	כּוֹר Kor	1	10	30	60	100	180	720
אֵיפָה Ephah	בַּת Bat	1/10	1	3	6	10	18	72
סְאָה Se'ah		1/30	1/3	1	2	3 1/3	6	24
תַּרְקַב Tarkav	הִין Hin	1/60	1/6	1/2	1	1 2/3	3	12
עִשָּׂרוֹן Isaron		1/100	1/10	3/10	3/5	1	1 4/5	7 1/5
קַב Kav		1/180	1/18	1/6	1/3	5/9	1	4
	לוֹג Log	1/720	1/72	1/24	1/12	5/36	1/4	1

Small Units

יָבֵשׁ Dry		קַב Kav	רוֹבַע Rova	תּוֹמֶן Tomen		עוּכְלָא Ukhlah	בֵּיצָה Egg's bulk		
	לַח Liquid		לוֹג Log		רְבִיעִית Revi'it			מְשׂוּרָה Mesurah	קוֹרְטוֹב Kortov
קַב Kav		1	4	8	16	20	24	144	256
רוֹבַע Rova	לוֹג Log	$1/4$	1	2	4	5	6	36	64
תּוֹמֶן Tomen		$1/8$	$1/2$	1	2	$2\,1/5$	3	18	32
	רְבִיעִית Revi'it	$1/16$	$1/4$	$1/2$	1	$1\,1/4$	$1\,1/2$	9	16
עוּכְלָא Ukhlah		$1/20$	$1/5$	$2/5$	$4/5$	1	$1\,1/5$	$7\,2/5$	$12\,4/5$
בֵּיצָה Egg's bulk		$1/24$	$1/6$	$1/3$	$2/3$	$5/6$	1	6	$10\,2/3$
	מְשׂוּרָה Mesurah	$1/144$	$1/36$	$1/18$	$1/9$	$5/36$	$1/6$	1	$1\,7/9$
	קוֹרְטוֹב Kortov	$1/256$	$1/64$	$1/32$	$1/16$	$5/64$	$3/32$	$9/16$	1

Coins

The currency systems in the Talmudic period are among the most complicated elements of weights and measures mentioned in the Talmud. All those factors that produced differing standards of length, area and volume were combined in the area of coinage. In the nature of things, legal tender passes from one country to another, so that there has to be some correlation between the monetary systems of different countries. Moreover, Eretz Israel, which was an international crossroads, and to which contributions from Jews all over the world were sent, was full of extremely diverse types of currency. Additional complications were created by the different monetary systems operating in various countries at various times, and the constant changes, for political and economic reasons, in the values of currencies, in the relationship between silver and gold coins, and in the relationship between these metals and copper coinage.

Furthermore, official exchange rates tended to be altered by the government through official and unofficial devaluations, and these changes help account for the controversies in the Talmudic literature itself concerning the values of different units of currency. Yet another factor should be mentioned here: sometimes a number of different coins shared the same name, depending on which system of measurement was used. Two different systems of coinage were used by the Jews: (1) "Tyrian money" (כֶּסֶף צוֹרִי), (largely equivalent to the coins mentioned in the Torah), and according to which those values mentioned in the Torah were calculated, and (2) "money of the state" (כֶּסֶף מְדִינָה), which had units with the same names as those in Tyrian money, but whose value was exactly one eighth of the corresponding coins in Tyrian money. Most of the payments specified by the Mishnah and the Talmud are reckoned according to the "sela of the state" (סֶלַע מְדִינָה), reflecting the latter system.

As with other measures, there was a systematic change of 20% in the larger coins during the Second Temple period. In the Bible a coin called a גֵּרָה is mentioned. The גֵּרָה was $1/20$ of the שֶׁקֶל הַקּוֹדֶשׁ (the "holy shekel," so called because it was used for payments made to the Sanctuary). During the Second Temple period, the שֶׁקֶל הַקּוֹדֶשׁ was revalued to equal 24 גֵּרָה, and all coins larger than one גֵּרָה were revalued accordingly. From this time the גֵּרָה was called מָעָה (see below) and the שֶׁקֶל הַקּוֹדֶשׁ was called סֶלַע. All payments required by the Torah to be made in units of שֶׁקֶל הַקּוֹדֶשׁ were thenceforth to be made in units of סֶלַע, thus increasing the amounts involved by one-fifth.

A list of units of currency in ascending value is given below, listed according to the value of each coin based on the rate of exchange normally used in the Talmud. Not all of these coins were in simultaneous use; some also have other names.

Many other types of currency are mentioned in the Talmud but have not been included here.

פְּרוּטָה   A copper coin; the smallest unit of currency. For Halakhic purposes, the פְּרוּטָה is defined as the value of half a barleycorn weight of pure silver. Traditionally this is about 24 milligrams of silver. The Halakhic value of all coins is linked to the price of silver. The value of a פְּרוּטָה approximates to one United States cent.

קוֹנְטְרַנְק   A coin worth two פְּרוּטוֹת, or ¼ of an אִיסָר.

מְסִימַס   4 פְּרוּטוֹת, or ½ an אִיסָר.

אִיסָר   8 פְּרוּטוֹת, or ½ a פּוּנְדְיוֹן.

פּוּנְדְיוֹן   (Roman dupondium); 16 פְּרוּטוֹת, or two אִיסָרִים.

מָעָה   A small silver coin, worth 32 פְּרוּטוֹת, or ⅙ of a דִינָר. The Biblical גֵּרָה. It had a weight of 16 barleycorns of silver, about 384 milligrams.

אִסְתְּרָא   טַרְפְּעִיק or ½ a דִינָר (= 96 פְּרוּטוֹת).

דִינָר or זוּז   A silver coin. To be differentiated from the golden dinar (דִינָר זָהָב) mentioned below. Worth — 6 מָעָה, or ¼ of a סֶלַע.

שֶׁקֶל   [in Rabbinic Hebrew] or בֶּקַע [in Biblical Hebrew] — two דִינָר, or ½ of a סֶלַע.

סֶלַע   [in Tyrian currency] or שֶׁקֶל [in the Torah, i.e., the שֶׁקֶל הַקּוֹדֶשׁ] — 4 דִינָר.

דִינָר זָהָב   A gold coin resembling the דִינָר in appearance, worth 25 דִינָרִים.

מָנֶה   100 דִינָר, four golden דִינָר.

מָנֶה שֶׁל קוֹדֶשׁ   200 silver דִינָר.

כִּיכָּר   60 מָנֶה (= 1,500 סֶלַע or 6,000 דִינָרִים).

כִּיכָּר שֶׁל קוֹדֶשׁ   3,000 סְלָעִים, or כִּיכָּרוֹת two regular.

Common Large Coins

	דִינָר Dinar	שֶׁקֶל Shekel	סֶלַע Sela	דִינָר זָהָב Golden dinar	מָנֶה Maneh	כִּיכָּר Kikkar
דִינָר Dinar	1	½	¼	1/25	1/100	1/6000
שֶׁקֶל Shekel	2	1	½	2/25	1/50	1/3000
סֶלַע Sela	4	2	1	4/25	1/25	1/1500
דִינָר זָהָב Golden dinar	25	12½	6¼	1	¼	1/240
מָנֶה Maneh	100	50	25	4	1	1/60
כִּיכָּר Kikkar	6000	3000	1500	240	60	1

Common Small Coins

	פְּרוּטָה Perutah	אִיסָר Isar	פּוּנְדְיוֹן Dupondium	מָעָה Ma'ah	אִסְתְּרָא Istera	דִּינָר Dinar
פְּרוּטָה Perutah	1	1/8	1/16	1/32	1/96	1/192
אִיסָר Isar	8	1	1/2	1/4	1/12	1/24
פּוּנְדְיוֹן Dupondium	16	2	1	1/2	1/6	1/12
מָעָה Ma'ah	32	4	2	1	1/3	1/6
אִסְתְּרָא Istera	96	12	6	3	1	1/2
דִּינָר Dinar	192	24	6	2	1	1

Weights

The units of weight in the Talmud are very closely related to the units of currency discussed in the previous section. This is particularly understandable when we recall that, during the Talmudic period, the primary factor in determining the value of any given coin was the amount of precious metal it contained. The different units of weight also varied in size from place to place; thus, the Judean סֶלַע weighed twice as much as the סֶלַע in Galilee. A list of the principal weights mentioned in the Talmud is given below.

כִּכָּר (pl. כִּיכָּרוֹת)   *The weight of a silver* כִּיכָּר. Approximately 27 kg. (there were also smaller כִּיכָּרוֹת).

מָנֶה (or מָנֶה אִיטַלְקִי; also called לִיטְרָא)   *One-sixtieth of a* כִּיכָּר. Approximately equal in weight to the U.S. pound (450 gm.). Weights of 1/2 of a לִיטְרָא and 1/4 of a לִיטְרָא are also mentioned in the Talmud.

תַּרְטֵימַר   *Half a* מָנֶה.

אוּנְקְיָא   *Two* סֶלַע *or* 8/100 *of a* מָנֶה.

סֶלַע   *Four* דִּינָרִים *or* 1/2 *of an* אוּנְקְיָא.

שֶׁקֶל   *Half a* סֶלַע *or* 2 דִּינָרִים.

דִּינָר (or זוּז)   *The equivalent in weight to* 1/100 *of a* לִיטְרָא. Also called זִין.

In addition, there were apparently smaller units of weight based on small coins or other units. Several of these measurements are mentioned in the Talmud as being part of other, larger units.

Coins

	כִּיכָּר Kikkar	מָנֶה Maneh	תַּרְטִימַר Tartimar	אוּנְקְיָא Unkeya	סֶלַע Sela	שֶׁקֶל Shekel	דִּינָר Dinar
כִּיכָּר Kikkar	1	60	120	750	1500	3000	6000
מָנֶה Maneh	$1/60$	1	2	$12\frac{1}{2}$	25	50	100
תַּרְטִימַר Tartimar	$1/120$	$1/2$	1	$6\frac{1}{4}$	$12\frac{1}{2}$	25	50
אוּנְקְיָא Unkeya	$1/750$	$2/25$	$4/25$	1	2	4	8
סֶלַע Sela	$1/1500$	$1/25$	$2/25$	$1/2$	1	2	4
שֶׁקֶל Shekel	$1/3000$	$1/50$	$1/25$	$1/4$	$1/2$	1	2
דִּינָר Dinar	$1/6000$	$1/100$	$1/50$	$1/8$	$1/4$	$1/2$	1

Rules Governing
Halakhic Decision-Making

Although the Talmud deals mainly with theoretical problems and discussions, and is not strictly speaking meant to be a compendium of Jewish law, it is nevertheless the primary source for Halakhic decisions. The use of the Talmud as a Halakhic source is based in part on those passages where the Talmud presents explicit Halakhic rulings on specific issues (...וְהִלְכְתָא — "and the Halakhah is..."). But Halakhic decisions are mainly arrived at by applying a wide range of rules of Halakhic decision-making. These rules are used to determine the Halakhic conclusion that is to be drawn from a particular Talmudic passage or difference of opinion. The principles of Halakhic decision-making are not meant to determine absolute and final truth, and the Talmudic discussion itself continues to consider views that have been rejected from the Halakhah, together with those that have been included within it. By contrast, a Halakhic decision is a practical definition of the way a person must actually behave in any situation.

The principles of Halakhic decision-making are of various kinds. Some of them relate to structural features of the Talmudic text, and rely on them in deriving the practical Halakhah from the wording of passages in the Mishnah or the Gemara. Other principles refer to specific subjects, and in particular there are numerous principles governing the ways to resolve differences of opinion between various Sages.

Some of the principles of Halakhic decision-making are explained by the Talmud itself, but these are insufficient to resolve all the problems left undecided in the Mishnah and the Gemara. The Saboraim (sixth century Talmud teachers in Babylon) and the Geonim (later Babylonian Rabbis) laid down many principles of Halakhic decision-making, and some of their observations and decisions found their way into the Talmudic text itself. Although most of these principles are generally accepted, differences of opinion still remain among the Geonim and the leading Rishonim (the medieval commentators who followed the period of the Geonim) as to the truth or full applicability of certain principles and also as to the relations of the principles to each other. For there are many instances in which two principles of decision-making lead to contradictory conclusions, and a decision must be made as to which of the two is preferable. Indeed, a significant proportion of the controversies among the Halakhic authorities, from the Rishonim until our own time, are a result of disagreement about the principles of decision-making in the Gemara.

Hundreds of rules are used in Halakhic decision-making. Some are general principles that apply everywhere, and some are decisions applying to isolated instances. Several leading Rabbis systematically collected these principles of Halakhic decision-making and many books have been written on these subjects, such as מָבוֹא לַתַּלְמוּד by Rabbi Shmuel HaNagid, who lived in Spain and was a contemporary of Rabbi Yitzhak Alfasi (eleventh century); סֵפֶר כְּרִיתוּת by Rabbi Shimshon of Kinon, one of the last French authors of the Tosafot; הֲלִיכוֹת עוֹלָם by Rabbi Yeshuah ben Yosef (fifteenth century, Spain) and the additions to that work by Rabbi Yosef Caro (sixteenth century, Eretz Israel); and יַד מַלְאָכִי by Rabbi Malachi HaKohen (eighteenth century, Italy). These works are based on traditional written sources, on explicit statements made in the works of the major Halakhic authorities, and on deductions from their statements.

Some of the major principles found in this literature are presented here.

The Authority of the Two Talmuds and of Other Sources

It is a major principle that, in making a Halakhic decision, one follows the Babylonian Talmud in preference to the Jerusalem Talmud or any other Rabbinic source. But where the case under discussion is not mentioned in the Babylonian Talmud, or where a problem discussed receives no clear solution in the Babylonian Talmud, the authority of the Jerusalem Talmud is relied upon. In general the Rabbis attempt to find as much agreement and consistency as possible between the approaches of the two Talmuds.

In the opinion of some of the greatest Halakhic authorities, especially Maimonides, the Jerusalem Talmud takes precedence over any other Tannaitic source such as Halakhic Midrashim or other sources, and even over the Tosefta. Nevertheless the Tosefta, the Halakhic Midrashim, and the Minor Tractates are all important Halakhic sources, and Halakhic rulings are based on them whenever they do not contradict other primary Halakhic sources. The major Aggadic compilations (such as *Midrash Rabbah* and *Tanḥuma*) also serve as authoritative Halakhic sources.

Most authorities, including those who were Kabbalists themselves, agree that where there is a difference of opinion between Halakhic decisions, mainly those in the Talmud, and statements found in Kabbalistic works, the Halakhah is in accordance with the non-esoteric sources. But wherever there is no contradiction or no clear decision in the works of the Halakhic authorities, one follows the Kabbalah.

These are the major principles involved in Halakhic decision-making, but there are certain exceptions to them in every area. For example, customs governing the weekly Torah reading do not follow the Talmud but rather מַסֶּכֶת סוֹפְרִים (the *Tractate of Scribes*), one of the minor tractates not included in the Talmudic canon. Similarly, in the scribal copying of Scripture one depends on the מְסוֹרָה (the Masoretic tradition consolidated in tenth century Tiberias) even where it contradicts the Talmud. Differences in custom in various places and among various Jewish communities are frequently based on decisions that do not necessarily follow the standard principles mentioned above.

Structural Principles

It is a basic principle that one decides the Halakhah according to סוּגְיָא דִּשְׁמַעְתָּא (the thrust of the argument). The fundamental axiom or Halakhic principle that appears to underly the words of a passage in the Gemara, even if not stated explicitly as a Halakhic decision, is regarded as the basis for arriving at such a decision. This principle is in fact an overriding one and is followed even when it contradicts other explicit principles of decision-making. Yet, although this principle is an accepted rule, the

Halakhic significance of a passage of Gemara is not always clear, and many differences of opinion among later Halakhic authorities result from conflicting understandings of the same passage, both with regard to the conclusions to be drawn from it and to the definition of the range of cases to which they are applicable.

When there are different versions of passages, as well as alternative readings, which reverse the names or basic assumptions of the Sages who are in disagreement, one generally relies on the passage from that tractate to which the given Halakhah naturally belongs.

הֲלָכָה כִּסְתַם מִשְׁנָה *The Halakhah follows an anonymous Mishnah.* Some Amoraim, such as Rabbi Yoḥanan, took this principle as a consistent basis for their decisions. It derives from the assumption that the anonymous presentation of a certain opinion in the Mishnah proves that Rabbi Yehudah HaNasi and his court decided that this was the Halakhah, and there was no court greater or more important than that of Rabbi Yehudah HaNasi in the following generations. This principle has a number of refinements. In some cases we find both an anonymous Mishnah and a difference of opinion between Tannaim. If the difference of opinion precedes the anonymous Mishnah, then the Halakhah agrees with the anonymous Mishnah. But if the anonymous Mishnah is followed by the difference of opinion, the Halakhah does not necessarily agree with the anonymous Mishnah. These principles regarding anonymous statements in the Mishnah are complicated by the fact that anonymous statements cited in various places occasionally disagree with each other, or a difference of opinion in connection with an anonymous statement may appear elsewhere in the Mishnah. The details of these matters are a matter of controversy among Rabbinical authorities.

אֵין לְמֵדִין מִן הַכְּלָלוֹת *One does not learn from generalizations.* One may not draw conclusions from generalizations, even in a passage where the expression "except" (חוּץ) is used. When the Mishnah presents a summary of the Halakhah in general terms, one may not draw practical Halakhic conclusions regarding all the details that belong to that generalization. This reservation applies not only to abstract generalizations, but even when the Mishnah explicitly gives a list of exceptions (חוּץ מִ...). This does not necessarily mean that one may rely on the general statement in *all* other cases.

אֵין הֲלָכָה כְּשִׁיטָה *The Halakhah is not in accordance with the approach of X and Y.* This principle is a Geonic tradition, meaning that when the Gemara cites a series of Sages, all of whom share the same line of thought ("Rabbi X, Rabbi Y, and Rabbi Z are all of the opinion..."), this is proof that the Halakhah does *not* follow that approach.

בֶּאֱמֶת אָמְרוּ *In truth they said.* A technical term in the Mishnah introducing a Halakhic decision. Where the Mishnah says בֶּאֱמֶת אָמְרוּ, this is the accepted Halakhah, and it is to be followed. Occasionally this term refers to הֲלָכָה לְמֹשֶׁה מִסִּינַי — a Halakhah given to Moses on Mount Sinai.

הֲלָכָה כְּלִישָׁנָא בַּתְרָא *The Halakhah is in accordance with the last version.* When the Gemara presents a number of versions of a statement or controversy, with changes in names or with changes in the details of the Halakhah or the like, the version that appears last in the Gemara is regarded as definitive. There are authorities such as Maimonides who followed this principle almost without exception, and in every instance where the Gemara presents two different versions of a statement or decision, no matter how they are formulated (whether the Gemara says לִישָׁנָא אַחֲרִינָא — "another version"; אִיבָּעֵית אֵימָא — "if you wish, say..."; or אִיכָּא דְּאָמְרִי — "others say"), they decided according to the expression appearing last.

הֲלָכָה כְּ"אִם תִּמְצֵי לוֹמַר" *The Halakhah is as* אִם תִּמְצֵי לוֹמַר — *"If you say."* When a number of linked questions are asked one after the other, using the expression אִם תִּמְצֵי לוֹמַר, even when the first questions in the series are not specifically resolved in the Talmud, it is assumed that the Halakhah is in accordance with the final אִם תִּמְצֵי לוֹמַר.

Principles on Various Subjects

From the basic Halakhic principle that סְפֵיקָא דְאוֹרַיְיתָא לְחוּמְרָא (when a doubt exists regarding the application of a Torah law, one makes a restrictive, stringent decision) and the converse principle, סְפֵיקָא דְרַבָּנָן לְקוּלָא (when a doubt exists regarding the application of a Rabbinical law, one makes a lenient, less stringent decision), important conclusions are to be drawn regarding Halakhic decision-making. In cases where a controversy among Sages has not been resolved, and no general principles are available to determine how to decide between them, this general principle may be invoked, and cases involving Torah commandments are decided severely, while cases involving Rabbinical laws are decided leniently. The most common use of this principle is in a case where a discussion in the Talmud is recorded as having ended without a decision (תֵּיקוּ). In civil law, however, where there can be no absolute standard of severity or leniency, since leniency towards one litigant is severity towards his opponent, the property in dispute is granted to the litigant who is in possession of it.

The Halakhah follows the lenient opinion in laws of Sabbath boundaries, since these laws are mainly of Rabbinical authority and origin. Hence this principle applies specifically to Sabbath boundaries but not to the laws of partitions (מְחִיצוֹת), which are of Torah authority.

The Halakhah is lenient in matters of mourning, because most of the laws involved are Rabbinic or matters of custom.

Principles Regarding Differences of Opinion Between Sages

The Sages of the Talmud set a number of rules regarding differences of opinion between Tannaim. But even those who accepted these principles of decision-making did not agree as to whether they are absolute or are to be regarded merely as guidelines.

One early rule is that the Halakhah agrees with the School of Hillel rather than with that of Shammai, going so far as to say, "The School of Shammai as against the School of Hillel does not have the status of an authoritative Mishnah." This principle holds in almost all situations, except in those cases in which the School of Hillel admitted that the School of Shammai was correct, and the eighteen cases mentioned in *Shabbat* 13b where a majority of the Sages decided in accordance with the viewpoint of the School of Shammai.

The Halakhah is in accordance with Rabbi Yehoshua where he differs with Rabbi Eliezer.

The Halakhah is in accordance with Rabbi Akiva in a difference of opinion between him and any other individual Sage of his generation.

The Halakhah is in accordance with every teaching of Rabban Shimon ben Gamliel (II), except for three cases.

The Halakhah is in accordance with Rabbi Yose as opposed to any other Sage who disagrees with him.

The Halakhah is in accordance with Rabbi Yehudah where he differs with Rabbi Shimon or Rabbi Meir.

The teachings of Rabbi Eliezer ben Ya'akov are few but excellent (מִשְׁנַת רַבִּי אֱלִיעֶזֶר בֶּן יַעֲקֹב קַב וְנָקִי). In other words, although he did not leave many Halakhic decisions, in every case his decisions are authoritative, even where many Sages disagree with him. This ancient principle, already cited by the Tanna Ben Azzai, nevertheless has certain exceptions.

The Halakhah is in accordance with Rabbi Yehudah HaNasi in a difference of opinion between him and any other individual Sage except his father.

Regarding the differences of opinion between the Sages of the Talmud, a number of principles are already mentioned in the Talmud itself, others were laid down and accepted during the period of the Saboraim, and others by later Halakhic authorities.

In differences of opinion between Rav and Shmuel, the Halakhah follows Rav in matters of ritual law (דִּינֵי אִיסּוּר וְהֶיתֵּר) and Shmuel in civil law (דִּינֵי מָמוֹנוֹת).

In differences of opinion between Rabbi Yoḥanan and Rav, the Halakhah follows Rabbi Yoḥanan. Likewise in differences of opinion between Rabbi Yoḥanan and Shmuel, the Halakhah follows Rabbi Yoḥanan. The Halakhah indeed usually follows Rabbi Yoḥanan even when he disagrees with both Rav and Shmuel together.

The Halakhah follows Rabbi Yoḥanan rather than Resh Lakish except in three instances (*Yevamot* 36a).

In differences of opinion between Rav Naḥman and Rav Sheshet, the Halakhah follows Rav Sheshet in ritual law and Rav Naḥman in civil law.

The Halakhah is in accordance with Rabbah as opposed to Rav Yosef in all cases except three.

The Halakhah is in accordance with Rava as opposed to Abaye in all their differences of opinion except for six matters, for which the mnemonic יע"ל קג"מ is used (see *Bava Metzia* 22b).

The Halakhah is in accordance with Mar bar Rav Ashi except for two (or three) instances.

In addition to detailed principles regarding differences of opinion between individual, named Sages, there are also more comprehensive principles according to which many decisions are made. One such principle is that the Halakhah does not follow a disciple when he disagrees with his teacher face to face. A greater and more comprehensive principle is that the Halakhah is in accordance with the later opinion (הֲלָכָה כְּבַתְרָאֵי).

This principle rests on the assumption that later authorities were familiar with the opinions of earlier ones and studied them carefully, and if they decided to rule in a different way, one must accept their decision. The Rishonim taught that this principle was even stronger with respect to differences of opinion that arose after the period of Abaye and Rava, and it was decided that, with regard to later generations, the Halakhah may even follow a disciple who disagrees with his teacher.

As noted, the detailed principles are subordinate to the more comprehensive ones. In other words, the principles are to be used as a basis for decision only where the Talmud contains no determination on a given subject; but where the Talmud does contain an explicit Halakhic decision, or where the conclusion of a passage disagrees with the principles, one does not take the principles into consideration.

Rashi Script

Rashi script is one of the most common forms of Hebrew writing in printed Hebrew texts. Almost all commentaries on the Talmud (and the Bible) and Halakhic works are printed in this script. The ability to read this script with ease is an essential skill for studying this literature. Actually, Rashi script is simply the printed version of the Sephardi cursive Hebrew script. Rashi and his students, the Tosafists (whose commentaries are normally printed in this script), did not use it; instead they used Ashkenazi cursive writing, from which contemporary cursive Hebrew script developed. Rashi script received its name because of its use in the history of Hebrew printing. The first books printed in Hebrew were published by Sephardi Jews, and when they printed the Hebrew Bible with commentary, in 1475, they distinguished between the Biblical text and its commentaries by printing the former in regular, square Hebrew letters, and the latter in a different typeface. Since Rashi's commentary was printed in this typeface it came to be called "Rashi script." Another typeface, very closely resembling Rashi script, was used among Ashkenazi Jews; this typeface, which has a somewhat Gothic appearance, is called "teitsch." Teitsch letters were used primarily in Germany, particularly for Yiddish-German translations and notes. As can easily be seen from the table of Rashi script that follows, there is little difference between printed Hebrew writing and Rashi script.

The most noticeable differences are to be found in the letters א, ב, צ, and ש. Certain letters in Rashi script are quite similar to one another, and it is therefore important to distinguish between them in order to avoid confusion:

א-ה These two letters are very similar; the difference between them is that א has a small projection on the upper left-hand side, whereas ה does not.

ה-ת The left foot of the ת has a small projection at the bottom facing outward, whereas ה does not.

ע-ט In certain typefaces, these letters look very similar; they can be distinguished, however, by the fact that the ע has a projection on the outward facing left-hand side.

ל-צ The similarity between these two letters is apt to be particularly confusing, as there is no similarity whatsoever between ל and צ in regular Hebrew script (or print). Note, therefore, that the upper part of the ל in Rashi script points straight up, whereas the upper part of the צ is tilted to the right.

ם-ס These two letters are similar not only in Rashi script, but in printed texts as well. The difference between ם and ס in Ashkenazi cursive writing is the opposite of the difference between these letters in Rashi script. Note, therefore, that the ם in Rashi script is round and smooth at the bottom, while ס has a small projection on the lower left side.

ע	ע		י	י		א	א	
פ	פ		כ	כ		ב	ב	
ף	ף		ר	ר		ג	ג	
צ	צ		ל	ל		ד	ד	
ץ	ץ		מ	מ		ה	ה	
ק	ק		ס	ם		ו	ו	
ר	ר		נ	נ		ז	ז	
ש	ש		ן	ז		ח	ח	
ת	ת		ס	ס		ט	ט	

Abbreviations

Initials and abbreviations are widely found in the Talmud and its commentaries, in the works of Halakhic authorities, and in Rabbinic literature in general. There are various reasons for this. In some cases, abbreviations were used to save time and writing materials, when books were copied by hand. In other cases, the use of an abbreviation was convenient, as it became a term in its own right, saving the constant repetition of recurring phrases. There were also cases where abbreviations were used to avoid writing a Biblical verse out in its entirety.

The following table includes the initials and abbreviations most commonly found in Talmudic literature, and some of the initials used by commentators on the Talmud and by Halakhic authorities. It should be noted that some abbreviations are coined for use only in reference to a certain topic, or within the framework of a well-defined issue. Most of the initials in this table omit the prepositional prefixes בכל"מ ("in," "like," "to," "from", as well as ו ("and"), and ה (the definite article.) When one encounters unfamiliar initials in a text one should ascertain whether they appear in this table without the prefix (this also applies to ד and שׁ ["for" or "that"] at the start of an abbreviation.) The names of books are indicated in this list by quotation marks to distinguish them from other entries. It should be remembered that the inverted commas used to mark an abbreviations are also used to distinguish foreign words (such as Old French words cited by Rashi) from Hebrew words, and that in some books this sign is used solely for emphasis.

א

א' — אלקים, אמר

א״א — אדוני אבי, אי אמרת, אי אפשר, אי אפשי, אשת איש

אא״א — אלא אי אמרת

אא״ב — אי אמרת בשלמא

אא״כ — אלא אם כן

א״ב — איכא ביניהו, אל״ף בי״ת, 'איסורי ביאה'

אב״א — אי בעית אימא, (ר') אברהם בן אשר

אב״ד — אב בית דין

אבה״ע — 'אבן העזר'

אבע״א — אי בעית אימא

א״ד — איכא דאמרי, או דילמא

אדר״נ — 'אבות דרבי נתן'

אה' — אהלות

א״ה — אי הכי, אמר הכתוב

אה״נ — אין הכי נמי

אה״ע — אומות העולם, 'אבן העזר'

אה״ק — ארץ הקודש

א״ו — אלא ודאי

או״א — אב ואם

או״ה — אומות העולם, איסור והיתר

אוה״ע — אומות העולם

או״ז — 'אור זרוע'

או״ח — 'אורח חיים'

אוצה״ג — 'אוצר הגאונים'

או״ת — 'אורים ותומים'

אא״ז — אדוני אבי זקני

אח״י — אחינו בית (בני) ישראל

אחז״ל — אמרו חכמינו זכרונם לברכה

אח״כ — אחר כך

אי' — איכא, איתא

א״י — ארץ ישראל, אינו יהודי, אינו (איני) יודע

איבע״א — אי בעית אימא

איכ״ר — 'איכה רבה'

א״כ — אם כן

אכי״ר — אמן כן יהי רצון

אכ״מ — אין כאן מקומו

אכמ״ל — אין כאן מקום להאריך

אכ״ע — אכולי עלמא

אל' — אלא

א״ל — אמר לו (ליה, להו), אמרו (לו) ליה, איכא למימר

אל״א — אין לי אלא

א״מ — אינו מובן, אבינו מלכנו, אבי מורי

אמ״ה — אלוהינו מלך העולם

אמ״ת — איוב, משלי תהלים

א״נ — אי נמי, אי נימא

אס' — אסתר

אסת״ר — 'אסתר רבה'

א״ע — את עצמו, את עצמה וכו'

אע״ג — אף על גב

אע״פ(י) — אף על פי

אעפי״כ — אף על פי כן

אפ״ה — אפילו הכי

אפי' — אפילו

א״צ — אין (אינו) צריך

אצ״ל — אין צריך (צורך) לומר

א״ק — אמר קרא, אלא קשיא

אקב״ו — אשר קדשנו במצוותיו וציוונו

א״ר — אמר רבי, אמר רב, 'אליהו רבה'

אר״א — אמר ר' אלעזר, אמר ר' אליעזר

אר״ג — אמר רבן גמליאל

ארז״ל — אמרו רבותינו זכרונם לברכה

אר״י — אמר ר' יוחנן, אמר ר' יהודה

א״ש — אתי שפיר

א״ת — אי תימא, אל תקרי, אם תאמר

את״ל — אם תמצא לומר

ב

ב״א — בן אדם, בני אדם

באה״ג — 'באר הגולה', 'ביאור הגר"א'

באה״ט — 'באר היטב'

בא״ח — 'בן איש חי'

בא״י — ברוך אתה י"י

ב״ב — בבא בתרא, בר ברוך, במהרה בימינו

בב״א — במהרה בימינו אמן

בב״ח — בר בר חנה

ב״ד — בית דין, בעל דין

בד״א — במה דברים אמורים

בד״ה — בדיבור המתחיל

בד״כ — בדרך כלל

בד״צ — בית דין צדק

ב״ה — בית הלל, ברוך הבא, בעל הבית, בית המקדש, 'בדק הבית', ברוך הוא, בעזרת השם

בה״א — בית הלל אומרים

בה״ב — בעל הבית, שני חמישי ושני

בה״ג — בעל 'הלכות גדולות', 'באר הגולה'

בה״ט — 'באר היטב'

בהמ״ז — ברכת המזון

ב״ו — בשר ודם

בו״ח — בשר וחלב

ב״ז — בן זומא, בן זכאי

בזה״ז — בזמן הזה

ב״ח — בעל חוב, בני חורין, 'בית חדש', בלי חשש

ב״י — 'בית יוסף', בית ישראל, בני ישראל, בן יומו

ביה״כ — בית הכנסת, בית הכבוד, בית הכיסא

ביהכ״נ — בית הכנסת

ביהמ״ד — בית המדרש

ביהמ״ק — בית המקדש

ביה״ס — בית הספר, בית הסתרים

ביה״ש — בין השמשות, בין השיטין

ב״כ — ברכת כהנים

בכו' — בכורות, ביכורים

בכ״ז — בכל זאת

בכ״מ — בכל מקום

בלא״ה — בלאו הכי

בל״ס — בלי (בלא) ספק

במ' — במדבר

ב״מ — בבא מציעא, בר מינן

במד(ב)״ר — 'במדבר רבה'

במ״מ — בורא מיני מזונות

ב״נ — בן נח, בורא נפשות

בנ״א — בני אדם, בנוסח אחר

בנ״ט — בנותן טעם

בנ״י — בני ישראל

בנ״ר — בורא נפשות

בנש״ק — בנן של קדושים

בס״ד — בסייעתא דשמיא

בס״ט — בסימן טוב, בסימנא טבא

בסי' — בסימן

בספ״י — בסבר פנים יפות

בע״ד — בעל דין, בעל דבר

בע״ה — בעל הבית, בעזרת השם

בעה״ב — בעל הבית

בעה״ת — בעלי התוספות

בעזהי״ת — בעזרת השם יתברך

בע״ח — בעל חוב, בעל חיים

בע״כ — בעל כורחו

בע״פ — בעל פה, בערב פסח

בע״ש — בערב שבת

בעש״ט — בעל שם טוב

ב״פ — ב' פעמים, בורא פרי

בפה״א — בורא פרי האדמה

בפה״ג — בורא פרי הגפן

בפה״ע — בורא פרי העץ

הנה"ח – הנץ החמה

הנ"ל – הנזכר לעיל

הנלע"ד – הנראה לעניות דעתי

הנ"מ – הכי נמי מסתברא, הני מילי

ה"פ – הכי פירושו, הכי פריך, 'הלכות פסוקות'

הק' – הקטן, הקשה

ה"ק – הכי קאמר, הכי קתני

הקב"ה – הקדוש ברוך הוא

הקמ"ל – הא קמשמע לן

הש"י, השי"ת – השם יתברך

ו

וא"א – ואי אפשר, ואי אמרת

ואצ"ל – ואין צריך לומר

וא"ת – ואם תאמר

ואת"ל – ואם תמצא לומר

וגו' – וגומר

ודו"ק – ודוק קצת

וד"ל – ודי למבין

ודפח"ח – ודברי פי חכם חן

והא"ר – והאמר רב(י)

וז"ל – וזה לשונו

וחכ"א – וחכמים אומרים

וי"א – ויש אומרים

וי"ג – ויש גורסין

וי"ל – ויש לומר, ויש לישב, ויש לתרץ, ויש להקשות

וי"מ – ויש מפרשים

ויק' – ויקרא

ויק"ר – 'ויקרא רבה'

וכד' – וכדומה

וכ"ה – וכן הוא

וכה"א – וכן הוא אומר

וכה"ג – וכהאי גוונא

וכו' – וכוליה

וכיו"ב – וכיוצא בו (בזה, בהם)

וכ"כ – וכל כך, וכמו כן, וכן כתב

וכ"ש – וכל שכן

וכ"ת – וכי תימא

ול"נ – ולי נראה

ול"פ – ולא פליגי, ולא פלוג

ולפע(נ)"ד – ולפי עניות דעתי

ונ"ל – ונראה לי

ועי' – ועיין

ועו"ש – ועיין שם, ועוד שם

וצ"ע – וצריך עיון

וצע"ג – וצריך עיון גדול

וקי"ל – וקיימא לן

וק"ל – וקל להבין, וקשה להבין

וש"נ – ושם נסמן

ז

ז' – זכר, שבעה, שבע

ז"א – זאת אומרת, זה אינו

ד"ט – ד' טפחים

ד"י – דפוס(ים) ישנ(ים)

דכ"ע – דכולי עלמא

ד"ל – די לחכימא, די למבין

ד"מ – דיני ממונות, 'דרכי משה', דרך משל

ד"נ – דיני נפשות, דפוס נאפולי

דני' – דניאל

ד"ס – דברי סופרים

ד"ע – דעת עצמו

דפו"י – דפוס(ים) ישנ(ים)

ד"ק – דפוס קושטא, דפוס קדמון

דק"ס – 'דקדוקי סופרים'

ד"ר – דברי רבי, דפוס ראשון, 'דברים רבה'

דרו"פ – 'דרישה ופרישה'

דר"מ – דברי רבי מאיר

דר"ע – דברי רבי עקיבא

דר"ש – דברי רבי שמעון

ד"ש – דפוס שונצינו

ד"ת – דברי תורה, דין תורה

ה

ה"א – הוה אמינא

ה"א, ה"ב – הלכה א, הלכה ב...

הב"ה – הקדוש ברוך הוא

הב"ע – הכא במאי עסקינן

ה"ג – הכי גרסינן, 'הלכות גדולות'

הג"א – 'הגהות אשרי'

הגה"מ – 'הגהות מיימוניות'

הגהמ"ר – 'הגהות מרדכי'

ה"ד – היכי דמי

הדה"ד – הדא הוא דכתיב

ה"ה – הוא הדין, היינו הך, הרב המגיד

הה"ד – הדא הוא דכתיב

הו' – הושע, הוא

הו"א – הוה אמינא

הו"ל – הוה ליה

הול"ל – הוה ליה למימר

הו(ש)"ר – הושענא רבה

ה"ז – הרי זה, הרי זו

ה"ט – האי טעמא

הי"ו – השם ישמרהו ויחייהו

היל"ל – היה לו לומר

הי"ת – ה' יתברך

ה"ל – הוה ליה, הוה להו

הל' – הלכה, הלכות

הלא"כ – הא לאו הכי

הל"ל – הוה ליה למימר

הל(מ)"מ – הלכה למשה מסיני

ה"מ – הני מילי, הוה מצי

המד"א – היך מה דאת אמר

המו"ל – המוציא לאור

המ"ל – הוה מצי למימר

המלבה"ד – המביא לבית הדפוס

המע"ה – המוציא מחבירו עליו הראיה

ה"נ – הכי נמי, הכא נמי

בפי' – בפירוש

בפ"נ ובפ"נ – בפני נכתב ובפני נחתם

בפ"ע – בפני עצמו

ב"ק – בבא קמא, בר קפרא, בן קרחה, בת קול, בעל קרי

בר' – ברייתא, בראשית, ברכות

ב"ר – בן רבי, בר רב, 'בראשית רבה'

ברא' – בראשית

ברה"מ – ברכת המזון

בר"ש – ברבי שמעון

ב"ש – בית שמאי, 'באר שבע'

בש"א – בית שמאי אומרים

בשו"מ – בשם ומלכות

בשכמל"ו – ברוך שם כבוד מלכותו לעולם ועד

בש"ר – בשם רב, בשם רבי

ב"ת – בן תימא

ג

ג"א – גירסה אחרת, ג' אלפים

ג"ד – גמר דין

גו' – גומר

ג"ז – גם זה

גז"ד – גזר דין

גז"ש – גזירה שווה, גם זה שם

ג"ח – גמילות חסד(ים)

ג"ט – ג' טפחים

גי' – גירסה

ג"כ – גם כן

גמ"ח – גמילות חסד(ים)

ג"ע – גילוי עריות, גן עדן

ג"פ – ג' פעמים, גט פיטורים

גפ"ת – גמרא, פירוש (רש"י), תוספות

גר"א – גאון ר' אליהו (מווילנא)

ג"ש – גזירה שווה, ג' שנים

ד

ד"א – דבר אחר, ד' אמות, דרך ארץ, ד' אלפים

דא"א – דאמרי אינשי, דאי אפשר

דא"ז – 'דרך ארץ זוטא'

דאלת"ה – דאי לא תימא הכי

דא"ר – דאמר רב(י), 'דרך ארץ רבה'

דב' – דברים

דב"ר – 'דברים רבה'

דגמ"ר – 'דגול מרבבה'

ד"ה – דברי הכל, דיבור המתחיל

דה"א – דברי הימים א

דה"ב – דברי הימים ב

דה"י, ד(ב)ה"י – דברי הימים

דה"כ – דברי הכל

ד"ו – דפוס ויניציא, דפוס וילנא

דו"ד – דין ודברים

ד"ח – דפוס(ים) חדש(ים), 'דברי חמודות', 'דרך חיים'

זא״ז — זה את זה, זה אחר זה
ז״ב — ׳זה בורר׳
זב״ז — זה בזה
זבח׳ — זבחים
זבל״א — זה בורר לו אחד
זה״ז — זמן הזה
זו״ז — זה וזה
זהש״ה — זה הוא שאמר הכתוב
זכ׳, זכר׳ — זכריה
ז״ל — זכרונו לברכה, זכור לטוב
זל״ז — זה לזה
זלהה״ה — זכרונו לברכה לחיי העולם הבא
זמ״ז — זה מזה
זמ״ן נק״ט — זרעים מועד נשים נזיקין קדשים טהרות
ז״נ — ז׳ נקיים
ז״פ — ז׳ פעמים
זצ״ל — זכר צדיק לברכה
זש״ה — זהו שאמר הכתוב

ח

ח״א — חד אמר, חכם אחד
ח״א, ח״ב — חלק א, חלק ב..., חד אמר
חב׳ חבק׳ — חבקוק
ח״ג — חילופי גרסאות, חלק ג
חגי׳ — חגיגה
חדר״ג — חרם דרבינו גרשום
חד״ת — חידושי תורה
ח״ה — ׳חזקת הבתים׳
ח״ו — חס ושלום, חס וחלילה
חוהמ״מ — חול המועד
חוהמ״ס — חול המועד סוכות
חוהמ״פ — חול המועד פסח
חו״ל — חוצה לארץ
חו״מ — ׳חושן משפט׳, ׳חובל ומזיק׳, ׳חמץ ומצה׳
חו״ק — חופה וקידושין
חו״ר — חכמי ורבני
חז״ל — חכמינו זכרונם לברכה
ח״ח — ׳חפץ חיים׳
ח״י — י״ח (שמונה עשרה)
חכ״א — חכמים אומרים, ׳חכמת אדם׳
ח״מ — חסורי מחסרא, ׳חושן משפט׳, ׳חלקת מחוקק׳
ח״נ — חצי נזק, חילופי נוסחאות
חסו״מ — חסורי מחסרא
ח״ק — חצי קדיש, חברא קדישא
חש״ו — חרש, שוטה וקטן
חת״י — חתימת יד
חת״ס — ׳חתם סופר׳

ט

ט״ב — ט׳ באב
ט״ג — טלית גדול
ט״ד — טעות דפוס

טה׳ — טהרות
טה״ד — טעות הדפוס
טואה״ע — ׳טור אבן העזר׳
טוא״ח — ׳טור אורח חיים׳
טוח״מ — ׳טור חושן משפט׳
טויו״ד — ׳טור יורה דעה׳
טו״נ — ׳טוען ונטען׳
טוש״ע — ׳טור שולחן ערוך׳
ט״ז — ׳טורי זהב׳
ט״י — טבול יום, טומאה ישנה
ט״מ — טעמא מאי
ט״ס — טעות סופר
טע״ט — טפח על טפח
ט״ק — טלית קטן

י

י״א — יש אומרים
יב״ח — י״ב (שנים עשר) חודש
יבמ׳ — יבמות
יב״נ — יהושע בן נון
יב״ע — יונתן בן עוזיאל
י״ג — יש גורסין
יד״ח — ידי חובה
יהו׳ — יהושע
יה״ר — יהי רצון
יהר״מ — יהי רצון מלפניך
יהש״ר — יהא שמיה רבא
יו״ד — ׳יורה דעה׳
יוה״כ — יום הכיפורים
יו״ט — יום טוב
יו״י — יעלה ויבוא
יו״כ — יום כיפור
יו״ל — יוצא לאור
י״ז — יש זמן
י״ח — ידי חובה, יש חולקין
יחז׳ — יחזקאל
י״ט — ימים טובים, י׳ טפחים
יי״נ — יין נסך
י״ל — יש לומר, יש ליישב, יש להקשות
יל׳ — ׳ילקוט (שמעוני)׳, ילף
יל(ק)״ש — ׳ילקוט שמעוני׳
י״מ — יש מפרשים, יש מקשים
ימה״מ — ימות המשיח
י״נ — יאיר נרו, יש נוהגין, יחיה נצח, יין נסך
י״ס — יש ספרים, י׳ ספירות
יעב״ץ — (ר׳) יעקב בן צבי (עמדין)
יעו״י — יעלה ויבוא
יעו״ש — יעוין שם
יפ״ת — יפת תואר, ׳יפה תואר׳
יצה״ט — יצר הטוב
יצה״ר — יצר הרע
יצ״ו — ישמרהו צורו ויחייהו
יצ״מ — יציאת מצרים
יקנה״ז — יין קידוש נר הבדלה זמן
י״ר — יהי רצון

ירו׳, ירוש׳ — ירושלמי
ירושת״ו — ירושלים תיבנה ותיכונן
ירמ׳ — ירמיה
יר״מ — יהי רצון מלפניך
יר״ש — ירא(ת) שמים
יש״ו — ימח שמו וזכרו
ישע׳ — ישעיה
יש״ש — ׳ים של שלמה׳
ית׳ — יתברך, יתעלה

כ

כ״א — כל אחד, כי אם
כ״א, כ״ב — כרך א, כרך ב...
כאו״א — כל אחד ואחד, כבוד אב ואם
כ״ג — כהן גדול, עשרים ושלושה
כד״א — כמה דאת אמר, כדקא אמרינן
כ״ה — כן הוא, כולי האי
כה״ג — כהאי גוונא, כנסת הגדולה, כהן גדול
כה״י — כתב(י) היד
כה״ק — כתבי הקודש
כו״כ — כך וכך, כאן וכאן, כמה וכמה
כו״ע — כולי עלמא, כלל ועיקר
כו״פ — כלל ופרט, ׳כפתור ופרח׳, ׳כרתי ופלתי׳
כ״ז — כל זמן, כל זה
כ״ח — כלי חרס
כ״י — כתב(י) יד, כנסת ישראל, כל יום, כן ירבו
כיו״ב — כיוצא בו (בזה)
כי״ל — כתב יד ליידן
כי״מ — כתב יד מינכן
כ״כ — כל כך, כמו כן, כן כתוב
כלו׳ — כלומר
כל״ח — כי לעולם חסדו
כ״מ — כל מקום, ׳כסף משנה׳, כל מה, כן משמע
כמ״ד — כמאן דאמר
כמד״א — כמה דאת אמר
כמהר״ר — כבוד מעלת הרב ר׳
כמוהר״ר — כבוד מורנו ורבנו הרב רבי
כמו״כ — כמו כן
כמ״ש — כמו שכת(ו)ב
כמש״ה — כמו שאמר הכתוב
כנה״ג — כנסת הגדולה, ׳כנסת הגדולה׳
כנ(י)״י — כנסת ישראל
כנ״ל — כנזכר לעיל, כן נראה לי
כ״ע — כולי עלמא, כל עיקר
כ״פ — כי פליגי, כמה פעמים, כך פסק, כך פירש
כצ״ל — כך צריך להיות
כרי׳ — כריתות
כ״ש — כל שכן, כל שהוא, כך שמעתי, כמו שכתוב
כ״ת — כי תימא, כתר תורה, כבוד תורתו
כת״ר — כבוד תורתו

ריב"ל – ר' יהושע בן לוי
ריב"מ – ר' יצחק בן מאיר
ריב"נ – ר' יוחנן בן נורי, ר' יהודה בן נתן
ריב"ס – ר' יהודה בר סימון
ריב"ק – ר' יהושע בן קרחה
ריב"ש – ר' יצחק בר ששת
ריה"ג – ר' יוסי הגלילי
רי"ף – ר' יצחק (אל)פסי, ר' יוסף פינטו
ריצב"א – ר' יצחק בן אברהם
ר"כ – רב כהנא, רובל כסף
ר"ל – רצונו לומר, ריש לקיש, ר' לוי, רחמנא ליצלן
רלב"ג – רבי לוי בן גרשם
ר"מ – ר' מאיר, ריש מתיבתא, רבינו משה
רמ"א – ר' מאיר אומר, ר' משה איסרלש
רמב"ם – ר' משה בן מימון
רמב"ן – ר' משה בן נחמן
רמ"ה – ר' מאיר הלוי
רמ"ז – ר' משה זכות
רמ"ך – ר' משה (ה)כהן
רמ"ע – ר' מנחם עזריה (מפאנו)
ר"נ – ר' נחמיה, ר' נחמן, ר' נתן, רב נסים (גאון)
ר"ן – רבינו נסים (בן ראובן)
רנב"י – רב נחמן בר יצחק
ר"ס – רב ספרא, ראש סימן, ראש סעיף
ר"ע – ר' עקיבא, רב עמרם, ר' עובדיה (מברטנורא)
רע"א – ר' עקיבא אומר, ראש עמוד א, ר' עקיבא איגר
רע"ב – ר' עובדיה (מ)ברטנורא, ראש עמוד ב
ר"פ – רב פפא, ר' פינחס, רבינו פרץ, ראש פרק, ראש פרשה
רפ"א, רפ"ב – ראש פרק א, ראש פרק ב...
רצ"ל – רוצה לומר
ר"ש – ר' שמעון, רב ששת, רבינו שמשון
רש"א – ר' שמעון אומר
רשב"א – ר' שמעון בן אלעזר (בגמרא), ר' שמשון בן אברהם (בתוספות), ר' שלמה בן אדרת (בפוסקים)
רשב"ג – רבן שמעון בן גמליאל
רשב"י – ר' שמעון בן יוחאי
רשב"ל – ר' שמעון בן לקיש
רשב"ם – ר' שמואל בן מאיר
רשב"נ – ר' שמואל בר נחמני
רשב"ץ – ר' שמעון בן צמח (דוראן)
רש"ג – רב שרירא גאון
רשד"ם – ר' שמואל די מדינה
רש"י – רבינו שלמה יצחקי, רבינו שיחיה
רשכבה"ג – רבן של כל בני הגולה
רש"ל – ר' שלמה לוריא
רש"ש – ר' שמואל שטראשון
ר"ת – ראשי תיבות, רבנו תם

ק"ש – קריאת שמע, קדיש שלם
ק"ת – קריאת תורה, קדיש תתקבל

ר

ר' – ראה, רבי, רבינו
ר"א – ר' אומר, ר' אליעזר, ר' אלעזר, ר' אבהו, רב אחא, רב אמי, רב אשי
רא"א – ר' אליעזר (ר' אלעזר...) אומר
ראב"ד – ראש אב בית דין, ר' אברהם בן דוד, ר' אברהם אב"ד
ראב"י – ר' אליעזר בן יעקב, ר' אברהם בן יצחק
ראבי"ה – ר' אליעזר בן יואל הלוי
ראב"כ – ר' אבא בר כהנא
ראב"ן – ר' אליעזר בר נתן
ראב"ע – ר' אלעזר בן עזריה, ר' אברהם (א)בן עזרא
ראב"צ – ר' אלעזר בן צדוק
ראב(ר)"ש – ר' אלעזר ברבי שמעון
רא"ה – ר' אהרן הלוי
רא"מ, רא"ם – ר' אליהו מזרחי
רא"ש – רבינו אשר
ר"ב – ר' (עובדיה מ)ברטנורא, ר' ברוך
רבב"ח – רבה בר בר חנה
רבש"ע – ריבונו של עולם
ר"ג – רבן גמליאל, ריש גלותא
רגמ"ה – רבינו גרשם מאור הגולה
רדב"ז – ר' דוד בן זמרה
רד"ק – רבי דוד קמחי
ר"ה – ראש השנה, רשות הרבים, רב הונא, רב המנונא
רה"ג – רב האי גאון, ראש הגולה
רה"י – רשות היחיד
רה"ק – רבינו הקדוש, רבותינו הקדושים
רה"ר – רשות הרבים
ר(ו)ה"ק – רוח הקודש
רו"ר – 'רות רבה', רוח רעה
ר"ז – ר' זירא, ר' (שניאור) זלמן
רז"ה – ר' זרחיה הלוי
רז"ל – רבותינו זכרונם לברכה
ר"ח – ראש חודש, רבי חייא, רבי חנינא, רב חסדא, רבנו חננאל, ר' חיים
רחב"א – רב חייא בר אבא
רחב"ד – ר' חנינא בן דוסא
ר"ט – ר' טרפון
רט"א – ר' טרפון אומר
ר"י – ר' יהודה, ר' יהושע, ר' יוחנן, רבי יוסי, רב יוסף, רב יצחק, ר' ישמעאל, רבינו יצחק (בתוספות), רבינו יונה
רי"א – ר' יהודה (יצחק...) אומר
רי"א – ר' יצחק בן אשר
ריב"ב – ר' יהודה בן בבא, ר' יהודה בן בתירא
ריבב"ן – ר' יהודה בן בנימין (בן הענוים)
ריב"ז – רבן יוחנן בן זכאי

פמ"ג – 'פרי מגדים'
פנ"י – 'פני יהושע'
פס"ד – פסק דין
פס"ז – 'פסיקתא זוטרתי'
פסח' – פסחים
פסידר"כ – 'פסיקתא דרב כהנא'
פסי(ק)"ר – 'פסיקתא רבתי'
פע(י)ה"ק – פה עיר הקודש
פ"פ – פתחון פה, פתח פתוח
פ"ק – פרק קמא
פקו"נ – פיקוח נפש
פרד"ס – פשט, רמז, דרש, סוד
פר"ח – 'פרי חדש', פירוש (פירש) רבינו חננאל
פר"מ – 'פרי מגדים'
פ"ת – 'פתחי תשובה'

צ

צ"ב – צריך ביאור, צאן ברזל
צעב"ח – צער בעלי חיים
צ"ה – צאת הכוכבים, צורת הפתח
צה"כ – צאת הכוכבים
צוה"פ – צורת הפתח
צ"ל – צריך לומר, צריכא למימר, צריך להיות
צ"ע – צריך עיון
צע"ג – צריך עיון גדול
צפ', צפנ' – צפניה

ק

קא"ל – קא אמר ליה
קב"ה – קודשא בריך הוא
קב"ו – קדשנו במצוותיו וציוונו
קב"ע – קבלת עדות, קבלת עול
קגא"ס – קנין גמור אגב סודר
קה' – קהלת
קה"ח – קידוש החודש
קה"ע – 'קרבן העדה'
קה"ק – קודש הקדשים
קה"ר – 'קהלת רבה'
קה"ש – קידוש השם
קה"ת – קריאת התורה
קו' – קושיה, קונטרס
ק"ו(ח) – קל וחומר
קוב"ה – קודשא בריך הוא
ק"י – קדיש יתום
קידו' – קידושין
קי"ל – קיימא לן
קק"ל – קשה לי, קל להבין
קמ"ל – קא משמע לן
ק"ס – קנין סודר
קס"ד – קא סלקא דעתך
ק"ע – 'קורבן העדה'
קצוה"ח – 'קצות החושן'
ק"ק – קצת קשה, קהל קדוש

ש

ש״א – שמואל א, שער א, ׳שאגת אריה׳,
שאר אחרונים
שאיל׳ – ׳שאילתות (דרב אחאי גאון)׳
ש״ב – שמואל ב, שאר בשר(י)
שבו׳ – שבועות
שבי׳ – שביעית
ש״ד – שפיכות דמים, שפיר דמי
שד״ר – שלוחא דרבנן
שה״ג – ׳שם הגדולים׳, שאר הגרסאות,
שבת הגדול
שהז״ג – שהזמן גרמא
שה״י פה״י – שבת היום פסח היום
שה״ל – ׳שבלי הלקט׳
שהע״ה – שלמה המלך עליו השלום
שהש״ש – שיר השירים
שהש״ר – ׳שיר השירים רבה׳
ש״ו – שתי וערב
שו״ב – שוחט ובודק
שו״ח – שומר חינם
שו(ח)״ט – ׳שוחר טוב׳
שוכ״ט – שלום וכל טוב
שו״מ – שפיירא ורמייזא מגנצא
שו״ע – ׳שולחן ערוך׳
שופ׳ – שופטים
שו״פ – שוה פרוטה
שו״ר – שוב ראיתי
שו״ש – שומר שכר
שו״ת – שאלות ותשובות
ש״ז – שכבת זרע, שנה זו
ש״ח – שומר חינם, שנאת חינם
ש״ט – שם טוב, ׳שוחר טוב׳
שט״ח – שטר חוב
שט״מ(ק) – ׳שיטה מקובצת׳
ש״י – של יד
שי׳ – שיחיה, שיטה
ש״ך – ׳שפתי כהן׳
שכ״מ – שכיב מרע
(ו)שכמ״ה – ושכרו כפול מן השמים
שלב״ל – שלא בא לעולם
של״ה – ׳שני לוחות הברית׳
שליט״א – שיחיה לאורך ימים טובים
אמן
שמ׳ – שמות
ש״מ – שמע מינה, שמעת מינה, שכיב מרע,
׳שיטה מקובצת׳

שמו״ת – שניים מקרא ואחד תרגום
שמח״ת – שמחת תורה
שמ״ע – שמיני עצרת, שחרית מנחה ערבית,
שמונה עשרה
שמ״ק – ׳שיטה מקובצת׳
שמ״ר – ׳שמות רבה׳
ש״נ – שם נסמן, שינויי נוסחאות
שנ״ב – שהכל נהיה בדברו
ש״ס – שישה סדרים, שיתא סדרי
ש״ע – שמונה עשרה, ׳שולחן ערוך׳, שמיני
עצרת
שע״ת – ׳שערי תשובה׳
ש״פ – שווה פרוטה, של פסח
ש״צ – שליח ציבור
ש״ק – שבת קודש, של קיימא
שק׳, שקל׳ – שקלים
שקה״ח – שקיעת החמה
שקו״ט – שקלא וטריא, שקיל וטרי
ש״ר – של ראש, שם רע
שר״י – שם רשעים ירקב
ש״ש – שם שמים, שומר שכר, ׳שב
שמעתתא׳
שש״פ – שביעי של פסח
ש״ת – שמחת תורה, שומע תפילה

ת

ת״א – תרג(ו)ם אונקלוס
תא״מ – תיבות אלו מחוקות (מוקפות)
ת״ב – תשעה באב
תג״ק – ׳תשובות גאונים קדמונים׳
תד״א – ׳תנא דבי אליהו׳
תד״ה – תוספות דיבור המתחיל
תדר״י – תנא דבי ר׳ ישמעאל
תהי, תהל׳ – תהלים
תה״ג – תשובות הגאונים
תה״ד – ׳תרומת הדשן׳
תה״מ – תחיית המתים
ת״ו – תם ונשלם, תיבנה ותיכונן
תו״א – תנאים ואמוראים, ׳תורה אור׳
תובב״א – תיבנה ותיכונן במהרה בימינו
אמן
תוד״ה – תוספות דיבור המתחיל
תוה״ק – תורתנו הקדושה
תוהרא״ש – ׳תוספות הרא״ש׳
תוה״ש – ׳תורת השלמים׳
תו״י – ׳תוספות ישנים׳

תוי״ט – ׳תוספות יום טוב׳
תו״כ – ׳תורת כהנים׳
תוכ״ד – תוך כדי דיבור
תו״מ – תרומות ומעשרות, תפילין ומזוזות
תומ״י – תיכף ומיד
תוס׳ – תוספות, תוספתא
תוס׳ רי״ד – תוספות רבנו ישעיה דטראני
תוס׳ הר״ף – תוספות הרב רבנו פרץ
תושב״כ – תורה שבכתב
תושבע״פ – תורה שבעל פה
תושלב״ע – תם ונשלם שבח לאל בורא
עולם
תז״מ – תיבה זו מחוקה
ת״ח – תלמיד חכם, תלמידי חכמים, תענית
חלום, תא חזי, תקנת חכמים, ׳תורת חטאת׳
ת(ק)חז״ל – תקנת חכמינו זכרונם לברכה
ת״י – תרגום יונתן, תרגום ירושלמי, תלמוד
ירושלמי, ׳תוספות ישנים׳, תחת ידי
ת״כ – תניא כוותיה, תקיעת כף, ׳תורת
כהנים׳
תכ״ד – תוך כדי דיבור
ת״ל – תלמוד לומר, תיפוק ליה
תמו׳ – תמורה
תנדב״א – ׳תנא דבי אליהו׳
תנדב״י – תנא דבי ר׳ ישמעאל
תנ״ה – תניא נמי הכי
תנ״ך – תורה, נביאים, כתובים
תע׳, תענ׳ – תענית
תע״ב – תבוא עליו ברכה
תפא״י – ׳תפארת ישראל׳
ת״צ – תענית ציבור
ת״ק – תנא קמא, חמש מאות
ת״ר – תנו רבנן, שש מאות
תרו׳ – תרומות
תרו״מ – תרומות ומעשרות
תר״י – ׳תלמידי רבנו יונה׳, תירץ ר״י
תר״ת – תקיעה תרועה תקיעה
ת״ש – תא שמע
תשב״כ – תורה שבכתב
תשב״ע – תורה שבעל פה
תשב״ר – תינוקות של בית רבן
תש״י – תפילה של יד
תש״ר – תפילה של ראש, ׳תורתן של
ראשונים׳
תשר״ת – תקיעה שברים תרועה תקיעה
תש״ת – תקיעה שברים תקיעה
ת״ת – תלמוד תורה, תנא תונא

USING THE INDEX

1. Each entry in those sections of the *Guide* that have been alphabetically arranged (Jewish Communities, Mishnaic Methodology, Talmudic Terminology, Halakhic Concepts and Terms, Talmudic Hermeneutics) is identified by a number in the index even though numbers are not printed alongside the entries in those sections. The purpose of this arrangement is to facilitate finding a particular entry on a page, which may contain more than a dozen entries.

In the Index a reference to an entry in one of the alphabetically arranged sections appears as a combined page and entry number — for example, 186(4) refers to entry number 4 on page 186. Sometimes reference is made to a number of entries on the same page — for example, 127(5,16).

To find an entry whose number has been cited in the Index, the reader should assign the number 1 to the first complete entry on the page referred to, and continue counting — following the alphabetical order of the entries — until the entry sought for is located. Please note that all entries on a page are included in the numbering scheme, including those that terminate with a *See* reference. The numbering of entries begins anew with the number 1 on each successive page of the alphabetically arranged sections. Where a new letter of the alphabet appears, the entries of the previous letter are counted first, and then the entries of the new letter.

2. Another feature of the Index concerning the alphabetically presented sections of the *Guide* is the division into primary, main, and ordinary references.

A primary reference appears entirely in boldface. It generally refers to an entry whose title is identical with the subject in the Index under which that primary reference is listed. For example, the reference **169(7)** under *Temple* refers to the entry of that name (בֵּית הַמִּקְדָּשׁ) in the section on Halakhic Concepts and Terms. A primary reference may also appear in one or more subheads of a subject in the Index. For example, the subhead *the four species* (under the subject *Sukkot*) is followed by a series of primary references, one for the composite term and one each for the constituent species listed as an extension of the subhead.

In a main reference only the number of the entry appears in boldface — for example, 133(**14**), 182(**3-5**), 193(**1,2,7**). A reference of this type usually refers to an entry that focuses on one particular aspect of the subject that lists that reference. For example, the entry אֲשֵׁרָה — *A tree worshipped as part of idolatrous rites* — in the section of Halakhic Concepts and Terms, appears as a main reference — 165(**2**) in the Index, under the subject *Idolatry*.

Ordinary references are printed entirely in lightface: 28(2), 151(3), etc. The entries they refer to have a partial or indirect bearing on the subject under which they appear in the Index.

3. Rabbinical titles (Morenu, Rabbenu, Rabbi, Rav, etc.) have been placed at the end of subject headings, for the sake of maintaining uniformity in the alphabetical system. Thus: Akiva, Rabbi; Huna, Rav; Tam, Rabbenu; etc. The only exception to this rule concerns the title *Mar*, which always precedes the name (Mar b. Rav Ashi, Mar Ukva, and Mar Zutra). The reason for this is that in the case of Mar b. Rav Ashi, *Mar* is a name as well as a title, and could not be detached like an ordinary title. To avoid separating the three Sages, all of them, Mar, Mar Ukva and Mar Zutra, were placed alphabetically with Mar b. Rav Ashi.

Index

139(**1,3**), 140(**9,14**), 141(**11**), 143(**11**)

Bikkurim 39, 162(16), 167(**9**), 232(6), 275(2)

tractate *Bikkurim* 39

Binyan av (conceptual analogy) **149(5)**, 154(2)

Birkat HaMazon. *See* Grace after Meals

Bivi b. Abaye, Rav 34

Blasphemy. *See under* God

Blessings. *See also* Priestly Benediction

38, 173(**3,4,6**), 182(**5,9**), 187(**7**), 201(3), 203(**4**), 225(2)

after eating and drinking 173(**1-3,5**), 192(7), 282

Blood **179(4)**, 179(**5-9**), 181(**10**), 182(**2**), 187(**11**), 188(**8**), 204(4), 207(9), 225(3,4,7), 228(12), 250(5), 266(**2**), 269(10)

Boaz, Rabbi Yehoshua 53-54, 59

Boethusians **249(2)**

Borrowing and lending (animals or objects) 215(3), 259(2), **262(4)**

Boundaries for the Sabbath and Festivals 39-40, 170(4), 208(1), 241(2), 247(**8**), 249(2), 255(**10**), 257(6), 261(10), 271(**8**), 289, 298

alleys 208(**6**), **210(4)**, 251(**12**), 266(3)

courtyards 167(7), 193(**8**), **240(9)**

domains 206(5), 223(3), 246(3), 253(8), **258(10)**

partitions 175(**1,2**), 198(1), 249(3)

Burial. *See* Funeral and burial rites

Caesarea **26(8)**

Calendar. *See also* Rosh Ḥodesh *and* Times of the day, *and the section on* Units of Time *in the chapter on* Talmudic Weights and Measures.

13, 23, 28(4), 40, 168(11), 189(4), 200(**5**), 249(1), 274(2)

commencement of a new year **256(5), 257(2)**

leap year 158(**14**), **240(1)**

months 158(**14**), 239(8), 252(4)

Camps of the Israelites (מחנה ישראל, מחנה לויה, מחנה שכינה) 213(**12-14**), 222(7), 242(10), 250(3), **267(5)**

Canaanites 217(3)

Capital punishment. *See also* Karet

13, 14, 42, 43, 93(3), 168(12), **179(1)**, 180(1), 181(9), 182(13), 185(7), 204(5), 218(4), 233(7,9), 237(3), 237(9)

administered by a "zealous person" **163(10)**, 185(5), 193(1), 233(**1**), 234(**9**), 269(14)

meted out by God ("at the hands of Heaven") 187(9), **216(4)**, 220(9), 252(7), 270(3), 275(2)

methods of execution 187(9), **216(4)**, 220(9), 252(7), 270(3), 275(2)

offenses carrying the death penalty 150(1), 151(1), 161(10), 165(3,5),

166(9), 172(1), 174(2), 174(9), 187(8,9), 206(6), 207(10), 209(7), 210(7), 216(5), 220(7), 223(6), 226(4), 230(10), 236(1), 242(9), 257(10), 261(5)

Caro, Rabbi Yosef 53, 296

Castration **233(4)**

Charity. *See also* Gemilut ḥasadim *and* Agricultural produce reserved for the poor

38, 84, 171(5), 173(6), 180(7), 198(7), 202(3), 214(1), 222(8), 227(2), 244(6), 272(**8**), 274(6)

Circumcision 177(1), 206(6), **215(5)**, 235(3), 242(**12**), 243(3), 248(**3**), 252(2)

Cities of refuge 43, 174(9), 176(**8**), 202(10), 236(3), **240(7)**, 242(8), 262(6)

Civil law (דיני ממונות). *See also* Damages

13, 14, 21, 42, 93(2), 95(6), 130(14), 158(13), 159(7), 164(8), 168(11), 172(**13**), 178(**11**), **178(12)**, 180(7,8), 181(9), 182(13), 183(5), 204(6), 209(2), 218(**6,7,10,11**), 231(4), 234(3), 236(6), 237(4), 243(7), 267(9), 298, 299

burden of proof (המוציא מחבירו) **183(7)**, 218(5)

Coinage. *See the sections on* Coins *and* Weights *in the chapter on* Talmudic Weights and Measures.

Commandments (mitzvot) 1-2, 42, 53, 93(2), 152(**3**), 154(1), 160(5), 160(**11**), 161(**3-5**,11), 171(7), 171(12), 178(8), 180(6), 187(7), 208(11), 209(1), 216(10), 220(**11**), 221(**1**), 222(**4**), 225(8), 233(3), 245(2), 252(2), 252(6), 261(5), 265(5), 267(7), 271(**1**)

commandments ordering the performance of an action 173(6), 222(8), 226(1), 235(3), **243(3)**, 243(4), 251(9)

commandments prohibiting an action 207(10), 226(1), 243(4), 259(7), 260(8)

intention in performance of **203(2)**, 205(5), 207(1), **222(5)**

Conditions (embodied in contracts, judicial decisions, etc.) 233(**8**), **272(11)**, 273(**1-3**)

Confession of sin **185(9)**, 199(10), 233(6)

Contracts and agreements 204(**7,8**), 211(6), 214(**8**), 272(**11**), 273(**2,3**)

Converts / conversion to Judaism 41, 47, 158(**10**), 173(6), 175(7), **177(1)**, 180(11), 184(7), 186(9), 194(10), 201(2), 215(5), 217(7), 218(9), 223(**1**), 225(9), 231(9), 235(4), 238(1), 238(4), 241(**6**), 243(6), 246(6)

Corporal punishment. *See* Lashes

Courts. *See also* Civil law; Judges; Oaths; Sanhedrin; Testimony

13, 14, 15, 17, 21-22, 42, 43, 112(2), 157(1), 158(9,15), 160(**13**), 164(8), **168(11)**, 169(7), 172(11), 174(**8**), 176(**11**), 178(**12**), 180(1), 183(9), 184(**8**), 187(**2**), 189(4), 192(2), 197(9), 198(7), 200(1), 202(9), 203(5), 204(6), 207(10), 211(**12**), 215(3), 216(11), 218(2-4), 218(**10**), 227(4), 232(**5**), 237(4), 243(**2**), 243(5), 247(5), 252(4), 253(**2**), 254(7), 255(3), 257(8), 258(8), 260(2), 261(**4,5,10**), 262(5), 263(**1,5**), 264(10),

266, 273(**1**), 273(6), 274(5)

of twenty-three judges (Lower Sanhedrin) 163(10), **168(12)**, 179(1), 232(**5**), 233(7), **233(9)**, 264(3)

Cursing 207(7), **223(5)**, 223(6), 232(3), 234(9), 254(3), 255(7)

Damages 42, 158(**12**), 159(2,11), 161(2,12), 178(**10**), 182(**6,7**), 193(4), 194(6,7), 197(**10**), 203(6), 212(1), 216(11), 218(7), 233(3), 240(4), 250(2), 254(7), 257(11), 259(1), 262(6), 272(6)

categories of compensation for injury 166(**12**), 179(**11**), 188(7), **192(6)**, 228(**11**), 249(8), 258(7), 261(9)

primary categories of agents that cause damage or injury 157(**6**), 164(**6**), 166(**11**), 255(**8**), 257(7), 264(2), 268(**10**)

Darkhei no'am ("ways of pleasantness") **180(6)**

Darkhei shalom (Rabbinic legislation to foster peace and amicable relations) **180(7)**

Darom **26(1)**

David, King 231(9), 232(6)

Davidic dynasty 14, 161(1), **218(2)**

Day of Atonement. *See* Yom Kippur

Dead Sea 199(9), 230(12)

Deaf-mute. *See also* Imbecile *and* Minor

96(1), 161(2), **194(6)**, 194(7), 214(7)

Demai. *See under* Tithes

Demai (tractate) 38

Derekh eretz (proper conduct) 47, **180(2)**

Derekh Eretz Rabba (tractate) 47, 180(2)

Derekh Eretz Zuta (tractate) 47, 180(2)

Diaspora 200(5), 259(4)

Dimi, Rav 33, 34

Dimi of Neharde'a, Rav 33, 34

Divorce 42, 93(6), 152(7), 159(11), 161(10), 177(4), 199(1), 202(9), 211(13), 212(4,7), 223(4), 233(8), 236(6), 248(13), 252(3), 268(13), 272(11)

get (bill of divorce) 42, 93(6), 159(2), 172(**11**), **175(8)**, 175(**9-11**), 189(4), 198(5), 203(5), 204(3), 209(8), 215(1), 225(2), 237(7), 264(10), 266(8)

Divrei soferim (legislation enacted by the Sages) **178(6)**

Dosa b. Harkinas, Rabbi 33, 34

Dowry 241(**3**)

Economic and financial matters 42, 163(6), 167(5), 178(4), 223(4), 224(**10**), 225(8), 240(5), 242(4,5), 245(3), 250(**6**), 255(8), 260(9), 263(3), 266(10), 270(5), 272(11)

acquisition (*kinyan*) and ownership 42, 159(1,13), 181(1), 183(8), 184(**7,8**), 189(9), 190(1), 192(**1**), 193(8), 195(7), 198(7), 205(6), 205(8), 214(5) 220(**6**), 223(8), 224(**6**), 225(11), 233(2), 253(8), **254(5)**, 254(**6**), 259(1), 263(1), 265(1), 265(8)

buying and selling 42, 159(7), 160(**3,4**),